IT Capability Maturity Framework™ (IT-CMF™)

The Body of Knowledge Guide

Other publications by Van Haren Publishing

Van Haren Publishing (VHP) specializes in titles on Best Practices, methods and standards within four domains:
- IT and IT Management
- Architecture (Enterprise and IT)
- Business Management and
- Project Management

Van Haren Publishing offers a wide collection of whitepapers, templates, free e-books, trainer materials etc. in the **Van Haren Publishing Knowledge Base**: www.vanharen.net for more details.

Van Haren Publishing is also publishing on behalf of leading organizations and companies: ASLBiSL Foundation, BRMI, CA, Centre Henri Tudor, Gaming Works, IACCM, IAOP, IPMA-NL, ITSqc, NAF, Ngi/NGN, PMI-NL, PON, The Open Group, The SOX Institute.

Topics are (per domain):

IT and IT Management	Architecture (Enterprise and IT)	Project, Program and Risk Management
ABC of ICT	ArchiMate®	A4-Projectmanagement
ASL®	GEA®	DSDM/Atern
CATS CM®	Novius Architectuur Methode	ICB / NCB
CMMI®	TOGAF®	ISO 21500
COBIT®		MINCE®
e-CF	**Business Management**	M_o_R®
ISO 20000	*BABOK® Guide*	MSP™
ISO 27001/27002	BiSL®	P3O®
ISPL	BRMBOK™	*PMBOK® Guide*
IT Service CMM	EFQM	PRINCE2®
ITIL®	eSCM	
MOF	IACCM	
MSF	ISA-95	
SABSA	ISO 9000/9001	
	Novius B&IP	
	OPBOK	
	SAP	
	SixSigma	
	SOX	
	SqEME®	

For the latest information on VHP publications, visit our website: www.vanharen.net.

IT Capability Maturity Framework™ (IT-CMF™)

The Body of Knowledge Guide

Edited by:
Martin Curley, Jim Kenneally, Marian Carcary

Contributing Authors:
Martin Curley, Jim Kenneally, Marian Carcary,
Eileen Doherty, Gerard Conway, Catherine Crowley,
Conor O'Brien, Clare Thornley,
Sinead Murnane, Louise Veling

Colophon

Title:	IT Capability Maturity Framework™ - IT-CMF™
Subtitle:	The Body of Knowledge Guide
Author:	IVI (Innovation Value Institute)
Editorial team:	Prof. Martin Curley, Jim Kenneally, Dr Marian Carcary
Content contributors:	Prof. Martin Curley, Jim Kenneally, Dr Marian Carcary, Dr Eileen Doherty, Gerard Conway, Catherine Crowley, Conor O'Brien, Dr Clare Thornley, Sinead Murnane, Louise Veling
Publisher:	Van Haren Publishing, Zaltbommel, www.vanharen.net
ISBN Hard copy:	978 94 018 0027 3
ISBN eBook (pdf):	978 94 018 0582 7
Edition:	First edition, first impression, September 2015
Editorial and design consultants:	Rédacteurs Limited, www.redact.ie.
Copyright:	© IVI / Van Haren Publishing, 2015

For any further enquiries about Van Haren Publishing, please send an e-mail to: info@vanharen.net

Trademarks

Innovation Value Institute, IVI, IT Capability Maturity Framework™, and IT-CMF™ are trademarks of the Innovation Value Institute.
All other trademarks used herein are the property of their respective owners. The use of any trademark in this text does not vest in the author or publisher any trademark ownership rights in such trademarks, nor does the use of such trademarks imply any affiliation with or endorsement of this book by such owners.

Printed in the Netherlands.

Preface

The software entrepreneur and internet pioneer, Marc Andreessen, famously wrote that 'software is eating the world'. As each day goes by, rapid developments in technology, as predicted by Moore's law, continue to enable disruptions that are changing and improving our world. As we continue to embrace computer and communications technology and the internet of things to enhance social, environmental and economic life, we become – as individuals and as organizations – increasingly dependent on distributed systems that operate at scale and contain many interconnected systems of systems – that is, large-scale distributed systems.

While many technology companies rush to create more sophisticated products and services, few have addressed the challenge of how such technologies and systems can be sustainably and reliably integrated and operated. A system that supports a city or an energy grid, for example, is as resilient only as its weakest link or component. While developing technology may be difficult, the organizational management of large-scale systems and IT functions presents challenges that are just as great – capabilities that are not strictly technology-related, such as risk management, governance, supply-demand management, and so on, are critical.

To help manage such systems, the IT Capability Maturity Framework™ (IT-CMF™) takes a systems-technology management and value-based perspective. It helps organizations to manage and improve their interconnected IT capabilities, by identifying areas needing improvement and showing how to make those improvements, based on industry best-known practice. This book publishes, for the first time, a catalogue of critical capabilities – capabilities we believe to be important in successfully managing large-scale systems and IT functions within large organizations.

The origins of IT-CMF lie in the successful transformation and development of the IT function within Intel Corporation in the early 2000s and subsequent research. The resulting set of artefacts was adopted by the Innovation Value Institute™ (IVI™) when the Institute was established, and has since been refined and extended to include additional practices, organizational assessment approaches and improvement roadmaps in a programme of research and experimentation conducted by the IVI in collaboration with a worldwide consortium of academic and industry partners.

IT-CMF does not seek to displace other useful IT frameworks – instead, it provides an umbrella under which other frameworks and methodologies can be understood and integrated to achieve synergy. It offers a coherent vision, a vocabulary, and a set of benchmarks that enable CIOs and other business leaders to identify their strengths and weaknesses, to set targets and to measure progress.

Sincere thanks are due to the many contributors who have helped evolve IT-CMF (from a nascent framework first described in the book - *Managing Information Technology for Business Value*) into the comprehensive body of knowledge that you are reading today. Very special thanks are due to my co-editors on this book, Jim Kenneally and Dr Marian Carcary, who led the team of contributing authors to transfer the IT-CMF body of knowledge into this uniform and cohesive volume. Thanks are due also to the many organizations and leaders who have adopted IT-CMF and supported its development, including the Boston Consulting Group, Chevron, BP, BNY Mellon, EY, and many others. Without their intellectual, resource and monetary support, IT-CMF would not have become what it is today.

The individuals from these organizations who graciously gave their time and insights to develop the IT-CMF body of knowledge are too many to mention here, but can be found on the Innovation Value Institute's website, www.ivi.ie/contributors. The core team at the IVI – led by Martin Delaney – have been, and continue to be, central to the development and adoption of IT-CMF. Martin deserves special thanks for the energy and enthusiasm he has brought to IVI's General Manager and Technology Leader position, as do successive Presidents of Maynooth University, John Hughes and Philip Nolan, for their support of the IVI initiative. Thanks are also due to Maynooth University, Enterprise Ireland, IDA Ireland and the European Commission for their respective support of the IVI and its research work.

This book can make significant contributions to how your organization manages IT for agility, innovation and value, and also to help professionalize across industries how we manage IT for agility, innovation and value.

To be part of the ongoing evolution of IT-CMF and its research and emerging services' ecosystem, I invite you to stay in touch with progress at www.ivi.ie.

Prof. Martin Curley
Vice President, Intel Labs
Senior Principal Engineer
Director, Intel Labs Europe
Intel Corporation
Co-Founder Innovation Value Institute

Contents

Managing the IT Budget

Managing the IT Capability

Managing IT for Business Value

Going forward with IT-CMF

Appendices

Foreword

Suresh Kumar, BNY Mellon

BNY Mellon is the oldest bank in the USA – founded in 1784, eight years before the NYSE. Today, we are recognized as a Global Systemically Important Financial Institution (G-SIFI) and play a critical role in the global financial markets. A significant portion of global finances passes through our IT infrastructure on a daily basis.

To ensure that our vast infrastructure and 13,000 technology employees deliver the functionality and value needed to support this global enterprise, we focus on Capability Excellence, which is also one of the priority areas of the IT Capability Maturity Framework (IT-CMF) from the Innovation Value Institute (IVI). IT-CMF provides us with a structured and systematic approach to identify the capabilities we need; a way to assess our strengths and weaknesses; and offers clear pathways to improve our performance.

Today, IT is at the heart of every business. When an organization's IT capability is mature, that organization can derive the full benefits promised by the technology. Without a mature IT capability, an organization can miss opportunities for value creation, and may put its very survival at risk.

The opportunity for value creation and the risk of loss needs to be understood and managed across the organization. IT-CMF enables a continual drive for operational excellence and accountability for business-value results.

Our focus on a capability management and excellence transformation program is organization-wide, and helps us to evolve our IT capabilities to fulfil business needs, ensuring that IT investment decisions are no longer made in a vacuum – rather they are evaluated in terms of their contribution to delivering business outcomes. Because IT-CMF adopts the language of business value, as opposed to a technical engineering language, it provides a solid basis for dialogue with business leaders and a solid understanding of the IT capabilities needed to support both day-to-day business operations and investment to cater for future requirements.

Improving Capability Excellence is an organizational priority, with top personnel accountable for its successful delivery. At BNY Mellon, we use a variety of management approaches, and IT-CMF enables us to holistically align the multiple aspects that relate to the management of technology. The program has already delivered significant, measurable benefits to BNY Mellon, contributing to solid improvement in key areas. From a cost perspective, we have saved millions of dollars since starting the program as well as increased business user satisfaction by over 10%. We have deepened client relationships, and strengthened the skills and engaged the passion of our people. We continue to deliver further improvements as we integrate capability excellence into our normal operations.

BNY Mellon is proud to be a Patron member of the Innovation Value Institute and a key contributor to the development and evolution of IT-CMF. This framework provides a consistent and organization-wide approach to managing the IT capability of our complex, global enterprise IT function, and a platform on which we can deliver enhanced business value and innovation from IT. I am really pleased to see this first edition of the body of knowledge guide to the IT Capability Maturity Framework published and hope it will help you and your organization achieve more value from IT.

Suresh Kumar
Senior Executive Vice President and Chief Information Officer, BNY Mellon

BNY Mellon

BNY Mellon is a global investments company, delivering investment management and investment services to institutions, corporations and individual investors in 35 countries and more than 100 markets, with a global workforce more than 50,000 strong.

BNY Mellon is dedicated to improving lives through investing, helping people realize their full potential by leveraging our distinctive expertise to power investment success.

Given our global presence and our role in servicing a significant portion of the world's financial assets, we are uniquely positioned to leverage our data and platform assets to alleviate many of our clients' challenges. Our scale and access to data provide rich analytics that help our company and the financial markets make evidence-based decisions, and effectively manage risk.

Under Suresh Kumar's leadership, the Client Technology Solutions organization is delivering innovative and exceptional technology solutions that power our business, secure the sensitive data entrusted to us, and help the company's clients and employees to succeed.

Visit us at www.bnymellon.com, or follow us on Twitter @BNYMellon.

Foreword

Christian Morales, Intel Corporation

Information Technology (IT) is becoming pervasive and already underpins a significant proportion of our societal, economic and industrial systems. In parallel, data and knowledge are being referred to as the new crude oil of the 21st century. Despite the exponential advances across the board in the development of IT and technology, driven by Moore's law advancements, similar progress has not been seen in practices for the management of information technology for value, and organizations often struggle to convert the high velocity of advances in IT into tangible business value. There was thus a need and an opportunity to create a cohesive framework and set of management tools that organizations can use to systematically design, deploy and operate integrated information systems for value.

In this context, Intel is proud to have co-founded the Innovation Value Institute (IVI) with Maynooth University. The core goal we set ourselves was to create an international ecosystem of learning, expertise and experience that could cooperate to research and develop an integrated framework and set of management tools that could be deployed globally.

I have been pleased to see the number of leading companies, such as the Boston Consulting Group, Chevron, BP, Cisco and many others, who joined us on the journey to create and validate the IT Capability Maturity Framework (IT-CMF). I am particularly pleased to see organizations around the globe use the framework to deliver higher levels of value. IVI's way of working is a great exemplar of Open Innovation 2.0, with the collective output and impact far greater than any one organization could achieve on its own.

As technology's influence becomes more and more pervasive throughout every aspect of organizational life, firms need to consider IT's role in shaping their competitiveness as a whole. To successfully respond to competitive forces, organizations continually need to review and evolve their existing IT practices, processes, and cultural norms across the entire organization. IT-CMF provides a structured framework for them to do that, and it gives me considerable pleasure to see this first edition of the body of knowledge guide published, so that the insights it incorporates can be used more widely.

I hope it helps you and your organization achieve even better results from using information technology.

Christian Morales
Corporate Vice President and General Manager Europe, Middle East, Africa
Intel Corporation

Foreword

Ralf Dreischmeier
The Boston Consulting Group

When I first met Martin Curley, Director of Intel Labs Europe, and discussed his vision for the IT Capability Maturity Framework, I quickly realized that this was something that would be tremendously valuable to CIOs and their management teams everywhere. In BCG's work with technology leaders at some of the world's largest and most successful companies, we have found that their biggest challenges often lie in building the management capabilities necessary to use technology to transform their businesses, in partnership with their business colleagues, technology suppliers, and ecosystems of partners.

There are, of course, other IT frameworks that have proved useful in helping professionals address specific challenges. Some are more domain-specific, some more industry-specific, some more controls-focused. The challenge of managing the contribution of IT to business value, however, has – until now – received less attention – probably because it was more of concern to other business unit leaders outside of IT, and perhaps also because it really is difficult.

Recognizing this need and opportunity, we were delighted to join Intel and Maynooth University as one of IVI's Steering Patrons, to help develop IT-CMF and to validate its relevance and business impact. BCG, along with other consortium members, contributed expert resources, intellectual property and experience to the project, and helped orchestrate some of the working groups that developed elements of the framework. Working group contributors typically drew on decades of real-world experience, and were also familiar with other IT frameworks – this ensured that IT-CMF neither reinvents nor competes with other frameworks, but rather augments them and facilitates integration between them. This allows companies that already have investment and skills in such frameworks to maximize the value of that investment.

The decision to use an open innovation development methodology for IT-CMF has clearly helped to keep the work relevant: practitioners from enterprise end users of IT (public and private sectors), from the high-tech and IT industry, from academia, and from professional services companies joined forces in these working groups to create something that would help bring IT and value generation closer together.

We have found IT-CMF to be a powerful tool to help technology and business leaders respond to questions such as:

- Which of our IT capabilities are ahead, on par with or behind our peers and competitors?
- Where are the most valuable opportunities to improve our IT capability?
- How ready is my IT function to exploit the new challenges and opportunities in the world of digital (or cloud computing, or the next technology trend)?

IT-CMF provides not only the diagnostic framework to assess an organization's current capability, but also the industry-specific benchmarking data to calibrate that assessment, and the toolkit of practices, outcomes and metrics to chart the way forward, along with valuable case studies of what others have done to improve their IT capability.

We have successfully applied IT-CMF in over 200 assignments for clients in diverse industries, including IT, financial services, telecommunications, medical technology, consumer goods, fashion, energy, natural resources, and the public sector. We've seen IT-CMF applied by a newly-appointed CIO of a European technology company looking to get a handle on what they inherited; a global chief enterprise architect for one of the world's largest energy firms use it to track and drive the transformation of the enterprise architecture function; and an experienced CIO use it to chart the journey to world class for a major bank. We've been privileged to be partners with these leaders and their teams in supporting them on their journey, and happy to be using and recommending a framework that fits with our philosophy of client enablement – helping our clients be more capable at the end of an engagement than when we started, and not be dependent on external support or a proprietary framework.

Many of our clients have gone on to become members of IVI and also make contributions to IT-CMF in their own right.

As IT-CMF has gained traction globally and across industries, demand has continued to increase for broader access to IT-CMF beyond IVI members and the clients of IVI and its partners. I am therefore delighted to see the first edition of the body of knowledge guide to the IT Capability Maturity Framework become more widely accessible to technology and business professionals as well as students across the globe. We believe this will help support IT-CMF's continuing journey to become the gold standard for managing IT for business value.

IT-CMF just works. Or, as our clients confirm, it helps them create more value from IT.

Ralf Dreischmeier
Senior Partner and Managing Director
Global Leader, Technology Advantage Practice
The Boston Consulting Group

Foreword

Philip Nolan, Maynooth University

Maynooth University traces its origins to the foundation of the Royal College of St. Patrick in 1795, and today draws inspiration from more than two centuries of tradition in education and scholarship. The university has earned an international reputation for its teaching and research in the humanities, and in social and physical sciences. The University has particular strengths in the areas of mathematics, computer science and electronic engineering. At Maynooth University, we are committed to tackling real-world problems and are proud of the impact that our research work has had throughout the world.

Within 25 km of the university campus are situated the European headquarters of many of the world's leading high-technology companies, who choose to locate in Ireland because of the high quality of our graduates and the excellence of our research. In this context, our partnership with Intel Corporation in establishing and supporting the Innovation Value Institute (IVI) is easy to understand. Intel's European base is located just 5 km from the university, and there is a constant flow of people, knowledge and ideas between the two institutions.

The model of cooperation and mutual learning between academia and industry that has been adopted by the IVI points the way for the future of university-enterprise cooperation. It shows how research results can be transferred into industry to create real value and innovation. And, equally important, it shows how real-world experience can be leveraged to inform teaching and further research.

IVI is a not-for-profit organization that supports and is supported by an international membership consortium of industry, academia, and public sector organizations, who collaborate in order to deepen their understanding and develop their abilities. The consortium includes many of the world's largest and most prestigious enterprises.

The research and development model in IVI is based on the principles of open innovation, in which IT practitioners and academic researchers jointly define the research agenda and validate the results. This collaborative model results in the rapid generation and adoption of new management approaches and perspectives that can be applied in different industries and contexts. This open, intensive and rich collaboration provides IVI with an essential feedback loop that ensures that its research continues to be both relevant and rigorous.

This book – *IT Capability Maturity Framework (IT-CMF): The Body of Knowledge Guide* – represents the early fruits of this collaborative model. It provides managers with direction and guidance to help them to understand what they need, to evaluate their current situation, and to make realistic, concrete plans for improvement.

Information technology is a defining element in today's business world. However, the technology is not an end in itself – it is of limited value unless it adds real value to business or the wider society. By using IT-CMF, business leaders can make sure that the tremendous potential of information technology is realized in their organization.

Professor Philip Nolan
President, Maynooth University
Chairman, Innovation Value Institute

Foreword

Colin Ashurst,
Newcastle University Business School

The focus of my work over the past 35 years, as consultant, IT manager and academic, has been deriving business value from IT. Although I had hoped that we would have tackled the IT attention deficit by now and developed both business-savvy IT leaders and IT-savvy business leaders, progress has been slow, but it is encouraging to see the issues and opportunities come sharply into focus now that every business is becoming a digital business, and exploiting waves of technology to enable business innovation is a strategic priority.

As a consequence, organizations need to focus more on developing their key capabilities, and this book presents an opportunity for doing so, along with practical guidance that is based in sound research and real-world experience. Based on experience, I can't stress enough that the need is for *organization-wide* capabilities and leadership, and so this book and the framework it sets out are just as relevant for the CEO and the wider business leadership as they are for the CIO and IT management team.

I have recently conducted an in-depth survey of organizations who have adopted IT-CMF, ranging in size from medium to very large, including, at the top end, organizations employing over 5,000 IT staff. Without exception, all said that IT-CMF was a valuable management tool, and that they recommend it to other organizations without hesitation. One CIO commented: 'we were able to take a hated function and create self-respect. We have an IT function that is relevant, that is respected and on a journey.'

I believe IT-CMF to be comprehensive and credible. The assessments it incorporates bring valuable insights for managing IT performance. Using the framework helps organizations to objectively identify and confirm priorities as the basis for driving improvements.

IT-CMF has been developed – and continues to be developed – with inputs from a group of major, industry-leading organizations, as well as academic research and insights from around the world. It can provide your organization with valuable and powerful resources for developing organization-wide IT capabilities. With these resources, there is no need for any organization to start from scratch, to reinvent the wheel – they can use IT-CMF to build on the hard-won experience of others. They can also participate in the IT-CMF community and share in further developments with other leaders.

Within an organization, IT-CMF can be the basis for a shared language, generating a broader understanding and improved practice – all with the object of delivering business value and innovation.

Dr Colin Ashurst
Senior Lecturer and Director of Innovation, Newcastle University Business School
Author, *Benefits Realization from Information Technology*, Palgrave Macmillan, 2011, and *Competing with IT: Leading a Digital Business,* Palgrave Macmillan, 2015

IT-CMF™

Introduction

The Management of IT Challenge

The rapid developments in information technology (IT) present a challenge for all organizations, large and small, public and private. While IT-enabled change and innovation are increasingly critical for their continued viability, many struggle to support and catalyse changes that will contribute value across the organization.

The rapid advances in IT have not been matched by developments in the management of information technology, and as a result many organizations fail to derive the full value from their investments – for example, over half of all large-scale technology deployments regularly fail to deliver the value and innovation expected of them [1][2]. With IDC estimating annual worldwide IT spending at around $2 trillion, such failures represent a significant loss of value and innovation.

Organizations must deploy and use IT effectively to remain relevant in an increasingly digital economy [3][4]. They need to continually innovate and differentiate themselves to keep pace and gain competitive advantage [5]. However, IT on its own does not provide competitive advantage – only an effective IT capability that delivers a steady stream of IT-enabled changes and innovations can provide sustainable competitive advantage [6].

The Innovation Value Institute™(IVI™) was founded to address these issues, as an open innovation ecosystem to research and develop an integrated management framework and set of tools for designing, deploying, and operating information systems to deliver sustainable business value and innovation.

The Innovation Value Institute™

The Innovation Value Institute (IVI) was established in 2006 as a non-for-profit, multi-disciplinary research and education institute within Maynooth University, Ireland. It was co-founded by Intel Corporation and the university with the objective of creating an international consortium of companies and public sector organizations to build on work already carried out in Intel and create an international standard for the management of information technology.

As well as the consortium's commitment of funding and in-kind resources, Enterprise Ireland and IDA Ireland, through the Technology Centre programme, support IVI's research agenda to focus on the creation and accumulation of knowledge and best-available practices in the management of IT.

Consortium Membership Profile

IVI supports and is supported by an international membership consortium of industry, academia, and public sector organizations who collaborate to deepen their understanding and develop their ability to manage their IT functions and realize the value of IT for their organizations. The consortium currently includes over 100 members, including many of the world's largest and most prestigious enterprises. Collaboration with the consortium members is a key part of IVI's research and development process.

Research and Development: Open Innovation and Design Science Research

The research and development process in IVI is based on the principles of open innovation, originally proposed by Henry Chesbrough [7] and extended to Open Innovation 2.0 by the EU Open Innovation Strategy and Policy Group [8]. In this approach, IT professionals across multiple industries, together with academic researchers jointly define the research agenda, perform the research, and validate the results. This collaborative, non-competitive way of sharing information and insights greatly accelerates the generation of new approaches, tools and techniques, helps to disseminate new practices among a diversity of organizations and to collate experimental results, and enables participants to quickly identify what works and what doesn't, and in what circumstances. It also provides IVI with an essential feedback loop that ensures that its research continues to be both relevant and rigorous.

The core research paradigm used by IVI is design science research [9][10][11]. Design science research 'creates and evaluates IT artefacts intended to solve organizational problems' [12], the main goal being to develop knowledge that professionals and practitioners can use to design solutions to problems experienced in their field [13]. While behavioural science dominated twentieth century information systems research, design science research is today becoming more mainstream, with IVI a leading adopter. A fundamental goal of design science in information systems research is utility – that is, that the resultant artefact should be useful in addressing a real-world problem or challenge. IVI addresses utility by making pragmatic validation an integral part of its research approach.

Research in IVI is overseen by a Steering Board, which includes both industry leaders and academic researchers. Research is conducted in an iterative and staged approach, in which artefacts and theory are generated and verified, using both inductive and deductive processes. Research work is carried out by workgroups that include industry-domain experts and academic subject-matter experts. Each workgroup is facilitated by a dedicated IVI researcher who manages the research direction within the workgroup, and the resultant research output is codified into standard artefacts.

The Origins of IT-CMF

In 2000, when Intel Corporation embarked on a programme of transformation of its IT function, they found that there was no comprehensive, integrated, CIO-level framework available [14]. Over the following years, they developed a maturity framework approach that proved to be highly successful. That approach, and the lessons learned from their experience of applying it, were captured in Prof. Martin Curley's book, *Managing IT for Business Value* [15].

When IVI was established in 2006, the Institute adopted the maturity framework from Intel Corporation, and continued to further develop and refine it. Since then, IVI has substantially enhanced and extended the framework with further research and feedback from users, to make it relevant to decision-makers in any industry (public or private) who need to manage key information technology capabilities to improve agility, innovation, and value.

IVI has also helped incubate a global professional-services ecosystem to satisfy the demand for IT-CMF training and consultancy. Certification programmes based on IT-CMF are available internationally; these equip suitably qualified individuals and organizations with the skills necessary to apply the framework to improve organizational performance.

What is IT-CMF?

Organizations that manage their IT capabilities better perform better [16]. However, many organizations regularly struggle to manage their IT capabilities in a systematic way. The IT Capability Maturity Framework™ (IT-CMF) enables decision-makers to identify and develop the IT capabilities they need in the organization to deliver agility, innovation and value for the organization.

Comprehensive Scope and Focus on Business Value

An analysis in 2011 of over 150 IT management tools revealed a significant gap in the available offerings, in that there was no framework that covered all IT domains and exhibited a significant value focus – see Figure 1 [10]. While each individual management tool or framework had the possibility of adding value in their specific area of focus, the complexity and inefficacy of using so many tools presented a challenge for organizations wishing to use them.

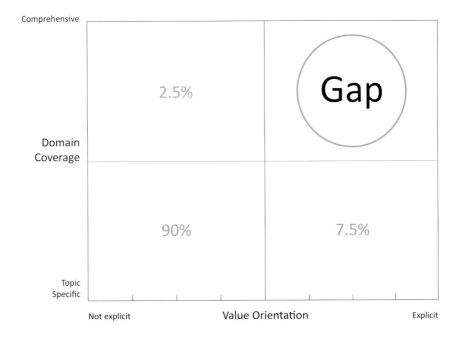

FIGURE 1. IT MANAGEMENT TOOLS: VALUE ORIENTATION AND DOMAIN COVERAGE

The lack of a holistic approach to managing IT for business value was similarly identified in a summary analysis of key academic papers on information systems research [17]. This failed to find a single paper dealing with business value as a significant or central theme.

Until IT-CMF, there was no single integrated enterprise IT approach for designing, operating, and supporting the increasingly integrated global computing and communications environment, particularly from a business value perspective. IT-CMF is explicitly designed to cover a range of IT capabilities needed in an IT function to deliver agility, innovation and value for the organization. It is also flexibly designed to allow new capabilities be captured and represented as they emerge.

IT-CMF and Other Industry Frameworks

There are a number of frameworks available to managers and practitioners that address the needs of specialist niches or specific aspects of managing IT. None, however, cover the full breadth of a CIO's responsibilities, nor do different frameworks integrate with one another seamlessly to provide a comprehensive solution. Many aim to optimize specific or local areas, without truly appreciating the possible unintended negative consequences for other areas of the organization.

By contrast, IT-CMF aims for comprehensive coverage of the components (or critical capabilities) needed to address a CIO's responsibilities. It leverages the concept of dynamic capabilities [18], by providing a mechanism not only for developing the capabilities, but also for enabling them to be reconfigured as necessary to adapt to changing circumstances and strategies. It provides a portfolio of options from which CIOs and other senior managers can design an improvement programme that is uniquely suited to their particular IT capability needs and their business environment.

IT-CMF builds on the maturity model conceptualization adopted by the Software Engineering Institute for the Software CMM model [19][20], but as well as focusing on process and capability maturity, IT-CMF also focuses on outcome maturity – that is, on the specific business outcomes expected at different levels of capability maturity.

What IT-CMF Provides

IT-CMF provides the basis for systematically and continually improving the performance of the IT function in an organization, and for measuring progress and value delivered. It enables organizations to devise more robust strategies, make better-informed decisions, and consistently deliver increased levels of agility, innovation and value.

IT-CMF offers:

▶ A holistic business-led approach that enables performance across the IT function to be managed consistently and comprehensively.
▶ Support for the development of enduring IT capabilities with a primary focus on achieving business agility, innovation and value.
▶ A platform and a common language for exchanging information between diverse stakeholders, enabling them to set goals, take action and evaluate improvements.
▶ An umbrella framework that complements other frameworks already in use in the organization to drive cohesive performance improvement.

The IT Capability Maturity Framework (IT-CMF) is currently used by hundreds of organizations worldwide, and is fast becoming the de facto standard for the management of IT in large organizations [21].

Core Concepts of IT-CMF

This section outlines the core principles and philosophy underpinning IT-CMF. A good understanding of these concepts will help the reader to navigate the remaining chapters of this book, and to see how IT-CMF improves management of IT for better agility, innovation and value.

What Is a Capability?

A capability is the *quality of being capable*, to have the capacity or ability to do something, to achieve pre-determined goals and objectives. Collectively, capabilities coordinate the activities of individuals and groups – linking individual actions into seamless chains of actions, leading to repeatable patterns of interaction that become more efficient and effective as they are practised and internalized. An organizational capability refers to an organization's ability to '*perform a set of co-ordinated tasks, utilizing organizational resources, for the purposes of achieving a particular end result*' [22].

Capabilities must work in a consistent manner. Having a capability means that the organization can perform an activity repeatedly and reliably. Organizations build their capabilities progressively in a cyclical process of trial, feedback, learning, and evolution. Organizations must be able to realign their resources in response to changes in strategy or the environment in which they operate. They must be able to embrace change, quickly innovating and reconfiguring resources to capture and exploit new, unforeseen opportunities. This is often referred to as 'dynamic' capabilities. IT-CMF facilitates this flexibility and responsiveness, and enables an organization to purposefully create, extend or modify its resource base to address rapidly changing circumstances [23].

Dynamic capabilities include the ability to search, explore, acquire, assimilate, and apply knowledge about resources and opportunities, and about how resources can be configured to exploit opportunities. Organizations with such capabilities have greater intensity of organizational learning, and are able to leverage feedback cycles more effectively, and thereby continually build stronger capabilities.

IT Capabilities

An organization's ability to orchestrate IT-based resources to create desired outcomes is a product of its IT capabilities. In IT-CMF, an IT capability is the *ability to mobilize and deploy (that is, integrate, reconfigure, acquire and release) IT-based resources to effect a desired end, often in combination with other resources and capabilities* (adapted [16]). Resources, in this context, can be either tangible (including financial, physical/infrastructural, human) or intangible (including software, data, intellectual property, branding, culture).

Relationships between Capabilities, Competences, and Processes

Business processes are sequences of actions that organizations engage in to accomplish specific tasks. They represent how an organization's resources are exploited, and can be thought of as the routines or activities that an organization develops to get something done [24][25]. Business processes require the competences of individual employees and groups for their effective execution. In turn, business processes help individual employees and groups develop competence in particular ways of working [26]. Processes and competences are thus mutually dependent and reinforcing.

Many organizations focus on process management, which has value, but may not equip them to respond to changing business strategies or environmental forces. While effective and efficient processes are critical for business operations, these processes must be regularly evaluated, modified and matured in anticipation of and in response to changing forces to deliver sustainable value [27].

Capability management provides the vital link between the business's strategy and environment and its business processes. It gives the organization *the ability to create patterns of learning and adjustment to establish and maintain synergetic relationships between competences (people), processes (routines), and resources (assets) to accomplish a desired end.*

Business Value

IT-CMF defines business value as *the contribution that IT-based resources and capabilities make to helping an organization achieve its objectives* [15]. Those objectives may be internal or external to the IT function; IT's greatest potential, however, lies in business enablement across the wider organization – that is, the organization's IT capability plays an important role in developing other business capabilities [16]. It is the resource configurations created with or enabled by IT capabilities that deliver value, rather than the IT capabilities themselves [28]. In addition, IT capabilities are just one part of the value creation process – they often need to be combined with non-IT-based resources and capabilities to fully realize value. IT-CMF helps organizations to continually enhance their capabilities to ensure that the resource (re)configurations are always aligned in support of business strategy and in response to environmental forces.

Design Patterns

Each organization has a unique starting point and a unique operating context. What works in one organization may not necessarily work to the same extent in another. The particular context can limit the efficacy of a given practice, even when it is applied in similar, but subtly different, problem and/or organizational situations. In recognition of this, IT-CMF is not a rigid, one-size-fits-all framework, but uses the flexibility of design patterns to allow an organization to effectively codify, adopt and share those practices that are most appropriate for them and are most likely to improve their overall performance.

The concept and use of design patterns originated in building architecture in the late 1970s, and were later adopted in software engineering and other disciplines as a way of dealing with recurring challenges. A design pattern *describes a problem which occurs over and over again in our environment, and then describes the core of the solution to that problem, in such a way that you can use this solution a million times over, without ever doing it the same way twice* [29]. Design patterns describe general reusable solutions and templates for dealing consistently and reliably with commonly occurring problems. The patterns are such that they can be applied in many different situations.

The various elements in IT-CMF are design patterns that can be combined in myriad ways: each organization can identify the patterns (critical capabilities, capability building blocks, practices, metrics, artefacts, etc.) that best address their particular needs, objectives and environment, and will enable them to deliver agility, innovation and value. Recognizing that each organization is different, the framework avoids an overly prescriptive approach, and instead provides guidance on good practice while enabling each organization to overcome its contextual challenges flexibly.

Maturity

Maturity frameworks are *conceptual models that outline anticipated, typical, logical, and desired evolution paths towards desired end-states* [30], where maturity is *an evolutionary progress in the demonstration of a specific ability or in the accomplishment of a target from an initial to a desired or normally occurring end stage* [31]. Maturity-based approaches for managing IT have been widely adopted – for example, the Software Engineering Institute's (SEI) Capability Maturity Model Integration (CMMI) is extensively used in the domain of software quality [19][20].

For each of the capabilities in the framework, IT-CMF defines five maturity levels, each of which characterizes a different level of efficiency and effectiveness. This facilitates a modular, systematic and incremental approach to capability improvement, by helping organizations to gauge how advanced they are in each area of activity, and identifying the actions they can take to improve over time.

While the definition of maturity levels is specific to each capability, the broad common characteristics of the five maturity levels, in terms of approaches, scope, and outcomes, are as shown in Table 1. (These are examples only – a wide diversity of maturity pillars is supported throughout IT-CMF.)

TABLE 1: GENERAL MATURITY LEVEL HEURISTICS

Level	Approaches Quality of routines / practices or activities	Scope Breadth of coverage / focus	Outcomes Predictability between actions and consequences
1 – Initial	Approaches are inadequate and unstable.	Scope is fragmented and incoherent.	Repeatable outcomes are rare.
2 – Basic	Approaches are defined, but inconsistencies remain.	Scope is limited to a partial area of a business function or domain area; deficiencies remain.	Repeatable outcomes are achieved occasionally.
3 – Intermediate	Approaches are standardized, inconsistencies are addressed.	Scope expands to cover a business function (typically IT) or domain area.	Repeatable outcomes are often achieved.
4 – Advanced	Approaches can systematically flex for innovative adaptations.	Scope covers the end-to-end organization / neighbouring domain areas.	Repeatable outcomes are very often achieved.
5 – Optimizing	Approaches demonstrate world-class attributes.	Scope extends beyond the borders of the organization / neighbouring domains.	Repeatable outcomes are virtually always achieved.

The Architecture of IT-CMF

Overview

IT-CMF is structured around four *macro-capabilities*, each of which embraces a number of *critical capabilities* (CCs) that can contribute to agility, innovation and value.

Each critical capability is made up of a number of *capability building blocks* (CBBs). The framework defines the different *maturity levels* for each CBB, and provides *evaluation questions* to assess their current state.

For each CBB, IT-CMF provides a series of representative practices to drive maturity, along with the outcomes that can be expected from implementing them and the metrics that can be applied to monitor progress (*Practices-Outcomes-Metrics*, or POMs).

The framework looks at typical *challenges* that the organization might face in attempting to develop maturity in each capability, and suggests *actions to overcome* them. And it identifies additional *management artefacts* that can be used in the development of maturity.

These elements are all described below.

Macro-Capabilities

At the top level, IT-CMF is structured around four key strategic areas, or macro-capabilities, for the management of IT [32]:

▶ Managing IT like a business.
▶ Managing the IT budget.
▶ Managing the IT capability.
▶ Managing IT for business value.

The effective management of technology within an organization focuses on these four macro-capabilites, all of which should be aligned with the overall business strategy, the business environment within which the organization operates, and the IT posture of the organization.

1. Managing IT like a business

To optimize the contribution of technology to the organization as a whole, the IT function needs to be managed using professional business practices. This involves shifting the focus away from technology as an end in itself towards the customers and the business problems to which IT can provide solutions. The **Managing IT Like a Business** macro-capability provides a structure within which the IT function can be repositioned from a cost centre to a value centre.

2. Managing the IT budget

There are many challenges associated with managing the IT budget, including, for example, unplanned cost escalation, the cost of maintaining legacy systems, and management reluctance to invest strategically in new technologies. The **Managing the IT Budget** macro-capability looks at the practices and tools that can be used to establish and control a sustainable economic funding model for IT services and solutions.

3. Managing the IT capability

The IT function was traditionally seen as the provider of one-off IT services and solutions. In order to fulfil its role as the instigator of innovation and continual business improvement however, the IT function has to proactively deliver – and be seen to deliver – a stream of new and improved IT services and solutions. This macro-capability provides a systematic approach to adopting that role, by effectively and efficiently maintaining existing services and solutions and developing new ones.

4. Managing IT for business value

Investments in IT must be linked to overall business benefits. This means that the investments should not be viewed simply as technology projects, but as projects that generate business value and innovation across the organization. The **Managing IT for Business Value** macro-capability provides a structure within which the IT function provides the rationale for investment in IT and measures the business benefits accruing from it.

Together these four macro-capabilities operate in a continuous feedback loop to optimize the way in which IT is managed [32].

- *Managing IT like a Business* sets the direction for the overall IT capability.
- In *Managing the IT Budget*, the strategic direction is translated into an IT budget to fuel activities and programmes.
- *Managing the IT Capability* is the production engine, where two primary activities are performed: maintaining existing IT services and developing new IT solutions.
- *Managing IT for Business Value* ensures that these activities and programmes deliver value.

Performance is fed back into *Managing IT like a Business*, to validate that the IT budget is being converted effectively into business value. This may result in tactical or strategic adjustments that feed through the cycle again [33]. (See Figure 2).

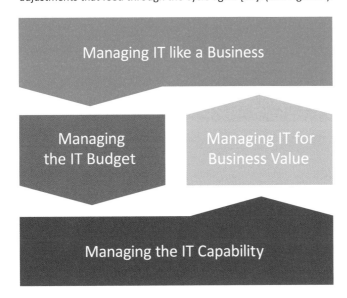

Managing IT like a Business

Managing the IT Budget

Managing IT for Business Value

Managing the IT Capability

FIGURE 2: IT-CMF'S MACRO-CAPABILITIES

The macro-capability feedback loop in IT-CMF ensures that the organization continually focuses on the IT capabilities needed to meet the challenges and opportunities presented by the changing business and operating environment.

Macro-capability strategies

When an organization is planning its capability improvement programme, it is helpful to decide on its strategic objectives in relation to each of the four macro-capabilities of IT-CMF, as depicted in Figure 3. This will help to identify the critical capabilities that the organization needs to focus on. Other factors that must be taken into account include IT posture, problem context, industry trends, business strategy, business context, and so on. (For further discussion of this topic, see [14][32].)

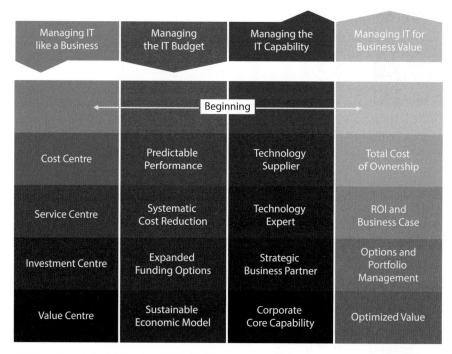

FIGURE 3: MAJOR STRATEGIES OF IT-CMF'S MACRO CAPABILITIES

Critical Capabilities

IT-CMF's four macro-capabilities encompass a modular library of 35 critical capabilities (adapted [33]) – see Figure 4. Critical capabilities are key management domains that need to be considered by an organization when planning and delivering IT-enabled business value and innovation.

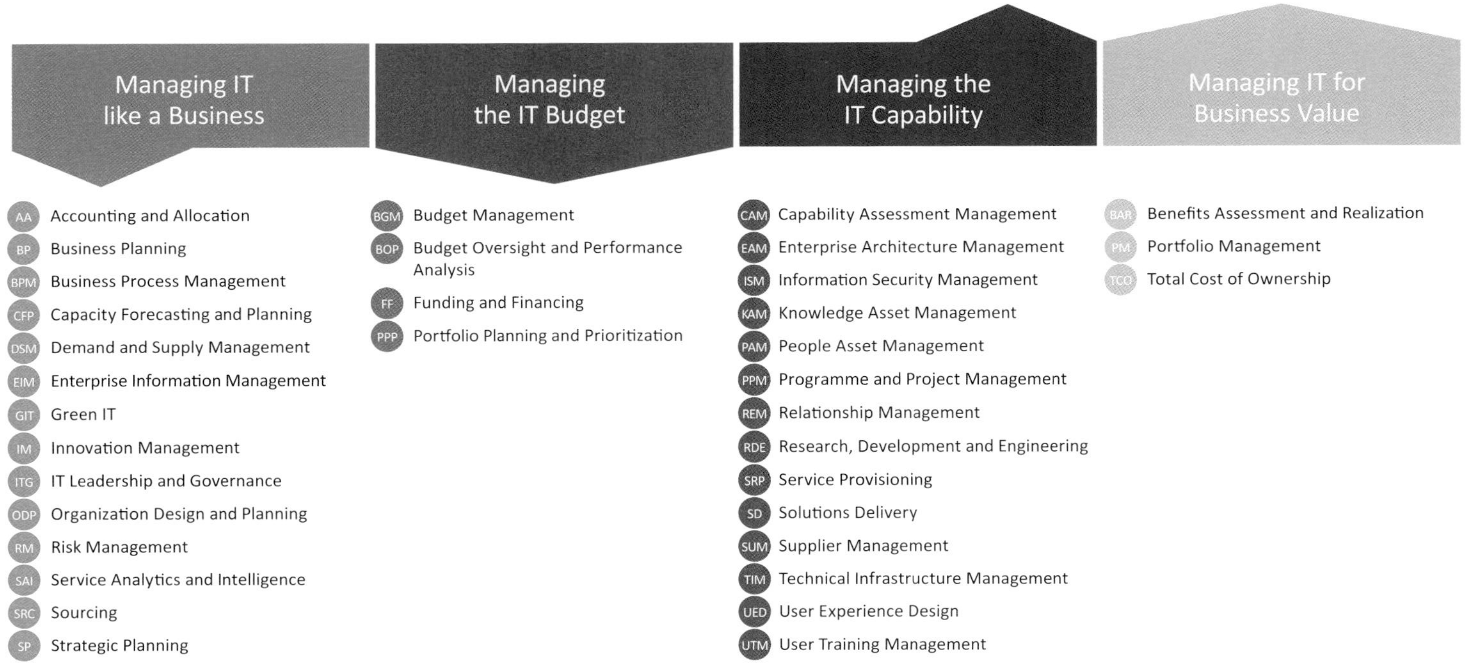

Managing IT like a Business

(AA) Accounting and Allocation
(BP) Business Planning
(BPM) Business Process Management
(CFP) Capacity Forecasting and Planning
(DSM) Demand and Supply Management
(EIM) Enterprise Information Management
(GIT) Green IT
(IM) Innovation Management
(ITG) IT Leadership and Governance
(ODP) Organization Design and Planning
(RM) Risk Management
(SAI) Service Analytics and Intelligence
(SRC) Sourcing
(SP) Strategic Planning

Managing the IT Budget

(BGM) Budget Management
(BOP) Budget Oversight and Performance Analysis
(FF) Funding and Financing
(PPP) Portfolio Planning and Prioritization

Managing the IT Capability

(CAM) Capability Assessment Management
(EAM) Enterprise Architecture Management
(ISM) Information Security Management
(KAM) Knowledge Asset Management
(PAM) People Asset Management
(PPM) Programme and Project Management
(REM) Relationship Management
(RDE) Research, Development and Engineering
(SRP) Service Provisioning
(SD) Solutions Delivery
(SUM) Supplier Management
(TIM) Technical Infrastructure Management
(UED) User Experience Design
(UTM) User Training Management

Managing IT for Business Value

(BAR) Benefits Assessment and Realization
(PM) Portfolio Management
(TCO) Total Cost of Ownership

FIGURE 4: IT-CMF's MACRO-CAPABILITIES AND CRITICAL CAPABILITIES

How IT-CMF Critical Capabilities Are Presented

The numbered chapters in this book (1–35) each relate to a particular Critical Capability (CC). In their layout and information design, these chapters are presented in a consistent manner, with the same content structure and headings. As you begin to use the book, you will become familiar with this structure and will find it easy to navigate through the different Critical Capabilities (CCs).

The structural components of each chapter are set out below.

1. Overview

The Overview provides the contextual background for each Critical Capability (CC), outlining the following in each case:

▸ **Goal**: The general purpose or end-state towards which the CC is directed.
▸ **Objectives**: Specifics regarding what the CC provides or enables. These provide the focus and the direction for the capability improvement effort.
▸ **Value**: How the effective management of this CC can contribute towards the organization's pursuit of business value – that is, what it delivers in a business context.
▸ **Relevance**: The importance of the CC in a business context.

2. Scope

The Scope defines the area that the CC deals with, in each case providing:

▸ **Definition**: a formal definition of the CC, its primary subject matter and the activities that it covers.
▸ **Other Capabilities**: activities that might be expected in this CC, but are covered in other CCs.

3. Understanding Maturity

This section describes the different levels of maturity associated with the Critical Capability (CC). It takes in a number of areas as described below.

Recognizing Excellence
This is a brief description of what performance in the CC might look like when it is operating well, and how good performance can be recognized. The main characteristics of high performance are summarized here.

Maturity at the Critical Capability (CC) Level
This provides a top-level summary of the CC across five successive and incremental levels of maturity. It describes the essential characteristics of the CC at each level. In doing so, it presents a picture of the transition from one maturity level to the next.

Maturity at the Capability Building Block (CBB) Level
This section describes the capability building blocks (CBBs) – the key components of the CC that enable its goals and objectives to be achieved efficiently and effectively. These are grouped into higher-order logical categories that are particular to each CC. For each CBB, there is a brief description of what it does, and an outline of the five progressive levels through which it passes as it matures. CBBs serve as the basis (the building blocks) upon which the CC's maturity is developed.

How to interpret maturity levels

The maturity levels described in the CCs and the CBBs are generally applicable in different contexts, but an individual organization may find that it does not fit neatly within any one level – it may, for example, exhibit characteristics of two or more maturity levels. Deciding which maturity level best describes the organization's current state depends on taking a common-sense approach that considers where the majority of the organization's time, resources and effort are being spent.

The maturity levels summarize the main characteristics that are generally observed at each level, but, for reasons of practicality, not all characteristics may be described.

Maturity levels are additive – each lower level provides the foundation for the next higher one, and capabilities are progressively enhanced in progressing from one level to the next. It can thus be unwise (and may not be possible) to skip levels – for example, to attempt to progress from level 1 directly to level 5. With proper planning, however, progress through the levels can be accelerated.

The maturity level that an organization should aim for depends on many factors, such as the organization's IT posture, business strategy, industry environment, current maturity, and so on. It may be unrealistic or inappropriate for every organization to automatically aim for maturity level 5 in every capability.

4. Improvement Planning

This section encourages the reader to reflect on their own organization's level of maturity in relation to the CC, and suggests some representative practices that might help them to develop.

Capability Evaluation

This consists of some high-level questions that help the reader to determine their current and desired maturity levels in relation to the CC. Each question has associated with it a series of corresponding maturity statements from which the organization selects the one that most closely matches their situation. In conjunction with the CBB maturity descriptions, these questions and answers can inform improvement planning discussions and help drive improvement across the areas under investigation.

Practices-Outcomes-Metrics (POMs)

This is a series of representative *practices* at each maturity level that an organization might adopt to help it stabilize its current maturity or progress to the next level of maturity. Each practice is accompanied by an *outcome* that states what benefits might result from following the practice, and one or more *metrics* against which the organization can gauge whether or not it has been successful in its efforts. The practices listed are indicative or representative, and are not exhaustive or mandatory – depending on organizational circumstances, alternative practices may yield the same results. Each organization should select the POMs that are most appropriate to their maturity circumstances and on which time, resources, and effort can be expended to maximum effect.

While the POMs are each described in association with a particular maturity level, this should not be seen as exclusive – it may be appropriate for an organization to implement, to a limited extent, POMs that are beyond its current maturity level. The key is to understand which POMs should command the majority of the organization's time, effort and focus in pursuit of capability improvement.

As with maturity levels, POMs are cumulative, in that lower-level POMs provide the foundation for adopting and succeeding with higher-level POMs.

Addressing Typical Challenges
This deals with general organizational challenges that may arise in attempting to develop maturity in the CC. For each challenge, there is a brief description of the context in which it is likely to occur, and a statement of the action that needs to be taken to meet or overcome the challenge.

Management Artefacts
These are artefacts that management might use to develop maturity in the CC. Although artefacts can be useful in more than one CC, in many cases they tend to be CC-specific. They include a range of tools, templates, documents, software applications, and other tools that have the potential to help practitioners develop their organization's capability.

5. Reference

There is a reference section at the end of each CC chapter as described below.

See Also
Capabilities are very often interdependent, and can rarely be improved in isolation. The maturity of the current CC may be constrained by the level of maturity in other CCs that have close and important relationships with it. When designing a capability improvement programme, the organizational context needs to be taken into account, and the related capabilities that are critical in that context identified. The CCs listed in the See Also section are the most likely candidates for consideration, but others should also be considered, depending on the organization's problem context and desired objectives.

Further Reading
This is a bibliography of material that relates directly to the current CC.

Notes
This is a list of published items referenced in the text of the chapter.

Notes

[1] British Computer Society, 2004. *The challenges of complex IT projects. The report of a working group from the Royal Academy of Engineering and the British Computer Society.* London: The Royal Academy of Engineering.

[2] Bloch, M., Blumberg, S., and Laartz, J., 2012. Delivering large-scale IT projects on time, on budget, and on value. McKinsey & Company. Available at: <http://www.mckinsey.com/insights/business_technology/delivering_large-scale_it_projects_on_time_on_budget_and_on_value>.

[3] Pavlou, P.A., and El Sawy, O.A., 2010. The 'third hand': IT-enabled competitive advantage in turbulence through improvisational capabilities. *Information Systems Research*, 21(3), 443–71.

[4] Granados, N., and Gupta, A., 2013. Transparency strategy: competing with information in a digital world. *MIS Quarterly*, 37(2), 637–42.

[5] Keen, P., and Williams, R., 2013. Value architectures for digital business: beyond the business model. *MIS Quarterly*, 37(2), 643–8.

[6] Ross, J.W., Beath, C.M., and Goodhue, D.L., 1996. Develop long-term competitiveness through information technology assets. *Sloan Management Review*, 38(1), 31–42.

[7] Chesbrough, H.W., 2003. The era of open innovation. *Sloan Management Review*, 44(3), 35–41.

[8] Curley, M., and Salmelin, B, 2014. Open innovation 2.0: a new milieu. In: *EU Open Innovation 2.0 Yearbook*. Luxembourg: European Commission.

[9] Curley, M., 2012. The emergence and initial development of a new design pattern for CIOs using design science. In: *Practical aspects of design science* (Communications in Computer and Information Science Series, Volume 286). Berlin: Springer.

[10] Curley, M., Kenneally, J., and Dreischmeier, R., 2012. Creating a new IT management framework using design science: a rationale for action and for using design science. In: *Practical aspects of design science* (Communications in Computer and Information Science Series, Volume 286). Berlin: Springer.

[11] Helfert, M., and Curley, M., 2012. Design science in action: researching and developing the IT-CMF. In: *Practical aspects of design science* (Communications in Computer and Information Science Series, Volume 286). Berlin: Springer.

[12] Van Aken J.E., 2005. Management research as a design science: articulating the research products of mode 2 knowledge production in management. *British Journal of Management*, 16(1), 19–36.

[13] Hevner, A., March, S., and Park, J., 2004. Design science in information systems research. *MIS Quarterly*, 28(1), 75–105.

[14] Curley, M., 2006. The IT transformation at Intel. *MIS Quarterly Executive,* 5(4).

[15] Curley, M., 2004. *Managing information technology for business value*. Hillsboro, OR: Intel Press.

[16] Mithas, S., Ramasubbu, N., and Sambamurthy, V., 2011. How information management capability influences firm performance. *MIS Quarterly*, 35(1), 237–56.

[17] Whitman, M., and Woszczynsk, A., 2003. *Handbook of information systems research.* Hershey, PA: Idea Group Publishing.

[18] Teece, D., and Pisano, G., 1994. The dynamic capabilities of firms: an introduction. *Industrial and Corporate Change*, 3(3), 537–56.

[19] Humphrey, W.S., 1988. Characterizing the software process: a maturity framework. *IEEE Software*, 5(2), 73–9.

[20] Paulk, M.C., Curtis, B., Chrissis, M.B., and Weber, C., 1993. Capability maturity model for software (Version 1.1). Software Engineering Institute. Available at <http://resources.sei. cmu.edu/library/asset-view.cfm?assetID=11955>.

[21] Costello, T., Langley, M.A., Botula, K., Forrester, E., Curley, M.,Kenneally, J., Delaney, M., and McLaughlin, S., 2013. IT frameworks. *IEEE IT Professional*, 15(5).

[22] Helfat, C.E., and Peteraf, M.A., 2003. The dynamic resource-based view: capability lifecycles. *Strategic Management Journal*, 24(10), 997–1010.

[23] Teece, D.J., 2007. Managers, markets, and dynamic capabilities. In C. Helfat, S. Finkelstein et al. (eds.), *Dynamic capabilities: understanding strategic change in organizations*. Oxford: Blackwell.

[24] Nelson, R.R., and Winter, S.G., 1982. *An evolutionary theory of economic change*. Cambridge, MA: Belknap Press.

[25] Porter, M.E., 1991. Towards a dynamic theory of strategy. *Strategic Management Journal*, 12, 95-117.

[26] Dosi, G., Nelson, R.R. and Winter, S.G. (eds.), 2000. *The nature and dynamics of organizational capabilities*. Oxford: Oxford University Press.

[27] Carcary, M., Doherty, E., and Thornley, C., 2015. Business innovation and differentiation: maturing the IT capability. *IT Professional*, 17(2), 46–53.

[28] Eisenhardt, K.M., and Martin, J.A., 2000. Dynamic capabilities: what are they? *Strategic Management Journal*, 21(10/11), 1105–21.

[29] Alexander, C., Ishikawa, S., and Silverstein, M., 1977. *A pattern language*. New York, NY: Oxford University Press.

[30] Becker, J., Niehaves, B., Poppelbus, J., and Simons, A., 2010. Maturity models in IS research. In: *Proceedings of the 18th European conference on information system.* Available at: <http://www.researchgate.net/publication/221408759_Maturity_Models_in_IS_ Research>.

[31] Mettler, T., 2009. A design science research perspective on maturity models in Information Systems. St Gallen: Institute of Information Management. University of St Gallen, CH.

[32] Curley, M., 2007. Introducing an IT capability maturity framework. In J. Cardos, J. Cordeiro and J. Filipe (eds.) *Enterprise Information Systems*. Berlin: Springer.

[33] Curley, M., 2008. *The IT capability maturity framework: A theory for continuously improving the value delivered from IT capability*. Ph.D. National University of Ireland, Maynooth.

Managing IT like a Business

To optimize the contribution of technology to the organization as a whole, the IT function needs to be managed using professional business practices. This involves shifting the focus away from technology as an end in itself towards the customers and the business problems to which IT can provide solutions. The **Managing IT Like a Business** macro-capability provides a structure within which the IT function can be repositioned from a cost centre to a value centre.

Contents: Managing IT like a Business

AA
01. Accounting and Allocation

01.1 OVERVIEW

Goal

The Accounting and Allocation (AA) capability aims to allocate the consumption of IT services to business units and to calculate the associated costs for chargeback/showback purposes.

Objectives

- Promote better understanding of the cost drivers for IT services.
- Enable business units to fund directly the provision of new IT services that might not otherwise have occurred because of a limited IT budget.
- Motivate managers across the organization to make sound economic decisions – for example, by subsidizing newer systems and imposing additional charges for the use of legacy systems.
- Encourage users to avoid expensive IT activities when slightly less convenient but far cheaper alternatives are available.

Value

The Accounting and Allocation (AA) capability assigns costs of IT services proportionally and transparently to the users of those services, improving cost awareness and responsible usage behaviours.

Relevance

IT functions regularly have to deal with reductions to their budgets, while at the same time maintaining ongoing operations, managing costs, and meeting an often fluctuating demand for IT services from other business units. For these reasons, strong financial management of the IT function is essential to ensure that funding for IT is based on the business demand for and usage of the services it provides [1]. When trying to fund IT services through the recovery of costs, IT leaders need to present strong financial data relating to the costs of the services they provide – otherwise, they run the risk of alienating their peers across the organization.

By developing an effective Accounting and Allocation (AA) capability, an organization is able to improve visibility into IT cost drivers and to assign costs to business units transparently and in proportion to their consumption. This enables the IT function to meter demand and to place funding for IT services on a sustainable footing.

01.2 SCOPE

Definition

The Accounting and Allocation (AA) capability is the ability to define and manage the policies, processes, and tools used for calculating the costs of IT and distributing them across the organization. The Accounting and Allocation (AA) capability covers:

▸ Establishing policies for measuring the consumption of IT services by business units in the organization, and for the chargeback/showback of associated IT costs to those units.
▸ Managing how the chargeback/showback for IT service consumption is allocated.
▸ Influencing the demand for IT services.

Other Capabilities

The following are addressed by other capabilities of IT-CMF:

For...	Refer to...
Determining sources of IT funding and planning IT funding levels	17. Funding and Financing (FF)
Understanding costs associated with IT services	35. Total Cost of Ownership (TCO)

01.3 UNDERSTANDING MATURITY

Recognizing Excellence

When the Accounting and Allocation (AA) capability is well-developed or mature:

▸ Service usage and cost recovery policies are transparent and communicated to relevant stakeholders.
▸ Costs of IT services (including essential, subscription, and discretionary services) are accurately and fairly allocated to business units based on usage.
▸ There is automated and centralized management of cost information from federated Human Resources (HR), Enterprise Resource Planning (ERP), and other financial systems of record.
▸ IT accounting and allocation is used in strategic decision-making – for example, for investment planning, and for balancing between the variable and fixed costs associated with the provisioning of IT services.

Maturity at the Critical Capability Level

The following statements provide a high-level overview of the Accounting and Allocation (AA) capability at successive levels of maturity:

Level 1	There is limited or no transparent allocation of IT consumption and associated costs to business units. Costs are typically allocated as overhead costs and are not linked to consumption.
Level 2	Transparent allocation of IT costs to business units is emerging for the largest IT projects and services only. Basic IT accounting is introduced. Fixed annual costs are allocated to business units based on an estimate of resource usage.
Level 3	Transparent allocation of IT costs to business units covers most IT services. The accounting framework is aligned across IT and accepted by Finance. Charges are allocated based on units of IT resources consumed, with some charges manipulated to drive desirable user behaviour (such as lower charges to encourage off-peak usage of network servers).
Level 4	Transparent allocation of IT costs to business units covers all IT services. The accounting framework is fully embedded in corporate systems. IT service fees are based on consumption of services as stated in the services catalogue. Fees are comparable to 'market' prices.
Level 5	Accounting and allocation enables business units to fully understand the costs of the IT services they consume, and enables them to optimize costs for their particular business units – for example, using metrics for unit price, volume, and quality.

Maturity at the Capability Building Block (CBB) Level

The Capability Building Blocks (CBBs) associated with the Accounting and Allocation (AA) capability fall into two categories:

▸ Category A: two CBBs associated with *Model Development* – these determine the scope for the accounting and allocation of IT costs.
▸ Category B: two CBBs associated with *Deployment* – these determine how the accounting and allocation of IT costs should be applied and overseen.

These are described below, together with a summary of the different maturity levels for each.

Category A: CBBs Associated with *Model Development*

CBB A1: Cost Coverage

Determine the scope of IT services (for example, essential, subscription, and discretionary services) whose costs are allocated to business units.

Level 1 — There is limited or no allocation of IT service costs to business units.

Level 2 — Cost allocation policies are applied only to a limited number of key IT projects and services.

Level 3 — Cost allocation policies are applied across the majority of IT projects and services.

Level 4 — Cost allocation policies are applied across all IT projects and services.

Level 5 — Cost allocation policies are continually reviewed and optimized for business environment conditions.

CBB A2: Accounting Policy and Cost Recovery Model

Develop policies for calculating costs associated with the consumption of IT services, and develop a model for cost allocation and recovery.

Level 1 — Policies and cost recovery models, if they exist, are based on a simple overhead cost allocation approach.

Level 2 — There is a defined accounting policy and a cost recovery model, both of which are accepted by Finance. However, they are not yet fully operational.

Level 3 — A standardized accounting policy and cost recovery model are fully operational and used by Finance and some other business units.

Level 4 — A comprehensive accounting policy and cost recovery model are fully operational across the entire organization.

Level 5 — The model for cost recovery is continually optimized to enable business units to fully control their costs.

Category B: CBBs Associated with *Deployment*

CBB B1: Decision-Making Transparency

Manage data on usage volumes and associated costs to provide visibility to inform decision-making across business units.

Level 1 — There is little or no availability of empirical data on which cost allocation or IT consumption decisions might be based.

Level 2 — There are high-level details of usage and cost projections for a limited number of key IT services to support decision-making, but these are not available at the business unit level.

Level 3 — Detailed usage data and unit costs are available for many IT services to support decision-making at the business unit level to enable cost reduction.

Level 4 — Comprehensive details of usage trends and unit costs are available for all IT services to support decision-making at the business unit level on investment prioritization.

Level 5 — The transparency of usage and cost data is continually reviewed in light of previous decision-making outcomes, and is regularly compared against relevant peers.

CBB B2: Governance and Communication

Apply appropriate oversight and communication approaches to ensure that business unit stakeholders understand and have buy-in to cost allocation and recovery policies.

Level 1   Governance and communication on cost allocation is non-existent or ad hoc.

Level 2   An informal governance forum is emerging with participants mostly from the IT and Finance functions. There is growing communication on cost allocation to a limited number of key business unit stakeholders.

Level 3   A central governance forum is fully operational with participation from the IT function, Finance, and other business unit stakeholders. Communication with stakeholders relating to cost allocation is planned and regular.

Level 4   Business unit liaison roles and sub-committees support two-way communication between the IT function and the whole organization to promote the idea of shared responsibility for controlling IT costs.

Level 5   Governance and communication relating to cost allocation and recovery are regularly reviewed for improvement based on feedback.

01.4 IMPROVEMENT PLANNING

Capability Evaluation

Two summary assessment questions are set out below, along with the typical response associated with each level of maturity.

How transparently are IT costs allocated across the business?

Level 1   IT cost allocation is limited or does not occur.

Level 2   Costs are allocated transparently for a limited number of larger IT services. Some costs are allocated using basic IT resource data, while other costs are estimates.

Level 3   Costs are allocated transparently for a growing number of IT services based on IT resource usage data. Charges may be manipulated to drive desired consumer behaviour.

Level 4   Costs are allocated transparently for nearly all IT services, using historical business consumption of IT service data.

Level 5   Costs are allocated transparently for all IT services, using near real time business consumption of IT service data.

How integrated is the IT service accounting system with strategic and operational decision-making?

Level 1   IT accounting seldom provides input to operational and strategic decisions.

Level 2   IT accounting provides defined high-level inputs to operational and strategic decisions for a limited number of IT services.

Level 3   IT accounting provides standardized inputs to operational and strategic decisions for most IT services.

Level 4   IT accounting provides comprehensive inputs to operational and strategic decisions for all IT services.

Level 5   The effectiveness of IT accounting integration into operational and strategic decision-making processes is continually reviewed.

Key Practices-Outcomes-Metrics (POMs)

Some useful POMs for developing the Accounting and Allocation (AA) capability are summarized below.

Level 2 POMs

Practice	Apply a cost allocation model to a prioritized list of IT services.
Outcome	Resource management is improved since IT accounting can track IT assets, expenses, and capital expenditures using transparent accounting logic.
Metric	Percentage of IT services covered by the cost allocation model.
Practice	Introduce governance of IT costs in collaboration with the Finance function.
Outcome	The IT function benefits from the Finance function's expertise.
Metric	IT function participation in an IT–Finance forum or governance body.
Practice	Report costs associated with the consumption of IT services.
Outcome	Business units can begin to understand usage patterns and cost drivers.
Metric	Percentage of IT costs that are covered by IT cost accounting and the cost allocation model.

Level 3 POMs

Practice	Expand the tracking and reporting of usage statistics to a wider scope of IT services using the accounting and cost allocation model.
Outcome	Business units gain better understanding of the relationship between IT consumption and IT costs when usage trends and unit costs are visible. Users are encouraged to adopt sustainable usage behaviours.
Metric	Percentage of IT costs charged back (or shown back) to business units.
Practice	Promote a standardized IT accounting and cost allocation model for formal adoption by corporate Finance.
Outcome	IT cost control can be more readily managed within existing corporate financial systems.
Metric	Yes/No adoption by corporate Finance.

Practice	Promote participation of stakeholders from IT, Finance, and other business units in governing cost accounting and the allocation model.
Outcome	Individual business units have a better understanding of IT consumption costs.
Metric	Percentage of business units represented in the governance forum.

Level 4 POMs

Practice	Promote responsible business unit behaviour by incentivizing desired IT service consumption patterns.
Outcome	Business units have more control over managing the costs of their IT service usage.
Metric	Percentage of IT services whose consumption patterns are influenced by incentivization schemes.
Practice	Make accounting and cost allocation a key component of the IT services catalogue, providing customers with full visibility on all charges.
Outcome	Business units are fully able to steer IT service usage based on price and on the required quality and volume of service.
Metric	Percentage of services in the IT service catalogue for which unit service costs are provided.

Level 5 POMs

Practice	Continually optimize cost accounting and allocation to ensure that it covers all IT services and their associated costs.
Outcome	The organization can continually evaluate and compare the costs of providing IT services.
Metric	Percentage of relevant costs charged back (or shown back) directly to business units.
Practice	Continually ensure that cost accounting and allocation forms a key input to operational and strategic decision-making regarding IT services.
Outcome	Investments to optimize the costs of various IT services will remain aligned to changes in business priorities.
Metric	Percentage of the discretionary IT budget devoted to cost optimization initiatives.

Addressing Typical Challenges

Some typical challenges that can arise in attempting to develop maturity in the Accounting and Allocation (AA) capability are set out below.

Challenge	Lack of necessary tools and skills to implement accounting and allocation practices.
Context	Translating data from the Finance function into IT-relevant structures may require integrating disparate data sets and complex formulas.
Action	Implement a pilot cost accounting and allocation project, and build on it to develop a case for automating accounting and allocation processes. The best place to start is likely to be the area that causes the organization the most pain, or costs the most, or where the quickest return can be derived.
Challenge	Resistance from either the IT function or other business unit stakeholders.
Context	IT cost accounting and allocation may be seen as an unnecessary burden on the rest of the business. Initially, IT personnel may perceive the additional workload in a negative way and business units may resent having to pay for IT services.
Action	Encourage the senior management team to raise awareness of how cost accounting and allocation can empower business units to optimize the value they derive from their consumption of IT services.
Challenge	Lack of financial and consumption data to determine IT unit costs and usage.
Context	The investment required to consolidate financial records is not available.
Action	Work with the Finance function to determine a satisfactory level of detail in relation to IT service costs and business unit consumption, such that the effort of collecting the data is worthwhile.

Management Artefacts

Management artefacts that may be used to develop maturity in the Accounting and Allocation (AA) capability include:

▸ An IT accounting model.
▸ A chargeback/showback model.
▸ An IT services catalogue.

IT Accounting Model

To generate a usage, chargeback, or showback report, the IT function needs to allocate consumption-based costs to the various business units for each month or reporting period. This requires IT to develop accounting models that can show specific links between the cost of an IT asset or service (the cost per unit of service consumed) and its consumption quantity, and from there calculate the total cost of the units consumed. The transparent and detailed breakdown of IT service provisioning costs is integral to the IT accounting model that enables chargeback/showback to the business units.

Chargeback/Showback Model

In a chargeback model, users are billed based on their consumption of IT products and services. In a showback model, they are kept informed of their levels of consumption, but are not charged directly. There are a number of different chargeback models, each of which will be appropriate in different circumstances:

▸ *Access Charges:* charges are based on the ability to access certain functions, usually for a flat fee. This may or may not be part of a subscription charge.

▸ *Subscription Charges:* charges are based on flat fees for various components that may be independently priced – for example, in a service menu. The fee is based on access rather than on usage; functionality and service levels are generally fixed.

▸ *Tiered Usage:* charges are based on pre-established ranges of use. If actual usage remains within the contracted tier, then a flat monthly fee is charged. Tiered usage is sometimes included in a subscription package.

▸ *Per Unit Usage:* charges are variable, depending on consumption quantity and the price per unit charged.

Whichever chargeback model (or combination) is used, it must be clear that the effort of collecting the data is worthwhile. Ultimately, the chargeback model should encourage purposeful use of IT services and ensure value for money for the organization.

IT Services Catalogue

The IT services catalogue is a list of customer-facing IT services provided by the IT function to the organization. It facilitates central registration of IT services, the finding and requesting of IT services by consumers, and service fulfilment tracking. Each service within the catalogue typically includes a description of the service, how it can be requested, how to get support, available service level options and associated costs (if applicable), details of who is responsible for the service, plus other information regarding the specific capabilities of the service. Increasingly, IT services catalogues are accessible via online self-service portals – for example, via cloud-based services. They can also be filtered and grouped in various ways – for example, by a particular theme (such as the most popular applications, CRM applications, desktop publishing software), by applicability to specific job functions, and so on. More sophisticated services catalogues may be automated to provide consumption reporting. Generally, as price increases, demand decreases, assuming all other factors remain constant. Therefore, price can be used as a lever to manage demand for IT services within the catalogue as long as the cost recovery principles (that is, the chosen chargeback/showback model) are transparent and business productivity is not constrained.

01.5 REFERENCE

See Also

Other capabilities of IT-CMF that have a particularly close relationship with the Accounting and Allocation (AA) capability include:

Capability	What it provides
04. Capacity Forecasting and Planning (CFP)	Insights on potential future resourcing scenarios for IT services
05. Demand and Supply Management (DSM)	Insights on how demand may react to changes in pricing strategies for IT services
09. IT Leadership and Governance (ITG)	Guidelines as input to establishing accounting and allocation governance
12. Service Analytics and Intelligence (SAI)	Insight into which IT-enabled business processes are driving infrastructure demand and by how much
35. Total Cost of Ownership (TCO)	Direct and indirect cost data on provision of IT services

Further Reading

Case, G., Du Moulin, T., and Spalding, G., 2007. *Service management strategies that work – guidance for executives*. Zaltbommel NL: Van Haren.

Datar, S.M., Rajan, M.V., Wynder, M., Maguire, W., and Tan, R., 2013. *Cost accounting: a managerial emphasis*. Melbourne, AU: Pearson Higher Education.

Notes

[1] Ryan, R., and Raducha-Grace, T., 2009. *The business of IT: how to improve service and lower costs*. Upper Saddle River, NJ: IBM Press.

BP
02. Business Planning

02.1 OVERVIEW

Goal

The IT function's Business Planning (BP) capability aims to link the IT strategy with IT operational planning. It represents the next level in planning detail following on from defining the IT strategy, ensuring that the necessary financial and other resources are allocated for implementation.

Objectives

- Break down the IT strategic plan into identifiable deliverables and required resources to achieve the medium- and long-term strategic objectives for the IT function.
- Build a robust process for allocating or reserving resources for IT programmes and operations in pursuit of strategic goals and objectives.
- Generate ownership and understanding among stakeholders of the critical success factors and the ways to monitor progress, so that the success of the IT business plan can be measured.
- Improve confidence that the IT function, through robust planning, can effectively deliver its goals and objectives within the specified planning period.
- Forecast the resources required to achieve the IT function's goals and objectives.
- Outline the financial and non-financial constraints within which the IT function operates.
- Focus and direct the IT effort by analysing actual against planned performance.

Value

The Business Planning (BP) capability links the IT strategy with operational delivery. It enables the development of multi-year investment roadmaps and plans to ensure that the IT strategy is successfully implemented.

Relevance

Significant efforts will typically be devoted to defining an IT strategy for the organization, only for it to 'sit on a shelf' unimplemented because of a lack of adequate resources. Evidence suggests there is a positive relationship between comprehensive forward planning by the IT function and that function's success [1]. Effective business planning delivers resource-feasible multi-year planning in support of the IT strategy, enabling the organization to extract maximum value from its strategic planning activities [2].

With an effective Business Planning (BP) capability, an organization is able to allocate the resources, roles, and responsibilities needed to ensure delivery of the goals and objectives set out in the IT strategic plan. The business plan clarifies the relationship between the organization's strategy and the IT function's shorter-term goals and objectives, and stakeholders as a result are better able to understand the resource requirements. They also have a tool for monitoring progress against the plan and can more easily modify the plan as business priorities change.

02.2 SCOPE

Definition

The Business Planning (BP) capability is the ability to produce an approved document that provides implementable detail for the IT strategy, setting out the IT function's tactical objectives, the operational services to be provided, and the financial and other resources and constraints that apply in the coming planning period. The Business Planning (BP) capability covers:

▸ Allocating responsibility to specific employees for IT business planning.
▸ Managing appropriate financial and non-financial resources and their capacities for ongoing IT business planning activities.
▸ Specifying the requirements for each activity in the IT business plan.
▸ Seeking the support of relevant stakeholders for the IT business plan.
▸ Reviewing the IT business plan against actual performance.

Other Capabilities

The following are addressed by other capabilities of IT-CMF:

For...	Refer to...
Defining the governance structure used to oversee IT decisions	09. IT Leadership and Governance (ITG)
Defining the strategic objectives of the IT function	14. Strategic Planning (SP)
Comparing actual spend with planned budget spend	16. Budget Oversight and Performance Analysis (BOP)
Setting funding levels and identifying funding sources for planned initiatives	17. Funding and Financing (FF)
Committing investment resources to specific programmes and projects	18. Portfolio Planning and Prioritization (PPP)
Executing the IT business plan	Other relevant IT-CMF Critical Capabilities, depending on the organizational need

02.3 UNDERSTANDING MATURITY

Recognizing Excellence

When the Business Planning (BP) capability is well-developed or mature:

▸ The IT business plan expands on the IT strategic plan by identifying the required activities, their value propositions, and the resources needed to deliver them in a timely and efficient manner.

▸ Stakeholders can see the projected resource requirements and can see how their deployment will address objectives of the IT strategic plan.

▸ IT has a prioritized plan for activities and resources, balanced between current operational and future strategic needs.

▸ Potential expenditure efficiencies across business units can be identified, and resources can be allocated to the activities that are best aligned to the IT strategic plan.

▸ The relevancy of the IT business plan is proactively monitored and adjusted as required.

▸ The IT business plan is disseminated throughout the organization to inform resource allocation decisions, and to help IT employees understand how their work contributes to objectives specified in the IT strategy.

Maturity at the Critical Capability Level

The following statements provide a high-level overview of the Business Planning (BP) capability at successive levels of maturity:

Level 1	The IT business plan is developed only for the purpose of budget acquisition, and offers little value beyond this to the organization.
Level 2	The IT business plan typically covers the resource requirements for a limited number of key areas that contribute to the objectives of the IT strategy.
Level 3	The IT business plan includes standardized details regarding required resources and identifies some of the ways in which the planned activities will contribute to the objectives of the IT strategy. Some input from some other business units is considered.
Level 4	The IT business plan is comprehensively validated by the IT function and all other business units, and identifies all required resources and the expected benefits.
Level 5	Relevancy of the IT business plan is continually reviewed, with regular input from relevant business ecosystem partners, to identify opportunities for organization-wide benefits.

Maturity at the Capability Building Block (CBB) Level

The Capability Building Blocks (CBBs) associated with the Business Planning (BP) capability fall into three categories:

▸ Category A: one CBB associated with **People** – this is concerned with allocating roles and responsibilities for IT business planning.

▸ Category B: five CBBs associated with **Process** – these deal with the development and implementation of an IT business planning process.

▸ Category C: four CBBs associated with **Content** – these deal with the content and characteristics of the IT business plan.

These are described below, together with a summary of the different maturity levels for each.

Category A: CBB Associated with *People*

CBB A1: Roles and Responsibilities

Select employees with the experience, knowledge, and authority needed to represent the interests of stakeholders.

Level 1   IT business planning doesn't exist or is not formally managed; employees do not have specific responsibility for this activity.

Level 2   Some IT employees are responsible for IT business planning. However, they may not have the authority or skills needed to ensure that IT business planning is effective.

Level 3   Employees from the IT function with the requisite experience, knowledge, and authority are allocated to IT business planning. Some employees from other business units are beginning to be involved.

Level 4   Employees from across the organization possessing adequate levels of knowledge and experience have responsibility for IT business planning and the authority to negotiate.

Level 5   The levels of experience and authorization of employees involved in IT business planning are continually reviewed and improved for effectiveness.

Category B: CBBs Associated with *Process*

CBB B1: Ongoing Operational Commitments

Determine the financial and other resources in the organization, and the extent to which they are already committed to ongoing contracts and obligations or are available to be deployed on new activities.

Level 1   There is limited resource usage and capacity data available for business planning purposes. The data available may rely on assumptions and incomplete data from previous planning periods.

Level 2   Verified resource usage and capacity data is increasingly becoming available, but estimates may be needed to fill basic baseline data gaps.

Level 3   Standardized usage and capacity data is available for many resources across the IT function.

Level 4   Comprehensive usage and capacity data is available for all IT resources in use across the organization. Information relating to potential future resource usage is also available.

Level 5   Usage and capacity data for all assets across the organization is continually reviewed for effectiveness.

CBB B2: Alignment Planning

Manage updates to the IT business plan to reflect changes in the IT strategy.

Level 1   Little or no effort is made to ensure that the IT strategy is reflected in IT business plans.

Level 2   Changes to the strategic plan, such as the mission statement and higher level strategic goals, are beginning to have a limited influence on aspects of the IT business plan.

Level 3   A standardized process, driven by the IT function, ensures that IT business planning is increasingly aligned with the IT strategy. The process includes input from some other business units.

Level 4   A comprehensive process that involves the IT function and all other affected business units ensures that IT business planning is clearly aligned with the IT strategy.

Level 5   Processes are continually reviewed for effectiveness to ensure the IT business plan remains fully synchronized with the IT strategy.

CBB B3: Business Plan Development

Formulate, review, revise, canvass support for, finalize, and sign-off the IT business plan.

Level 1   Any IT business plan that exists is of uncertain quality and relevance.

Level 2   Deliverables specified in the IT business plan are defined at a high level. The plan is broadly consistent with the IT strategy and some attempt has been made to prioritize elements within it. The content is typically based on inputs from the IT function only.

Level 3   The structure and format of the IT business plan are developed by the IT function. However, some other business units are involved in specifying deliverables, assumptions, and estimates.

Level 4   Priorities, assumptions, and estimates in the IT business plan are agreed jointly by the IT function and all other business units. Industry trend simulation and economic forecasting models are consistently used to produce and validate assumptions and estimates in the plan.

Level 5   The IT business plan is developed to the level of detail needed for accurate estimation of delivery times and resources. Quality reviews and checks are regularly undertaken and opportunities for improvement are identified.

CBB B4: Business Plan Communication

Communicate the IT business plan and its implications to stakeholders.

Level 1   Any communication of the IT business plan is ad hoc and one-way (such as bulletins or emails).

Level 2   Communication of the IT business plan is emerging in a limited number of employee forums (such as monthly staff meetings). However, significant numbers of relevant stakeholders are unlikely to be represented in these forums.

Level 3   The IT business plan is increasingly communicated in a more consistent manner across the IT function and some other business units, and increasingly reaches more stakeholders.

Level 4   Communication of the IT business plan occurs across IT and all other business units, reaching all stakeholders. There are effective and timely feedback mechanisms in place.

Level 5   Continual validation is conducted on communication of the IT business plan through various channels. Stakeholders may include those from relevant business ecosystem partners.

CBB B5: Business Plan Review and Control

Monitor planned against actual performance, so that the plan can be adapted appropriately as business priorities change.

Level 1	If there is any monitoring process, it is informal, perhaps limited to tracking start and due dates.
Level 2	A defined approach to monitoring progress is emerging. It is largely confined to the IT/technical delivery dimensions for a limited number of key projects.
Level 3	A standardized approach is used by the IT function to monitor all aspects of progress on the IT business plan, including budget, resources, services, capability, capacity, timeliness, and value of delivery. There is emerging collaboration with some other business units on this activity.
Level 4	The IT function and all other business units jointly conduct control and progress reviews of the IT business plan.
Level 5	The approach for reviewing the IT business plan is continually evaluated for improvement. Input from relevant business ecosystem partners is regularly sought to enhance the quality of the reviews and the review approach itself.

Category C: CBBs Associated with *Content*

CBB C1: Business Plan Objectives

Define IT objectives, including those relating to ongoing operational needs, new initiatives, and opportunities that the business wishes to pursue.

Level 1	If there are any explicit objectives, these are defined in an ad hoc manner.
Level 2	An IT team sets quantifiable objectives for parts of the IT function.
Level 3	Quantifiable objectives are set across the IT function, with input from some other business units.
Level 4	The IT function and all other business units jointly collaborate in setting quantifiable objectives.
Level 5	Objectives are continually reviewed for alignment with the organization's strategic direction, with input from relevant business ecosystem partners, where appropriate.

CBB C2: Planned Resource Utilization

Forecast resources required to achieve the objectives set out in the IT business plan, including finance, equipment, facilities, energy, people, telecommunications, services, and so on.

Level 1   Planning of resources is non-existent or ad hoc.

Level 2   Resource requirements are forecast for a limited number of major strategic objectives; internal or external resource peaks or conflicts are rarely addressed.

Level 3   Forecasts are made for most resource requirements across the IT function, with well-defined schedules showing how the objectives set out in the IT business plan can be achieved. Remedial plans are in place to deal with most foreseeable resource peaks and conflicts within the IT function.

Level 4   All resources across the IT function and all other business units are planned with well-defined usage schedules. Tools and techniques are used to proactively manage resources and avoid under- or over-utilization – for example, resource smoothing.

Level 5   Resources across the IT function, all other business units, and relevant business ecosystem partners are planned to achieve the objectives of the IT business plan effectively and efficiently. Innovative resource management methods, tools, and techniques are used. These may include using partner resources, when necessary, to deal with peaks in the workload or specialist skills requirements.

CBB C3: Success Criteria

Specify success criteria and associated metrics for determining the effectiveness of IT business planning.

Level 1   Success criteria are not defined. The IT function relies on informal or anecdotal feedback.

Level 2   Success criteria and metrics are defined by the IT function for key components of IT business planning (such as technology-focused delivery criteria).

Level 3   Success criteria and metrics are increasingly set by the IT function together with some other business units, with an emerging emphasis on service levels, asset utilization, and business value.

Level 4   Success criteria and metrics are set by the IT function together with all other business units, with service levels, asset utilization, and business value at their core.

Level 5   Success criteria and metrics are continually reviewed for effectiveness and opportunities for improvement.

CBB C4: Planning Assumptions

Document the scope and provenance of the assumptions and estimates that underlie the IT business plan – for example, an internally generated sales forecast that is informed by market and customer feedback.

Level 1	Planning assumptions are not explicit, and can usually only be inferred.
Level 2	A limited number of overarching macro or non-specific business planning assumptions are described.
Level 3	Assumptions regarding the IT element of key programmes are described. Input from some other business units regarding wider business assumptions is beginning to be taken into account.
Level 4	Assumptions are described and verified at the level of individual projects, and are developed by the IT function together with all other business units.
Level 5	Assumptions are continually reviewed for accuracy and improvement.

02.4 IMPROVEMENT PLANNING

Capability Evaluation

Two summary assessment questions are set out below, along with the typical response associated with each level of maturity.

How are employees selected for IT business planning activities – in terms of experience, knowledge, authority, and business focus?

Level 1	IT business planning is not formally managed; employees do not have formal responsibility for this activity.
Level 2	Employees from the IT function typically have the required experience and knowledge, but lack sufficient authority to deliver a complete plan.
Level 3	Employees typically have the prerequisite levels of experience, knowledge, and authority. While there is emerging input from some other business units, the majority come from the IT function.
Level 4	Employees are appropriately drawn from the IT function and other business units. They have sufficient experience, knowledge, and authority.
Level 5	The levels of experience and authorization of employees involved in IT business planning are continually reviewed and improved for effectiveness.

What process is in place to develop, communicate, and review the organization's IT business plan?

Level 1	IT business planning processes are non-existent or ad hoc.
Level 2	A defined IT business planning process is beginning to emerge within some areas of the IT function.
Level 3	There is a standardized IT business planning process in place across the IT function, with input from some other business units.
Level 4	There is a comprehensive IT business planning process applied organization-wide.
Level 5	The IT business planning process is continually reviewed to identify opportunities for improvement. It regularly incorporates input from relevant business ecosystem partners.

Key Practices-Outcomes-Metrics (POMs)

Some useful POMs for developing the Business Planning (BP) capability are summarized below.

Level 2 POMs

Practice	Assign resources from within the IT function to undertake IT business planning activities.
Outcome	A basic IT business plan can be made available.
Metric	Assignment of IT employees to IT business planning.
Practice	Identify and prioritize the key initiatives in the IT business plan, particularly those relating to ongoing operations and major technology programmes.
Outcome	Key initiatives can be validated as supporting the IT strategy.
Metric	Percentage of IT budget expenditure allocated to key initiatives in the IT business plan.
Practice	Disseminate the IT business plan across the IT function.
Outcome	Employees understand the IT business plan and can discuss its potential impacts.
Metric	Percentage of employees from the IT function who are familiar with the IT business plan.
Practice	Hold meetings to review progress against the IT business plan.
Outcome	Implementation challenges can be discussed and remedied.
Metric	Frequency of review meetings.
Practice	Establish success criteria, focusing initially on technology implementation aspects of the IT business plan.
Outcome	There is increased clarity regarding what success means.
Metric	Number of success criteria identified.

Level 3 POMs

Practice	Include employees from other business units in IT business planning activities.
Outcome	The plan is developed with greater organizational coverage and input, resulting in the plan being more effective.
Metric	Percentage of other business units engaged in IT business planning activities.
Practice	Increase communication of the IT business plan across the wider organization.
Outcome	Improvements can be made to the IT business plan based on feedback from the wider organization.
Metric	Number of items that are refined in the IT business plan arising from feedback from the wider organization.
Practice	Establish a standardized quality checklist for the IT business plan.
Outcome	Inputs to the IT business plan can be objectively assessed for quality and managed transparently.
Metric	Number of reworks/resubmissions required for the IT business plan.
Practice	Balance peaks and troughs in requirements for IT resources across initiatives in the IT business plan.
Outcome	Resource conflicts can be resolved during the planning stage, and resource utilization can be optimized across initiatives.
Metric	Number and percentage of objectives for which resource levelling is performed.

Level 4 POMs

Practice	Develop priorities and assumptions for the IT business plan on an organization-wide basis.
Outcome	The wider organization has greater confidence that the IT business plan addresses real needs and is based on valid fundamentals.
Metric	Percentage of business units satisfied with the IT business plan.
Practice	Use multiple and diverse communication channels to communicate the proposed IT business plan to stakeholders.
Outcome	The proposed IT business plan can be further refined based on diverse feedback from stakeholders across the organization.
Metric	Percentage of business units familiar with the proposed IT business plan.
Practice	Involve key stakeholders from across the entire organization in reviews of progress against the IT business plan.
Outcome	Impediments to implementing the IT business plan can be more easily remedied if relevant stakeholders are involved.
Metric	Percentage of relevant stakeholders present at review meetings.

Practice	Mandate the use of preferred scenario modelling tools to validate estimates and assumptions in the IT business plan.
Outcome	Sensitivity of the key variables underlying the IT business plan can be more consistently analysed, understood, and managed.
Metric	Percentage of estimates in the IT business plan that are vigorously stress-tested.

Level 5 POMs

Practice	Continually engage relevant parts of the wider business ecosystem in IT business planning activities.
Outcome	The IT business plan is informed by knowledgeable and authoritative employees from the business ecosystem.
Metric	Number of business goals that are recently validated.
Practice	Continually incorporate leading practices from relevant business ecosystem partners into IT business planning activities.
Outcome	The IT business plan is comprehensively and continually improved to amplify organization-wide benefits.
Metric	Number of improvements to IT business planning adopted from external sources.

Addressing Typical Challenges

Some typical challenges that can arise in attempting to develop maturity in the Business Planning (BP) capability are set out below.

Challenge	The funding and resourcing provided are inadequate to support effective business planning.
Context	The organization does not see the value of IT business planning as the link between IT plans and the organization's strategic objectives is considered difficult to articulate.
Action	Demonstrate to management that business planning of IT is critical to realizing the organization's strategic objectives, and should be resourced accordingly.
Challenge	Limited availability of employees with sufficient experience and knowledge, and with sufficient authority to conduct IT business planning.
Context	There is a general shortage of employees suitable for IT business planning, often through a lack of focus on recruitment or poor in-house training and development.
Action	Initiate an awareness campaign on the importance of building skills in IT business planning using targeted recruitment and/or in-house training.

Challenge	Ensuring IT business planning serves the needs of other business units, as well as the IT function.
Context	At the requirements gathering stage, emphasis is exclusively placed on the needs of the IT function, with little consideration of the needs of other business units.
Action	When gathering requirements, involve stakeholders from both the IT function and other business units. This can help maintain a balanced and representative consideration of business unit perspectives.
Challenge	It may not be possible to meet expectations of deliverables with existing resources.
Context	Resource capacity is poorly understood throughout the organization, resulting in unrealistic expectations.
Action	Promote wider discussion among senior management on improving transparency into available resource capacity in order to set more realistic expectations for deliverables contained within the IT business plan.

Management Artefacts

Management artefacts that may be used to develop maturity in the Business Planning (BP) capability include:

- An IT business plan.
- A business-as-usual commitments database.
- A global requirements catalogue.

IT Business Plan

The IT business plan breaks down the IT strategy into implementable deliverables that will satisfy ongoing operations and new initiatives. The plan typically illustrates how deliverables will be realized using a multi-year investment roadmap (typically covering a three- to five-year time horizon) showing the expected high-level financial and other resource requirements and constraints, and implications for related areas such as enterprise architecture, operations and infrastructure, and programme management. The plan may also set out the metrics that will be used to track progress – for example, adherence to planned budget and resources, timeliness of delivery, improvement in service quality levels, and business value impact of business capabilities enabled. An agreed review methodology helps ensure that the IT business plan is proactively adapted, based on actual progress and/or when business priorities change. The agreed IT business plan becomes the basis for budget recommendations or requests for the following financial period.

Business-as-Usual Commitments Database

The business-as-usual commitments database provides an overview of the key IT services required to keep the organization functioning, the ongoing contracts and obligations, and the financial and other resources in IT (both committed and available). The data may be gathered from, for example, a review of current costs/run rate, data on hardware and software obsolescence, and contractual commitments.

Global Requirements Catalogue

The global requirements catalogue sets out very high-level requirements for new functionality, and amendments to or removal of existing functionality across the organization's IT systems. The emphasis is on having a central repository to facilitate more rounded planning discussions. At a minimum, the following should typically be recorded in a global requirements catalogue:

▶ Project/system affected.
▶ Source/origin of requirement.
▶ Priority assigned to requirement – for example, high, medium, or low.
▶ Description of functional requirements.
▶ Description of non-functional requirements.
▶ Proposed action.

These requirements, along with the strategic plan, project prioritization, and the business-as-usual commitments, feed into defining the IT business plan.

02.5 REFERENCE

See Also

Other capabilities of IT-CMF that have a particularly close relationship with the Business Planning (BP) capability include:

Capability	What it provides
04. Capacity Forecasting and Planning (CFP)	Help with scenario modelling of utilized and available resource capacity
14. Strategic Planning (SP)	Strategic objectives and high-level programme propositions from which business plans can be derived
16. Budget Oversight and Performance Analysis (BOP)	Reviews of expenditure and variance analysis on actual versus planned spending
17. Funding and Financing (FF)	Information on the source, nature, and details of potential funds available
25. Relationship Management (REM)	Facilitation of communication regarding developments across the business that may impact the IT business plan

Further Reading

Hope, J., 2009. *Target-setting: focus on medium-term stretch goals that drive continual improvement.* [pdf] IBM, Actions in Innovation Series. Available at: <ftp://ftp.software.ibm.com/software/data/sw-library/cognos/pdfs/articles/art_target_setting_focus_on_mediumterm_stretch_goals_that_drive_continuous_improvement.pdf>.

Kaplan, R.S., and Norton, D.P., 1996. *The balanced scorecard: translating strategy into action.* Boston, MA: Harvard Business School Press.

Kaplan, R.S., and Norton, D.P., 2004. *Strategy maps: converting intangible assets into tangible outcomes.* Boston, MA: Harvard Business School Press.

Notes

[1] Kraus, S., Reiche, S.B., and Henning Reschke, C., 2007. Implications of strategic planning in SMEs for international entrepreneurship research and practice. In M. Terziovski (ed.) 2007. *Energizing management through innovation and entrepreneurship: European research and practice.* London: Routledge. pp 110–27.

[2] Zwass, V., 2015. Planning for Information Systems. In: W.R. King (ed.), 2015. *Planning for information systems (Advances in Management Information Systems).* London: Routledge.

BPM
03. Business Process Management

03.1 OVERVIEW

Goal

The Business Process Management (BPM) capability helps create an understanding of business activity flows so that they can be more readily understood and developed, and so that errors can be reduced and risks mitigated.

Objectives

- Enable the organization to be more capable of change.
- Drive a holistic approach to process improvement using a cross-functional and organization-wide perspective.
- Correct and improve complex, people-intensive processes before (potentially) automating them.
- Support a better understanding of processes and their objectives, which in turn leads to a more reliable and efficient execution of these processes.
- Provide graphical representations of processes to facilitate more effective discussion and collaboration between process performers, and between performers and managers.
- Make the strategic objectives of the organization more explicit and visible (for example, reliability and efficiency, product or service quality, business agility, and so on).

Value

The Business Process Management (BPM) capability helps to make business activity flows more effective, more efficient, and more responsive to evolving business objectives.

Relevance

Business environments are becoming increasingly turbulent and unpredictable, driven by many different factors, including, for example, changing customer needs, globalization of supply chains, new business models, innovative and disruptive technologies, and so on. In cases where organizational processes span functional departments, these challenges can be even greater – especially if the processes are not visible across departments and where it is not clear who owns each process. To compete successfully, organizations must find ways to respond quickly, adopting, changing and upgrading their processes to align with evolving business requirements. There are countless examples showing significant gains when an organization implements a business process management programme [1] [2] [3].

By establishing an effective Business Process Management (BPM) capability, an organization can make work less costly, design more sustainable processes that are flexible and easier to change, increase speed to market, embed a culture of continuous improvement, and deliver better returns from organizational resources.

03.2 SCOPE

Definition

The Business Process Management (BPM) capability is the ability to identify, design, document, monitor, optimize, and assist in the execution of both existing and new organizational processes. The Business Process Management (BPM) capability covers:

▶ Implementing process improvement initiatives and driving cultural change for business process improvement.

▶ Selecting, developing, and applying methods, governance models, technologies, skills, roles, and communication materials that support management of the organization's processes.

▶ Developing and applying graphical representations of processes – for example, process architecture diagrams.

▶ Adopting technologies that automate and assist with the execution of business process management.

Other Capabilities

The following are addressed by other capabilities of IT-CMF:

For...	Refer to...
Determining the relationship between business processes and underlying IT infrastructure and IT services	12. Service Analytics and Intelligence (SAI)
Providing recommendations on specific architecture specification methods	20. Enterprise Architecture Management (EAM)

03.3 UNDERSTANDING MATURITY

Recognizing Excellence

When the Business Process Management (BPM) capability is well-developed or mature:

▸ Continual adaptation is seen as a natural condition, where organizational processes are modified in response to internal and external events.

▸ All organizational processes are owned, governed, and measured by clearly identified process owners; and the process owners are given the appropriate authority and are held accountable for process improvement and performance.

▸ Organizations can describe and quantify the impact of business process management practices on organizational performance.

Maturity at the Critical Capability Level

The following statements provide a high-level overview of the Business Process Management (BPM) capability at successive levels of maturity:

Level 1   Business process improvement efforts are non-existent, or ad hoc and sporadic.

Level 2   Business process improvement is beginning to be coordinated by an emerging group of knowledgeable business process practitioners.

Level 3   Common business process methods, standards, and technologies are readily accessible, and are used by an established community of knowledgeable business process practitioners.

Level 4   Effective management of business processes is culturally embedded across the whole organization.

Level 5   Business process management and continual improvement are sources of competitive advantage, and empower personnel at all levels.

Maturity at the Capability Building Block (CBB) Level

The Capability Building Blocks (CBBs) associated with the Business Process Management (BPM) capability fall into two categories:

▸ Category A: five CBBs associated with *Foundation* – these define how to establish business process management strategy, and stimulate development of enabling standards, methods, models, technologies, training, and communication approaches.

▸ Category B: six CBBs associated with *Implementation* – these determine and manage how business process management will be put into practice for the organization.

These are described below, together with a summary of the different maturity levels for each.

Category A: CBBs Associated with *Foundation*

CBB A1: Strategy and Leadership

Establish strategies and plans to lead the development of process management activities.

Level 1   There is little or no coherent planning to drive process improvement, or to increase process understanding.

Level 2   Planning of process improvement activities is emerging in limited areas.

Level 3   Process improvements are increasingly planned as cross-functional activities.

Level 4   Process improvements are consistently planned across the entire organization.

Level 5   Process improvement plans are continually reviewed to ensure business process management remains a competitive differentiator for the organization.

CBB A2: Support Organization and Personnel

Establish the structure, competences, roles, responsibilities, and resource levels to support process improvement activities.

Level 1   Initiatives tend to be individually driven. Roles and competence criteria are ad hoc.

Level 2   Some business process management competences are present in localized pockets, but there is no recognized group providing broad-based business process management support for the organization.

Level 3   A business process management group is emerging with proven expertise in some key areas.

Level 4   A recognized business process management group with organization-wide scope is in place. Structured process management career paths and skills development are present.

Level 5   The business process management group has a reputation for excellence across the organization, and among relevant business ecosystem partners.

CBB A3: Standards and Methods

Establish a set of standards and methods for managing processes. These could include modelling standards, process notations, definitions of terminology to be used, improvement methods, process governance structures, and measures for determining value and the effectiveness of implementation.

Level 1	Any standards and methods that are in place are project-specific or are used in isolation.
Level 2	There are instances emerging of common standards and methods being applied to a limited number of key projects.
Level 3	A fundamental suite of common standards and methods are formally adopted, and approaches are established to ensure compliance.
Level 4	An expanded or comprehensive suite of standards and methods is implemented and used across the organization.
Level 5	Standards and methods are continually reviewed to ensure they are fit-for-purpose and that they can adapt to evolving needs.

CBB A4: Technologies

Identify and implement technologies for documenting, organizing, and evaluating process improvements.

Level 1	Some generic technologies with simple functionality may be used in an ad hoc manner.
Level 2	Discrete business process management technologies are used locally, limiting effective sharing and reuse of information across the organization.
Level 3	A preferred suite of business process management technologies is emerging, supported by a central repository of tools and documentation to aid information sharing and reuse.
Level 4	A preferred suite of business process management technologies is adopted across the organization, amplifying information sharing and reuse.
Level 5	Business process management technologies and repositories are continually reviewed for improvement, and support the sharing and reuse of information with relevant business ecosystem partners.

CBB A5: Stakeholder Management

Generate understanding, motivation, and commitment to process management. This may include communication about process management approaches, success stories, lessons learned, potential value opportunities, and value realized.

Level 1	There is no or ad hoc communication with stakeholders on process improvement projects.
Level 2	A limited number of stakeholders are regularly contacted regarding business process management activities.
Level 3	A standardized stakeholder management plan communicates the activities of business process management across the IT function.
Level 4	A comprehensive stakeholder management plan communicates the activities of business process management across the entire organization.
Level 5	Stakeholder input and feedback are continually evaluated to improve the business process management capability.

Category B: CBBs Associated with *Implementation*

CBB B1: Scope of Implementation

Establish the breadth of processes to be managed. This is guided by the organizational context – for example, by the structure, strategies, priorities, and culture of the organization.

Level 1	The scope of process management is limited (typically) to meeting compliance-related process changes.
Level 2	In addition to addressing compliance, a limited number of operational processes are being managed.
Level 3	Compliance and operational processes are consistently managed, and process management is beginning to extend into non-operational processes.
Level 4	Most processes are being managed across the organization, and can readily interface with key customers and suppliers.
Level 5	All processes are being managed across the organization, including those that interface with relevant business ecosystem partners.

CBB B2: Process Architecture

Document the organization's process architecture, using consistent terminology, precise definition of objectives, roles, flows, and relationships, and agreed protocols for process naming.

Level 1 — Documentation of individual processes, to the extent it exists, is unmanaged, static, and has varying formats and levels of detail.

Level 2 — There is documentation of a limited number of processes. Typically, however, attention to their fit within a larger process architecture is lacking.

Level 3 — Many of the key processes are documented; and the documentation is easily accessible and is a basis for collaboration.

Level 4 — Most organizational processes have up-to-date documentation that presents their architecture and shows how they interface with key external entities.

Level 5 — There is comprehensive documentation of all process architecture, including process components that extend beyond the organization – for example, to relevant business ecosystem partners.

CBB B3: Process Governance

Establish a governance structure for the processes being addressed. This might cover process ownership, decision rights, and measures to evaluate progress against process objectives.

Level 1 — There is informal governance for only the most critical of compliance-related processes.

Level 2 — Governance is in place for all compliance-related processes, and for a limited set of business-critical processes.

Level 3 — Governance is in place for most business-critical processes.

Level 4 — Governance is in place for all processes in accordance with their criticality, and is integrated with the broader organizational governance structures and mechanisms.

Level 5 — Governance is continually reviewed for effectiveness across the organization and also covers process interfaces with relevant business ecosystem partners.

CBB B4: Process Improvement

Identify and use available methodologies for evaluating, redesigning, and improving how the organization works towards its desired outcomes.

Level 1 — There is no coordinated or formal approach to process improvement. The approach is typically entirely reliant on individual or local experience.

Level 2 — Formal improvement methodologies are occasionally used, but a dominant methodology is lacking.

Level 3 — A dominant improvement methodology is mandated and applied to most process improvement initiatives.

Level 4 — A suite of improvement methodologies (for example, Lean, Six Sigma, Total Quality Management, and so on) can be coherently blended to maximize improvement opportunities.

Level 5 — The organization readily experiments with and adapts the most appropriate improvement methods to address the needs of the business ecosystem.

CBB B5: Process Automation

Use technologies to simulate, integrate, operationalize, and monitor business processes.

Level 1   There is little or no process automation.

Level 2   Instances of process automation are emerging.

Level 3   Many high-volume operational processes are automated.

Level 4   Most operational and management processes are automated.

Level 5   Process automation and optimization are widespread and extend to relevant business ecosystem partners.

CBB B6: The IT Contribution

Use the IT function's organization-wide perspective to drive the effectiveness of business process management.

Level 1   Any involvement by the IT function in process improvements is ad hoc.

Level 2   The IT function is increasingly consulted regarding the analysis and design of a limited number of process improvement initiatives.

Level 3   The IT function facilitates most process improvement initiatives on behalf of the organization, providing holistic insight into process relationships and dependencies.

Level 4   The IT function promotes leading practices and tools that enhance outcomes for all process improvement initiatives.

Level 5   The IT function is recognized for its thought leadership in proactively identifying areas of business process improvement and innovation.

03.4 IMPROVEMENT PLANNING

Capability Evaluation

Two summary assessment questions are set out below, along with the typical response associated with each level of maturity.

To what extent are common approaches (such as standards, methods, governance models, and technologies) applied to managing business processes across the organization?

Level 1   Process management, to the extent it exists, uses local approaches which are typically incompatible with each other.

Level 2   An emerging business process team promotes common approaches for pockets of the organization.

Level 3   An established business process team supports the adoption of common approaches across most of the organization.

Level 4   Common approaches are used across the entire organization, and are supported by a dedicated business process function.

Level 5   Industry leading approaches are embedded across the entire organization.

How are process improvement opportunities managed for their business value contribution?

Level 1   Potential business value is not prioritized as a criterion for process improvement opportunities.

Level 2   Process improvement opportunities are occasionally prioritized within pockets of the organization.

Level 3   Process improvement opportunities are regularly prioritized based on their potential business value contribution across most of the organization.

Level 4   Process improvement opportunities are systematically prioritized to deliver business value across the whole organization.

Level 5   Process improvement opportunities are continually managed to optimize business value across relevant business ecosystem partners.

Key Practices-Outcomes-Metrics (POMs)

Some useful POMs for developing the Business Process Management (BPM) capability are summarized below.

Level 2 POMs

Practice	Evaluate appropriate business process management technologies for the organization.
Outcome	The need for coordinated approaches towards the use of business process management technologies emerges to enable greater levels of sharing and reuse.
Metric	Number of initiatives complying with a preferred suite of business process management technologies.
Practice	Define owners for some of the highest priority processes.
Outcome	There is increased accountability for managing the most critical business processes.
Metric	Percentage of business-critical processes with defined owners.
Practice	Establish a process improvement practice – such as Lean, Six Sigma, or Total Quality Management.
Outcome	Effectiveness in the application of a process improvement methodology gradually increases, and frequent tactical improvements in organizational performance are delivered.
Metric	The aggregated value of process improvement projects.

Level 3 POMs

Practice	Form a business process management governing body with employees from multiple business units to track metrics and milestones.
Outcome	A business process management capability is established with appropriate accountability and oversight.
Metric	Percentage of business units represented on the business process management governing body.
Practice	Create a business process management community of practice that is accountable for the development of business process management.
Outcome	There is improved sharing of proven practices, and deepening of skills.
Metric	Number of relevant personnel belonging to a business process management community of practice.
Practice	Ensure that process improvement projects that span multiple business units have the backing of senior management and are adequately resourced.
Outcome	Process improvement projects generate significant value for the organization.
Metric	The value created from process improvement projects as a percentage of organizational costs (or revenues).

Level 4 POMs

Practice	Promote the process improvement strategy organization-wide.
Outcome	An organization-wide focus can be prioritized over local or functional priorities, yielding higher value returns.
Metric	Percentage of process improvement initiatives spanning multiple business units.
Practice	Establish a central business process management support group to take organization-wide responsibility for standards, methods, and models, and so on.
Outcome	A common set of practices for driving process improvement becomes deeply embedded in the culture of the organization.
Metric	Percentage of business process initiatives that use a common set of practices.
Practice	Ensure that all relevant processes are owned and managed.
Outcome	Process ownership and accountability across the organization help eliminate and/or reduce bottlenecks, poor hand-offs, and so on.
Metric	Percentage of relevant processes with assigned ownership.
Practice	Take a portfolio approach to process improvement so that individual process improvement projects are prioritized and sequenced by reference to the entire portfolio or suite of process improvement projects.
Outcome	The organization's process improvement portfolio is designed to deliver optimal financial and strategic value, and is considered a major contributor to business value.
Metric	Year-on-year improvements in return on investment (ROI) from the process improvement portfolio.

Level 5 POMs

Practice	Make knowledge of business processes a core competency for all managers.
Outcome	Managers understand business process management and know how to derive value from it.
Metric	The business process management training and experience levels of managers.
Practice	Manage and continually improve processes that involve relevant business ecosystem partners.
Outcome	Process management and optimization beyond the boundaries of the organization deliver recognizable competitive advantages.
Metric	Number of agreements with third parties for integrated management of processes.
Practice	Regularly review how the portfolio of process improvement opportunities can influence the development of the business model.
Outcome	The organization can articulate the strategic value of its process improvements.
Metric	Number of independently verified process improvements or innovations that raise the organization's performance for a given function.

Addressing Typical Challenges

Some typical challenges that can arise in attempting to develop maturity in the Business Process Management (BPM) capability are set out below.

Challenge	The prevalence of a silo culture with poor communication across business functions.
Context	Some organizations tend to be defined in functional silos or separate business units that can limit the return on investment from business process management efforts at an organizational level.
Action	Develop an organizational culture that encourages different business units to work in harmony, so that they eliminate potential competition between them, and overcome obstacles to cooperation.
Challenge	The failure of business process management to deliver tangible value, with the consequent risk that investment in it will be cut.
Context	Implementing business process management across the organization is a complex undertaking that requires considerable commitment of financial and other resources.
Action	Encourage senior management to commit to overcoming bureaucratic and cultural obstacles to business process management. Ensure the required expertise is in place for business process management implementation.

Challenge	Over-emphasis on process tools and methods, rather than on business value.
Context	Because of the complexity and scope of business process management there can be a tendency to focus on tools and methods, rather than on adding value to the organization. This can be particularly challenging when business process management is led by or biased towards a single business unit.
Action	Ensure business process management teams are representative of the wider organizational interests. Monitor process performance and prioritize a programme of process changes based on objective value contributions.
Challenge	Volatility or fragmentation of the working environment arising from significant organizational change – as can happen, for example, with start-ups, or with organizations undergoing significant change or crisis management.
Context	An organization that is living 'hand to mouth' is not usually in a position to give organizational priority to required medium- or longer-term changes.
Action	Start with simple and tactically focused management of the organization's processes. Concentrate on improvements that deliver quick wins and build upon early successes.

Management Artefacts

Management artefacts that may be used to develop maturity in the Business Process Management (BPM) capability include:

▸ A business process management policy.
▸ A business process management governance model.
▸ A business process management technology suite.
▸ A business process model and notation.

Business Process Management Policy

The business process management policy identifies the scope and objectives of business process management, and how it is aligned to the organization's strategic plans. It describes how to develop a process improvement culture and documents the business process management training topics and priorities. It also provides detailed procedures for prioritization, and protocols for business process management reporting and communication.

Business Process Management Governance Model

A business process management governance model sets out the rules and structures regarding the management of business processes, and it defines the standards and priorities for business process management across the organization. It identifies the governance leaders and defines the roles and responsibilities of the business process management participants. The governance model's primary goal is to ensure that the organization's business processes are optimized and that the organization's workflows are efficient and effective.

Business Process Management Technology Suite

Business process management requires appropriate technologies and tools for visual modelling, simulation, automation, integration, and the control and monitoring of business processes, together with the information systems that support them. A business process management technology suite helps ensure that the appropriate technologies and tools are used to manage the improvement cycle, from process design to process monitoring and optimization, and to enhance the organization's ability to change business processes so that it can adjust rapidly to changing circumstances. It also helps to facilitate greater levels of sharing and reuse of business process information.

Business Process Model and Notation

A business process model is an analytical representation of the organization's business processes. It is generally regarded as a critical component of business process management that should be used to map out the organization's current processes and that should act as the basis for the design and management of any changes that are required by process improvement efforts, organizational changes, and so on. Process modelling uses a standard method of illustrating processes with flowchart-like diagrams that can be easily understood by both IT and other business managers.

03.5 REFERENCE

See Also

Other capabilities of IT-CMF that have a particularly close relationship with the Business Process Management (BPM) capability include:

Capability	What it provides
02. Business Planning (BP)	A business plan with potential areas of improvements, and baseline and target metrics
11. Risk Management (RM)	Risk metrics and areas where processes may be improved with a view to reducing risk
12. Service Analytics and Intelligence (SAI)	Analysis of how to meet business process performance objectives
20. Enterprise Architecture Management (EAM)	The architecture framework, including the business architecture, in which business process management operates

Further Reading

Boots, J., 2012. *BPM boots on the ground: how to implement strategic business process management*. Tampa, FL: Meghan Kiffer Press.

Davenport, T.H., 1993. *Process innovation: reengineering work through information technology*. Boston, MA: Harvard Business School Press.

La Rosa, M., and Soffer, P., 2015. Special issue on best papers from the 'BPM 2012' workshops. *Information Systems and e-Business Management,* 2015 (13), 1–3.

Notes

[1] Harry, M., and Schroeder, R., 2006. *Six Sigma: the breakthrough management strategy revolutionizing the world's top corporations*. New York, NY: Crown Business.

[2] Gartner, 2005. Business process management's success hinges on business-led initiatives. Available at: <http://www.gartner.com/doc/483847/business-process-managements-success-hinges>.

[3] Westerman, J., 2009. *The case for business process management*. [pdf] BPTrends. Available at: <http://www.bptrends.com/publicationfiles/04-09-CS-Case-for-BPM-TIBCO.doc.pdf>.

CFP

04. Capacity Forecasting and Planning

04.1 OVERVIEW

Goal

The Capacity Forecasting and Planning (CFP) capability aims to understand what resources will be required to support IT services based on current and projected organizational demands.

Objectives

- ▸ Increase knowledge about the IT resource capacity in order to predict bandwidth constraints.
- ▸ Scenario-model the impact of business strategies and forecasts on IT resources.
- ▸ Inform management of IT strategies – for example, about over- or under- capacity utilization, or about reassigning underutilized resources.

Value

The Capacity Forecasting and Planning (CFP) capability anticipates the shifting needs for IT resources so that capacity can be cost-effectively added or reduced in a timely manner to meet changes in demand.

Relevance

The IT function needs to anticipate business needs rather than just react to them as they arise, to avoid potentially compromising business operations. An effective approach to IT capacity forecasting and planning can help ensure that the IT function can meet current organizational demand and is geared for its future requirements.

By developing an effective Capacity Forecasting and Planning (CFP) capability, an organization can manage its resources more efficiently and effectively, ensuring capacity insights are available so that IT resources can be readily delivered or withdrawn as appropriate.

04.2 SCOPE

Definition

The Capacity Forecasting and Planning (CFP) capability is the ability to model and forecast demand for IT services, infrastructure, facilities, and people. The Capacity Forecasting and Planning (CFP) capability covers:

▶ Collecting capacity-related strategic and operational information.
▶ Designing and advancing IT capacity forecasting models to demonstrate how business forecasts might impact the resources required by the IT function.
▶ Modelling the current and future capacity requirements across all IT-related resources – for example, services, infrastructure, facilities, and people.
▶ Communicating insights from capacity planning to the relevant stakeholders.

Other Capabilities

The following are addressed by other capabilities of IT-CMF:

For...	Refer to...
Matching business demand with IT services	05. Demand and Supply Management (DSM)
Modelling the performance of IT infrastructure and related services to supported business processes	12. Service Analytics and Intelligence (SAI)
Making investment decisions to close capacity gaps	18. Portfolio Planning and Prioritization (PPP)
Tracking the direct and indirect costs associated with IT services and assets	35. Total Cost of Ownership (TCO)

04.3 UNDERSTANDING MATURITY

Recognizing Excellence

When the Capacity Forecasting and Planning (CFP) capability is well-developed or mature:

▶ Credible data is available on current capacity utilization.
▶ Transparent and objective assumptions can be agreed when determining the possible spectrum of future demand scenarios.
▶ A comprehensive set of integrated models is used to forecast future capacity requirements across all IT resources.
▶ Forecasting models can be continually calibrated for accuracy and efficiency.
▶ Key stakeholders have a clear understanding of what actions are required to address capacity issues.

Maturity at the Critical Capability Level

The following statements provide a high-level overview of the Capacity Forecasting and Planning (CFP) capability at successive levels of maturity:

Level 1
Capacity forecasting and planning efforts are made on an ad hoc basis, with little or no standardization or alignment of assumptions or methodologies with business requirements planning.

Level 2
Some basic capacity forecasting and planning approaches are in place. Capacity plans are used in parts of the IT function.

Level 3
Capacity forecasting and planning approaches are standardized, and capacity plans increasingly underpin the dialogue between the IT function and some other business units.

Level 4
Comprehensive capacity forecasting and planning activities are in place across the whole organization. Capacity plans are jointly verified by IT and the rest of the business.

Level 5
Capacity forecasting and planning activities are continually refined to maintain sustainable long-term strategic and operational alignment between IT and other business units.

Maturity at the Capability Building Block (CBB) Level

The Capability Building Blocks (CBBs) associated with the Capacity Forecasting and Planning (CFP) capability fall into two categories:

▸ Category A: two CBBs associated with *IT Capacity Modelling* – these forecast the utilization of IT resources and services.
▸ Category B: three CBBs associated with *IT Capacity Planning* – these aim for agreement on the required IT resources.

These are described below, together with a summary of the different maturity levels for each.

Category A: CBBs Associated with *IT Capacity Modelling*

CBB A1: Model Design

Define a model or set of models to forecast resource utilization across IT services, infrastructure, facilities, and people. Agree on assumptions and methodology, as well as error tolerances for each resource type.

Level 1	Available headroom monitoring is non-existent or conducted on an ad hoc basis. There is little or no alignment of underlying model assumptions or methodologies with business requirements planning.
Level 2	Underlying assumptions and methodologies are documented, but alignment with business requirements planning may not yet be fully standardized. Open dialogue is emerging within IT to decide which resources should be covered by the forecast models.
Level 3	A consistent approach is taken across the IT function to ensure complete standardization of the underlying assumptions and methodologies that are used, and to decide which resources should be covered by any modelling.
Level 4	A comprehensive set of underlying assumptions and methodologies are agreed across the organization and form the criteria used to decide which resources are modelled.
Level 5	The capacity forecasting model is continually improved and optimized.

CBB A2: Model Maintenance

Monitor the modelling accuracy (for example, by comparing actual to forecast resource utilization) and manage efficiency (for example, automation and data availability) of IT capacity modelling. Refine and recalibrate the model's structure, parameters, and assumptions, as required to improve performance.

Level 1	There is limited or no maintenance of any capacity model.
Level 2	The maintenance of capacity modelling is defined, but, typically, it is not yet fully adopted.
Level 3	A standardized approach is adopted across the IT function for the maintenance of the capacity model.
Level 4	Capacity models are comprehensively maintained based on error tolerances agreed with most business units.
Level 5	Model behaviour that results in errors outside agreed limits triggers automatic maintenance of capacity modelling approaches across the entire organization.

Category B: CBBs Associated with *IT Capacity Planning*

CBB B1: Input Management

Identify inputs required for IT capacity forecasting. Gather and validate input data for forecast scenarios.

Level 1   Input data is captured on an ad hoc basis, if at all.

Level 2   Input data is collected for a limited number of services and resources; however, data quality is not always validated.

Level 3   There is a consistent method of collecting input data. Plans are in place to rectify data quality issues.

Level 4   Collected input data is verified for all IT services and resources using quantitative approaches. There is an escalation process in place if data is not available or if data quality is not sufficient.

Level 5   The method of collecting input data is continually improved to reflect changing business needs.

CBB B2: Production of Capacity Plans

Compile capacity plans to inform decision-making.

Level 1   Capacity plans are inconsistent; typically they only review the headroom of monitored resources.

Level 2   Capacity plans are produced for a limited number of key IT services and resources, and reflect resource forecasts as well as available headroom. Scenario options are typically only included by explicit request.

Level 3   Capacity plans are produced for most IT services and resources, with standardized scenario options regularly reported.

Level 4   There is a consolidated capacity plan produced across all IT services and resources. Bespoke business-framed scenarios can be readily included alongside standardized scenario options.

Level 5   The production of the capacity plan is continually improved based on feedback.

CBB B3: Communication

Communicate the IT capacity plan to relevant stakeholders, and facilitate action to resolve shortages and/or over-capacity.

Level 1   Any communication of the capacity plan occurs on an ad hoc basis. Actions to resolve resource shortages or over-capacity are typically reactive and slow.

Level 2   Communication of the capacity plan typically happens in parts of the IT function. Action is taken to address forecasted resource shortages or over-capacity, but not yet on a consistent basis.

Level 3   The capacity plan is regularly reported across the entire IT function and to some other business units. There are standardized approaches within the IT function to deal with forecasted resource shortages or over-capacity.

Level 4   The capacity plan is regularly reported across the entire organization, and involves organization-wide involvement in addressing forecasted resource shortages or over-capacity.

Level 5   The communication of the capacity plan is regularly optimized based on stakeholder feedback.

04.4 IMPROVEMENT PLANNING

Capability Evaluation

Two summary assessment questions are set out below, along with the typical response associated with each level of maturity.

How well is capacity forecasting of IT services and resources conducted in your organization?

Level 1   IT capacity forecasting is non-existent or ad hoc.

Level 2   There is basic forecasting in parts of the IT function, typically requiring considerable manual effort, and the output is not always reliable.

Level 3   There is standardized and partially automated forecasting across the IT function, which produces increasingly reliable and repeatable results.

Level 4   Forecasting is standardized across the organization and automated where appropriate, producing results that are reliable and predictable.

Level 5   Forecasting is continually reviewed based on outcomes from previous forecasting activities and inputs from relevant business ecosystem partners.

How are IT capacity forecasts and plans produced and communicated to the relevant stakeholders?

Level 1	IT capacity forecasts and plans are produced in an ad hoc manner with limited communication reach.
Level 2	IT capacity forecasts and plans are produced for a limited number of key IT services and resources. Communication is limited to parts of the IT function only.
Level 3	IT capacity forecasts and plans are produced for most IT services and resources. There is communication across the entire IT function and with some other business units.
Level 4	IT capacity forecasts and plans are produced for all IT services and resources. Bespoke communications target different audiences across the entire organization.
Level 5	IT capacity forecasts and plans are continually reviewed for effectiveness and communicated to relevant business ecosystem partners as appropriate.

Key Practices-Outcomes-Metrics (POMs)

Some useful POMs for developing the Capacity Forecasting and Planning (CFP) capability are summarized below.

Level 2 POMs

Practice	Prioritize which resources should be covered by the capacity forecast models, and document any assumptions and methodologies that are used.
Outcome	Initial forecasting efforts are targeted at areas that are likely to deliver the most benefit.
Metric	Percentage of IT resources covered by capacity forecast models.
Practice	Develop and maintain IT capacity models.
Outcome	Increasing the quality of IT capacity models will increase the likelihood of them being used consistently in decision-making.
Metric	Number of IT capacity models created. Percentage level of IT capacity model reuse. Refresh frequency of IT capacity models.
Practice	Collect usage data on key IT resources.
Outcome	Capacity modelling for key IT resources is based on up-to-date empirical data.
Metric	Percentage of resources with up-to-date empirical usage data. Frequency of data collection.
Practice	Produce and communicate IT capacity plans, including resource forecasts.
Outcome	Transparency is provided on the actual and future capacity of the reported IT resources.
Metric	Percentage of resources covered by the IT capacity plan. Refresh frequency of the IT capacity plan.

Practice	Ensure action is taken on forecasted shortages or over-capacities in IT resources.
Outcome	The organization can proactively avoid any negative impacts from over- and under-capacity forecasts.
Metric	Number of IT capacity-related issues identified and number resolved.

Level 3 POMs

Practice	Ensure there are regular reviews to improve capacity forecast models based on ongoing comparison between forecasted and actual capacity.
Outcome	Improving the accuracy of capacity forecast models helps ensure actual outcomes are in line with what was forecasted.
Metric	Actual capacity versus plan.

Practice	Working with other business units, implement approaches to collate the organization's strategic direction, vision, business forecasts, and operational objectives as inputs into IT capacity forecasting.
Outcome	A more valid suite of possible scenarios informs IT capacity forecasts.
Metric	Number of IT capacity scenarios agreed between IT and other business units.

Practice	Adopt standardized, semi-automated approaches to produce regular IT capacity plans.
Outcome	The production of IT capacity plans is more timely, efficient, and repeatable.
Metric	Cost and time to produce an IT capacity plan. Percentage level of IT capacity model automation.

Practice	Regularly communicate the IT capacity plan across key stakeholders within the IT function and to some other business units.
Outcome	IT and business stakeholders know about the capacity forecasts and their implications.
Metric	Frequency of IT capacity reporting. Percentage of key stakeholders receiving the IT capacity reports.

Level 4 POMs

Practice	Establish and advocate the use of an escalation process for issues relating to data availability and data quality.
Outcome	Forecasts of capacity requirements are more likely to be accurate when there is a process to improve the quality of data inputs.
Metric	Actual capacity versus plan. Percentage of inputs checked for quality.

Practice	Regularly incorporate data on macro trends and patterns (such as industry and global economic trends) as input to capacity forecasting.
Outcome	The IT capacity plans are informed by input from outside the organization to provide more robust forecasts.
Metric	Number of external macro trends included in IT capacity planning.
Practice	Plan regular meetings with all key stakeholders (for example, from HR, technical infrastructure management, facility management, service provisioning, and portfolio management) to take appropriate action over potential IT resource shortages or over-capacities.
Outcome	Proactive discussions take place across the organization to ensure IT capacity is aligned to current and future needs.
Metric	Number of IT capacity-related outages and performance issues.

Level 5 POMs

Practice	Regularly review and optimize the IT capacity models to improve the assumptions and modelling methodologies used – for example, based on agreed error tolerances.
Outcome	IT capacity plans are continually validated for accuracy to meet current and future business demands.
Metric	Frequency of IT capacity model reviews. Percentage deviation of actual capacity from forecasted capacity.
Practice	Regularly review the communication approaches with all key stakeholders to identify improvement opportunities.
Outcome	Refined, business-centred capacity plans are clearly and regularly communicated to all key stakeholders, with tailored communications for each discrete audience.
Metric	Frequency of review with key stakeholders.

Addressing Typical Challenges

Some typical challenges that can arise in attempting to develop maturity in the Capacity Forecasting and Planning (CFP) capability are set out below.

Challenge	Poor communication on IT capacity forecasting and planning between different parts of the IT function, and between the IT function and the rest of the business.
Context	There are fragmented short-term and localized capacity forecasting and planning approaches across the IT function and the broader organization. Facilitating centralized capacity planning is not prioritized by the organization.
Action	Promote awareness of the need for accurate forecasting and communication of the IT capacity plan, and encourage proactive collaborations and feedback on the plan from all levels of the organization.

Challenge	Poor understanding of the patterns of business demand for IT services, and this limits the effectiveness of IT capacity planning.
Context	The IT function does not take the time or does not have the expertise to understand the patterns of demand across the organization. Further, the rest of the business might not provide the required information in a timely manner.
Action	Focus on recruiting/developing people with the expertise to understand, interpret, and communicate historic, current, and likely future patterns of demand in the organization. Encourage business units to work with the IT function to share their knowledge, and to jointly collaborate on translating patterns of demand into realistic and flexible capacity plans that the organization can afford.
Challenge	Lack of an effective business planning cycle across the organization.
Context	The senior management team regard business planning as a low priority activity, and this has knock-on impacts on the availability of suitable inputs for IT capacity planning.
Action	Encourage senior management to take the lead to ensure an effective and integrated planning cycle is in place, one that proactively considers the need for IT capacity forecasting and planning.

Management Artefacts

Management artefacts that may be used to develop maturity in the Capacity Forecasting and Planning (CFP) capability include:

▶ An IT forecast plan.
▶ An IT utilization report.
▶ A capacity management information system (CMIS).

IT Forecast Plan
The IT forecast plan specifies resources that are required to support future demand for IT services. For each IT service, it typically describes the agreed capacity availability and performance thresholds, the forecast usage levels, and a trend analysis of the expected increase/decrease for each IT service over defined time periods. The plan describes scenarios for forecasts based on different levels of business demand, and options with cost estimates on how to deliver the agreed target levels. It also may contain details of the actions necessary to address shortfalls or over-provision of IT services and resources.

IT Utilization Report
The IT utilization report provides IT management with information relating to current service and resource utilization rates and performance. Typically, it identifies which resources are under- or over-utilized, which projects and IT services are consuming the most resources, where there are bottlenecks, and opportunities for switching or consolidating resources. Typically, the report feeds into the IT forecast plan.

Capacity Management Information System (CMIS)

A capacity management information system is a collection of information relating to IT infrastructure usage, capacity, and performance that has been gathered and stored in one or more repositories. It is the single book of record complete with associated statistics and visualization tools. Note that a single system for complete resource capacity management may require considerable integration development to connect across heterogeneous IT infrastructures and other resources. A CMIS typically feeds into production of the IT utilization report.

04.5 REFERENCE

See Also

Other capabilities of IT-CMF that have a particularly close relationship with the Capacity Forecasting and Planning (CFP) capability include:

Capability	What it provides
02. Business Planning (BP)	The business plan to deliver the IT strategy as input to the design of possible scenarios
05. Demand and Supply Management (DSM)	Information on business demand as input for IT capacity forecasting and modelling assumptions
12. Service Analytics and Intelligence (SAI)	Capacity planning and infrastructure right-sizing, based on business activity
13. Sourcing (SRC)	Supplier capacity information
18. Portfolio Planning and Prioritization (PPP)	Current and future project resource requirements
23. People Asset Management (PAM)	Information on current hiring plans and attrition rates
35. Total Cost of Ownership (TCO)	Current and future cost data to help improve the efficiency of IT capacity forecasting and planning

Further Reading

Browning, T., 2014. *Capacity planning for computer systems*. London: Academic Press.

Gunther, N.J., 2006. *Guerrilla capacity planning: a tactical approach to planning for highly scalable applications and services*. Secaucus, NJ: Springer-Verlag.

Klosterboer, L., 2011. *ITIL capacity management.* Boston, MA: Pearson Education.

DSM
05. Demand and Supply Management

05.1 Overview

Goal

The Demand and Supply Management (DSM) capability aims to balance the business demand for IT services and the supply of those services.

Objectives

- Strive for equilibrium between the demand for and the supply capacity of IT services.
- Arrive at an understanding of the total or aggregate demand for IT services, and meet this with a supply capacity that is fit for purpose and cost-effective.
- Forecast the impact of demand for IT services on the scalability of the supply pipeline.
- Maintain a balanced IT services portfolio so that current requirements for IT can be managed, and expected future requirements can be provided for.
- Understand how emerging technologies can replace or substitute current technologies, and open up new supply options.

Value

The Demand and Supply Management (DSM) capability can improve the business value that IT services deliver by reducing or eliminating supply surpluses and missed fulfilment opportunities.

Relevance

In today's business landscape, organizations need to be increasingly dynamic and responsive to fluctuating customer demand for IT products and services. Peak demands can be triggered by a combination of predictable and unpredictable factors, including advertising, social media, competitor moves, industry regulation, weather, natural events, and even market rumours. To thrive in turbulent business environments, organizations need to focus on meeting shifting demand with agile approaches to ensuring supply.

By developing an effective Demand and Supply Management (DSM) capability, an organization can support and enable business services while keeping costs as low as possible across different demand and supply scenarios. Organizations that consistently balance demand and supply can do so because they are either able to anticipate and address small-scale imbalances before they become larger problems, or because they are capable of responding very quickly, after the fact, when inevitable spikes or dips in demand or supply occur.

05.2 SCOPE

Definition

The Demand and Supply Management (DSM) capability is the ability to manage the IT services portfolio in such a way that there is a balance between the demand for and the supply of IT services. The Demand and Supply Management (DSM) capability covers:

▸ Analysing and managing the existing and future business demand for IT services.

▸ Analysing and managing the existing and future supply of IT services.

▸ Proposing responses to address gaps between the demand for and supply of IT services, for both the short term and the long term.

▸ Fostering collaboration between IT and other business units to manage the IT services portfolio.

▸ Understanding trade-offs between satisfying demand and the cost of supply – for example, by using emerging technologies or by changing the nature of the demand.

Other Capabilities

The following are addressed by other capabilities of IT-CMF:

For...	Refer to...
Scenario modelling regarding availability of IT resources to satisfy potential demand patterns	04. Capacity Forecasting and Planning (CFP)
Sourcing and contracting of IT services and processes	13. Sourcing (SRC)
Enhancing relationships between the IT function and other business units	25. Relationship Management (REM)
Managing service introduction, service performance, and service decommissioning	27. Service Provisioning (SRP)
Measuring the performance of suppliers and operational supplier management	29. Supplier Management (SUM)
Calculating the direct and indirect costs associated with IT services and assets	35. Total Cost of Ownership (TCO)

05.3 UNDERSTANDING MATURITY

Recognizing Excellence

When the Demand and Supply Management (DSM) capability is well-developed or mature:

▶ The IT function's ability to predict and meet demand for current and future IT services is enhanced.

▶ Shortfalls and surpluses of IT services are minimized – this occurs through the use of a balanced IT services portfolio that facilitates cost-effective development of new IT services and retirement of those that are no longer required.

▶ Decision-making in relation to demand and supply is informed by what-if analysis that assesses likely impact of different scenarios on demand or supply.

▶ Emerging technologies are rapidly and systematically applied to alleviate demand bubbles or supply shortfalls in IT service provision.

Maturity at the Critical Capability Level

The following statements provide a high-level overview of the Demand and Supply Management (DSM) capability at successive levels of maturity:

Level 1   Analysis of information regarding gaps between demand and supply is non-existent or ad hoc.

Level 2   There is a defined approach emerging for analysing current levels of demand and supply for a limited number of IT services. Gaps tend to be identified after the event and managed reactively.

Level 3   There is a standard approach in place for most IT services to understand projected levels of demand and supply. Management of gaps is becoming more proactive but results may still vary in places.

Level 4   A well-established approach provides a comprehensive picture regarding levels of demand and supply for all IT services. Across the organization, there is a proactive effort to balance demand and supply.

Level 5   Demand and supply management is continually improved to minimize both shortfalls and surpluses in IT service provision.

Maturity at the Capability Building Block (CBB) Level

The Capability Building Blocks (CBBs) associated with the Demand and Supply Management (DSM) capability fall into three categories:

▶ Category A: two CBBs associated with *Demand Management* – these identify changes in business demand and opportunities for emerging technologies that might have an impact on demand.

▶ Category B: two CBBs associated with *Supply Management* – these relate to how the supply of IT services and technologies can meet demand.

▶ Category C: two CBBs associated with *Equilibrium Management* – these aim to balance supply with demand to minimize shortages or surpluses in IT service provision.

These are described below, together with a summary of the different maturity levels for each.

Category A: CBBs Associated with *Demand Management*

CBB A1: Demand Analysis and Management

Analyse business demand for and consumption of IT services to anticipate future demand and how it might be provided for.

Level 1   Business consumption of IT services tends to be uncontrolled, and information gathering relating to demand is typically ad hoc.

Level 2   Basic information is gathered on business demand for and consumption of a limited number of IT services, and a defined demand analysis approach is emerging.

Level 3   Information is gathered on business demand for and consumption of most IT services, and a standardized demand analysis approach is followed.

Level 4   Information is gathered on business demand for and consumption of all IT services, and is systematically analysed. This enables demand to be dynamically adjusted in line with expected supply capacity. Where necessary, demand-side incentives are in place.

Level 5   Demand analysis approaches are continually reviewed for effectiveness.

CBB A2: Technology Impact Assessment

Comprehend the impact that changes in emerging technologies could have on business demand for IT services.

Level 1   There is little or no evaluation of emerging technologies for the purposes of understanding their impact on the business demand for IT services.

Level 2   Evaluation of emerging technologies is carried out for a limited number of IT services, focused mostly on technical feasibility rather than understanding their potential to affect business demand.

Level 3   Evaluation of emerging technologies' potential to affect business demand is conducted for most IT services.

Level 4   Evaluation of emerging technologies' potential to affect business demand is conducted for virtually all IT services across the whole organization.

Level 5   Approaches for evaluating potential changes to business demand for IT services based on emerging technologies are continually reviewed and improved to be highly responsive.

Category B: CBBs Associated with *Supply Management*

CBB B1: Supply Analysis and Management

Gather and analyse information on the supply capacity of IT services to arrive at optimum supply solutions.

Level 1	Information gathering and analysis relating to the supply capacity of IT services are non-existent or ad hoc.
Level 2	Basic information relating to supply capacity of IT services is gathered, and some approaches are emerging on how to influence supply of IT services.
Level 3	Analysis and management of the IT services supply capacity follow a standardized approach, and supply can be increased or reduced with greater ease.
Level 4	There is a comprehensive approach to the analysis and management of the IT services supply capacity. Scenario models are used to proactively identify supply solutions.
Level 5	The approaches taken to analysing and managing IT services supply capacity are continually refined and optimized.

CBB B2: Technology Application

Analyse existing and emerging technologies with a view to determining what are the most cost-effective supply solutions.

Level 1	Review of existing and emerging technologies is non-existent or ad hoc.
Level 2	A defined approach is evolving for the evaluation of existing and emerging technologies for a limited number of IT services.
Level 3	There is a standardized approach for the evaluation of existing and emerging technologies, and this informs understanding of the likely impact of technology change for most IT services.
Level 4	A comprehensive evaluation approach for existing and emerging technologies is proactively applied to drive value across the entire IT services portfolio.
Level 5	New strategies for evaluating existing and emerging technologies are proactively evaluated and implemented, where appropriate. Relevant business ecosystem partners are systematically consulted as part of the evaluation.

Category C: CBBs Associated with *Equilibrium Management*

CBB C1: Gap Management

Ensure IT services meet business needs by addressing projected gaps between the supply of IT services and likely business demand. This might include measures such as capacity expansion, changes in charging structures, product or service substitutions, training programmes for end users, and the association of incentives and penalties with particular usage patterns.

Level 1	There is little or no management of demand–supply gaps.
Level 2	A common approach to identify gaps is emerging for a limited number of IT services. However, these gaps are addressed in a way that is typically fragmented and reactive.
Level 3	A standardized approach for most IT services ensures that most gaps are identified. Strategies for proactively addressing them are emerging.
Level 4	There is a comprehensive approach for predicting and addressing gaps across all IT services.
Level 5	Gap management is continually improved, with a focus on how best to continue to meet business needs.

CBB C2: Service Portfolio Management

Manage the IT services portfolio to include setting deployment schedules for new services, making changes to existing services, and removing redundant services.

Level 1	Management of the IT services portfolio is ad hoc and reactive.
Level 2	The IT services portfolio is managed tactically for a limited number of the more significant IT services.
Level 3	A common service portfolio management approach is used for most IT services, with emerging input from some other business units.
Level 4	The IT function and the rest of the business units proactively collaborate to support a balanced IT services portfolio.
Level 5	The service portfolio management approach regularly incorporates input from relevant business ecosystem partners to dynamically meet demand for IT services.

05.4 IMPROVEMENT PLANNING

Capability Evaluation

Two summary assessment questions are set out below, along with the typical response associated with each level of maturity.

What is known about the business demand for IT services?

Level 1	Information on business demand for IT services is gathered in an ad hoc manner, if at all.
Level 2	A common approach is emerging for gathering information on business demand across a limited number of IT services, but the frequency of collection is not standardized.
Level 3	A standardized approach specifies the frequency and manner in which business demand information is gathered for most IT services.
Level 4	There is a comprehensive approach to the collection of business demand information across all IT services.
Level 5	The collection of business demand information can be systematically translated into IT requirements. The collection approach is regularly reassessed and optimized.

What is known about the range of services that the IT function has the capacity to supply should there be business demand for them?

Level 1	Information on the supply capacity of IT services is non-existent or ad hoc.
Level 2	There is information on the supply capacity for a limited number of IT services. Supply gaps tend to be reactively managed.
Level 3	There is a standardized approach to gathering information on supply capacity for most IT services. Supply gaps are increasingly managed in a proactive manner.
Level 4	Information on supply capacity is comprehensively gathered for all IT services. Supply gaps are always proactively managed between the IT function and the rest of the business.
Level 5	Information on supply capacity is proactively optimized with regular involvement of relevant business ecosystem partners.

Key Practices-Outcomes-Metrics (POMs)

Some useful POMs for developing the Demand and Supply Management (DSM) capability are summarized below.

Level 2 POMs

Practice	Maintain information on business consumption levels for a subset of key IT services.
Outcome	Information helps make the case for resource assignment and validates the relevance of current IT services.
Metric	Number and percentage of IT services analysed within the IT services catalogue.
Practice	Develop a methodology for consistently conducting evaluations of existing and emerging technologies on a scheduled basis.
Outcome	Technologies are evaluated periodically with a view to building a case for introducing, retaining, upgrading, or replacing them.
Metric	Number of technology evaluations per annum.
Practice	Create a formal documented record of the IT services portfolio.
Outcome	A formal documented record represents the menu of available IT services, and facilitates planning discussions on how best to manage business demand for IT services.
Metric	Frequency of reviews and updates to the IT services portfolio record.

Level 3 POMs

Practice	Document the gaps between current demand for and supply of existing IT services, and how these could be addressed with new or emerging technologies.
Outcome	A robust business case can be made for investment in appropriate technologies.
Metric	Percentage of identified gaps in demand–supply where new or emerging technologies have the potential to deliver positive return on investment (ROI).
Practice	Activate a formal process of dialogue between IT and the other business units to develop a shared understanding of business demand.
Outcome	Business requirements can be centrally documented and catalogued, enabling more holistic discussions regarding how to satisfy business demand.
Metric	Number of business requirements that are centrally documented.
Practice	Engage key stakeholders across IT and some other business units to discuss the balance of supply and demand across the IT services portfolio.
Outcome	The IT services portfolio is periodically reviewed and where necessary realigned to meet business demand.
Metric	Percentage of IT services reviewed per annum to assess their alignment with business demand.

Level 4 POMs

Practice	Institute an organization-wide policy to moderate the demand for IT services, without negatively impacting business productivity.
Outcome	Gaps between demand and supply are smaller, and faster re-alignment with respect to demand-supply variances is possible.
Metric	Average time taken to address demand–supply variances for IT services.
Practice	Conduct discussions between the IT function and the rest of the business regarding fluctuations and variations in business demand for IT services.
Outcome	There is greater organization-wide understanding of business demand fluctuations, their underlying drivers, and how necessary supply adjustments can be proactively planned.
Metric	Percentage of business demand opportunities fulfilled.
Practice	Collate information from various sources on current and future supply capacities to support IT services. Monitor industry trends and innovate accordingly.
Outcome	There is a coherent picture of current and future supply capacity, and this forms the basis for discussion between the IT function and the rest of the business, and between the IT function and external suppliers.
Metric	Percentage of IT services whose supply capacities are known and documented.
Practice	Make sure that proactive and structured communication takes place with all relevant stakeholders, and that this is an integral part of service portfolio management.
Outcome	Stakeholders collaborate in keeping the IT services portfolio up to date, and are in turn kept up to date regarding planned operational peaks and troughs, as well as planned events – and this helps prevent shortages or service outages.
Metric	Frequency of communication with stakeholders relating to the IT services portfolio.

Level 5 POMs

Practice	Regularly review and optimize strategies for collecting and processing information relating to business demand for IT services, and for translating such information into defined IT requirements.
Outcome	Knowledge about business demand for IT services is continually kept up to date, thereby reducing the possibility of unexpected demand spikes or falls.
Metric	Number of updates to the services portfolio per annum.
Practice	Review strategies for investment in emerging and existing technologies on a regular basis.
Outcome	IT can better meet business needs using an appropriate blend of technologies.
Metric	Percentage of business customers who are satisfied that they are being offered appropriate technologies and services.

Practice	Continually review and optimize strategies for collecting and processing information on supply capacities.
Outcome	Information on supply capacities is optimized to ensure that appropriate solutions can be offered in a timely manner to meet demand for IT services.
Metric	Number of updates to the IT services portfolio per annum to meet demands for IT services.
Practice	Integrate IT services portfolio management as a key element of organizational strategy planning.
Outcome	The IT services portfolio is continually optimized to balance supply with demand.
Metric	Number of supply–demand mismatches for key IT services.

Addressing Typical Challenges

Some typical challenges that can arise in attempting to develop maturity in the Demand and Supply Management (DSM) capability are set out below.

Challenge	There are regular gaps between the anticipated demand and the actual supply of IT services.
Context	Identifying business demand levels doesn't involve the IT function.
Action	Indicate the adverse business and IT reputational damage that shortages or outages of services might have – for example, value at risk. Promote cross-functional collaboration, communication, and the use of shared operations diaries for the effective supply management of IT services to meet business demand.
Challenge	Other business units assume the supply of IT services to be instantaneous and infinite.
Context	IT service supply interdependencies are poorly understood by stakeholders, and this leads regularly to shortfalls or oversupply, and incurs costs that could be avoided.
Action	Promote collaboration between the IT function and the rest of the business on how best to ensure that the supply of IT services is cost-effective.
Challenge	Satisfying all of the business demand for IT services potentially inflates IT costs beyond what is appropriate to support business operations.
Context	Other business units may not understand the IT function's role in proposing effective and efficient IT service solutions.
Action	Promote cross-functional discussions on the strategies that other business units use to cope with volume fluctuations, and how the IT function could adapt some of these appropriately.

Management Artefacts

Management artefacts that may be used to develop maturity in the Demand and Supply Management (DSM) capability include:

▸ Demand models.
▸ An IT services portfolio.
▸ An IT services catalogue.
▸ A shared operations calendar.
▸ Supply models.

Demand Models
Demand models are sets of mathematical equations that aggregate demand across all business units to generate demand forecasts for IT services. More sophisticated models can analyse pattern-based demand data to improve forecasting accuracy.

IT Services Portfolio
The IT services portfolio is the range of IT services offered to the business. It includes the service pipeline (all services under consideration or development), the services catalogue (all live services and those available for deployment), and retired services (those services not available to new customers). The services portfolio can act as a basis for discussions around long-term planning [1].

IT Services Catalogue
The IT services catalogue is a list of customer-facing IT services provided by the IT function to the organization. It facilitates central registration of IT services, the finding and requesting of IT services by consumers, and service fulfilment tracking. Each service within the catalogue typically includes a description of the service, how it can be requested, how to get support, available service level options and associated costs (if applicable), details of who is responsible for the service, plus other information regarding the specific capabilities of the service. Increasingly, IT services catalogues are accessible via online self-service portals – for example, via cloud-based services. They can also be filtered and grouped in various ways – for example, by a particular theme (such as the most popular applications, CRM applications, desktop publishing software), by applicability to specific job functions, and so on. More sophisticated services catalogues may be automated to provide consumption reporting. Generally, as price increases, demand decreases, assuming all other factors remain constant. Therefore, price can be used as a lever to manage demand for IT services within the catalogue as long as the cost recovery principles (that is, the chosen chargeback/showback model) are transparent and business productivity is not constrained.

Shared Operations Calendar
A shared operations calendar is one where all business units share information on future events, particularly those that impact demand or supply of operational capacity in any business unit. Collaboration across the organization is needed to avoid excesses in supply or unfulfilled demands.

Supply Models
Supply models are sets of mathematical equations that aggregate accessible supply from within the organization and across all vendors and qualified suppliers. They help identify optimum supply solutions to satisfy particular demands for a particular planning period.

05.5 REFERENCE

See Also

Other capabilities of IT-CMF that have a particularly close relationship with the Demand and Supply Management (DSM) capability include:

Capability	What it provides
02. Business Planning	Information on planned initiatives to satisfy business demand for IT services
08. Innovation Management (IM)	Promotion of innovation campaigns to find better alternatives over existing technologies to address supply and demand issues
14. Strategic Planning (SP)	Insights into drivers of business demand for IT services
20. Enterprise Architecture Management (EAM)	Plans for architecture consolidation, alignment, and reuse
25. Relationship Management (REM)	Information on business demand that is gathered during interaction with the other business units
26. Research, Development and Engineering (RDE)	Information about new technological offerings
27. Service Provisioning (SRP)	Information on service introduction and decommissioning, and respective costs

Further Reading

Mark, D., and Rau, D.P., 2006. Splitting demand from supply in IT. *The McKinsey Quarterly*, September 2006, 22–9.

Wisner, J., Tan, K.C., and Leong, G., 2015. *Principles of supply chain management: a balanced approach*. Boston, MA: Cengage Learning.

Notes

[1] Cannon, D., Wheeldon, D., Lacy, S., and Hanna, A., 2011. *ITIL service strategy*. London: The Stationery Office.

EIM

06. Enterprise Information Management

06.1 OVERVIEW

Goal

The Enterprise Information Management (EIM) capability ensures that quality data is available to support the business activities of the organization.

Objectives

▸ Improve the quality of information available at all levels of the organization to support improved decision-making and business insights.

▸ Improve the efficiency of business processes by making data and information available that is fit for purpose.

▸ Provide flexible, dynamic, and centralized data platforms that enable stakeholders to access, interpret, and manipulate data as appropriate to their roles.

▸ Enable the analysis of data and information to improve the identification and exploitation of new business opportunities by the provision of an appropriate linked data platform.

▸ Safely and effectively manage data and information throughout their life cycles.

Value

The Enterprise Information Management (EIM) capability provides appropriate operational data for business transactions, and consistently enables timely and informed decision-making.

Relevance

Data is the lifeblood of any business. It is obtained from many disparate, often discrete, sources: emails, business transactions, operational processes, websites, and so on. In this era of big data, the volume, speed, and variety of data and information continue to increase. In addition, the regulatory and legal requirements relating to data retention and privacy are becoming more complex. For data to be of benefit, it has to address the needs of the organization's employees and customers. It has to be accurate, understandable, and accessible. A life cycle approach to managing data and information [1] can be effective, as this can help inform an understanding of what data is currently stored where and its value to the organization [2] [3].

By establishing an effective Enterprise Information Management (EIM) capability, an organization can manage potential information risks, support ongoing business operations, and enable the strategic development of the organization [4]. It can lead to employee and customer productivity improvements, as better knowledge leads to improved decision-making [5], fewer mistakes, deeper insights, and identification of new opportunities.

06.2 SCOPE

Definition

The Enterprise Information Management (EIM) capability is the ability to establish effective systems for gathering, analysing, disseminating, exploiting, and disposing of data and information. The data can be held in any medium – all forms of digital storage, film, paper, or any other recording mechanism used by the organization. The Enterprise Information Management (EIM) capability covers the strategic, operational, and security aspects of information management:

▶ Establishing an information management strategy.
▶ Establishing data and information governance mechanisms.
▶ Establishing information management standards, policies, and controls.
▶ Performing information valuations.
▶ Defining and maintaining master- and metadata – for example, metadata for information security classifications and continuity management.
▶ Making infrastructure and storage decisions.
▶ Managing data and information life cycles, including data and information tracking.
▶ Establishing information quality with inputs from stakeholders.
▶ Measuring how frequently information is accessed and assessing its value to the business.
▶ Analysing information, including exploratory and confirmative data analysis.
▶ Developing the skills and competences of information management and analytics practitioners.

Other Capabilities

The following are addressed by other capabilities of IT-CMF:

For...	Refer to...
Managing organizational risk related to technology	11. Risk Management (RM)
Designing infrastructure architecture	20. Enterprise Architecture Management (EAM)
Managing information security	21. Information Security Management (ISM)
Addressing the cultural and organizational aspects of knowledge and information sharing	22. Knowledge Asset Management (KAM)
Designing and building solutions or applications	28. Solutions Delivery (SD)
Selecting and managing storage infrastructure	30. Technical Infrastructure Management (TIM)

06.3 UNDERSTANDING MATURITY

Recognizing Excellence

When the Enterprise Information Management (EIM) capability is well-developed or mature:

▷ Enterprise information is used strategically to support the goals and objectives of the organization, and its effective management is recognized as a top priority for business success.

▷ Business, technical, forensic, and operational information is maintained consistently and efficiently across the organization. Data is available to those who need it on a timely and cost-effective basis.

▷ There is an accessible data and information platform that facilitates analytics and business intelligence.

▷ The management and security of information is facilitated by appropriate metadata that classifies the data, specifies how it is to be managed through its life cycle, controls access to it, logs all access to it, and provides an audit trail.

Maturity at the Critical Capability Level

The following statements provide a high-level overview of the Enterprise Information Management (EIM) capability at successive levels of maturity:

Level 1	Management has limited awareness of information management opportunities.
Level 2	Basic and discrete information management approaches are in place, typically by function or line of business.
Level 3	Standardized information management policies, standards, and controls are in place across the IT function, enabling formal oversight of all aspects of information management.
Level 4	Comprehensive information management policies, standards, and controls are in place across the organization. Business intelligence and analysis are recognized as key to organizational success.
Level 5	Information management policies, standards, and controls are continually reviewed based on agreed risk tolerance factors. Their scope effectively extends to key business ecosystem partners.

Maturity at the Capability Building Block (CBB) Level

The Capability Building Blocks (CBBs) associated with the Enterprise Information Management (EIM) capability fall into four categories:

▶ Category A: four CBBs associated with **Strategy and Organization** – these set out the objectives of information management in the organization, and the governance and organizational framework for the information management activities.

▶ Category B: two CBBs associated with **Standards, Policies, and Controls** – these identify and review applicable legislation and standards, and develop and implement compliant policies and controls for the management of information.

▶ Category C: seven CBBs associated with **Information Management** – these address the day-to-day activities of collecting, processing, storing, securing, and managing the end of life of data and information.

▶ Category D: three CBBs associated with **Enabling Business Analytics** – these promote the development and use of competences and applications to support the analytical use of data and information for business intelligence.

These are described below, together with a summary of the different maturity levels for each.

Category A: CBBs Associated with *Strategy and Organization*

CBB A1: Information Management Strategy

Define the long-term value and competitive positioning objectives for the management, sources, and uses of information.

Level 1	There is minimal or no evidence of an information management strategy. Information management activities are ad hoc, and are not aligned with the business strategy.
Level 2	An information management strategy is under development. It is typically largely independent of business strategy, or it may be focused on a function or line of business.
Level 3	The IT function and some other business units develop, support, and implement a joint information management strategy.
Level 4	The information management strategy is aligned with all business requirements, and is adopted organization-wide, with senior executive oversight.
Level 5	The information management strategy is fully participative and continually improved, involving multiple levels of management, and functional and governance oversight teams.

CBB A2: Information Governance

Develop and implement authorization and decision-making approaches that are executed through organizational structures and activities.

Level 1	Data and information ownership and governance is non-existent or ad hoc.
Level 2	Parts of the IT function are beginning to develop data and information ownership rules and governance plans.
Level 3	IT and business data and information ownership and stewardship roles are well defined and implemented. Rules are defined and managed for data and information owners, stewards, administrators, and users.
Level 4	Senior business executives and data owners are involved in establishing information governance mechanisms, and in monitoring and evaluating their implementation.
Level 5	Management of data and information is participative, involving multiple levels of senior management and functional experts. Information management is recognized as a priority for business success.

CBB A3: Communities of Practice

Build, foster, and maintain the sharing of good information management practices among employees.

Level 1	Knowledge of what constitutes good practice is non-existent or confined to isolated pockets in the organization.
Level 2	There are communities of practice around a limited number of key business solutions, where informal sharing of good practices takes place.
Level 3	Communities of practice span the IT function and include some other business units, with structured sharing of good practices.
Level 4	Communities of practice span the organization, and are recognized as valuable sources of expertise.
Level 5	Communities of practice actively engage across the business ecosystem to provide up-to-date information on tools, practices, and expertise.

CBB A4: Leadership

Promote the adoption of information management practices.

Level 1	There is little or no awareness of, or interest in, information management.
Level 2	Local leaders and champions promote information management, but their efforts are typically not connected to each other.
Level 3	Business unit leaders in parts of the organization support the establishment and development of enterprise information management practices.
Level 4	Senior management across the entire organization promotes enterprise information as an asset and a platform for both explorative activities (those designed to identify new insights) and exploitative activities (those designed to leverage new insights).
Level 5	Enterprise information management practices are continually reviewed and seen as a competitive tool.

Category B: CBBs Associated with *Standards, Policies, and Controls*

CBB B1: Standards and Policies

Develop and communicate standards and policies for information management (including data definitions, taxonomies, models, usage patterns, archiving policies and schedules, information policies, roles and rights), and key process indicators (such as service levels for all data and information-based services, and cost of ownership).

Level 1	Standards and policies are determined in an ad hoc manner; some may be available as documents.
Level 2	Standards and policies are being developed by a cross-functional information management team.
Level 3	Standards and policies are in place and are in use across the IT function and some other business units.
Level 4	Standards and policies are adopted organization-wide and are regularly reviewed in light of changing regulations and risk profiles.
Level 5	Standards and policies are adapted to evolving strategic, risk, and technical factors, and are improved based on experience and lessons learned. Application of standards and policies may be automated, based on agreed risk tolerance factors and recognized external standards.

CBB B2: Controls

Establish a control framework for information management, which may include ways to monitor effectiveness and efficiency, manage change, and control access, as well as guidance on data and information use.

Level 1	Controls are defined and implemented in an ad hoc manner, with few tests or reviews.
Level 2	A defined approach to developing and implementing controls is emerging, and some testing of controls and audit trails occasionally takes place.
Level 3	A standardized approach is used to establish relevant controls, and its application is monitored for consistency. A comprehensive set of test cases to invoke exceptions and violations can be used for regression testing and validation.
Level 4	Comprehensive controls are established and tested on an ongoing basis, and there are systematic mechanisms in place to uncover and rectify breaches and quantify risks.
Level 5	Controls are continually reviewed to reflect evolving business objectives, risks, and technical factors, and application and testing of them is adequately automated.

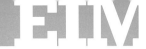

Category C: CBBs Associated with *Information Management*

CBB C1: Information Valuation

Establish and update the value of data and information assets based on criteria such as economic, financial, reputational, and technical risk, age, frequency of use, and position within the information life cycle.

Level 1   Data and information asset valuations are ad hoc.

Level 2   Guidelines are emerging for eliciting stakeholders' views on the value of a limited number of data and information assets. Top-down data and information valuations are available.

Level 3   There are standardized guidelines for assessing the value of most data and information assets (those prioritized by senior management). Top-down and some bottom-up methods of evaluating data are used.

Level 4   Comprehensive valuations of data and information assets are available to a level of granularity suitable for virtually all business stakeholder roles. Stakeholders understand the value of their data at each stage of the life cycle. Valuation methods include top-down, bottom-up, and value-at-risk analysis.

Level 5   Data and information asset valuation approaches are readily and continually adapted in response to changes in the business context. Relevant data and information valuation methods are used. Some valuations are automatically calculated from different perspectives – for example, marketing, sales, reputational damage if data is lost, compromised or disclosed, and so on.

CBB C2: Master Data Management

Define and maintain one or more master datasets, and synchronize them across relevant processes and systems. Define the data patterns and the quality standards to which data must conform in each stage of its life cycle.

Level 1   Master data management efforts are ad hoc.

Level 2   There are some elements of master data management in place – for example, there are isolated master data glossaries at function or department level for a limited number of services.

Level 3   Master data descriptions are in place for core business data items, and some efforts are being made to synchronize data from different sources.

Level 4   Master data descriptions are in use for all data items and are synchronized using batch and real-time automated processes across the organization.

Level 5   Master data descriptions are available to relevant business ecosystem partners, thus enabling enhanced cooperation. Most master data synchronizations are real-time and batch systems are available for some systems recovery scenarios.

CBB C3: Metadata Management

Define and update metadata that indicates the information life cycle stage and access control criteria for both business and technical data.

Level 1	Metadata management is ad hoc.
Level 2	Metadata is provided for some data, but typically this is not done in a coordinated way across the organization.
Level 3	Metadata is provided for data items across the IT services catalogue.
Level 4	Metadata is provided for all data items across the IT services catalogue, and there is agreement on the structure and protocols for metadata. Metadata is mapped to business processes for context, and dependencies between metadata are identified.
Level 5	Metadata enables the optimized use and control of data and information across the organization, and also with relevant business ecosystem partners.

CBB C4: Information Quality

Establish policies that promote data and information quality.

Level 1	Data and information quality policies are implemented on an ad hoc basis.
Level 2	Data and information quality policies identify issues for a limited number of areas that are particularly data quality-sensitive within the IT function. Training on data and information quality policies is emerging for selected employees.
Level 3	Data and information quality roles are defined and training programmes are in place across the IT function and some other business units. Employees are trained on data and information quality, and advised on how the policies and standards impact on their roles and those of others.
Level 4	Data and information quality policies are applied throughout the organization. Regular audits ensure high levels of compliance.
Level 5	Data and information quality policies, processes, and techniques are regularly reviewed and updated as appropriate, with regular input from relevant business ecosystem partners.

CBB C5: Information Life Cycle Management

Define and manage the life cycle for business, technical, and forensics data and information to ensure that it is accurate, available, and accessible, and that it is removed at the end of its useful life. Life cycle management extends to archive maintenance.

Level 1   Information life cycles are non-existent or are defined in an ad hoc manner.

Level 2   Some basic information life cycles are defined at the process or function level to satisfy a limited number of business transaction needs.

Level 3   Information life cycles are defined for all key assets, and are agreed between the IT function and some other business units. Managing information across multiple life cycles is emerging.

Level 4   The management of information life cycles supports the needs of most stakeholders across the organization. There is a multi-life cycle management approach in place – the organization can typically manage data and information along more than one life cycle.

Level 5   Information life cycle management is continually improved, giving users insight into data layer costs, transaction throughput, volume of access, and quality criteria at each stage.

CBB C6: Business Continuity Management

Provide information to business continuity planning on the data and information that is needed to support various business functions and activities.

Level 1   The provision of inputs to business continuity planning is non-existent or ad hoc.

Level 2   Information is provided to business continuity planning for a limited number of events, such as emergency response governance guidelines, or the processes and procedures for restoring IT systems from backups.

Level 3   Governance processes are in place that enable any site to manage a recovery. Business continuity planning and testing is conducted regularly, with defined targets for recovery times and recovery points.

Level 4   Detailed and regularly tested recovery plans are in place. The plans include prioritized recovery goals that may affect the order or manner in which systems are backed up and restored.

Level 5   Business continuity plans are regularly reviewed based on business recovery priorities, business cycles, and operations criticality.

CBB C7: Information Security

Provide oversight, processes, and tools to enable the security, availability, integrity, and accessibility of information throughout its life cycles.

Level 1   Information security is ad hoc, and lacks granularity – for example, in relation to different permissions for create, read, update, and delete (CRUD).

Level 2   Basic data and information security is emerging for a limited number of function and department levels.

Level 3   Data security, based on agreed roles and classifications, is designed into architecture, code, databases, networks, access controls, and so on.

Level 4   Security discrepancies detected in test and live environments systematically help to improve the application of data security and compliance with governance.

Level 5   Security oversight, tools, and processes are consistent across the organization and regularly reviewed. Data security is applied consistently across relevant business ecosystem partners.

Category D: CBBs Associated with *Enabling Business Analytics*

CBB D1: Competences and Tools

Develop competences and tools for information management, business intelligence, and analytics to support decision-making.

Level 1   There is little or no awareness of, or interest in, information management, business intelligence, or analytics.

Level 2   Local efforts promote information management, business intelligence, and analytics, but these efforts are typically not connected.

Level 3   Leaders across the IT function support the establishment and development of enterprise information management practices, business intelligence, and analytics.

Level 4   Senior management across the entire organization promotes an evidence-based culture that uses business intelligence and analytics for decision-making.

Level 5   Competences and tools for business intelligence and analytics are continually reviewed for improvement, taking into account inputs from key business ecosystem partners.

CBB D2: Data Provision

Provide data for reporting and analysis purposes.

Level 1   Data extract preparation is ad hoc and resource-intensive.

Level 2   Some functions and business processes have a limited range of preformatted data extracts available for analysis purposes.

Level 3   Data extracts are available for analysis purposes across most business data at agreed levels of quality.

Level 4   Data extracts are available across the organization for numerous business intelligence and analysis purposes. External data sources can be used as required, and could include national/regional statistics office data, geospatial data, weather data, and so on.

Level 5   The provision of data and information for business intelligence and analysis purposes is continually reviewed, with input from relevant business ecosystem partners.

CBB D3: Reports and Analytics

Provide reports for representing and interpreting business information.

Level 1   Reports are typically provided on an ad hoc basis.

Level 2   Defined data exports and reports incorporating basic statistics are available for a limited number of departments or functions.

Level 3   Standardized intelligence and analytics reports, typically based on standard commercial packages, are available across the IT function.

Level 4   Comprehensive intelligence and analytics reports inform decision-making organization-wide. Tools facilitate the production of role- and function-specific reports.

Level 5   Decision-making is supported with intuitive self-service tools for analytics and reporting. The effectiveness of intelligence and analytics reports are continually reviewed for improvement.

06.4 IMPROVEMENT PLANNING

Capability Evaluation

Two summary assessment questions are set out below, along with the typical response associated with each level of maturity.

To what extent is information management recognized as a core activity that facilitates business operations?

Level 1	Information management is not generally recognized as a core activity and is typically in place only for isolated activities and solutions.
Level 2	Information management activities are conducted for a limited number of key projects and business needs.
Level 3	A common enterprise-level approach is adopted for information management across the IT function and some other business units using defined policies, standards, and governance.
Level 4	A comprehensive organizational approach to information management is adopted, with well-defined and regularly improved policies, standards, and governance.
Level 5	There is support across all management levels for information management approaches that are cross-functional and cross-business ecosystem.

To what extent has an evidence-based culture been established in which major decisions are supported by data-driven intelligence and analytics?

Level 1	Some operational decisions are supported by data. Strategic decisions, however, are typically not supported by readily available data.
Level 2	Intelligence and analytics are emerging to support decision-making in limited parts of the IT function.
Level 3	The IT function is enabling the provision of standardized analytical data and tools. Appropriate processes, policies, and procedures are in place to support decision-making across the IT function.
Level 4	Comprehensive tools and analytical data are enabling improved decision-making and innovations at operational, tactical, and strategic levels organization-wide.
Level 5	Intelligence and analytics are continually revised and enhanced based on outcomes of past decisions and inputs from the organization and key business ecosystem partners.

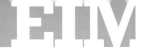

Key Practices-Outcomes-Metrics (POMs)

Some useful POMs for developing the Enterprise Information Management (EIM) capability are summarized below.

Level 2 POMs

Practice	Ensure management is involved in the development of information management policies, standards, and controls.
Outcome	Confidence in a business-focused Enterprise Information Management (EIM) capability grows.
Metric	Percentage of relevant stakeholders participating in the approval of information management policies, standards, and controls.
Practice	Clearly define information management roles, and provide training for data stewardship, quality, and security.
Outcome	Employee competences are improved, and employees take ownership of, and responsibility for, data and information services.
Metric	Stakeholder satisfaction with data and information availability. Number of roles identified. Number of training programmes offered.
Practice	Develop and implement a life cycle approach for the management of the most critical and voluminous data and information.
Outcome	Data begins to be properly curated and deleted as appropriate – that is, the organization knows when it is safe to delete data (all uses are complete) and what data is due for deletion (for example, a personal data retention policy states the data must be deleted).
Metric	Percentage of data sets managed following a life cycle approach. Data sets assigned to a life cycle phase as a percentage of all data sets.
Practice	Encourage business unit leaders and champions to promote business intelligence and analytics.
Outcome	Local business intelligence and analytics activities deliver local gains and enhance expertise. The application of statistics to support decision-making is growing.
Metric	Percentage of employees with formal enterprise information management, business intelligence, or analytics training and qualifications. Number of reports using analytics. Number of decisions routinely supported by business intelligence and analytics.

Level 3 POMs

Practice	Promote regular alignment of information management, business intelligence, and analytics activities with business objectives.
Outcome	Information management services meet the needs of most stakeholders.
Metric	Number of major business intelligence goals and analytics-specific goals set by the business and met by using IT-enabled analytical services.

Practice	Promote metadata and master data management to improve information quality.
Outcome	Information quality issues can be systematically addressed and improved.
Metric	Transaction data quality – for example, the number of transactions needing rework. Analytical data quality – quality should be looked at in terms of fitness for purpose. For example, marketing may be happy with a 10 per cent accuracy variance, whereas inventory management may want less than 1 per cent variance.
Practice	Ensure employees that are assigned to information management roles are suitably qualified and their performance is managed.
Outcome	Reliable and professional information management services develop.
Metric	Stakeholder satisfaction with data and information management services, as indicated by survey results.
Practice	Apply a life cycle approach for information management to most data and information.
Outcome	The organization moves from a reactive to a proactive approach to managing key quality attributes of data and information.
Metric	Data sets whose life cycles are defined and managed as a percentage of all data sets throughout the organization. Number of systems requirements, policy, and process documents referring to information life cycles.

Level 4 POMs

Practice	Develop a rolling multi-year planning cycle for the information management strategy.
Outcome	Adopting a longer term strategic focus will help deliver greater value over time.
Metric	Number of years covered by the rolling information management strategy.
Practice	Use cross-functional teams to collectively manage data and information acquisition, storage, and retrieval costs.
Outcome	Investment decisions can be more holistic and business value-focused.
Metric	Percentage of data sets assigned to life cycles with associated acquisition, storage, and retrieval costs. This can be measured at architectural, database, file, view, transaction, or field level.
Practice	Implement data classifications and access controls in metadata.
Outcome	The management of information artefacts is facilitated.
Metric	Percentage of data with associated classification and access control metadata. This can be measured at architectural, database, file, view, transaction, or field level.

Practice	Design, implement, and manage life cycles for business, technical, and forensics information.
Outcome	Cost-effective, well-managed information life cycles ensure information is available when, where, and how it is needed.
Metric	Percentage of data assigned to life cycles with associated acquisition, storage, and retrieval costs. Number of storage platform moves related to life cycles – that is, does data need to be located in the fastest (usually most expensive) storage or is there a phased movement of data to secondary and lower tier (archival storage) over its life cycles to manage cost?
Practice	Encourage management to set ambitious organization-wide business intelligence and analytics targets.
Outcome	Business intelligence and analytics efforts are focused on issues identified as important by senior management. This focus helps to develop relevant skills, tool usage, and problem solving techniques.
Metric	Number of business intelligence and analytics targets.

Level 5 POMs

Practice	Regularly review and update information management policies, standards, and controls.
Outcome	Continually validating compliance with legal, regulatory, and industry standards reduces risk and enhances reputation.
Metric	Number of compliance issues raised per reporting period.
Practice	Review information life cycles to maintain their extensibility and flexibility.
Outcome	New opportunities can be more readily seized where there are flexible data platforms that enable access, interpretation, and manipulation of data by stakeholders. Extensible life cycles can easily be expanded to include new features or life cycle steps.
Metric	Number of business opportunities that can be pursued because of the availability of flexible data platforms.

Addressing Typical Challenges

Some typical challenges that can arise in attempting to develop maturity in the Enterprise Information Management (EIM) capability are set out below.

Challenge	Returns from investing in enterprise information management take time and are often not immediately realized.
Context	Organizational inertia may exist due to the perception that large efforts are needed to develop information management services.
Action	Work with key stakeholders to identify a small number of areas for quick wins with visible returns on investment. Continue with plans to incrementally build expertise, tools, and processes across the organization. Develop and win support for an enterprise information management strategy.
Challenge	Locally focused optimization efforts may yield quick savings but can impair a coherent approach to information management across the organization.
Context	An overarching strategy is lacking and funding is made available for individual projects, rather than at a portfolio level.
Action	Acknowledge localized work, but emphasize with senior management the need to develop an organization-wide approach. Define roles and assign owners and data stewards with organization-wide responsibilities.
Challenge	There is little support for the multi-year planning approach needed to resolve data and information issues.
Context	Designing and implementing master data and metadata sets can take a number of years.
Action	Seek senior management support for strategic data and information management goals by developing win-win scenarios across business units. Ensure employee rewards are not adversely affected by their work on longer-term strategic objectives.
Challenge	Difficulty in gaining consensus and support for data and information management activities that span the entire organization.
Context	Different parts of the organization own different data sets, and the ownership of data may change as it moves along its various life cycles. Access rights, data format needs, and other attributes may differ, depending on the intended use and purpose of the data.
Action	Build discussions and trust amongst key stakeholders as to the benefits of sharing data across the organization, and how it will lead to improved decision-making and insights. Identify and illustrate some quick wins to gain support.

Management Artefacts

Management artefacts that may be used to develop maturity in the Enterprise Information Management (EIM) capability include:

▸ An information management strategy.
▸ An information governance policy.
▸ An access controls policy.

Information Management Strategy

An information management strategy documents the overarching approach taken by the organization to the management of information. The strategy lists the information types used and how the information should be managed and exploited by the business. It also deals with data and information quality, security, valuation, and the use of master data and metadata sets. It may also specify the methods and practices to be used within the organization to facilitate the sharing and adoption of identified good practice.

Information Governance Policy

An information governance policy sets out the rules by which administration and access rights are assigned. It identifies the data owners, controllers, and all data information roles and responsibilities. It outlines what audit trails are required for changes to access rights and what levels of evidence must be retained as proof of authorized changes to access or administrative rights.

Access Controls Policy

An access controls policy describes how access to enterprise information is controlled. It sets operational limits, alert limits, and actions to correct or bring about good governance and control of data and information items.

06.5 REFERENCE

See Also

Other capabilities of IT-CMF that have a particularly close relationship with the Enterprise Information Management (EIM) capability include:

Capability	What it provides
09. IT Leadership and Governance (ITG)	Guidance on oversight requirements
11. Risk Management (RM)	Guidelines on information risk management activities
20. Enterprise Architecture Management (EAM)	Data architecture guidelines
21. Information Security Management (ISM)	Guidance on information security classifications for metadata to control administration and access
22. Knowledge Asset Management (KAM)	A catalogue of knowledge assets
28. Solutions Delivery (SD)	Solution dependent data views or database stored functionality that modifies the view (field combinations), access rights (CRUD), or access permissions. These changes can affect architectural integrity, security integrity, or validation and consistency of the data view

Further Reading

DAMA, 2009. *The DAMA guide to the data management body of knowledge* (DMBOK), 1st ed. Bradley Beach, NJ: Technics Publications.

Eppler, M., and Helfert, M., 2004. A classification and analysis of data quality costs. In: *Proceedings of the ninth international conference on information quality (ICIQ-04)*. Cambridge, MA. November 5th–7th, 2004.

Seddon, P.B., Calvert, C., and Yang, S., 2010. A multi-project model of key factors affecting organizational benefits from enterprise systems, *MIS Quarterly,* 34, 305–328.

Notes

[1] Tallon. P., and Scannell, R.W., 2007. Information life cycle management, *Communications of the ACM,* 50(11), 65–9.

[2] Wixom, B.H. and Markus, M.L., 2015. Data value assessment: recognizing data as an enterprise asset. *Centre for Information Systems Research (CISR) Research Briefing,* vol. XV.

[3] Tallon P., and Short, D.J., 2010. *Data migration practices and tiered storage management: challenges and opportunities*. [webinar paper]. Available at: <http://hmi.ucsd.edu/pdf/DataMigrationSept_2010_webinar.pdf>.

[4] Anderson, K., 2010. Implementing enterprise information management: a research-based approach in two Swedish municipalities: Part 2. *IQ (InfoRMAA Quarterly),* 26, 34–7.

[5] Davenport, T.H., Harris, J., and Morison, R., 2010. *Analytics at work: how to make better decisions*. Boston, MA: Harvard Business School.

GIT
07. Green Information Technology

07.1 OVERVIEW

Goal

The Green Information Technology (GIT) capability aims to manage IT operations in an environmentally sensitive manner, and to leverage IT to minimize the environmental impact of the wider business activities.

Objectives

▷ Enable the organization to meet its goals of minimizing its environmental impact by:
  ▷ Developing the IT capabilities to minimize the impact of computing activities on the environment – for example, sourcing/designing, operating, and disposing of the computing infrastructure efficiently and effectively with minimal or no impact on the environment.
  ▷ Enabling hi-tech/low-carbon business operations – for example, redesigning business operations using environmentally sensitive IT solutions.
▷ Enable the organization to comply with environmental regulations.
▷ Enhance its brand reputation by minimizing the organization's environmental impact.
▷ Demonstrate leadership in information technology practices that have environmental benefits (planet), social benefits (people), and financial benefits (profit).

Value

The Green Information Technology (GIT) capability enables organizations to minimize their impact on the environment by using IT to deliver Triple Bottom Line (TBL) results – environmental (planet), social (people), and financial (profit).

Relevance

It is estimated that collectively the IT industry accounts for yearly global emissions of 830m tonnes of carbon dioxide (CO_2). This equates to approximately 2 per cent of the total yearly global emission levels and is roughly the same as that produced by the aviation industry [1]. Furthermore, IT-related emissions are rising five times faster than global CO_2 emission levels [2]. Therefore, if action isn't taken, IT activities are set to drive global CO_2 emissions even higher. With the introduction of environmental taxes on business activities, offending organizations can expect to face increased carbon tax levies and a negative impact on their public image.

By establishing an effective Green Information Technology (GIT) capability, an organization can reduce the environmental impact of its activities, improve its brand value, and contribute to its bottom line. Typically, such an approach will focus on reducing the power consumed by data centres and other computing equipment; and then moving beyond internal IT infrastructure to where the IT function can enable environmentally sustainable business practices across the entire organization.

07.2 SCOPE

Definition

The Green Information Technology (GIT) capability is the ability to minimize the environmental impact of IT, and to make the best use of technology to minimize environmental impact across the organization. The Green Information Technology (GIT) capability covers:

▶ Developing a green information technology strategy for IT and aligning it to business requirements.
▶ Planning how to define and meet the IT function's goals for environmental sustainability.
▶ Implementing an IT governance structure that includes common policies on compliance with environmental regulation.
▶ Providing measurement and reporting to enable environmental sustainability across the IT life cycle and the business value chain.
▶ Managing the people and cultural issues associated with the adoption of environmental sustainability practices enabled through technology.
▶ Aligning organizational capabilities that are most important for ensuring environmentally sustainable computing.

Other Capabilities

The following are addressed by other capabilities of IT-CMF:

For...	Refer to...
Redesigning business operations to minimize environmental impact	03. Business Process Management (BPM)
Incentivizing environmentally sensitive consumption of IT services	05. Demand and Supply Management (DSM)
Ensuring environmentally sensitive sourcing practices across the supply chain	13. Sourcing (SRC)
Applying design guidelines for implementing environmentally sensitive IT services	20. Enterprise Architecture Management (EAM)
Managing the computing infrastructure	30. Technical Infrastructure Management (TIM)

07.3 UNDERSTANDING MATURITY

Recognizing Excellence

When the Green Information Technology (GIT) capability is well-developed or mature:

▸ Green information technology practices and solutions become increasingly integrated into the organization and are part of the overall business strategy.

▸ Achievement of environmental sustainability goals is both supported and influenced by IT.

▸ The organization consistently reviews its IT investment priorities to minimize environmental impact.

▸ Environmentally sustainable IT capabilities are adopted across the IT supply chain and business ecosystem, and suppliers are assessed against environmental sustainability goals.

Maturity at the Critical Capability Level

The following statements provide a high-level overview of the Green Information Technology (GIT) capability at successive levels of maturity:

Level 1   There is little or no awareness of environmental sustainability issues, and any IT-related environmental sustainability actions tend to be ad hoc.

Level 2   There is an emerging awareness of environmental sustainability principles and priorities being applied to parts of the IT function's activities.

Level 3   The design and operation of IT activities take account of environmental sustainability guidelines and impact criteria that are agreed across the IT function, and include inputs from some other business units.

Level 4   Environmental sustainability principles and impact criteria are adopted across the organization. The IT function provides key enabling technologies to achieve the organization's sustainability goals.

Level 5   Environmental sustainability is regarded as a key success factor by key business ecosystem partners. The IT function provides the key enabling technologies to achieve the ecosystem's sustainability goals.

Maturity at the Capability Building Block (CBB) Level

The Capability Building Blocks (CBBs) associated with the Green Information Technology (GIT) capability fall into four categories:

▸ Category A: two CBBs associated with **Strategy and Planning** – these deal with the strategy and objectives for green information technology.

▸ Category B: three CBBs associated with **Process Management** – these manage approaches to enabling green information technology across the IT life cycle and the business value chain.

▸ Category C: two CBBs associated with **People and Culture** – these manage the people and cultural issues associated with the adoption of a green information technology approach.

▸ Category D: two CBBs associated with **Governance** – these deal with mechanisms to ensure compliance with policies and reporting protocols.

These are described below, together with a summary of the different maturity levels for each.

Category A: CBBs Associated with *Strategy and Planning*

CBB A1: Objectives

Define the green information technology objectives for the IT function.

Level 1   Any objectives that might be defined tend to be limited and inconsistent.

Level 2   A minimal set of short-term objectives and a rudimentary execution roadmap meet basic requirements.

Level 3   Objectives and a medium-term execution roadmap regularly exceed minimum requirements.

Level 4   Objectives and the execution roadmap regularly meet advanced requirements.

Level 5   Objectives and the execution roadmap are continually reviewed to meet advanced requirements always.

CBB A2: Alignment

Align green information technology objectives between the IT function and the rest of the business.

Level 1   Any sustainability alignment that takes place is informal and inconsistent.

Level 2   The alignment of green information technology objectives with those of the wider organization is beginning to be considered. Formal endorsement of alignment may still be lacking.

Level 3   A set of medium-term sustainability objectives that IT can readily influence is agreed with some other business units.

Level 4   A longer-term vision for how IT can favourably influence sustainability objectives is agreed and integrated across the entire organization.

Level 5   Sustainability objectives are regularly reviewed to cover end-to-end business activities, including relevant business ecosystem partners.

Category B: CBBs Associated with *Process Management*

CBB B1: Operations and Life Cycle

Source/design, operate, and dispose of IT systems in an environmentally sensitive manner.

Level 1   Any green information technology criteria included in the management of IT operations are typically inconsistent and ad hoc.

Level 2   Green information technology criteria, policies, and life cycle management are implemented for some IT assets within the IT function.

Level 3   Green information technology criteria, policies, and life cycle management are implemented for most IT assets within the IT function, and there is emerging evidence of this happening in some of the wider business operations.

Level 4   Green information technology criteria, policies, and life cycle management are fully implemented for all IT assets across the wider business.

Level 5   The organization continually reviews its green information technology operations and life cycle management for adherence to good industry practices, and regularly seeks input from relevant business ecosystem partners.

CBB B2: Technology-Enhanced Business Processes

Identify IT solutions that enable environmentally sensitive business operations.

Level 1   Any application of IT to reduce the environmental impact of operations is ad hoc.

Level 2   The application of IT to reduce the environmental impact of operations tends to be short-term and one-off project-based.

Level 3   IT and some other business units are dedicated to identifying and progressing new technology-enabled solutions that target reducing the environmental impact of operations.

Level 4   Technology enablement of operations for environmental sensitivity is embedded in the long-term strategy and annual planning approaches across the whole organization.

Level 5   The organization is considered a business ecosystem leader in the technology-enablement of environmentally sensitive business solutions.

CBB B3: Performance and Reporting

Demonstrate progress against objectives for green information technology concerning the IT function or technology-enabled solutions across business operations.

Level 1   There is little or no performance measurement and reporting for green information technology.

Level 2   Some operationally focused green information technology metrics are emerging for parts of IT. However, reporting may still be fragmented within local and one-off projects.

Level 3   Green information technology performance is reported across the IT function and some other business units. IT's green objectives are increasingly aligned with corporate sustainability objectives.

Level 4   Green information technology performance is consistently reported across the whole organization, and there is good alignment with corporate sustainability objectives.

Level 5   Reporting on green information technology performance is aggregated to include that of relevant business ecosystem partners.

Category C: CBBs Associated with *People and Culture*

CBB C1: Language

Define, communicate, and use language and vocabulary for green information technology that are understood by all stakeholders.

Level 1   There is little or no consistency in the language and terminology used to discuss green information technology.

Level 2   Basic principles are emerging relating to how the IT function performs in relation to green information technology.

Level 3   Standardized communication initiatives regularly take place across the IT function and some other business units to drive a common awareness of key concepts and practices concerning green information technology.

Level 4   Communication, using multiple channels, takes place across the organization to continually improve awareness of advanced concepts and practices concerning green information technology.

Level 5   A common language for green information technology is used for all key communications and is part of the organization's mind-set – it is used, for example, to reinforce the goals for green information technology explicitly within statements of the organization's core values and mission, and also in communications with employees and customers.

CBB C2: Adoption

Promote principles and behaviours that support green information technology.

Level 1   Principles and behaviours relating to green information technology are adopted on an ad hoc basis and are limited to individual project initiatives.

Level 2   Sharing of basic principles and behaviours relating to green information technology is increasingly encouraged through team events, informal training, and other communication channels.

Level 3   Principles for green information technology behaviours are defined across the IT function, with regular reviews undertaken to assess progress. An informal community of practice network is emerging.

Level 4   Common principles for green information technology behaviours are defined across most business units of the organization. A formally supported community of practice encourages people to develop and share innovative technology-enabled practices for sustainability.

Level 5   Principles are agreed with relevant business ecosystem partners to reinforce the widespread adoption of green information technology behaviours.

Category D: CBBs Associated with *Governance*

CBB D1: Regulatory Compliance

Enable and demonstrate compliance with external standards and regulations concerning the environmental impact of computing and business operation activities.

Level 1	Compliance with external standards and regulations is incomplete and ad hoc.
Level 2	A common contact point is emerging within the IT function to assess the relevance of a limited number of external standards and regulations. There may still be significant time lags in the implementation of proposed remedial actions.
Level 3	A centre of excellence is emerging that regularly advises the IT function and some other business units on standards and regulations concerning the environmental impact of computing and business operations. Most proposed remedial actions are implemented within agreed time-frames.
Level 4	A centre of excellence works across the organization to conduct regular audits of organizational compliance with external standards and regulations relating to the environmental impact of computing and business operations. The implementation of proposed remedial actions is a priority for senior management.
Level 5	The organization is considered a leader in adhering to external standards and regulations concerning the environmental impact of computing and business operations. The organization is regularly invited to provide inputs on new or revised standards and regulations.

CBB D2: Corporate Policies

Establish corporate policies to support a green information technology strategy.

Level 1	Corporate policies, where they exist, are ad hoc.
Level 2	Responsibility is informally assigned for defining a limited number of consistent policies.
Level 3	Responsibility is formally assigned for defining a standard set of policies to apply to all IT activities. Some policies are reviewed with a limited number of other business units.
Level 4	All policies are reviewed across the organization and agreed by all business units with a view to meeting longer-term sustainability objectives.
Level 5	Corporate policies for green information technology are in place across the organization and are actively managed to ensure they continue to be appropriate. The organization is recognized as an industry leader in green information technology by relevant business ecosystem partners.

07.4 IMPROVEMENT PLANNING

Capability Evaluation

Two summary assessment questions are set out below, along with the typical response associated with each level of maturity.

What approach is taken by your organization to ensure there is a strategy for green information technology?

Level 1	There is little if any evidence of a coherent strategy in place.
Level 2	There is emerging evidence of strategy planning and a definition of a basic execution roadmap. However, approaches may still be incomplete.
Level 3	A unifying strategy for green information technology and a coherent execution roadmap is applied to a prioritized list of IT programmes and activities.
Level 4	Green information technology is a core consideration in planning cycles for IT and other business units.
Level 5	The organization actively collaborates with relevant business ecosystem partners on a common business ecosystem strategy for green information technology.

How does your organization measure the impact of green information technology activities?

Level 1	Performance measurement and reporting, where they exist, are ad hoc.
Level 2	Basic performance measurement and reporting are emerging in parts of the IT function for a limited number of activities.
Level 3	Performance is measured and reported for most activities in the IT function and some other business units.
Level 4	Common goals and targets are agreed across the organization for measuring and reporting performance.
Level 5	The organization actively collaborates with relevant business ecosystem partners to define a common measurement and reporting programme for green information technology.

Key Practices-Outcomes-Metrics (POMs)

Some useful POMs for developing the Green Information Technology (GIT) capability are summarized below.

Level 2 POMs

Practice	Develop an initial vision and objectives for green information technology, placing greater emphasis on short-term targets.
Outcome	An agreed green information technology vision with clear objectives can help mobilize the organization into action.
Metric	Percentage of employees who can describe the objectives.

Practice	Agree targets for the establishment of key roles, policies, and compliance goals to support green information technology.
Outcome	Visible targets help mobilize the organization towards fulfilment.
Metric	Percentage of policies available. Number of roles operationalized. Compliance goals published.
Practice	Agree the green information technology policies in compliance with key regulations and standards.
Outcome	Any organizational non-compliance is known and remedial actions can be defined.
Metric	Number of compliance breaches. Time taken to remedy compliance breaches.
Practice	Promote a common language/vocabulary for discussing the impact of green information technology activities and how to measure it.
Outcome	Stakeholders share a common understanding of what green information technology means for the organization.
Metric	Percentage of green information technology activities with defined outcomes using the approved organizational language/vocabulary – for example preferred or agreed metrics.
Practice	Assess the environmental impact of IT infrastructure and services at different stages of the life cycle – for example, production, transportation, use, maintenance, and disposal.
Outcome	Quantifying the environmental impact of IT activities can widen stakeholder buy-in to the green information technology strategy.
Metric	Percentage reduction in the IT function's carbon footprint. Percentage reduction in the use of hazardous materials/components.

Level 3 POMs

Practice	Ensure that the strategy for green information technology is applied to a prioritized list of projects and activities.
Outcome	The organization's sustainability agenda and activities have greater influence across the organization.
Metric	Percentage improvement in the IT function's carbon footprint. Percentage improvement in the overall organization's carbon footprint.
Practice	Provide employee incentives to improve awareness of green information technology and encourage use in business operations.
Outcome	Awareness and acceptable behaviours grow among individual employees.
Metric	Percentage of employees with green information technology and business operations targets. Number of communications showcasing model employee behaviours.

Practice	Mandate environmental sustainability policies across the IT asset life cycles, IT operations, and processes.
Outcome	The environmental impact of IT activities becomes a formal mandate across the IT function.
Metric	Percentage reduction in the IT function's carbon footprint. Percentage reduction in the use of hazardous materials.
Practice	Benchmark the outcomes from green information technology initiatives.
Outcome	The improved environmental sustainability performance of the entire organization is known, and this can lead to the wider promotion and take-up of better practices.
Metric	Number of practices shared across business domains.
Practice	Encourage all suppliers (current or prospective) to provide details of their green information technology practices.
Outcome	A more sustainable IT procurement process is encouraged.
Metric	Percentage of suppliers who provide sustainability reports.

Level 4 POMs

Practice	Conduct joint reviews with other business units to evaluate the performance of green information technology initiatives.
Outcome	The green information technology performance of the entire organization is known, and any performance gaps in it are clear.
Metric	Percentage of business units' environmental sustainability targets achieved.
Practice	Jointly review green information technology objectives across the whole organization.
Outcome	There is a single forum for discussing green information technology initiatives.
Metric	Number of joint business unit initiatives involving green information technology enablement.
Practice	Leverage the success of green information technology initiatives in corporate communications – for example, by communicating sustainability performance and progress to stakeholders.
Outcome	Employees, customers, and partners better appreciate the organization's endeavours regarding green information technology.
Metric	Number of industry awards received for green information technology. Number of times the organization is mentioned externally – for example in media outlets – for its green information technology credentials.

Level 5 POMs

Practice	Continually promote the green information technology strategy at the executive board level.
Outcome	The organization maintains its focus on achieving its environmental objectives.
Metric	Percentage reduction in carbon footprint across the organization.
Practice	Advocate green information technology throughout the extended value chain.
Outcome	The impact on the triple bottom line (people, planet, profit) can be amplified by leveraging relevant business ecosystem partners.
Metric	Percentage reduction in carbon footprint across the organization. Percentage reduction in carbon footprint across the value chain.
Practice	Maintain a continual engagement with standards and regulation setting bodies.
Outcome	The IT function has an insight into evolving trends and can influence future compliance, government programmes, and industry targets.
Metric	Number of active engagements with industry, regulation, and standards bodies.

Addressing Typical Challenges

Some typical challenges that can arise in attempting to develop maturity in the Green Information Technology (GIT) capability are set out below.

Challenge	Lack of organizational commitment and resources to support green information technology initiatives.
Context	Green information technology is seen as a low priority item by senior management – for example, because it might cost too much.
Action	Identify a sustainability champion who can demonstrate to senior management how green information technology can reduce costs, and enhance business reputation.
Challenge	Lack of confidence to deliver the green information technology strategy.
Context	Management and personnel do not have the required knowledge of green information technology, or struggle to see how it can be applied within the organization.
Action	Discuss how to increase expertise across the organization using training, HR policies, mentoring networks, a dedicated green information technology centre of excellence, and so on.

Challenge	Absent or limited involvement across the organization in planning and priority-setting for green information technology.
Context	Historically, sustainability approaches may have been considered too IT-centric and inadequately aligned with the objectives of the wider organization.
Action	Make senior management aware of the benefits that can accrue to the entire organization from planning and setting sustainability objectives – for example, through aggregating and sharing resources, eliminating duplication of effort, uncovering hidden opportunities for technology-enabled solutions, and so on.
Challenge	There is organization-wide apathy among employees towards the achievement of sustainability goals.
Context	While sustainability goals and initiatives may have been agreed at senior levels, individual employees don't feel engaged, motivated, or incentivized to help achieve them.
Action	Promote discussions on how individual employees can feel more ownership of the sustainability agenda through their engagement in shaping goals and initiatives, and by linking the achievement of sustainability goals to job performance appraisals. Provide employees with information on individual behaviours (for example, on energy and print consumption), organize regular seminars/training on environmentally sensitive behaviours, and so on.

Management Artefacts

Management artefacts that may be used to develop maturity in the Green Information Technology (GIT) capability include:

▸ An environmental sustainability strategy.
▸ A green information technology roadmap.
▸ Green information technology targets.

Environmental Sustainability Strategy

An environmental sustainability strategy addresses the entire organization at every level, and is not specific to the IT function. It provides the guiding principles for how technology should be employed to reduce environmental impact, and typically it covers:

▸ How environmental sustainability will drive business value.
▸ IT policies for procurement, reuse, recycling, and disposal of IT devices, and for energy efficient use of end-user IT devices.
▸ Organizational change management and training policies to raise awareness and skills in environmentally sustainable computing practices.
▸ Governance and oversight of initiatives exploiting IT services and solutions to improve the sustainability of the organization's processes and practices.
▸ Measuring performance and communicating results.

Green Information Technology Roadmap

A green information technology roadmap provides implementation details on how to achieve the strategy – for example, the scope of the required activities, the associated costs, the expected benefits, the implementation schedules, and so on. Typically it covers how the organization is planning to address the following:

▸ *Computer monitors* – for example, procurement of energy efficient devices, setting of brightness levels and screensavers, powering down monitors when they are not in use, and so on.

▸ *Computer workstations* – for example, activating energy saving functions (sleep and hibernation standby modes) during short periods of inactivity, completely powering down when not in use for extended periods, procurement of energy efficient devices, and so on.

▸ *Printers* – for example, use of standby mode when inactive during daytime and powered down overnight, not automatically printing submitted jobs (such as requesting the employee PIN when at the printer to release the print job), printing double-sided and in black and white, use of recycled paper and toners, procurement of multi-functional devices encompassing functions for printing, scanning, faxing, and copying, use of networked printers versus individual printers, and so on.

▸ *Network services* – for example, switching off channels and using available power saving modes to reduce energy consumption outside office hours, turning off excess Wi-Fi access points when not in use, use of telephony and wireless device management software, and so on.

▸ *Data centres, servers and storage* – for example, addressing the balance between the IT electrical load (the electrical consumption of the IT equipment) and the facilities' electrical load (the mechanical and electrical systems that support the IT electrical load).

▸ *Specific technology-enabled initiatives that reduce the environmental impact of the organization's processes and practices* – for example, the use of e-conferencing services to reduce employee travel, and so on.

Green Information Technology Targets

Green information technology targets specify the desired set of results expected from the organization's ambitions or efforts. Agreed targets can help the organization collectively understand what is expected – that is, if it's not measurable, it's not manageable. Targets are typically composed of two elements – a measurable criterion and a defined threshold. Examples can include:

▸ Reduce the IT function's CO_2 emissions by 5 per cent year on year.

▸ Ensure that more than 30 per cent of energy needs are from renewable sources.

▸ Reduce waste to less than 20 per cent in five years.

▸ Eliminate all hazardous materials and components within three years.

07.5 REFERENCE

See Also

Other capabilities of IT-CMF that have a particularly close relationship with the Green Information Technology (GIT) capability include:

Capability	What it provides
08. Innovation Management (IM)	Themes, ideas, and opportunities to facilitate the introduction of new technologies and processes to meet green information technology objectives and priorities
11. Risk Management (RM)	Understanding of the potential risks associated with green information technology – for example, auditing for breaches of standards and regulations, or the risks associated with continuity of supply in renewable energy
14. Strategic Planning (SP)	The high-level strategic direction that will guide and influence the green information technology strategy and implementation roadmap
27. Service Provisioning (SRP)	The impact of sustainability requirements on IT service management – for example, the impact on SLAs if the financial close is moved to take place at a quiet time, or if it is decided to move to a virtual environment
30. Technical Infrastructure Management (TIM)	Details on managing the physical IT infrastructure (and related software) components in an environmentally sensitive manner

Further Reading

Curry, E., Guyon, B., Sheridan, C., and Donnellan, B., 2012. Developing a sustainable IT capability: lessons from Intel's journey. *MIS Quarterly Executive*, 11(2), 61–74.

Esty, D., and Winston, A., 2009. *Green to gold: How smart companies use environmental strategy to innovate, create value, and build competitive advantage*. Hoboken, NJ: Wiley.

International Organization for Standardization (ISO), 2004. *ISO 14001:2004 Environmental management systems – requirements with guidance for use*. ISO. Available at: <http://www.iso.org/iso/home/store/catalogue_tc/catalogue_detail.htm?csnumber=31807>.

Notes

[1] *The Economist* (green.view), 2009. Computing climate change. 24 August 2009. Available at: <http://www.economist.com/node/14297036>.

[2] Energy Information Administration (US), 2009. *Annual energy outlook 2009 – with projections to 2030.* [pdf] DOE/EIA-0383. Available at: <http://www.eia.gov/forecasts/archive/aeo09/pdf/0383(2009).pdf>.

08. Innovation Management

08.1 OVERVIEW

Goal

The Innovation Management (IM) capability helps exploit IT in new and pioneering ways to satisfy business objectives.

Objectives

▶ Increase innovation throughput from the IT function by fostering a pioneering culture informed by approaches, methods, and tools for innovative thinking and problem solving.

▶ Incentivize collaboration with other business units to identify novel uses of IT to support business operations, products, and services.

▶ Improve accountability for innovation management by measuring business value and other meaningful metrics.

▶ Promote informed risk taking – for example, by:

    ▶ Harvesting key learnings from unsuccessful innovation initiatives using non-accusatory approaches.

    ▶ Supporting innovative performance of teams and individual employees.

    ▶ Providing more control over how employees approach solving business challenges.

Value

The Innovation Management (IM) capability helps improve the throughput of and yield from novel uses of IT and technology-driven innovation to solve business challenges.

Relevance

Innovation has long been recognized as a driver of sustainable competitive advantage in business [1]. The topic of innovation is increasingly high on the agenda of senior business leaders and, now more than ever, they are looking to the CIO and senior IT managers to support and drive business innovation. The IT function is perhaps uniquely positioned for this challenge because of its connected view of the organization, and its requirement to continually employ strategic technological advancement to keep the organization secure and competitive.

The IT function is, however, regularly accused of holding back business innovation because it does not always share the same cultural, managerial, and practical perspectives as the rest of the organization [2]. By developing an effective Innovation Management (IM) capability, an organization can implement appropriate innovation practices that fit with its specific context, allowing the IT function to facilitate technology-driven business innovation.

08.2 SCOPE

Definition

The Innovation Management (IM) capability is the ability to identify, fund, and measure technology-driven business innovation, which can be:

▶ Applied within the IT function.
▶ Applied to the organization's operations.
▶ Applied to the organization's products and services.

Other Capabilities

The following are addressed by other capabilities of IT-CMF:

For...	Refer to...
Managing IT employees' skillsets	23. People Asset Management (PAM)
Testing new technologies	26. Research, Development and Engineering (RDE)
Assessing and realizing benefits	33. Benefits Assessment and Realization (BAR)

08.3 UNDERSTANDING MATURITY

Recognizing Excellence

When the Innovation Management (IM) capability is well-developed or mature:

▶ The IT function demonstrates excellence in IT services and operations, and has won the right to own the agenda for technology-driven business innovation.
▶ There is a focus on continual improvement using a combination of business change and the power of IT to deliver technology-driven business innovation.
▶ The IT function understands the rest of the business from the perspective of the business leaders, and is proactive about promoting the capabilities of various technologies.
▶ There are enabling innovation management approaches that filter and nurture the ideas that have the best chance of breakthrough success – for example, through ideation, screening, rapid failure testing, and so on.
▶ The organization actively promotes a culture of innovation by the way in which it allocates resources such as funding, time, and people to improve innovation practices, by its strong leadership support of innovation, and by other means, including employee incentives. Informed risk-taking is regarded as an organizational strength; and nurturing technology-driven business innovation is considered part of everyone's job.
▶ Technology-driven business innovation enhances the reputation of the organization.

Maturity at the Critical Capability Level

The following statements provide a high-level overview of the Innovation Management (IM) capability at successive levels of maturity:

Level 1   While local 'heroes' may innovate without any formal organizational support, their efforts are largely on an ad hoc basis. At the organizational level, there is little understanding of the potential impact and value of technology-driven business innovation.

Level 2   Technology-driven business innovation is increasingly observed in parts of the IT function, where efforts are primarily focused on improving IT efficiency. The impact of technology-driven business innovation is measured and communicated via anecdotal metrics.

Level 3   There is visible leadership support for technology-driven business innovation across the IT function, with the emergence of formal and informal networks to facilitate collaboration, ideation, and knowledge exchange, and the use of targeted innovation frameworks, tools, and defined approaches. The value of technology-driven business innovation is beginning to be understood and business value starts to be regularly quantified.

Level 4   There is visible leadership support for technology-driven business innovation across the whole organization, and targeted innovation frameworks, tools, and defined approaches are widely used. Formal and informal cross-functional networks are encouraged. Reporting of technology-driven business innovation consistently demonstrates clear business value returns.

Level 5   Organizational leaders visibly reinforce an innovative and entrepreneurial culture. Collaborative networks beyond organizational boundaries are systematically encouraged. Innovation frameworks, tools, and defined approaches are integrated and extended across the business ecosystem and continually reviewed. Business value, enabled by technology-driven innovation, influences collaboration with the wider business ecosystem.

Maturity at the Capability Building Block (CBB) Level

The Capability Building Blocks (CBBs) associated with the Innovation Management (IM) capability fall into three categories:

▶ Category A: four CBBs associated with **Strategy and Management** – these determine the technology-driven business innovation approach to be adopted.
▶ Category B: six CBBs associated with **People and Culture** – these determine how technology-driven innovation practices, skills, and roles are actualized on a day-to-day basis.
▶ Category C: three CBBs associated with **Methods and Measurement** – these determine how technology-driven innovation is measured and its impact reported.

These are described below, together with a summary of the different maturity levels for each.

Category A: CBBs Associated with *Strategy and Management*

CBB A1: Vision

Define, communicate, and realize the vision and goals for technology-driven innovation.

Level 1	The vision and goals for technology-driven innovation are non-existent or ad hoc.
Level 2	The vision and goals for technology-driven innovation are partly defined in areas of the IT function, but they are not standard across the entire IT function.
Level 3	The vision and goals for technology-driven innovation are defined consistently for the IT function, and are shared with some other business units.
Level 4	The vision and goals for technology-driven innovation are shared and aligned across the organization.
Level 5	The vision and goals for technology-driven innovation are shared and aligned with relevant business ecosystem partners.

CBB A2: Scope

Define the scope and nature of technology-driven innovation.

Level 1	Technology-driven innovation occurs on an ad hoc basis, mostly limited to addressing break-fix issues.
Level 2	The majority of technology-driven innovation efforts are typically targeted at efficiency improvements within the IT function.
Level 3	A significant amount of technology-driven innovation effort focuses on pursuing operational excellence across the organization.
Level 4	Technology-driven innovation efforts are balanced between pursuing efficiency improvements within the IT function, ensuring operational excellence across the organization, and enabling new products and services.
Level 5	The scope of technology-driven innovation includes pursuing new business and operating models to continually deliver competitive advantage.

CBB A3: Funding and Resource Allocation

Identify sources of funding for technology-driven innovation and allocate resources appropriately based on prioritization.

Level 1	There are little to no explicit funding or resources available for technology-driven innovation.
Level 2	Funds and resources for technology-driven innovation are typically allocated on a once-off or individual project basis.
Level 3	Dedicated funds and resources for technology-driven innovation are allocated on a recurring basis from the IT budget.
Level 4	Funds and resources for technology-driven innovation are co-sponsored from budgets of the IT function and other business units.
Level 5	Flexible funding sources and resources are applied to technology-driven innovation, including funding sources from relevant business ecosystem partners.

CBB A4: Portfolio Management

Manage decision-making relating to technology-driven innovation projects through an innovation pipeline or portfolio.

Level 1   Technology-driven innovation projects are typically managed on an individual basis with no common oversight.

Level 2   A defined portfolio or pipeline is in place. However, only a limited number of technology-driven innovation projects are included.

Level 3   A standardized portfolio or pipeline is used to manage most technology-driven innovation projects within the IT function.

Level 4   A comprehensive portfolio or pipeline is used to manage all technology-driven innovation projects organization-wide.

Level 5   The portfolio or pipeline of technology-driven innovation projects is continually reviewed based on outcomes from previous experiences.

Category B: CBBs Associated with *People and Culture*

CBB B1: Management Leadership

Provide visible leadership support for technology-driven innovation activities.

Level 1   There is little or no evidence of leadership support for technology-driven innovation.

Level 2   Leadership support is visible only for a limited number of technology-driven innovation projects.

Level 3   Leadership promotes an innovative culture, primarily among all IT employees.

Level 4   Leadership empowers employees organization-wide and encourages desired behaviours.

Level 5   Leadership and employees are fully engaged in driving continual improvement in technology-driven innovation activities.

CBB B2: Acceptance of Risk Taking

Promote a positive attitude towards informed risk-taking.

Level 1   The consequences of 'failure' from innovation are typically not viewed as learning opportunities and might be punished.

Level 2   Informed risk taking is beginning to be accepted in some parts of the IT function, and 'failure' starts to be seen as a learning opportunity.

Level 3   Informed risk-taking is actively encouraged across the IT function to contain the potential cost of failure and to generate learning opportunities.

Level 4   While reckless action is not encouraged anywhere in the organization, taking informed risks is considered better than always 'playing it safe'.

Level 5   Informed risk-taking methods, training, and incentive programmes are continually reviewed, and shared with relevant business ecosystem partners.

CBB B3: Collaboration

Enable employee collaboration on technology-driven innovation – for example, task forces, cross-functional teams, collaboration networks, communities of practice, and so on.

Level 1   Little or no employee collaboration occurs on technology-driven innovation.

Level 2   Collaboration is typically limited to a small group of employees from the IT function.

Level 3   Employees are encouraged to build networks and leverage them across the IT function as a way of driving innovation. However, collaborative initiatives are not always staffed by an appropriate mix of employees.

Level 4   Diversity of participation is appreciated as a key enabler of innovation. Employees are encouraged to seek out and build collaborative initiatives across the organization.

Level 5   Employees are continually encouraged to seek out and build collaborative initiatives with relevant business ecosystem partners.

CBB B4: Innovation Skills Development

Develop employees' skills to enable and leverage technology-driven innovation.

Level 1   There are few, if any, innovation training or development programmes available.

Level 2   Innovation training is available in areas of the IT function.

Level 3   There is a standardized innovation training programme available to all IT employees, which is shared with some other business units.

Level 4   Comprehensive innovation training is available to all employees across the organization.

Level 5   Innovation training is continually reviewed based on technology-driven innovation objectives and results from previous activities.

CBB B5: Roles and Responsibilities

Define roles and responsibilities within the organization to empower ownership of technology-driven innovation and promote engagement with innovation practices.

Level 1   There are few, if any, defined innovation roles or responsibilities.

Level 2   An explicit role for innovation is acknowledged for a limited number of specific positions. Champions or 'evangelists' for technology-driven innovation are identified within the IT function; however, they may have limited resources.

Level 3   Roles and responsibilities for driving and enabling technology-driven innovation are defined across the IT function. IT employees are encouraged to engage more proactively with technology-driven innovation, perhaps by a centrally coordinated group within the IT function.

Level 4   Innovation roles are aligned across business units. Champions or 'evangelists' are identified across the organization to promote engagement with technology-driven innovation among all employees.

Level 5   Job descriptions and performance review criteria are continually reviewed to reinforce an affirmative culture in which innovation is seen as part of everyone's job.

CBB B6: Rewards and Recognition
Incentivize people to contribute to technology-driven innovation.

Level 1   There are little or no incentives offered for technology-driven innovation.

Level 2   Incentives for technology-driven innovation are applied in limited parts of the IT function.

Level 3   Incentives for technology-driven innovation are applied in the IT function and extended to some other business units.

Level 4   Incentives for technology-driven innovation are applied across the entire organization.

Level 5   Incentives for technology-driven innovation are applied to relevant business ecosystem partners.

Category C: CBBs Associated with *Methods and Measurement*

CBB C1: Methods and Processes
Leverage methodologies and tools (such as idea management tools, innovation prototyping workshops, and project management methodologies) to facilitate an innovation management life cycle – for example, from idea generation and development to implementation and end-of-life.

Level 1   Processes and tools for facilitating technology-driven innovation are used in an ad hoc manner, if at all.

Level 2   Basic innovation tools, methods, frameworks, and processes are catalogued in parts of the IT function.

Level 3   Innovation tools, methods, frameworks, and processes for facilitating technology-driven innovation are catalogued in a standardized manner for use across the IT function and shared with some other business units.

Level 4   Innovation tools, methods, frameworks, and processes for facilitating technology-driven innovation are integrated and used organization-wide.

Level 5   Innovation tools, methods, frameworks, and processes for facilitating technology-driven innovation are continually reviewed, updated, and optimized.

CBB C2: Measurement of Impact
Measure the impact from technology-driven innovation.

Level 1   Measurement of technology-driven innovation is non-existent or ad hoc.

Level 2   Technology-driven innovation metrics are assigned owners within the IT function. However, such owners are not always held accountable for achieving metric targets.

Level 3   Those with responsibility for achieving innovation metric targets are consistently held accountable, and performance metrics are managed in a standardized manner across the IT function.

Level 4   Measurement of technology-driven innovation is managed comprehensively across the entire organization, with a core focus on business impact or outcomes.

Level 5   Measurement of technology-driven innovation is continually reviewed based on its historical effectiveness.

CBB C3: Communication of Value

Communicate the value generated from technology-driven innovation.

Level 1   The value generated from technology-driven innovation is communicated on an ad hoc basis, if at all.

Level 2   The value generated from technology-driven innovation is communicated in areas of the IT function, focusing primarily on innovation activities (as opposed to outcomes).

Level 3   The value generated from technology-driven innovation is regularly communicated throughout the IT function and shared with some other business units, with an increasing focus on business impact or outcomes.

Level 4   The value generated from technology-driven innovation is consistently communicated across the organization.

Level 5   The communication of the value generated from technology-driven innovation is continually reviewed for improvement opportunities.

08.4 IMPROVEMENT PLANNING

Capability Evaluation

Two summary assessment questions are set out below, along with the typical response associated with each level of maturity.

How is technology-driven innovation supported by appropriate processes, tools, and funding?

Level 1   Processes, tools, and funding for technology-driven innovation are non-existent or ad hoc.

Level 2   Basic processes and tools are available. Funding tends to be allocated on a once-off or individual project basis.

Level 3   Processes and tools are catalogued in a standardized manner for use across the IT function. There is dedicated recurring funding available from the IT budget.

Level 4   Technology-driven innovation processes and tools are integrated and used organization-wide. Technology-driven innovation is co-funded by the IT function and other business units.

Level 5   Technology-driven innovation tools and processes are continually reviewed for improvement. Funding of technology-driven innovation regularly includes sources external to the organization – for example, national research programmes, or business ecosystem partners.

How well does the organizational culture support technology-driven innovation?

Level 1   The vision and values of technology-driven innovation are undefined or not shared.

Level 2   The vision and values of technology-driven innovation are beginning to be communicated to a limited number of employees within the IT function. However, employee adherence to them may be lagging.

Level 3   The vision and values of technology-driven innovation are communicated to and embraced by most employees across the IT function.

Level 4   The vision and values of technology-driven innovation are collaboratively developed with the rest of the business, and embraced across the organization.

Level 5   The vision and values of technology-driven innovation are continually reviewed so that they remain fully integrated with the organization's culture.

Key Practices-Outcomes-Metrics (POMs)

Some useful POMs for developing the Innovation Management (IM) capability are summarized below.

Level 2 POMs

Practice	Focus innovation efforts on cost reductions and/or process efficiency improvements or gains.
Outcome	Cost reduction from innovation efforts can be readily visible and can make a strategic contribution to the business.
Metric	Financial savings through cost reductions and/or efficiency gains.
Practice	Create and encourage development of multi-disciplinary teams within the IT function.
Outcome	Increased collaboration on innovation efforts is fostered across the IT function.
Metric	Number and percentage of teams with appropriate levels of multi-disciplinary representation.
Practice	Provide mentoring and training on technology-driven innovation.
Outcome	Initial training helps primarily with understanding what technology-driven innovation is. More in-depth development helps build deeper skills and expertise in technology-driven innovation practices.
Metric	Percentage of the work force trained in technology-driven innovation.
Practice	Promote the use of collaborative tools and platforms to support technology-driven innovation.
Outcome	The collective power of employees can be harnessed by providing more inclusive and comprehensive collaboration and innovation platforms.
Metric	Levels of user activity on various tools and platforms. Number of technology-driven innovation ideas supported.

Practice	Communicate the impact of technology-driven innovation activities within the IT function.
Outcome	There is growing recognition for innovative efforts.
Metric	Number of technology-driven innovation case studies captured for communication.

Level 3 POMs

Practice	Broaden technology-driven innovation efforts to include enhancing business operations.
Outcome	The IT function is seen to drive operational excellence and deliver value.
Metric	Number of innovative solutions that improve operational excellence. Cumulative business value of technology-driven innovation solutions.

Practice	Encourage and support development of cross-functional teams between the IT function and some other business units.
Outcome	Collaborative capability is extended within and between the IT function and key business units, increasing potential to share knowledge and identify opportunities to develop innovative business solutions.
Metric	Percentage of teams with appropriate levels of cross-functional representation.

Practice	Offer career development opportunities, such as technical leadership career tracks, job rotations, or special assignments to other parts of the organization.
Outcome	Cross-fertilization of ideas and practices allows employees to develop the technical expertise and/or business acumen to identify and deliver technology-driven business innovation.
Metric	Percentage of total employees on technical leadership career paths. Number of job rotations available.

Practice	Catalogue innovation tools for use across the IT function, and share them with the rest of the organization.
Outcome	Employees have access to proven innovation tools and practices.
Metric	Utilization rate of innovation tools. User rating assigned to each tool.

Practice	Validate that innovation metrics communicate the business impact of technology-driven innovation.
Outcome	Sharing results increases understanding regarding the impact of technology-driven innovation across the organization.
Metric	Return on investment of innovation spending. Cumulative total of business costs eliminated by technology-driven innovation.

Level 4 POMs

Practice	Broaden innovation efforts to enable the development of new products, services, or business processes.
Outcome	The credibility of the IT function to creatively solve business problems is increased.
Metric	Number of new products or services developed through technology-driven innovation. New revenue from technology-driven innovation as a percentage of total revenue.
Practice	Support and leverage cross-functional and inter-disciplinary teams across the organization for technology-driven innovation projects.
Outcome	A collaborative culture is reinforced and the perception of 'siloed' innovation efforts across the organization is less prevalent.
Metric	The number of distinct functions or disciplines adequately represented in the cross-functional/inter-disciplinary teams.
Practice	Formalize innovation champion/evangelist positions across the organization.
Outcome	A culture of technology-driven innovation is shared at the organizational level.
Metric	Number of job descriptions containing defined roles and responsibilities for innovation.
Practice	Integrate and widely use tools and best-known methods for technology-driven innovation across the organization.
Outcome	The integration of tools and practices is comprehensive across the organization, so that employees have access to appropriate and relevant supports for enabling technology-driven innovation.
Metric	Rate of utilization of innovation tools. Effectiveness ratings for each tool/practice.
Practice	Ensure technology-driven innovation proposals that have co-funding from multiple business units receive due consideration.
Outcome	The business value of technology-driven innovation proposals receives strong upfront validation and endorsement if they are sponsored by multiple business units.
Metric	Percentage of technology-driven innovation projects that are co-funded by other business units.
Practice	Communicate the impact of technology-driven innovation activities across the organization.
Outcome	Credibility of technology-driven innovation activities is enhanced and generates higher levels of support for engaging in future activities.
Metric	Frequency, breadth, and diversity of communications across the organization.

Level 5 POMs

Practice	Broaden the focus of technology-driven innovation to include organizational transformation opportunities.
Outcome	The potential to create strategic advantage over industry peers using technology-driven innovation is heightened.
Metric	Number of new products or services enabled through technology-driven innovation. The financial value derived from technology-enabled innovation.
Practice	Implement organization-wide guidelines to systematically encourage external alliances for technology-driven innovation – for example, with suppliers, customers, academia, external labs, and so on.
Outcome	The IT function is seen as a broker of technology-driven innovation between external parties and internal beneficiaries.
Metric	Number of innovations adopted that originated externally. Return on investment from external innovations adopted.
Practice	Continue to reinforce desirable innovative behaviours across the wider organization by, for example, providing appropriate incentives, eradicating disincentives, implementing mentoring and coaching programmes, and so on.
Outcome	Organizational culture around technology-driven innovation is fully embedded and embraced by all employees.
Metric	Number of technology-driven innovation ideas submitted per number of employees, per quarter.
Practice	Reinforce a culture of continual improvement regarding application of proven practices and tools that can support technology-driven innovation.
Outcome	Constantly seeking and testing novel methods ensures the most effective approaches are adopted.
Metric	Frequency of reviews on technology-driven innovation practices. Number of updates to technology-driven innovation practices.
Practice	Systematically prioritize win–win opportunities for co-funding IT innovation projects with other business units.
Outcome	The business relevance of IT innovation projects receives strong upfront validation and endorsement by business units.
Metric	Percentage of IT innovation projects co-funded by other business units.

Addressing Typical Challenges

Some typical challenges that can arise in attempting to develop maturity in the Innovation Management (IM) capability are set out below.

Challenge	Scepticism that the IT function can credibly deliver a technology-driven innovation agenda.
Context	It can be difficult to own a technology-driven innovation agenda if the IT function is viewed merely as a utility provider, especially where the IT function struggles to provide basic IT services of an adequate quality.
Action	Build credibility with key stakeholders by ensuring IT operations are 'rock-solid' and reliably support stable IT services. Capitalize upon the IT function's growing reputation during strategic planning discussions to help grow a technology-driven innovation mandate.
Challenge	Lack of employee buy-in for technology-driven innovation.
Context	Technology-driven innovation is not always appropriately incentivized. Indeed, there may be significant deterrents that discourage employees from wanting to engage in innovation – for example, a negative career impact for ideas that don't work, or inappropriate performance metrics geared solely around day-to-day operations.
Action	Create an environment where innovation and innovative behaviours are encouraged (for example, by providing appropriate rewards) and enabled (for example, by ensuring there are no disincentives to engage in innovation).
Challenge	Potentially breakthrough technology-driven innovations fail to gain traction with key stakeholders.
Context	More radical ideas may not be understood by key stakeholders, who might not appreciate their potential value or who might consider them implausible, and this could result in missed business opportunities.
Action	Harness the commitment and energy of 'idea/innovation evangelists' to generate support for innovative ideas across the organization, and in doing so help key stakeholders to comprehend how such breakthrough technology-driven innovations could be realized. Additionally, stakeholder support for innovative initiatives can be increased by including them from the outset, getting their input at every phase so that the final outcome has been designed with the stakeholders' needs in mind.
Challenge	Striking the right balance between structured and unstructured approaches to managing technology-driven innovation.
Context	While guidelines, tools, and methods can help channel purposeful technology-driven innovation, imposing a structure that is too rigid may stifle ingenuity and creativity.
Action	Make a selection of approaches and frameworks available to manage technology-driven innovation, allowing flexibility in the type of approaches and frameworks that may be followed. Base such flexibility on the specific context of the various innovation efforts being undertaken.

Challenge	Reluctance to fund promising ideas that may be risky.
Context	There can be significant risks associated with innovation, with uncertain returns and unpredictable outcomes that may deter support for risky but potentially breakthrough ideas.
Action	Develop multiple funding sources and pipeline management strategies for technology-driven innovation projects, which will share investments and potential risks, and spread the intensity of innovation-related activities. For example, this could be achieved by staging investments so that they are tied to particular achievements, and thus lower risk incrementally.
Challenge	Unwillingness to increase funding (or stay the course) with promising or breakthrough innovations.
Context	While return on investment for technology-driven innovation may be promising, it might not materialize fast enough to satisfy the organization's financial criteria for current revenue flows.
Action	Create safe havens (for example, 'incubators', or even 'spin-offs') for relevant technology-driven innovation efforts that have potentially greater return on investment but over a longer time period. This will give the innovations a chance to get established and be protected from the organization's shorter-term financial analysis criteria.

Management Artefacts

Management artefacts that may be used to develop maturity in the Innovation Management (IM) capability include:

▸ An innovation lab.
▸ An innovation pipeline dashboard.
▸ Innovation recognition rewards.
▸ An innovation facilitation portal.
▸ A social collaboration platform.

Innovation Lab
An innovation lab is a platform for the IT function to evaluate and showcase novel or unique approaches to how emerging technologies and technology-driven innovations can enable business units overcome specific challenges. Innovation labs can take numerous forms, such as product demonstrations, presentations, focus groups, or town hall-style forums. The purpose is to provide an opportunity for the IT function to engage with other business units (relationship building), while engaging in mutual knowledge exchange – understanding business challenges and the potential of IT to address them.

Innovation Pipeline Dashboard
An innovation pipeline dashboard allows an organization to have an overview of what is happening in its innovation portfolio, and the stage of development for each of the innovation projects. The pipeline approach ensures that there is a spread of projects at each stage, so that the intensity of effort is scaled and distributed.

Innovation Recognition Rewards

Innovation recognition rewards are a way to give recognition for innovative efforts, to acknowledge significant learnings, and to reward successes. They may take the form of specific 'contribution to innovation' criteria in performance or promotion evaluations, 'innovator of the month'-type awards, or even special showcase or competition events. Such recognition raises awareness of innovation and promotes a learning environment across the organization. Rewards for discovering learning points also normalizes risk-taking within the organizational culture.

Innovation Facilitation Portal

An innovation facilitation portal contains a selection of guides, tools, templates, and methods to facilitate innovative thinking and practices for solving business problems. Individuals and teams are free to choose the most appropriate guides, tools, templates, and methods that best fit with their available resources and skills and desired outcomes. Such portals help ensure that innovation is not stifled by overly-prescriptive approaches and that they allow a degree of autonomy regarding the choice of the most appropriate guides, tools, templates, and methods to apply to each particular innovation effort.

Social Collaboration Platform

A collaboration platform is a category of business software that adds broad social networking capabilities to work processes. The goal of a collaboration software application is to foster innovation by incorporating knowledge management into business processes so that employees can share information and solve business problems more efficiently. They typically come with a common set of functions that support collaborative work spaces – these include issue tracking, messaging, videoconferencing, storage and exchange of files, and facilities for jointly creating and modifying documents.

A popular type of social collaboration platform is an *ideation platform*, which is a way of collecting innovative ideas from a wide variety of sources, including employees, customers, and partners, who are encouraged to contribute their own ideas and discuss and develop those of others. Ideas are typically ranked according to a number of criteria, including the reputation of the individual submitting the idea, responses to that idea, and the feasibility of acting on the suggestion. Ideation platforms often make use of behavioural science methods, software algorithms, and game mechanics to encourage participation and collaboration.

08.5 REFERENCE

See Also

Other capabilities of IT-CMF that have a particularly close relationship with the Innovation Management (IM) capability include:

Capability	What it provides
14. Strategic Planning (SP)	The IT vision and strategy from which to derive the vision for technology-driven innovation
17. Funding and Financing (FF)	Allocation of funding for technology-driven innovation
18. Portfolio Planning and Prioritization (PPP)	Practices for prioritizing technology-driven innovation activities
22. Knowledge Asset Management (KAM)	Details on the availability of knowledge that can enhance problem solving and understanding when conducting technology-driven innovation
25. Relationship Management (REM)	Promotion of greater collaboration, understanding of business issues, and development of networks across the organization and beyond to support technology-driven innovation
26. Research, Development and Engineering (RDE)	Validation of the potential of new technologies to support innovative business solutions
33. Benefits Assessment and Realization (BAR)	Benefits assessment of technology-driven innovation projects

Further Reading

Baldwin, E., and Curley, M., 2007. *Managing IT innovation for business value: practical strategies for IT and business managers* (IT Best Practices Series). Hillsboro, OR: Intel Press.

Chesbrough, H.W., 2003. *Open innovation: the new imperative for creating and profiting from technology.* Boston, MA: Harvard Business School Publishing.

Christensen, C.M., 1997. *The innovator's dilemma: when new technologies cause great firms to fail.* Boston, MA: Harvard Business Review Press.

Tidd, J., and Bessant, J., 2013. *Managing innovation: integrating technological, market and organizational change.* Chichester: Wiley.

Notes

[1] Keeley, L., Walters, H., Pikkel, R., and Quinn, B., 2013. *Ten types of innovation: the discipline of building breakthroughs*. Hoboken, NJ: Wiley.

[2] Allen, T., and Henn, G., 2007. *The organization and architecture of innovation: managing the flow of technology*. New York, NY: Routledge.

ITG
09. IT Leadership and Governance

09.1 OVERVIEW

Goal

The IT Leadership and Governance (ITG) capability establishes a leadership style, and ensures that distributed IT decisions are supportive of the organization's strategic goals and objectives.

Objectives

▸ Establish the IT leadership competences required to drive organizational progress and win stakeholder support.
▸ Enhance the business orientation and engagement of IT leaders.
▸ Establish IT governance as a central component of effective corporate governance.
▸ Improve confidence in, and the agility and transparency of IT decision-making.
▸ Establish appropriate IT accountability mechanisms.
▸ Establish oversight structures to support compliance with ethical, legislative, and/or regulatory obligations.
▸ Provide broad oversight on the performance of IT in the organization.

Value

The IT Leadership and Governance (ITG) capability can improve the direction and consistency of leadership and distributed IT decision-making throughout the organization, and accelerate realization of the organization's strategic goals and objectives.

Relevance

Emerging and disruptive technologies can transform an entire organization and change its relationships with its customers, partners, and suppliers. However, without clear IT leadership and governance approaches, the organization may be exposed to heightened risk, inappropriate resource allocation, and poor performance from IT. Effective IT leadership is necessary to encourage commitment to the purpose and value proposition of IT, and to set accountabilities for value delivery. Appropriate governance (including decision rights and oversight mechanisms) is required to enable the IT function to move swiftly and as a cohesive unit so that it can extract full business value from technology-enabled business investments.

By establishing an IT Leadership and Governance (ITG) capability, an organization can effectively and efficiently deploy IT in pursuit of its business goals. The IT leadership team steers the IT function in a direction supportive of the organization's goals and best interests. IT governance is integrated with the wider corporate governance function, with IT decisions jointly and consistently taken by the IT function and other business unit leaders [1]. The ability of the IT function to demonstrate leadership and governance through improved accountability mechanisms and structures will help ensure that the IT function takes appropriate decisions in support of the business strategy, reacts to legislative demands, manages IT resources and risks effectively, and contributes value to the organization [2].

09.2 SCOPE

Definition

The IT Leadership and Governance (ITG) capability is the ability to motivate employees towards a common strategic direction and value proposition, and to establish appropriate IT decision-making bodies and processes, including mechanisms for IT escalation, accountability, and oversight. While the leadership aspect establishes the IT function's direction, it cannot directly affect all IT decisions distributed across the various levels in the organization. The governance aspect addresses this by establishing appropriate IT decision rights, and mechanisms for accountability and oversight. The IT Leadership and Governance (ITG) capability covers:

▸ Uniting the IT function around a shared IT value proposition, vision, and direction.
▸ Determining the effectiveness of the partnership between IT and other business units.
▸ Determining the effectiveness of IT leadership.
▸ Establishing governance/decision-making bodies and processes, including decision rights, accountabilities, and escalation paths.

Other Capabilities

The following are addressed by other capabilities of IT-CMF:

For...	Refer to...
Implementing organization design	10. Organization Design and Planning (ODP)
Managing organizational risks	11. Risk Management (RM)
Developing a strategic plan for the IT function	14. Strategic Planning (SP)
Prioritizing and selecting programmes and projects for the IT investment portfolio	18. Portfolio Planning and Prioritization (PPP)
Developing leadership skills of individual employees	23. People Asset Management (PAM)
Managing individual programmes and projects	24. Programme and Project Management (PPM)

The IT Leadership and Governance (ITG) capability provides the overarching context for many of the above capabilities.

09.3 UNDERSTANDING MATURITY

Recognizing Excellence

When the IT Leadership and Governance (ITG) capability is well-developed or mature:

- ▸ IT leadership steers the IT function in a direction that supports the organization's strategic goals and objectives.
- ▸ IT leadership drives a culture within the IT function that distributes decision-making and accountability to high-performing individuals and teams.
- ▸ The IT function works effectively with other business units. IT governance decisions are jointly taken by IT and other business unit leaders.
- ▸ IT governance bodies employ transparent decision-making structures and approaches to support organizational objectives.
- ▸ Accountabilities for value delivery are defined and assigned for all projects across the organization, are systematically tracked with respect to individual and group performance, and are continually optimized.

Maturity at the Critical Capability Level

The following statements provide a high-level overview of the IT Leadership and Governance (ITG) capability at successive levels of maturity:

Level 1   IT leadership and governance are non-existent or are carried out in an ad hoc manner.

Level 2   Leadership with respect to a unifying purpose and direction for IT is beginning to emerge. Some decision rules and governance bodies are in place, but these are typically not applied or considered in a consistent manner.

Level 3   Leadership instils commitment to a common purpose and direction for IT across the IT function and some other business units. IT decision-making forums collectively oversee key IT decisions and monitor performance of the IT function.

Level 4   Leadership instils commitment to a common purpose and direction for IT across the organization. Both the IT function and other business units are held accountable for the outcomes from IT.

Level 5   IT governance is fully integrated into the corporate governance model, and governance approaches are continually reviewed for improvement, regularly including insights from relevant business ecosystem partners.

Maturity at the Capability Building Block (CBB) Level

The Capability Building Blocks (CBBs) associated with the IT Leadership and Governance (ITG) capability fall into two categories:

▸ Category A: five CBBs associated with *Leadership* – these are designed to encourage commitment to the purpose and value proposition of the IT function.

▸ Category B: three CBBs associated with *Governance* – these deal with the structures and supporting mechanisms needed for effective IT decision-making, escalation, and oversight.

These are described below, together with a summary of the different maturity levels for each.

Category A: CBBs Associated with *Leadership*

CBB A1: Value Orientation

Advocate for delivery of the expected business value from IT.

Level 1	Accountabilities for value delivery are not considered, or may be vague and inconsistently assigned.
Level 2	Accountabilities for value delivery are partly defined and assigned for parts of the IT function.
Level 3	Accountabilities for value delivery are defined and assigned for major projects within the IT function; however, systematic tracking is often absent.
Level 4	Accountabilities for value delivery are defined and assigned for all projects across the organization, and systematic tracking is growing.
Level 5	Accountabilities for value delivery are systematically tracked for individual and group performance, and are continually optimized.

CBB A2: Business Interaction

Build a high-quality and effective partnership between the IT function and other business units. Build an understanding of business requirements and how they can be met or enabled by IT.

Level 1	The IT function is typically isolated from other business units. Interaction is non-existent or ad hoc in nature.
Level 2	Individuals in the IT function and some other business units interact on a case-by-case basis, as required.
Level 3	Representatives of the IT function and most other business units meet at standard intervals to discuss each other's current plans.
Level 4	A comprehensive interaction approach ensures that the plans of the IT function and all other business units are readily known and aligned.
Level 5	The approaches adopted by the IT function for interacting with other business units are continually reviewed and optimized, and new interaction tools and approaches are adopted as required.

CBB A3: Communication

Establish mechanisms for dialogue with stakeholders such as IT colleagues, other business units, and third parties.

Level 1	Communication is non-existent or top-down and ad hoc.
Level 2	Most communication is top-down, but some areas encourage two-way communication.
Level 3	Two-way communication is the norm across the IT function. Feedback is generally encouraged, but may not always be acted upon.
Level 4	Communication is a well-functioning, dynamic, two-way process, and feedback is consistently shared and acted upon.
Level 5	The two-way communication process is seen as a major success factor by the IT leadership. It is continually reviewed, and improved as required.

CBB A4: IT Vision

Promote the role of the IT function and its strategic direction.

Level 1	The concept of an 'IT vision' is non-existent or defined in an ad hoc manner.
Level 2	An IT vision is defined. However, it has yet to be embraced among relevant IT employees.
Level 3	IT employees are committed to the IT vision, and are motivated to contribute to its realization.
Level 4	The IT vision is universally recognized as underpinning all IT activities, and is promoted throughout the organization.
Level 5	IT employees use the IT vision as a reference point to drive superior IT performance when collaborating with business ecosystem partners.

CBB A5: Style, Culture, and Collaboration

Create a style of IT leadership that is effective in driving progress, winning support from stakeholders, and fostering a culture of credibility, accountability, and teamwork.

Level 1	IT leaders are typically viewed as lacking the appropriate professional management skills.
Level 2	IT leaders provide clear direction to the IT team, but their direction is often constrained by a limited understanding of the wider organizational needs.
Level 3	IT leaders have a growing comprehension of the wider organizational needs, and they work with some other business units to respond to them.
Level 4	IT leaders have a comprehensive understanding of the business requirements, and work closely across all business units to anticipate and meet them.
Level 5	IT leaders are viewed as leaders in an industry-wide context, and proactively seek to improve the organization's realization of business value.

Category B: CBBs Associated with *Governance*

CBB B1: Decision Bodies and Escalation

Establish IT governance bodies, defining their composition, scope, and decision rights, stating their role in complying with regulatory obligations, and setting out protocols for escalation between them and their organizational units.

Level 1	The IT management team meets occasionally. Escalation processes are ad hoc or are not considered.
Level 2	Working groups are established for important IT projects and are responsible for decision-making in relation to the project. Some escalation processes are defined and applied in specific areas.
Level 3	An IT steering committee, predominantly staffed by IT team members, oversees all important IT decisions and monitors performance of the IT function. Escalation processes are defined and are increasingly applied in a consistent manner.
Level 4	An IT governance council is established as a subset of the senior management team, chaired by the CEO (or highest-ranking person in the organization). It devolves its authority through a cascade of subsidiary committees or working groups at the business unit and programme/project levels. Escalation processes are defined, consistently applied, and periodically tested.
Level 5	IT governance is clearly established as a subset of corporate governance and is directed by the board of directors. Appropriate escalation processes are continually reviewed for improvement.

CBB B2: Decision-Making Processes

Implement decision-making processes based on, for example, principles of transparency and accessibility. Document decisions and translate them into action plans.

Level 1	Transparent decision-making is non-existent or ad hoc. Decision-making processes are not documented or are documented in an unstructured manner.
Level 2	Some decision-making rules are in place, but are not consistently applied. Some important decision-making processes are documented, facilitating the translation of decision outcomes into action plans.
Level 3	Consistent decision-making processes are in place that clarify who is involved in making a decision. Most decision outcomes are documented and translated into action plans.
Level 4	Comprehensive decision-making processes are defined that specify the relevant personnel involved, the information needed, and the decision criteria. All decision outcomes are documented and translated into action plans.
Level 5	The decision-making processes are regularly reviewed and optimized for agility.

CBB B3: Reporting and Oversight

Monitor the status of essential IT capabilities and desired outcomes, including key performance indicators (KPIs) and accountabilities.

Level 1	Reporting and oversight are non-existent or ad hoc.
Level 2	Basic reporting and oversight approaches are established, but their effectiveness is typically not adequately validated.
Level 3	Standardized reporting and oversight approaches are in place within the IT function. There is a growing focus on the contribution that the IT function can make to the objectives of other business units.
Level 4	Comprehensive reporting and oversight approaches are in place focused on the contribution that the IT function makes to the objectives of the entire organization.
Level 5	Reporting and oversight practices are continually reviewed for improvement opportunities.

09.4 IMPROVEMENT PLANNING

Capability Evaluation

Two summary assessment questions are set out below, along with the typical response associated with each level of maturity.

To what extent does IT leadership emphasize the delivery of business value as a key objective of the IT function?

Level 1	Limited focus or no focus is placed on business value.
Level 2	Emerging focus is placed on business value, through target-setting and identifying KPIs for a limited number of larger projects.
Level 3	Core focus is placed on business value, through assigning accountability, target-setting, and measuring KPIs across many projects.
Level 4	Business value delivery is emphasized across all projects organization-wide, through comprehensively assigning accountability, target-setting, and through measuring KPIs.
Level 5	There is a continual focus on business value, evidenced by reviews of targets and KPIs, in line with changes to the business environment and with latest industry practices.

To what extent are structures and processes in place to support IT decision-making?

Level 1   Decision-making is ad hoc, with no formal rules or guidelines.

Level 2   There are basic decision-making processes emerging in parts of the IT function, supported by defined decision-making criteria. However, these are not always applied consistently.

Level 3   There is a structured decision-making process within the IT function that incorporates inputs from some other business units. This is supported by well-defined decision-making criteria that are increasingly applied in a consistent manner.

Level 4   A comprehensive decision-making process is in place that incorporates participation from the entire organization. Decision-making criteria are consistently applied.

Level 5   The decision-making process and associated criteria are regularly reviewed and adapted as required.

Key Practices-Outcomes-Metrics (POMs)

Some useful POMs for developing the IT Leadership and Governance (ITG) capability are summarized below.

Level 2 POMs

Practice	Promote a common IT vision within the IT function and inspire commitment to it.
Outcome	Emerging buy-in to the IT vision is evident, particularly among key stakeholders and influencers in the IT function.
Metric	Percentage of IT employees who see the connection between their work and the IT vision.
Practice	Ensure there is effective two-way dialogue across the IT leadership team.
Outcome	The leadership team can constructively challenge the perspectives and decisions of the management team, leading to more robust decision-making outcomes.
Metric	Yes/No indicator regarding facilitation of diverse contributions and perspectives at team meetings.
Practice	Establish basic decision-making criteria in the areas most critical for the functioning of the IT function.
Outcome	Consistent decision-taking is ensured for the most important decisions.
Metric	Yes/No indicators regarding the involvement of appropriate individuals in relevant decisions.

Level 3 POMs

Practice	Ensure members of the IT leadership team collaborate with other business units to develop a sound grasp of the business and to anticipate key business requirements.
Outcome	The IT team responds promptly and efficiently to key requests from the other business units.
Metric	Percentage of IT service change requests not meeting customer expectations.
Practice	Expand the IT decision-making process to clearly define which individuals across the IT function need to be involved in what decisions.
Outcome	Decisions are increasingly taken in a transparent manner by appropriate individuals.
Metric	Yes/No indicators regarding the involvement of appropriate individuals in relevant decisions.
Practice	Define a comprehensive escalation process for troubleshooting key IT decisions.
Outcome	Key IT decisions can be readily escalated and addressed in a consistent manner.
Metric	Percentage of decisions escalated that follow the defined IT escalation process.
Practice	Establish an IT steering committee, which is co-chaired by the CIO and senior representatives from other business units (such as the Chief Financial Officer) to oversee all important IT decisions and monitor performance of the IT function.
Outcome	Senior representatives from the business can influence important IT decisions, resulting in greater alignment with the business objectives.
Metric	Relative proportion of executives from the IT function and executives from other business units on the IT steering committee.

Level 4 POMs

Practice	Promote the IT vision throughout the organization, with an emphasis on enabling business objectives rather than delivering technical objectives.
Outcome	Stakeholders across the organization can see that the primary focus of the IT vision supports strategic business objectives.
Metric	Level of agreement among business unit leaders regarding whether the IT vision enables the organization's objectives.
Practice	Expand the IT decision-making process to involve appropriate individuals across the organization and ensure the availability of all relevant information and well-defined criteria for making decisions.
Outcome	All decisions are based on factual information, and are taken in a transparent manner by appropriate individuals.
Metric	Yes/No indicators regarding the involvement of appropriate individuals in relevant decisions.

Practice	Periodically stress test the escalation process to confirm its ability to deal with all potential IT decisions.
Outcome	All IT-related decisions can be readily escalated and addressed in a consistent and timely manner.
Metric	Percentage of decisions escalated that follow the defined IT escalation process.
Practice	Ensure the IT governance council is a subset of the executive board, and is chaired by the CEO or the highest-ranking person in the organization.
Outcome	IT governance is anchored at the organization's executive level. The IT governance council can devolve its authority with confidence through a cascade of subsidiary committees or working groups at business unit and programme/project levels.
Metric	Percentage of top executives on the IT governance council.
Practice	Ensure monitoring systems for IT governance are focused on business outcomes and are operating effectively.
Outcome	The governance monitoring systems enable the outcomes of organization-wide IT-supported activities to be transparently reviewed, and agile corrective decisions made.
Metric	Number of upheld complaints submitted against governance decisions.

Level 5 POMs

Practice	Reflect accountabilities for value delivery as a major category in all individual and group performance scorecards.
Outcome	Business value goals are reflected in the performance assessments of IT leaders.
Metric	Percentage of bonuses related to business value delivery.
Practice	Empower the IT leadership team to proactively engage with business ecosystem partners on the improvement of business processes and business value.
Outcome	IT leaders are to the fore in driving the success of the business. The IT function is viewed positively by the rest of the organization and is perceived as an exemplar by business ecosystem partners, competitors, and other external parties.
Metric	Percentage of IT leaders collaborating with business ecosystem partners and engaging in industry-relevant activities.
Practice	Ensure IT governance is rooted in corporate governance, is directed by the board of directors, and regularly incorporates insights from the business ecosystem to improve the governance structures.
Outcome	IT governance reflects industry best known practice, and its importance is recognized by its position within the corporate governance structures.
Metric	Frequency of reviews of the IT governance structures (and updates as appropriate).

Addressing Typical Challenges

Some typical challenges that can arise in attempting to develop maturity in the IT Leadership and Governance (ITG) capability are set out below.

Challenge	Undervaluing the importance of inspiring employees with the IT vision.
Context	Promotion of the IT function's direction and vision is not considered important by other organizational stakeholders.
Action	Stimulate senior management awareness and discussion on the importance of providing clarity, motivation, and buy-in in relation to the vision for the IT function and its connection to wider business objectives.
Challenge	Evidence of inadequate IT leadership to support the organization's goals and objectives.
Context	IT leadership lacks credibility within the IT function and with the wider organization due to an inability to deliver projects, foster teamwork, and define accountability.
Action	Stimulate senior management discussion on how the IT leadership style can support organizational progress, fostering a culture of commitment and accountability.
Challenge	Poor understanding of the IT function's value proposition and the business value that it can deliver.
Context	The IT function's image is one of a technology implementer, rather than a contributor to the broader organization's strategic direction and business value realization.
Action	Promote widespread awareness and visibility across the senior management team of how the IT function has contributed and can contribute to business success.
Challenge	Lack of alignment between the IT function's activities and the business objectives.
Context	The IT function's role in supporting business objectives is not clearly defined. The IT function's activities are often considered in isolation from the objectives of the business.
Action	Promote a partnership-type relationship between the IT function and other business units, in which they both recognize the importance of developing a shared understanding of business requirements and how they can be enabled by IT.
Challenge	Underestimating the importance of IT governance structures.
Context	IT governance is isolated from corporate governance structures. Transparent IT reporting lines, decision-making processes, roles, responsibilities, and accountabilities are not evident.
Action	Initiate an awareness campaign on the importance of IT governance in consistently supporting day-to-day activities to deliver successful outcomes.

Challenge	A lack of senior business management support and buy-in to IT governance.
Context	Current IT governance structures are too complex or have little or no transparency. Control aspects are over-emphasized, and too little focus is placed on deriving business value.
Action	Foster a senior management mind-set that recognizes effective and agile IT governance as central to the organization's competitiveness and business success.
Challenge	Lack of an escalation process to support effective IT decision-making.
Context	IT decisions are not escalated to an appropriate individual or level in the organization. Hence, the decisions made may not be the most effective for enabling the organization to achieve its goals.
Action	Raise awareness of the importance of establishing escalation structures and supporting mechanisms to enable IT decisions to be made in a consistent and timely manner.

Management Artefacts

Management artefacts that may be used to develop maturity in the IT Leadership and Governance (ITG) capability include:

▸ An IT vision statement.
▸ A documented IT decision-making process.
▸ A decision-making responsibility and accountability matrix.
▸ Formal constitution for an IT corporate steering committee.
▸ Formal constitution for an IT enterprise governance council.

IT Vision Statement

An IT vision statement reflects the desired future state of the IT function in a small number of sentences or a concise paragraph. The starting point for its development is an examination of the organization's current industry positioning, its realistic ambitions for the medium and long-term, and the role of IT in realizing these ambitions. It presents a series of precise aspirational value statements outlining how the IT function will effectively contribute to the organization's future success. These statements typically focus on a number of key themes, such as organizational culture, management style, business unit partnership, and IT service provision. However, while an IT vision statement presents the high-level aspirations pertaining to IT for the organization, it doesn't detail a plan to achieve these aspirations. Rather, it provides direction and serves as a reference or guideline to support goal-setting and inspire strategic decisions, such as investment decision-making. It also serves as a motivational device for employees who can work in a unified, cohesive manner towards achieving a desired 'end state'. While an IT vision statement is long-term in nature, it will be revised over time to reflect changing business goals, objectives, and culture.

IT Decision-Making Process

The document detailing the IT decision-making process describes how a course of action is selected from the available alternatives in a consistent and transparent manner. All IT decisions involve consideration of multiple tangible and intangible factors, such as risk, cost, business value, alignment with business objectives, compliance requirements, and future IT trends. These factors have to be evaluated and translated into a set of facts and assumptions to support selecting the option with the best possible outcome. The process may describe how resources are allocated, who has decision-making responsibility, how to ensure the availability of relevant information and supporting tools and techniques, and how decision criteria and decision rules are established. A documented decision-making process results in improved stakeholder consensus and buy-in, and improved decision outcomes.

Decision-Making Responsibility and Accountability Matrix

A decision-making responsibility and accountability matrix supports an organization in allocating IT decision rights and accountabilities, with a view to aligning individual IT decisions with strategic objectives. The matrix outlines key decision domains on one axis, and governance archetypes on the other. Key IT governance decision domains include:

- ▷ *IT principles* – high-level decisions pertaining to the strategic role of IT in the business.
- ▷ *IT architecture* – the technical choices which enable business needs to be satisfied.
- ▷ *IT infrastructure* – the shared IT services providing the foundation for the IT capability.
- ▷ *Business application needs* – the organization's requirements for IT applications.
- ▷ *Prioritization and investment decisions* – the focus areas of investment for IT.

Archetypal approaches to IT decision-making range from centralized to decentralized, and include:

- ▷ *Business monarchy* – senior business executives, sometimes including the CIO, make all IT-related decisions.
- ▷ *IT monarchy* – IT executives make all IT-related decisions.
- ▷ *Federal system* – C-level executives and business unit representatives collaborate with the IT function in decision-making.
- ▷ *IT duopoly* – IT executives and business unit leaders both participate in decision-making.
- ▷ *Feudal system* – business unit leaders make the decisions based on their business unit requirements.
- ▷ *Anarchy* – each individual or small group pursues its own IT agendas.

A matrix positioning these decision domains against the decision-making archetype approaches provides a useful tool for specifying where IT-related decisions are made [3] [4].

IT Corporate Steering Committee

The constitution of the IT corporate steering committee should cover its composition and terms of reference. The committee typically includes a cross functional group of executives from the IT function and other business units, chaired by the CEO. The committee oversees important IT-related decisions, including, for example, the funding levels for IT, alignment between IT and the organization's strategic direction, principles for technology use, and the general sourcing strategy. It also monitors and reviews the overall performance of the IT function by, for example, tracking the status of major programmes.

IT Enterprise Governance Council

The constitution of the IT enterprise governance council should cover its composition and terms of reference. The council typically includes the IT senior management team and selected representatives of other business units, chaired by the CIO. The council may be responsible for determining the general allocation of the IT budget, establishing the principles for compliance and risk management, and monitoring KPIs. It may also advise on the selection of technology and infrastructure products, ensure that the vulnerability of new technologies is assessed, and verify technology compliance with relevant standards and guidelines.

09.5 REFERENCE

See Also

Other capabilities of IT-CMF that have a particularly close relationship with the IT Leadership and Governance (ITG) capability include:

Capability	What it provides
02. Business Planning (BP)	The IT business plan that describes tactical and operational service objectives
10. Organization Design and Planning (ODP)	The current organization design as input to governance design
14. Strategic Planning (SP)	The IT vision and strategy

Further Reading

Holt, A.L., 2013. *Governance of IT – an executive guide to ISO/IEC 38500*. Swindon: BCS.

International Organization for Standardization (ISO), 2015. *Information technology – governance of IT for the organization (ISO/IEC 38500)*. Available at: <http://www.iso.org/iso/home/store/catalogue_tc/catalogue_detail.htm?csnumber=62816>.

IT Systems Audit and Control Association (ISACA), 2012. *COBIT 5.0 – A business framework for the governance and management of enterprise IT*. Available at: <http://www.isaca.org/COBIT/Pages/COBIT-5-Framework-product-page.aspx>.

Notes

[1] International Organization for Standardization (ISO), 2015. *Information technology – governance of IT for the organization (ISO/IEC 38500).* Available at: <http://www.iso.org/iso/home/store/catalogue_tc/catalogue_detail.htm?csnumber=62816>.

[2] Turel, O., and Bart, C., 2014. Board-level IT governance and organizational performance. *European Journal of Information Systems,* 23, 223–39.

[3] Weill, P., and Ross, J., 2004. *IT governance: how top performers manage IT decision rights for superior results.* Boston, MA: Harvard Business School Press.

[4] Weill, P., and Ross, J., 2005. A matrixed approach to designing IT governance. *MIT Sloan Review.* Available at: <http://sloanreview.mit.edu/article/a-matrixed-approach-to-designing-it-governance/>.

ODP
10. Organization Design and Planning

10.1 Overview

Goal

The Organization Design and Planning (ODP) capability aims to organize the IT function by establishing lines of authority, defining roles and functions, and specifying their interrelationships, so that IT employees can collectively deliver the objectives of the IT function.

Objectives

▸ Promote effective decision-making and follow-on action by removing organizational bureaucracy and structural inefficiencies.
▸ Ensure that the organization design of the IT function is appropriate to the wider organization it serves.
▸ Promote IT employees' acceptance of organizational change.
▸ Clarify reporting lines, roles, responsibilities, and accountabilities.
▸ Organize the IT function so that it can develop and leverage core IT capabilities.

Value

The Organization Design and Planning (ODP) capability enables the IT function to readily adapt its organization structure in response to business needs, strategic leadership goals, and the operating environment.

Relevance

Organization design and planning involves structuring the IT function in such a way that it is aligned with and responsive to all other functions, processes, and strategies within the business. When looking at organization design and planning, the context within which the business operates must be taken into consideration. If this capability is weak, the IT function needs to be continually restructured, which can be inefficient, confusing, and demoralizing for its employees. If the capability is well developed, it can enhance coordination, accountability, decision-making, and responsiveness, and enable work activities to be conducted efficiently in support of the IT function's strategy and objectives. The IT function's internal structures should be sufficiently flexible to allow it to deal with business challenges and goals as they arise [1].

By establishing an effective Organization Design and Planning (ODP) capability, an organization can structure and organize its IT function to effectively support its goals and objectives. The IT function is able to adapt (using comprehensive change management processes), and can proactively respond to changes in the business strategy or operating environment, easily integrate new organizational elements, incentivize organization-wide collaboration, and promote operational efficiency and flexibility.

10.2 SCOPE

Definition

The Organization Design and Planning (ODP) capability is the ability to manage the IT function's internal structure and its interfaces with other business units, suppliers, and business partners. The Organization Design and Planning (ODP) capability covers:

▸ Defining the internal structure of the IT function, including reporting lines, span of control, roles, responsibilities, and accountabilities.
▸ Defining the interfaces with other parts of the business, suppliers, and business partners.
▸ Defining IT roles and key performance indicators (KPIs).
▸ Managing the process for (re)organizing and (re)structuring the IT function.
▸ Documenting, communicating, and gaining commitment to the organization design.
▸ Communicating and gaining commitment to organizational change.
▸ Monitoring the effectiveness and efficiency of the organization design.

Other Capabilities

The following are addressed by other capabilities of IT-CMF:

For...	Refer to...
Executing IT governance	09. IT Leadership and Governance (ITG)
Defining the IT strategy	14. Strategic Planning (SP)
Managing roles and career progression, and implementing incentives	23. People Asset Management (PAM)
Managing project delivery	24. Programme and Project Management (PPM)

10.3 UNDERSTANDING MATURITY

Recognizing Excellence

When the Organization Design and Planning (ODP) capability is well-developed or mature:

▶ The IT function's organization structure is arranged in such a way that it supports the strategic direction of the wider organization.

▶ The IT function's organization structure is highly responsive to business and operating environment changes, and to strategic leadership goals.

▶ The IT function is able to adopt different organization structures to meet business needs, and the structures are regularly optimized.

▶ All interfaces between the IT function and other business units, suppliers, and business partners are formally designed, monitored, and adapted as required.

▶ Decision rights, accountabilities, and responsibilities are documented.

▶ KPIs are agreed for measuring the effectiveness of the organization design of the IT function, and regular monitoring occurs.

Maturity at the Critical Capability Level

The following statements provide a high-level overview of the Organization Design and Planning (ODP) capability at successive levels of maturity:

Level 1   The organization structure of the IT function is not well defined or is defined in an ad hoc manner. Internal structures are unclear, as are the interfaces between the IT function and other business units, suppliers, and business partners.

Level 2   A basic organization structure is defined for the IT function, focused primarily on internal roles, responsibilities, and accountabilities. A limited number of key interfaces between IT and other business units, suppliers, and business partners are designed.

Level 3   The IT function's organization structure is harmonized across internal functions, with a primary focus on enabling the mission and values of the business. Most interfaces between IT and other business units, suppliers, and business partners are designed.

Level 4   The IT function is able to adopt a range of organization structures simultaneously, from industrialized IT to innovation centres, in support of the organization's strategic direction. All interfaces to entities external to the IT function are designed.

Level 5   The organization structure(s) adopted by the IT function are continually reviewed, taking into account insights from industry benchmarks. All interfaces are continually reviewed and adapted in response to changes in the business environment.

Maturity at the Capability Building Block (CBB) Level

The Capability Building Blocks (CBBs) associated with the Organization Design and Planning (ODP) capability fall into two categories:

▶ Category A: three CBBs associated with **Organization Design** – these determine the internal structure of the IT function and its interfaces with the rest of the business, key suppliers, and business partners.

▶ Category B: three CBBs associated with **Organization Planning** – these ensure that the organization design is effective, with strong stakeholder buy-in.

These are described below, together with a summary of the different maturity levels for each.

Category A: CBBs Associated with *Organization Design*

CBB A1: Internal Structure

Define the internal structure of the IT function so that it supports the organization's strategic direction and culture. The definition includes, for example, reporting lines, roles, responsibilities, accountabilities, and span of control (that is, the number of employees reporting to each manager).

Level 1	The organization structure of the IT function is not well defined or is defined in an ad hoc manner. Staffing and management layers have accumulated without strategic consideration.
Level 2	A basic organization structure is defined for the IT function, focusing primarily on internal roles, responsibilities, and accountabilities.
Level 3	The IT function's organization structure is harmonized across internal functions, with a primary focus on enabling the business's mission and values. Roles, responsibilities, accountabilities, and related KPIs are defined for all sub-units of the IT function.
Level 4	The IT function is able to adopt a range of organization structures simultaneously, from industrialized IT to innovation centres, in support of the organization's strategic direction. The span of control is defined for all sub-units of the IT function.
Level 5	The organization structure(s) adopted by the IT function are continually reviewed, taking into account changes to the business and operating environment, as well as insights from industry benchmarks.

CBB A2: Business Interfaces

Manage the interfaces between the IT function and other business units.

Level 1   There is no formal process for identifying or designing interfaces between the IT function and other business units.

Level 2   A limited number of key interfaces between the IT function and other business units are formally designed. There may, however, be structural inconsistencies across interfaces.

Level 3   Most interfaces between the IT function and other business units are designed to a common standard.

Level 4   All interfaces between the IT function and other business units are comprehensively designed with shared objectives, incentives, and KPIs.

Level 5   All interfaces between the IT function and other business units are continually reviewed and adapted in response to changes in the business and operating environment.

CBB A3: Supplier Interfaces

Manage the interfaces between the IT function and its suppliers.

Level 1   There is no formal process for identifying or designing interfaces between the IT function and its suppliers.

Level 2   A limited number of key interfaces between the IT function and its suppliers are formally designed. There may, however, be structural inconsistencies across interfaces.

Level 3   Most interfaces between the IT function and its suppliers are comprehensively designed to a common standard.

Level 4   All interfaces between the IT function and its suppliers are designed with shared objectives, incentives, and KPIs.

Level 5   All interfaces between the IT function and its suppliers are continually reviewed and adapted to changes in the business and operating landscape.

Category B: CBBs Associated with *Organization Planning*

CBB B1: Planning Process

Manage the organizational planning process for the IT function and the outcomes of that process, for example by involving stakeholders, and securing commitment to change.

Level 1   Planning is typically conducted in an ad hoc manner, with no structured stakeholder involvement.

Level 2   A defined planning process is emerging, but responsibilities for organizational planning may not be clear. There is increasing involvement of key stakeholders.

Level 3   The planning process is standardized with clear responsibilities allocated for organizational planning. A standardized process is in place for identifying and involving relevant stakeholders.

Level 4   Comprehensive planning processes regularly evaluate business changes and their implications for the IT function. The rationale for any changes made to the organization structure of the IT function is based on the business strategy.

Level 5   The planning process is regularly revised, taking into account lessons learned from previous planning initiatives.

CBB B2: Documentation and Communication

Document the IT function's organization design (including, for example, an organization chart showing links between units and interfaces), and communicate it to relevant stakeholders.

Level 1   Any documentation and communication of the IT function's organization design is ad hoc.

Level 2   Basic results from the IT function's organization design activities are documented, and typically made available only on a limited basis.

Level 3   Key responsibilities and accountabilities are centrally documented. The organization chart, including names, roles, and responsibilities, is widely available to all employees (for example, via an intranet).

Level 4   The internal structure and interfaces of the IT function are comprehensively documented, including all decision rights, responsibilities, and accountabilities. Regular communication on the organization design is proactively provided (for example, via employee forums).

Level 5   Documentation and communication approaches are continually reviewed and improved.

CBB B3: Monitoring

Monitor the effectiveness of the IT function's organization design.

Level 1   The effectiveness of the IT function's organization design is not monitored or is monitored only in an ad hoc manner.

Level 2   A basic set of KPIs for measuring the effectiveness of the IT function's organization design is emerging. However, monitoring is limited.

Level 3   KPIs for measuring the effectiveness of the IT function's organization design are standardized within the IT function. A specific role/unit is tasked with monitoring the effectiveness of the design.

Level 4   KPIs for measuring the effectiveness of the IT function's organization design are agreed across the whole organization. The effectiveness of the design is systematically monitored.

Level 5   A process is in place to continually review and revise KPIs and measurement approaches based on organizational performance, and regular insights from relevant business ecosystem partners.

10.4 IMPROVEMENT PLANNING

Capability Evaluation

Two summary assessment questions are set out below, along with the typical response associated with each level of maturity.

To what extent is the organization design of the IT function appropriate to the needs of the wider organization it serves?

Level 1	The organization design of the IT function does not effectively support business needs.
Level 2	An organization design is defined for parts of the IT function, and may support some high-level business needs.
Level 3	An organization design is standardized for the entire IT function, and supports general organizational needs.
Level 4	The IT function's organization design is tailored to support the needs of the individual business units.
Level 5	The IT function's organization design is continually reviewed to ensure that it remains fit for purpose.

To what extent is the IT function able to adapt to changing business needs and strategies?

Level 1	The IT function has limited or no ability to adapt.
Level 2	The IT function can adapt, using basic change management processes – if given an extended period of time and significant resources to enable change.
Level 3	The IT function can adapt, within reasonable time periods, using standardized change management processes and resources.
Level 4	The IT function can swiftly adapt, using a comprehensive suite of change management processes and minimal resources.
Level 5	The IT function is considered to be dynamic in its ability to adapt and anticipate impending changes.

Key Practices-Outcomes-Metrics (POMs)

Some useful POMs for developing the Organization Design and Planning (ODP) capability are summarized below.

Level 2 POMs

Practice	Decide on a standard organization structure for the IT function. Make sure that hierarchical levels and sizing reflect current business needs and take predictions of expected changes into account.
Outcome	An appropriate organization structure and sizing will lead to greater efficiencies in key areas.
Metric	Yes/no indicator on whether or not there is a standard organization structure for the IT function.

Practice	Introduce a formal process to identify and design interfaces between the IT function and other business units and suppliers.
Outcome	Key interfaces between the IT function and the rest of the organization and its suppliers are in place, facilitating improved coordination and collaboration.
Metric	Number of business interfaces formally designed. Number of supplier interfaces formally designed.
Practice	Define roles, responsibilities, accountabilities, and related KPIs for all sub-units of the IT function.
Outcome	There is improved understanding and transparency with respect to the roles, responsibilities, accountabilities, and KPIs for all sub-units of the IT function.
Metric	Number of line functions that have written role descriptions, including responsibilities, accountabilities and KPIs, as a percentage of all line functions.
Practice	Ensure that major organizational changes are proactively communicated to employees.
Outcome	Employees are well informed about all major organizational changes, enhancing their sense of ownership and buy-in to those changes.
Metric	Frequency of communications regarding major organizational changes.

Level 3 POMs

Practice	Ensure that formal mechanisms and processes allow the standard organization structure to be adapted to the needs of sub-units within the IT function.
Outcome	The organization structure can be tailored to accommodate local requirements where it makes sense.
Metric	Number of sub-units within the IT function adapting the standard organization structure to their particular needs, as a percentage of those who need to do so.
Practice	Centrally document the deliverables between the IT function and other business units, specifying key responsibilities and accountabilities for each deliverable.
Outcome	Deliverables, responsibilities, and accountabilities are clarified and potential confusion can be prevented.
Metric	Number of major IT deliverables documented, with responsibilities and accountabilities specified.
Practice	Make the organization chart widely available to all employees.
Outcome	The organization chart effectively clarifies and communicates the key roles and responsibilities of employees.
Metric	Percentage of employees who know how to access the organization chart.

Practice	Introduce standardized organization design and planning processes for the IT function, with clear allocation of responsibilities.
Outcome	Clear processes and responsibilities help to secure stakeholders' commitment to change.
Metric	Yes/No indicator regarding the presence of standardized organization design and planning processes.
Practice	Ensure that KPIs for measuring the IT function's organization design effectiveness are defined and regularly monitored.
Outcome	The effectiveness of the IT function's organization design is validated, allowing adjustments to be made if necessary.
Metric	Frequency of KPI reporting.

Level 4 POMs

Practice	Formalize a range of pre-approved organization structures (ranging from industrialized IT to innovation centres), that the IT function is able to adopt to address business needs.
Outcome	The availability of alternative organization structures allows the IT function to respond more flexibly to business needs.
Metric	Number of different organization structures pre-approved for adoption within the IT function. Effectiveness with which different organization structures coexist.
Practice	Ensure that IT line managers work with peers in other business units to define shared objectives.
Outcome	Greater organizational relationships/partnerships are fostered between the IT function and the rest of the organization through shared objectives.
Metric	Percentage of common objectives shared between the IT function and other business units.

Level 5 POMs

Practice	Continually review the effectiveness of roles, responsibilities, accountabilities, and KPIs across the IT function.
Outcome	Employee behaviour is continually aligned with the IT function's organization structure.
Metric	Frequency of reviews (and updates as appropriate).
Practice	Continually review interfaces to ensure that the IT function adapts to changes in the business and operating environment.
Outcome	The IT function is flexible and responsive to changing needs.
Metric	Percentage of business interfaces redesigned to adapt to business environment changes. Percentage of supplier interfaces redesigned to adapt to business environment changes. Survey results on stakeholder satisfaction with business interfaces.

Addressing Typical Challenges

Some typical challenges that can arise in attempting to develop maturity in the Organization Design and Planning (ODP) capability are set out below.

Challenge	Poor awareness of the factors that influence the design of an effective organization structure.
Context	The importance of the business context and operating environment is not recognized when designing new organization structures – for example, political influences can dictate new organization structures.
Action	Stimulate discussion among senior management on how organization design needs to take the business context into account if it is to be effective.
Challenge	Inability to formalize the design of interfaces with other business units, suppliers, and business partners.
Context	A lack of shared responsibilities and poorly defined task descriptions make it more difficult to design and operationalize interfaces.
Action	Promote greater collaboration between relevant stakeholders in the IT function, other business units, suppliers, and business partners on the effective design of key interfaces.
Challenge	Resistance to organizational change and a desire to maintain the legacy organization structure of the IT function.
Context	The organization design does not engage sufficiently with stakeholders, resulting in lack of ownership and poor buy-in among employees.
Action	Initiate an awareness campaign on the rationale for organizational change. Seek appropriate stakeholder involvement in designing the new organization structure for the IT function. Communicate roles, responsibilities, and accountabilities to affected employees at the earliest opportunity.

Management Artefacts

Management artefacts that may be used to develop maturity in the Organization Design and Planning (ODP) capability include:

▶ Organization structure templates.
▶ Organization design guidelines.
▶ Organization charts.
▶ Documented organization design effectiveness indicators.

Organization Structure Templates

The way in which an organization is structured can help or hinder its progress toward accomplishing its goals. In the context of this document, the organization structure refers to the internal structure of the IT function and how it connects/interfaces with external entities. An organization structure template specifies the key factors to consider in establishing the organization structure, and includes, for example, lines of authority, roles, responsibilities, accountabilities, number of employees, skill sets, and resource allocation. The reporting structure or chain of command, including span of control, may also be outlined. Organization structures for which templates may be constructed are typically classified as functional, divisional, or matrix.

- In a *Functional (or Centralized) Structure*, all IT infrastructure and application services for all lines of business (or business units) in the organization are delivered by a single internal IT function, which is internally organized according to specific purposes, such as plan, build, run, and manage.
- In a *Divisional (or Decentralized) Structure* (typically used in larger organizations), each line of business potentially has its own dedicated internal IT function, with devolved decision-making. The IT functions could be geographically dispersed, and could each be highly specialized to deal with the needs of the business unit(s) they serve.
- In a *Matrix (or Federated) Structure* (commonly adopted in organizations that are very project-based), some IT services (usually infrastructure services) are provided centrally to the entire organization, and some services (usually application services) are provided by dedicated IT functions embedded in individual lines of business.

Where a number of different organization structures are adopted within a single organization, the term 'multi-mode organization structure' is sometimes used.

Organization Design Guidelines

In designing an organization structure, choices have to be made in relation to:

- *Division of labour* – the extent to which jobs should be specialized.
- *Delegation of authority* – the amount of authority delegated to each job.
- *Departmentalization* – combining jobs into logical groupings (sub-units, teams, departments) according to some shared characteristic(s).
- *Span of control* – number of individuals who report to each specific manager.

The challenge is to devise guidelines that will help design an organization structure to motivate managers and employees, coordinate actions for efficiency and effectiveness, and fit the environment within which the IT function operates. The guidelines should take into account the business strategy, the business operating environment, the business processes, the size of the organization, the levels of employee professionalism, performance measures, and how IT is used to coordinate and control organizational activities, as well as external factors such as trade unions, suppliers and customers, industry regulations, and culture.

Organization Charts

An organization chart is a diagrammatic representation of an organization's structure, showing the position/rank of roles/jobs in the organizational hierarchy. It visually depicts key reporting lines, and the relationships between various positions, as well as the relationships between business units.

Documented Organization Design Effectiveness Indicators

While bottom-line results, such as cost-efficiency, revenue, or profit targets, are perhaps the clearest indicators for measuring the effectiveness of organizational design, such indicators can often take a year or more to respond to a redesign and are unlikely to provide interim feedback if a redesign is not performing to expectations. Interim indicators that can be taken and documented to provide more timely indication of success or otherwise include:

▸ Levels of conflict within and between internal groups arising, for example, from confusion over roles and responsibilities, or allocation of resources.

▸ Ability of resources to be allocated and reallocated quickly when needed.

▸ Speed of decision-making – the right information getting to the right people; removal of cumbersome decision-making processes.

▸ Efficiency of work – removal of cumbersome work flows.

▸ Employee morale – willingness to adapt to change; employee turn-over.

While these indicators may be influenced by factors other than organizational design, having appropriate monitoring granularity can help with root-cause analysis and enable organizational design issues to be remedied at the earliest opportunity.

10.5 REFERENCE

See Also

Other capabilities of IT-CMF that have a particularly close relationship with the Organization Design and Planning (ODP) capability include:

Capability	What it provides
02. Business Planning (BP)	Planned major initiatives to inform the IT function's organization structure
03. Business Process Management (BPM)	Insights on the organization's business processes
09. IT Leadership and Governance (ITG)	Guidelines on decision structures, bodies, and escalation paths
14. Strategic Planning (SP)	The strategic context for designing and planning the organization structures of the IT function
25. Relationship Management (REM)	Insights on interfaces between the IT function and other business units
29. Supplier Management (SUM)	Insights on interfaces to IT service suppliers

Further Reading

Agarwal, R., and Sambamurthy, V., 2002. Principles and models for organizing the IT function. *MIS Quarterly Executive*, 1(1), 1–16.

Bhattacharyya, D.K., 2009. *Organizational systems, design, structure and management*. Mumbai, IN: Himalaya Publishing House.

Brynjolfsson, E., 1998. Information technology and organizational design – evidence from micro data. MIT Sloan School of Management. Available at: <http://digital.mit.edu/erik/ITOD.htm>.

Burton, R.M., Obel, B., and DeSanctus, G., 2011. *Organizational design: a step-by-step approach*. 2nd ed. Cambridge: Cambridge University Press.

Notes

[1] Chan, Y.E., 2002. Why haven't we mastered alignment? The importance of the informal organization structure. *MIS Quarterly Executive,* 1(2), 97–112.

RM

11. Risk Management

11.1 OVERVIEW

Goal

The Risk Management (RM) capability aims to protect the organization from risk exposures associated with Information Technology (IT).

Objectives

▹ Identify and assess the IT-related risks that present vulnerabilities to the business, determine appropriate risk handling strategies, and monitor their effectiveness.

▹ Manage the exposure to IT-related risks such as those related to IT security, IT sabotage, data protection, information privacy, product and project life cycles, and IT investment; and protect the business from the impact of risk incidents.
NOTE: For detailed technical analysis and technical mitigation actions pertaining to information security-related risks, see chapter 21, **Information Security Management (ISM)**.

▹ Increase compliance with external regulations and ethics policies relating to the deployment and use of technology.

▹ Increase transparency around how IT-related risks could affect business objectives and decisions.

▹ Contribute to improving the organization's reputation as a trusted supply chain business partner.

Value

The Risk Management (RM) capability can reduce the frequency and the severity of risks associated with IT negatively impacting the organization's business operations.

Relevance

While the replacement of traditional business models by technology-enabled models (as in, for example, the replacement of 'bricks and mortar' stores by e-commerce stores) supports improved operational efficiency, it can also increase the exposure of the organization to IT-related risk if not managed appropriately. Risks pertaining to cloud computing, analytics, mobile, and social technologies continue to evolve, and these could potentially impact business-critical operations [1]. Hence, an effective approach to managing these and other IT-related risks is required to enable organizations to reduce their exposure and the potential negative consequences [2].

By establishing an effective Risk Management (RM) capability, an organization can identify and understand current and emerging IT-related risks, including the likelihood of their occurrence and the magnitude of their impact. Stakeholders can then take steps to protect IT assets proportionate to their organizational value through prioritizing, handling, and monitoring those risks. Integrating the management of risks associated with IT with wider Enterprise Risk Management (ERM) practices promotes a greater understanding by the IT function of business priorities and critical business services, thereby enabling more effective risk treatment, avoidance of risk oversights, and better return on IT investments [3] [4].

11.2 SCOPE

Definition

The Risk Management (RM) capability is the ability to assess, prioritize, handle, and monitor the exposure to and the potential impact of IT-related risks that can directly impact the business in a financial or reputational manner. Risks include those associated with (among others) IT security, data protection and information privacy, operations, continuity of business and recovery from declared disasters, IT investment and project delivery, and IT service contracts and suppliers. The Risk Management (RM) capability covers:

▶ Establishing an IT risk management programme and policies.
▶ Establishing risk management roles and responsibilities.
▶ Communicating and training in the area of risk management.
▶ Understanding the organization's tolerance for IT-related risks.
▶ Defining risk profiles.
▶ Assessing and prioritizing different types of risks.
▶ Defining risk handling strategies for identified IT risks (accept, avoid, mitigate, or transfer).
▶ Monitoring IT risk exposures.
▶ Integrating IT risk management with wider ERM practices such as business continuity planning, disaster recovery, information security, audit and assurance.

Other Capabilities

The following are addressed by other capabilities of IT-CMF:

For...	Refer to...
Managing information security and managing the detailed technical analysis and treatment of specific information security-related risks	21. Information Security Management (ISM)
Resolving IT service incidents	27. Service Provisioning (SRP)

11.3 UNDERSTANDING MATURITY

Recognizing Excellence

When the Risk Management (RM) capability is well-developed or mature:

▶ The risk management programme and framework are continually refined and updated in cooperation with other business units and relevant business ecosystem partners.

▶ Key IT risks are known, their likelihood and potential business impact are quantified, and appropriate risk handling strategies are in place (that is, the decision has been taken to accept, avoid, mitigate, or transfer them).

▶ Risks are effectively identified, tracked, and monitored, and lessons learned are incorporated into future risk management activities.

▶ Risk management is built into all relevant processes within the organization. The risk management of IT is integrated into wider ERM practices.

▶ Current and emerging risks associated with IT are continually identified and effectively managed.

▶ Risk management budget and resources are allocated effectively and efficiently.

▶ The efficacy of the Risk Management (RM) capability is confirmed at regular intervals.

Maturity at the Critical Capability Level

The following statements provide a high-level overview of the Risk Management (RM) capability at successive levels of maturity:

Level 1
The risk management programme and framework are considered in an ad hoc manner, if at all. No risk-related roles are defined, or they are defined in an ad hoc manner. Risks are not actively or systematically managed.

Level 2
The risk management programme sits within the IT function, and a basic framework is established. Responsibility and accountability for risk management are assigned to persons/roles in the IT function. Some basic risk management approaches are established but these may not be consistently adhered to.

Level 3
The risk management programme and supporting framework are established and consistently referenced in the IT function and some other business units. Responsibility and accountability for risk management are assigned to dedicated persons/roles in the IT function and other business units. Most risk management activities adhere to defined and documented approaches.

Level 4
The risk management programme and framework are established through the cooperation of, and in consultation with, the IT function and the rest of the business. The risk management of IT is integrated into wider ERM practices. Explicit risk management responsibility and accountability are assigned to employees across the organization. Compliance with the approaches, principles, and guidance for all risk management activities is mandated and enforced organization-wide.

Level 5
The risk management programme and framework are continually refined and updated, and involves regular cooperation with business ecosystem partners. Responsibility and accountability for risk management are dynamically assigned to the appropriate organization level, and regularly reviewed. Risk management approaches, principles, and guidance are continually reviewed and improved based on changes in the risk landscape, and learning from previous risk incidents.

Maturity at the Capability Building Block (CBB) Level

The Capability Building Blocks (CBBs) associated with the Risk Management (RM) capability fall into three categories:

▸ Category A: four CBBs associated with *Governance* – these are designed to establish how IT risk management should be executed.
▸ Category B: two CBBs associated with *Profiling and Coverage* – these are designed to ensure that IT-related risks are assessed effectively.
▸ Category C: four CBBs associated with *Process* – these are designed to address the day-to-day activities of identifying and protecting the organization from IT-related risks.

These are described below, together with a summary of the different maturity levels for each.

Category A: CBBs Associated with *Governance*

CBB A1: Policies for Risk Management

Define, implement, review, and make accessible risk management policies. Incorporate compliance requirements into risk management approaches.

Level 1	Risk management policies are defined in an ad hoc manner, if at all, and are seldom reviewed.
Level 2	Risk management policies are developed by the IT function, and are reviewed typically after major incidents.
Level 3	Risk management policies are developed by the IT function and some other business units, and are regularly reviewed.
Level 4	Risk management policies are developed via organization-wide collaboration, and are systematically reviewed for alignment with business objectives.
Level 5	Risk management policies are continually reviewed for organization-wide effectiveness and efficiency, and reflect consultation with relevant business ecosystem partners.

CBB A2: Integration

Integrate IT risk management with IT leadership and governance structures, and with overall ERM policies and approaches.

Level 1	IT risk management is either not integrated with wider ERM and governance, or is integrated only on an ad hoc basis.
Level 2	IT risk management is integrated with some limited aspects of wider ERM and governance structures on a reactive basis – for example, after incidents occur.
Level 3	IT risk management is mostly integrated with ERM and governance structures in some other business units.
Level 4	IT risk management is comprehensively integrated with ERM and governance structures organization-wide.
Level 5	The extent to which IT risk management is integrated into organizational ERM and governance is continually reviewed and improved.

CBB A3: Risk Management Programme and Performance Management

Identify risk management leadership responsibilities and accountability. Define risk management roles, responsibilities, and accountabilities in support of the programme's principles and guidance. Measure and report on the effectiveness and efficiency of risk management activities.

Level 1	No risk-related roles are defined, or they are defined in an ad hoc manner. There is little or no evidence of tracking or reporting on the programme's performance.
Level 2	The risk management programme sits within the IT function. Responsibility and accountability for risk management are assigned to persons/roles in the IT function. There is basic tracking and reporting on the programme's performance.
Level 3	The risk management programme is established and consistently referenced across the IT function and some other business units. Responsibility and accountability for risk management are assigned to dedicated persons/ roles in the IT function and some other business units. The consistency of performance tracking and reporting with broader ERM functions is improving.
Level 4	The risk management programme is established through the cooperation of and in consultation with IT and the rest of the business, and a dedicated organization-wide function is accountable for risk management. Explicit risk management responsibility and accountability are assigned to employees across the organization. Performance tracking and reporting are standardized across the organization, providing transparency on the programme's effectiveness.
Level 5	The risk management programme is continually refined and updated, and includes cooperation with relevant business ecosystem partners. Responsibility and accountability for risk management are dynamically assigned to the appropriate organization level, and regularly reviewed and improved based on learning from experience. Performance tracking and reporting are consolidated into a single dashboard and used to support continual improvement.

CBB A4: Communication and Training

Disseminate risk management approaches, policies, and results. Train stakeholders in risk management practices. Develop a risk management culture and risk management knowledge and skills.

Level 1	There is no formal training or communication relating to risk management, although there may be some informal knowledge transfer.
Level 2	There is an emerging risk management training programme in areas of the IT function, and risk management concepts are beginning to be communicated.
Level 3	There is standardized risk management training and communication across the IT function and some other business units, with on-demand training provided for selected employees.
Level 4	Comprehensive risk management training and communication is provided organization-wide.
Level 5	Risk management training is continually optimized for various risk management roles, and the risk management policy is continually reviewed, and regularly involves inputs from relevant business ecosystem partners.

Category B: CBBs Associated with *Profiling and Coverage*

CBB B1: Definition of Risk Profiles

Define the risk profiles by their potential impact on business continuity and performance. Apply risk profiles in risk management activities.

Level 1	Risk profiles are defined in an ad hoc manner, if at all, and are used in an ad hoc manner for identification and treatment of risks.
Level 2	A limited number of basic risk profiles are defined and used within the IT function to identify and categorize risks, but there is no consistent methodology in place.
Level 3	A standardized approach is in place for defining risk profiles, and the risk profiles are used across the IT function and some other business units for risk assessment and treatment activities.
Level 4	A comprehensive organization-wide approach is in place for defining risk profiles, and the risk profiles are systematically used in the organization's risk assessment and treatment activities.
Level 5	The effectiveness of the risk profiles in risk assessment and treatment is regularly reviewed and optimized, and there is regular input from relevant business ecosystem partners.

CBB B2: Risk Coverage

Establish the breadth of IT risk categories and asset classes that are addressed by risk management activities.

Level 1	Risk coverage is ad hoc or unknown.
Level 2	There is an emerging approach in areas of the IT function to identifying the critical risk categories and asset classes to be addressed in risk management activities.
Level 3	The IT function and some other business units jointly identify the risk categories and asset classes to be addressed in risk management activities.
Level 4	There is a comprehensive organization-wide approach to identifying the risk categories and asset classes to be addressed in risk management activities.
Level 5	The approaches for identifying the risk categories and asset classes to be included in risk management activities are regularly reviewed and optimized.

Category C: CBBs Associated with *Process*

CBB C1: Assessment

Identify subject matter experts for risk assessments. Run risk assessments to identify, document, and quantify or score risks and their components. Assessments include the evaluation of exposure to risks and measurement of their potential impact.

Level 1	Risk management assessments are ad hoc, and no measures or metrics are defined.
Level 2	A risk management assessment approach is emerging in the IT function (including an approach to scoring identified risks), and assessments include IT-specific measures.
Level 3	The risk management assessment approach is standardized between IT and some other business units, and assessments include IT and business measures.
Level 4	The risk management assessment approach is comprehensively adopted across the organization, and the risk measures used are linked to the potential impact on business processes.
Level 5	Risk management assessments and risk measures are continually reviewed to ensure they are sufficiently adaptable and agile to address the needs of the business.

CBB C2: Prioritization

Prioritize inherent and residual risks and risk handling strategies, based on the organization's risk tolerance – that is, what risk levels are acceptable.

Level 1	Risk prioritization is not conducted or is conducted in an ad hoc manner. For example, it may be reactive based on recent incidents or current headlines.
Level 2	A basic risk prioritization approach is emerging in the IT function. Potential impacts are expressed mostly in IT-based metrics.
Level 3	There is a standardized risk prioritization approach across the IT function and some other business units. Potential impacts are increasingly expressed in terms of business metrics.
Level 4	A comprehensive risk prioritization approach is adopted across the organization. Potential impacts are expressed in terms of business value.
Level 5	The risk prioritization approach is regularly reviewed for improvement, and the accuracy of estimates is regularly assessed.

CBB C3: Handling

Assign ownership to identified risks, and responsibility and accountability for developing risk handling strategies. Initiate implementation of risk handling strategies, where risks can be transferred, absorbed, or mitigated. Interact with incident management functions – see chapter 27, Service Provisioning (SRP).

Level 1	Risks are handled and risk ownership is assigned in an ad hoc manner, if at all.
Level 2	There is a basic approach emerging for handling prioritized risks in the IT function, and a basic risk ownership policy is also emerging.
Level 3	Prioritized risks are handled across the IT function and some other business units using standardized approaches, and there is a defined risk ownership policy, with risk owners allocated in the IT function and some other business units.
Level 4	Prioritized risks are comprehensively handled organization-wide, and there is a systematic approach for assigning risk ownership.
Level 5	The approach for handling and assigning ownership to prioritized risks is continually reviewed for improvement and regularly extends to relevant business ecosystem partners.

CBB C4: Monitoring

Establish a risk register. Track and report risks and risk incidents, and validate the effectiveness of risk controls.

Level 1	Risks are reported in an ad hoc manner, if at all, and risks are not monitored.
Level 2	Risks are beginning to be monitored and reported consistently within the IT function.
Level 3	Risks are monitored consistently, and detailed risk reports are published by the IT function and some other business units.
Level 4	Organization-wide risk monitoring results can trigger preset activities, and risk reporting is comprehensively integrated into organization-wide reporting.
Level 5	Risk monitoring is continually reviewed for improvement based on past incidents, and reporting mechanisms are reviewed and improved where appropriate.

11.4 IMPROVEMENT PLANNING

Capability Evaluation

Two summary assessment questions are set out below, along with the typical response associated with each level of maturity.

How are risk management policies and a governance framework developed and implemented?

Level 1	Policies and a governance framework are considered in an ad hoc manner, if at all.
Level 2	Basic policies (for example covering risk avoidance or legal requirements) and a governance framework are emerging within the IT function.
Level 3	Detailed policies (for example covering assets, people, approaches, and emerging risks) are developed by the IT function, with some inputs from other business units. These policies and a supporting governance framework are implemented across the IT function and in some other business units.
Level 4	Policies and a governance framework are developed through the cooperation of and in consultation with the IT function and the rest of the business, and are comprehensively implemented organization-wide.
Level 5	Policies and a governance framework are continually refined as appropriate, and there is regular cooperation with relevant business ecosystem partners.

What approaches are in place for assessing, prioritizing, handling, and monitoring IT-related risks?

Level 1	Approaches are considered in an ad hoc manner, if at all.
Level 2	Some basic risk management approaches are established within the IT function, but these may not be consistently adhered to.
Level 3	Standardized and documented approaches are in place across the IT function and some other business units, and most risk management activities adhere to these approaches.
Level 4	The approaches are comprehensively rolled out organization-wide. Compliance with the approaches for all risk management activities is mandated and systematically enforced.
Level 5	The approaches are continually reviewed for improvement based on changes in the risk landscape, and learning from previous risk incidents.

Key Practices-Outcomes-Metrics (POMs)

Some useful POMs for developing the Risk Management (RM) capability are summarized below.

Level 2 POMs

Practice	Identify regulatory compliance policies and frameworks.
Outcome	Confidence grows regarding the consistent implementation of measures to satisfy regulatory requirements.
Metric	Number of instances of non-compliance with external regulations. Number of compliance issues identified as business-critical.
Practice	Set up initial employee training in risk management principles, tools, and techniques, initially focusing on the IT function.
Outcome	There is high-level user awareness of, and proficiency in, risk management for operational and decision-making processes.
Metric	Number of mandatory risk management training sessions per annum. Percentage of IT employees trained in risk management. Number of IT employees with industry certifications in risk management.
Practice	Create basic risk profiles for prioritized areas across the IT function.
Outcome	Basic risk profiles support the IT function's risk assessment and treatment in a number of high-risk areas.
Metric	Number of risk areas covered by the risk profiles. Percentage of projects and operational systems in the various risk categories and asset classes.
Practice	Assess risk exposure to high-profile incidents within the IT function.
Outcome	A basic risk overview is provided, with particular emphasis on major pain-points/sensitivities and current trends.
Metric	Risk exposure for each identified risk. Percentage of identified risks whose potential impact or likelihood of being realized exceeds the organization's risk tolerance.

Level 3 POMs

Practice	Implement a consistent set of risk management principles and guidelines across the IT function and some other business units.
Outcome	A consistent and holistic risk management policy is in place covering assets, approaches, people, risk identification, and risk treatment, and it is increasingly relevant to more and more business unit needs.
Metric	Percentage of functional groups within the IT function and other business units that have participated in the risk management programme.
Practice	Communicate the risk management policy and approaches across the IT function and to some other business unit stakeholders.
Outcome	There is a growing awareness of risk management principles and guidelines. Communication ensures that a risk management culture emerges across key areas of the organization.
Metric	Percentage of functional groups that align to the overall ERM policies.

Practice	Allocate risk management ownership and accountability across roles in the IT function and some other business units.
Outcome	Points of contact exist for risk management, and the necessary time and skills are invested in the risk management programme.
Metric	Distribution of employees with allocated risk management responsibility and accountability.
Practice	Establish a central risk register.
Outcome	The recording of risks in a central register provides consistent information on risks, and supports efficient management and reporting.
Metric	Number of risks actively managed in a central risk register.
Practice	Conduct regular risk assessments, using dimensions and information provided by the risk profiles. Assess violations, missed opportunities, and response times.
Outcome	Data on risks can be consistently gathered, and used to support risk prioritization and handling.
Metric	Risk exposure for each identified risk. Percentage of identified risks whose potential impact or likelihood of being realized exceeds the organization's risk tolerance.

Level 4 POMs

Practice	Benchmark risk management practices against industry best-known practice on a regular basis.
Outcome	The risk management policy reflects latest industry practice insights. Risk management principles and guidelines are more robust and complete.
Metric	Percentage of identified risks within the tolerance levels of broader ERM guidance.
Practice	Broaden training on risk management approaches to include all stakeholders and teams.
Outcome	Teams have the knowledge and tools needed for risk management activities. Risk management becomes more embedded in the organization's culture.
Metric	Number of mandatory risk management training sessions per annum. Percentage of executives, IT employees, and business unit employees trained in risk management. Number of executives, IT employees, and business unit employees with industry certifications in risk management.
Practice	Incorporate benchmark data from industry sources into the risk profiles.
Outcome	Incorporating benchmark data enables risks to be evaluated in an industry context, with meaningful placement of risks along the risk profile's dimensions, and supports validity and quality assurance.
Metric	Percentage of projects and operational systems in the various risk categories and asset classes.

Practice	Integrate the risk management of IT into overall ERM approaches and decision-making.
Outcome	The risk management of IT is on the agenda of all stakeholders, and is accepted as a key component in the management of business risks.
Metric	Percentage of IT risk management principles that align with ERM approaches.
Practice	Extend risk identification and assessment approaches organization-wide, and embed risk assessment into IT service life cycles and investment appraisals.
Outcome	There is a consistent organization-wide approach to risk management assessment. Risks in relation to IT service life cycles and proposed investments are consistently understood, enabling more informed investment decisions to be made.
Metric	Percentage of IT risk categories and asset classes covered by risk management measures.

Level 5 POMs

Practice	Establish a collaborative network of risk managers across the business ecosystem.
Outcome	Collaboration of risk managers and external experts across the business ecosystem supports optimized visibility and management of risks.
Metric	Percentage of business units that have a dedicated risk management role.
Practice	Review risk profiles in regular collaboration with relevant business ecosystem partners, and update them as required.
Outcome	Risk profiles are kept up to date and relevant through collaborative input and review.
Metric	Frequency of risk profile reviews and updates (as appropriate).
Practice	Ensure that ERM tools share data across the organization and that decision criteria relating to risk are uniform across the IT function and the rest of the business.
Outcome	Tools and data that support risk management are consistent.
Metric	Number of occurrences of non-compliance with risk management policies.
Practice	Optimize training programmes for specific stakeholder groups/risk management roles.
Outcome	The most up-to-date training and tools are available, in line with policies and techniques. Risk management knowledge and skills can be specialized.
Metric	Number of employees completing mandatory risk management training courses per annum. Percentage of executives, IT employees, and business unit employees trained in risk management. Number of executives, IT employees, and business unit employees with industry certifications in risk management. Frequency of updates to training programmes.

Addressing Typical Challenges

Some typical challenges that can arise in attempting to develop maturity in the Risk Management (RM) capability are set out below.

Challenge	Provision of adequate funding and resourcing for an effective Risk Management (RM) capability.
Context	Identified risks can be difficult to quantify, and the value of risk management activities is measurable only in relation to the impacts of incidents that might never materialize. This may undermine the recognition of the need or desire for a Risk Management (RM) capability.
Action	Effective risk management of IT should be viewed as a necessary management activity, and should be funded as a component of the organization's overall approach to ERM.
Challenge	A lack of senior management ownership of risk management.
Context	Risk management is considered a low priority by the senior management team, seen as 'insurance' or an activity that does not add value to the core business.
Action	Stimulate a mind-set whereby effective risk management of IT is viewed as a value-add (or value-protection) activity and is funded as a component of the organization's overall approach to ERM.
Challenge	A general lack of awareness towards how risks associated with IT should be managed.
Context	There is limited understanding of risk management principles, tools, and techniques, or the skills required to manage risk effectively. Risk assessment, prioritization, handling, and monitoring approaches may or may not be in use.
Action	Initiate an awareness raising campaign on the importance of risk management in day-to-day activities to protect the organization.
Challenge	Difficulties in understanding and keeping up-to-date with current and emerging risks.
Context	The risks associated with IT are continually changing and evolving, sometimes remaining unknown until a breach is reported.
Action	Stimulate organizational commitment to proactively conducting outreach and horizon scanning initiatives with a view to understanding current and emerging risks.
Challenge	Risk management of IT is isolated from general business risk management.
Context	A reactionary, survivability stance prevails with respect to the risk management of IT.
Action	Promote greater collaboration between general business risk managers and those responsible for the management of risk associated with IT.

Management Artefacts

Management artefacts that may be used to develop maturity in relation to the Risk
Management (RM) capability include:

- A risk management policy.
- A risk profiling and scoring approach.
- A risk register.

Risk Management Policy

A risk management policy identifies risk management's scope, objectives, and mapping to
strategic objectives. It documents the attitudes and the level and nature of acceptable risk. It
details mechanisms for managing IT risks, and identifies mechanisms to develop a risk-aware
culture. The policy also documents training topics and priorities, and details procedures for
risk assessment, prioritization, handling, and monitoring, and protocols for risk reporting and
communication. Further, it identifies sample areas for which specific IT risk policies should be
developed – for example, security, data protection, emerging risks, and disaster recovery.

Risk Profiling and Scoring Approach

A risk profiling and scoring approach is used to ensure that the organization's risk tolerance
is reflected in its decision-making processes. The risk profile outlines the various risks
associated with IT that the organization may be exposed to, and for each risk estimates
the likelihood of it being realized and its corresponding impact. Such risks may include, for
example, IT security risks, data protection and information privacy risks, operations/business
continuity risks, IT investment risks, IT service contracts/supplier risks, IT reputation/brand
risks, and regulatory/legal and ethics policy compliance risks. Numerical values can be
assigned to both likelihood and impact, and the product of these values used for risk ranking
and prioritization. In some cases, financial quantification of the risk, in terms of cost to the
business, may serve as the basis for risk ranking.

Risk Register

The risk register is a record of known risks associated with IT, recorded in one or more
databases. It records risk descriptions, and estimates of their potential impact and
likelihood. It also records risk handling options and the individuals who are responsible for
implementing the identified response. It supports risk prioritization by ranking risk scores
or by quantifying potential cost to the business. It enables risks to be tracked over time to
determine the effectiveness of the mitigation approach. The underlying data in a risk register
may be viewed in a variety of ways – to enable financial experts to manage financial risks,
IT security experts to manage information security risks, supply managers to manage supply
risks, and so on.

11.5 REFERENCE

See Also

Other capabilities of IT-CMF that have a particularly close relationship with the Risk Management (RM) capability include:

Capability	What it provides
04. Capacity Forecasting and Planning (CFP)	Understanding of potential exposures regarding resourcing requirements to satisfy demand for current and future IT services
06. Enterprise Information Management (EIM)	Alerts of potential risks and risk events, such as unauthorized data access, compromised data, or theft of proprietary information
09. IT Leadership and Governance (ITG)	Overarching guidance on governance protocols, compliance with regulatory obligations, escalation processes and procedures, and risk documentation
12. Service Analytics and Intelligence (SAI)	Details on the probability of failure or degraded performance of infrastructure components and their effect on business activities
13. Sourcing (SRC)	Details on sourcing activities that could carry potential risk exposures
19. Capability Assessment Management (CAM)	Details on shortcomings in IT capabilities that could impact the organization, plus continual improvement activities
20. Enterprise Architecture Management (EAM)	Updates on risks stemming from implementing enterprise architecture roadmaps
21. Information Security Management (ISM)	Detailed technical analysis and technical mitigation actions pertaining to information security-related risks
30. Technical Infrastructure Management (TIM)	Updates on risks associated with the technical infrastructure, such as infrastructure outages, infrastructure refresh rates, or planned maintenance, and their need to be evaluated from an overall business perspective
34. Portfolio Management (PM)	Updates on risks stemming from the portfolio of programmes and projects, such as delivery schedule slippages, possible cost over-runs, or potential impact on operations during deployments

Further Reading

International Organization for Standardization (ISO), 2009. *ISO 31100 – Risk management.* Available at: <http://www.iso.org/iso/home/standards/iso31000.htm>.

ISACA, 2009. *Risk IT framework*. Available at: <http://www.isaca.org/Knowledge-Center/Research/ResearchDeliverables/Pages/The-Risk-IT-Framework.aspx>.

ISACA, 2013. *COBIT 5 for risk*. Available at: <http://www.isaca.org/cobit/pages/risk-product-page.aspx>.

Office of Government Commerce, 2011. *Management of risk – guidance for practitioners.* 3rd ed. London: The Stationery Office.

Notes

[1] Ernst and Young, 2013. *Under cyber attack: EY's global information security survey.* [pdf]. Available at: <http://www.ey.com/Publication/vwLUAssets/EY_-_2013_Global_Information_Security_Survey/$FILE/EY-GISS-Under-cyber-attack.pdf>.

[2] Elky, S., 2006. *An introduction to information systems risk management.* [pdf] SANS Institute. Available at: <http://www.sans.org/reading_room/whitepapers/auditing/introduction-information-system-risk-management_1204>.

[3] *Silicon Republic*, 2010. Closing the gaps between ICT and enterprise risk management. Available at: <http://www.siliconrepublic.com/news/item/16901-closing-the-gaps-between-ic>.

[4] Fraser, J., Simkins, B., and Narvaez, K., 2014. *Implementing enterprise risk management: case studies and best practices.* Hoboken, NJ: Wiley.

SAI

12. Service Analytics and Intelligence

12.1 OVERVIEW

Goal

The Service Analytics and Intelligence (SAI) capability aims to clarify the link between the performance of business processes and the performance of the underlying IT infrastructure and services – that is, to provide an end-to-end view of IT services.

Objectives

- Provide a quantified view of the end-to-end performance of IT services – that is, define and measure the relationship between IT infrastructure and services, and the business processes and services enabled by IT.
- Map performance data from discrete IT systems (including networks, finance, voice, data, storage, processing speeds, data centres, and applications) to performance data from business processes and services, to highlight business value-at-risk, gain insights into ways of optimizing IT infrastructure and service configurations, and prioritize future investments.
- Establish proactive approaches to resolving IT infrastructure and service quality problems by maintaining profiles of normal infrastructure operational characteristics, and automatically detecting deviations from norms.
- Support improved decision-making on the performance of IT services at all levels of the organization – that is:
  - Inform operational decision-making relating to service delivery by providing insight into matters such as performance, capacity, availability, cost, and use.
  - Inform strategic decision-making by providing insight into matters such as profiling of user populations, understanding the business impact of change, and contingency planning.

Value

The Service Analytics and Intelligence (SAI) capability helps identify how best to configure IT infrastructure and services to meet business demand.

Relevance

Many organizations have installed tools and processes to monitor the performance of individual IT components (such as, for example, storage, network, or processing speeds). However, it is often more difficult to achieve an end-to-end view of IT services performance, based on the collective performance of underlying infrastructure components. And it can be equally, if not more, difficult to understand how the organization's business processes are impacted by the performance (or underperformance) of the IT infrastructure and services. Relevant information can often lie hidden in different formats across technology stacks and software layers. If properly analysed and understood, this data, which is generated at the infrastructure level by IT systems, can reveal emerging trends before they become problems, and help to identify ways of addressing their causes. Appropriate data collection and analytical approaches can enable the modelling of IT services (at all levels) to inform better decision-making [1].

By establishing an effective Service Analytics and Intelligence (SAI) capability, an organization can facilitate a data-driven decision-making culture [2]. Service analytics and intelligence enhances the detail and scope of IT insight, and goes beyond a one-to-one mapping between the different technology stacks and software layers to reveal the true nature of the relationships between different performance variables. Understanding performance relationships between IT services and business services can enable more timely responses to emerging service issues or potential outages. The IT function can act as an exemplar for the whole organization in adopting business intelligence data and analytics to improve operational and strategic decision-making.

12.2 SCOPE

Definition

The Service Analytics and Intelligence (SAI) capability is the ability to define and quantify the relationships between IT infrastructure, IT services, and IT-enabled business processes. The Service Analytics and Intelligence (SAI) capability covers:

▶ Service Analytics: Monitoring, modelling, and analysing service performance to:
  ▶ Measure, sustain, and optimize the delivery of IT services for business value.
  ▶ Provide the data that planning activities require.
▶ Service Intelligence: Applying insights from service analytics to:
  ▶ Identify risks associated with IT infrastructure and services that could impact on the business.
  ▶ Identify business risks and changes that could impact on IT infrastructure and services.
  ▶ Identify opportunities for business growth and IT innovation.

Other Capabilities

The following are addressed by other capabilities of IT-CMF:

For...	Refer to...
Modelling IT architecture in general	20. Enterprise Architecture Management (EAM)
Real-time monitoring of Service Level Agreements (SLAs)	27. Service Provisioning (SRP)
Managing infrastructure assets	30. Technical Infrastructure Management (TIM)

12.3 UNDERSTANDING MATURITY

Recognizing Excellence

When the Service Analytics and Intelligence (SAI) capability is well-developed or mature:

▹ There is a clear understanding of the relationship between the performance of business processes and the performance of the underlying IT infrastructure and services.

▹ Emerging trends can be identified and responded to before they become problems across the portfolio of IT services.

▹ Service analytics and intelligence is leveraged as part of strategic planning organization-wide (including in risk management, and investment planning).

Maturity at the Critical Capability Level

The following statements provide a high-level overview of the Service Analytics and Intelligence (SAI) capability at successive levels of maturity:

Level 1	Ad hoc monitoring of individual IT components occurs, with limited reporting. There is little or no modelling of IT infrastructure performance as it relates to business activity levels. There are frequent outages and major performance degradations.
Level 2	Rudimentary modelling is carried out on individual IT components, typically limited to identifying potential failure or latency.
Level 3	Standardized monitoring of IT services is in place, with the ability to drill down to component layers for precise root-cause analysis. Individual risks associated with most IT services can be modelled based on the performance of the underlying infrastructure.
Level 4	Business processes are comprehensively monitored and most are mapped to their enabling IT services. Modelling of demand from business processes directly influences the sizing of the IT services and infrastructure on which they depend.
Level 5	Business processes are monitored organization-wide. The relationships between all IT infrastructure, IT services, and business processes are clearly understood. Continual scenario modelling ensures that the IT infrastructure is always aligned with business goals.

Maturity at the Capability Building Block (CBB) Level

The Capability Building Blocks (CBBs) associated with the Service Analytics and Intelligence (SAI) capability fall into three categories:

▸ Category A: three CBBs associated with **Profiling** – these validate the relationships between various business and IT layers to support reliable forecasting.

▸ Category B: three CBBs associated with **Planning** – these are used to align IT capacity with business requirements.

▸ Category C: two CBBs associated with **Business Interaction** – these build relationships between the IT function and other business units to facilitate the planning and management of IT assets.

These are described below, together with a summary of the different maturity levels for each.

Category A: CBBs Associated with *Profiling*

CBB A1: Empirical Model

Define and quantify the relationships between IT infrastructure (for example, CPU load or latency) and IT services, business processes, and ultimately, the organization. Populate models with data to act as a basis for all analysis (including historical and projected).

Level 1	No formal models are in place for managing IT infrastructure performance. Any modelling that occurs is ad hoc.
Level 2	Models are emerging for most infrastructure component groupings – for example, storage, computer network, and so on.
Level 3	Standardized models express the relationships between most IT services and their underlying IT infrastructure components.
Level 4	Comprehensive models connect most business processes to IT underlying services, which in turn are tied to IT infrastructure components.
Level 5	Models provide an integrated view of all IT-enabled business processes across the organization, extending to relevant business ecosystem partners where appropriate.

CBB A2: Performance Monitoring

Measure, record, and track various service performance indicators for IT infrastructure, end-to-end IT services, business processes, and the organization (based on empirical models).

Level 1	Any monitoring is ad hoc, typically only instigated to investigate the failure of specific components.
Level 2	Monitoring is done on specific infrastructure components, primarily focused on proactively identifying hardware failure patterns.
Level 3	Monitoring increasingly provides a service-oriented view, helping achieve high availability levels for most services.
Level 4	The business processes that depend on IT services are monitored, enabling early identification of underperforming IT services and limiting their business impact.
Level 5	Aggregated service performance indicators for each business unit continually provide insight into new opportunities for improvement.

CBB A3: Results Analysis

Identify the key issues relating to IT infrastructure and how they impact or are impacted by IT services, business processes, and the organization, based on empirical model outputs.

Level 1	There is no formal analysis of infrastructure data, apart from occasional investigations into the cause of outages.
Level 2	A limited number of critical business/IT processes and services are regularly analysed, enabling identification of specific trends and causes of problems, and facilitating preventative or corrective action.
Level 3	Most IT service metrics are analysed, helping to ensure that services are maintained at or above performance goals. Improvement plans are increasingly targeted at alleviating service constraints.
Level 4	Analysis is focused on performance correlations between IT services and business processes, helping to identify mismatches and prevent their recurrence. Improvement planning focuses on systematically prioritizing IT service enhancements to deliver business impact.
Level 5	Business scenario planning is regularly used to determine the implications for IT infrastructure and IT services arising from potential business initiatives. This ensures that IT resources are optimally allocated for maximum business impact.

Category B: CBBs Associated with *Planning*

CBB B1: Capacity Trend Analysis

Size the infrastructure based on current and expected business demand – for example, by examining current performance trends or deducing expected capacity needs from the business strategy.

Level 1	The approach to capacity planning is non-existent or ad hoc – for example, new servers are acquired only after the capacity of existing servers is exhausted (in which case the time taken to install the new servers results in business activities being curtailed), or server capacity is overprovided to avoid such constraints (thereby incurring the costs associated with the redundant capacity).
Level 2	IT infrastructure is typically sized according to component-specific capacity planning models – for example, current bandwidth plus 20 per cent headroom.
Level 3	A standardized capacity planning model is used to link infrastructure components to most IT services they support. Services can be cost-effectively scaled horizontally (for example, by adding more nodes to the system) or vertically (for example, by adding additional capacity to existing nodes), depending on requirements.
Level 4	A comprehensive capacity planning model links infrastructure components to all IT services, providing insight into the effect of expected business growth or contraction on IT applications and infrastructure.
Level 5	Capacity trend analysis provides a fully integrated view across the organization, and provides the information needed to ensure that IT infrastructure and applications can support current and future business requirements.

CBB B2: Risk Assessment

Assess the probability and impact of IT-related risks on organizational activities – for example, quantification of IT-enabled business value-at-risk.

Level 1	Risk assessments are non-existent or ad hoc.
Level 2	The risk of service level agreements being breached is beginning to be assessed for individual IT components. Contingency options are developed for a limited number of priority IT applications/services.
Level 3	Standardized risk assessments are in place for most IT services. Similarly, contingency options are developed for most IT applications/services.
Level 4	Comprehensive risk assessments are in place for all IT-supported business processes. Contingency options are developed for all IT applications/services.
Level 5	Risk assessment approaches are continually reviewed.

CBB B3: Investment Scenario Planning

Understand existing capacity and identify the need for additional/new IT infrastructure to support growth of business processes.

Level 1	Scenario planning is non-existent or ad hoc.
Level 2	Scenario planning is beginning to be used to extrapolate capacity requirements for a limited number of infrastructure components, with a focus on infrastructure robustness.
Level 3	Scenario planning is routinely used to extrapolate capacity requirements for most IT infrastructure and services, with a focus on service resilience.
Level 4	Comprehensive scenario planning is used to model various business process demand loads, with a view to understanding the impact on all related IT infrastructure and services.
Level 5	Scenario planning activities are continually reviewed to ensure that they capture the impact on IT infrastructure and services of business initiatives and options under consideration.

Category C: CBBs Associated with *Business Interaction*

CBB C1: Communication Management

Establish lines of communication between the IT function and other business units regarding the management of IT infrastructure and services.

Level 1	Communication between the IT function and other business units focuses mainly on problems and corrections.
Level 2	Communication is increasing between the IT function and other business units, but tends to be technically framed, dealing with usage and capacity limits relating to isolated aspects of technology – for example, storage, bandwidth, and processing capacity.
Level 3	Communication between the IT function and other business units is business-unit framed, dealing with the impact of trends in business process throughput on the capacity of IT services and infrastructure.
Level 4	Communication is organization-wide, facilitating the systematic prioritization of investments in IT services based on the collective needs and projections of the entire organization.
Level 5	Communication is aimed at securing mutual benefits by continually identifying new opportunities to optimize the organization.

CBB C2: Partnership Management

Establish ways of managing and maintaining interactions with business units and stakeholders – these could include informal approaches, such as phone calls, emails, and courtesy visits, and formal written, signed agreements reviewed periodically.

Level 1	Partnership management is non-existent or ad hoc, resulting in limited trust in the performance and predictability of IT services and infrastructure.
Level 2	The IT function has a relationship akin to a utility supplier to other business units. A robust and predictable IT environment is emerging through the use of analytics.
Level 3	The IT function is perceived as a preferred supplier of cost-effective IT services to other business units. This relationship is enabled through the use of increasingly more business-focused analytics.
Level 4	The IT function is perceived as a strategic partner to other business units, based in part on its ability to analyse relationships between business events/transactions and IT services.
Level 5	The IT function is perceived as a true business partner, based on its ability to lead business scenario modelling discussions and advise on suitable options.

12.4 IMPROVEMENT PLANNING

Capability Evaluation

Two summary assessment questions are set out below, along with the typical response associated with each level of maturity.

How are usage patterns for IT services monitored and modelled?

Level 1   Monitoring is limited to infrastructure component points. Capacity is poorly understood due to ad hoc modelling approaches.

Level 2   Monitoring and modelling policies and tool sets are defined for a limited number of critical points across core IT services.

Level 3   Monitoring and modelling policies and tool sets are fully implemented for most IT services and all network attached devices.

Level 4   Monitoring and modelling policies and tool sets are fully implemented for virtually all IT-enabled business processes and services.

Level 5   IT-enabled business processes and services are continually monitored, modelled, and improved.

How is the impact of planned business demand for IT services and infrastructure understood?

Level 1   There is limited or no forecasting of IT service demand.

Level 2   Service forecasting is carried out in parts of the IT function. Service level breaches are declining but still occur frequently.

Level 3   Standardized service forecasting is carried out across the IT function. Service levels are routinely met.

Level 4   Comprehensive service forecasting is carried out across the organization. Service levels are met most of the time.

Level 5   Service forecasting is continually reviewed for improvement based on accuracy of past forecasts. Service levels are always met.

Key Practices-Outcomes-Metrics (POMs)

Some useful POMs for developing the Service Analytics and Intelligence (SAI) capability are summarized below.

Level 2 POMs

Practice	Apply component-level Service Level Agreements (SLAs).
Outcome	The performance of IT infrastructure components is monitored and improved.
Metric	Mean time between failures (MTBF). Mean time to resolution (MTTR).

Practice	Implement component monitoring processes to identify when actual performance deviates from the normal. Escalate if the level of deviation breaches the limits set in the corresponding service level agreement.
Outcome	Infrastructure performance metrics improve, leading to overall better predictability.
Metric	Number of incidents/SLA breaches per type/component.
Practice	Map the infrastructure component landscape. Perform root cause analysis for each incident.
Outcome	Recurring incidents are minimized, with the result that the performance of the infrastructure is more predictable.
Metric	Number of incidents by type or service. IT components' availability/response time/capacity.

Level 3 POMs

Practice	Map IT services to infrastructure components. Undertake root-cause analysis of IT service problems, examining the underlying IT infrastructure component issues that impact on IT service performance, and taking remedial actions to avoid recurrence.
Outcome	The performance of the IT environment is more predictable, and potential threats to performance are identified before they impact users.
Metric	Service latency/availability/utilization. Mean time between failures (MTBF). Mean time to resolution (MTTR).
Practice	Explore flexible options for sizing the IT infrastructure to match the demand for IT services.
Outcome	Investments and divestments are prioritized based on business demand and cost per service.
Metric	IT service cost per user. IT asset utilization. Frequency with which a risk threshold is breached.
Practice	Conduct regular service performance reviews between IT service owners and business customers. Include discussions on expected business demand.
Outcome	Collaboration results in increased understanding of the business needs of the customer, and ensures that fulfilment plans are mutually agreed.
Metric	Business customer satisfaction levels with IT services.

Level 4 POMs

Practice	Map business processes to underlying IT services to develop understanding of performance interdependencies and to facilitate root cause analysis.
Outcome	Areas are identified where IT services are constraining business performance.
Metric	Business process hours/transactions lost due to IT failures or breaches of service level agreements.

Practice	Develop the business case for investment in IT by emphasizing the relationship between business processes and the underlying IT services and infrastructure.
Outcome	Investments are prioritized to meet business process requirements.
Metric	Business process hours/transactions gained because of addition/expansion of IT services and infrastructure.
Practice	Conduct scenario planning of business value-at-risk, based on IT service and infrastructure data.
Outcome	Investments in IT can be prioritized according to their potential for mitigating business risk.
Metric	Cost per transaction. Business process hours/transactions lost due to IT failures or breaches of service level agreements.

Level 5 POMs

Practice	Conduct ongoing validation of monitoring and modelling, comparing actual with forecasted, and amending models as required to improve accuracy.
Outcome	Planning is continually improved to support optimized resource allocation.
Metric	Cost of excess capacity. (Opportunity) cost of under capacity.
Practice	Develop an enterprise-level model of all IT-enabled business processes, thereby establishing the link from the organization and its business processes to the IT services and infrastructure.
Outcome	Business-level scenario planning across the entire organization is facilitated. This enables the impact of IT investments on the business and the impact of business plans on IT services to be holistically understood and quantified.
Metric	Percentage of enterprise processes covered by the model.

Addressing Typical Challenges

Some typical challenges that can arise in attempting to develop maturity in the Service Analytics and Intelligence (SAI) capability are set out below.

Challenge	Analytical initiatives fail to gain traction across the wider organization.
Context	Senior management support is lacking in other business units owing to a lack of understanding regarding what can be achieved. Furthermore, analytical skills and expertise are inadequate to deliver such initiatives.
Action	In discussions with management, highlight business framed scenarios where analytics can help overcome existing business challenges or anticipate emerging trends before they pose significant business challenges. Prioritize recruitment and employee development programmes targeting appropriate analytical skills.
Challenge	Difficulty in accessing sufficient data for analysis and modelling.
Context	Infrastructure performance data can be difficult to compile, as it can reside deep inside technology stacks, in varying formats across heterogeneous systems and organizational boundaries.
Action	Initiate dialogue on the business value of extracting the required data either by in-house development or by using commercial off-the-shelf applications.
Challenge	It is difficult to achieve a consistent organization-wide approach to analytics.
Context	Analytics is largely viewed as an individual or business unit activity, with responsibility allocated to disparate groups or employees across the organization. This results in localized or fragmented approaches, leading to short-term local gains but hindering potentially larger organization-wide gains.
Action	Generate dialogue on the benefits of managing analytics at an organizational level, ensuring no one business process is optimized at the expense of another – unless it is strategically important to do so. Ensure proper care is taken to manage data and its analysis across the organization.

Management Artefacts

Management artefacts that may be used to develop maturity in the Service Analytics and Intelligence (SAI) capability include:

▸ Service level agreements (SLAs).
▸ Analytics software.
▸ Business process to IT service maps.
▸ A configuration management database (CMDB).

Service Level Agreements (SLAs)

A service level agreement (SLA) provides a formalized record of the customer's expectations regarding the level of service from a supplier. Typically, it can include:

▸ A general definition of the service to be provided.
▸ Service level measurement methods for capacity, response time (latency), availability (up-time), reliability (mean-time between failures and mean-time to resolution), control limits on process variances, and so on.
▸ Remedies or penalties that apply if service levels are not achieved.
▸ Responsibilities of each party – for example, support and escalation procedures.
▸ A service performance reporting process, its contents and frequency.
▸ A dispute resolution process.
▸ Indemnification against third-party costs resulting from service level breaches.
▸ A process for updating the agreement.

Having effective SLAs defined for IT services will help manage expectations of both the supplier and the customer.

Analytics Software

Analytics software facilitates techniques such as:

▸ Data importing (collating data from different sources – for example, service availability records, helpdesk calls, transaction histories, financials, process owner feedback).
▸ Pre-analytics (data harmonizing – time synchronization, nomenclature alignment, data cleansing, data extrapolation, and so on).
▸ Autonomous machine learning (searching for patterns).
▸ Statistical analysis (including mathematical techniques for identifying correlations and causalities in patterns).
▸ Automatic alerting (notifying when something unexpected occurs).
▸ Pre-computation of queries (pre-emptive analysis in anticipation of likely questions).
▸ Ad hoc scenario modelling (multi-criteria what-if analysis).
▸ Intuitive visualization (ways of presenting the analysis).

Analytics software can help eliminate guesswork and quickly identify areas for cost optimization, identify opportunities to streamline operations, and improve business outcomes.

Business Process to IT Service Maps

Business process to IT service maps provide graphical illustrations of the relationships between business processes and the underlying IT services. They are useful for articulating how business processes relate to IT services and vice-versa. These maps can be used to develop business-level performance monitoring indicators, to clarify performance interdependencies, and to facilitate root cause analysis.

Configuration Management Database (CMDB)

The configuration management database is a repository of information or metadata on all significant IT components. Typically a CMDB includes details of:

- IT assets and applications, collectively referred to as configuration items (CIs).
- The relationships between the CIs.
- The CIs' life cycle stage – for example, whether it is active or retired.
- Changes made – for example, changes to a CI's status or relationship to other CIs.

The CMBD is useful in tracing any change whose introduction causes a problem in a complex IT environment. It can also be useful in identifying the last known 'good state' or 'operational state' of the IT environment.

12.5 REFERENCE

See Also

Other capabilities of IT-CMF that have a particularly close relationship with the Service Analytics and Intelligence (SAI) capability include:

Capability	What it provides
02. Business Planning (BP)	Insight into planning initiatives and projected demand for IT services, which can inform likely demand on IT
03. Business Process Management (BPM)	Definition/documentation of business processes, which helps support relationship mapping between processes and IT services
11. Risk Management (RM)	Visibility across various IT-related risks that could impact business activity
14. Strategic Planning (SP)	High-level overview of likely IT demand and strategic options being considered
20. Enterprise Architecture Management (EAM)	Architectural mappings of business processes to specific IT applications that support those processes, which can inform the creation of an end-to-end view of IT service performance
27. Service Provisioning (SRP)	Data points on IT services for further analysis
30. Technical Infrastructure Management (TIM)	Visibility into activity and status of IT assets

Further Reading

DAMA, 2009. *The DAMA guide to the data management body of knowledge (DMBOK)*, 1st ed. Bradley Beach, NJ: Technics Publications.

Kiron, D., Prentice, P.K., and Ferguson, R.B., 2014. The analytics mandate. *MIT Sloan Management Review,* 55, 29–33.

Schniederjans, M.J., Schniederjans, D.G., and Starkey, C.M., 2014. *Business analytics principles, concepts, and applications: what, why, and how*. Upper Saddle River, NJ: Pearson Education.

Notes

[1] Davenport, T.H., 2006. Competing on analytics. *Harvard Business Review,* 84, 98–107.

[2] Kiron, D., Prentice, P.K., and Ferguson, R.B., 2014. The analytics mandate. *MIT Sloan Management Review,* 55, 29–33.

SRC
13. Sourcing

13.1 OVERVIEW

Goal

The Sourcing (SRC) capability aims to streamline the strategic planning and development of the IT supply base to optimize the contribution of the supply base to the organization's strategic objectives.

Objectives

▷ Establish a common approach to selecting IT suppliers for their operational contribution and potential strategic impact, instead of awarding contracts only or mainly on the basis of lowest bid price.

▷ Assess the value and relevance of current and potential sourcing opportunities and relationships according to long-term goals and overall business and supply management objectives.

▷ Achieve both cost reduction and improvement in IT supplier performance.

▷ Ensure continuity of supply if a supplier's operations are unexpectedly disrupted or when switching suppliers.

▷ Leverage good practice and innovations from the supply base to support business innovation.

▷ Increase organizational effectiveness by simplifying, automating, and integrating sourcing processes across the organization.

Value

The Sourcing (SRC) capability fosters mutually beneficial partnerships with the supply base by developing appropriate sourcing relationships based on market knowledge and the business objectives.

Relevance

A rapidly evolving business environment continually challenges organizations to reduce costs, increase productivity, and deliver innovation. Many organizations turn to external IT service providers, who offer economies of scale and technical know-how, to address some or all of their IT service needs [1]. Additionally, the rise of 'everything-as-a-service' (XaaS) means that external IT services can be procured more easily than ever before. Research indicates, however, that organizations without an overarching IT sourcing strategy can experience significant difficulties, including vendor lock-in, rigid contracts, and security and service level concerns, leading to an erosion of the original sourcing benefits. Equally, organizations that rely exclusively on their internal IT functions to provide all IT services can suffer complacency, high costs, and lack of innovation. This points to the need for a balanced, incremental, and selective approach to sourcing IT services [2].

With an effective Sourcing (SRC) capability, an organization is able to define an appropriate sourcing strategy, manage the selection of IT service providers, integrate internal and external services, and ensure the delivery of innovation and business value.

13.2 SCOPE

Definition

The Sourcing (SRC) capability is the ability to evaluate, select, and integrate IT service providers according to a defined strategy and sourcing model, which could include service providers both inside and outside the organization. The Sourcing (SRC) capability covers:

▸ Defining the strategy for sourcing IT services and the high-level business cases for sourcing initiatives.

▸ Defining the sourcing model, including, for example, considering internal or third-party sourcing arrangements, on-shoring, near-shoring, or far-shoring, and single or multiple IT service providers.

▸ Developing criteria for selecting providers and processes for choosing the most advantageous provider.

▸ Defining approaches for preparing, negotiating, closing, and re-evaluating contracts with IT service providers.

▸ Establishing a win-win culture to promote enduring and successful relationships with the supply base.

▸ Managing potential operational impacts when transitioning to a new provider.

Other Capabilities

The following are addressed by other capabilities of IT-CMF:

For...	Refer to...
Balancing business demand and IT supply including the IT services portfolio	05. Demand and Supply Management (DSM)
Managing service performance levels for individual IT services	27. Service Provisioning (SRP)
Managing suppliers from an operational perspective	29. Supplier Management (SUM)

13.3 UNDERSTANDING MATURITY

Recognizing Excellence

When the Sourcing (SRC) capability is well-developed or mature:

▶ There is an IT sourcing strategy that is aligned with the organization's overall business sourcing strategy.

▶ Rather than always demanding the lowest possible price, the organization can innovate with suppliers to transform the underlying cost structure of IT services.

▶ The intellectual capital of the supplier base is leveraged to develop new solutions, helping to influence – not just support – the organization's business strategy.

▶ The IT function protects the business from risk by working with stakeholders to determine the best mitigation strategy when a risk exposure is identified.

▶ Sourcing options for a range of IT services are regularly evaluated.

▶ The process for selecting IT service providers is aligned with an organization-wide sourcing approach to realize synergies.

▶ Commercial terms with IT service providers incentivize actions that are mutually beneficial.

▶ The sourcing governance model promotes sustainable, cooperative, and amicable relationships with IT service providers.

Maturity at the Critical Capability Level

The following statements provide a high-level overview of the Sourcing (SRC) capability at successive levels of maturity:

Level 1   Sourcing decisions are uncoordinated, and made on an ad hoc basis, driven by tactical criteria and localized needs.

Level 2   Sourcing decisions for a limited number of IT services are driven by a defined sourcing approach.

Level 3   A standardized approach for sourcing decisions is used for most IT services – including, for example, common evaluation criteria, aggregated purchasing power, and evaluation of legacy providers.

Level 4   Sourcing decisions for all IT services are driven by a comprehensive, organization-wide sourcing approach to exploit potential synergies.

Level 5   Sourcing decisions are always driven by the sourcing strategy and supporting approaches, which are continually reviewed with input from relevant business ecosystem partners to improve effectiveness and innovation.

Maturity at the Capability Building Block (CBB) Level

The Capability Building Blocks (CBBs) associated with the Sourcing (SRC) capability fall into three categories:

▶ Category A: six CBBs associated with ***Sourcing Strategy*** – these establish the key components of the IT sourcing strategy.

▶ Category B: two CBBs associated with ***Contracting*** – these determine how provider selection is managed.

▶ Category C: two CBBs associated with ***Sourcing Execution*** – these address how IT service providers are integrated into and governed in the organization.

These are described below, together with a summary of the different maturity levels for each.

Category A: CBBs Associated with *Sourcing Strategy*

CBB A1: Strategy Alignment

Align IT sourcing options and activities with the IT strategy for organizational impact.

Level 1	Consideration of sourcing options and activities in the IT strategy is non-existent or ad hoc.
Level 2	The IT strategy incorporates a limited number of sourcing options and activities, typically focused on cost management within the IT function – for example, replacing existing services with cheaper substitutes.
Level 3	The IT strategy consistently incorporates sourcing options and activities, typically focused on enhancing certain business processes outside the IT function – for example, supplementing existing services with more flexible options.
Level 4	The IT strategy systematically incorporates sourcing options and activities, typically focused on transforming end-to-end business processes across the organization.
Level 5	The IT strategy incorporates sourcing options and activities with a continual focus on enabling agility and innovation.

CBB A2: Objectives and Scoping

Specify the sourcing objectives (for example, quality, cost, flexibility, risk, innovation, agility), the scope of IT services, and the criteria used to evaluate and select service providers.

Level 1	Sourcing objectives, scope, and selection criteria are rarely, if ever, explicitly specified.
Level 2	Sourcing objectives, scope, and selection criteria are specified for a limited number of IT services.
Level 3	Sourcing objectives, scope, and selection criteria are specified for most services that are facilitated by the IT function.
Level 4	Sourcing objectives, scope, and selection criteria are agreed with stakeholders across the organization to include services not directly facilitated by the IT function.
Level 5	Sourcing objectives, scope, and selection criteria are continually cross-checked with input from relevant business ecosystem partners to ensure they remain effective.

CBB A3: Sourcing Model Selection

Choose appropriate sourcing model(s) to support delivery of IT services (for example, internal or third-party providers, single or multiple providers).

Level 1 Selection of sourcing model(s) is made on a subjective, tactical, and case-by-case basis.

Level 2 For a limited number of IT services, the sourcing model(s) are selected based on emerging common criteria.

Level 3 For most IT services that the IT function facilitates, the sourcing model(s) are selected based on standardized criteria, and with input from some other business units.

Level 4 For all IT services, the sourcing model(s) are selected using an approach that is endorsed organization-wide.

Level 5 The approaches used to select sourcing model(s) are continually refined and improved to take into account lessons learned from previous sourcing decisions, changes in corporate strategy, and regular input from relevant business ecosystem partners.

CBB A4: Business Case Creation

Create and review business cases for evaluating sourcing options for IT services.

Level 1 Any business case that is created is informal and ad hoc.

Level 2 Business cases are occasionally created for evaluating a limited number of sourcing options. They generally only consider tactical cost factors.

Level 3 Business cases are consistently created for evaluating most sourcing options. They include key strategic objectives and factors (including cost).

Level 4 Business cases are a part of a comprehensive decision-making process for evaluating sourcing options. They include an appropriate balance of quantitative and qualitative aspects.

Level 5 Business case templates for sourcing decisions are continually reviewed and improved to enhance their effectiveness.

CBB A5: Organizational Readiness

Assess and review the organization's readiness for sourcing initiatives. Such an assessment might take into account, for example, the extent of process standardization, the adaptability of the organizational structure and culture, the methods and media used for communication, and the policies and practices relating to resourcing and skills transfer and retention.

Level 1 Any assessments of organizational readiness for sourcing initiatives are conducted without reference to formal guidelines, and are individually driven.

Level 2 An emerging set of critical success factors is used to assess organizational readiness for a limited number of larger sourcing initiatives.

Level 3 A standardized assessment model is used to assess organizational readiness for most sourcing initiatives.

Level 4 A comprehensive assessment model is used organization-wide to evaluate organizational readiness for all sourcing initiatives.

Level 5 The organizational readiness assessment model is continually reviewed and optimized to take into account the outcomes of previous sourcing initiatives.

CBB A6: Re-evaluation

Assess legacy sourcing decisions and consider alternative sourcing options. Consider, for example, changes that have taken place in the business context, new opportunities and risks that have arisen, and costs associated with vendor lock-in or switching.

Level 1	Any legacy sourcing decisions that are re-evaluated are done so in an ad hoc manner.
Level 2	A limited number of legacy sourcing decisions are re-evaluated using an emerging set of criteria. Corrective actions are occasionally implemented.
Level 3	Increasingly more legacy sourcing decisions are re-evaluated using a standardized set of criteria. Corrective actions are implemented most of the time.
Level 4	The majority of legacy sourcing decisions are re-evaluated using a comprehensive set of criteria. Corrective actions are implemented in all instances.
Level 5	All legacy sourcing decisions are continually re-evaluated to maintain alignment with the business context and strategic objectives.

Category B: CBBs Associated with *Contracting*

CBB B1: Provider Selection

Ensure that the approach used for selecting IT service providers adheres to and influences the organization's procurement procedures.

Level 1	Providers are selected informally, and no formal selection approach is applied.
Level 2	Providers are typically selected based only on their responses to a Request for Information (RFI). Most IT service provider selection procedures are conducted without specific input from the organization's procurement function.
Level 3	There is a standardized provider selection approach in place, which involves an initial list of candidates, a Request for Information (RFI), a short list, a Request for Proposal (RFP), and a final selection, and this approach is consistently followed. The approach taken to selecting IT service providers occasionally involves input from the organization's procurement function.
Level 4	There are comprehensive provider selection approaches tailored for first-time and renewal bids. IT service provider selection is fully integrated into the organization's procurement process.
Level 5	The approach to IT service provider selection, and its interaction with the organization's procurement process, is continually reviewed and optimized to maintain synergies.

CBB B2: Contract Preparation and Closing

Develop IT's own contract negotiation position in advance (for example, by identifying negotiable and non-negotiable items, and considering incentives). Understand the IT service provider's success criteria to create win-win situations.

Level 1	Contracts are prepared and closed informally, with little consideration for any formal process.
Level 2	Contract preparation and closing are predominantly focused on a limited set of primary variables, such as cost, security, quality, and legal recourse.
Level 3	Contract preparation and closing include an expanded set of secondary variables, including inter-provider Operational Level Agreements (OLAs). The IT service provider's own success criteria are beginning to be accommodated.
Level 4	Contract preparation and closing consistently strike a balance between incentivizing innovation by the IT service provider and ensuring cost-effective IT service delivery.
Level 5	Contract preparation and closing activities are continually reviewed for improvement opportunities.

Category C: CBBs Associated with *Sourcing Execution*

CBB C1: Transition

Support the introduction of new IT services or the migration of legacy IT services between the IT service provider and the organization, considering, for example, staffing the project team, identifying and informing affected employees, employee placement, preparing technical interfaces, migrating data, security protocols, defining access rights, and validating availability.

Level 1	Any preparation for transitioning IT services is ad hoc, and is not part of a formal approach.
Level 2	A limited number of larger transitions are managed using an emerging approach.
Level 3	Most transitions across the IT function are managed using a standardized approach with explicit critical success factors.
Level 4	A suite of comprehensive approaches that are endorsed organization-wide are used to effect transitions, enabling timely and reliable delivery.
Level 5	The transition approaches are regularly reviewed in the light of experience from previous sourcing initiatives.

CBB C2: Provider Integration and Governance

Integrate IT service providers into organizational activities with appropriate governance and performance oversight structures.

Level 1   Responsibilities and accountabilities are unclear, as there is no formal governance or performance oversight structure in place.

Level 2   A limited number of governance structures are emerging that cover the activities of some IT service providers.

Level 3   Most of the IT service providers are included within formal governance and performance oversight structures.

Level 4   Comprehensive structures for managing all IT service providers are in place and consistently adhered to. These extend to inter-provider relationships.

Level 5   Structures are continually reviewed and revised based on ongoing integration effectiveness.

13.4 IMPROVEMENT PLANNING

Capability Evaluation

Two summary assessment questions are set out below, along with the typical response associated with each level of maturity.

To what extent does the IT sourcing strategy support overall IT and business strategies?

Level 1   An IT sourcing strategy is not clearly defined or is informal in nature.

Level 2   Multiple IT sourcing strategies are in use across the IT function. They may be uncoordinated and at times may conflict.

Level 3   There is a single IT sourcing strategy for the entire IT function, which is primarily focused on satisfying the IT function's objectives.

Level 4   The IT function's sourcing strategy is integrated with the organization's sourcing strategy, and has a balanced focus between IT and business objectives.

Level 5   The IT sourcing strategy is continually reviewed based on performance and on regular input from relevant business ecosystem partners.

How are internal and external IT service providers selected and governed to ensure that they deliver on required objectives?

Level 1   Providers are typically selected on an ad hoc basis, using informal governance structures.

Level 2   A defined provider selection process is used in parts of the IT function, and key governance roles are emerging.

Level 3   A standardized provider selection process is used across the IT function with input from some other business units, and a consistent governance structure is in place.

Level 4   Provider selection processes and governance structures are comprehensively integrated organization-wide, supporting and influencing the business strategy.

Level 5   Provider selection processes and governance structures are continually reviewed based on effectiveness, and on regular input from relevant business ecosystem partners.

Key Practices-Outcomes-Metrics (POMs)

Some useful POMs for developing the Sourcing (SRC) capability are summarized below.

Level 2 POMs

Practice	Check that legacy sourcing decisions remain relevant to the IT strategy.
Outcome	Previous sourcing opportunities are assessed for value and relevance to current organizational needs.
Metric	Percentage of legacy sourcing decisions evaluated.
Practice	Within the IT function, apply a consistent process to select IT service providers.
Outcome	Transparency and objectivity guide selection of the most suitable candidate.
Metric	Percentage of providers selected, using the preferred selection process.
Practice	Identify necessary interfaces between the retained organization (people, skills, and so on) and the IT service providers.
Outcome	Smoother transitions and ongoing cooperation are facilitated.
Metric	Number of defined interfaces between the retained organization and the IT service providers.
Practice	Use defined criteria to translate sourcing objectives into contract terms and conditions.
Outcome	Expectations of providers can be explicitly managed.
Metric	Percentage of contracts that are based on an approved template. Percentage of contracts where providers meet expectations during the term of the contract.

Level 3 POMs

Practice	Mandate standard criteria for selecting the appropriate sourcing model. Such criteria might include, for example, business criticality, capability of the provider, risk associated with physical location, quality, and cost.
Outcome	Appropriate sourcing models can be consistently selected, minimizing potentially negative outcomes from sourcing selections.
Metric	Percentage of selected sourcing models that have to be changed because they turn out to be inappropriate.
Practice	Determine organizational readiness for sourcing, by assessing, for example, the extent of process standardization, the availability of resources and skills, and design of the retained organization's structure.
Outcome	The organization's readiness for a sourcing initiative is clarified, and realistic transition plans can be considered before deciding on a sourcing deal.
Metric	Organizational scope and depth of readiness assessment. Number of recurring issues relating to transition initiatives.
Practice	Ensure provider selection processes and criteria regularly incorporate input from the corporate procurement function.
Outcome	The selection process can be enhanced by inputs from the organization's procurement function.
Metric	Percentage of providers selected with the cooperation of corporate procurement.
Practice	Issue guidance on adapting sourcing contracts to reflect the specific requirements and circumstances of each individual sourcing context.
Outcome	A standardized approach to managing contract flexibility enables different sourcing objectives to be realized, while contract consistency is maintained within acceptable tolerance levels.
Metric	Percentage of sourcing contract templates that are modified within specified tolerance limits.

Level 4 POMs

Practice	Require all sourcing decisions to reference the established sourcing model.
Outcome	Sourcing decisions are made in a consistent manner, based on a comprehensive set of criteria.
Metric	Percentage of sourcing decisions that adhere to the appropriate sourcing model.
Practice	Fully integrate IT service provider selection into the organization-wide procurement process.
Outcome	Full synergies can be realized. Compliance with procurement guidelines is maximized.
Metric	Percentage of IT service providers selected using the organization's standard procurement approach.

Practice	Consider positive incentive clauses across relevant sourcing contracts.
Outcome	Sourcing contracts provide win-win opportunities for the organization and the service provider.
Metric	Number of innovations jointly realized. Number of chargeable activities not charged by IT service providers.

Level 5 POMs

Practice	Maintain continual reviews of sourcing objectives, the scope of services/processes being sourced, and the governance model.
Outcome	The adaptation of sourcing approaches to remain current with business needs is encouraged.
Metric	Frequency of reviews. Percentage of actions completed following each review.

Practice	Regularly assess IT service delivery against original business case objectives.
Outcome	Results can feed into the process of re-evaluating the sourcing of IT service providers.
Metric	Percentage of IT service providers re-evaluated against original business case objectives and contracts.

Practice	Continually review the provider selection process and criteria, and their integration with the organization-wide procurement process.
Outcome	Synergies are optimized.
Metric	Percentage of audit suggestions implemented.

Addressing Typical Challenges

Some typical challenges that can arise in attempting to develop maturity in the Sourcing (SRC) capability are set out below.

Challenge	The IT sourcing model cannot adequately facilitate the central sourcing of all IT services across the entire organization, leading to rising 'shadow' IT expenditure.
Context	The IT function focuses primarily on stable sourcing arrangements that deliver robust and efficient back-office systems, while the other business units focus primarily on flexible sourcing arrangements that facilitate agile prototyping of front-office digital technologies, such as data analytics, mobility, and social media.
Action	Stimulate cross-organization discussions on how best to adopt IT sourcing models that can cater for both traditional and emerging business requirements for IT services – for example, by embracing a greater diversity of vendors, ranging from traditional hardware suppliers and system integrators to more innovative cloud service providers and entrepreneurial vendors.

Challenge	There is a fear that, once the organization selects a vendor, it will be *locked in* and unable to take advantage of innovations coming from other sources without incurring high switching costs, because of proprietary or non-standard vendor technologies.
Context	In many instances, there are, as yet, no widely accepted standards that promote interoperability between vendor offerings. This often means choosing between vendors of proprietary technologies (with the risk that the chosen vendor will take advantage of the arrangement) or choosing a consortium that is building open source technologies, in the hope that these will become dominant in the market.
Action	Investigate how the prospective vendor's technology can interface with external technologies, and the implications of migrating off it at a later point if it proves to be unsatisfactory. Factors to consider include data export formats, application programming interfaces (APIs), level of customization options, and use of open standards and protocols.
Challenge	Inability to conduct appropriate due diligence of commercial arrangements with potential IT service providers.
Context	The role of procuring IT services is not adequately resourced to deal with complex legal issues, sustainability concerns, or regulatory or ethical considerations.
Action	Canvass senior business leaders for their support for an adequately resourced IT procurement approach by highlighting the benefits in terms of managing and anticipating risk, and increasing transparency.
Challenge	Despite having been selected following rigorous evaluation, an IT service provider may fail to deliver against the stated business case, resulting in premature contract termination or renegotiation.
Context	With the shift to sourcing a significant proportion of IT services externally, the IT function lacks the skills required to manage external vendors effectively.
Action	Initiate discussions with senior management on such things as the methods, structures, incentives, and competences that are needed to proactively manage IT service providers so that they deliver innovation and business value.

Management Artefacts

Management artefacts that may be used to develop maturity in the Sourcing (SRC) capability include:

▶ A strategic IT sourcing plan.
▶ A documented IT sourcing methodology.
▶ A sourcing readiness checklist.
▶ A sourcing contract.
▶ Sourcing model templates.

Strategic IT Sourcing Plan

The strategic IT sourcing plan documents the circumstances under which the sourcing of IT services will be considered, the requirements for an initial high-level business case, the high-level guidelines for determining the sourcing model, and the high-level transition planning. The strategic IT sourcing plan is ideally enabled by the IT sourcing methodology.

IT Sourcing Methodology

A documented IT sourcing methodology outlines how sourcing activities are organized. It covers:

- Selecting the appropriate sourcing model – how new providers of IT services are engaged.
- Developing the transition plan – how IT services are migrated.
- Preparing the various procurement stages – how the organization engages with the marketplace – for example, by issuing an RFI, an RFP, and/or an RFQ.
- Evaluating and selecting IT service providers.
- Agreeing commercial terms with chosen IT service providers.
- Overseeing the actual migration/introduction of IT services.

The objective of the IT sourcing methodology is to effectively deliver the strategic IT sourcing plan.

Sourcing Readiness Checklist

The sourcing readiness checklist is used to evaluate organizational and cultural readiness to execute a sourcing decision. It specifies a variety of characteristics, such as organizational structure, cultural philosophy, available skills and required learning curve, technical environment stability and complexity, business process understanding, and vendor security/connectivity. Readiness scores can yield a better perspective on how to develop the transition plan to execute sourcing decisions.

Sourcing Contract

The sourcing contract sets out the agreement between the organization and the supplier in relation to the IT services that will be delivered over a fixed time period. The contract may include a description of the services to be provided, service levels, security requirements, base and incremental pricing, hardware and software assets and configurations required, change control procedures, intellectual property management, business continuity requirements, compliance requirements, subcontractor agreements, termination clauses, termination assistance services, and so on. Evaluation criteria to determine the success or otherwise of a sourcing initiative may also be specified. The more forthright both parties are regarding the contract parameters, the greater the likelihood that they will have a shared understanding of the terms and conditions and the expected outcomes. This will reduce the risk of issues arising during the lifetime of the contract.

Sourcing Model Templates

There are a number of ways in which an organization can source its IT services, including:

▶ *Traditional* – a single service provider delivers a service to the client. This model is typically used for self-contained work with minimum dependencies, or for a contract covering a broad range of services where there is a requirement to minimize sourcing overheads. Also called 'full/sole sourcing', or, if the services are provided by an internal IT function, 'in-house/internal delivery', in which case the IT function may in turn act as a broker between external service providers and internal business units.

▶ *Co-sourcing* – a combination of external and in-house people, processes, and technologies working in collaboration to provide a service. This model is typically used when the scope of services is too broad to be addressed internally, but the client wants to retain control and so engages subcontractors to complement the internal resources.

▶ *Multi-sourcing* – the client directly chooses numerous service providers and is responsible for managing them on a day-to-day basis. This model is typically used when there is a strong need to ensure that different elements are sourced from the best possible service providers. Also called 'selective' or 'best of breed' sourcing.

▶ *Off-shoring* – using service providers in locations that are distant from where the service is likely to be consumed. This model is typically used to take advantage of market arbitrage – for example, labour costs.

▶ *On-shoring* – using service providers located in the same country as the contracting organization.

▶ *Near-shoring* – using service providers in locations that are near to where the service is likely to be consumed. This model is typically used to minimize communication and management barriers, such as language, culture, time differences, or distance.

▶ *In-sourcing* – using internal service providers to supply services to internal business units under market conditions. Such providers compete with external service providers, and may also provide services to third parties in the marketplace. Also called 'shared services', 'captive off-shoring' or 'global delivery centre'.

▶ *Joint-venture* – a legal arrangement between two or more parties in which they agree to form a new company to work together to provide services. This model is typically used where more favourable terms can be secured from such an arrangement than if each party operated independently.

▶ *Strategic alliance* – an agreement between multiple service providers to provide, on a contractual basis, services to a client that neither would be able to provide on their own. This model is typically used when there is a desire to benefit from shared assets, expertise, costs, business risk, markets, flexibility, demand, and so on, but without forming a legal partnership or separate company.

Selecting the appropriate sourcing model(s) will depend on the situation, and the goals and objectives behind the sourcing decision, and will take into consideration factors such as governance and oversight, contract flexibility, cost savings, access to expertise, and vendor lock in.

13.5 REFERENCE

See Also

Other capabilities of IT-CMF that have a particularly close relationship with the Sourcing (SRC) capability include:

Capability	What it provides
03. Business Process Management (BPM)	An understanding of how sourcing arrangements may affect business processes (both within the IT function and across the organization)
04. Capacity Forecasting and Planning (CFP)	Scenario modelling and forecasting of IT resources
05. Demand and Supply Management (DSM)	Forecasts of demand for IT services, some of which may be appropriately sourced externally
09. IT Leadership and Governance (ITG)	Guiding principles for a sourcing governance model between the IT function and third parties
11. Risk Management (RM)	A framework for managing the business risk in sourcing decisions
14. Strategic Planning (SP)	The business and operational strategy, as the context for strategic sourcing decisions
19. Capability Assessment Management (CAM)	An understanding of (potential) IT capability gaps that may inform sourcing options
21. Information Security Management (ISM)	Security requirements that need to be taken into account in selecting IT service providers
27. Service Provisioning (SRP)	Service performance levels for IT services
29. Supplier Management (SUM)	Day-to-day management of IT service providers/suppliers, such as assessing performance against SLAs

Further Reading

Ali, S., and Green, P., 2012. Effective information technology (IT) governance mechanisms: an IT outsourcing perspective. *Information Systems Frontiers*, 14(2), 179–193.

International Association of Outsourcing Professionals (IAOP), 2014. *The outsourcing professional body of knowledge (OPBOK)*. Zaltbommel, NL: Van Haren.

ITSQC, 2015. *The eSourcing capability model for service providers (eSCM-SP) v2*. Available at: <http://www.itsqc.org/models/escm-sp/>.

Notes

[1] Lacity, M., and Hirschheim, R., 1993. *Information systems outsourcing: myths, metaphors, and realities*. Chichester: Wiley.

[2] Lacity, M., Willcocks, L., and Feeny, D., 1996. The value of selective outsourcing. *MIT Sloan Management Review*. Spring 1996. Available at: <http://sloanreview.mit.edu/article/the-value-of-selective-it-sourcing/>.

SP
14. Strategic Planning

14.1 OVERVIEW

Goal

The Strategic Planning (SP) capability aims to specify ways in which technology can enable and influence the business strategy.

Objectives

- Outline key strategic issues and options for how technology can support and influence the business strategy.
- Clarify the purpose and goals of IT activities, thus enabling more consistent decision-making.
- Align the IT function and other business units on the strategic value of technology to amplify the creation of business value.
- Translate strategy and decisions into a set of programmes calculated to deliver desired objectives.
- Clearly communicate strategic goals and targets to all stakeholders.
- Promote more effective and efficient technology deployments.

Value

The Strategic Planning (SP) capability clarifies the purpose and goals of using technology to optimize value generation.

Relevance

IT resources must be aligned with organizational needs if they are to play a strategic role in the organization's success [1]. The more closely they are aligned, the more likely it is that the resultant IT-enabled business capabilities will be valuable, rare, inimitable, and non-substitutable (VRIN) [2], contributing to a sustainable competitive advantage for the organization [1] [3]. However, many organizations fail at the first stage of resource alignment – the strategic planning stage [4] [5].

By establishing an effective Strategic Planning (SP) capability, an organization can better enable and inform its overall business strategy, using a unifying vision for the IT function to identify suitable strategic options and programmes.

14.2 SCOPE

Definition

The Strategic Planning (SP) capability is the ability to formulate a long-term vision and translate it into an actionable strategic plan for the IT function. The Strategic Planning (SP) capability covers:

▶ Developing a long-term (typically 3-5 year) orientation or vision for the IT function, and high-level strategic options, and outlining programmes to implement these options.

▶ Aligning IT and business strategies.

▶ Identifying and analysing business challenges and opportunities to which IT can contribute.

▶ Involving key stakeholders in IT strategic planning.

▶ Evaluating and adjusting strategy and targets as appropriate.

▶ Developing relevant long-term roadmaps, such as for technology roll-out.

Other Capabilities

The following are addressed by other capabilities of IT-CMF:

For...	Refer to...
Developing lower level tactical and operational plans	02. Business Planning (BP)
Establishing governance structures	09. IT Leadership and Governance (ITG)
Prioritizing, initiating, or stopping programmes and projects	18. Portfolio Planning and Prioritization (PPP)
Undertaking detailed programme and project planning for individual initiatives	24. Programme and Project Management (PPM)
Undertaking detailed benefits assessment	33. Benefits Assessment and Realization (BAR)
On-going monitoring of programmes and projects	34. Portfolio Management (PM)

14.3 UNDERSTANDING MATURITY

Recognizing Excellence

When the Strategic Planning (SP) capability is well-developed or mature:

▶ The IT function effectively contributes to enabling and informing the business strategy.

▶ The IT vision is intrinsic to the business vision.

▶ The strategic plan for technology deployment has the clear objective of supporting the generation of business value.

▶ Strategic planning integrates seamlessly with operational planning.

▶ The IT strategic planning activity is embedded in the roles and responsibilities of dedicated IT and business stakeholders.

▶ Funding of IT strategic planning is recognized as an organization-level responsibility, and budgets are constructed with this in mind.

Maturity at the Critical Capability Level

The following statements provide a high-level overview of the Strategic Planning (SP) capability at successive levels of maturity:

Level 1	Any IT strategic planning that exists or resources allocated to it are informal, and opportunities and challenges are identified only in an ad hoc or informal way.
Level 2	An IT strategic planning approach is emerging. Limited resources are made available for IT planning purposes. An IT strategy is beginning to be formalized, but may not yet be adequately aligned with basic business needs.
Level 3	The IT strategic planning approach is standardized. Sufficient IT resources are allocated to IT strategic planning activities. The IT strategy is developed increasingly in consultation with planners from other business units to satisfy a wider array of business needs.
Level 4	The IT strategic planning approach is an integral part of wider organizational planning processes. Dedicated resources from the IT function and other business units are allocated to IT strategic planning, enabling the IT strategy to comprehensively support and influence the business strategy.
Level 5	The IT strategic planning approach is reviewed and improved using process improvement methods and tools. A strong symbiotic relationship exists between the IT and business strategic plans to such an extent that it can be difficult to distinguish between them.

Maturity at the Capability Building Block (CBB) Level

The Capability Building Blocks (CBBs) associated with the Strategic Planning (SP) capability fall into two categories:

▶ Category A: three CBBs associated with **Embedding IT Strategic Planning in the Organization** – these create the environment within which IT strategic planning can be undertaken.

▶ Category B: five CBBs associated with **Strategy Process** – these outline the planning activities involved in formulating the IT strategic plan.

These are described below, together with a summary of the different maturity levels for each.

Category A: CBBs Associated with *Embedding IT Strategic Planning in the Organization*

CBB A1: Resourcing

Allocate and coordinate roles, responsibilities, accountabilities, and resources for the IT strategic planning function.

Level 1	Any specific resources that are allocated for IT strategic planning are done so on an informal basis.
Level 2	Limited resources are formally allocated from within the IT function to support the IT strategic planning cycle.
Level 3	Dedicated resources are allocated from within the IT function and from some other business units to support the IT strategic planning cycle.
Level 4	Dedicated resources are allocated from within the IT function and from all other relevant business units to support the IT strategic planning cycle.
Level 5	The allocation of resources to IT strategic planning is continually reviewed as part of the wider organization's approach to strategic planning.

CBB A2: Related Planning Processes

Align and integrate IT strategic planning with relevant IT and business planning processes, such as budget and operational planning, resource allocation, business planning, and performance measurements.

Level 1	Any alignment or integration between IT strategic planning and other IT or business planning processes is coincidental rather than deliberate.
Level 2	IT strategic planning is starting to be aligned with other IT or business planning processes across the IT function.
Level 3	IT strategic planning is explicitly agreed by all stakeholders within the IT function and integrated with the business planning cycles of some other business units.
Level 4	IT strategic planning is comprehensively integrated with the business planning cycles of all other relevant business units.
Level 5	Specific roles and responsibilities have been assigned for IT strategic planning and there are review mechanisms in place to assist in continual planning process improvement.

CBB A3: Stakeholder Management and Communication

Communicate all aspects of IT strategic planning with stakeholders, including key individuals in the IT function, and business unit heads. Manage stakeholder expectations, engagement, and sponsorship.

Level 1	Any communication with stakeholders on IT strategic planning is informal and ad hoc.
Level 2	There is formal communication emerging with some stakeholders regarding IT strategic planning, for example through circulations to the executive board, Finance, and Human Resources.
Level 3	There is regular two-way communication with the majority of stakeholders regarding IT strategic planning. Stakeholder communications are increasingly becoming part of corporate business planning activities.
Level 4	Stakeholder communication of IT strategic planning is an intrinsic part of wider corporate business planning and communication.
Level 5	Stakeholder communication of IT strategic planning is continually reviewed for improvement.

Category B: CBBs Associated with *Strategy Process*

CBB B1: Alignment with Business

Mutually align and integrate IT and business strategic plans. Determine the IT strategy's contribution to business objectives. Influence the formation of the business strategy regarding the use of technology-enabled solutions to overcome business challenges.

Level 1	Any IT strategic planning that is performed is informal and ad hoc, with no formal input from or into business strategy planning.
Level 2	An IT strategy is emerging but it is developed largely independently of business strategy planning.
Level 3	Whilst driven by the IT function, the IT strategy is developed increasingly in consultation with business strategy planners from other business units.
Level 4	The IT strategy is driven within the overall business strategy planning process.
Level 5	IT and business strategic plans are continually reviewed for improvement. A strong symbiotic relationship exists between the IT and business strategic plans to such an extent that it can be difficult to distinguish between them.

CBB B2: IT Vision and Principles

Formulate the long-term scope and objectives for IT value generation (IT vision), and create high-level guidelines for deploying technology-enabled services (IT design principles).

Level 1 — Formulation or documenting of a long-term vision or design principles for IT is non-existent or ad hoc.

Level 2 — A high-level statement of long-term IT goals and plans, together with a more detailed statement covering the first two to three years, is prepared as part of the annual IT planning process. Design principles are formulated and published for widely-used technologies although compliance may be patchy.

Level 3 — A statement of the IT vision, linking IT goals to key business goals, is prepared by the IT function as part of the wider organization's planning cycle. Design principles are formulated and published by the IT function in relation to all of IT. Compliance is increasing across the organization.

Level 4 — A joint statement of the IT vision is prepared by the IT function together with all other business units as part of the organization's planning cycle. Design principles are also formulated jointly and compliance is high.

Level 5 — The IT vision is an intrinsic part of the business vision, and is continually reviewed for relevance. Design principles are formulated, published, and continually enforced for all levels of IT usage. A 'sense and respond' process monitors the evolution of externally-originating artefacts and protocols, to ensure ongoing compliance and internal cohesion among the different elements.

CBB B3: Strategic Options

Identify challenges and opportunities in the IT function and other business units, where IT can enhance performance. Identify options for action, and evaluate, prioritize, and select these options based on their potential contribution to business value.

Level 1 — Any challenges and opportunities are identified on an ad hoc or informal basis.

Level 2 — Technology trends are reviewed intermittently to identify challenges and opportunities.

Level 3 — Business challenges and opportunities for the IT function, and occasionally for some other business units, feed into IT planning workshops.

Level 4 — Business challenges and opportunities are comprehensively identified in close collaboration with the rest of the business at periodic intervals.

Level 5 — The approach taken to identifying business challenges and opportunities is continually reviewed for improvement with regular input from relevant business ecosystem partners.

CBB B4: Plan Development

Translate the selected strategic options into an approved strategic plan, encompassing high-level IT goals, programmes, timeframes, manpower planning, skills development, and long-range technology planning. Outline programme ownership, business goals, business value/benefits, and an outline business case at the programme level.

Level 1   Any IT strategy document that exists is informal.

Level 2   The IT strategy document consists only of an outline business case for some of the major IT programmes.

Level 3   The IT strategy document is driven by the IT function, but with increasing input from some other business units. It includes details of most approved IT programmes.

Level 4   The IT strategy document is jointly developed by the IT function and the rest of the business. It has a strong emphasis on programme sponsorship, ownership, and governance across all IT programmes.

Level 5   The IT strategy document is seen as a living artefact, and is continually reviewed in light of business ecosystem, industry, and regulatory dynamics.

CBB B5: Tracking and Evaluation

Assess the extent to which strategic targets are being achieved. Review all relevant programmes using qualitative and quantitative measures (such as satisfaction surveys, programme progress, and KPIs), and generate input for strategy reviews.

Level 1   The tracking and evaluation of IT strategic programmes to ascertain their contribution to business value is non-existent or informal.

Level 2   There is a basic tracking and evaluation process emerging, which is used occasionally to review the delivery of the intended results of major strategic IT programmes.

Level 3   A standardized tracking and evaluation process is in place with regular reviews of benefit and risk-focused metrics.

Level 4   A comprehensive tracking and evaluation process exists. Key IT strategic programmes are systematically reviewed post-implementation to assess whether or not they delivered the intended business value or results.

Level 5   The tracking and evaluation process is continually reviewed to ensure all IT strategic programmes remain valid and on course to deliver the intended business value or results.

14.4 IMPROVEMENT PLANNING

Capability Evaluation

Two summary assessment questions are set out below, along with the typical response associated with each level of maturity.

How embedded is IT strategic planning within the organization?

Level 1	IT strategic planning is not recognized as an activity and any effort by management in this area is ad hoc.
Level 2	Some basic IT strategic planning practices are emerging within the IT function, covering roles and responsibilities, and communication with stakeholders. However, these practices are primarily developed and used within the IT function without reference to other business units.
Level 3	Standardized IT strategic planning practices exist. These practices are developed with increasing input from some other business units.
Level 4	Comprehensive IT strategic planning practices are developed jointly by the IT function and all other business units.
Level 5	IT strategic planning practices are regularly reviewed for improvement, and include regular input from relevant business ecosystem partners.

To what extent are IT strategy processes (such as defining the IT vision and principles, strategic planning, tracking, and evaluation) operating within the organization?

Level 1	IT strategy processes are either not defined, or are defined and used in an ad hoc manner.
Level 2	Within the IT function, some basic IT strategy processes are emerging but may be inconsistently applied.
Level 3	IT strategy processes are consistently defined and applied by the IT function and some other business units.
Level 4	Comprehensive IT strategy processes are developed jointly by key stakeholders from the IT function and all other business units, and are applied organization-wide.
Level 5	The IT strategy processes are reviewed on a periodic and timely basis, and refined by key stakeholders, including those from relevant business ecosystem partners.

Key Practices-Outcomes-Metrics (POMs)

Some useful POMs for developing the Strategic Planning (SP) capability are summarized below.

Level 2 POMs

Practice	Allocate appropriately qualified IT personnel to key IT strategic planning duties.
Outcome	Resources are allocated for the most important planning duties.
Metric	Yes/No indicator regarding adequate resourcing of key IT strategic planning duties.
Practice	Hold formal and informal forums and discussions on IT strategic planning.
Outcome	Stakeholders have a forum in which they can influence the creation of the IT strategic plan.
Metric	Breadth of stakeholders involved in discussions held on IT strategic planning.
Practice	Outline key IT design principles, and show how they relate to the IT vision.
Outcome	Decisions within the IT function begin to follow common design principles that support the IT strategy.
Metric	Number of IT design principles traceable back to the IT vision.
Practice	Develop a high-level IT strategic plan and distribute it to key stakeholders.
Outcome	A documented IT strategy exists to guide how key domains are supported by the IT strategic plan.
Metric	Number of IT and business unit employees on the strategic plan circulation list.

Level 3 POMs

Practice	Distribute responsibility for IT strategic planning between the IT function and some other business units as appropriate.
Outcome	Broader participation will help ensure more effective strategic planning activities.
Metric	Representation of business units formally involved in IT strategic planning activities.
Practice	Ensure the IT budget includes an allocation to support IT strategic planning.
Outcome	IT strategic planning duties receive adequate resourcing and become more effective.
Metric	Percentage of IT resources formally assigned to IT strategic planning.
Practice	Prepare a high-level business case for each programme in the IT strategic plan.
Outcome	All major assumptions underpinning the IT strategy are recorded and validated.
Metric	Percentage of the programmes in the IT strategic plan for which a business case is developed.

Level 4 POMs

Practice	Gather stakeholder input on IT strategic planning through regular and structured reviews.
Outcome	There is increased stakeholder ownership of the IT strategy.
Metric	Number of joint review meetings held between the IT function and all other business units.
Practice	Validate an IT vision statement jointly between the IT function and all other business units, with a core focus on enabling business capabilities.
Outcome	An understanding of what constitutes IT value is shared throughout the organization.
Metric	Representation of stakeholders from the IT function and other business units involved in the validation of the IT vision.
Practice	Revisit the IT strategy for comprehensiveness at agreed intervals or conditional triggers.
Outcome	Lessons learned can inform the alignment of IT strategic planning with other relevant processes.
Metric	Frequency of review meetings. Number of programme change requests approved. Number of programmes terminated before completion.

Level 5 POMs

Practice	Ensure IT strategic planning remains an integral part of wider business strategic planning.
Outcome	There is minimal risk of misalignment between IT and business planning, or of missing opportunities for the strategic use of IT.
Metric	Number of business strategic goals addressed in the IT vision.
Practice	Ensure IT management and key stakeholders, including relevant business ecosystem partners, develop a single strategic plan.
Outcome	A single, integrated strategic plan replaces separate IT and business strategic plans.
Metric	Evidence of an integrated IT and business strategic plan.
Practice	Leverage the IT vision to drive the continual identification of new business opportunities to benefit from technology in meaningful ways.
Outcome	Potentially 'game-changing' business opportunities are identified and acted upon.
Metric	Number of potentially 'game-changer' strategies directly influenced by IT.
Practice	Align the strategic intent for leveraging technology across key suppliers and business partners.
Outcome	Key alliances and relationships can enhance how the IT strategy is formed.
Metric	Number of key alliances or relevant stakeholders in the business ecosystem who provide input to the IT strategy.

Addressing Typical Challenges

Some typical challenges that can arise in attempting to develop maturity in the Strategic Planning (SP) capability are set out below.

Challenge	Inadequate engagement of IT leadership and stakeholders on IT strategic planning activities.
Context	IT strategic planning may not be considered a distinct area of activity for the organization. As a result, IT leadership and other stakeholders fail to commit to it, and do not allocate adequate resources, such as time, budget and personnel.
Action	Advocate among senior management that effective IT strategic planning is a key enabler of business value generation within the organization, and that it is deserving of adequate time, funding and resourcing.
Challenge	Lack of involvement by relevant business stakeholders in IT strategic planning and priority setting.
Context	Other business units may not know how they can be involved in IT strategic planning.
Action	Raise awareness on how other business units can participate in IT strategic planning activities, to ensure that IT plans and priorities reflect business needs and goals.
Challenge	Ineffective translation of IT strategic goals into actionable projects.
Context	IT strategic goals may not be truly understood or defined in actionable ways that enable them to be successfully achieved.
Action	Encourage development of an actionable project roadmap, with clearly defined deliverables, demonstrating what successful achievement of the IT strategic goals should look like.
Challenge	Programmes in the IT strategic plan are not systematically tracked and evaluated for their delivered value.
Context	Programmes may not be tracked frequently enough to determine whether or not they are achieving the desired objectives or require 'course corrections'.
Action	Promote the ongoing monitoring of programmes for achievement of intended objectives. Incorporate results into the strategy review process.
Challenge	Lack of alignment between IT strategic planning and planning elsewhere in the organization.
Context	The degree of alignment between business and IT plans may depend on the extent to which the IT planners are familiar with wider business strategy plans and vice-versa.
Action	Promote the adoption and implementation approaches that encourage joint evaluation, approval, and sign-off of IT and business strategic plans.

Management Artefacts

Management artefacts that may be used to develop maturity in relation to the Strategic Planning (SP) capability include:

▸ A business strategic plan.
▸ An IT strategic plan.
▸ An IT vision statement.
▸ An outline business case.
▸ IT strategic options.

Business Strategic Plan

The business strategic plan is a statement of the long-term plan to achieve the organization's high-level business objectives. It integrates component plans from each key function within the organization (such as marketing, finance, production, and IT). An effective business strategic plan can incorporate the various component plans (including the IT strategy plan) in a harmonious and unifying manner.

IT Strategic Plan

The IT strategic plan sets out the ways in which the IT function will support the business. It is the synthesis of the following:

▸ The *IT strategic objectives* (what the IT function wants to do to support the business).
▸ The *IT vision and principles* (the architectural and other constraints within which the IT function must work).
▸ The *IT strategic options* (the technology solutions available).

The IT strategic plan outlines all approved IT programmes, and for each summarizes the outline business case, technology implications, resource requirements, indicative timeframes, relationships and dependencies, change implications, and risk management challenges. It also outlines the programmes of work which, when delivered, will achieve the IT strategic objectives. The IT strategic plan also references the IT vision and principles statement (see below), which represents the realistic ambitions of the IT function for the medium- and long-term (1-5 years). A key output is the IT strategic options (see below) which describe *actionable* programmes and technology solutions that may play a role in achieving the strategic objectives.

IT Vision Statement

An IT vision statement reflects the desired future state of the IT function in a small number of sentences or a concise paragraph. The starting point for its development is an examination of the organization's current industry positioning, its realistic ambitions for the medium and long-term, and the role of IT in realizing these ambitions. It presents a series of precise aspirational value statements outlining how the IT function will effectively contribute to the organization's future success. These statements typically focus on a number of key themes, such as organizational culture, management style, business unit partnership, and IT service provision. However, while an IT vision statement presents the high-level aspirations pertaining to IT for the organization, it doesn't detail a plan to achieve these aspirations. Rather, it provides direction and serves as a reference or guideline to support goal-setting and inspire strategic decisions, such as investment decision-making. It also serves as a motivational device for employees who can work in a unified, cohesive manner towards achieving a desired 'end state'. While an IT vision statement is long-term in nature, it will be revised over time to reflect changing business goals, objectives, and culture.

Outline Business Case

An outline business case is a document that provides the preliminary justification for a programme or project, based on a strategic assessment of business needs. It documents major assumptions, results of initial research, and options considered, and provides a high-level assessment of the likely costs of the programme or project. The outline business case is used as the starting point for development of the detailed business case if the programme or project is approved in principle.

IT Strategic Options

IT strategic options describe the alternative ways in which technology could be used in the future to support the business. It identifies challenges and opportunities across business units in which technology has the potential to enhance performance. It sets out the feasible options, assesses them, and prioritizes the best possible options, based on their potential value contribution.

14.5 REFERENCE

See Also

Other capabilities of IT-CMF that have a particularly close relationship with the Strategic Planning (SP) capability include:

Capability	What it provides
04. Capacity Forecasting and Planning (CFP)	Scenario modelling of required IT resources for proposed strategic options
05. Demand and Supply Management (DSM)	Business demand and supply patterns, identifying mismatches that might put strategic goals at risk
07. Green Information Technology (GIT)	Augmenting of strategies to incorporate sustainability principles for triple bottom-line value impact
08. Innovation Management (IM)	Promotion of innovation campaigns to support and shape strategic objectives
10. Organization Design and Planning (ODP)	Insights on the appropriateness of the IT function's current organizational design to effectively execute the IT strategy
11. Risk Management (RM)	Insights on IT-related risks that could inform the shaping of strategic opportunities and programmes
12. Service Analytics and Intelligence (SAI)	Insight into strategic opportunities for IT-enabled business processes
13. Sourcing (SRC)	Information on how the innovative capabilities of key suppliers can help shape strategic opportunities and programmes
17. Funding and Financing (FF)	Validation of various funding options to adequately resource IT strategic plan options
19. Capability Assessment Management (CAM)	An understanding of (potential) IT capability gaps to adequately execute the IT strategy plan
20. Enterprise Architecture Management (EAM)	Information on the trends, choices, and optimal roadmap to execute the organization's business vision and strategy
25. Relationship Management (REM)	Communication of developments in business units that may impact the strategic plan

Further Reading

Kaplan, R.S., and Norton, D.P., 1996. *The balanced scorecard: translating strategy into action.* Boston, MA: Harvard Business School Press.

Kaplan, R.S., and Norton, D.P., 2004. *Strategy maps: converting intangible assets into tangible outcomes.* Boston, MA: Harvard Business School Press.

Ward, J.L., and Peppard, J., 2002. *Strategic planning for information systems,* 3rd ed. Hoboken, NJ: Wiley.

Notes

[1] Nevo, S., and Wade, M.R., 2010. The formation and value of IT-enabled resources: antecedents and consequences of synergistic relationships. *MIS Quarterly,* 34(1), 163–83.

[2] Barney, J.B., 1991. Firm resources and sustained competitive advantage. *Journal of Management,* 17(1), 99–120.

[3] Nevo, S., and Wade, M.R., 2011. Firm-level benefits of IT-enabled resources: a conceptual extension and an empirical assessment. *Journal of Strategic Information Systems,* 20, 403–18.

[4] Mentzas, G., 1997. Implementing an IS strategy – a team approach. *Long Range Planning,* 1(1), 84–95.

[5] Bustin, G., 2014. Why most company strategic plans fail. *Forbes.* Available at: <http://www.forbes.com/sites/forbesleadershipforum/2014/09/15/why-most-company-strategic-plans-fail/>.

Managing the IT Budget

There are many challenges associated with managing the IT budget, including, for example, unplanned cost escalation, the cost of maintaining legacy systems, and management reluctance to invest strategically in new technologies. The **Managing the IT Budget** macro-capability looks at the practices and tools that can be used to establish and control a sustainable economic funding model for IT services and solutions.

Contents: Managing the IT Budget

BGM
15. Budget Management

15.1 OVERVIEW

Goal

The Budget Management (BGM) capability aims to ensure that the allocated IT budgets are spent appropriately and within expectations.

Objectives

▸ Make budget allocation decisions in a deliberative, participatory, and transparent manner.

▸ Achieve predictable IT financial performance by establishing responsible fiscal management and clear lines of accountability.

▸ Maintain the flexibility to respond to short-term challenges and opportunities by allowing managers to reallocate IT funds across budget categories and projects at their discretion.

▸ Make sure that expenditure matches the allocated budget. Identify and plan for any likely overrun in advance.

Value

The Budget Management (BGM) capability helps ensure that IT budget planning is transparent and participatory, and that it responds to changing needs and unanticipated opportunities.

Relevance

At a time when most organizations rely on IT to grow and innovate, managing the IT budget is of critical but sometimes under-rated importance [1]. The IT budget facilitates implementation of the IT strategic plan by providing funding for the required resources and activities. It also provides the means of initiating corrective action when business conditions change, by allowing budgets to be reallocated as necessary. However, if IT budgets are arbitrarily managed, problems can occur, such as erratic over- or under-spending, inability to reallocate previously committed budgets to more productive activities, and so on.

By establishing an effective Budget Management (BGM) capability, an organization can improve business outcomes by enabling rapid response to changing business needs and unanticipated expenses. Money saved by managing the IT budget effectively can be reinvested in IT innovation programmes to drive further savings, creating a virtuous cycle.

15.2 SCOPE

Definition

The Budget Management (BGM) capability is the ability to oversee and adjust the IT budget to ensure that it is spent effectively. The Budget Management (BGM) capability covers:

▸ Planning the IT budget.
▸ Tracking actual expenditure and variances from the budget.
▸ Establishing budget accountability, oversight structures, and decision rights.
▸ Predicting future expenditure and out-of-tolerance variances.

Other Capabilities

The following are addressed by other capabilities of IT-CMF:

For...	Refer to...
Allocating the costs of provisioning IT services to consumers	01. Accounting and Allocation (AA)
Trending of projects and budget expenditure categories on a multi-year basis	16. Budget Oversight and Performance Analysis (BOP)
Determining various sources of potential IT funding	17. Funding and Financing (FF)
Selecting individual programmes/projects for funding	18. Portfolio Planning and Prioritization (PPP)
Understanding direct and indirect costs for IT services and assets	35. Total Cost of Ownership (TCO)

15.3 UNDERSTANDING MATURITY

Recognizing Excellence

When the Budget Management (BGM) capability is well-developed or mature:

▸ IT budgets are transparently linked to broader strategic priorities and business planning cycles, there is participation by key stakeholders in the budgeting process, and there is budget flexibility that allows the organization to respond to unanticipated opportunities.
▸ The IT budget covers the full scope of IT spending, and forms the basis for monitoring expenditure and taking corrective actions.
▸ Budget expenditure patterns are predictable, and variances are actively managed with well-defined approaches that control cost and risk.
▸ Robust budget oversight and accountability structures are in place.

Maturity at the Critical Capability Level

The following statements provide a high-level overview of the Budget Management (BGM) capability at successive levels of maturity:

Level 1	Budget management approaches are ad hoc, and budgets are not actively reviewed.
Level 2	There are defined budget management approaches emerging in parts of the IT function. The frequency of significant budget variances is reducing.
Level 3	Standardized budget management approaches cover all key IT operations, services, and projects. Actual spending is increasingly managed to the IT budget plan.
Level 4	Comprehensive IT budget management approaches are fully integrated with the organization's financial management approaches. There is a transparent and fully embedded escalation path for taking action on budget variances.
Level 5	IT budget management approaches are continually improved to reliably predict budget run rates, and ensure that spending varies from budget only within defined tolerances.

Maturity at the Capability Building Block (CBB) Level

The Capability Building Blocks (CBBs) associated with the Budget Management (BGM) capability fall into three categories:

▸ Category A: three CBBs associated with *Planning* – these deal with the creation of the IT budget.

▸ Category B: three CBBs associated with *Performance Management* – these deal with the monitoring of spending against the IT budget plan.

▸ Category C: two CBBs associated with *Governance* – these address the responsibilities and accountabilities for managing the IT budget.

These are described below, together with a summary of the different maturity levels for each.

Category A: CBBs Associated with *Planning*

CBB A1: Budget Scope

Manage the scope and depth of information relating to the categories of expenditure in the IT budget (for example, capital expenses, operations expenses, shadow IT, and so on).

Level 1	The IT budget typically covers expenditure associated only with parts of IT operations for the current year.
Level 2	The IT budget covers expenditure associated with key IT operations and significant discretionary projects for the current year.
Level 3	The IT budget covers expenditure associated with most IT operations and discretionary projects, with a one- to two-year time horizon.
Level 4	The IT budget covers the full IT spend, and incorporates multi-year expenditure plans.
Level 5	The scope of the IT budget is continually monitored for improvement opportunities.

CBB A2: Budget Processes

Develop processes to manage budget planning and expenditure (such as processes to manage stakeholder involvement, processes to align the budget planning with business planning cycles, processes to manage payments, and so on).

Level 1	IT budget processes are ad hoc, and are not clearly defined.
Level 2	IT budget processes are defined, but they may be inconsistently applied across the IT function.
Level 3	IT budget processes are consistently followed by all stakeholders across the IT function.
Level 4	IT budget processes are executed in full alignment with other planning cycles, with the involvement of stakeholders across the organization.
Level 5	IT budget processes are continually improved based on lessons learned from past experiences and industry good practice.

CBB A3: Business Alignment

Engage stakeholders from the wider business in setting the IT budget to ensure that strategic priorities are reflected in the IT budget priorities.

Level 1	Budget allocations are driven by day-to-day tactical IT operational needs, with little or no involvement by stakeholders.
Level 2	Budget allocations are made with the involvement of a limited number of IT stakeholders. Results are sometimes, but not always, aligned with strategic priorities.
Level 3	Budget allocations reflect the involvement of relevant stakeholders in the IT function and some other business units. The IT budget is increasingly aligned with strategic priorities.
Level 4	Budget allocations reflect the involvement of relevant stakeholders from across the entire organization. The IT budget is fully aligned with strategic priorities.
Level 5	Budget allocations are continually reviewed for improvement and regularly reflect input from relevant business ecosystem partners.

Category B: CBBs Associated with *Performance Management*

CBB B1: Budget Monitoring

Monitor and report to stakeholders on actual performance against planned expenditure.

Level 1	Ad hoc monitoring of spending may be conducted. Little or no effort is made to compare actual with planned expenditure.
Level 2	Basic approaches for monitoring IT spending are defined but are not consistently applied in all instances.
Level 3	Standardized approaches for monitoring IT spending are adopted, primarily between the IT and finance functions. Actual expenditure can be compared with planned expenditure with increasing ease.
Level 4	Actual expenditure is comprehensively monitored and reviewed against planned expenditure and the results are shared across the organization.
Level 5	Expenditure is regularly monitored and reviewed, with inputs from relevant business ecosystem partners.

CBB B2: Variance Management

Manage deviations of expenditure from the planned budget (by, for example, establishing escalation channels, and taking corrective actions).

Level 1   Deviations of IT expenditure from the planned budget are managed in an ad hoc manner, if at all.

Level 2   A defined approach is emerging for dealing with major expenditure variances. The impact of corrective action may, however, be limited, as this approach is not yet consistently applied.

Level 3   A standardized and systematic approach is in place for dealing with most variances based on post hoc analysis. The impact of corrective actions to reduce costs or rebalance the budget is increasing.

Level 4   A proactive approach to reviewing and managing variances is adopted based on spending patterns and trends. Corrective action is almost always effective.

Level 5   Variances are managed automatically using predefined policies, leading to a continual focus on managing expenditure and business value.

CBB B3: Predictability

Manage IT expenditure within budget targets and variance ranges.

Level 1   The ability to meet IT budget targets is ad hoc and unpredictable.

Level 2   The IT function has a basic ability to predict run rates for key parts of its IT expenditure. Budget targets are, however, still occasionally missed.

Level 3   The IT function is able to reliably predict run rates for most of its IT expenditure, with the result that budget targets are rarely missed.

Level 4   The IT function is able to reliably predict run rates for all of its IT expenditure, and continually hits budget targets within tightly defined variance ranges.

Level 5   The approaches for managing IT expenditure are continually reviewed for improvement based on past experience and the corresponding expenditure patterns of relevant business ecosystem partners.

Category C: CBBs Associated with *Governance*

CBB C1: Budget Governance

Establish oversight structures and decision rights to set IT budgets and manage allocations.

Level 1   Oversight of the IT budget is typically informal.

Level 2   Compliance/audit-orientated oversight structures are in place, primarily driven by the finance and/or legal functions.

Level 3   Performance orientated governance structures are in place, staffed by the finance and IT functions.

Level 4   Governance of the IT budget has cross-functional staffing and is fully integrated with appropriate governance functions of the wider organization.

Level 5   Governance structures are continually improved based on prior experience and on regular input from relevant business ecosystem partners.

CBB C2: Accountability Assignment

Establish accountability for managing the expenditure of IT budgets.

Level 1   Accountability for maintaining expenditure within planned IT budgets is unclear.

Level 2   Managers are typically accountable for their own budgets; however, there are limited operational data or tools to support their decision-making.

Level 3   Managers have ready access to data, and sensitivity analysis and scenario modelling tools to support their decision-making.

Level 4   Managers can automatically escalate out-of-tolerance deviations from the planned budget for corrective action and follow-up investigation.

Level 5   The accountability approach is continually reviewed to ensure that transparent and real-time budget decisions can be facilitated.

15.4 IMPROVEMENT PLANNING

Capability Evaluation

Two summary assessment questions are set out below, along with the typical response associated with each level of maturity.

To what extent is the IT budget planned, monitored, and adjusted to meet the demands of the business and minimize IT costs?

Level 1   Any IT budgets are ad hoc in nature, typically resulting in misalignment with the IT function's business planning.

Level 2   Defined IT budgets are emerging. However, they are typically static and only partially aligned with the IT function's business planning.

Level 3   IT budgets are becoming increasingly flexible and more aligned with the IT function's business plans and with the plans of a number of other business units.

Level 4   IT budgets are considered dynamic and fully aligned with business plans across the organization.

Level 5   IT budgets are continually reviewed for improvement opportunities and are influenced by inputs from relevant business ecosystem partners.

To what extent does the IT function actively manage variances between budgeted and actual expenditure?

Level 1   Expenditure is typically not controlled in an active manner, with the result that significant budget variances may remain hidden for a long time.

Level 2   There is an emerging focus on IT expenditure control in parts of the IT function. The more significant budget variances can be identified in advance. Consistent remediation approaches are, however, still emerging.

Level 3   A standardized approach to IT expenditure control is adopted across all of the IT function. Proactive approaches are in place for dealing with variances.

Level 4   A comprehensive approach to IT expenditure control is adopted across the organization. Variances are controlled to within narrow tolerance ranges.

Level 5   The approaches for IT expenditure control and variance remediation are continually reviewed for improvement. Inputs are provided by relevant business ecosystem partners.

Key Practices-Outcomes-Metrics (POMs)

Some useful POMs for developing the Budget Management (BGM) capability are summarized below.

Level 2 POMs

Practice	Explicitly define the approach for relevant stakeholders to participate in planning the IT budget for the coming year.
Outcome	Participatory planning of the IT budget is likely to lead to higher levels of support for it.
Metric	Percentage of identified key stakeholders who are involved in defining IT budget planning approaches.
Practice	Prioritize which IT budget items should carry the highest levels of expenditure monitoring (for example, include major IT projects and significant business-as-usual expenditure activities).
Outcome	Expenditure monitoring allows greater levels of visibility, planning, and predictability.
Metric	Extent to which actual expenditure matches budgeted expenditure.
Practice	Establish formal IT budget oversight structures with the support of the corporate finance function.
Outcome	Budget oversight benefits from corporate finance's expertise.
Metric	Percentage of IT expenditure approved using IT budget oversight structures.

Level 3 POMs

Practice	Designate managers accountable for forecasting and managing actual expenditure.
Outcome	By assigning individual accountability and authority, there is greater likelihood that budgets will be effectively managed.
Metric	Percentage of IT budget and associated expenditure assigned to designated managers.
Practice	Ensure budget allocations across IT projects are fully aligned with the IT strategy.
Outcome	Confidence increases that the IT budget supports the implementation of the IT strategy.
Metric	Percentage of projects funded that are aligned with the IT strategy.
Practice	Review deviations of expenditure from the IT budget, and take corrective action as required.
Outcome	Run rates for IT expenditure are more reliably predicted, and budget targets are increasingly met.
Metric	Percentage of IT budget targets that are met. Percentage of IT budget variances satisfactorily resolved.
Practice	Ensure that the potential impact of proposed IT budget expenditure is taken into account in the budget for future years (for example, the effect of this year's capital expenditure on future depreciation and maintenance costs).
Outcome	The knock-on demands of the current IT budget commitments can be better predicted to increase future budget flexibility.
Metric	Budget split between predetermined (often longer-term) versus discretionary budget expenditure.

Level 4 POMs

Practice	Expand IT budgeting to include all of 'shadow IT' expenditure.
Outcome	Total IT expenditure across the organization is clarified, enabling identification of more synergies and variances.
Metric	Percentage of total IT expenditure accounted for by the IT function.
Practice	Involve all relevant stakeholders in IT budgeting and ensure that the budgeting process is aligned with business planning cycles.
Outcome	There is increasing stakeholder participation in recognizing and resolving budget variances.
Metric	Percentage of identified relevant stakeholders participating in IT budget planning and management. Number of unresolved budget variances.
Practice	Broaden the IT budget governance structures to authorize appropriate individuals to facilitate budget reallocation.
Outcome	Flexible governance structures facilitate appropriate responses to unanticipated events.
Metric	Number of IT budget changes per quarter. Number of budget reassignments.

Practice	Automatically escalate expenditure that deviates from the IT budget plan.
Outcome	Key stakeholders are immediately informed of variances to encourage a timely response.
Metric	Number of unresolved budget variances.

Level 5 POMs

Practice	Advocate and identify budget management improvement opportunities across the organization.
Outcome	The IT budget is predictable, inclusive, and continually improved.
Metric	Planned budget versus actual expenditure.
Practice	Ensure that the IT budget continues to be actively managed for flexibility, so that the organization can capitalize on emerging opportunities to invest in innovation.
Outcome	Budget management is seen to enable innovation.
Metric	Percentage of IT expenditure invested in innovation.

Addressing Typical Challenges

Some typical challenges that can arise in attempting to develop maturity in the Budget Management (BGM) capability are set out below.

Challenge	Senior management is reluctant to support or approve the proposed IT budget allocations.
Context	Proposed IT budget allocations can often be contentious, especially if allocations are considered ambiguous.
Action	Link the proposed IT budget allocations to strategic business objectives, and demonstrate that IT investments represent good value for money.
Challenge	Significant shadow IT expenditure exists across the organization.
Context	The use of technology across the organization, without the formal approval or control of the IT function, poses risks to data security, IT systems compatibility and/or duplication, as well as impacting IT operational budgets.
Action	Raise awareness amongst senior management of the risks posed by uncontrolled shadow IT. Collaborate with shadow IT proponents to use a coordinated and common approach wherever possible.
Challenge	Inadequate time to fully review IT requirements and the associated costs prior to submission of the IT budget.
Context	A last-minute approach to specifying IT requirements prevails in the rest of the business.
Action	Be proactive and request plans well ahead of budgetary deadlines, giving ample time for business units to accurately prepare IT budget submissions so that they can be analysed, and the viability of shared solutions considered.

Challenge	A general lack of understanding of the business value of IT, with the IT function often being perceived as a cost centre.
Context	The value of IT is not always understood and its benefits are not evident to many employees.
Action	Engage in communication across the business, and inform, in simple and straightforward terms, the business reasons for, and the implications of, IT expenditure.

Management Artefacts

Management artefacts that may be used to develop maturity in the Budget Management (BGM) capability include:

▸ An IT budget plan.
▸ An IT budget review charter.
▸ An IT financial audit report.
▸ A cash flow/operating budget statement.

IT Budget Plan

An IT budget plan is a financial statement of proposed IT expenditure for a defined period of time. It usually includes details relating to salaries, IT hardware, software, licensing, maintenance, professional services, and so on. Normally it is drawn up annually and reviewed a number of times during the year. Depending on the philosophy of the organization, the budget, once established, may or may not be adjusted within the budget period. It is important that actual expenditure be as close as possible to the budget.

Under-runs indicate that proposed expenditure did not materialize within the budget time frame – for example, a project/activity was not initiated or is moving at a slower than planned pace. An under-run may also represent an opportunity cost for other projects that could otherwise have been funded.

Over-runs typically indicate unforeseen expenditures, which could mean a project/activity is terminated, or they could lead to cuts to funding of other projects/activities if an increase to the original IT budget is not possible. An over-run could also undermine the original business case for the project.

IT Budget Review Charter

The IT budget is the basis for obtaining funding for the IT function and subsequently for controlling IT expenditure. The purpose of the IT budget review charter is to establish a framework for reviewing actual expenditure, assessing the extent to which it conforms to the budget, and making any necessary adjustments. The charter defines the purpose of the review, the participants, the frequency with which they meet, and the required inputs and expected outputs of their meetings. The review is normally attended by senior management from across the organization, and the results are ideally published organization-wide to promote transparency and understanding.

IT Financial Audit Report

An IT financial audit report is a periodic and independent evaluation of the financial statements of the organization. Financial auditors conduct an audit to examine the responsibility of the organization with respect to IT expenditure and the accuracy of financial statements. The auditors normally review budget policies, rules, standards or criteria, and they report on the level of conformity to these, making recommendations on improvements where necessary. The information contained in IT financial audit reports can be used to track the effectiveness of the IT budget process over time.

Cash Flow/Operating Budget Statement

A cash flow/operating budget statement shows where funding is coming from and where it is going to, typically on a month-by-month basis. It normally covers cash inflows and outflows for both operations and capital financing. Cash flow budgeting is concerned only with money movement, and not with net income or profitability. A cash flow budget is a useful management tool that enables the organization to plan and monitor its cash flows. It enables the IT function to test the viability of its budget plans for the year ahead, to verify that its expenditure needs can be met.

15.5 REFERENCE

See Also

Other capabilities of IT-CMF that have a particularly close relationship with the Budget Management (BGM) capability include:

Capability	What it provides
01. Accounting and Allocation (AA)	Details of cost accounting and chargeback models, which may impact on the budget management process
02. Business Planning (BP)	Details of how strategic objectives should be supported
09. IT Leadership and Governance (ITG)	Guidelines for governance structures to link budgeting decisions to key activities
16. Budget Oversight and Performance Analysis (BOP)	Analysis of budget performance data, which can be used to improve future budgeting activities
17. Funding and Financing (FF)	Details of IT funding allocations for capital expenditure and operating expenditure
33. Benefits Assessment and Realization (BAR)	Benefit assessments of IT services and solutions, which can be used as input to budgeting
35. Total Cost of Ownership (TCO)	Full understanding of direct and indirect costs to inform accurate budget decisions, and enable tracking of actual expenditure against budget plans

Further Reading

Harris, M.D., Herron, D., and Iwanicki, S., 2008. *The business value of IT: managing risks, optimizing performance and measuring results*. Boca Raton, FL: CRC Press.

Notes

[1] McGittigan, J., 2014. *IT budgeting key initiative overview*. Gartner Research. Available at: <https://www.gartner.com/doc/2701817/it-budgeting-key-initiative-overview>.

BOP

16. Budget Oversight and Performance Analysis

16.1 OVERVIEW

Goal

The Budget Oversight and Performance Analysis (BOP) capability aims to compare actual IT expenditure against planned IT expenditure over extended time periods, and in doing so provides management with the stimulus to confirm or reset budget allocations, where appropriate.

Objectives

▶ Improve visibility of actual IT expenditure over extended time periods.
▶ Better inform decisions regarding future funding levels and allocations.
▶ Improve the quality of future budgets, and identify favourable budget trends and areas of concern.
▶ Increase confidence that budget allocations can avoid unplanned adjustments midway through a financial cycle.

Value

The Budget Oversight and Performance Analysis (BOP) capability analyses past budgeting and expenditure patterns to inform decision-making on current planning for budget forecasts and allocations.

Relevance

Better quality plans, budgets, and forecasts facilitate smart decisions that can help organizations react to challenges, grasp opportunities, and grow. Decision-makers who have access to relevant IT budget performance and trend information are in a better position to understand past performance and, with appropriate analysis, they can understand what is likely to occur in the future [1]. It is within this dynamic landscape that the Budget Oversight and Performance Analysis (BOP) capability helps decision-makers to manage the IT budget so that it remains in synch with and responsive to evolving business activities, strategies, and KPIs. By applying pattern analytics to understanding how budgets perform over extended time periods, organizations can identify how best to drive planned improvements [1].

By establishing an effective Budget Oversight and Performance Analysis (BOP) capability, an organization can have access to more accurate and timely IT budget analysis data, and can significantly reduce the guesswork from its decision-making processes. The Budget Oversight and Performance Analysis (BOP) capability looks across a series of budgets and financial planning timeframes to determine their effectiveness, to recognize historical IT budget expenditure patterns and emerging trends, and to use the analysis to support better forecasts and decision-making regarding the financial management of IT [2]. Investing in appropriate financial planning, budgeting, and forecasting approaches can accelerate the decision-making process, even when underlying assumptions and conditions change.

16.2 SCOPE

Definition

The Budget Oversight and Performance Analysis (BOP) capability is the ability to compare actual IT expenditure against budgeted IT expenditure over extended time periods. Where appropriate, it offers management the opportunity to reprofile or reprioritize budget forecasts and allocations. The Budget Oversight and Performance Analysis (BOP) capability covers:

▸ Developing approaches and tools for budget performance analysis.
▸ Performing multi-year tracking and trend analysis of expenditure patterns in IT projects and IT budget categories.
▸ Reviewing IT budget plans versus actual expenditure.
▸ Providing a stimulus for rebalancing and reprioritizing budgets.
▸ Forecasting future IT funding levels, allocation requirements, and prices for IT services.
▸ Determining the impact of historical budget performance on future budget planning and on general cost management.
▸ Communicating IT budget performance metrics to key stakeholders.

Other Capabilities

The following are addressed by other capabilities of IT-CMF:

For...	Refer to...
Establishing alignment between the IT function and the rest of the business	14. Strategic Planning (SP)
Determining funding and financing for IT investments	17. Funding and Financing (FF)
Prioritizing the IT investment portfolio	18. Portfolio Planning and Prioritization (PPP)
Monitoring budget expenditure on a day-to-day basis	35. Total Cost of Ownership (TCO)

16.3 UNDERSTANDING MATURITY

Recognizing Excellence

When the Budget Oversight and Performance Analysis (BOP) capability is well-developed or mature:

▶ The organization has defined and automated approaches that can pull budget expenditure data from coherent up-to-date sources, to analyse and link it to broader organizational activities and metrics.

▶ The organization is able to conduct sophisticated multi-year tracking and trending across the full range of budget categories; and this is likely to lead to improved budget performance, reprioritizing and rebalancing of budgets, more accurate forecasts, and better decisions on consumption of IT resources and services.

Maturity at the Critical Capability Level

The following statements provide a high-level overview of the Budget Oversight and Performance Analysis (BOP) capability at successive levels of maturity:

Level 1   There is no or ad hoc tracking of actual against planned IT budget expenditure.

Level 2   Budget expenditure analysis begins to inform trends in some selected IT budget categories. However, this is a highly manual approach based on data taken from multiple and perhaps unstructured or duplicate sources.

Level 3   There is in-period tracking and trending of all IT budget categories and projects (for example, for the current year), and this level of detail helps to identify any issues.

Level 4   There is multi-year tracking of IT budget trends and performance; and a comprehensive set of metrics can be transparently applied to IT performance targets.

Level 5   Real-time information on IT budget performance is readily available for analysis and reporting (for example, via management dashboards), which enables IT budgets to be monitored and adjusted as required.

Maturity at the Capability Building Block (CBB) Level

The Capability Building Blocks (CBBs) associated with the Budget Oversight and Performance Analysis (BOP) capability fall into three categories:

▶ Category A: three CBBs associated with **Analysis** – these define the tracking and modelling approaches, tools, sources, and data structures required to conduct budget performance analysis.

▶ Category B: three CBBs associated with **Impact and Value** – these define metrics for reporting the impact of budget performance analysis on planning and cost management.

▶ Category C: one CBB associated with **Alignment** – this promotes understanding of IT budget management practices.

These are described below, together with a summary of the different maturity levels for each.

Category A: CBBs Associated with *Analysis*

CBB A1: Scope, Granularity, and Sophistication

Establish budget tracking and forecasting approaches (for example, single versus multi-year analysis).

Level 1	There is no or only ad hoc tracking of specific projects and individual budget categories, with occasional simplified trend analysis of some specific budget categories.
Level 2	There is in-period (for example, current year) tracking, forecasting analysis, and oversight for a limited number of larger projects and budget categories.
Level 3	There is in-period tracking, forecasting analysis, and oversight of most projects and budget categories.
Level 4	There is multi-year tracking and forecasting (using appropriate automation) for all qualifying projects and budget categories.
Level 5	The multi-year tracking and forecasting approach is continually optimized across all budget categories and projects.

CBB A2: Tools and Processes

Develop tools and processes to generate budget performance analyses.

Level 1	Any budget performance analysis reporting is undertaken on an ad hoc basis.
Level 2	A defined performance analysis reporting process is in place for parts of the IT function, typically using manual approaches to conduct performance analysis. There is awareness emerging that an IT budget performance analysis tool should be considered.
Level 3	A standardized performance analysis reporting process is agreed across IT and some other business units, with partial automation in places.
Level 4	The performance analysis reporting process is sufficiently automated across the organization, but analysis may not be always available in real time.
Level 5	Performance analysis is continually improved, can provide real-time or up-to-the-minute analysis, and incorporates inputs from relevant business ecosystem partners.

CBB A3: Data Consistency

Develop the sources of data, and structure the data required to conduct budget performance analyses. Develop a common budget management terminology in the organization to enable wider comparisons to be made.

Level 1   Multiple, unstructured sources of data restrict IT budget performance evaluation to rudimentary analysis only. Budget terminology is undefined or ad hoc.

Level 2   A common budget terminology is emerging within the IT function, allowing first steps to be taken to resolve potential conflicts between multiple IT data sources.

Level 3   Common budget terminology is in use across all of IT and some other business units, allowing a greater range of data sources to be utilized for budget performance analysis.

Level 4   Common budget terminology is in use across the whole organization, allowing a coherent suite of data sources to be used for budget performance analysis.

Level 5   A single data source (or a coherent suite of multiple sources) exists with real-time budget performance analysis. A universal budget terminology is shared with relevant business ecosystem partners, to enable comparisons of budget performance.

Category B: CBBs Associated with *Impact and Value*

CBB B1: Metrics Reporting

Develop a suite of metrics to enable reporting on a range of budget performance criteria (for example, over/under expenditure and expenditure run-rates), and the relationships between them.

Level 1   Reporting on the IT budget is typically ad hoc and based on inconsistent metrics.

Level 2   A limited set of IT budget performance metrics is reported for a limited number of budget categories.

Level 3   A standardized set of IT budget performance metrics is reported for most budget categories.

Level 4   A comprehensive suite of IT budget performance metrics is reported for all budget categories and linked to performance targets both for individuals and for the IT function.

Level 5   The budget performance metrics systematically feed senior management dashboards and are continually reviewed based on their effectiveness.

CBB B2: Future IT Expenditure

Inform decision-making for planning of future IT expenditure.

Level 1
Budget performance analysis has limited or no impact on IT expenditure planning.

Level 2
Analysis is beginning to be used by the IT function to predict future IT expenditure for a limited number of budget allocation categories and larger projects.

Level 3
Analysis is consistently used by the IT function to inform planning of future expenditure for most budget allocation categories, and, with input from some other business units, to adjust IT budgets accordingly.

Level 4
Analysis is used jointly by IT and the rest of the business to inform planning of future expenditure for all budget allocation categories, and to develop business cases based on predicted future savings from budget performance analysis.

Level 5
The impact of budget performance analysis on IT expenditure planning is continually reviewed, and extends to business ecosystem partners, where appropriate.

CBB B3: Management of Unit Costs

Inform decision-making regarding unit cost adjustments – for example, those relating to pricing and consumption.

Level 1
Budget performance analysis does not normally lead to unit cost adjustments or to management decisions regarding consumption and pricing.

Level 2
Budget performance analysis occasionally leads to adjustment of unit costs in a limited number of circumstances and occasionally informs discussion with other business units about their consumption of IT services.

Level 3
Budget performance analysis regularly leads to adjustment of unit costs, and routinely informs discussion with other business units about their consumption of IT services and prices.

Level 4
Budget performance analysis leads to constant adjustment of unit costs, and is constantly used as a basis for agreement on IT service consumption and pricing with the rest of the business.

Level 5
Budget performance analysis is used to optimize unit cost management, informing levels of IT consumption, and optimizing pricing decisions for business value.

Category C: CBB Associated with *Alignment*

CBB C1: Awareness and Communication

Communicate IT budget management practices and methods, and details of their business impact to stakeholders.

Level 1	Any communication of IT budget management practices and methods, and IT budget performance to stakeholders is ad hoc.
Level 2	IT budget management practices and methods are communicated to a limited number of key stakeholders. There is a defined approach emerging for reporting of IT budget performance against the IT function's objectives.
Level 3	Budget management practices and methods are communicated to most stakeholders. There is a standardized approach for reporting regularly on IT budget performance against the objectives of the IT function.
Level 4	Budget management practices and methods are communicated to all relevant stakeholders. Reporting of IT budget performance is comprehensively integrated into the wider organization's reporting of budget performance against objectives.
Level 5	Reporting and communication approaches are continually reviewed for improvement opportunities.

16.4 IMPROVEMENT PLANNING

Capability Evaluation

Two summary assessment questions are set out below, along with the typical response associated with each level of maturity.

How are variances and trends in IT budget performance tracked and analysed with a view to minimizing deviations?

Level 1	Some ad hoc analysis may occur. However, variances and trends are not easily identified.
Level 2	Manual analysis identifies historical variances and trends for a limited number of budget categories.
Level 3	Partially automated analysis can identify historical variances and trends in most budget categories.
Level 4	Fully automated analysis can readily identify historical variances and trends in all budget categories, with growing identification of emerging variances.
Level 5	Historical and emerging variances and trends can be readily identified across all budget categories.

To what extent is historical budget performance reporting used as an input to budget planning?

Level 1   Where there is historical budget performance reporting, it is typically ad hoc and not linked to budget planning.

Level 2   Some basic historical budget performance is used to inform allocations for larger projects or budget categories.

Level 3   Increasingly structured historical budget performance reports inform allocations for the majority of budget categories across the IT function.

Level 4   Comprehensive historical budget performance reports are used to inform planned allocations for all budget categories across the IT function, and to improve the accuracy of project business cases organization-wide.

Level 5   Historical budget performance reports inform the continual optimization of all future expenditure in IT budgets, and are shared with relevant business ecosystem partners to improve the wider budget planning effort.

Key Practices-Outcomes-Metrics (POMs)

Some useful POMs for developing the Budget Oversight and Performance Analysis (BOP) capability are summarized below.

Level 2 POMs

Practice	Track IT budget performance within the current period at operations and project levels.
Outcome	Data begins to be accrued on actual versus planned expenditure.
Metric	Percentage of projects and operational activities with budget analysis reported.
Practice	Adjust IT budgets based on budget performance analysis.
Outcome	IT budgets become more realistic and transparent.
Metric	Percentage of projects and operational activities that meet their original IT budget allocations. Percentage of those that meet their adjusted IT budget allocations.
Practice	Use extrapolations from historical patterns to stress-test planned IT expenditure for larger IT projects and IT budget categories.
Outcome	Confidence levels for budget planning can be improved by more formally leveraging past experience.
Metric	Percentage deviation from planned to actual expenditure by budget category. Percentage deviation from planned to actual expenditure for larger projects.
Practice	Establish basic reporting of IT budget performance at operational and project levels.
Outcome	IT personnel are aware of the role that budget performance plays in meeting business objectives.
Metric	Percentage of relevant IT personnel who are aware of IT budget performance.

Level 3 POMs

Practice	Expand in-period tracking and trend analysis to cover most IT budget categories.
Outcome	Oversight and performance analysis can be performed, and it becomes easier to identify issues across broader budget categories.
Metric	Percentage of IT budget categories with budget metrics reported each period.
Practice	Facilitate IT budget analysis, with partial automation of the reporting approach.
Outcome	Partial automation allows for more timely budget analysis and decision-making.
Metric	Number of days after month end that the monthly budget analysis report is produced.
Practice	Report a standardized set of budget performance metrics (for example, cost per unit or earned value) for all budget categories and link them to IT targets.
Outcome	A standard set of budget performance metrics can be compared across budget categories, thereby facilitating deeper analysis. Management have a suite of metrics and understand the strategic alignment of these metrics.
Metric	Percentage of budget categories with budget metrics reported. Survey of stakeholder confidence in fiscal management by the IT function conducted.
Practice	Use budget analysis to predict future IT expenditure for all budget categories.
Outcome	The inclusion of all budget categories enables more accurate scenario-modelling and planning.
Metric	Percentage deviation from planned budget for each reporting period.
Practice	Report IT budget performance against the objectives of business units.
Outcome	There is wider visibility into how the IT budget performance can positively and negatively affect business goals.
Metric	Frequency of communication on budget performance to stakeholders in other business units.

Level 4 POMs

Practice	Sufficiently automate multi-year budget tracking and trending analysis.
Outcome	More accurate and more timely analysis is available to management across the organization.
Metric	Percentage of IT projects and operation activities with budget tracking and trending analysis.
Practice	Promote organization-wide reuse of the IT budget performance analysis to inform planning on future expenditure.
Outcome	There are better discussions regarding organization-wide buy-in to how best to balance between *run the business* IT expenditure and *change the business* IT expenditure.
Metric	Year-on-year percentage change in budget allocations by category.

Practice	Establish regular reporting cycles to communicate IT budget performance against the organization-wide objectives – for example, via management dashboards.
Outcome	There is increasing awareness across the organization of IT expenditure patterns, which in turn informs planning activities.
Metric	Percentage of the IT budget aligned with business units' objectives.

Level 5 POMs

Practice	Continually review the scope of real-time gathering, analysis, and reporting of budget performance data.
Outcome	Management will have the ability to make better informed decisions more quickly – for example, budgets can be adjusted immediately based on trend data.
Metric	Percentage of IT projects where corrective actions lead to budget adjustments.

Practice	Continually use budget performance analysis to optimize unit cost management.
Outcome	Budget analysis identifies opportunities to optimize unit cost management decisions for improved business value.
Metric	Percentage improvement in business value that results from unit cost adjustments.

Addressing Typical Challenges

Some typical challenges that can arise in attempting to develop maturity in the Budget Oversight and Performance Analysis (BOP) capability are set out below.

Challenge	The IT function resists being measured solely on budget performance.
Context	Management may regard IT budget monitoriong as an unnecessary burden.
Action	Promote greater collaboration between general business unit budget managers and those responsible for the management of the IT budget. Facilitate discussions regarding how reporting of the IT budget performance to senior management should occur.

Challenge	Lack of transparency relating to accountability for adhering to planned IT budgets.
Context	IT budget oversight is typically viewed as the exclusive responsibility of a narrow group of people within the IT function.
Action	Link adherence to planned budgets with individual performance management throughout the organization.

Challenge	There is a question mark over the accuracy and integrity of the data quality and performance reporting of the IT budget.
Context	There is a perception that the quality of the IT budget data is not accurate or there are instances where it has been shown to be unreliable. This may lead to resistance regarding any changes to the IT budget, even when there is strong evidence to suggest that it needs to be modified.
Action	Improve the quality and address any misconceptions regarding the quality of the IT budget data. Have open and organization-wide discussions to address when changes to the IT budget are needed. These should be based on criteria other than just data quality, possibly following a weighting system until data quality issues are addressed.
Challenge	Difficulty in making the necessary changes to previously approved IT funding levels and budget category allocations in the middle of the financial year.
Context	IT funding levels and budget category allocations typically use simplistic planning methods (for example, increase or decrease over the previous year) and decisions are typically locked in for each financial planning cycle.
Action	Promote discussion on the need for increased flexibility in cases where resetting IT funding and budget category allocations is required between financial planning milestones.

Management Artefacts

Management artefacts that may be used to develop maturity in the Budget Oversight and Performance Analysis (BOP) capability include:

- ▸ An IT budget plan.
- ▸ An IT budget analysis tool.
- ▸ An IT financial audit report.

IT Budget Plan

An IT budget plan is a financial statement of proposed IT expenditure for a defined period of time. It usually includes details relating to salaries, IT hardware, software, licensing, maintenance, professional services, and so on. Normally it is drawn up annually and reviewed a number of times during the year. Depending on the philosophy of the organization, the budget, once established, may or may not be adjusted within the budget period. It is important that actual expenditure be as close as possible to the budget.

Under-runs indicate that proposed expenditure did not materialize within the budget time frame – for example, a project/activity was not initiated or is moving at a slower than planned pace. An under-run may also represent an opportunity cost for other projects that could otherwise have been funded.

Over-runs typically indicate unforeseen expenditures, which could mean a project/activity is terminated, or they could lead to cuts to funding of other projects/activities if an increase to the original IT budget is not possible. An over-run could also undermine the original business case for the project.

IT Budget Analysis Tool

While the purpose of the IT budget plan is to control IT expenses, by contrast the purpose of the IT budget analysis tool is to compare actual against planned expenditure, and to understand any variances or expenditure trends that are emerging. The tool draws data from a centralized financial database that provides a single view of IT expenditure across teams, projects, and business activities. Output from the IT budget analysis tool provides information to relevant management to help them make decisions on budget performance, and to allow them to make any adjustments to the projected expenditure that are necessary to achieve optimum business value.

IT Financial Audit Report

An IT financial audit report is a periodic and independent evaluation of the financial statements of the organization. Financial auditors conduct an audit to examine the responsibility of the organization with respect to IT expenditure and the accuracy of financial statements. The auditors normally review budget policies, rules, standards or criteria, and they report on the level of conformity to these, making recommendations on improvements where necessary. The information contained in IT financial audit reports can be used to track the effectiveness of the IT budget process over time.

16.5 REFERENCE

See Also

Other capabilities of IT-CMF that have a particularly close relationship with the Budget Oversight and Performance Analysis (BOP) capability include:

Capability	What it provides
15. Budget Management (BGM)	Data on actual expenditure across all budget categories, costs centres, and projects
17. Funding and Financing (FF)	Details on the management of funding for various types of budget expenditure
27. Service Provisioning (SRP)	The IT services catalogue that defines and prices the IT services that are available
35. Total Cost of Ownership (TCO)	A full understanding of total costs to ensure accurate comparison of actual with predicted expenditure

Further Reading

Brown, E.J., and Yarberry, W.A., 2008. *The effective CIO: how to achieve outstanding success through strategic alignment, financial management, and IT gover*nance. Boca Raton, FL: CRC Press.

Hallinan, E., 2004. Tracking your cost management performance. *Reeves Journal,* 84.

Notes

[1] Castellina, N., 2014. Improving planning, budgeting, and forecasting with advanced analytics. The Aberdeen Group. Available at: <http://www.aberdeen.com/research/9565/RR-planning-budgeting-forecasting-analytics.aspx/content.aspx>.

[2] Harris, M.D., Herron, D., and Iwanicki, S., 2008. *The business value of IT: managing risks, optimizing performance, and measuring results*. Boca Raton, FL: CRC Press.

17. Funding and Financing

17.1 OVERVIEW

Goal

The Funding and Financing (FF) capability aims to generate reliable and flexible sources of funding for an organization, so that it can provide adequate investment and enable the IT function to deliver services and solutions to the organization.

Objectives

▶ Set appropriate funding levels for IT to maximize development of the business capabilities that drive strategic or operational advantage.

▶ Consider alternative sources for technology funding, and understand their associated costs and expected benefits.

▶ Ensure transparent practices and objective governance when agreeing options for funding and financing.

▶ Benchmark IT funding against that of peer organizations to inform funding and financing decisions.

Value

The Funding and Financing (FF) capability enables improved decision-making in selecting appropriate funding sources, in determining adequate funding levels, and in the initial assigning of funds for IT.

Relevance

Possessing an array of flexible funding options to support technology expenditure can be important to facilitate business growth [1], especially when organizations seek to leverage technologies to support business strategy and operations, but lack the necessary financial resources. An effective approach to managing and governing both the acquisition of capital (financing) and the investment of capital (funding) in IT can enable organizations to deliver technology-enabled business capabilities that drive strategic or operational advantage [2].

By establishing an effective Funding and Financing (FF) capability, an organization can ensure that sufficient funds are consistently available to allocate to technology investments. An effective Funding and Financing (FF) capability is informed by a thorough understanding of possible funding options, and of how to generate alternative options when necessary.

17.2 SCOPE

Definition

The Funding and Financing (FF) capability is the ability to determine the funding level required for IT and to allocate it appropriately. The Funding and Financing (FF) capability covers:

▸ Setting the overall levels of IT funding.
▸ Establishing leadership understanding regarding issues and options for IT funding and financing.
▸ Establishing funding and financing governance structures and decision-making processes.
▸ Allocating IT funds to broad categories of IT activities – for example, for capital and operational expenditure.

Other Capabilities

The following are addressed by other capabilities of IT-CMF:

For...	Refer to...
Managing day-to-day budget accounting	15. Budget Management (BGM)
Understanding IT financial performance	16. Budget Oversight and Performance Analysis (BOP)
Governing the benefits to be derived from funding allocations	33. Benefits Assessment and Realization (BAR)
Determining the cost of owning IT assets and running IT services	35. Total Cost of Ownership (TCO)

17.3 UNDERSTANDING MATURITY

Recognizing Excellence

When the Funding and Financing (FF) capability is well-developed or mature:

▸ The funding and financing of IT is regarded as a strategic activity.
▸ IT funding and financing decision-making and governance are clear, transparent, and aligned with business priorities.
▸ Funding from multiple internal and external sources is investigated.
▸ The level of funding is adequately set based on aspirations for strategic development, operational excellence, levels of innovation, and comparison with industry benchmarks.
▸ Initial allocations of funding are objectively balanced against operational, business improvement, and innovation priorities.

Maturity at the Critical Capability Level

The following statements provide a high-level overview of the Funding and Financing (FF) capability at successive levels of maturity:

Level 1   Funding levels and allocations are determined in an ad hoc manner.

Level 2   Funding levels are based on broad adjustments made to the previous year's funding levels, with a limited number of funding allocations based on the requirements of specific projects. Funding for IT typically comes from central corporate budgeting.

Level 3   An IT investments portfolio view is emerging, enabling an increasing number of funding allocations to be directly linked to defined IT initiatives. Funding for IT is available from internal sources other than the central corporate budget – for example, from other business units.

Level 4   Funding levels and allocations for IT can readily change in response to business strategies. Funding can be obtained from multiple internal and external sources.

Level 5   Funding levels and allocations for IT can be dynamically adjusted based on continual review cycles and an array of possible funding options.

Maturity at the Capability Building Block (CBB) Level

The Capability Building Blocks (CBBs) associated with the Funding and Financing (FF) capability fall into two categories:

▶ Category A: four CBBs associated with *Process* – these determine IT financing sources and the appropriate level of funding to allocate.

▶ Category B: two CBBs associated with *Alignment and Oversight* – these determine how funding decisions are made, governed, and communicated.

These are described below, together with a summary of the different maturity levels for each.

Category A: CBBs Associated with *Process*

CBB A1: Funding Sources

Establish sources of IT financing, which may include a centrally allocated IT budget, allocations from other business units, and external sources (for example, joint ventures, industry consortia, vendors, suppliers, clients, and so on). Understand the costs of financing and the expected benefits to be derived from each funding source.

Level 1   Financing is typically obtained in an ad hoc manner from a central internal source.

Level 2   Financing is obtained in a more proactive manner from a central internal source – for example, through the organization's financial planning cycle.

Level 3   Financing is obtained from multiple internal sources, including central allocation and some business unit financing – for example, for specific projects.

Level 4   Financing obtained from external sources is emerging. There is an organization-wide understanding that the effective use of funds needs to be objectively measured – for example, cost of funds vs. benefits.

Level 5   Financing is obtainable from multiple internal and external sources, based on capital cost efficiency.

CBB A2: Funding Levels

Set the overall level of IT funding for the organization based on, for example, strategic priorities and competitive benchmarks.

Level 1   Funding levels are determined in an ad hoc manner.

Level 2   Funding levels are based on those of the previous year with some adjustments. The IT function has limited involvement in determining the funding levels.

Level 3   Most funding levels are reviewed annually, based on the IT strategy and predominantly cost-only benchmarking.

Level 4   Funding levels are determined by analysing IT and business strategies, and by regular cost–quality benchmarking.

Level 5   There are consistent funding levels that are continually reviewed for relevance.

CBB A3: Allocation

Allocate funding to broad categories of IT activity (for example, infrastructure/product improvements, capability development) to align with objectives and derive business value.

Level 1   Funding allocations are determined in an ad hoc manner.

Level 2   A limited number of funding allocations are made, primarily based on the requirements of individual projects.

Level 3   Most funding allocations to major activities are aligned with the IT strategy.

Level 4   All funding allocations to major activities are aligned with IT and business strategies.

Level 5   Funding allocations to major activities are flexible and adaptable to changes, and are consistently reviewed for optimization opportunities.

CBB A4: Performance Measurement

Use metrics to track, evaluate, and improve funding-related outcomes – for example, cost of funds, spend by category/initiative/business unit, return on investment (ROI), return on assets (ROA), and so on. Link funding to the benefits derived to determine the impact of funding.

Level 1	Funding performance measurement is informal and ad hoc.
Level 2	There is emerging use of defined funding metrics (for example, spend by category). Results are rarely reviewed.
Level 3	A standardized set of IT funding metrics is established and, increasingly, results are reviewed.
Level 4	A comprehensive set of IT funding metrics (for example, ROI, ROA, spend by category) is used to communicate performance, and results are reviewed periodically. The comparative costs of funds from different sources are considered up front in decision-making.
Level 5	Metrics are continually reviewed and acted upon to drive efficiencies and improvements in funding decisions.

Category B: CBBs Associated with *Alignment and Oversight*

CBB B1: Governance Model and Alignment

Define guidelines and decision rights for funding governing bodies and promote decision-making alignment with organization-wide decision-making cycles.

Level 1	Funding governance happens on an ad hoc basis, if at all.
Level 2	A defined funding governance model is emerging within the IT function, with a limited number of key decision-making processes defined.
Level 3	A standardized funding governance model is agreed across the IT function. Decision-making processes regarding funding are consistently applied within the IT function and within some other business units.
Level 4	The IT function and the rest of the business agree to share and apply a consistent funding governance model across the organization. Decision-making processes regarding funding are consistently applied organization-wide.
Level 5	There is evidence of continual improvement in funding governance and decision-making performance.

CBB B2: Communication

Discuss funding and financing decisions with stakeholders.

Level 1   IT funding and financing decisions are generally not communicated, or are communicated in an ad hoc manner.

Level 2   The published IT budget serves as the only mechanism through which IT funding and financing decisions are communicated. Communication guidelines are published; typically, however, these are inconsistently applied.

Level 3   Funding and financing decisions plus underlying rationales are communicated to key stakeholders in the IT function and some other business units, using published communication guidelines.

Level 4   Funding and financing decisions plus underlying rationales are communicated to all stakeholders across the organization. Use of published communication guidelines is mandatory.

Level 5   Communication is improved based on continual refinement of communication guidelines and practices.

17.4 IMPROVEMENT PLANNING

Capability Evaluation

Two summary assessment questions are set out below, along with the typical response associated with each level of maturity.

To what extent are IT funding levels flexible and aligned with IT and business strategies?

Level 1   Funding levels are set on an ad hoc basis. The IT function is typically not actively involved in funding and financing-related decisions.

Level 2   Funding levels are set using historical levels, rather than in alignment with current strategic goals. Parts of the IT function are involved in making funding and financing decisions.

Level 3   Funding levels are aligned with the IT strategy. Most of the relevant IT function areas are involved in funding and financing decisions.

Level 4   Funding levels are aligned with IT and business strategies. The IT function proactively collaborates with other relevant business units in funding and financing decisions.

Level 5   Funding levels are driven by the business strategy and are continually reviewed for appropriate levels of alignment and flexibility. The IT function is regarded as a strategic partner in funding and financing decision-making.

How does IT funding allocation contribute to the achievement of IT and business strategic objectives?

Level 1	Funding allocation is determined in an ad hoc manner.
Level 2	There is a defined funding allocation approach emerging in parts of the IT function, with a limited number of allocations occurring based on the requirements of specific projects.
Level 3	Standardized funding allocation practices across the entire IT function balance spend by category to align with the IT strategy.
Level 4	Comprehensive funding allocation practices across the organization balance spend by category to align fully with both IT and business strategies.
Level 5	The funding allocation practices are readily adaptable to the business environment and to the strategies of relevant business ecosystem partners.

Key Practices-Outcomes-Metrics (POMs)

Some useful POMs for developing the Funding and Financing (FF) capability are summarized below.

Level 2 POMs

Practice	Perform due diligence to ensure key projects are adequately funded.
Outcome	The likelihood of key projects achieving a successful outcome is increased by the allocation of sufficient funding.
Metric	Percentage of key projects with validated funding allocations. Percentage of funded projects that don't require additional funding or have cost over-runs.
Practice	Assess IT funding levels based on the previous year's budget, allowing for some adjustments based on uncontrollable increases.
Outcome	At a minimum, IT funding keeps pace with cross-industry cost increases.
Metric	Percentage increase/decrease in IT funding over the previous year's budget.
Practice	Establish a governance model for approving IT funding – for example, involving the executive offices of CEO, CFO, COO, CIO, and so on.
Outcome	IT funding decisions are made at the highest level, promoting consideration of short- and long-term perspectives when approving IT funding.
Metric	Percentage of funding expenditure approved within the defined decision-making process.

Level 3 POMs

Practice	Design multiple scenarios with predefined triggers to prepare the IT function for changes in funding allocation or demand.
Outcome	Funding plans will have greater flexibility if predicted scenarios emerge.
Metric	Percentage by which IT funding could readily increase or decrease.

Practice	Expand the ability of the IT function to receive funds from other sources beyond the central corporate source.
Outcome	In order to meet funding shortfalls, the IT function can integrate other funding streams in pursuit of the supporting business strategy.
Metric	Percentage and amount of IT funds by source.
Practice	Promote transparent and objective funding decisions.
Outcome	Clear and explicit decision criteria enable funding applicants to develop better proposals and/or funding applications.
Metric	Percentage of funding decisions that occur within an approved funding process.
Practice	Standardize the criteria for conducting due diligence on alternative funding sources.
Outcome	Unexpected consequences can be avoided post funding agreements.
Metric	Percentage of IT expenditure from alternative funding sources found to be in compliance with due diligence reviews.

Level 4 POMs

Practice	Use benchmark comparisons to validate the organization's corporate strategies, information intensity regarding the organization's products/services, IT expenditure levels, corporate revenue, geographical locations, the preferred sourcing strategy, and so on.
Outcome	The use of benchmarking approaches doesn't misrepresent IT funding analysis, either favourably or unfavourably.
Metric	Percentage of IT expenditure benchmarked using a balanced multi-criteria approach.
Practice	Mandate a portfolio approach to provide visibility on organization-wide technology expenditure.
Outcome	All technology-related expenditure by the IT function and other business units can be understood, allowing opportunities for consolidation and the rerouting of funds to new opportunities.
Metric	Ratio of IT function expenditure on technology to other business unit expenditure on technology.
Practice	Ensure that funding performance measurement includes both tangibles and intangibles such as risk adjusted return on capital (RAROC) and shareholder value.
Outcome	There is a holistic understanding of the costs of financing and the expected benefits to be derived from these funds.
Metric	RAROC. Shareholder value.

Level 5 POMs

Practice	Continually review the alignment of IT funding levels with business objectives.
Outcome	Funding is aligned to maximize development of business capabilities that drive strategic or operational advantage.
Metric	Percentage of overall IT funding aligned to specific business strategic priorities/objectives.
Practice	Demonstrate that funding and financing of IT can be a strategic lever for the organization.
Outcome	All senior stakeholders understand the strategic value of funding IT correctly and from different sources, thus ensuring capital cost efficiency.
Metric	Percentage of senior stakeholders who understand funding and options available.

Addressing Typical Challenges

Some typical challenges that can arise in attempting to develop maturity in the Funding and Financing (FF) capability are set out below.

Challenge	Difficulty in convincing business leaders of the strategic value of increased IT investment.
Context	IT is viewed as a cost centre, with costs to be reduced over time. Typically, there is limited transparency in how IT funding decisions are made, where funds come from, and how they are used.
Action	Clearly communicate funding and financing decisions and underlying rationales to ensure they are transparent to and accepted by relevant stakeholders.
Challenge	IT funding and financing governance oversight is limited to annual budget approval discussions.
Context	There is little appetite for expanding governance beyond initial budget approvals, as this is likely to require more time and administration.
Action	Advocate to senior management the benefits and flexibility to be expected from the continual oversight of funds between approval cycles. These benefits include the ability to reprioritize initial allocations and to adjust funding levels in response to rapidly emerging opportunities and challenges.
Challenge	Difficulty in engaging business leaders in funding allocation decisions, as the technical language used to describe IT projects can be cumbersome and confusing.
Context	There is a general lack of appreciation of how funding of the IT function supports business initiatives.
Action	Using plain, business-level language, highlight the impact that funding of the IT function can have on business initiatives.

Management Artefacts

Management artefacts that may be used to develop maturity in the Funding and Financing (FF) capability include:

▸ An IT budget plan.
▸ IT funding benchmark data.
▸ IT funding models.
▸ Cash flow/operating budget statement.

IT Budget Plan

An IT budget plan is a financial statement of proposed IT expenditure for a defined period of time. It usually includes details relating to salaries, IT hardware, software, licensing, maintenance, professional services, and so on. Normally it is drawn up annually and reviewed a number of times during the year. Depending on the philosophy of the organization, the budget, once established, may or may not be adjusted within the budget period. It is important that actual expenditure be as close as possible to the budget.

Under-runs indicate that proposed expenditure did not materialize within the budget time frame – for example, a project/activity was not initiated or is moving at a slower than planned pace. An under-run may also represent an opportunity cost for other projects that could otherwise have been funded.

Over-runs typically indicate unforeseen expenditures, which could mean a project/activity is terminated, or they could lead to cuts to funding of other projects/activities if an increase to the original IT budget is not possible. An over-run could also undermine the original business case for the project.

The Funding and Financing (FF) capability provides input on broad funding allocations to the IT budget to enable the realization of the intended business value.

IT Funding Benchmark Data

When using benchmarked data, organizations should be mindful to consider items other than IT expenditure. For example, factors such as organizational strategies, business scale, information intensity of the organization's products/services, IT expenditure levels, corporate revenue, geographical locations, and the preferred sourcing strategy often dictate long-term requirements for IT services, with consequent effects on IT funding levels. Such factors should be taken into account when interpreting benchmarking data.

Some typical benchmark comparisons can include:

▸ IT expenditure as a percentage of revenue and/or operating expenses.
▸ IT capital and operational expenditure.
▸ Strategic IT spending categories.
▸ Business-led technology expenditure.
▸ IT spending distribution – for example, hardware, software, personnel, outsourcing.

Benchmarking is typically used as a high-level directional indicator in planning IT funding (rather than an absolute limit or target).

IT Funding Models

Once the IT function can demonstrate budgetary control (often a good sign of improved business alignment), alternative funding options to enhance business value are likely to be more readily considered – as credibility is often built on successful budget expenditure control. Options for IT funding models can include:

▶ Internal Models:
  ▸ *Corporate budget:* the primary funding model often tied to the annual budgeting cycle.
  ▸ *Other business units:* the business unit(s) that primarily benefit from the technology investment put up some or all of the funds.
  ▸ *Pay-per-view/use:* business units fund IT budgets based on their consumption of IT services.
  ▸ *IT funded:* the IT function itself collects an acceptable margin on the IT services it provides, which it uses to fund additional IT solutions and services.
  ▸ *Venture:* a loan, based on market/commercial terms, from corporate finance to fund riskier propositions with potentially higher benefits.
▶ External Models:
  ▸ *Vendor*: funds provided by a technology vendor in return for regular scheduled repayments.
  ▸ *Government grants and incentives*: funds from national and local jurisdictions for projects that have potential for employee upskilling, job creation, intellectual property generation, and generation of further commercial investment.
  ▸ *Consortium*: funding from consortia to develop a common and shared solution – for example, those formed under the European Commission's Horizon 2020 programme.
  ▸ *Direct revenue*: IT services or solutions are sold on the open market to generate revenue and profit. Leasing of intellectual property rights from internally developed software (for example, via patents) is also an option here.
  ▸ *Leasing:* assets are leased in order to avoid capital expenditure – for example, infrastructure as a service (IaaS) and software as a service (SaaS).
  ▸ *Borrowing*: a commercial loan is obtained from an external bank or other lender.

Before making the decision to expand funding options, the scale of the project, the timescale for realization of the investment, and the level of risk should be considered, as well as the pros and cons attached to the possible IT funding models.

Cash Flow/Operating Budget Statement

A cash flow/operating budget statement shows where funding is coming from and where it is going to, typically on a month-by-month basis. It normally covers cash inflows and outflows for both operations and capital financing. Cash flow budgeting is concerned only with money movement, and not with net income or profitability. A cash flow budget is a useful management tool that enables the organization to plan and monitor its cash flows. It enables the IT function to test the viability of its budget plans for the year ahead, to verify that its expenditure needs can be met.

17.5 REFERENCE

See Also

Other capabilities of IT-CMF that have a particularly close relationship with the Funding and Financing (FF) capability include:

Capability	What it provides
02. Business Planning (BP)	Identification of IT activities that may require funding
04. Capacity Forecasting and Planning (CFP)	Scenario modelling of business strategy and operations to ensure future capacity needs are accommodated in the funding process
16. Budget Oversight and Performance Analysis (BOP)	Analysis of actual expenditure versus original forecasts to improve future funding and financing decisions
33. Benefits Assessment and Realization (BAR)	An evaluation of the potential benefits and risks associated with investment opportunities which may require funding
35. Total Cost of Ownership (TCO)	Details of direct and indirect costs associated with an IT service or asset

Further Reading

Cao, L., Mohan, K., Ramesh, B., and Sarkar, S., 2013. Adapting funding processes for agile IT projects: an empirical investigation. *European Journal of Information Systems,* 22, 191–205.

Harris, M.D., Herron, D., and Iwanicki, S., 2008. *The business value of IT: managing risks, optimizing performance and measuring results.* Boca Raton, FL: CRC Press.

Schwienbacher, A., 2014. Financing the business. In T. Baker and F. Welter, *The Routledge companion to entrepreneurship.* Abingdon: Routledge, 193–206.

Notes

[1] Brinckmann, J., Salomo, S., and Gemuenden, H.G., 2011. Financial management competence of founding teams and growth of new technology-based firms. *Entrepreneurship Theory and Practice,* 35, 217–43.

[2] Teichroew, D., Robichek, A.A., and Montalbano, M., 1965. An analysis of criteria for investment and financing decisions under certainty. *Management Science,* 12, 151–79.

PPP
18. Portfolio Planning and Prioritization

18.1 Overview

Goal

The Portfolio Planning and Prioritization (PPP) capability aims to establish the investment portfolio composition for technology-related programmes and projects.

Objectives

▸ Increase the likelihood that organizational resources are applied in accordance with the organization's strategy.

▸ Improve consistency and transparency in programme and project selection, based on agreed evaluation and prioritization criteria.

▸ Prioritize technology-related programmes and projects that have the greatest potential for value delivery in alignment with the organization's strategic direction, while managing potential downsides.

▸ Dynamically reprioritize the portfolio based on strategy change – for example, mergers, acquisitions, and business environment changes.

▸ Provide insight into financial, people, and technical resource requirements for execution of the IT investment portfolio.

▸ Improve the perception of IT as a catalyst or enabler of the business, by delivering positive returns on the IT investment portfolio.

Value

The Portfolio Planning and Prioritization (PPP) capability helps ensure that the investment portfolio of technology-related programmes and projects is aligned to and optimized for the organization's strategic direction.

Relevance

Where multiple programmes and projects compete for a limited investment fund, portfolio selection and prioritization is a critical factor in establishing and maintaining organizational competitiveness. The number of IT programmes and projects seeking investment will typically exceed the number that can be funded and executed, owing to limited resources and capacity. Organizations thus have to systematically prioritize those IT programmes and projects that have the best potential benefit for the organization as a whole, and avoid selection based on bias. Further, with the acceleration of business change, the selected portfolio needs to be managed dynamically and reprioritized whenever necessary, to ensure ongoing alignment with the organization's strategic direction. However, many IT functions over-promise and under-deliver on their IT investment portfolios, with frequent reports of IT project failures. An effective approach to prioritizing and planning the portfolio is required, to ensure that a balanced investment portfolio is chosen that can deliver optimal value to the business.

By developing an effective Portfolio Planning and Prioritization (PPP) capability, an organization can create a synchronized and balanced portfolio that supports the organization's pursuit of its strategic goals and objectives [1]. The priority attached to each programme and project should guide the financial, people, and technical resource allocations [1], thus minimizing the likelihood of resourcing issues during the execution phase. Achieving consensus among key stakeholders using a transparent approach to portfolio selection minimizes the influence of organizational politics, and increases the likelihood of making organizational investments that deliver positive returns.

18.2 SCOPE

Definition

The Portfolio Planning and Prioritization (PPP) capability is the ability to select, prioritize, approve, and terminate programmes and projects that are seeking organizational resources. The Portfolio Planning and Prioritization (PPP) capability covers:

▶ Establishing a framework for selecting and prioritizing programmes and projects.
▶ Involving key personnel in selecting programmes and projects.
▶ Assessing and prioritizing programmes and projects based on their alignment with business objectives and operational needs.
▶ Approving and terminating programmes and projects.
▶ Maintaining oversight of financial, people, and technical resources for portfolio resource planning purposes.

Other Capabilities

The following are addressed by other capabilities of IT-CMF:

For...	Refer to...
Creating a roadmap of projects targeting internal improvements within the IT function	19. Capability Assessment Management (CAM)
Methodologies for managing individual programmes and projects	24. Programme and Project Management (PPM)
Managing the IT services portfolio	27. Service Provisioning (SRP)
Evaluating the performance of individual programmes and projects	33. Benefits Assessment and Realization (BAR)
Reviewing the ongoing performance of the investment portfolio for technology-related programmes and projects.	34. Portfolio Management (PM)

18.3 UNDERSTANDING MATURITY

Recognizing Excellence

When the Portfolio Planning and Prioritization (PPP) capability is well-developed or mature:

▶ Programmes and projects are selected using transparent assessment criteria and a prioritization framework that are continually reviewed and adjusted to provide optimal value to the business.

▶ A central committee, comprising senior management representatives across the organization, is recognized as the sole authority for selecting, prioritizing, approving, and terminating programmes and projects.

▶ The organization's strategic goals are key determinants in defining the portfolio's selection criteria and evaluation framework.

▶ The success (or otherwise) of previous programmes and projects informs decisions regarding the prioritization and approval of similar or related new programmes and projects, and the termination of programmes and projects in progress.

Maturity at the Critical Capability Level

The following statements provide a high-level overview of the Portfolio Planning and Prioritization (PPP) capability at successive levels of maturity:

Level 1   Programmes and projects are prioritized by management in a reactive and ad hoc manner. The resource allocations needed to implement the prioritized programmes and projects are considered in an informal and ad hoc manner.

Level 2   There is emerging use of a prioritization framework when considering new programmes and projects. However, the framework may not be consistently applied and the legacy investment portfolio is rarely fully considered. Only a limited number of the key resource allocations needed to implement the prioritized programmes and projects are taken into account during portfolio planning.

Level 3   Most programmes and projects are prioritized according to a common prioritization framework that reflects a standardized set of criteria. However, reprioritization may still be reactive. Most resource allocations needed to implement the prioritized programmes and projects are taken into account during portfolio planning.

Level 4   All programmes and projects are proactively prioritized and reprioritized at regular intervals, with a central focus on business value contribution. Any required re-allocation of resources is taken into account during portfolio planning.

Level 5   The prioritization approach for all programmes and projects is optimized based on internal feedback and external comparisons. Planning for the resource allocations needed to implement the prioritized programmes and projects is continually improved, as there is real-time visibility into the availability of key resources.

Maturity at the Capability Building Block (CBB) Level

The Capability Building Blocks (CBBs) associated with the Portfolio Planning and Prioritization (PPP) capability fall into two categories:

▸ Category A: two CBBs associated with **Governance** – these outline the decision-making mechanisms for determining the portfolio's composition.
▸ Category B: two CBBs associated with **Process** – these outline the operational activities of assessing, prioritizing, and planning for the portfolio's programmes and projects.

These are described below, together with a summary of the different maturity levels for each.

Category A: CBBs Associated with *Governance*

CBB A1: Prioritization Framework

Use an evaluation framework and a set of criteria to select and prioritize programmes and projects for the portfolio.

Level 1	There is no formal portfolio prioritization framework defined. The prioritization of programmes and projects is non-existent or ad hoc.
Level 2	A portfolio prioritization framework, with a few fundamental criteria (such as acquisition costs), is emerging within the IT function.
Level 3	The portfolio prioritization framework includes standardized criteria (such as risk, value, resource availability, and technology mix). Input is sought from some other business units.
Level 4	A single, comprehensive portfolio prioritization framework is adopted organization-wide. The framework includes value-oriented criteria (such as benefits, ROI, value at risk, and project interdependencies).
Level 5	The portfolio prioritization framework is optimized, based on feedback, and reflects industry best-known practice.

CBB A2: Authority

Involve key personnel in decisions regarding the selection and prioritization of programmes and projects. Approve and terminate the selected programmes and projects as required.

Level 1	There is no recognized authority for selecting, prioritizing, approving, or terminating programmes and projects. Resourcing conflicts typically arise because of ad hoc decisions taken by individuals.
Level 2	Functional managers track and manage their individual programmes and projects, and may directly approve new programmes and projects.
Level 3	A central committee (such as a Portfolio Investment Board), with representatives from the IT function and some other business units, has oversight of the portfolio. Some programmes and projects, however, may still be selected, prioritized, and approved directly by line management, and there is still a reluctance to terminate non-performing programmes and projects.
Level 4	The central committee has senior management representatives from all business units and is the sole authority for selecting, prioritizing, approving, and terminating programmes and projects.
Level 5	The cross-functional composition of the central committee is regularly reviewed for effectiveness based on lessons learned from previous programme and project selection, prioritization, approval, and termination activities.

Category B: CBBs Associated with *Process*

CBB B1: Assessment and Prioritization

Assess programmes and projects against explicit criteria, such as alignment with strategic vision, business objectives, operational needs, desired portfolio mix and scope, and resource availability. Prioritize programmes and projects based on the assessment results.

Level 1	Programmes and projects are assessed and prioritized by management in a reactive and ad hoc manner.
Level 2	Key programmes and projects are typically prioritized using locally defined assessment criteria and a basic portfolio prioritization framework.
Level 3	A formal approach to prioritization is used across the IT function, with clearly defined and standardized assessment criteria and a portfolio prioritization framework. However, reprioritization may still be reactive.
Level 4	A comprehensive assessment approach is adopted organization-wide to regularly assess and re-assess all programmes and projects, with a major focus on business value contribution. Changes in the business environment are systematically considered, as well as current portfolio performance.
Level 5	The assessment approach is regularly revised and optimized, based on lessons learned from previous programme and project selection decisions. The portfolio prioritization approach for all programmes and projects is optimized based on internal feedback and external comparisons.

CBB B2: Planning

Develop a high-level plan for aligning the portfolio with the organization's strategy. Acquire information on financial, people, and technical resources to plan their allocation to the portfolio.

Level 1	The organization's strategy is rarely considered in any portfolio planning and prioritization activities.
Level 2	A basic approach to portfolio planning and prioritization is emerging within the IT function, aimed at ensuring that the portfolio is aligned with the organization's strategy. Major strategic changes are recognized and acted upon.
Level 3	A standardized approach to portfolio planning and prioritization, aimed at ensuring that the portfolio is aligned with the organization's strategy, is established within the IT function and some other business units.
Level 4	Comprehensive engagement with senior management across the whole organization helps ensure that portfolio planning and prioritization activities result in the portfolio being quickly adapted to changing business requirements.
Level 5	Input from the strategies of relevant business ecosystem partners is consistently captured and considered in portfolio planning and prioritization activities.

18.4 IMPROVEMENT PLANNING

Capability Evaluation

Two summary assessment questions are set out below, along with the typical response associated with each level of maturity.

To what extent is there a recognized authority within your organization to select, approve, and terminate programmes and projects, and to make decisions on prioritization?

Level 1   There is no recognized authority for selecting, prioritizing, approving, or terminating programmes and projects. Resourcing conflicts typically arise because of ad hoc decisions taken by individuals.

Level 2   Functional managers track and manage their individual programmes and projects, and may directly approve new programmes and projects.

Level 3   A central committee (such as a Portfolio Investment Board), with representatives from the IT function and some other business units, has oversight of the portfolio. Some programmes and projects, however, may still be selected, prioritized, and approved directly by line management, and there is still a reluctance to terminate non-performing programmes and projects.

Level 4   A central committee has senior management representatives from all business units and is the sole authority for selecting, prioritizing, approving, and terminating programmes and projects.

Level 5   The cross-functional composition of a central committee is regularly reviewed for effectiveness based on lessons learned from previous programme and project selection, prioritization, approval, and termination activities.

How are programmes and projects prioritized?

Level 1   Programmes and projects are prioritized by management in a reactive and ad hoc manner.

Level 2   There is emerging use of a prioritization framework when prioritizing new programmes and projects. However, the framework may not be consistently applied and the legacy investment portfolio is rarely considered in full.

Level 3   Most programmes and projects are prioritized according to a common prioritization framework that reflects a standardized set of criteria. However, reprioritization may still be reactive.

Level 4   All programmes and projects are proactively prioritized and reprioritized at regular intervals, with a central focus on business value contribution.

Level 5   The prioritization approach for all programmes and projects is optimized, based on internal feedback and external comparisons.

Key Practices-Outcomes-Metrics (POMs)

Some useful POMs for developing the Portfolio Planning and Prioritization (PPP) capability are summarized below.

Level 2 POMs

Practice	Define a basic portfolio prioritization framework for the IT function that reflects a limited number of key criteria (such as fundamental acquisition costs).
Outcome	A transparent ranking methodology is available.
Metric	Yes/No indicator regarding the existence of a portfolio prioritization framework. Number of framework criteria defined.
Practice	Encourage functional managers to directly prioritize and approve new programmes and projects for their individual portfolios.
Outcome	Visibility into investments is emerging, with potential to identify and escalate local conflicts.
Metric	Percentage of programmes and projects that are approved by functional managers.

Level 3 POMs

Practice	Establish a central committee (for example, a Portfolio Investment Board) with representatives from the IT function and some other business units, to maintain oversight of the portfolio.
Outcome	Programmes and projects approved by the central committee are more likely to be aligned with the organization's strategic direction.
Metric	Percentage of programmes and projects that are approved by a central committee.
Practice	Expand the portfolio prioritization framework to incorporate several criteria (such as risk, value, resource availability, and technology mix).
Outcome	A clear and consistent ranking of key programmes and projects is available within the IT function and some other business units.
Metric	Number of framework criteria defined.
Practice	Run the portfolio planning activity annually, using a dedicated team.
Outcome	The success rate for programmes and projects in the portfolio improves, and interconnections between most projects can be proactively planned.
Metric	Frequency of portfolio planning activities. Assignment of IT and business unit employees with dedicated responsibility for portfolio planning.

Practice	Consider the financial, people, and technical resources needed to implement the prioritized programmes and projects. Replan the portfolio if required, according to resource availability.
Outcome	Prioritized programmes and projects in the portfolio are less likely to be impacted by resource constraints.
Metric	Percentage of prioritized programmes and projects that have resource allocation issues.

Level 4 POMs

Practice	Recognize a central committee, comprising senior management representatives from across the whole organization, as the sole authority for selecting, prioritizing, approving, and terminating programmes and projects.
Outcome	Senior management representation on the central committee helps ensure that all programmes and projects are aligned with the organization's strategic direction.
Metric	Percentage of programmes and projects that are approved by a central committee (such as a central Portfolio Investment Board).

Practice	Adopt a formal approach to regularly assess and re-assess all programmes and projects organization-wide.
Outcome	Organization-wide programme and project assessments help ensure that the investment portfolio remains relevant to the organization's needs.
Metric	Percentage of programmes and projects that are evaluated against an agreed set of criteria. Percentage of programmes and projects that are re-assessed.

Practice	Build value-oriented criteria (such as benefits, ROI, value at risk, and project interdependencies) into the portfolio prioritization framework, and regularly check that the framework is aligned with the organization's strategies.
Outcome	A clear, consistent, and transparent ranking approach is available. The portfolio is better aligned with the organization's strategic direction, and the portfolio is revised in line with changing business requirements.
Metric	Percentage of programmes and projects that are prioritized using agreed criteria. Number of reviews of alignment with the organization's strategies per planning cycle.

Practice	Fully integrate portfolio planning into the organization's overall planning activities.
Outcome	Portfolio planning is recognized as a key component of the organization's overall planning. The success rates for all programmes and projects are improved.
Metric	Yes/No indicator regarding the integration of IT portfolio planning activities with the organization's general planning activities.

Level 5 POMs

Practice	Regularly review the effectiveness of the cross-functional composition of the central committee, based on lessons learned from previous programme and project selection, prioritization, approval, and termination activities.
Outcome	Relevant management stakeholders are involved in all programme and project prioritizations, increasing their commitment to the prioritization outcomes.
Metric	Frequency of central committee staffing reviews.
Practice	Continually update the portfolio prioritization framework and approach, based on feedback and industry best-known practice.
Outcome	The portfolio prioritization framework is adjusted, based on lessons learned from previous prioritization cycles and industry best-known practice, to meet the organization's needs.
Metric	Frequency of framework reviews (and updates as appropriate).
Practice	Capture and consider input from the strategies of relevant business ecosystem partners for portfolio planning activities.
Outcome	The portfolio is regularly aligned with changing business requirements.
Metric	Number of key business partners providing input to portfolio planning.
Practice	Maintain clear and up-to-date visibility of all resource allocations and their utilization rates across the portfolio.
Outcome	The planning of resources required to implement the prioritized programmes and projects is optimized.
Metric	Percentage of programmes and projects that have resource allocation issues. Percentage of programmes and projects completed successfully within resource forecasts.

Addressing Typical Challenges

Some typical challenges that can arise in attempting to develop maturity in the Portfolio Planning and Prioritization (PPP) capability are set out below.

Challenge	Lack of senior management support and buy-in for portfolio planning and prioritization activities.
Context	Planning and prioritizing the IT investment portfolio is not perceived as being of strategic importance.
Action	Foster a senior management mind-set in which the selection of appropriate IT programmes and projects is recognized as important to the organization's success, and critical to using the organization's scarce resources effectively.

Challenge	Resources provided for planning and prioritizing programmes and projects are inadequate.
Context	Willingness to invest in portfolio planning and prioritization activities is limited, as this is perceived as an unnecessary and bureaucratic overhead.
Action	Promote dialogue on the merits of portfolio planning and prioritization, and how it should be funded as an important contributor to the realization of the organization's overall goals and objectives.
Challenge	Unwillingness to assign (or accept) responsibility for participating in the portfolio planning, prioritization, and oversight activities.
Context	IT investments are made predominantly based on the siloed interests or agendas of individual business units.
Action	Recognize that assigning responsibility for portfolio planning and prioritization is a way of ensuring that programmes and projects are assessed and prioritized in a consistent and transparent manner, in line with the organization's overall best interests, and that participation in the decision-making process increases stakeholder buy-in to the selected portfolio.
Challenge	Difficulty in reprioritizing the portfolio in response to poor portfolio performance or changes in the business environment.
Context	There is no transparent approach for concluding that legacy programmes or projects are failing, or that they no longer align with the organization's goals.
Action	Stimulate organizational commitment to proactively remaining abreast of business environment changes, reviewing existing programmes and projects, and terminating those that are no longer necessary or fail to meet expectations.
Challenge	Poor understanding of the benefits of effective portfolio planning and prioritization.
Context	The value of systematically optimizing the selection of programmes and projects is poorly communicated.
Action	Promote widespread awareness and visibility among stakeholders on the portfolio's successes and quick wins, and its contribution to overall business value.

Management Artefacts

Management artefacts that may be used to develop maturity in the Portfolio Planning and Prioritization (PPP) capability include:

▸ Portfolio prioritization criteria.
▸ A portfolio prioritization framework.
▸ A portfolio plan.

Portfolio Prioritization Criteria

Portfolio prioritization criteria are the basis for evaluating programmes and projects for investment. The criteria and their relative importance should be developed with input from key organization stakeholders. Emphasis should be placed on criteria that can be objectively and easily measured. Criteria may include risk, estimated cost, estimated financial return and benefits, resource availability, complexity, technical feasibility, desired portfolio mix and scope, operational needs, strategic alignment, competitive advantage, and stakeholder satisfaction. The organization may also choose to decompose some criteria to support portfolio prioritization at a more granular level. For example, the 'risk' criterion may have sub-criteria such as the 'risk of cost overrun' and the 'risk of failure'.

Portfolio Prioritization Framework

A portfolio prioritization framework outlines the way in which the prioritization criteria are applied to evaluate programmes and projects. This helps the organization to determine the programmes and projects most likely to deliver the best returns for the business. It also helps to minimize selection based on instinct, local preference, or bias.

Criteria should be weighted in terms of their importance to the business – for example, on a scale of 1 to 5. The impact of each programme and project being evaluated should then be rated with respect to each criterion. The product of the criterion weighting and the impact rating provides a total score for the programme or project against that criterion. The aggregate of all criteria scores is then the total score for the programme or project.

The portfolio prioritization framework thus provides a clear, consistent, and transparent way of ranking the programmes and projects in the IT portfolio. Those programmes or projects with the highest scores reflect those with the greatest potential benefit for the business.

Portfolio Plan

A portfolio plan includes an overview of all approved programmes and projects in the portfolio, and outlines their interconnections and any reprioritizations over time. The plan reflects existing financial, people, and technical resource allocations and availability. It provides visibility into potential resource constraints for executing the prioritized set of programmes and projects within a given timeframe. It may also inform decisions pertaining to programme and project scheduling, resource hiring and development, sourcing of material and equipment, and workload re-balancing. Clearer visibility into resourcing across the portfolio minimizes the risk of attempting to execute programmes and projects with scheduling conflicts, excessive budget constraints, excessive over- or under-allocations of people, or inadequate infrastructure capacity/bandwidth. Availability of a portfolio plan improves programme and project success rates. It further supports consideration of the alignment between the portfolio's components and the organization's strategic objectives, and the performance of each portfolio component in the context of strategic goals.

18.5 REFERENCE

See Also

Other capabilities of IT-CMF that have a particularly close relationship with the Portfolio Planning and Prioritization (PPP) capability include:

Capability	What it provides
04. Capacity Forecasting and Planning (CFP)	The current capacity plan and scenarios for future resources based on current and proposed programmes and projects
09. IT Leadership and Governance (ITG)	The organization's decision-making policies to support portfolio prioritization
14. Strategic Planning (SP)	The strategic vision and objectives to support programme and project prioritization
17. Funding and Financing (FF)	Determination of appropriate sources of funds for IT investment portfolio initiatives
19. Capability Assessment Management (CAM)	A roadmap of projects aimed at improvements within the IT function
33. Benefits Assessment and Realization (BAR)	The business case for each proposed programme and project
34. Portfolio Management (PM)	Status reports and decisions to be taken on the current IT investment portfolio

Further Reading

Maizlish, B., and Handler, R., 2008. *IT (information technology) portfolio management step-by-step: unlocking the business value of technology*. Hoboken, NJ: Wiley.

Pendharkar, P.C., 2014. A decision-making framework for justifying a portfolio of IT projects. *International Journal of Project Management,* 32(4), 625–39.

Pennypacker, J., and Retna, S. eds., 2009. *Project portfolio management: a view from the management trenches*. Hoboken, NJ: Wiley.

Project Management Institute, 2013. *The standard for portfolio management*. 3rd ed. Newtown Square PA: Project Management Institute.

Notes

[1] Project Management Institute, 2013. *The standard for portfolio management.* 3rd ed. Newtown Square PA: Project Management Institute.

Managing the IT Capability

The IT function was traditionally seen as the provider of one-off IT services and solutions. In order to fulfil its role as the instigator of innovation and continual business improvement however, the IT function has to proactively deliver – and be seen to deliver – a stream of new and improved IT services and solutions. This macro-capability provides a systematic approach to adopting that role, by effectively and efficiently maintaining existing services and solutions, and developing new ones.

Contents: Managing the IT Capability

CAM
19. Capability Assessment Management

19.1 OVERVIEW

Goal

The Capability Assessment Management (CAM) capability aims to provide the organization with an accurate picture of its current IT management capabilities, and to identify areas needing improvement.

Objectives

▶ Improve the organization's ability to identify strengths and weaknesses in key IT capabilities.
▶ Establish a consistent approach to assessing IT capabilities and selecting areas for IT capability improvement that are aligned with the organization's strategic direction.
▶ Identify over-investment in IT capabilities that are of lower strategic importance.
▶ Establish a credible and achievable approach to managing a continual improvement programme, which can be used to verify improvements over time.

Value

The Capability Assessment Management (CAM) capability helps ensure reliability, repeatability, and validity in assessing IT capabilities and implementing improvement initiatives.

Relevance

The creation, deployment, and exploitation of distinct and inimitable IT capabilities can be among an organization's key competitive differentiators [1] [2] [3], as they determine the pace and manner by which it can use technology to innovate and deliver value [4]. However, to optimize IT capabilities, an organization needs to know which IT capabilities are strategically important, how mature they currently are, and in what areas they need to be developed further [4]. The organization thus needs reliable, repeatable, and valid approaches for assessing the strengths and weaknesses of various IT capabilities and developing dependable improvement roadmaps.

By developing an effective Capability Assessment Management (CAM) capability, the organization can conduct capability assessments, set capability targets, and implement improvement initiatives in a consistent and transparent manner. This enables the organization to develop the core IT capabilities that support its strategy, and to identify non-core capabilities that may be stood-down and resources diverted elsewhere.

19.2 SCOPE

Definition

The Capability Assessment Management (CAM) capability is the ability of the organization to conduct current state evaluations and plan improvements for its portfolio of IT capabilities. Current state evaluations involve gathering and documenting data about the specific IT capabilities in the organization. The results then inform the planning and execution of improvement actions to deal with any deficiencies. The Capability Assessment Management (CAM) capability covers:

▸ Selecting an overarching capability framework and mapping other frameworks used in the organization to it.

▸ Managing continuous improvement of the organization's IT capabilities.

▸ Securing appropriate senior management sponsorship for IT capability improvement.

▸ Promoting organizational buy-in and incentivizing participation in capability improvement evaluation and planning.

▸ Planning, preparing, and conducting capability evaluations.

▸ Setting IT capability targets and defining development roadmaps for key IT capabilities.

Other Capabilities

The following are addressed by other capabilities of IT-CMF:

For...	Refer to...
Approving business cases for individual capability improvement initiatives	18. Portfolio Planning and Prioritization (PPP)
Executing capability improvement projects	24. Programme and Project Management (PPM)
Specific guidance regarding individual IT capabilities	The relevant IT-CMF Critical Capability (CC)

19.3 UNDERSTANDING MATURITY

Recognizing Excellence

When the Capability Assessment Management (CAM) capability is well-developed or mature:

▸ An integrated and organization-wide continual capability improvement approach is in place, with adequate resourcing.

▸ There is an up-to-date and holistic view of the strengths and weaknesses across the portfolio of IT capabilities.

▸ IT capability targets are aligned with business goals and are informed by industry benchmarks, previous assessment results, and organizational challenges.

▸ Development roadmaps have executive sponsors assigned to them.

▸ Improvement initiatives are consistently prioritized and acted upon. Key areas are regularly re-assessed to check progress.

▸ Stakeholders are sufficiently involved and adequate resources are available to identify and address IT capability deficiencies or gaps.

Maturity at the Critical Capability Level

The following statements provide a high-level overview of the Capability Assessment Management (CAM) capability at successive levels of maturity:

Level 1	No specific IT capability framework is selected. Assessments and target-setting are non-existent or ad hoc.
Level 2	IT capability frameworks are used in parts of the IT function. A basic assessment approach is in place within the IT function, with limited IT capability target-setting.
Level 3	A lead or dominant IT capability framework is emerging, covering all of the IT function and some other business units. A systematic assessment approach is beginning to be used, with consistent IT capability target-setting.
Level 4	A lead or dominant IT capability framework is comprehensively aligned with the organization-wide strategy and business goals. The assessment approach is deployed organization-wide, and IT capability targets are fully aligned with business requirements.
Level 5	The lead IT capability framework and IT capability targets are continually optimized. Feedback is continually acted upon to improve the IT capability assessment and target-setting approach.

Maturity at the Capability Building Block (CBB) Level

The Capability Building Blocks (CBBs) associated with the Capability Assessment Management (CAM) capability fall into two categories:

▸ Category A: three CBBs associated with *Governance* – these create the oversight mechanisms for managing capability assessment programmes.

▸ Category B: four CBBs associated with *Process* – these reflect the operational activities involved in conducting individual IT capability assessments.

These are described below, together with a summary of the different maturity levels for each.

Category A: CBBs Associated with *Governance*

CBB A1: Framework

Determine the capability framework(s) to be used for assessment. Define an integration and mapping approach in cases where a number of frameworks are used simultaneously.

Level 1   There is no formally selected IT capability framework; individual capability elements may be informally defined. Multiple frameworks may be in use with little or ad hoc integration.

Level 2   A number of IT capability frameworks are in use across the IT function. Any linkages between these frameworks are basic and do not follow a specific approach.

Level 3   A standardized approach is emerging for consistently mapping or integrating the IT capability frameworks in use.

Level 4   The IT capability frameworks in use are mapped to a lead or dominant framework. The lead framework is aligned with business needs and with the organization's strategic direction.

Level 5   There is an approach in place to ensure continual review and fine tuning of the IT capability framework(s), based on past performance and future business needs.

CBB A2: Commitment

Promote management sponsorship and stakeholder commitment. Provide the required resources for capability assessments.

Level 1   Stakeholders for IT capability assessment and improvement activities are identified in an informal manner.

Level 2   An approach is defined to involve a limited set of key IT function stakeholders in IT capability assessment and improvement activities. Other business unit stakeholders are involved on rare occasions.

Level 3   All relevant stakeholders from the IT function are involved in IT capability assessment and improvement activities. Some other business units are beginning to participate more consistently.

Level 4   Roles and responsibilities for IT capability assessment and improvement activities are assigned to a specific function, with full organization-wide stakeholder involvement.

Level 5   Feedback on IT capability assessment and improvement activities is continually sought and acted upon systematically. Business ecosystem partners are regularly involved when necessary.

CBB A3: Culture

Promote organizational buy-in to targets by, for example, highlighting the reasons for change and identifying the owners of improvement initiatives.

Level 1	There is little or no communication on or organizational buy-in to IT capability assessment and improvement activities.
Level 2	Basic awareness events are held to inform a limited number of IT function stakeholders of IT capability assessment and improvement activities.
Level 3	There is a standardized approach to raising awareness of and encouraging participation in IT capability assessment and improvement activities by all relevant IT function stakeholders and some stakeholders from other business units.
Level 4	Communication around IT capability assessment and improvement activities is embedded in organization-wide communication, to facilitate broad participation across all business units.
Level 5	Communication activities around IT capability assessment and improvement activities are continually reviewed for improvement.

Category B: CBBs Associated with *Process*

CBB B1: Assessment Planning

Plan and prepare the approach for conducting capability assessments – examine the organization's needs and business goals, establish assessment objectives, and agree assessment scope, team members, participants, and logistics.

Level 1	Planning and preparation for assessments, if any, is ad hoc.
Level 2	There is basic assessment planning and preparation emerging in parts of the IT function, with limited examination of the business needs and goals.
Level 3	A standardized planning approach or blueprint is present across the IT function. Assessments are consistently planned, including identification of the capability framework, the assessment scope, the team responsible, and the supporting logistics.
Level 4	A comprehensive planning approach or blueprint is deployed organization-wide; compliance with the approach is mandated and enforced.
Level 5	The planning and preparation approach is continually reviewed and is connected as appropriate with relevant business ecosystem partners.

CBB B2: Assessment Execution

Conduct the assessment, including such activities as running awareness campaigns, employing assessment tools, conducting evaluation interviews, and gathering information about existing practices in the organization.

Level 1	Any assessments tend to be heterogeneous, employing ad hoc methods.
Level 2	Standardization is emerging, but predominantly manual assessment methods are employed.
Level 3	Partly automated standardized assessment methods are employed.
Level 4	An integrated and appropriately automated central assessment method is adopted.
Level 5	Assessment methods are continually reviewed based on feedback and lessons learned from previous assessment activities.

CBB B3: Evaluation

Analyse the assessment results, and determine strengths and areas for improvement.

Level 1	Evaluation is non-existent or ad hoc. Evaluation scope and depth depend on the subjectivity of individuals carrying out the evaluation.
Level 2	A basic evaluation approach is emerging within areas of the IT function.
Level 3	A standardized evaluation approach is present across the IT function and some other business units, and most evaluations are conducted in line with this approach.
Level 4	A comprehensive evaluation approach is established organization-wide, and virtually all evaluations are conducted in line with this approach.
Level 5	The evaluation approach is regarded as industry-leading and is continually reviewed based on stakeholder feedback.

CBB B4: Target-Setting and Development Roadmap

Identify IT capability areas in need of improvement. Develop plans to close the gap between the current state and the target. Obtain support for implementing improvement initiatives. Communicate with stakeholders about assessment results, targets, gaps, and roadmap progress.

Level 1	Target-setting is non-existent or ad hoc. There is little or no accountability for implementing improvements.

Level 1 — Target-setting is non-existent or ad hoc. There is little or no accountability for implementing improvements.

Level 2 — IT capability targets tend to be aligned to technical deliverables. Responsibility for addressing deficiencies or gaps is generally assigned to line managers in the IT function. The provision of adequate resources for capability improvement is not formally considered.

Level 3 — There is a consistent approach to identifying IT capability targets, and a support structure is emerging to enable improvements. Dedicated financial and stakeholder resources are provided from within the IT function to support improvements.

Level 4 — IT capability targets are comprehensively aligned with business goals. Dedicated financial and stakeholder resources are jointly provided from across the wider organization.

Level 5 — IT capability targets are continually reviewed for improvement opportunities. The support structure for managing improvement seeks and responds to input from business ecosystem partners.

19.4 IMPROVEMENT PLANNING

Capability Evaluation

Two summary assessment questions are set out below, along with the typical response associated with each level of maturity.

To what extent are frameworks and governance structures in place to support capability assessment management?

Level 1 — Multiple IT capability frameworks may be in use, with little or ad hoc integration. Sponsorship of capability evaluation is limited and resources provided for the activity tend to be inadequate.

Level 2 — Some parts of the IT function use basic IT capability frameworks with occasional linkages between them. Responsibility for capability assessment and improvement activities is assigned on top of the normal workload.

Level 3 — A standardized approach is emerging for integrating multiple frameworks into a lead framework for the IT function. Dedicated resources from IT and some other business units are responsible for capability assessment and improvement activities.

Level 4 — All frameworks in use are integrated into a lead framework. Sponsors from the IT function and the rest of the business have oversight and ownership of capability assessment and improvement activities.

Level 5 — There are continual reviews to ensure capability assessment and improvement activities remain effective.

To what extent are approaches for planning and executing assessments, evaluating results, setting targets, and developing improvement roadmaps in place?

Level 1	Any approaches used are ad hoc. Any assessments that are conducted are not comparable with each other.
Level 2	Some basic approaches are emerging within some areas of the IT function.
Level 3	Defined and documented approaches are in place across the IT function, and most assessments that are conducted comply with these approaches.
Level 4	Comprehensive approaches are consistently adopted organization-wide. Compliance with the approaches for all assessments is mandated and enforced.
Level 5	The approaches are continually reviewed based on regular feedback, input from relevant business ecosystem partners, and on lessons learned from previous capability assessment activities.

Key Practices-Outcomes-Metrics (POMs)

Some useful POMs for developing the Capability Assessment Management (CAM) capability are summarized below.

Level 2 POMs

Practice	Determine if any IT capability frameworks are already in use, and establish basic relationships/linkages between them.
Outcome	Clear mapping between frameworks supports greater transparency in IT capability assessments.
Metric	Number of discrete frameworks in use.
Practice	Run awareness campaigns across the IT function to inform employees of IT capability assessment activities and the reasons for change.
Outcome	There is increased awareness of and buy-in to IT capability assessment and improvement.
Metric	Number of communications formats used to inform relevant employees.
Practice	Establish a basic IT capability assessment approach to evaluate key IT capabilities, and to identify areas for improvement in key parts of the IT function.
Outcome	Basic planning and preparation activities can begin to identify the capabilities needed to address the organization's needs and business goals.
Metric	Percentage of IT capability assessments adhering to an emerging approach or blueprint for conducting assessments.
Practice	Make IT line managers responsible for addressing identified gaps.
Outcome	Responsibility for realizing improvement is clearly assigned, increasing the likelihood of successful improvement action.
Metric	Percentage of identified capability gaps assigned to IT line managers. IT capability improvement funding as a percentage of total IT expenditure.

Level 3 POMs

Practice	Select and agree one lead framework for IT capabilities, and establish an approach for consistently mapping, integrating, or migrating other frameworks that were previously used to this lead framework.
Outcome	The lead framework acts as a central reference under which any other frameworks can be organized or mapped. The mapping of all frameworks and methodologies in use to this lead framework provides capability assessments with greater transparency, consistency, and comparability.
Metric	Percentage of legacy/discrete frameworks that are retired, integrated or mapped onto the lead framework.
Practice	Introduce assessment cycles for key IT capabilities.
Outcome	Time series comparisons and benchmarking over time become more reliable.
Metric	Percentage of targeted IT capabilities that were assessed per annum. Percentage of targeted survey participants who provided current-state evaluations of IT capabilities.
Practice	Take industry benchmarks and results of previous assessments into account when setting improvement goals.
Outcome	Improvement goals are more likely to be realistic, resource feasible, and aligned with business needs.
Metric	Percentage of IT capability targets that are achieved.
Practice	Establish a standardized support structure for implementing prioritized IT capability improvements, including senior management commitment and guidance, and adequate resourcing for improving IT capabilities.
Outcome	Fundamental requirements for implementing improvements are in place, increasing confidence in the delivery of business value and in achieving targets.
Metric	Percentage of identified IT capability improvement initiatives that have adequate financial and stakeholder resources explicitly assigned to them. IT capability improvement funding as a percentage of total IT expenditure. Percentage of IT capability improvement initiatives with explicit senior stakeholder sponsorship.

Level 4 POMs

Practice	Evaluate the effectiveness and efficiency of the lead framework against the on-going needs of the broader IT function and all other business units, and establish a consistent organization-wide mapping of all subservient frameworks to this lead framework.
Outcome	The framework is comprehensively aligned with the broader organization's needs and strategic direction, and is supported by all business stakeholders. The IT capability assessments are regarded as highly credible.
Metric	Percentage of legacy or subservient frameworks that are integrated or mapped to the lead framework.

Practice	Foster broader awareness of, and support for, IT capability assessments through organization-wide communications.
Outcome	There is increased support for IT capability assessment and improvement initiatives.
Metric	Percentage of relevant employees in each business unit involved in IT capability assessments.
Practice	Ensure organization-wide compliance with the standardized IT capability assessment planning approach or blueprint.
Outcome	A holistic and reliable IT capability assessment across the organization is possible.
Metric	Percentage of IT capability assessments adhering to a standardized blueprint.
Practice	Implement formal training and incentive schemes organization-wide to encourage employee participation in driving capability improvements (including appropriate capability training, improvement suggestion schemes, and integration with employee incentive schemes for promotion, recognition, and reward).
Outcome	Greater employee support for capability assessment and improvement is fostered, increasing the likelihood of successful capability improvements.
Metric	Percentage of relevant employees in each business unit receiving training. Percentage of relevant employees in each business unit receiving additional compensation/recognition based on their contribution to IT capability improvements.

Level 5 POMs

Practice	Continually review and improve framework integration by taking into account insights and lessons learned from previous IT capability assessments.
Outcome	The framework continues to support required IT capability evaluations.
Metric	Frequency of review of the framework integration approach (and update as appropriate).
Practice	Regularly review the support structure for managing IT capability improvement (including, for example, levels of senior management commitment and guidance, training, and resource provisioning), based on feedback and lessons learned.
Outcome	The support structure continues to enable IT capability improvements.
Metric	IT capability improvement funding as a percentage of total expenditure. Distribution of employees with capability improvement responsibilities across business units.

Practice	Reflect contributions to improving IT capability in employee performance reviews.
Outcome	Capability assessment and improvement is recognized as an important aspect of employees' work.
Metric	Distribution of employees with defined roles and responsibilities in capability assessment and improvement across business units.
Practice	Regularly include relevant business ecosystem partners when reviewing and updating IT capability planning activities and improvement targets.
Outcome	Capability planning activities and improvement targets reflect insights of the business ecosystem.
Metric	Frequency of IT capability planning reviews. Percentage of total expenditure allocated to capability improvements.

Addressing Typical Challenges

Some typical challenges that can arise in attempting to develop maturity in the Capability Assessment Management (CAM) capability are set out below.

Challenge	A lack of senior management support and key stakeholder buy-in for capability assessment management.
Context	The senior management team places a low priority on conducting IT capability assessments and identifying areas for improvement. Key stakeholders view capability assessments as having limited credibility and adding little value.
Action	Promote continual IT capability review and improvement to senior management and key stakeholders, emphasising the value of the activity as a key contributor to the organization's competitiveness.
Challenge	Lack of clarity on the IT capabilities most critical to the organization.
Context	The IT landscape is continually evolving, resulting in a reactionary and short-sighted approach to targeting IT capabilities.
Action	Commit the organization to proactively remaining abreast of technological developments, and to identifying both near- and longer-term IT capabilities that are critical for the organization to succeed.
Challenge	Inadequate financial and stakeholder resources allocated to IT capability assessments and improvement initiatives.
Context	The necessary IT capability improvements identified are difficult to implement because the organization is unable or unwilling to provide the required funds and human resources.
Action	Promote IT capability assessments and the improvement initiatives as enablers of business innovation and differentiation. Position the funding and resourcing of IT capability assessments as part of enabling the organization's IT strategy.

Challenge	Lack of alignment between IT capability targets and business objectives.
Context	IT capability targets are considered in isolation from business objectives.
Action	Stimulate senior management discussion on the importance of IT capabilities supporting the organization's overall strategic direction, and promote greater collaboration between business unit managers when agreeing IT capability targets.
Challenge	Isolated approaches are taken to identifying and prioritizing IT capability improvement initiatives.
Context	Individual improvement initiatives are not coordinated, resulting in conflicts and missed opportunities.
Action	Promote greater discussion and collaboration between business unit managers and key stakeholders to agree the improvement initiatives that contribute most to the achievement of the IT capability targets.
Challenge	Poor understanding of the motivation for IT capability change.
Context	The reasons why change is required and the value expected from implementing IT capability improvement initiatives are poorly communicated to stakeholders.
Action	Promote widespread awareness and visibility among stakeholders of how IT capability improvements will contribute to business success.

Management Artefacts

Management artefacts that may be used to develop maturity in the Capability Assessment Management (CAM) capability include:

▸ A capability-based framework.
▸ An assessment guideline document.
▸ An assessment methodology.
▸ A development roadmap.

Capability-Based Framework

A capability-based framework identifies and organizes the management elements that are needed to ensure that capability assessments and improvement initiatives are successful. When multiple discrete frameworks are in use in an organization at the same time, they can all be mapped onto IT-CMF (a capability-based framework) to provide management with a single coherent view of current capabilities and the needed improvements, while retaining the benefits of legacy discrete frameworks.

Assessment Guideline Document

An assessment guideline document provides a checklist of activities in an IT capability evaluation, and identifies the fundamental requirements at each stage of the process. It covers evaluation planning and preparation (activities such as identifying the assessment sponsor, selecting the capability-based framework, agreeing assessment scope, objectives and logistics, forming the assessment team, and performing an assessment readiness check).

It also covers the approach to executing evaluations (activities such as running assessment meetings, distributing pre-assessment information to participants, providing access to assessment tools, gathering and documenting assessment data, and interviewing assessment participants). The document may also provide guidelines on evaluating and analysing assessment data, validating assessment results, prioritizing areas for improvement, and setting IT capability targets.

Assessment Methodology

The documented assessment methodology describes how the stakeholders' evaluations of current and target IT capabilities are conducted. This might be by way of questionnaires or surveys, either manual or online. Evaluations collected using closed questions (such as multiple-choice) can be analysed quantitatively. Open questions (for example, asking participants to identify the key successes arising from IT capability improvement over the past five years) can be analysed using a qualitative approach. The assessment methodology may also include interview schedules, and outline the focus areas for in-depth discussion with key stakeholders, to support the generation of rich, context-specific insights.

Development Roadmap

A development roadmap shows the sequence in which the IT capability improvement initiatives will be implemented. It lists the initiatives, along with the time-lines and resources required, and the person or persons responsible. The roadmap serves as an important communication aid, and a mechanism for achieving consensus on the planned IT capability improvement activities.

19.5 REFERENCE

See Also

Other capabilities of IT-CMF that have a particularly close relationship with the Capability Assessment Management (CAM) capability include:

Capability	What it provides
02. Business Planning (BP)	Planned initiatives and the likely capabilities required to deliver those initiatives
08. Innovation Management (IM)	Themed innovation campaigns to support a continual improvement programme across the IT function
10. Organization Design and Planning (ODP)	Information about the capabilities embedded in the IT function's current organization design
14. Strategic Planning (SP)	Strategic priorities and objectives that serve as the foundation for long-term capability planning

Further Reading

Evans, J., and Lindsay, W., 2015. *An introduction to Six Sigma and process improvement.* 2nd ed. Boston, MA: Cengage Learning.

International Organization for Standardization (ISO), 2012. *ISO/IEC 15504-5:2012. Information technology – process assessment – part 5: an exemplar software life cycle process assessment model.* Available at: <http://www.iso.org/iso/catalogue_detail.htm?csnumber=60555>.

Software Engineering Institute, 2011. Standard CMMI appraisal method for process improvement (SCAMPISM) A. Version 1.3. Method definition document. [pdf]. Available at: <http://www.sei.cmu.edu/reports/11hb001.pdf>.

Notes

[1] Pavlou, P.A., and El Sawy, O.A., 2010. The 'third hand': IT-enabled competitive advantage in turbulence through improvisational capabilities. *Information Systems Research*, 21(3), 443–71.

[2] Mithas, S., Ramasubbu, N., and Sambamurthy, V., 2011. How information management capability influences firm performance. *MIS Quarterly*, 35(1), 237–56.

[3] Lu, Y., and Ramamurthy, K., 2011. Understanding the link between information technology capability and organizational agility: an empirical examination. *MIS Quarterly,* 35(4), 931–54.

[4] McLaughlin, S., 2012. Positioning the IT-CMF: a capability versus process perspective. [pdf] IVI executive briefing. Available at: <http://ivi.nuim.ie/sites/ivi.nuim.ie/files/publications/IVI%20Exec%20Briefing%20-%20Positioning%20IT-CMF,%20v0.5%20(no%20mark-ups).pdf>.

EAM

20. Enterprise Architecture Management

20.1 OVERVIEW

Goal

The Enterprise Architecture Management (EAM) capability aims to deliver an overarching approach within which the IT function can design, deploy, and execute the organization's business strategy.

Objectives

▶ Enable the IT function to align its strategy with the needs of the business strategy.
▶ Define the technical standards and operating principles for guiding business solution design and technology choices.
▶ Ensure consistency and integration across process, information, application, and infrastructure for optimal business performance.
▶ Reduce business complexity through the reuse and sharing of functional components, and through standardization of technologies and infrastructure.
▶ Improve business processes and enhance productivity across the organization by unifying and integrating data linkages.
▶ Promote sound architecture management practices and governance.
▶ Minimize and manage business, IT, and project-level risks through more informed portfolio and solutions planning.

Value

The Enterprise Architecture Management (EAM) capability helps determine how the organization can most effectively plan the use of technology to achieve its current and future objectives.

Relevance

The IT function adds value to the organization by enabling it to perform more cost-effectively and efficiently [1]. This requires the continual adoption of new technologies while evolving the existing IT portfolio.

By developing an effective Enterprise Architecture Management (EAM) capability, an organization can ensure that its IT systems can respond to the organization's changing business needs in a coherent and planned manner [2].

20.2 SCOPE

Definition

The Enterprise Architecture Management (EAM) capability is the ability to plan, design, manage, and control the conceptualization of systems, processes, and/or organizations, and the relationships between them. The conceptualization may be layered to represent specific types of relationships – for example, those between applications, business services, internal IT services, security, networking, data storage, and so on. The Enterprise Architecture Management (EAM) capability covers:

▶ Establishing principles to guide the design and evolution of systems, processes, and/or organizations.
▶ Providing a framework, including models or templates, that articulates the business, the technical architecture, and the relationships between them.
▶ Providing the architecture vision, roadmap, and governance, together with the approaches required for managing their life cycle.
▶ Managing the architectural skills and architecture resourcing.
▶ Communicating the impact of enterprise architecture activities.

Other Capabilities

The following are addressed by other capabilities of IT-CMF:

For...	Refer to...
Identifying or selecting a specific business process management methodology and framework	03. Business Process Management (BPM)
Identifying or selecting a specific information architecture management methodology and framework	06. Enterprise Information Management (EIM)
Defining a project delivery approach	24. Programme and Project Management (PPM)
Designing and building IT services and solutions	28. Solutions Delivery (SD)
Defining the infrastructure operations and management methodology	30. Technical Infrastructure Management (TIM)

20.3 UNDERSTANDING MATURITY

Recognizing Excellence

When the Enterprise Architecture Management (EAM) capability is well-developed or mature:

▸ Enterprise architecture planning is integrated with business planning, and uses approved roadmaps to manage change across the business.

▸ Enterprise architecture artefacts are consistently defined and regularly used by individual programmes.

▸ The development of careers for enterprise architecture practitioners is actively supported.

▸ The value derived from good enterprise architecture practices is measured and recognized by stakeholders.

Maturity at the Critical Capability Level

The following statements provide a high-level overview of the Enterprise Architecture Management (EAM) capability at successive levels of maturity:

Level 1   Enterprise architecture is conducted within the context of individual projects, by applying one-off principles and methods within those projects.

Level 2   A limited number of basic architecture artefacts and practices are emerging in certain IT domains or key projects.

Level 3   A common suite of enterprise architecture principles and methods are shared across the IT function, allowing a unifying vision of enterprise architecture to emerge.

Level 4   Planning by the IT function and the rest of the business consistently leverages enterprise-wide architecture principles and methods to enable efficiency and agility across the organization.

Level 5   Enterprise architecture principles and methods are continually reviewed to maintain their ability to deliver business value.

Maturity at the Capability Building Block (CBB) Level

The Capability Building Blocks (CBBs) associated with the Enterprise Architecture Management (EAM) capability fall into three categories:

▸ Category A: four CBBs associated with *Practices* – these deal with the framework, processes, governance, and value relating to enterprise architecture.

▸ Category B: three CBBs associated with *Planning* – these define the architectural strategy and funding model, the architectural roadmap, and the underlying technical direction required to meet current and new business requirements.

▸ Category C: two CBBs associated with *People* – these develop leadership and enterprise architecture engagement across the business.

These are described below, together with a summary of the different maturity levels for each.

Category A: CBBs Associated with *Practices*

CBB A1: Architecture Framework

Provide the overarching framework of standards, templates, and specifications for organizing and presenting a description of the business and technical architectures.

Level 1	The process to select an architectural framework may have started, but typically there is no useful architectural framework in place.
Level 2	There is a basic architectural framework used in pockets of the IT function.
Level 3	A standardized architectural framework covers the IT function and some other business units.
Level 4	A comprehensive architectural framework is used organization-wide, and is based on a version of an established architectural framework that is tailored to meet the organization's needs.
Level 5	The architectural framework is continually reviewed for improvement and regularly reflects input from relevant business ecosystem partners, when appropriate.

CBB A2: Architecture Processes

Provide the methodology to define, develop, and maintain the architecture components, and their interrelationships.

Level 1	Architectural methodologies, if they are used, are limited to individual one-off projects.
Level 2	There are defined internal architectural methodologies that are primarily focused on the infrastructure.
Level 3	There are standardized architectural methodologies established in most domains – for example, desktop, server, mobile, and so on.
Level 4	There are comprehensive architectural methodologies in use across the organization.
Level 5	The architectural methodologies are continually reviewed to ensure that they remain adaptable to business changes, and that they integrate, where appropriate, with relevant business ecosystem partners.

CBB A3: Architecture Governance

Determine the principles, decision rights, rules, and methods that are used to give direction to and monitor the development of enterprise architecture and its alignment with wider organizational governance.

Level 1   Architectural governance is non-existent or ad hoc.

Level 2   Architectural governance defines the review principles for a limited number of architectural components.

Level 3   A standardized architectural governance board is established as part of the overall IT governance. Its membership includes senior IT managers and representatives from some other business units.

Level 4   Architectural governance is comprehensively embedded as part of an organization-wide governance model. Responsibility for it is shared by senior managers and key stakeholders from across the whole organization.

Level 5   Architectural governance is continually reviewed and improved as necessary, with regular input from key business ecosystem partners.

CBB A4: Architecture Value

Define, measure, and communicate the business value of enterprise architecture.

Level 1   The measurement and reporting of the value of enterprise architecture is non-existent or ad hoc.

Level 2   The value of enterprise architecture is reported, but only in the wider context of shared IT infrastructure, or of specific technical initiatives, or of general architecture management activities.

Level 3   The value of enterprise architecture is recognized and reflected within the reporting of IT metrics for the overall IT function. This involves using outcome measures (such as TCO) and in-process measures (such as percentage of on-time delivery), at both IT portfolio and individual project levels.

Level 4   The value of enterprise architecture is measured and reported in terms of business objectives and defined functional metrics. This is validated jointly by senior IT managers and business stakeholders.

Level 5   The value of enterprise architecture is defined, measured, and reported in terms of tangible business outcomes, business innovation, business models, top-line growth, and the reach of products and services.

Category B: CBBs Associated with *Planning*

CBB B1: Architecture Funding

Develop approaches to funding enterprise architecture management and architecture improvement initiatives.

Level 1	Architecture funding, if it is provided, occurs on an individual project basis.
Level 2	There is cross-project funding for a limited number of architecture capabilities.
Level 3	Funding mechanisms provide for a central enterprise architecture function, enabling economies to be achieved across the IT function.
Level 4	Funding mechanisms support an expanded suite of architecture capabilities, enabling innovation and value across the whole organization.
Level 5	A sustainable architecture funding model is in place, and can regularly leverage the capabilities of key business ecosystem partners.

CBB B2: Architecture Planning

Define the enterprise architecture vision and the implementation roadmap and anticipate business needs and trends.

Level 1	Architecture planning is project-based and ad hoc.
Level 2	Architecture planning has a limited vision and a limited implementation roadmap for parts of the IT function.
Level 3	An architecture planning approach has been standardized covering most domains (for example, desktop, server, mobile, and so on). Increasingly more projects deliver expanded architecture capabilities.
Level 4	The architecture planning approach is comprehensively aligned with the business planning cycle and its objectives.
Level 5	The architecture planning approach is continually reviewed to anticipate and respond to changes within the business, industry, and technologies.

CBB B3: Architecture Alignment

Use architecture principles and blueprints to align business needs and IT capabilities. Define the strategy guidelines for selecting IT investments.

Level 1   There is little or no recognition of the value of enterprise architecture management in strategic IT planning.

Level 2   Enterprise architecture roadmaps are the basis for selecting and prioritizing capabilities in some IT domains – for example, using shared infrastructure and establishing dependencies for project plans. The impact on strategic plans tends to be limited to areas of particular technical focus.

Level 3   Enterprise architects are active participants in the strategic planning process. The selection and prioritization of the IT project portfolio is regularly informed by defined architecture principles and roadmaps.

Level 4   The architecture roadmap guides the strategic planning process for the IT function, and drives alignment between the IT function and the rest of the business. IT planning for budget, financing, the workforce, and capability portfolios always leverages architecture principles and roadmaps.

Level 5   IT and business planning are integrated and continually reviewed to enable business efficiency, increase the agility of the organization so that it can rapidly respond to change, and help differentiate the organization's products and services from those of its competitors.

Category C: CBBs Associated with *People*

CBB C1: Organization Structure and Skills

Define the roles, responsibilities, and skills required for enterprise architecture management.

Level 1   Few, if any, roles, responsibilities, and skills have been defined.

Level 2   Formal technical roles are defined within specific projects.

Level 3   Formal roles and responsibilities are centrally defined within the IT function and some other business units.

Level 4   A comprehensive and clear professional career path is defined across the organization for people with expertise in enterprise architecture management.

Level 5   There is a professional career structure within which enterprise architects are continually developed.

CBB C2: Communication and Stakeholder Management

Manage communication with stakeholders who are interested in, or are influenced by, enterprise architecture management, and manage their expectations of what it can deliver.

Level 1   Communication is project-based and inconsistent.

Level 2   A limited number of key IT project stakeholders are kept informed about aspects of enterprise architecture management.

Level 3   For stakeholders in the IT function and some other business units, there is regular and standardized communication in relation to enterprise architecture.

Level 4   There is proactive and comprehensive communication with relevant stakeholders across all of the IT function and the rest of the business, and there is a feedback mechanism for incorporating their views.

Level 5   There is regular collaboration and communication with relevant partners across the business ecosystem.

20.4 IMPROVEMENT PLANNING

Capability Evaluation

Two summary assessment questions are set out below, along with the typical response associated with each level of maturity.

To what extent is there a current and target architecture for infrastructure, applications, and information to support business processes?

Level 1   Any attempt to generate and document the current and target architecture is ad hoc and informal.

Level 2   The current and target architecture is defined for selected IT areas – for example, infrastructure, applications, data, or for other specific IT services. The primary focus of architecture definition is on technology and/or physical implementation.

Level 3   The current and target architecture is defined for all IT areas and services, and is reviewed and maintained on a regular basis. The architecture definition extends beyond technology into data and business processes, and considers the business context. There is an architectural roadmap that is accepted and used by IT decision makers.

Level 4   An enterprise architecture vision and the enterprise architecture roadmaps are jointly developed by the IT function and the rest of the business, for all business and technical areas, and services.

Level 5   The enterprise architecture vision and roadmaps extend across the business ecosystem and take into account the enterprise architecture requirements of relevant business ecosystem partners.

To what extent does the IT architecture reflect the organization's requirements for standardization (same or different business processes), and integration (high or low linking of data across the organization)?

Level 1   Architecture standardization and integration are ad hoc.

Level 2   Architectural decisions relating to a limited number of larger projects are reviewed against a basic collection of architecture standardization and integration principles.

Level 3   Architectural decisions relating to most projects across the IT function are reviewed against a common set of architecture standardization and integration principles.

Level 4   Architectural decisions for all projects across the whole organization are reviewed against a comprehensive set of architecture standardization and integration principles.

Level 5   Architecture standardization and integration principles are continually reviewed for improvement opportunities based on internal and external feedback.

Key Practices-Outcomes-Metrics (POMs)

Some useful POMs for developing the Enterprise Architecture Management (EAM) capability are summarized below.

Level 2 POMs

Practice	Define the architecture framework for use in prioritized areas of IT.
Outcome	A consistent architecture framework will guide IT developments, promoting complexity reduction and greater reuse of the resultant architectures.
Metric	Percentage of the project portfolio adhering to the architecture framework.
Practice	Using common technical architecture standards, carry out architecture reviews of key IT projects and services.
Outcome	Improved architectural governance starts to deliver a more standardized IT infrastructure, with a reduction in the total cost of ownership.
Metric	Percentage of projects that are compliant with the defined technical architecture.
Practice	Include subject matter experts and key stakeholders in architecture workshops to establish enterprise architecture goals and technology roadmaps.
Outcome	There is joint ownership of the resultant architecture plan.
Metric	Number of architectural goals and roadmaps that are defined and jointly agreed.

Practice	Define and establish the architecture roles required for specific projects and domains.
Outcome	A formalized enterprise architecture structure is emerging with defined roles and responsibilities. Across the IT function, architects attempt to use a broad perspective that incorporates industry best-known practices and approaches.
Metric	Percentage of IT domains with architects in place in defined roles.

Level 3 POMs

Practice	Put processes in place to monitor compliance with the agreed target architecture (as designed), and report on any conflicts or design exceptions. This could be achieved, for example, by the establishment of an Architecture Governance Board.
Outcome	Projects consistently deliver quality solutions and the linkage from business requirements to design decisions is clearly traceable.
Metric	Percentage of projects approved that are compliant with the target architecture.
Practice	Map key business processes to specific IT applications that support those processes.
Outcome	There is improved visibility of the business risks associated with using unsupported or outdated technology.
Metric	Percentage of key business processes mapped to the applications that support them.
Practice	Map business processes to the costs of IT services required to support them for each technology domain.
Outcome	There is improved visibility of the costs of IT services and what business processes they enable. These insights can help justify investment and retirement strategies for IT services.
Metric	Percentage of business processes whose underlying IT services have been costed.
Practice	Formalize roles and responsibilities for enterprise architecture across the IT function.
Outcome	A formal enterprise architecture structure is in place, promoting economies of scale through a concentration of skills and expertise.
Metric	Percentage of projects with staffed architecture roles.

Level 4 POMs

Practice	Extend the architecture framework to facilitate increased use of common or shared patterns for enterprise system architecting. Within this framework, define process model templates for all key business areas.
Outcome	There is greater consistency and reusability of IT/systems artefacts across the organization.
Metric	Number of shared, reusable components or services. Percentage of artefacts failing certification against the architecture framework.

Practice	Promote projects that deliver cross-functional or cross-domain benefits, and encourage the development of shared services across all business areas where it makes sense.
Outcome	The architecture approach is integrated across the IT function and the rest of the business so that it increases both the agility and adaptability of the business operating model.
Metric	Number of shared services and their degree of adoption.
Practice	Involve a broader collection of business stakeholders in architecture planning and in the definition of an enterprise capability model. Describe architecture roadmaps for each business unit in terms of the business capabilities delivered.
Outcome	Architecture planning becomes even more business-oriented and business-driven, and maximizes the return on IT investment.
Metric	Number of business stakeholders who participate in architecture planning.
Practice	Ensure that there is a clearly defined career path for enterprise architects, and that this is fully supported by Human Resources. This path should include career progression, formal evaluations, appropriate training, and certification programmes.
Outcome	Enterprise architecture is viewed favourably as a career choice. Continuing professional development is available to architects to ensure that they can continue to meet the organization's requirements.
Metric	Percentage of architects with formal career development plans.

Level 5 POMs

Practice	Establish a common planning cycle within which relevant enterprise architects can influence each other.
Outcome	There is an open and robust planning cycle that has enterprise architecture at its core, and that can deliver an increased return on investment (ROI) for all technology investments.
Metric	Business value contribution from enterprise architecture.
Practice	Require the architecture team to participate actively in external architecture bodies. Challenge the architecture team to match and exceed the achievements of their peers in external organizations.
Outcome	Enterprise architecture is considered a thought leader within the organization, and a source of competitive advantage.
Metric	Number of enterprise architecture papers published. Number of enterprise architecture recognition awards.

Addressing Typical Challenges

Some typical challenges that can arise in attempting to develop maturity in the Enterprise Architecture Management (EAM) capability are set out below.

Challenge	Lack of organizational commitment and/or resources for enterprise architecture management.
Context	Enterprise architecture can have difficulty securing adequate organizational commitment and resources due to the supporting nature or role of enterprise architecture within other programmes.
Action	Facilitate discussions on what are adequate levels of commitment and resourcing so that enterprise architecture can more effectively coordinate the transition strategy between current and future state architectures, and can effectively sequence the implementation of IT solutions to achieve the business strategies.
Challenge	Lack of suitably qualified enterprise architects.
Context	The development of enterprise architecture within the organization is hampered by the perception that enterprise architect practitioners have poor career prospects.
Action	Implement a training and mentoring network to help make enterprise architecture an attractive career choice. Enable architects to make good professional and personal choices, and in doing so, increase the level of enterprise architecture expertise across the organization.
Challenge	Lack of understanding regarding the benefits that enterprise architecture management can deliver for the organization.
Context	Management and personnel do not understand how enterprise architecture management can help reduce costs, enhance business opportunities, and deliver on business objectives.
Action	Communicate the value of enterprise architecture to senior management. Demonstrate how enterprise architecture can reduce costs, increase flexibility, and enhance new business opportunities.

Management Artefacts

Management artefacts that may be used to develop maturity in the Enterprise Architecture Management (EAM) capability include:

▶ Documented enterprise architecture deliverables.
▶ A documented architecture development methodology.
▶ An enterprise architecture tool set and repository.

Documented Enterprise Architecture Deliverables

Enterprise architecture deliverables articulate and describe the different elements of the enterprise architecture and how they are organized. Common deliverables include strategic and reference models, typically expressed across architecture domains of business, information, application, and infrastructure.

Documented Architecture Development Methodology

An architecture development methodology describes practices for developing and managing the life cycle of enterprise architecture deliverables (for example, results of as-is and to-be architecture analysis). It may also contain enterprise architecture principles for decision-making and self-governance. It is typically overseen by an enterprise architecture review board.

Enterprise Architecture Tool Set and Repository

A common enterprise architecture tool set is essential to make the architectural information available in a consistent, reusable form across projects, architectures, and functional areas. In conjunction with this, a common knowledge repository can ensure the accessibility of the standardized enterprise architecture templates and tools. Standardization and accessibility makes it easier to reuse and share architectural artefacts such as diagrams and reports across the organization. This promotes reuse and improves the quality and consistency of all of the deliverables.

20.5 REFERENCE

See Also

Other capabilities of IT-CMF that have a particularly close relationship with the Enterprise Architecture Management (EAM) capability include:

Capability	What it provides
03. Business Process Management (BPM)	Information on the design of current business processes which can help shape cross-function mapping
05. Demand and Supply Management (DSM)	Details of long-term demand that needs to be catered for by future architectures
09. IT Leadership and Governance (ITG)	The governance model that is reflected in architecture governance
11. Risk Management (RM)	Items to be considered in future architecture decisions in order to mitigate risk
14. Strategic Planning (SP)	Input on the IT strategy to help design the enterprise architecture framework
35. Total Cost of Ownership (TCO)	Cost data on IT services, which can help prioritize enterprise architecture initiatives

Further Reading

Ahlemann, F., Stettiner, E., Messerschmidt, M., and Legner, C., 2012. *Strategic enterprise architecture management: challenges, best practices, and future developments.* Berlin, DE: Springer.

Blevins, T.J., Spencer, J., and Waskiewicz, F., 2004. *TOGAF ADM and MDA.* [pdf] The Open Group and OMG. Available at: < http://www.opengroup.org/cio/MDA-ADM/MDA-TOGAF-R1-070904.pdf>.

Giachetti, R.E., 2004. A framework to review the information integration of the enterprise. *International Journal of Production Research.* 42(6), 1147–66.

Notes

[1] Niemann, K.D., 2006. *From enterprise architecture to IT governance.* Wiesbaden, DE: Vieweg & Sohn.

[2] Open Group, 2011. *TOGAF Version 9.1.* Zaltbommel, NL: Van Haren Publishing.

ISM

21. Information Security Management

21.1 OVERVIEW

Goal

The Information Security Management (ISM) capability aims to protect the information held by the organization from damage, to prevent its harmful use (to people or organizations), and to facilitate its legitimate operational and business use.

Objectives

- Facilitate information security approaches, policies, and controls, both during normal business operations and in the event of significant information security incidents, to safeguard the organization's information resource's:
  - Integrity (that is, its accuracy and completeness).
  - Confidentiality (that is, its protection from theft or unauthorized disclosure).
  - Accountability (that is, its traceability and authenticity).
  - Usability (that is, its fitness for purpose).
  - Availability (that is, its accessibility and access controls).
- Ensure that all information security incidents and suspected security weaknesses are reported through suitable channels, so that they are appropriately investigated and dealt with.
- Help employees maintain appropriate levels of awareness and skills to minimize the occurrence and severity of information security incidents.
- Provide assurance to stakeholders and regulators that information security approaches, policies, and controls function as intended – that is, they help discover, prevent, and minimize threats and breaches.
- Ensure key stakeholders are accepting of the residual risk remaining after the information security technical analysis and mitigation actions for identified security threats have been taken.

Value

The Information Security Management (ISM) capability can help reduce the frequency and limit the adverse effects of information security breaches.

Relevance

With the rise of mobile computing, cloud computing, and social media usage, and the increased digitization of business processes, information security threats are also increasing [1]. Poor oversight, and inadequate protocols and procedures are the main causes of information security incidents. Organizations vary in their approaches to preventing such security breaches: some are overly restrictive, making even routine business activities difficult, while others are too relaxed, creating unnecessary exposures. Implementing overly restrictive or excessively weak information security controls can result in the loss of trust, reputation, and money. The organization has to find the right balance in order to secure its information resources without impeding effective business operations.

By developing an effective Information Security Management (ISM) capability, an organization can develop the structures and language necessary for discussing, analysing, and addressing security considerations, thereby helping to protect its information resources and to ensure their confidentiality, integrity, accountability, and availability [2] [3].

21.2 SCOPE

Definition

The Information Security Management (ISM) capability is the ability to manage approaches, policies, and controls that safeguard the integrity, confidentiality, accessibility, accountability, and usability of digitized information resources [4]. The Information Security Management (ISM) capability covers:

▸ Preventing unauthorized access, use, disclosure, disruption, modification, or destruction of digitized information resources.
▸ Establishing an information security governance model, including allocating roles, responsibilities, and accountabilities.
▸ Measuring the effectiveness of existing security approaches, policies, and controls – for example, by applying security standards and conducting internal audits.
▸ Managing security-related communications and training of employees.
▸ Assessing, prioritizing, responding to, and monitoring information security risks and incidents.
▸ Securing physical IT components and IT areas.
▸ Providing expertise to protect, preserve, and/or destroy data in line with business, regulatory, and/or other security requirements.
▸ Reporting on information security activities and compliance levels.

Other Capabilities

The following are addressed by other capabilities of IT-CMF:

For…	Refer to…
Establishing IT governance structures	09. IT Leadership and Governance (ITG)
Managing the broader risks associated with the potential impact of IT on the organization	11. Risk Management (RM)

21.3 UNDERSTANDING MATURITY

Recognizing Excellence

When the Information Security Management (ISM) capability is well-developed or mature:

▸ There is awareness and understanding across the organization of the role that effective information security plays in business success – security is recognized as an enabler rather than a disabler.

▸ Business-focused information security measures are defined, monitored, and acted upon by the IT function and the rest of the business.

▸ Senior management's sponsorship of information security is evident, and clear responsibilities are allocated for security activities.

▸ The IT function and other business units agree on the required security levels.

▸ The organization is able to rapidly identify and address new and emerging security risks and threats.

▸ The organization's approach to information security enhances its reputation and builds trust with its customers and business partners.

Maturity at the Critical Capability Level

The following statements provide a high-level overview of the Information Security Management (ISM) capability at successive levels of maturity:

Level 1 The approach to information security tends to be localized. Incidents are typically not responded to in a timely manner.

Level 2 Defined security approaches, policies, and controls are emerging, primarily focused on complying with regulations.

Level 3 Standardized security approaches, policies, and controls are in place across the IT function, dealing with access rights, business continuity, budgets, toolsets, incident response management, audits, non-compliance, and so on.

Level 4 Comprehensive security approaches, policies, and controls are in place and are fully integrated across the organization.

Level 5 Security approaches, policies, and controls are regularly reviewed to maintain a proactive approach to preventing security breaches.

Maturity at the Capability Building Block (CBB) Level

The Capability Building Blocks (CBBs) associated with the Information Security Management (ISM) capability fall into five categories.

▶ Category A: six CBBs associated with *Governance* – these establish the oversight structures to support the execution of information security management.

▶ Category B: three CBBs associated with *Technical Security* – these are concerned with securing IT components and the physical environment.

▶ Category C: five CBBs associated with *Security Risk Control* – these assess and prioritize risks so that appropriate handling and monitoring activities can be put in place.

▶ Category D: three CBBs associated with *Security Data Administration* – these classify data and information into security groupings, and provide guidance for managing their access rights and life cycles.

▶ Category E: two CBBs associated with *Business Continuity Management* – these are concerned with managing security inputs into incident management and business continuity planning and testing.

These are described below, together with a summary of the different maturity levels for each.

Category A: CBBs Associated with *Governance*

CBB A1: Information Security Strategy

Develop, communicate, and support the organization's information security objectives.

Level 1	There is no or ad hoc coordination between the IT function and the rest of the business on the information security strategy.
Level 2	Agreement on a basic information security strategy is emerging, primarily focused on tactical security concerns in a limited number of areas.
Level 3	The IT function increasingly collaborates with other business units to define an information security strategy that represents common objectives.
Level 4	The published information security strategy represents shared objectives across the entire organization.
Level 5	The objectives of the information security strategy are continually aligned and re-aligned with changes in business/IT strategies, regulations, and risk appetite.

CBB A2: Security Policies and Controls

Establish and maintain security policies and controls, taking into account relevant security standards, regulatory and legislative security requirements, and the organization's security objectives.

Level 1   The development and use of security policies and controls are ad hoc.

Level 2   Mandatory standards are identified and reviewed to inform policy development. Compliance audits are emerging in response to major incidents.

Level 3   Information security policies and controls are standardized across assets, processes, and people for many business units. Standardized approaches for auditing compliance with the policies and standards are also in place.

Level 4   Comprehensive reviews of standards, legal requirements, incident reports, and security risk assessments regularly inform security policies across the entire organization. Compliance with the policies and standards is consistently and regularly audited organization-wide.

Level 5   Information security policies and controls are continually improved, with regular input from relevant business ecosystem partners, where appropriate.

CBB A3: Security Roles, Responsibilities, and Accountabilities

Establish responsibilities and accountabilities for information security roles, and check enforcement.

Level 1   Information security roles are not defined or are defined in an ad hoc manner.

Level 2   Information security roles and training needs are defined, primarily within the IT function. Monitoring of security responsibilities and accountabilities may be inconsistent.

Level 3   Suitably qualified employees from the IT function and some other business units are increasingly sharing information security roles. Monitoring of security responsibilities and accountabilities is standardized, but non-compliance is not always identified or dealt with appropriately.

Level 4   Information security roles are allocated organization-wide to balance business efficiency and security needs. Non-compliance with security responsibilities and accountabilities is almost always dealt with appropriately.

Level 5   The responsibilities and accountabilities for information security are continually reviewed, along with enforcement approaches, for improvement.

CBB A4: Communication and Training

Disseminate security approaches, policies, and other relevant information to develop security awareness and skills.

Level 1 — Any communication and training on information security is ad hoc.

Level 2 — Information security activities are typically communicated to a limited number of IT stakeholders only. Basic training programmes are established, but employee participation in them may not be mandatory or monitored.

Level 3 — Communication of information security activities is standardized to stakeholders across the IT function and some other business units. There is on-demand training and mandatory testing for prioritized at-risk employees.

Level 4 — Communication and training have established a security-aware culture across the entire organization, with communication appropriate to individual stakeholder needs, and tailored training is provided for all employees across the organization.

Level 5 — Communication and training approaches are monitored for effectiveness, and are continually improved to reinforce an information security culture.

CBB A5: Security Performance Reporting

Report on the effectiveness and efficiency of information security policies and activities, and the level of compliance with them.

Level 1 — Any information security performance reporting is ad hoc.

Level 2 — Reporting on the performance of security policies and activities is limited to parts of the IT function.

Level 3 — Reporting on the performance of security policies and activities extends across the IT function and some other business units.

Level 4 — Reporting on the performance of security policies and activities extends organization-wide.

Level 5 — The performance of security policies and activities is regularly reviewed to identify improvement opportunities.

CBB A6: Supplier Security

Define security requirements pertaining to the procurement and supply of hardware, software, services, and data.

Level 1 — Information security requirements are not defined in procurement activities, or are defined only in an ad hoc manner. Similarly, audits of supplier compliance are non-existent or ad hoc.

Level 2 — Information security requirements are beginning to be defined in some of the IT function's procurement activities. Some supplier compliance audits are conducted, but typically only following an incident.

Level 3 — Standardized information security requirements are defined in most of the IT function's procurement activities. Audits of supplier compliance are increasingly structured and proactive.

Level 4 — Comprehensive information security requirements are defined for all IT-related procurement activities across the organization. Audits of supplier compliance increasingly include indirect suppliers.

Level 5 — Information security requirements are reviewed and updated regularly in conjunction with key business ecosystem partners and in response to changing threat profiles.

Category B: CBBs Associated with *Technical Security*

CBB B1: Security Architecture

Build security criteria into the design of IT solutions – for example, by defining coding protocols, depth of defence, configuration of security features, and so on.

Level 1 — A security architecture is not defined, or is defined only in an ad hoc manner.

Level 2 — A defined security architecture is emerging. While new solutions and services conform to this architecture, many legacy ones may not conform.

Level 3 — A standardized security architecture is used for all new and most legacy IT solutions and services.

Level 4 — A comprehensive security architecture is used across the IT solutions and services catalogue.

Level 5 — The security architecture is continually reviewed for efficiency and effectiveness.

CBB B2: IT Component Security

Implement measures to protect all IT components, both physical and virtual, such as client computing devices, servers, networks, storage devices, printers, and smart phones.

Level 1   IT component security measures are not defined, or are defined only in an ad hoc manner.

Level 2   IT component security guidelines are emerging within the IT function, but only basic security measures are implemented.

Level 3   The IT function and some other business units jointly agree on IT component security measures, which are then consistently implemented across these areas.

Level 4   IT component security measures are systematically and comprehensively implemented for all systems and devices across the organization.

Level 5   IT component security measures are regularly reviewed for effectiveness and improvement opportunities.

CBB B3: Physical Infrastructure Security

Establish and maintain measures to safeguard the IT physical infrastructure from harm. Threats to be addressed include extremes of temperature, malicious intent, and utility supply disruptions.

Level 1   Any consideration of securing the IT physical infrastructure from harm is ad hoc.

Level 2   Measures for ensuring the security of the physical infrastructure are limited to access restrictions, and monitoring systems for temperature control, and fire and flood detection. Resilience capabilities are limited to a few critical systems.

Level 3   Measures for ensuring the security of the physical infrastructure are extended to cover utility supply continuity and site disaster recovery planning. Responses to environmental issues are mostly automated, and entry and exit logs are robustly maintained. Most on-site IT services are protected with fault-tolerant designs, uninterruptable power supplies, and wide area network redundancy. Restorations can be managed and achieved locally.

Level 4   Physical infrastructure security measures are fully integrated with organization-wide business continuity planning and incident management plans, including power and network infrastructure outages. Backup systems have been developed and tested to maintain critical systems online even if a site and its IT infrastructure are taken offline. IT systems restoration can be completed and/or managed locally or remotely.

Level 5   The security measures for the physical infrastructure are continually tested and reviewed to identify opportunities for improvement.

Category C: CBBs Associated with *Security Risk Control*

CBB C1: Security Threat Profiling

Gather intelligence on IT security threats and vulnerabilities to better understand the IT security threat landscape within which the organization operates – including, for example, the actors, scenarios, and campaigns that might pose a threat.

Level 1   Any information security threat profiling is ad hoc.

Level 2   A defined approach to information security threat profiling is emerging and is applied to the most critical IT services and key infrastructure components.

Level 3   A standardized approach to information security threat profiling is implemented across all critical IT services and most non-critical IT services. It increasingly addresses architecture layers (such as storage, networking, applications, and database servers), infrastructure components, and end devices (including a limited bring-your-own-device (BYOD) set).

Level 4   A comprehensive information security threat profiling approach is implemented to comprehensively address all architecture layers, solutions and services, devices (including an expanded BYOD set), and infrastructure components, both physical and virtual.

Level 5   Information security threat profiling is continually reviewed to identify opportunities for improvement.

CBB C2: Security Risk Assessment

Identify exposures to security-related risks, and quantify their likelihood and potential impact.

Level 1   Any information security risk assessments are ad hoc.

Level 2   A basic approach to information security risk assessment is defined for the more common threat types.

Level 3   Standardized information security risk assessments are conducted for most types of information security risk. New risk types are handled as exceptions that warrant further investigation.

Level 4   Comprehensive information security risk assessments are conducted in line with organization-wide risk assessment approaches. Risk avoidance and mitigation measures are consistently proportionate to the potential impact on business processes.

Level 5   Information security risk assessments are continually adapted to changes in business objectives and the threat landscape.

CBB C3: Security Risk Prioritization

Prioritize information security risks and risk handling strategies based on residual risks and the organization's risk appetite.

Level 1   Information security risks are not prioritized or are prioritized in an ad hoc manner. For example, prioritization may be reactive, based on recent incidents or current headlines.

Level 2   Information security risks are beginning to be prioritized more objectively, but only by the IT function, and only based on the potential impact on IT operations, the probability of occurrence, and the time period during which security breaches are regarded as being more likely.

Level 3   A standardized approach to information security risk prioritization is taken jointly by the IT function and some other business units. Potential impacts are expressed in terms of business operations.

Level 4   A comprehensive approach to information security risk prioritization is adopted across the organization. Potential impacts are expressed in terms of business value.

Level 5   The information security risk prioritization approach is regularly reviewed, and the accuracy of estimates regarding likelihood and impact is regularly validated.

CBB C4: Security Risk Handling

Implement strategies for handling information security risk, including risk acceptance, transfer, absorption, and mitigation, as appropriate. Promote interaction with incident management functions.

Level 1   Information security risks are handled in an ad hoc manner, if at all. Risk management and incident management generally operate independently, in isolation from one another – although they may occasionally interact after a major incident.

Level 2   A defined approach for handling information security risks is emerging in parts of the IT function. Interaction between risk management and incident management is growing, but not yet standardized.

Level 3   The IT function and some other business units follow a standardized approach for handling information security risks. Interaction between information security risk management and incident management is standardized.

Level 4   A comprehensive approach for handling information security risks is followed organization-wide. Information security risk management and incident management collaborate proactively.

Level 5   The approach for handling information security risks is continually reviewed, as are interactions between information security risk management and incident management.

CBB C5: Security Risk Monitoring

Manage the on-going efficacy of information security risk handling strategies and control options.

Level 1   The efficacy of security risk handling is rarely, if ever, monitored.

Level 2   Approaches for monitoring the efficacy of security risk handling are documented for a limited number of threat types. Risk handling approaches can be adjusted.

Level 3   The efficacy of most IT security risk handling is monitored using standardized approaches. Changes in information security risk that are not covered by standardized approaches are escalated for remedial action using established approaches.

Level 4   Monitoring the efficacy of security risk handling approaches and adjusting them as necessary is comprehensive and increasingly automated.

Level 5   Monitoring the efficacy of security risk handling approaches and adjusting them as necessary are adequately automated. Improvements are continually made, based on lessons learned, research, and updates from external sources.

Category D: CBBs Associated with *Security Data Administration*

CBB D1: Data Identification and Classification

Define information security classes, and provide guidance on protection and access control appropriate to each class.

Level 1   Information security classes are not defined, or are defined only in an ad hoc manner.

Level 2   Information security classes and guidelines for the associated protection levels and access controls are emerging for a limited number of highly sensitive datasets, such as financial records and employee records.

Level 3   Information security classes are standardized for most data sets, and guidelines are in place for protection levels and access controls for architecture layers, networks, IT services, and data stores, such as network-attached storage and databases.

Level 4   Information security classes are comprehensive for virtually all datasets, information fragments, and incomplete data groupings. Comprehensive protection levels and access control guidelines are in place for architecture layers, networks, IT services, and data stores.

Level 5   Information security classes and their associated protection and access control guidelines are regularly reviewed for improvement opportunities.

CBB D2: Access Rights Management

Manage user access rights to information throughout its life cycle, including granting, denying, and revoking access privileges.

Level 1   Access rights are managed in an ad hoc manner using informal procedures, if at all.

Level 2   Within the IT function, there are defined guidelines for access rights management (for example, access rights are withdrawn if abused; access rights are matched to job needs; personnel are discouraged from sharing credentials). Access rights management controls and tools are also defined. Enforcement may, however, still be inconsistent.

Level 3   A standardized authorization approach is used to grant data access rights across the IT function and some other business units. Access rights are granted only to formally approved applicants, and there is documentary evidence to support most existing access rights.

Level 4   Changes to access rights are synchronized with the organization's human resources system, to cater for new employees, movers/promotions, and leavers, and their corresponding privileges. Authorizations and revocations are based on approved changes or those triggered by changes in the scope of an employee's responsibilities or by an employee moving to a different job role.

Level 5   Data, systems, applications, and network access activity is continually reviewed to identify opportunities for improving access control.

CBB D3: Data Life Cycle Management

Provide the security expertise and guidance to ensure that data throughout its life cycle is appropriately available, adequately preserved, and/or destroyed to meet business, regulatory, and/or other security requirements.

Level 1   Data and information life cycles tend not to be managed, or to be managed only in an ad hoc manner.

Level 2   There are defined guidelines for managing the life cycles of a limited number of business-critical and sensitive data sets.

Level 3   There are standardized guidelines for managing the life cycles of most datasets.

Level 4   There are comprehensive guidelines for managing life cycle states and life cycle state transitions for virtually all datasets. For example, when data is moved from processed to archived, a security measure might be to delete the data from the processed storage area only after the archive storage has been backed up.

Level 5   Guidelines for managing data through its life cycle are continually reviewed to identify opportunities for improvement.

Category E: CBBs Associated with *Business Continuity Management*

CBB E1: Business Continuity Planning

Provide stakeholders throughout the organization with security advice to assist in the analysis of incidents and to ensure that data is secure before, during, and after the execution of the business continuity plan.

Level 1	Any contribution to business continuity planning is ad hoc.
Level 2	Information security guidance for backup, archiving, and systems recovery is in place only for a limited number of key data sets and business-critical support systems.
Level 3	Information security guidance is standardized and implemented for most aspects of business continuity planning and testing. Business continuity can be implemented and managed locally.
Level 4	Information security guidance is comprehensive and implemented for all aspects of business continuity planning and testing. Business continuity can be implemented or managed remotely from other designated sites.
Level 5	The security of business continuity is continually reviewed, based on lessons learned, research, and input from relevant business ecosystem partners.

CBB E2: Incident Management

Manage security-related incidents and near incidents. Develop and train incident response teams to identify and limit exposure, manage communications, and coordinate with regulatory bodies as appropriate.

Level 1	Incident management approaches are considered in an ad hoc manner, if at all.
Level 2	There are defined approaches for incident detection and handling for a limited number of incident types (such as virus infections, denial of service attacks, or known caller scams).
Level 3	Standardized approaches are in place for tracking and closing most IT security incidents (such as virus infection, spam, phishing, unusual real-time usage patterns, user or system profile variations, or data access violation). Security awareness ensures that most employees can recognize and report anomalous patterns.
Level 4	Comprehensive approaches to incident management are adopted organization-wide. A culture of security awareness and compliance helps to ensure that incidents are handled efficiently and effectively.
Level 5	The approaches to incident management are continually reviewed, in consultation with relevant business ecosystem partners.

21.4 IMPROVEMENT PLANNING

Capability Evaluation

Two summary assessment questions are set out below, along with the typical response associated with each level of maturity.

How are information security policies, approaches, and controls agreed?

Level 1   Information security policies, approaches, and controls are developed in an ad hoc manner, or they are ignored in favour of just getting things working, rather than working securely.

Level 2   Basic information security policies and approaches are developed within the IT function, with little input from other business units.

Level 3   Standardized information security policies, approaches, and controls are agreed between the IT function and some other business units.

Level 4   Comprehensive information security policies, approaches, and controls are agreed across the organization, aligning with business risk appetite, culture, and legislative and regulatory requirements.

Level 5   Security policies, approaches, and controls are continually reviewed by all relevant stakeholders to enhance the security of information.

To what extent is a security-compliant culture evident?

Level 1   The organization lacks a coherent culture of information security compliance.

Level 2   A culture of information security compliance is emerging with the availability of basic training and awareness campaigns. Security compliant behaviour is increasing; non-compliance, however, is not always identified or addressed.

Level 3   Standardized information security awareness and training ensure that most employees are aware of their responsibilities in relation to security compliance. Occurrences of non-compliance are increasingly known and addressed most of the time.

Level 4   Comprehensive information security awareness and training are delivered across the organization. Adherence to security compliant behaviour is the norm. Security violations are systematically detected and swiftly addressed.

Level 5   The effectiveness of information security awareness and training is continually reviewed. Deviations from security compliant behaviour are rare.

Key Practices-Outcomes-Metrics (POMs)

Some useful POMs for developing the Information Security Management (ISM) capability are summarized below.

Level 2 POMs

Practice	Establish an intelligence gathering and threat profiling process that identifies information security threat levels and new and emergent threat types.
Outcome	There is greater awareness of emerging and recurring information security threats.
Metric	Number of preventive measures adopted in response to identified security threats.
Practice	Implement security classifications in metadata for data life cycle management and data access control.
Outcome	Data can be more reliably managed using metadata.
Metric	Number of security classes defined. Percentage of data sources that have associated security metadata.
Practice	Establish information security training and awareness raising campaigns, starting in the IT function.
Outcome	A growing information security awareness promotes good practices by employees.
Metric	Percentage of employees who have attended information security training.
Practice	Measure the efficacy of key information security activities.
Outcome	The security measures that are most effective in protecting the business can be understood, while inadequate security measures can be addressed.
Metric	Time taken from the identification of a security threat to the implementation of a suitable counter measure. Number of security incidents causing service interruption or reduced availability. Number of virus infections attempted (detected and prevented). Number of infections that had to be cleaned.

Level 3 POMs

Practice	Specify security requirements for suppliers.
Outcome	Suppliers increasingly understand and meet consistent security requirements, reducing the risk of security breaches.
Metric	Person hours expended on validating security protocols for new IT components and services.
Practice	Define data security classes for data sets – for example, 'trade secret' (for competitive information such as know-how, or product development information), 'confidential' (for sensitive information such as financials, or employee records), 'internal business use only' (for sales figures and financially sensitive data until/unless published), or 'public' (for company publicity collateral).
Outcome	Appropriate levels of security can be applied consistently to business data, helping to ensure its protection and appropriate use.
Metric	Number of security classes supported at each architecture layer (network, storage, database, applications, and so on). Number of security classes supported in each IT service. Number of security classes supported at each device type.
Practice	Ensure information security is an integral part of business continuity planning.
Outcome	Business continuity planning is increasingly more security aware.
Metric	Number of information security management recommendations adopted and implemented in business continuity plans.
Practice	Integrate the security management of IT infrastructure sites with facilities security management.
Outcome	Appropriate IT infrastructure sites are increasingly more secure and monitored appropriately.
Metric	Percentage of locations with integrated management plans. Percentage of systems covered by uninterruptable power supplies (UPS) and managed shutdown processes in the event of a power outage.
Practice	Audit the process for prioritizing and handling security risks.
Outcome	Prioritized security risks are increasingly handled more reliably.
Metric	Percentage of prioritized security risks mitigated using audited risk handling strategies.

Level 4 POMs

Practice	Check all devices (physical, virtual, and user), architecture layers, networks, applications, and storage systems for compliance with recommended security features.
Outcome	Security features are deployed consistently, and the risk from weak links is reduced.
Metric	Percentage of applications and devices complying with recommended security features.

Practice	Use software tools to monitor account usage, system usage, network usage, and component usage, to detect variances from the norm and issue alerts.
Outcome	Breaches can increasingly be detected in real time, contained and fixed quickly, with fewer false alerts.
Metric	Percentage of false triggers (or false positives – suggesting over-sensitivity to variance). Percentage of systems, applications, solutions, and services with real-time variance monitoring. Number of (attempted) breaches, intrusions, and compromised accounts detected by real-time monitoring.

Practice	Promote active membership of appropriate security forums and associations.
Outcome	The organization is kept abreast of new and emerging security threats and security practices, and is better able to make decisions on security investments and the deployment of security resources.
Metric	Percentage of threats in the risk register identified through security special interest groups, forums, or associations. Number of new practices brought in from security special interest groups, forums, or associations.

Practice	Audit account usage and use real-time systems to detect compromised accounts (user and administrative) organization-wide.
Outcome	There are fewer security violations and greater security vigilance among employees at all levels.
Metric	Number of employee security lapses and deliberate security violations. Number of security issues detected by employees. Number of breach attempts targeted at users, such as email, telephone, or personal contact attempts to gain passwords or information pertaining to security measures.

Level 5 POMs

Practice	Continually review security policies and controls to identify improvement opportunities and to keep up with latest practices.
Outcome	Security policies and controls are continually refreshed to combat latest security threats.
Metric	Number and severity of security breaches resulting from previously unknown security vulnerabilities. Number of security breaches prevented. Number of denial of service attacks thwarted. Number of virus/spyware incidents prevented or cleaned.

Practice	Implement measures to record any attempt to tamper with compliance verification data in prioritized areas. Use time-stamps and checksums to help ensure the integrity of audit log files.
Outcome	Confidence in security compliance is increased. The audit logs accurately reflect actions on the data and (failed) attempts to tamper with it.
Metric	Number of false positives regarding security compliance.
Practice	Systematically collaborate with relevant business ecosystem partners to detect compromised accounts (user and administrative).
Outcome	There are fewer security audit violations and greater security vigilance among employees and business partners at all levels.
Metric	Number of account security violations. Number of security issues detected by an account holder.

Addressing Typical Challenges

Some typical challenges that can arise in attempting to develop maturity in the Information Security Management (ISM) capability are set out below.

Challenge	Insufficient resources are available to implement effective information security management.
Context	The return on investment in information security is difficult to calculate, and as a result there may be a reluctance to provide adequate funding for security-related activities.
Action	Consider approaches such as value-at-risk analysis to help justify funding for information security.
Challenge	The level of information security awareness is low among employees.
Context	Information security education and training is rarely given the priority it deserves.
Action	Persuade senior management to encourage employees to comply with the organization's security policies. Conduct information security awareness briefings that highlight the complexity of security threats, their potential impact on the organization, and the measures that can be taken to combat them.
Challenge	Lack of ownership and responsibility for information security across the organization.
Context	IT security management is perceived as not adding value, and as a result the security of the organization's information assets is not actively managed.
Action	Encourage senior management to develop an effective information security governance policy, with clearly defined roles, responsibilities, and accountabilities. Specify audit expectations and remediation actions for non-compliance.

Management Artefacts

Management artefacts that may be used to develop maturity in the Information Security Management (ISM) capability include:

- ▶ An incident log.
- ▶ A risk register.
- ▶ IT security management software.
- ▶ An information security management policy.
- ▶ A vulnerabilities and patch availability database.

Incident Log

An incident log itemizes all incidents, how they were detected/reported, actions taken to neutralize them, and measures taken to prevent their recurrence. Statistical analysis of this log can identify patterns that can help in future planning. The incident log should also be viewed from perspectives such as time, weather, business cycle, and so on when attempting to identify patterns. Incident logs should also note highly publicized incidents in other businesses, and the organization should be on the alert for similar attacks.

Risk Register

The risk register is a record of known risks associated with IT, recorded in one or more databases. It records risk descriptions, and estimates of their potential impact and likelihood. It also records risk handling options and the individuals who are responsible for implementing the identified response. It supports risk prioritization by ranking risk scores or by quantifying potential cost to the business. It enables risks to be tracked over time to determine the effectiveness of the mitigation approach. The underlying data in a risk register may be viewed in a variety of ways – to enable financial experts to manage financial risks, IT security experts to manage information security risks, supply managers to manage supply risks, and so on.

IT Security Management Software

IT security management software facilitates high-level management of security settings on all connected IT assets – for example, enabling the anti-virus settings on PCs to be checked, the firewall status on different devices to be updated, and summary details for all devices in a building to be viewed.

Information Security Management Policy

An information security management policy typically takes account of relevant legislation and regulations, as well as IT and security standards that apply to managers and employees. The document addresses IT security governance and allocates responsibilities for all aspects of information security. It identifies external sources to be used for security information and advice, and provides guidelines for risk monitoring and management.

Vulnerabilities and Patch Availability Database

Patch management software gathers patch-level information for operating systems, databases, and other back-office services, and for user devices and network-attached end-points. In many cases, these tools can be used to automate the roll out of patches.

21.5 REFERENCE

See Also

Other capabilities of IT-CMF that have a particularly close relationship with the Information Security Management (ISM) capability include:

Capability	What it provides
06. Enterprise Information Management (EIM)	Details on information critical to the business and its ownership. Critical information can be afforded enhanced security features and prioritized for business recovery purposes
09. IT Leadership and Governance (ITG)	The overarching IT governance framework, to guide how information security management should operate
11. Risk Management (RM)	General IT risk-related management approaches, policies, standards, and risk handling strategies for consideration in the management of information security-related risks
14. Strategic Planning (SP)	The IT function's strategic plan, which the information security strategy should seek to facilitate and not restrict
20. Enterprise Architecture Management (EAM)	Standards, directions, policies, frameworks, and roadmaps to guide technical infrastructure planning and solution design, which may trigger information security considerations

Further Reading

Estall., H. 2012. *Business continuity management systems: implementation and certification to ISO 22301*. Swindon: BCS

Jaquith, A., 2007. *Security metrics: replacing fear, uncertainty, and doubt*. Upper Saddle River, NJ: Pearson Education.

Sing, A.N., Gupta, M.P., and Ojha, A., 2014. Identifying factors of 'organizational information security management'. *Journal of Enterprise Information Management Decision*, 27.

Stamp, M. 2011. *Information security: principles and practice*. Hoboken, NJ: Wiley.

Notes

[1] Stamp, M., 2011. *Information security: principles and practice*. Hoboken, NJ: Wiley.

[2] Suby, M., 2013. The 2013 (ISC)2 Global information security workforce study. [pdf] Frost and Sullivan. Available at: <https://www.isc2.org/giswsrsa2013>.

[3] Council on CyberSecurity, 2013. Critical controls for effective cyber defense. Available at: <http://www.counciloncybersecurity.org/critical-controls/>.

[4] Joint Task Force Transformation Initiative, 2013. *Security and privacy controls for federal information systems and organizations.* Gaithersburg, MD: National Institute of Standards and Technology. Available at: <http://dx.doi.org/10.6028/NIST.SP.800-53r4>.

KAM
22. Knowledge Asset Management

22.1 OVERVIEW

Goal

The Knowledge Asset Management (KAM) capability enables employees to capture, share, develop, and leverage their collective knowledge to improve the performance of knowledge-based business activities and decision-making.

Objectives

▶ Get the right knowledge, to the right people, at the right time, and thereby improve the quality of decision-making.

▶ Promote access to formalized documented knowledge and also to tacit, contextual knowledge by facilitating collaboration and communication between employees and, where appropriate, between employees and external experts.

▶ Scan the business environment to identify knowledge that is relevant to the organization.

▶ Organize and index knowledge assets so that they can be easily found and accessed.

▶ Measure the use and impact of knowledge assets for relevant organizational activities including, for example, research and development, operations, and training.

Value

The Knowledge Asset Management (KAM) capability facilitates better learning and decision-making by leveraging relevant knowledge.

Relevance

Knowledge-based activities form an increasing proportion of work activities, even in manufacturing environments, where large amounts of knowledge, cognitive work, and collaboration are required. Competitiveness often depends on how efficiently employees leverage knowledge and expertise to generate ideas, solve problems, and make decisions. This is becoming increasingly crucial as the rate of change in all business environments continues to accelerate.

Despite its importance, knowledge management initiatives can often fail [1] [2] – this can be due to the fact that knowledge management is a challenging task that cannot be implemented piecemeal. It requires the support of a technological infrastructure, a change in organizational culture, and the management of different types of knowledge [3]. Organizations may fail in their efforts if they do not know how or where to start, or they lack the guidance of a cohesive implementation framework [4].

A significant challenge in knowledge management lies in changing organizational culture and people's habits, but efforts are most often focused on technological infrastructure and the management of different types of knowledge, without addressing the ways in which these systems interact with how people actually work [5].

By establishing an effective Knowledge Asset Management (KAM) capability, an organization can ensure that its knowledge assets are organized in a way that enables them to be effectively created, shared, and used in support of the organization's strategic objectives. Value is gained by effectively using knowledge in the provision of products and services or in the development of new products and services, where ideas are developed, used, or combined in innovative ways.

22.2 SCOPE

Definition

The Knowledge Asset Management (KAM) capability is the ability to identify, capture, profile, classify, store, maintain, protect, and exploit the organization's knowledge assets in pursuit of business outcomes. The Knowledge Asset Management (KAM) capability covers:

▶ Establishing a knowledge management policy, strategy, and programme.
▶ Assigning roles and accountabilities, and determining requisite employee skills.
▶ Fostering a knowledge-sharing culture.
▶ Providing tools, technologies, and other resources to support knowledge management activities.
▶ Managing the knowledge asset life cycle, from identifying, capturing, profiling, classifying, storing, and maintaining, to archiving or discarding, as appropriate.
▶ Assessing the impact of knowledge asset management activities.

Other Capabilities

The following are addressed by other capabilities of IT-CMF:

For...	Refer to...
Managing the quality of enterprise information and data for business value	06. Enterprise Information Management (EIM)
Managing data and information security	21. Information Security Management (ISM)
Managing employee skills and development	23. People Asset Management (PAM)

22.3 UNDERSTANDING MATURITY

Recognizing Excellence

When the Knowledge Asset Management (KAM) capability is well-developed or mature:

▸ It is easier to leverage relevant information, knowledge, and resources (such as ideas, documents, and expertise) to support better and faster decision-making.

▸ Loss of know-how is reduced by capturing both explicit and tacit knowledge.

▸ The organizational culture reinforces knowledge-sharing behaviour.

▸ Knowledge can be readily leveraged by others in similar contexts – those experiencing a problem or challenge that has previously arisen can easily find and tailor the previous solution.

▸ Appropriate roles, responsibilities, and accountabilities for managing knowledge assets are assigned.

▸ Supporting tools and technologies are in place. Knowledge repositories are up-to-date, relevant, and complete, ensuring timely and continued availability of knowledge.

▸ Employees across the organization collaborate in the creation, use, and sharing of knowledge.

▸ Knowledge is effectively managed throughout the entire knowledge life cycle.

Maturity at the Critical Capability Level

The following statements provide a high-level overview of the Knowledge Asset Management (KAM) capability at successive levels of maturity:

Level 1   Knowledge management is ad hoc. Knowledge is not shared across the organization or maintained after projects finish.

Level 2   Defined knowledge management activities are emerging in a limited number of areas within the IT function. A supporting toolset is emerging but not yet fully in place.

Level 3   Standardized knowledge management activities are promoted across the IT function, supported by standardized IT toolsets. Knowledge management is increasingly becoming a valued ingredient in the organization's culture.

Level 4   Comprehensive work structures and practices foster knowledge management behaviour organization-wide, and are supported by comprehensive IT toolsets that are integrated across the organization. Knowledge management is valued throughout the organization.

Level 5   Knowledge management activities and toolsets are continually reviewed to identify opportunities for improvement. The organization expects and rewards positive knowledge management behaviour.

Maturity at the Capability Building Block (CBB) Level

The Capability Building Blocks (CBBs) associated with the Knowledge Asset Management (KAM) capability fall into three categories:

▸ Category A: three CBBs associated with **Governance** – these determine how knowledge asset management activities are controlled.

▸ Category B: four CBBs associated with **Structures and Resources** – these provide the systems for recording and indexing knowledge assets in order to facilitate and support a culture of knowledge sharing and use.

▸ Category C: four CBBs associated with **Life Cycle** – these provide for the capture, classification, storage, and analysis of knowledge assets.

These are described below, together with a summary of the different maturity levels for each.

Category A: CBBs Associated with *Governance*

CBB A1: Strategy for Knowledge Asset Management

Develop and communicate knowledge asset management goals and objectives. Develop high-level action plans to implement the strategy.

Level 1   Knowledge asset management goals and objectives are not explicit, or are stated only in an ad hoc manner.

Level 2   Some generic knowledge asset management goals and objectives are emerging, but they are only treated as priorities by some parts of the organization.

Level 3   Knowledge asset management goals and objectives are agreed and prioritized across many of the business units.

Level 4   Knowledge asset management goals and objectives are agreed and prioritized across the entire organization.

Level 5   Knowledge asset management goals and objectives are continually reviewed for improvement and to remain aligned with the business strategy.

CBB A2: Roles and Skills

Determine accountability for knowledge asset management activities, along with requisite employee skills and obligations.

Level 1   There is limited understanding of the skills required for knowledge management.

Level 2   Knowledge management roles, skills, and training requirements are emerging in parts of the IT function. However, training and recruitment to fulfil those roles are often inadequate.

Level 3   Standardized knowledge management training is in place for many of the roles identified across the IT function, along with recruitment, where appropriate, into key knowledge management roles in some other business units.

Level 4   Knowledge management roles across the organization are appropriately staffed. There is tailored training in knowledge management for all relevant employees.

Level 5   Accountability for knowledge management, along with the associated employee skills and obligations, are continually reviewed to ensure employees drive knowledge-based competitive advantage.

CBB A3: Value Impact Measurement

Identify and measure the impact of knowledge asset management activities in the organization. Examples include the numbers of new products or services delivered based on knowledge management activities, improvements in existing products or services, ability to identify knowledge activities that support improved decision-making, and so on.

Level 1   Any impact indicators that exist are defined in an ad hoc manner, and are rarely used consistently.

Level 2   Activity-based (input) indicators are emerging for a limited number of areas within the IT function.

Level 3   Standardized value-based (output) indicators are present across the IT function.

Level 4   Comprehensive value-based impact indicators are used across the entire organization.

Level 5   Impact indicators are continually reviewed to improve the value of knowledge management for the organization.

Category B: CBBs Associated with *Structures and Resources*

CBB B1: Knowledge Culture

Incentivize a culture in which employees communicate, coordinate, work together, and engage in the creation, use, and sharing of knowledge assets. For example, motivate employees by rewarding innovation and expertise in knowledge asset management activities.

Level 1	Knowledge asset management activities are not generally valued in the organization's culture.
Level 2	Knowledge asset management activities are valued in a limited number of parts of the organization.
Level 3	A culture that values knowledge asset management activities is shared across most of the organization.
Level 4	A culture that values knowledge asset management activities is shared across the entire organization.
Level 5	The organization's culture regarding knowledge asset management activities is continually reviewed and strengthened based on lessons learned.

CBB B2: Enabling Methods

Provide enabling methods (such as tools and techniques) to support the creation, capture, access, and sharing of knowledge assets.

Level 1	Enabling methods for knowledge management are non-existent or ad hoc.
Level 2	Enabling methods are emerging in limited areas of the organization.
Level 3	Enabling methods are standardized across most parts of the organization.
Level 4	Comprehensive enabling methods are in place across the entire organization.
Level 5	Enabling methods are continually reviewed to identify opportunities for improvement.

CBB B3: Knowledge Asset Repository

Design, develop, and adopt a knowledge asset repository (including a defined structure and a method for content representation) to facilitate access to knowledge assets. Record and communicate the location of available knowledge assets.

Level 1   There may be local silos of knowledge, but these are not organized into formal repositories.

Level 2   One or more knowledge asset repository projects are defined and sponsored, but implementation may not yet be complete.

Level 3   There is a standardized knowledge asset repository (or interoperable repositories) in place, supporting increasing levels of consistent knowledge capture, indexing, and retrieval.

Level 4   Comprehensive knowledge taxonomies and indexing services assist in locating knowledge assets. Usage patterns and search terms are evaluated to guide improvements.

Level 5   The knowledge asset repository is continually reviewed for improvement opportunities, and can be adapted to the specific search procedures across different users.

CBB B4: Knowledge Domain Experts Register

Capture information about knowledge domain experts to make their areas of expertise and experience discoverable.

Level 1   Information on knowledge domain experts is either not formalized or is held in incomplete lists on a localized basis.

Level 2   A basic register is emerging which documents current roles.

Level 3   A standardized register reflecting competences and proficiency levels, domains of expertise, and contact details is in place across the IT function.

Level 4   A comprehensive register reflecting competences and proficiency levels, domains of expertise, methods of contact, and mentoring opportunities is in place covering the entire organization.

Level 5   The register is extended to include relevant business ecosystem partners, and is continually reviewed for accuracy and relevance.

Category C: CBBs Associated with *Life Cycle*

CBB C1: Identification and Capture

Manage the identification and collection of knowledge assets.

Level 1   Knowledge assets are identified and collected in an ad hoc manner.

Level 2   Knowledge assets are identified and collected using basic methods, for limited areas of the organization.

Level 3   Knowledge assets are identified and collected using standardized methods for many areas of the organization.

Level 4   Knowledge assets are identified and collected using comprehensive methods for virtually all areas of the organization.

Level 5   The methods in which knowledge assets are identified and collected are continually reviewed to find opportunities for improvement.

CBB C2: Profiling and Classification

Manage profiling and classification schemes for knowledge assets and the relationships between them.

Level 1   There is no agreed profiling or classification scheme. Any methods for labelling or organizing knowledge assets are ad hoc – for example, they are local to particular business units or are personal to individuals.

Level 2   Basic profiles of individual knowledge assets are in place (indicating, for example, the age of the data, the volume of the data, and the manner in which it is encoded) and/or there is a basic classification scheme for knowledge assets, which is used only in parts of the organization.

Level 3   A knowledge asset profiling and/or classification scheme is used by most of the organization. Some progress is being made towards automating the profiling or classification of assets, where appropriate.

Level 4   Knowledge asset profiling and/or classification schemes are aligned with organizational processes and priorities across the organization. Profiling or classification of assets is adequately automated.

Level 5   Knowledge asset profiling and/or classification schemes, as appropriate, are regularly reviewed to reinforce their alignment with organizational priorities and processes.

CBB C3: Knowledge Storage Management

Manage policies and procedures for storage media maintenance.

Level 1 — Knowledge storage management, if performed at all, is localized within business units.

Level 2 — Common policies and procedures for storage media maintenance are emerging for a limited number of knowledge repository management processes. For example, storage tiers may be matched to access times, retention periods, and media refresh criteria.

Level 3 — Policies and procedures for storage media maintenance are standardized for the majority of knowledge repository management processes. For example, media maintenance may be done on a batch basis.

Level 4 — Policies and procedures for storage media maintenance are comprehensive for all knowledge repository management processes across the entire organization. For example, data rewrites may be semi-automated as low-priority background tasks.

Level 5 — Policies and procedures for storage media maintenance are continually reviewed for improvement opportunities. For example, knowledge assets may be automatically removed based on life cycle stage, relevance, or quality.

CBB C4: Knowledge Usage Analytics

Analyse the use of knowledge assets by, for example, user, search terms, and/or knowledge asset category, to improve knowledge asset management activities.

Level 1 — There are no reliable usage analytics available. Improvements tend to be made only in reaction to user complaints.

Level 2 — Basic knowledge asset usage analytics are emerging within the IT function, but use of the resultant insights may be limited.

Level 3 — Knowledge asset usage analytics are standardized, and regularly inform improvement efforts within the IT function.

Level 4 — Knowledge asset usage analytics are comprehensive, and drive systematic improvement efforts across the organization.

Level 5 — Knowledge asset usage analytics are continually reviewed to identify opportunities for improvement.

22.4 IMPROVEMENT PLANNING

Capability Evaluation

Two summary assessment questions are set out below, along with the typical response associated with each level of maturity.

How do IT services and solutions support the capture and use of knowledge?

Level 1 — IT services and solutions to perform or assist in knowledge asset capture and use have not been identified, or they are identified in an ad hoc manner.

Level 2 — Basic IT services and solutions have been defined to assist in knowledge asset capture and use. Results, however, typically show only minimally acceptable performance levels.

Level 3 — Standard IT services and solutions for knowledge asset capture and use are applied in most parts of the organization. Results, however, show moderate performance levels.

Level 4 — Comprehensive IT services and solutions for knowledge asset capture and use are applied throughout the organization. Results, however, show good performance levels.

Level 5 — IT services and solutions for knowledge asset capture and use are continually reviewed to identify opportunities for improvement. Results consistently show industry-leading performance levels.

How are the benefits of knowledge asset management practices tracked?

Level 1 — There is little or no understanding of how knowledge asset management practices contribute to business value.

Level 2 — Basic knowledge asset management practices are emerging in parts of the IT function to demonstrate their impact on business value.

Level 3 — Standardized knowledge asset management practices are followed across the IT function and some other business units to demonstrate their impact on business value.

Level 4 — Knowledge asset management practices are comprehensively adopted across the organization, with organization-wide tracking of business benefits.

Level 5 — Knowledge asset management practices are continually reviewed to maintain their contribution to business value.

Key Practices-Outcomes-Metrics (POMs)

Some useful POMs for developing the Knowledge Asset Management (KAM) capability are summarized below.

Level 2 POMs

Practice	Develop policies and procedures for knowledge asset management activities, in line with the organization's strategic use of knowledge.
Outcome	The knowledge asset management strategy increasingly supports the organization's strategy and is translated into actionable items for employees.
Metric	Number of knowledge asset management goals being pursued. Percentage of strategic knowledge asset management objectives that are delivered.
Practice	Identify roles, responsibilities, and required competences for knowledge asset management.
Outcome	Knowledge asset management roles can be filled by employees with the necessary skills and competences.
Metric	Percentage of employees in knowledge asset management roles who have received appropriate training/development.
Practice	Identify indicators to measure the impact of knowledge asset management activities in targeted areas.
Outcome	There is emerging awareness of the impact of knowledge asset management activities.
Metric	Cumulative impact (such as speed of execution, or error avoidance) of knowledge asset management activities.
Practice	Analyse processes to identify delays or failures that result from relevant knowledge not being available or used appropriately.
Outcome	Identifying gaps in the quality of the organization's knowledge can help improve the effectiveness and efficiency of business processes.
Metric	Percentage of relevant processes reviewed and subsequently improved.

Level 3 POMs

Practice	Establish standardized approaches for identifying, capturing, profiling, classifying, storing, and analysing knowledge assets.
Outcome	Knowledge assets can be effectively managed throughout their life cycles.
Metric	Number of knowledge assets managed using defined approaches.
Practice	Form an organization-wide knowledge asset management steering team.
Outcome	The goals and objectives for knowledge asset management are no longer defined locally, but seek to identify synergistic opportunities at an organization-wide level.
Metric	Representation of business units on the steering committee.

Practice	Identify standardized toolsets to support flexible knowledge management practices (for example, distributed, centralized, or federated) appropriate to the needs of the business.
Outcome	The use of standardized tools and technologies promotes interoperability, facilitates training, and reduces support and vendor management costs.
Metric	Costs of IT services and solutions associated with knowledge management practices.
Practice	Create a register of knowledge domain experts, detailing their competences and proficiency levels, domains of expertise, and contact details.
Outcome	The register facilitates access to individuals who are knowledgeable in specific work domains, thereby enabling their knowledge to be exploited for business purposes.
Metric	Number of experts listed in the knowledge domain experts register. Percentage of relevant employees accessing the register.

Level 4 POMs

Practice	Promote automation in relation to the capture and indexing of knowledge assets.
Outcome	Cost, effort, and number of defects associated with the capture and indexing of knowledge assets can be reduced. Reliability and confidence in how the knowledge assets are indexed are increased. Appropriate use of the organization's knowledge assets is more likely.
Metric	Extent of user satisfaction. Increase regarding the accuracy of retrieval for relevant knowledge assets. Percentage reduction in costs and number of errors associated with capture and indexing of knowledge assets.
Practice	Formalize the improvement of knowledge asset management based on metrics and analysis of usage patterns.
Outcome	Defined metrics can help identify what is working well, and what requires improvement.
Metric	Percentage of major knowledge asset management activities that include metrics to reveal use and impact. Percentage of needed improvements that are actioned.
Practice	Ensure that relevant employees have access to knowledge management conferences, events, publications, and leading industry insights.
Outcome	The latest proven practices across a variety of industries and business sectors can be evaluated and adopted if appropriate.
Metric	Number of events that knowledge management employees attend. Number of updates to existing knowledge management approaches. Number of new knowledge management approaches adopted.

Level 5 POMs

Practice	Evaluate new technologies that support knowledge management activities and processes, and adopt those that are appropriate to the organization.
Outcome	New technologies that are better able to support knowledge asset management practices can be identified and put in place.
Metric	Impact (in terms of business value) of new technologies that support knowledge management practices.
Practice	Use knowledge asset usage analytics organization-wide to drive continual improvements in knowledge asset management.
Outcome	Ineffective knowledge management practices are continually upgraded or replaced by more effective practices.
Metric	Number of knowledge management practices that are improved or replaced.
Practice	Continually review the culture of the organization from the perspective of knowledge asset management.
Outcome	Required changes to the organization's culture can be identified and implemented to embed and normalize knowledge asset management.
Metric	Frequency of reviews. Percentage of improvement objectives achieved.

Addressing Typical Challenges

Some typical challenges that can arise in attempting to develop maturity in the Knowledge Asset Management (KAM) capability are set out below.

Challenge	Lack of senior management sponsorship and buy-in to resource a knowledge asset management programme.
Context	Due to the perceived intangibility of knowledge, there can sometimes be a difficulty in articulating the business impact of knowledge asset management activities.
Action	Stimulate senior management discussion on how day-to-day critical business activities depend on the effective sharing and use of knowledge assets.
Challenge	Knowledge asset management programmes can be overwhelmed by complexity.
Context	The cost and scope of knowledge asset management projects are underestimated, and employees with the requisite roles, experience, skills, and accountabilities are not assigned.
Action	Ensure adequate time and resources are given to conducting upfront feasibility studies, to minimize the risks involved, and to act as a basis for allocating resources appropriately and effectively.

Challenge	It can be difficult to foster a knowledge-sharing culture across the organization.
Context	Resistance to the cultural change may be due, in part, to the notion that knowledge is organizational power and that sharing potentially reduces individual power, control or influence. Additionally, knowledge often depends on inputs and contributions from many parts of the organization, making it difficult to track individual employee contributions. Metrics that focus only on use, without looking at who contributes to the creation and refinement of the knowledge assets, can act as a disincentive to further employee contributions. An overly hierarchical culture can dissuade more junior employees from engaging in knowledge sharing activities.
Action	Incentivize a learning culture in which personal development encourages the sharing of know-how and knowledge. Recognize or reward employees contributing to and sharing knowledge.

Management Artefacts

Management artefacts that may be used to develop maturity in the Knowledge Asset Management (KAM) capability include:

▸ A knowledge strategy document.
▸ A knowledge asset repository.
▸ A knowledge domain experts register.

Knowledge Strategy Document

A knowledge strategy document sets out the goals and objectives for knowledge asset management, indicating how the organization plans to invest in knowledge assets and how it will exploit them over time. It forms the basis for the organization's knowledge asset management programme (that is, the translation of the strategy into specific actions) and its knowledge policy (that is, the set of guiding principles, such as 'our organization bases its practices on leading-edge scientific evidence'). The strategy includes an integrated set of actions intended to deliver specific business outcomes – for example, the identification of valuable knowledge assets and the use of those assets with a view to improving an organization's performance.

Knowledge Asset Repository

A knowledge asset repository is a computerized system that helps to capture, organize, categorize, store, retrieve, and preserve an organization's knowledge assets. These can include content in a range of different media, such as video, text, numerical data and images with different degrees of structure. Repositories can index their contents in different ways, with some using standardized classification schemes and/or allowing user input, such as tagging, to label items. Different search capabilities (for example through defined terms/ keywords or potential uses) can be provided depending on the nature of the content and needs of the users.

Knowledge Domain Experts Register

A knowledge domain experts register helps with locating experts (predominantly internal, but can include external) to leverage their insights and expertise. Potentially it can include details of domain expertise, references to any published work, key projects worked on, office location, time-zone working hours, and contact details. More sophisticated solutions can build social networks and social-media functionality on top of a basic register to assist in speedier and more meaningful contacts for knowledge asset management purposes.

22.5 REFERENCE

See Also

Other capabilities of IT-CMF that have a particularly close relationship with the Knowledge Asset Management (KAM) capability include:

Capability	What it provides
06. Enterprise Information Management (EIM)	Data analytics to inform knowledge management activities
08. Innovation Management (IM)	Mechanisms to turn knowledge assets into new forms of value – for example, new products and services
14. Strategic Planning (SP)	The strategic goals and objectives that knowledge asset management can support
21. Information Security Management (ISM)	Guidance on keeping knowledge assets secure
23. People Asset Management (PAM)	Reinforcement of employee behaviours regarding sharing of knowledge across the organization, and an environment of continuous learning

Further Reading

Alavi, M., and Leidner, D.E., 2001. Review: knowledge management and knowledge management systems: conceptual foundations and research issues. *MIS Quarterly*, 25(1), 107–36.

Hislop, D., 2013. *Knowledge management in organizations: a critical introduction*. Oxford: Oxford University Press.

North, K., and Kumta, G., 2014. *Knowledge management: value creation through organizational learning*. Cham, CH: Springer.

Pasher, E., and Ronen, T., 2011. *The complete guide to knowledge management: a strategic plan to leverage your company's intellectual capital*. Hoboken, NJ: Wiley.

Notes

[1] Perrin, A., Vidal, P., and Mc Gill, J., 2004. *Valuing knowledge management in organizations, from theory to practice: the case of Lafarge Group*. [pdf]. Available at: <http://km.typepad.com/index/files/valuing_km_in_organizations_the_lafarge_case_perrin_vidal_mcgill.pdf>.

[2] Quintas, P., Lefrere, P., and Jones, G., 1997. Knowledge management: a strategic agenda. *Long Range Planning*, 30, 385–91.

[3] Davenport, T.H., De Long, D.W., and Beers, M.C., 1998. Successful knowledge management projects. *Sloan Management Review*, 39, 43–57.

[4] Fahey, L., and Prusak, L., 1998. The eleven deadliest sins of knowledge management. *California Management Review*, 40, 265.

[5] McDermott, R., 2000. Why information technology inspired but cannot deliver knowledge management. *Knowledge and Communities*, 41, 21–35.

PAM
23. People Asset Management

23.1 OVERVIEW

Goal

The People Asset Management (PAM) capability aims to manage the IT workforce's employment life cycle to ensure adequate availability of competent employees.

Objectives

▸ Establish an effective recruitment process that attracts the best qualified candidates.
▸ Identify, manage, and retain talented and high-potential employees.
▸ Incentivize employee productivity, satisfaction, and motivation, and reduce turnover rates.
▸ Link employee compensation and incentives to performance goals.
▸ Promote career development by providing mentoring, training, and education.
▸ Proactively plan for employee succession to provide continuity in key organizational positions.

Value

The People Asset Management (PAM) capability helps ensure that the employees with the right skills and competences are available to support the achievement of organizational objectives.

Relevance

Employees' skills, knowledge, and expertise are significant organizational assets [1]. Given the global shortage of key IT skills [2], any loss of valued employees is costly for an organization. An effective approach to managing the IT workforce supports the recruitment and retention of the right skills, in support of the organization's strategic direction [3].

By developing an effective People Asset Management (PAM) capability, the organization can recruit, deploy, evaluate, develop, promote, and retain competent employees, and manage succession planning for key organizational positions. Knowledge transfer between employees can be promoted, thereby improving the availability of competent employees and reducing knowledge loss when employees leave [4] [5]. The resulting competent and motivated workforce is better positioned to execute operational plans, and satisfy critical business requirements.

23.2 SCOPE

Definition

The People Asset Management (PAM) capability is the ability to meet the organization's requirements for an effective IT workforce. The People Asset Management (PAM) capability covers:

▶ Defining and implementing an IT workforce strategy.

▶ Implementing Human Resources (HR) policies.

▶ Defining IT job families and career development models.

▶ Establishing a compensation and incentive system.

▶ Defining and managing organizational culture.

▶ Monitoring and managing employee satisfaction.

▶ Defining and managing the IT function's branding and the IT employee recruitment process.

▶ Managing IT employee deployment into specific roles.

▶ Managing the evaluation of IT employee performance.

▶ Managing IT employee development.

▶ Establishing an IT employee promotion process.

▶ Succession planning for key IT roles.

▶ Managing IT employee turnover, termination, and post-employment relations (for example through alumni networking).

Other Capabilities

The following are addressed by other capabilities of IT-CMF:

For...	Refer to...
Scenarios for future workforce requirements based on current and proposed initiatives	04. Capacity Forecasting and Planning (CFP)
Managing knowledge that may reside across the workforce	22. Knowledge Asset Management (KAM)
Building and managing relationships within the IT function and between it and other entities	25. Relationship Management (REM)

23.3 UNDERSTANDING MATURITY

Recognizing Excellence

When the People Asset Management (PAM) capability is well-developed or mature:

- ▸ The IT workforce strategy is aligned with the organization-wide HR strategy.
- ▸ The required skilled and competent employees can be effectively recruited.
- ▸ Job families, career development models, the training catalogue, the compensation system, and the promotion policy are aligned.
- ▸ Well-functioning approaches are in place to develop and promote employees, including high-potential employees.
- ▸ IT employee satisfaction is monitored and managed. Appropriate action is taken to improve satisfaction levels, when required.
- ▸ The organization has the ability to attract and retain the most qualified, high-potential, and high-performing employees.
- ▸ There are well-functioning approaches for managing employee departures and integrating their successors.

Maturity at the Critical Capability Level

The following statements provide a high-level overview of the People Asset Management (PAM) capability at successive levels of maturity:

Level 1	The IT workforce and employment life cycle activities are managed on an ad hoc basis.
Level 2	The IT workforce is actively managed in some areas only. Basic job families and development models are defined, and basic employment life cycle management approaches may be in place.
Level 3	An integrated IT workforce strategy addresses long-, medium-, and short-term needs, and there are job families and development models in place for most areas. The employment life cycle is managed in a standardized way.
Level 4	The IT workforce strategy is fully aligned with organization-wide HR strategies. There are stable and reliable approaches for managing the IT workforce and the employment life cycle effectively and efficiently.
Level 5	The IT workforce and employment life cycle management approaches are continually refined for improvement opportunities.

Maturity at the Capability Building Block (CBB) Level

The Capability Building Blocks (CBBs) associated with the People Asset Management (PAM) capability fall into two categories:

▶ Category A: five CBBs associated with ***Strategic Workforce Management*** – these define human resource plans, policies, and other structures that support the establishment and maintenance of a productive workforce.

▶ Category B: seven CBBs associated with ***Employment Life Cycle Management*** – these define how activities across an employee's career, from recruitment through to termination, are addressed.

These are described below, together with a summary of the different maturity levels for each.

Category A: CBBs Associated with *Strategic Workforce Management*

CBB A1: IT Workforce Strategy

Define an IT workforce strategy, outlining long-term needs regarding, for example, the quantity, skill level, and geographic location of employees. Communicate strategic decisions to the workforce.

Level 1	There is no documented IT workforce strategy, and strategic workforce decisions are communicated informally or in an ad hoc manner.
Level 2	A basic IT workforce strategy is defined, and employees may be only informed of significant strategic workforce decisions.
Level 3	An integrated IT workforce strategy outlines long-, medium-, and short-term needs, and most strategic workforce decisions are communicated to relevant employees in an increasingly timely manner.
Level 4	The IT workforce strategy is aligned with the organization-wide HR strategies, and all strategic workforce decisions are proactively communicated to employees in an appropriate manner.
Level 5	Requirements for implementing the annual IT workforce strategy are continually reviewed for improvement opportunities and include regular input from key business ecosystem partners and the organization's HR function. Communications regarding strategic workforce decisions are continually improved.

CBB A2: HR Policies

Draw up and implement HR policies for IT employees, covering topics such as health and safety, annual leave, code of conduct, discipline procedures, workplace diversity, performance evaluation, compensation, hiring, terms and conditions of employment, and so on.

Level 1   HR policies are expressed in an ad hoc manner, if at all.

Level 2   HR policies are increasingly used to guide management practice, and are made available to IT employees when required or requested.

Level 3   HR policies guide management practice, and IT employees are informed of them via induction and ongoing communications.

Level 4   The availability and the implementation of HR policies are comprehensively monitored.

Level 5   HR policies are continually benchmarked against those of relevant business ecosystem partners, and are readily adapted to reflect changing requirements.

CBB A3: Job Families and Development Models

Define IT-specific job families and the corresponding skill requirements. Establish IT-specific career development models that outline the career paths open to IT employees.

Level 1   Job families and career development models are defined in an ad hoc manner, if at all.

Level 2   Basic job families and career development models are defined for a limited number of areas within the IT function.

Level 3   Job families are defined for most areas across the IT function, and career development models are based on the structure of job families.

Level 4   Job family definitions are comprehensive in all areas of the IT function. Career development models address all relevant career paths, including, for example, technical and management paths.

Level 5   Job family definitions are continually benchmarked against those of relevant business ecosystem partners and with the IT workforce strategy. Career development models are similarly reviewed.

CBB A4: Compensation

Establish a compensation, benefits, and incentive system based on job families and the performance evaluation system.

Level 1   Employees receive a fixed salary. Variable performance-related compensation is typically not provided.

Level 2   The compensation system includes fixed salary and benefits, and may include variable salary components, although these are typically not linked to formal employee performance evaluation reviews.

Level 3   Compensation decisions are based on job families, career level, and comparison to market rates. Variable salary components are linked to 'on the job' performance against individual goals.

Level 4   Variable salary components are linked to 'on the job' performance against individual, team, and organization-wide goals.

Level 5   The compensation system is continually monitored and adapted as required.

CBB A5: Culture and Satisfaction

Define and manage the culture of the IT function. Monitor and manage employee job satisfaction, including employee motivation.

Level 1   The culture of the IT function is expressed in an ad hoc manner. Employee satisfaction may have ad hoc monitoring.

Level 2   The importance of the IT function's culture is increasingly recognized by senior IT management. Employee satisfaction surveys are conducted at increasingly frequent intervals.

Level 3   The IT function's culture is regularly validated with the organization's HR function, and measures are derived to manage its development. Employee satisfaction polls are conducted at standard intervals, and follow-up action is taken on most occasions.

Level 4   The measures to manage culture development and improve employee satisfaction in the IT function are fully aligned with wider organization approaches. Follow-up actions are always taken.

Level 5   Culture development and employee satisfaction in the IT function are continually monitored and acted upon.

Category B: CBBs Associated with *Employment Life Cycle Management*

CBB B1: Recruitment

Manage the recruitment of IT employees.

Level 1   IT line managers rarely collaborate with the HR function regarding recruitment, and do so only in an ad hoc, informal manner.

Level 2   A basic and tactical recruitment approach is emerging for the IT function.

Level 3   Transparent, standardized and objective recruitment practices are in place for most vacancies within the IT function, based on defined job families.

Level 4   The process for filling vacancies within the IT function is comprehensively aligned with the organization-wide recruitment process, with localized flexibility allowed within specified tolerances.

Level 5   The process for filling vacancies within the IT function is continually reviewed based on learning from previous recruitment activities and insights into the recruitment practices of relevant business ecosystem partners.

CBB B2: Deployment

Manage IT employee deployment into specific roles.

Level 1   Employee deployment into roles is ad hoc or reactive.

Level 2   Employee deployments are based on basic criteria, and adherence to these is growing.

Level 3   Standardized criteria are used to prioritize staffing needs and deploy resources for most IT roles across the IT function and some other business units that have embedded IT employees.

Level 4   Comprehensive criteria are used to prioritize staffing needs and deploy resources for all IT roles across the organization.

Level 5   The deployment approach is continually reviewed in line with feedback from stakeholders.

CBB B3: Performance Evaluation

Define and manage the performance evaluation approach.

Level 1   Performance evaluations are conducted on an ad hoc basis, if at all.

Level 2   A basic performance evaluation approach is emerging within the IT function. It may be informally part of compensation negotiations or based on subjective impressions.

Level 3   A standardized performance evaluation approach is in place across the IT function to measure employee performance against set goals.

Level 4   Performance evaluation approaches are expanded to include comprehensive upward feedback and 360 degree feedback.

Level 5   Performance evaluation approaches are continually monitored and adjusted to meet changing business needs, and may reflect input from relevant business ecosystem partners.

CBB B4: Development

Manage training and education programmes, developmental job assignments, mentoring, and coaching.

Level 1   Development needs are identified in an ad hoc manner, if at all. There is limited or no training, coaching, or mentoring available.

Level 2   Development needs are typically identified by the IT line manager usually in a tactical manner, or when explicitly highlighted by individual employees. Basic training, coaching, and mentoring programmes are emerging.

Level 3   Development needs are identified in a standardized manner, drawing from job families, career paths, organizational strategy, and employee performance evaluations. Standard training, coaching, and mentoring programmes are established.

Level 4   Tailored training, coaching, and mentoring programmes are provided to address the individual requirements of, for example, high-potential employees and those on specific career paths.

Level 5   Development needs and skill gaps are continually reviewed. Training is continually adjusted to minimize gaps, and coaching and mentoring programmes are evaluated against those of relevant business ecosystem partners.

CBB B5: Promotion

Define and manage the way in which employees are promoted.

Level 1   Promotions, if they occur, are typically decided subjectively by line managers.

Level 2   Some objective criteria and procedures are emerging for justifying promotions across the IT function.

Level 3   A standardized promotion process is in place, based on clearly defined criteria and procedures for each career level, and it is aligned with job family definitions.

Level 4   Decisions on promotions beyond certain career levels are taken by a designated committee, in line with the standardized promotion process.

Level 5   Promotion criteria are periodically checked for alignment with the IT workforce strategy, and may reflect input from relevant business ecosystem partners.

CBB B6: Succession Planning

Define and implement a succession plan to identify and develop employees capable of filling key organizational positions and maintain continuity. Manage knowledge transfer to support succession planning and prevent knowledge loss in the event of employees leaving.

Level 1   Succession planning is non-existent or ad hoc.

Level 2   A basic approach towards succession planning is emerging for a limited number of key roles within the IT function.

Level 3   Succession planning is in place for many key roles within the IT function and some other business units that have embedded IT roles.

Level 4   Succession planning is in place for all key IT roles across the organization.

Level 5   Succession planning is monitored for effectiveness, and adapted accordingly. It regularly includes input from relevant business ecosystem partners.

CBB B7: Turnover Management

Manage employee exits and post-employment relations.

Level 1   Employee turnover and post-employment relations are managed in an ad hoc, reactive manner.

Level 2   A defined approach to managing employee turnover and post-employment relations is emerging in some areas of the IT function.

Level 3   Procedures for active exit management are established in relation to most IT roles, and are applied across the IT function and some other business units that have embedded IT roles. A standard approach for managing post-employment relations is emerging within the IT function, but may not always be consistently followed.

Level 4   Procedures for active exit management are applied in relation to IT roles across the whole organization, allowing employee turnover to be effectively and holistically managed. A comprehensive approach for managing post-employment relations is consistently followed, facilitating effective management of post-employment relations.

Level 5   Management approaches to employee turnover and post-employment relations are continually revised, and may reflect input from relevant business ecosystem partners.

23.4 IMPROVEMENT PLANNING

Capability Evaluation

Two summary assessment questions are set out below, along with the typical response associated with each level of maturity.

To what extent are strategies and mechanisms in place to support the strategic management of the IT workforce?

Level 1 There is no documented IT workforce strategy. Any employee management mechanisms are ad hoc.

Level 2 A basic IT workforce strategy is emerging within the IT function. Basic job families and career development models are defined in a limited number of areas. The compensation system is primarily based on fixed salary and benefits, but may include some limited variable salary components.

Level 3 A standardized IT workforce strategy identifies long-, medium-, and short-term needs for employees. Job families and career development models (based on the structure of job families) are defined for most areas. Compensation decisions are linked to job families, career level, and performance against individual goals.

Level 4 The IT workforce strategy is aligned with organization-wide HR strategies, while still offering flexibility. Comprehensive job families and career development models are defined for all areas. Compensation decisions are transparently linked to performance against individual, team, and organization-wide goals.

Level 5 The IT workforce strategy is continually reviewed, and regularly includes consultation with relevant business ecosystem partners and the organization's HR function. Job families, career development models, and the compensation system are continually benchmarked and adapted as required.

To what extent are approaches in place for managing the IT employment life cycle, including recruitment, deployment, performance evaluation, training and development, promotion, and succession planning?

Level 1 Approaches are non-existent or ad hoc.

Level 2 Some basic approaches are emerging within parts of the IT function, but these may not be consistently adhered to.

Level 3 Standardized and documented approaches are in place across the IT function and in some other business units. Most employment life cycle management activities adhere to these approaches.

Level 4 Approaches across the IT function are aligned with organization-wide approaches, while still allowing for flexibility. All employment life cycle management activities adhere to these approaches.

Level 5 Approaches are continually reviewed based on lessons learned and changes in the business landscape.

Key Practices-Outcomes-Metrics (POMs)

Some useful POMs for developing the People Asset Management (PAM) capability are summarized below.

Level 2 POMs

Practice	Define and document a basic workforce strategy for the IT function.
Outcome	Consistent recruitment planning emerges according to an agreed IT workforce strategy.
Metric	Comprehensiveness of dimensions reflected in the IT workforce strategy – for example, quantity, skill level, and geographic location of employees.
Practice	Establish a defined and repeatable process for recruiting IT employees.
Outcome	The ability to consistently recruit employees with the required skills for specific job profiles is improved.
Metric	Percentage of applicants hired following the defined recruitment process.
Practice	Introduce a basic training catalogue for employees within the IT function.
Outcome	Employee development can be directed via the training catalogue.
Metric	Number of training courses listed in the training catalogue. Number of training courses delivered.
Practice	Roll out a basic and repeatable performance evaluation approach within the IT function.
Outcome	There is a growing understanding of employee performance levels by both the employees and their line managers.
Metric	Percentage of employees whose performance is reviewed at specified intervals – for example, quarterly.

Level 3 POMs

Practice	Further refine the IT workforce strategy to include long-, medium-, and short-term needs, specifying the numbers, skill levels, and geographic location of employees, and indicate how these needs should be addressed.
Outcome	More holistic planning is possible, based on the detailed IT workforce strategy. There is increased likelihood that the required number of employees with the required skills will be available in the required locations.
Metric	Yes/No indicator regarding the explicit inclusion in the IT workforce strategy of details regarding the organization's long-, medium-, and short-term needs for employees with specified skill levels, and details of the specific geographic locations where they are needed.
Practice	Define job families for key areas, each family to include a series of progressively more advanced competences, experience levels, responsibilities, duties, and so on.
Outcome	Transparent groupings of related jobs are defined for most areas.
Metric	Percentage of roles that can be mapped onto job family descriptions.

Practice	Define a career development model based on the structure of job families.
Outcome	The model clarifies the career development that can take place within each job family.
Metric	Percentage of job families covered by the career development model.
Practice	Base the fixed component of employee compensation on a combination of job family, career level, and comparison to market rates. Link variable salary components to performance against individual goals.
Outcome	Fixed and variable compensation becomes increasingly more consistent and transparent.
Metric	Percentage of positions for which a blended approach is used to set compensation levels.
Practice	Establish a standardized promotion process based on an objective set of criteria, and that is in line with the definition of job families.
Outcome	Transparent promotion criteria are in place.
Metric	Percentage of employees that become candidates for promotion based on set criteria.

Level 4 POMs

Practice	Ensure full alignment of the IT workforce strategy with organization-wide HR strategies.
Outcome	Greater synergies will be possible through alignment.
Metric	Frequency of formal alignment reviews.
Practice	Tailor training to address the requirements of high-potential employees who are following specific career paths.
Outcome	Development of high-potential employees is increasingly accommodated.
Metric	Percentage of training programmes customized to address the requirements of high-potential employees.
Practice	Develop job family descriptions for all IT roles.
Outcome	Comprehensive job family descriptions are available for all areas, thereby supporting employee career planning and increasing visibility of employee deployment.
Metric	Percentage of jobs that can be mapped onto job family descriptions.
Practice	Expand the career development model to include all relevant career paths, including, for example, technical, programme, and team management career paths.
Outcome	A wider array of development paths is incorporated into the career development model, thereby better enabling employees to achieve their career goals. This may include, for example, a technical career ladder to reward and retain experienced individuals who work in an individual contributor capacity.
Metric	Percentage of jobs with explicit career paths defined.

Practice	Expand the variable salary components of compensation to take account of performance against individual, team, and organization-wide goals.
Outcome	High-performing employees are better incentivized and retained.
Metric	Percentage of roles with compensation related to performance against individual, team, and organization-wide goals.
Practice	Take upward and 360 degree feedback into account when evaluating the performance of IT employees.
Outcome	Evaluations are more holistic, as the perspectives of employees at the same level and lower levels are taken into account.
Metric	Percentage of jobs for which upward and 360 degree feedback is taken into account.
Practice	Roll out succession planning for all key IT roles. Maintain succession plans up-to-date in line with changes to key roles and responsibilities.
Outcome	There is smooth succession transition for all key IT roles.
Metric	Percentage of key roles for which there are succession plans.

Level 5 POMs

Practice	Continually benchmark the definition of job families and career development models against those of relevant business ecosystem partners.
Outcome	Job families and career development models are up-to-date and industry-relevant.
Metric	Number of benchmark exercises. Frequency of updates to job families and career development models.
Practice	Adjust the training catalogue as required to reflect trends in skills requirements.
Outcome	Long-term training needs remain satisfied via the training catalogue, and skills shortages are minimized.
Metric	Number of revisions to the training catalogue per specified time interval.
Practice	Continually compare the organization's criteria, practices, and rewards for managing employee performance with those of relevant business ecosystem partners.
Outcome	Performance evaluation and compensation are kept in line with latest industry practices.
Metric	Number of employee performance criteria, practices, and rewards revised based on industry peer comparisons per annum.

Addressing Typical Challenges

Some typical challenges that can arise in attempting to develop maturity in the People Asset Management (PAM) capability are set out below.

Challenge	Inadequate funding provided to support the management of people and their skills.
Context	The organization is unable to recruit, develop, and retain sufficiently competent IT employees because of budget constraints.
Action	Promote discussion with senior management regarding recruiting, developing, and retaining appropriate IT employees, and how best it can support the organization to remain competitive and innovative.
Challenge	The value of a formal IT workforce strategy and long-term IT workforce planning is underestimated.
Context	A reactionary and short-term view is taken of IT workforce planning requirements.
Action	Stimulate senior management awareness and discussion on the importance of maintaining balanced workforce planning objectives in the short-, medium-, and long-term to support current and future business activities.
Challenge	The skills available in the IT workforce are static and do not evolve rapidly enough over time to support the organization's changing goals and objectives.
Context	The organization does little to encourage employee training and education, and provides little opportunity to engage in developmental job assignments, mentoring, and coaching.
Action	Initiate an awareness campaign, with support from senior management, on the importance of employee career development and advancement. Offer on-the-job support for employees to develop their skills and experience in-line with organizational needs.
Challenge	The approach to employee performance evaluation is considered highly subjective.
Context	Compensation systems are not transparently linked to individual, team, and organization-wide performance.
Action	Use objective performance assessments to identify and encourage development of motivated employees and future leaders.
Challenge	Critical knowledge is lost when an employee leaves.
Context	The organization does not engage in succession planning or effective exit management to minimize knowledge loss and disruption.
Action	Raise senior management awareness of the importance of proactively identifying and developing candidates for key positions, so as to provide continuity in the event of employee turnover. Initiate discussions on how best to manage employee exits regarding the retention of critical knowledge.

Management Artefacts

Management artefacts that may be used to develop maturity in the People Asset Management (PAM) capability include:

- An IT workforce strategy.
- HR policies.
- Job families.
- A career development model.
- A training catalogue.

IT Workforce Strategy

An IT workforce strategy documents the organization's medium- and long-term needs with respect to the IT workforce, to support its strategic objectives and operational plans. The strategy identifies the number, skill level, and geographic location of employees needed throughout the term of the strategy. It may also cover issues such as training and development, organizational restructuring, and outsourcing. The IT workforce strategy documents key assumptions and responsibilities with respect to these areas. It also provides information on the costs associated with managing employees throughout the employment life cycle, which is an important input to the organization's operating budget.

HR Policies

HR policies provide a formal statement of the organization's rules and guidelines to support activities throughout the employment life cycle. HR policies typically deal with issues such as annual leave, overtime, health and safety, equal employment opportunities, payroll deductions, sick leave, dress code, ethical conduct, and termination (among others). The policies specify the employee obligations and expected standards of behaviour in these areas, and the disciplinary procedures associated with breaches. These policies support the organization in:

- Ensuring that employees know what is expected of them.
- Demonstrating both internally and externally the organization's commitment to, and compliance with, employment legislation.
- Consistently adopting good practices.
- Developing the organization's culture.
- Supporting consistent, fair, and transparent treatment of all employees.

Job Families

Job families are groupings of related job descriptions, which have graduated levels of skills, knowledge, expertise, and responsibility. Each family includes jobs where similar types of work are performed, where similar skills, knowledge, expertise, and training are required, and where there are comparable responsibilities, salary ranges, and duties. The jobs within a job family are ranked according to the level of competence required at each level. Each specific job exists within only one job family, but the jobs in a family may span any number of business units or functions within the organization. Job families help to clarify career paths and promotional opportunities for employees within or between job families. They may also support employee career planning, career advancement, and participation in training and development. Further, job families can improve employee retention and performance, and provide managers with a wider range of options when deciding on employee deployment into specific job roles.

Career Development Model

A career development model outlines the career paths open to IT employees. It supports the proactive planning and implementation of actions enabling IT employees to achieve their career goals. The model is often based on the structure of job families, and it outlines various alternative career paths, such as technical, programme, and project management career paths. The career paths identify the possible sequences or progressions of jobs through which an employee can move during his/her employment. While performing one job, the employee develops the skills needed to progress to the next position. A project management career path, for example, might include progression from junior IT project manager, to IT project manager, to senior IT project manager – at each level, the career path would specify the level of skills, experience, qualifications required, and so on.

Training Catalogue

A training catalogue provides an overview of the IT-related training courses or modules available to support employee development. It includes details such as subject areas covered, prerequisite course requirements, duration, qualification costs, and medium of delivery. The courses may align with job family definitions, and may be tailored to address the requirements of employees who are following specific career paths.

23.5 REFERENCE

See Also

Other capabilities of IT-CMF that have a particularly close relationship with the People Asset Management (PAM) capability include:

Capability	What it provides
04. Capacity Forecasting and Planning (CFP)	Scenarios for future workforce requirements based on current and proposed initiatives
08. Innovation Management (IM)	Requirements with respect to employees' competences required to embrace innovation
13. Sourcing (SRC)	Information about employee competences available through IT service providers
14. Strategic Planning (SP)	High-level input on how the IT strategy impacts the IT workforce strategy
22. Knowledge Asset Management (KAM)	Details on how knowledge critical to organizational success can be better managed across employees
32. User Training Management	Training to improve user proficiency levels on business applications and other IT supported services

Further Reading

Ariss, A., 2014. *Global talent management: challenges, strategies and opportunities*. Cham: Springer.

Curtis, B., Hefley, W.W., and Miller, S.A., 2009. *The people capability maturity model (P-CMM)*. Version 2. [pdf] Software Engineering Institute. Available at: <http://www.sei.cmu.edu/reports/09tr003.pdf>.

Sparrow, P., Scullion, H., and Tarique, I., 2014. *Strategic talent management: contemporary issues in an international context*. Cambridge: Cambridge University Press.

Notes

[1] Scullion, H., Collings, D.G., and Caligiuri, P., 2010. Global talent management. *Journal of World Business*, 45(2), 105–8.

[2] McLaughlin, S., Sherry, M., Doherty, E., Carcary, M., Thornley, C., Wang, Y., CEPIS, IDC, and Empirica, 2014. European Commission DG Enterprise and Industry. e-Skills: the international dimension and impact of globalization. [pdf]. Available at: <http://www.eskills-international.com/files/FINAL_INTERNATIONAL_e_Skills_report_Aug_14.pdf>.

[3] Sparrow, P., Scullion, H., and Tarique, I., 2014. *Strategic talent management: contemporary issues in an international context.* Cambridge: Cambridge University Press.

[4] Hills, A., 2009. Succession planning – or smart talent management? *Industrial and Commercial Training*, 41(1), 3–8.

[5] Whelan, E., and Carcary, M., 2011. Integrating talent and knowledge management: where are the benefits? *Journal of Knowledge Management,* 15(4), 675–87.

PPM
24. Programme and Project Management

24.1 OVERVIEW

Goal

The Programme and Project Management (PPM) capability provides a methodical approach to achieving business objectives when planning, executing, and closing programmes and projects.

Objectives

▸ Increase predictability in programme and project outcomes with respect to schedule, cost, and quality parameters.
▸ Improve consistency in handling programme and project changes and risks.
▸ Improve ability to drive strategic change and establish new capabilities in the organization, through effective programme and project delivery.
▸ Improve business value realization from programmes and projects, with effective utilization of capital investments.

Value

The Programme and Project Management (PPM) capability helps ensure that programmes and projects are run in an agile and consistent manner to support the timely and predictable realization of expected business benefits.

Relevance

The completion of programmes and projects that support the organization's objectives is critical to the achievement of its goals. However, programmes and projects are often complex in nature, with multiple and interdependent tasks, finite resources drawn from multiple disciplines, defined durations, and fixed budgets. Many programmes and projects are challenged by risks, issues, changes in scope, and lack of stakeholder buy-in and support [1] [2] [3]. For these reasons, an effective approach to managing programmes and projects is necessary to fully institutionalize the changes or transformations that they aim to achieve.

By developing an effective Programme and Project Management (PPM) capability, an organization can initiate, plan, execute, monitor, control, and close programmes and projects, track their performance impact, and take corrective action where required. Developing a proficiency in programme and project management tools, techniques, and methodologies ensures that the most appropriate approaches are applied. Consequently, the organization can be better positioned to deliver programmes and projects that are on schedule, within budget, and aligned with the original specifications/objectives, thereby contributing to the realization of business value [4] [5].

24.2 SCOPE

Definition

The Programme and Project Management (PPM) capability is the ability to initiate, plan, execute, monitor, control, and close programmes and projects in line with the business objectives, and to manage associated risks, changes, and issues. The Programme and Project Management (PPM) capability covers:

▸ Establishing governance structures, such as programme/project reporting lines, stage gate reviews, and the roles, responsibilities, and accountabilities required to support programme and project management.

▸ Establishing and adopting approaches to initiate, plan, execute, monitor, control, and close individual programmes and projects.

▸ Identifying and using appropriate programme/project management methodologies, tools, and techniques.

▸ Defining and developing the necessary programme/project management competences of individuals.

▸ Managing programme/project risks, changes, and other issues.

▸ Implementing lessons learned from programme and project execution.

Other Capabilities

The following are addressed by other capabilities of IT-CMF:

For...	Refer to...
Understanding the current allocation of IT resources and scenario modelling future needs	04. Capacity Forecasting and Planning (CFP)
Selecting programmes and projects for investment, or deciding whether to continue (maintain, accelerate, slow-down) or cease investment into projects that have already started	18. Portfolio Planning and Prioritization (PPP)
Assessing the benefits of individual programmes/projects	33. Benefits Assessment and Realization (BAR)
Monitoring the overall programme and project portfolio	34. Portfolio Management (PM)

24.3 UNDERSTANDING MATURITY

Recognizing Excellence

When the Programme and Project Management (PPM) capability is well-developed or mature:

▸ Programmes and projects are managed with a business value focus.

▸ An organization-wide or central body (for example, a Project Management Office (PMO)), with clearly defined and documented roles, responsibilities, accountabilities, and reporting lines, is established to support consistency and best practices in programme and project planning, execution, monitoring, and reporting.

▸ Programme and project management methodologies are agile and adaptive to changing business needs, and have the flexibility to incorporate input from relevant business ecosystem partners.

▸ Programme and project risk management and change management approaches are transparent and effective.

▸ Best practices and key lessons learned are always used to optimize the running of future programmes and projects.

Maturity at the Critical Capability Level

The following statements provide a high-level overview of the Programme and Project Management (PPM) capability at successive levels of maturity:

Level 1   Approaches for programme/project management are inconsistent, or may not exist at all. Performance of programmes and projects is unpredictable.

Level 2   Basic programme/project management approaches are emerging within the IT function. Performance is tracked within the IT function for a limited number of key programmes and projects.

Level 3   Standardized management approaches are present for most parts of a programme/project life cycle, and they are increasingly used across the IT function. Performance is tracked for most programmes and projects.

Level 4   Management approaches are comprehensive across the entire programme/project life cycle, and are adopted organization-wide. Performance is tracked for all programmes and projects.

Level 5   Programme/project management approaches are adaptive to business and technology changes, and are regularly reviewed based on input from lessons learned internally and from relevant business ecosystem partners. Performance management is continually reviewed to minimize variances in performance.

Maturity at the Capability Building Block (CBB) Level

The Capability Building Blocks (CBBs) associated with the Programme and Project Management (PPM) capability fall into two categories:

▸ Category A: four CBBs associated with **Foundation** – these define the overarching methodology within which programmes and projects will be delivered.

▸ Category B: four CBBs associated with **Control and Evaluation** – these create a feedback loop in relation to the management of programme and project performance.

These are described below, together with a summary of the different maturity levels for each.

Category A: CBBs Associated with *Foundation*

CBB A1: Governance Structures

Establish a governance framework or approach to support programme/project management decision-making and involvement of stakeholders. Define associated reporting lines, and roles, responsibilities, and accountabilities.

Level 1	Roles, responsibilities, and accountabilities are assigned in an ad hoc manner.
Level 2	Basic roles, responsibilities, accountabilities, and reporting lines are emerging within the IT function for a limited number of key programmes and projects.
Level 3	Standardized roles, responsibilities, accountabilities, and reporting lines are clearly defined and documented across the IT function for most programmes and projects.
Level 4	An organization-wide or central body (for example, a PMO) is established encapsulating comprehensively defined and documented roles, responsibilities, accountabilities, and reporting lines, and supporting improved consistency and use of best practices when planning, executing, monitoring, and reporting on all programmes and projects.
Level 5	Executive sponsors and project managers proactively drive the optimization of outcomes from each programme and project.

CBB A2: Processes and Methods

Adopt appropriate methodologies to guide the management of the full programme/project life cycle – that is, initiate, plan, execute, monitor, control, and close.

Level 1 Programme/project management methodologies are not used, or are considered in an ad hoc manner.

Level 2 Basic programme/project management methodologies, outlining objectives, roles, responsibilities, deliverables, mandatory approvals, and stage gate reviews, are applied with increasing frequency within limited areas of the IT function – for example, for larger projects.

Level 3 Standardized programme/project management methodologies, covering the full life cycle, are consistently applied across the IT function and in some other business units.

Level 4 Comprehensive programme/project management methodologies are adopted across the organization.

Level 5 Programme/project management methodologies are adaptive to changing business needs, including those of relevant business ecosystem partners. The choice of what specific methodologies to use is regularly reassessed.

CBB A3: Tools and Techniques

Apply tools and techniques to manage individual programme/project activities – for example, risk and issue management, schedule management, budget management, document sharing and collaboration, root cause analysis, and calculating earned value.

Level 1 Tools and techniques for programme/project management are chosen in an ad hoc manner.

Level 2 Basic programme/project management tools and techniques are emerging within the IT function, but typically are not consistently applied.

Level 3 Programme/project management tools and techniques are standardized across the IT function and some other business units.

Level 4 Comprehensive tools and techniques are integrated across the programme/project life cycle and are adopted organization-wide.

Level 5 The use of tools and techniques is continually reviewed for improvement opportunities, based on lessons learned from previous programmes and projects.

CBB A4: Competences

Define the skills required for various programme and project roles. Develop a training curriculum to support skills development – for example, skills in relation to leadership, stakeholder management, programme and project management approaches, and technologies.

Level 1   Limited training may be available.

Level 2   A basic training curriculum has been defined across the IT function, and is typically delivered in response to individual requests.

Level 3   A standard training curriculum is proactively delivered to the IT function and to some other business unit stakeholders.

Level 4   A comprehensive training curriculum, offering tailored training for various roles and competence levels, is proactively delivered to stakeholders across the organization.

Level 5   The training curriculum is continually reviewed for improvement opportunities, based on feedback and lessons learned from monitoring the effectiveness of previous programmes and projects.

Category B: CBBs Associated with *Control and Evaluation*

CBB B1: Performance Management

Define, track, and report on the performance of programmes and projects and on how they are managed.

Level 1   Performance management metrics are identified in an ad hoc manner.

Level 2   A basic set of metrics is defined to track progress against scope, schedule, and cost baselines for a limited number of key programmes and projects.

Level 3   A standardized set of metrics is defined to track performance, quality, and benefits across most programmes and projects.

Level 4   A comprehensive set of metrics is applied for all programmes and projects.

Level 5   The performance management approaches are continually improved based on industry insights and lessons learned from previous programmes and projects.

CBB B2: Risk Management

Establish an approach to manage programme and project risks, and to monitor their impact on performance.

Level 1   Obvious risks may be discussed informally when the programme/project is initially planned. Typically, no further consideration is given to them unless they trigger an event that impacts the programme/project.

Level 2   Risks and risk treatment strategies are formally evaluated for a limited number of key programmes/projects. These are periodically reviewed throughout the programme/project life cycle.

Level 3   There is a standardized approach to identifying and documenting risks and risk treatment strategies for most programmes and projects. Risks and risk treatment strategies are increasingly reviewed at more frequent intervals.

Level 4   Programme and project risk management is formally integrated with Enterprise Risk Management (ERM). Risks and risk treatment strategies are reviewed for all programmes and projects on an ongoing basis.

Level 5   Programme and project risks, contingencies, and risk treatment strategies are regularly improved as required, based on, for example, the past experiences and the input of relevant business ecosystem partners.

CBB B3: Change Management

Establish an approach to manage changes within programmes and projects, and monitor their impact on performance.

Level 1   Changes may be discussed informally with the programme or project sponsor and approved. However, their potential impact on the delivery of the programme/project is rarely understood until they are implemented.

Level 2   There is a basic approach to identifying, documenting, and approving changes for a limited number of major programmes and projects. The potential impact of change on performance is more systematically investigated, although significant variances from forecasts may still occur.

Level 3   There is a standardized approach to identifying, documenting, and approving changes for most of the key programmes and projects across the IT function. Variance in forecasted performance arising from changes is reducing.

Level 4   A comprehensive change management approach is followed for all programmes and projects. Variances in forecasted performance arising from changes is rare.

Level 5   The change management approach is continually evaluated against external best-known practices, and improved accordingly.

CBB B4: Post-programme and Post-project Learning

Manage lessons learned to improve the execution of future programmes and projects.

Level 1   Lessons learned from previous programmes and projects are not captured, or are captured in an inconsistent and ad hoc manner.

Level 2   Basic lessons from a limited number of key programmes and projects are retained and used.

Level 3   There are standardized post-programme and post-project reviews for most of the portfolio. Changes in scope, schedule, and cost can be more readily understood through ex-post analysis.

Level 4   There are in-depth post-programme and post-project reviews for the full portfolio. Changes in scope, schedule, and cost can be more readily planned for with ex-ante analysis.

Level 5   Key lessons learned are routinely used to optimize future programmes and projects.

24.4 IMPROVEMENT PLANNING

Capability Evaluation

Two summary assessment questions are set out below, along with the typical response associated with each level of maturity.

To what extent does an overarching methodology exist for managing the full programme and project life cycle – initiating, planning, executing, monitoring, controlling, and closing programmes and projects?

Level 1   Approaches are inconsistent, or may not exist at all.

Level 2   Basic approaches are emerging and are typically adopted for a limited number of programmes and projects within the IT function.

Level 3   Approaches are standardized covering most aspects of the programme and project life cycle, and are adopted across the IT function and some other business units.

Level 4   Approaches are comprehensive and adopted across the organization, addressing the entire programme and project life cycle.

Level 5   Approaches are adaptive to business and technology changes, and are regularly reviewed using input from past experience and relevant business ecosystem partners.

To what extent is the performance of individual programmes and projects managed?

Level 1   Performance management is non-existent or ad hoc.

Level 2   Basic performance management approaches are used for a limited number of key programmes and projects within the IT function.

Level 3   Standardized performance management approaches are used across the IT function for most programmes and projects.

Level 4   Comprehensive performance management approaches are proactively adopted organization-wide for all programmes and projects.

Level 5   Performance management approaches are continually reviewed to minimize variances while allowing appropriate levels of flexibility where needed, using prior lessons learned and regular input from business ecosystem partners.

Key Practices-Outcomes-Metric (POMs)

Some useful POMs for developing the Programme and Project Management (PPM) capability are summarized below.

Level 2 POMs

Practice	Establish basic approaches for initiating, planning, executing, monitoring, controlling, and closing programmes and projects, and apply them across key programmes and projects within the IT function.
Outcome	Consistency in programme and project management is emerging within the IT function.
Metric	Percentage of targeted programmes and projects following defined approaches.
Practice	Establish programme and project roles, responsibilities, accountabilities, and reporting lines, for key programmes and projects within the IT function.
Outcome	Ownership of roles, responsibilities, and accountabilities is understood, enabling better accountability.
Metric	Percentage of project members with identified roles.
Practice	Apply basic programme and project management methodologies for key programmes and projects – for example, defining objectives, agreeing deliverables, and planning stage gate reviews.
Outcome	Execution of some of the larger programmes/projects begins to follow consistent methodologies.
Metric	Percentage of programmes and projects run in conformance with defined methodologies. Number of programmes and projects failing their stage gate reviews.
Practice	Define a basic set of metrics to track progress against schedule, scope, cost, and quality baselines for key programmes and projects.
Outcome	The initial building blocks for performance tracking are put in place.
Metric	Number of projects completed on time. Number of projects completed within scope. Number of projects delivered within cost. Number of projects completed within quality parameters. Number of cancelled projects.

Level 3 POMs

Practice	Expand the scope for defining programme/project roles, responsibilities, accountabilities, and reporting lines to include all of the IT function and some other business units.
Outcome	A more comprehensive definition of roles, responsibilities, and accountabilities increases transparency and speeds up decision-making.
Metric	Percentage of programmes and projects with identified gaps in defined roles, responsibilities, accountabilities, and reporting lines.
Practice	Define a standard training curriculum in relation to programme and project management, and proactively deliver it to the IT function and to some other business unit stakeholders.
Outcome	Most stakeholders can avail of standard training that improves proficiencies in programme and project management.
Metric	Percentage of employees with formal training in programme and project management. Percentage of employees with certification in programme and project management.
Practice	Operationalize governance oversight measures for key programmes/projects. Identify, document, and approve changes for prioritized key programmes and projects. Consider the knock-on impact of changes on other programmes and projects in the portfolio.
Outcome	Proposed changes in scope for most programmes and projects are traceable, and are considered prior to any changes being decided.
Metric	Number of approved and rejected changes per programme/project. Percentage of programmes and projects that follow a defined change management approach. Percentage of proposed changes whose impact on related programmes and projects is considered.
Practice	Develop ways of keeping stakeholders informed about the overall status of programmes and projects – for example, an online dashboard/KPI tracking.
Outcome	Reporting and visibility on the status of programmes and projects are improved.
Metric	Percentage of programmes and projects reported on.

Level 4 POMs

Practice	Introduce an organization-wide or central body that oversees all programmes and projects – for example, a Project Management Office (PMO).
Outcome	The central body supports consistency and best practices in programme and project planning, execution, monitoring, and reporting.
Metric	Number of successful projects as a percentage of all projects.

Practice	Validate governance protocols across the organization to deal with recurring programme/project management decisions such as scope changes, additional funding, and modification of the programme or project team.
Outcome	The transparency and speed of decision-making are increased.
Metric	Percentage of decisions processed by authorized decision-makers – for example, a Change Advisory Board. Average time to process a change.
Practice	Allow tailoring of industry-recognized programme and project management methodologies, where appropriate and within defined limits.
Outcome	There is improved control over what programme/project methods should be standardized and customized.
Metric	Number of incidences of non-conformance to defined methodologies per programme/project.
Practice	Fully integrate the risk management of programmes and projects with Enterprise Risk Management (ERM).
Outcome	Risks for key programmes and projects have appropriate levels of corporate-wide visibility and management oversight.
Metric	Yes/No indicators regarding alignment of programme and project risk management policies with ERM policies.
Practice	Compare performance management across all programmes and projects with industry standards.
Outcome	The performance standard for programme and project performance is informed by external comparisons to remain abreast of latest practices.
Metric	Percentage of programmes/projects whose performance data is benchmarked against industry standards.

Level 5 POMs

Practice	Ensure the central programme and project body reports to the executive board or sponsors.
Outcome	Executive sponsors and project managers can readily troubleshoot programmes and projects with a view to achieving the organization's strategic objectives.
Metric	Percentage of programmes and projects reporting to a central body.
Practice	Regularly re-evaluate programme and project methodologies, and adapt them as required to reflect changing business needs. Include input from relevant business ecosystem partners.
Outcome	Methodologies can evolve to satisfy the changing needs of the organization.
Metric	Number of incidences of non-conformance to defined methodologies per programme/project.

Practice	Capture and implement key lessons learned from the management of existing programmes and projects.
Outcome	The continual improvement of approaches will benefit the management of future programmes and projects.
Metric	Number of recommendations captured and fed into future programmes and projects.

Addressing Typical Challenges

Some typical challenges that can arise in attempting to develop maturity in the Programme and Project Management (PPM) capability are set out below.

Challenge	A lack of commitment to developing a good Programme and Project Management (PPM) capability.
Context	Having a formalized approach to programme and project management is perceived as an impediment to agility. The value of having competent project managers, and investing in consistent methodologies, tools and techniques, is subsequently undervalued.
Action	Stimulate a mind-set in which a robust programme and project management approach is viewed as an important contributor to the realization of the organization's overall goals and objectives. Stimulate senior management awareness and discussion on the importance of developing an appropriate organizational structure, competent programme and project managers, and providing appropriate resources and supporting mechanisms to enable timely delivery of programmes and projects.

Challenge	Lack of transparency in programme and project management governance structures.
Context	Decision-making within and across programmes/projects is unclear and impacts delivery.
Action	Promote to the senior management the value of establishing appropriate reporting lines, decision-making processes, roles, responsibilities, and accountabilities within and across programmes/projects.

Challenge	Weak recognition of programme and project management activities.
Context	The value delivered from programme and project management activities is poorly evaluated, reviewed, and communicated.
Action	Promote widespread awareness and visibility among stakeholders on programme and project management successes.

Management Artefacts

Management artefacts that may be used to develop maturity in the Programme and Project Management (PPM) capability include:

▸ A project schedule/Gantt chart.
▸ A programme performance dashboard.
▸ A programme/project risk scorecard.
▸ A programme/project issues log.

Project Schedule/Gantt Chart

A project schedule/Gantt chart is useful for planning the timing, sequencing, and resourcing of project activities. In essence, it acts as a map or navigation tool throughout the project. It clearly outlines all tasks, including those that are linear or sequential in nature, those that can be completed in parallel, and those that form part of the project's critical path. It also outlines the order in which tasks should be performed, the timeframe within which they should be completed, and the allocation of resources. The schedule serves as a basis to monitor and control project activities, and evaluate 'what if' scenarios in relation to project risks and scope changes. As the schedule is informed by estimates of activities, it should be reviewed and updated regularly throughout the project's life cycle.

Programme Performance Dashboard

A dashboard provides a clear snapshot of the current status of programmes and projects within the organization, and can quickly convey overall programme/project status to stakeholders. The effectiveness of this tool depends on ensuring that the most appropriate measures are tracked, and that each measure is accurately classified. A simple and useful visual approach is to adopt red (critical), amber (attention required), and green (on target) status indicators for the dimensions being measured. These may include budget, schedule, and specified deliverables. In addition, allocated responsibilities and accountabilities in relation to each aspect may be tracked. The tool gives stakeholders a quick visual summary of status, so that detailed status reports need to be read only for those programmes or projects that require attention.

Programme/Project Risk Scorecard

A programme/project risk scorecard or risk impact/probability chart serves as a visual tool that helps identify levels of risk: critical, moderate, or low level. For each risk, the scale of impact and likelihood of occurrence are estimated and are plotted on a chart. Risk probability is depicted on one axis and scale of impact is depicted on the other. Those risks with the highest scale of impact and likelihood of occurrence are flagged as requiring the most urgent attention. Resources can be allocated and strategies assigned accordingly to manage those risks. Numerical values can be assigned to both the potential scale of impact and likelihood of occurrence, the product of which can serve as an input to risk prioritization. Financial quantification, in terms of cost to the business or value at risk, may also serve as the basis for risk prioritization.

Programme/Project Issues Log

An issues log serves as a communication tool with respect to unexpected problems related to programmes or projects, and enables them to be tracked while they are being investigated and resolved. While some risks can be identified in advance, issues may materialize without warning, and must be addressed as they arise to avoid conflicts and delays. An issues log template can be created easily (using a spreadsheet or database) to record the nature of the issue (for example, technical, resource, business process, or third-party), the issue identifier and date, its description, priority, assigned responsibility, resolution for action and resolution date. The issues log can also be a useful tool for improving how future programmes and projects are managed.

24.5 REFERENCE

See Also

Other capabilities of IT-CMF that have a particularly close relationship with the Programme and Project Management (PPM) capability include:

Capability	What it provides
09. IT Leadership and Governance (ITG)	Definitions of governance structures for managing programmes and projects
15. Budget Management (BGM)	Reports on budget variances to inform the current and future management of programmes and projects
18. Portfolio Planning and Prioritization (PPP)	Evaluations on whether to fund individual programmes and projects
28. Solutions Delivery (SD)	Guidance on IT solutions development methodologies
33. Benefits Assessment and Realization (BAR)	Benefits estimation and tracking for individual programmes and projects
34. Portfolio Management (PM)	Oversight on the portfolio of programmes and projects to be managed

Further Reading

Kerzner, H., 2005. *Using the project management maturity model: strategic planning for project management.* 2nd ed. Hoboken, NJ: Wiley.

Kerzner, H., 2013. *Project management: a systems approach to planning, scheduling, and controlling.* 11th ed. Hoboken, NJ: Wiley.

Marchewka, J., 2014. *Information technology project management: providing measurable organizational value.* 5th ed. Hoboken, NJ: Wiley.

Project Management Institute, 2013. *A guide to the project management body of knowledge.* 5th ed. Newtown Square, PA: Project Management Institute.

Notes

[1] Kerzner, H., 2013. *Project management: a systems approach to planning, scheduling, and controlling*. 11th ed. Hoboken, NJ: Wiley.

[2] Schwalbe, K., 2013. *Information technology project management*. 7th ed. Boston, MA: Cengage Learning.

[3] Brock, J., Saleh, T., and Iyer, S., 2015. Large-scale IT projects – from nightmare to value creation. *BCG Perspectives*. Available at: <https://www.bcgperspectives.com/content/articles/technology-business-transformation-technology-organization-large-scale-it-projects/>.

[4] Marchewka, J., 2014. *Information technology project management: providing measurable organizational value*. 5th ed. Hoboken, NJ: Wiley.

[5] Project Management Institute., 2013. *A guide to the project management body of knowledge*. 5th ed. Newtown Square, PA: Project Management Institute.

REM
25. Relationship Management

25.1 OVERVIEW

Goal

The Relationship Management (REM) capability aims to ensure that liaison and long-term interaction between the IT function and other business units foster business awareness, mutually align interests, and help minimize issues of conflict.

Objectives

▸ Increase the opportunities for innovation and collaboration by fostering openness and knowledge-sharing between the IT function and other business units.

▸ Use collaborative engagement approaches to guide business units through the technology element of projects.

▸ Overcome internal organizational politics by championing mutual interests.

▸ Earn the IT function a trusted-adviser and honest-broker status with other business units.

Value

The Relationship Management (REM) capability enhances goodwill, trust, and confidence between the IT function and the rest of the business.

Relevance

Disharmony between the IT function and the rest of the organization is a frequently documented feature of many organizations [1][2][3][4]. This arises particularly where organizations seek more strategic ways to apply technology (for example, to support new products/services, to attract new customers, or to streamline processes), and lack the necessary liaison channels to broker the complex relationships between the IT function and other business units.

If the organization is viewed as a network, then the IT function is ideally placed as a primary node, connecting with all business units. By establishing an effective Relationship Management (REM) capability, an organization can leverage all the formal and informal networks and relationships between the IT function and the rest of the organization [5], and this can be a first step towards overcoming any disharmony.

25.2 SCOPE

Definition

The Relationship Management (REM) capability is the ability to analyse, plan, maintain, and enhance relationships between the IT function and the rest of the business. It covers:

▸ Understanding the IT function's web of formal and informal relationships across the organization.

▸ Developing programmes to enhance relationships between the IT function and the rest of the business.

▸ Acting as a conduit for real-time, bi-directional knowledge transfer between the IT function and the rest of the business.

Other Capabilities

The following are addressed by other capabilities of IT-CMF:

For...	Refer to...
Adapting the organizational structure of the IT function	10. Organization Design and Planning (ODP)
Organizing knowledge embedded in organizational activities	22. Knowledge Asset Management (KAM)
Managing IT employees and the job roles they perform	23. People Asset Management (PAM)
Fostering relationships with external suppliers	29. Supplier Management (SUM) and 13. Sourcing (SRC)

25.3 UNDERSTANDING MATURITY

Recognizing Excellence

When the Relationship Management (REM) capability is well-developed or mature:

▸ Open and frequent communications help ensure there is a good understanding between the IT function and other business units.

▸ Potentially negative events can be openly discussed in a productive manner between the IT function and other business units (rather than being considered something to be hidden or disregarded).

▸ There is a deep understanding of organizational structures across business units, and this allows key relationships to be systematically identified, developed, and monitored.

▸ Both formal and informal relationships are used to ensure effective communications.

▸ Different communications channels are used as appropriate to the audience and the message being communicated.

Maturity at the Critical Capability Level

The following statements provide a high-level overview of the Relationship Management (REM) capability at successive levels of maturity:

Level 1	There is no formal or organized relationship management, nor are there any formal communications or information gathering structures in place.
Level 2	A basic understanding of the organization's networks and how to leverage them begins to emerge. Defined communications and information gathering processes are emerging at a managerial level between the IT function and other business units.
Level 3	Standardized approaches to relationship management are in place across the IT function. There are robust communications and information gathering processes between the IT function and many of the other business units, and these enable increasingly timely communication of issues.
Level 4	There are dedicated relationship management teams in place within the IT function for all key business units. There are communications and information gathering processes between the IT function and all other business units, and these enable rapid communication of issues as they arise.
Level 5	There is a comprehensive and up-to-date understanding of the formal and informal networks and information flows within the organization. The IT function and the rest of the business always communicate effectively with each other.

Maturity at the Capability Building Block (CBB) Level

The Capability Building Blocks (CBBs) associated with the Relationship Management (REM) capability fall into two categories:

▶ Category A: four CBBs associated with *Relationship Management Strategy* – these determine the IT function's overarching approach to understanding, managing, and leveraging its relationships with other business units.
▶ Category B: four CBBs associated with *Relationship Management Practice* – these describe how the IT function actively engages with other business units to create, enhance, and leverage their relationships.

These are described below, together with a summary of the different maturity levels for each.

Category A: CBBs Associated with *Relationship Management Strategy*

CBB A1: Relationship Profiles

Understand the formal and informal networks in the organization and how these can provide insight into relationship characteristics, behaviours, and information flows. This includes an understanding of the organization's structures and culture, its strategic goals, the business models it uses, and the degree of operational autonomy that individual business units have.

Level 1	Any documentation or analysis of the organization occurs on an ad hoc basis.
Level 2	There is a basic mapping of formal networks for a limited number of entities in the organization.
Level 3	Standardized documentation and analysis approaches are used to describe most entities in the organization.
Level 4	Comprehensive documentation and analysis approaches examine both formal and informal relationship network characteristics across all entities in the organization.
Level 5	A continually updated view of relationships across the organization is maintained.

CBB A2: Relationship Management Methodology

Define goals, objectives, and targets for the relationship management function/role. Design the relationship management approach to be taken; this includes details of roles and responsibilities, governance, policies, processes, and tools, and also any required support mechanisms such as skills development.

Level 1	Any relationship management methodology in place is ad hoc.
Level 2	A defined relationship management methodology is emerging for a limited number of entities, usually prioritized by the CIO (or by someone in a similar role).
Level 3	A standardized relationship management methodology consistently applies common roles, governance, policies, processes, and tools to manage relationships in most entities.
Level 4	A comprehensive methodology for managing relationships is in place for all relevant relationships between the IT function and the rest of the business.
Level 5	The relationship management approach is regularly monitored for improvement opportunities.

CBB A3: Capturing Business Awareness

Design information collation principles so that the IT function can recognize and comprehend relevant changes as they occur in the rest of the business – for example, this could include new business plans or project reports. Identify and develop tools and approaches to support this feedback loop.

Level 1	There are no or only ad hoc approaches to capturing business awareness information.
Level 2	Business awareness is emerging, but is captured primarily by consulting formal, published communications.
Level 3	There are standardized formal approaches to capturing business awareness that enable the IT function to understand the opportunities and threats other business units may be facing. These are supplemented by informal channels.
Level 4	There are comprehensive approaches to capturing and understanding opportunities and threats across all of the business units. These are a fully embedded set of formal and informal channels.
Level 5	Approaches for capturing information from the rest of the business are regularly monitored for improvement opportunities.

CBB A4: Communication Programme

Design the communication programme to be used to keep stakeholders informed of IT developments, future plans, and other issues – for example, through the use of annual IT reports, IT strategy forums, and IT briefing papers. The frequency of communication is likely to vary depending on issues such as the target audience and message criticality.

Level 1	No formal approaches are established for planning communications.
Level 2	Communication programmes are emerging for a limited number of IT projects and activities.
Level 3	Communication programmes are standardized across all IT projects and activities. Formal communication channels and appropriate communication formats and/or approaches are agreed across the IT function.
Level 4	Comprehensive communication programmes are jointly planned and developed between the IT function and the rest of the business. An agreement on how to use a combination of formal and informal communication channels is reached.
Level 5	Communication programmes are continually reviewed and take account of the needs of the different audiences to be addressed – down to the level of a key individual, where appropriate.

Category B: CBBs Associated with *Relationship Management Practice*

CBB B1: Advocate IT

Advocate for IT by disseminating information to assist stakeholders (primarily outside the IT function) to understand the role IT currently plays and potentially could play in supporting the organization – for example, demonstrating the value of IT activities and promoting the identification of new opportunities.

Level 1	The IT function is typically not viewed as an enabler of business value to the organization.
Level 2	A limited number of business units understand how IT can help the organization address key challenges.
Level 3	Most business units regularly request the IT function to propose how technology can support the organization.
Level 4	The IT function is regularly championed to other parts of the organization by stakeholders from other business units.
Level 5	The entire organization views the IT function as a strategic enabler that delivers business value to the organization.

CBB B2: Advocate Business

Collate information to assist stakeholders (primarily inside the IT function) to understand where technology can best contribute to enabling business value and supporting the organization.

Level 1	The IT function has little or no understanding of the business challenges facing the organization.
Level 2	A few IT managers understand the challenges facing a limited number of business units. Understanding of how technology can assist may still be limited.
Level 3	IT managers have an understanding of the challenges facing most business units. Credible IT solutions can be proposed in many circumstances.
Level 4	There is an understanding across the entire IT function of the challenges facing all business units. Credible IT solutions can be proposed in virtually all circumstances.
Level 5	The IT function continually proposes effective solutions to meet emerging business challenges across the organization before they become significant.

CBB B3: Relationship Prioritization

Prioritize relationships with stakeholders and business units (for example, depending on previous, current, and upcoming business initiatives) to minimize negative impacts of competing priorities.

Level 1   Prioritizing relationships is non-existent or ad hoc, often resulting in a dysfunctional or adversarial relationship culture between the IT function and the rest of the business.

Level 2   A defined prioritization approach exists for managing a limited number of key relationships. A 'workmanlike' relationship culture is growing between the IT function and some other business units. However, goals may not yet be totally aligned.

Level 3   A standardized prioritization approach is applied to most relationships. A 'professional' relationship culture exists between the IT function and many other business units, with goal alignment increasing.

Level 4   A comprehensive prioritization approach is applied to all relationships. A 'collaborative and open' relationship culture with aligned goals exists between the IT function and the rest of the organization.

Level 5   The effectiveness of relationship prioritization is continually monitored. A 'win-win and synergistic' relationship culture prevails.

CBB B4: Awareness and Responsiveness to Business Intelligence

Maintain awareness of what is happening within relationships to track and act on business intelligence. Route business intelligence (for example, that relating to emerging risks, opportunities, and exceptions) to the attention of appropriate individuals/forums to enable suitable responses.

Level 1   Approaches to tracking and acting on business intelligence are non-existent or ad hoc. Issues occur frequently.

Level 2   Defined approaches are emerging in limited areas of the organization to track and react to business intelligence. Issues are decreasing but still likely to occur.

Level 3   Standardized approaches are present in many areas of the organization to track and act on business intelligence. Issues are less frequent but occasionally occur.

Level 4   Comprehensive approaches exist across the organization to track and act on business intelligence. Issues seldom occur.

Level 5   The effectiveness of tracking and acting on business intelligence is continually reviewed. Issues are virtually non-existent.

25.4 IMPROVEMENT PLANNING

Capability Evaluation

Two summary assessment questions are set out below, along with the typical response associated with each level of maturity.

To what extent does the IT function actively manage relationships with stakeholders and other business units?

Level 1   Relationships are managed on an ad hoc basis.

Level 2   A defined approach is used to manage a limited number of relationships. Most relationship management occurs informally.

Level 3   A standardized approach is used to manage relationships across most of the organization.

Level 4   A comprehensive combination of informal and formal approaches is used to systematically manage relationships across the entire organization.

Level 5   Management of relationships between the IT function and the rest of the business is continually reviewed for improvement opportunities.

How are relationship management activities monitored to build trust, confidence, and goodwill?

Level 1   There is no or only ad hoc monitoring of relationships.

Level 2   There is basic monitoring of a limited number of relationships. Trust, confidence, and goodwill are growing but are limited to a few areas.

Level 3   There is standardized monitoring of most relationships. Trust, confidence, and goodwill are growing between the IT function and some other business units.

Level 4   There is comprehensive monitoring of all relationships. There are high levels of trust, confidence, and goodwill between the IT function and the rest of the organization.

Level 5   There is continual monitoring of all relationships. Trust, confidence, and goodwill create a virtuous circle relationship between the IT function and the rest of the organization.

Key Practices-Outcomes-Metrics (POMs)

Some useful POMs for developing the Relationship Management (REM) capability are summarized below.

Level 2 POMs

Practice	Communicate a responsibility matrix so that general IT employees (for example, business analysts, developers, and helpdesk colleagues), and those with specific relationship management duties clearly understand their roles and how to deal with the grey areas of overlap that may occur when dealing with other business units.
Outcome	IT employees are apprised of current and previous engagements with specific business units, and clearly understand that a relationship management initiative is under way.
Metric	Frequency of briefing sessions held across the IT function. Percentage of IT employees attending briefing sessions.
Practice	Prioritize stakeholder relationships across business units.
Outcome	Stakeholders are prioritized in order to focus initial relationship management efforts most effectively, while initial successes will facilitate the approval of the additional resources required to run relationship management activities full time.
Metric	Percentage of relationships that are prioritized.
Practice	Measure customer satisfaction regarding IT service quality – building to include impact on business productivity variables.
Outcome	A performance baseline is created from which to improve.
Metric	Results of customer satisfaction surveys.
Practice	Define the IT function's requirements for business intelligence on business units and identify likely sources of such intelligence.
Outcome	An understanding of business units' opportunities and challenges emerges.
Metric	Percentage of IT's relationships with other business units with defined information requirements.
Practice	Hold regular meetings between IT executives and other business units to share concepts and points of view.
Outcome	The IT function and other business units build trusting relationships and additional dialogue is encouraged.
Metric	Number of regularly scheduled communication sessions between senior IT and other business unit management.

Level 3 POMs

Practice	Move from a reactive to a more proactive process for dealing with business unit concerns.
Outcome	A friendly, courteous, and responsive process resolves problems, and satisfactorily closes the loop with clients.
Metric	Mean time to resolve problems.

Practice	Use stakeholder expectations of the IT function as a basis for defining a formal suite of KPIs.
Outcome	The performance improvement of the IT function can be measured with more business-framed criteria.
Metric	Percentage of KPIs agreed between the IT function and other business units.
Practice	Establish an intra-organizational forum to discuss business requirements for new IT projects and changes to existing systems.
Outcome	The IT function is aware of the business requirements across all areas of the organization.
Metric	Percentage of prioritized business requirements jointly agreed between the IT function and other business units.
Practice	Keep business units informed of the way emerging technologies can help their business units.
Outcome	New usage models emerge demonstrating the strategic value of technology.
Metric	Proximity of CIO to CEO/CFO in the organizational hierarchy. New revenue enabled by technology as a percentage of total revenue.
Practice	Plan regular meetings between the IT function and stakeholders from other business units.
Outcome	Better relationships between the IT function and other business units can be nurtured and maintained.
Metric	Percentage of stakeholders who have regularly scheduled meetings with the IT function. Satisfaction levels of surveyed stakeholders.

Level 4 POMs

Practice	Formalize account management roles for key relationships.
Outcome	Dedicated account manager roles are responsible for all aspects of a stakeholder's relationship with the IT function, and ensure that each stakeholder receives the highest standards of service.
Metric	Percentage of key relationships for which there is an account management plan.
Practice	Develop regular communication plans jointly with other business units for key projects and events.
Outcome	Communications are jointly validated as 'fit-for-purpose', and are released in a timely manner.
Metric	Number of IT communication plans defined jointly with other business units.
Practice	Process and disseminate key information captured across business units to support the IT function's decision-making.
Outcome	Business intelligence is routed to appropriate employees for consideration and, if necessary, action.
Metric	Number of negative events that arise from poor communications.

Practice	Regularly hold customer advocacy sessions to ensure that the entire IT function understands evolving customers' requirements and can respond with the right quality of service.
Outcome	By working with product development teams, for example, the IT function can ensure that the IT services portfolio reflects changing customer needs.
Metric	Number of updates to the IT services portfolio attributable to customer advocacy sessions.

Level 5 POMs

Practice	Keep understanding of the business intelligence current through regular updates.
Outcome	Decisions are based on an up-to-date understanding of business units and their challenges.
Metric	Refresh frequency of business intelligence across business units. Number of issues arising from poor business intelligence.
Practice	Establish a cross-organizational forum of senior employees with responsibility for optimizing long-term relationships.
Outcome	There is a higher chance of defining win-win objectives, and of preventing the emergence of a 'them and us' culture.
Metric	Percentage of objectives shared between the IT function and other business units.
Practice	Continually monitor the health status of relationships to identify improvement opportunities.
Outcome	Improvements in relationship management activities are enabled, giving confidence that stakeholders across business units are receiving proper levels of customer attention.
Metric	Percentage of relationships with regular health status reviews conducted.

Addressing Typical Challenges

Some typical challenges that can arise in attempting to develop maturity in the Relationship Management (REM) capability are set out below.

Challenge	Limited resources and time allocated to develop a proficient Relationship Management (REM) capability.
Context	The IT function is typically consumed by daily fire-fighting of issues, leaving relationship management as a 'nice-to-have' activity.
Action	Leverage influencers within the organization to act as advocates and raise awareness of the importance of having a strong Relationship Management (REM) capability that can help to defuse crises or prevent them from occurring in the first place.

Challenge	Over-emphasis on the formal mapping of the organization's relationship networks.
Context	Putting undue emphasis on these efforts can mean that more subtle connections across the organization are overlooked or even undermined; these include informal networks, hidden information flows, and stakeholders with informal interconnections who span multiple parts of the organization.
Action	View the formal mapping of the organization's structure as a stepping-stone to a more thorough understanding of how information flows throughout the organization and who its key influencers are. It is essential that the map does not drive relationship management, but rather is an ever-changing by-product of developing a clearer understanding of the organization.
Challenge	Only technical competences are valued within the IT function.
Context	The bias towards technical qualifications for IT employees can result in a workforce that is highly skilled in very specific technical domains, but lacks the business skills to communicate the potential value of technical solutions to other business unit audiences.
Action	Broaden the hiring/recruitment and development practices, to ensure that there is a balanced repertoire of skills and competences available within the IT function.
Challenge	The IT function has little influence or input into the strategic business discussions of other business units.
Context	While business users may be invited to partake in management committees of the IT function, there is little or no reciprocation, and IT is not represented in other parts of the organization, particularly at the senior management and C-suite levels.
Action	Actively involve the CIO (supported by his/her direct reports) in informing how IT can support the organization's strategic goals and objectives. Promote the embedding of IT representatives throughout the organization.
Challenge	Organizational politics and 'turf wars' continually undermine relationships between the IT function and other business units.
Context	Friction between business units may originate from a lack of clarity or inconsistencies regarding roles and responsibilities in the management of IT – for example, in governance, role definition, and the scope of responsibility.
Action	Work with senior executives to provide transparency and clarity across the organization about roles and responsibilities for management of IT.

Management Artefacts

Management artefacts that may be used to develop maturity in the Relationship Management (REM) capability include:

- An account management plan.
- An innovation lab.
- An IT annual report.
- Business (unit) profiles.
- Business relationship call logs.
- An IT services catalogue.

Account Management Plan

The account management plan is designed to help the relationship management team stay focused on the business units' objectives and goals to ensure they achieve the planned results. It will typically contain:

- A list of key business unit contacts.
- Business unit objectives and significant developments regarding the business environment.
- IT services and solutions that are currently availed of.
- A roadmap of active and planned projects.
- Key performance indicators (KPIs).
- Potential opportunities.

Innovation Lab

An innovation lab is a platform for the IT function to evaluate and showcase novel or unique approaches to how emerging technologies and technology-driven innovations can enable business units overcome specific challenges. The actual representation of innovation labs can take numerous forms, such as product demonstrations, presentations, focus groups, or town hall-style forums. The purpose is to provide an opportunity for the IT function to engage with other business units (relationship building), while engaging in mutual knowledge exchange – understanding business challenges and the potential of IT to address them.

IT Annual Report

The IT annual report is primarily a performance report on the IT function's contribution to business value and to the organization's success. It can serve as an effective marketing tool, promoting the next phase of the IT strategy and other important initiatives. It may also draw specific attention to any adjustments in the IT strategic plan that are required to satisfy changed business priorities. The more effective reports typically:

- Are orientated along the lines of stakeholder's interests.
- Are co-written between the IT function and relevant business units.
- Give an open account of good practices and lessons learned.
- Use short, crisp narratives along with complementary graphics.

Business (Unit) Profiles

Business (unit) profiles are representations of the organization as a whole that show how the different business units connect with each other and with the IT function. They include information on organizational structures such as formal reporting lines and hierarchies, designated contact people, and official sources of information pertaining to business units. Network maps and business relationship call logs can contribute to well-rounded and sufficiently detailed profiles.

Business Relationship Call Logs

Business relationship call logs can be designed around a simple document template, or on a more complex customer relationship management (CRM) type system. The call logs can be used to summarize business unit interactions with the IT function across all levels. Such summaries are typically available in a knowledge repository, which IT management and relevant IT employees can query to achieve an understanding regarding the totality of business unit relationships. The repository can also be a good source of information on how the IT function is viewed by other business units.

IT Services Catalogue

The IT services catalogue is a list of customer-facing IT services provided by the IT function to the organization. It facilitates central registration of IT services, the finding and requesting of IT services by consumers, and service fulfilment tracking. Each service within the catalogue typically includes a description of the service, how it can be requested, how to get support, available service level options and associated costs (if applicable), details of who is responsible for the service, plus other information regarding the specific capabilities of the service. Increasingly, IT services catalogues are accessible via online self-service portals (for example, via cloud-based services) and can be filtered and grouped in various ways – for example, by a particular theme (most popular applications, CRM applications, desktop publishing software, and so on), by applicability to specific job functions, and so on. Such catalogues can simplify business units' connections with the IT function by directing them to appropriate contacts and by setting realistic expectations, thereby establishing a solid foundation for future relationships.

25.5 REFERENCE

See Also

Other capabilities of IT-CMF that have a particularly close relationship with the Relationship Management (REM) capability include:

Capability	What it provides
05. Demand and Supply Management (DSM)	Options on possible demand and supply management strategies
08. Innovation Management (IM)	Guidance on stimulating innovation to deepen relationships between entities
10. Organization Design and Planning (ODP)	Understanding of how the IT function is structured and interfaces with other entities
14. Strategic Planning (SP)	Details of the IT function's strategic goals as the basis for aligning the relationship strategy
27. Service Provisioning (SRP)	Information on service quality, incidents, and problems
29. Supplier Management (SUM)	Information on interactions with IT service providers

Further Reading

Cross, R., and Parker, A., 2004. *The hidden power of social networks: understanding how work really gets done in organizations*. Boston, MA: Harvard Business School Publishing.

Patching, K., and Chatham, R., 2000. *Corporate politics for IT managers.* Oxford: Butterworth Heinemann.

Reich, B.H., and Benbasat, I., 2000. Factors that influence the social dimension of alignment between business and information technology objectives. *MIS Quarterly* 24(1), 81–113.

Venkatraman, N.N., and Loh, L., 1994. The shifting logic of the IS organization: from technical portfolio to relationship portfolio. *Information Strategy: The Executive's Journal.* 10(2), 5–11.

Notes

[1] Ward, J., and Peppard, J., 1996. Reconciling the IT/business relationship: a troubled marriage in need of guidance. *Journal of Strategic Information Systems,* 5(1), 37–65.

[2] Peppard, J., and Ward, J., 1999. 'Mind the gap': diagnosing the relationship between the IT organization and the rest of the business. *Journal of Strategic Information Systems,* 8(1), 29–60.

[3] Coughlan, J., Lycett, M., and Macredie, R.D., 2005. Understanding the business–IT relationship. *International Journal of Information Management,* 25(4), 303–19.

[4] Manfreda, A., and Štemberger, M.I., 2011. Partnership between top management and IT personnel: is it really beyond the reach? In *Proceedings of European, Mediterranean & Middle Eastern Conference on Information Systems, May 30–31, Athens, Greece,* 523–30.

[5] Jarratt, D., 2008. Testing a theoretically constructed relationship management capability. *European Journal of Marketing,* 42(9/10), 1106–32.

RDE
26. Research, Development and Engineering

26.1 OVERVIEW

Goal

The Research, Development and Engineering (RDE) capability aims to identify new technologies that can deliver business value to the organization.

'New' in this context means things that are new to the organization, including technologies, solutions, and usage models. These could be well established elsewhere (outside the organization) but would be considered new if they had not already been applied within the organization. Of course, 'new' also includes technologies that are universally new or emerging.

Objectives

▸ Identify the promising technologies and usage models that are likely to deliver value.
▸ Limit investments in potentially unpromising technologies through phased investment decisions.
▸ Increase organizational awareness of the accepted approach for identifying and developing new technologies and usage models that are likely to deliver business value.
▸ Manage the pipeline of new technologies and usage models so that business value returns are optimized.

Value

The Research, Development and Engineering (RDE) capability enables the organization to investigate how best to use new technologies and usage models to deliver business value.

Relevance

Organizations are often challenged by the speed at which new technologies emerge, and many struggle to determine which technologies are the most suitable for their particular business needs [1] [2]. How prepared an organization is to leverage new technologies can be influenced by several factors, such as being able to spot the significance of emerging technology trends, internal resistance to technological change, or the influence of external stakeholders [2].

To address such factors, an effective approach to the investigation of new technologies and how they might help support organizational objectives can offer significant value to an organization. By establishing an effective Research, Development and Engineering (RDE) capability, an organization can systematically investigate what new technologies and usage models could help it more readily achieve its objectives.

26.2 SCOPE

Definition

The Research, Development and Engineering (RDE) capability is the ability to investigate, acquire, develop, and evaluate technologies, solutions, and usage models that are new to the organization and might offer value. The Research, Development and Engineering (RDE) capability covers:

▸ Ensuring that research into new technologies is managed appropriately, so that risk to the organization is minimized, while opportunities are maximized.

▸ Linking research into new technology to potential usage models that can benefit business units.

▸ Coordinating a research pipeline of promising new technology projects, through a series of phased investment decisions, as understanding of feasibility and relevance is enhanced.

▸ Managing the research portfolio to better align with business goals.

▸ Instilling an organizational culture that promotes research and innovation.

▸ Measuring the value contributed by technology research activities.

Other Capabilities

The following are addressed by other capabilities of IT-CMF:

For...	Refer to...
Facilitating broad-scale IT-enabled innovation activities	08. Innovation Management (IM)
Developing technologies beyond the proof of concept stage	28. Solutions Delivery (SD)

26.3 UNDERSTANDING MATURITY

Recognizing Excellence

When the Research, Development and Engineering (RDE) capability is well-developed or mature:

▸ Resources are used to best effect for investigating new technologies and usage models. This is achieved through the adoption of a 'fail fast/fail cheap' mentality that balances the investment of resources by considering risk and realistic opportunity potential.

▸ A constant pipeline of research project outcomes is produced to enable innovation, solutions delivery, and an enhanced knowledge base.

▸ There is an open, collaborative, and business-aware environment in which investigators have the motivation, time, means, knowledge, and skills to research and develop appropriate projects.

▸ Appropriate business and external partners are actively engaged in research into new technologies.

Maturity at the Critical Capability Level

The following statements provide a high-level overview of the Research, Development and Engineering (RDE) capability at successive levels of maturity:

Level 1   The value of research into new technologies is not recognized by the organization.

Level 2   IT management begins to recognize the value of research into new technologies. However, research outcomes are primarily focused on internal goals of the IT function (as opposed to other business units' goals).

Level 3   The IT function and some other business units jointly adjudicate on specific research projects, which are increasingly focused on identifying new technologies with the potential to address defined business objectives.

Level 4   Across the organization, regular business-driven reviews assess new technology research projects and how well they could potentially meet business objectives.

Level 5   Business strategy is actively informed by new technology research.

Maturity at the Capability Building Block (CBB) Level

The Capability Building Blocks (CBBs) associated with the Research, Development and Engineering (RDE) capability fall into three categories:

▶ Category A: two CBBs associated with *Alignment* – these define how research into new technology opportunities is aligned with the organization's needs.

▶ Category B: three CBBs associated with *Process* – these define how research into new technologies is carried out.

▶ Category C: three CBBs associated with *Management* – these define the day-to-day management of new technology research within the organization.

These are described below, together with a summary of the different maturity levels for each.

Category A: CBBs Associated with *Alignment*

CBB A1: Business Alignment

Align new technology research projects/activities with organizational goals.

Level 1   There may be some new technology research projects, but they are not actively aligned with business goals.

Level 2   Most of the new technology research effort is focused on internal goals of the IT function, and not on wider business goals.

Level 3   The research pipeline for new technologies increasingly reflects the goals of a growing proportion of other business units beyond the IT function.

Level 4   Regular business-driven reviews assess new technology research projects and how well they could potentially meet business objectives.

Level 5   Business strategy is actively informed by the new technology research, and business needs are proactively anticipated by IT-enabled solutions that originated in the IT function's research activities.

CBB A2: Intelligence Gathering

Identify and categorize information on new technologies and the potential they offer – for example, through competitive analysis, industry networking, and technology scanning activities.

Level 1   Where intelligence on new technologies is gathered, it is done so in a sporadic manner and without focus.

Level 2   There is some awareness of the value of gathering intelligence on new technologies. Consideration of business needs is emerging.

Level 3   There is a systematic approach to gathering intelligence on new technologies and making it available. Business needs are addressed based on specific requests.

Level 4   There is a comprehensive and proactive approach to gathering intelligence on new technologies. A variety of sources is used, and business needs constantly inform the intelligence gathering.

Level 5   Gathering intelligence on new technologies systematically includes involvement with external research programmes, standards bodies, industry networks, and industry thought-leaders. Business needs are anticipated and appropriate intelligence is continually gathered.

Category B: CBBs Associated with *Process*

CBB B1: Governance

Have management and governance approaches in place to align new technology research activities.

Level 1   Any management and governance process that exists is informal.

Level 2   There are basic management and governance processes emerging for some but not for all new technology research projects.

Level 3   There are standardized project management methodologies across the IT function for management and governance of new technology research activities.

Level 4   Comprehensive project management methodologies are in place across the organization to proactively address technical uncertainty – for example, a 'fail-fast, fail-cheap, but learn' philosophy.

Level 5   The management and governance of new technology research activities are continually improved and adapted where necessary.

CBB B2: Up-front Analysis

Assess possible new technology research proposals in the light of customer needs, market analysis, financial analysis, and alignment with the technical strategy; and produce a clear product or solution definition that reduces the risk of spending on inappropriate research projects.

Level 1	Any analysis of new concepts or initial assessments is ad hoc.
Level 2	A semi-formal analysis process is presented at project proposal, but is seldom re-examined after that.
Level 3	A standardized business case is prepared within the IT function at project proposal for most new technology research projects, and this is re-examined occasionally during the life of the project.
Level 4	There is organization-wide involvement in preparing a comprehensive business case. The quality of specific deliverables is jointly examined at each investment decision point.
Level 5	Activities for development of business cases are continually reviewed for improvement opportunities.

CBB B3: Phased Delivery

Move approved new technology research projects to conclusion through defined project phases such as initial research, prototyping, proof-of-concept testing, and so on.

Level 1	In managing new technology research projects to a conclusion, only informal approaches are used.
Level 2	Standard project management approaches, artefacts, and tools are emerging, but are only applied to a limited number of new technology research projects.
Level 3	For most new technology research projects, there is a standard approach covering research, prototype development, proof of concept testing, and so on.
Level 4	The approach to researching new technology is universal across the organization and is consistently applied across all projects.
Level 5	The approach to researching new technology is continually reviewed to ensure that it is fit for purpose, and takes advantage of latest management practices.

Category C: CBBs Associated with *Management*

CBB C1: Culture

Promote a management culture within which research into new technology is incentivized and can thrive.

Level 1	The management culture incentivizes research into new technology only in an informal or ad hoc manner.
Level 2	A culture of research into new technology is promoted in limited areas within the IT function.
Level 3	A culture of research into new technology is supported by senior management across the IT function and in some other business units.
Level 4	A culture of research into new technology is supported and explicitly endorsed by the IT function and all other business-units.
Level 5	A culture of research into new technology is shared with key business ecosystem partners, facilitating a continual drive for excellence in research activities.

CBB C2: Resource and Portfolio Management

Balance the new technology research portfolio in terms of opportunity, resources, risk, and focus areas to best serve the organization.

Level 1	Resources are allocated on an ad hoc basis, and there is no formal approach to the portfolio management of research projects.
Level 2	Resources may be formally assigned for major research projects within the IT function, and a basic portfolio management approach is followed for a limited number of new technology research projects.
Level 3	There is a standardized approach to allocating resources, and a portfolio management approach is used to manage most of the new technology research projects. This is driven primarily by the IT function.
Level 4	An oversight team consisting of stakeholders from the IT function and all other business unit leaders jointly allocates resources to new technology research projects. An organization-wide portfolio management process is also in place.
Level 5	There is continual evaluation of the practices for managing the new technology research portfolio to optimize resource allocation and research opportunities.

CBB C3: RDE Impact Measurement

Develop methods, tools, and other artefacts to define and apply metrics that can be used to monitor and evaluate the impact and performance of new technology research projects.

Level 1   Any approaches in place to measure the impact of new technology research are informal.

Level 2   There is a basic approach emerging to measure the impact of new technology research within the IT function, where it typically leverages traditional project management metrics.

Level 3   Metrics specific to monitoring and evaluating the impact and performance of new technology research are used across the IT function and some other business units.

Level 4   The impact of new technology research is systematically measured across the entire organization.

Level 5   Metrics relating to the impact of new technology research are continually analysed for trends and improvement opportunities.

26.4 IMPROVEMENT PLANNING

Capability Evaluation

Two summary assessment questions are set out below, along with the typical response associated with each level of maturity.

How are new technology research projects aligned with business goals?

Level 1   Any alignment of new technology research projects with business goals is coincidental.

Level 2   IT management begins to recognize the value of research into new technologies. However, research outcomes are primarily focused on internal goals of the IT function (as opposed to other business units' goals).

Level 3   The IT function and some other business units jointly adjudicate on specific research projects, which are increasingly focused on identifying new technologies with the potential to address defined business objectives.

Level 4   Across the organization, regular business-driven reviews ensure that the goals of the new technology research portfolio are aligned with the wider business goals.

Level 5   There are continual reviews conducted on alignment activities to maintain business value from technology research projects.

How are new technology research projects governed?

Level 1   Any governance that may occur is largely informal.

Level 2   Some basic governance practices (for example, those relating to project approval, project review, and project cancellation) are in place, and are applied to key projects.

Level 3   The governance of new technology research projects is standardized, with defined roles and responsibilities established across the IT function.

Level 4   There is a collaborative governance model adopted across the organization covering all new technology research projects.

Level 5   The technology research governance model is continually reviewed for improvement opportunities.

Key Practices-Outcomes-Metrics (POMs)

Some useful POMs for developing the Research, Development and Engineering (RDE) capability are summarized below.

Level 2 POMs

Practice	Maintain a repository of intelligence sources for comprehending new technologies in targeted areas of interest.
Outcome	The repository of intelligence sources helps ensure the organization is up to date with technology trends.
Metric	Number of new technologies that are flagged for further investigation.
Practice	Implement basic governance practices for major new technology research projects – for example, those relating to project approval, project review, and project cancellation.
Outcome	There is visibility on the status and resourcing of major new technology research projects.
Metric	Number of new technology research projects analysed by project stage – for example, basic research, prototype, business case, recommendation.
Practice	Assign formal responsibility to specific employees from the IT function for the analysis of major new technology research projects and for the identification of likely benefits.
Outcome	A formal mandate is assigned to ensure consistent consideration of the benefits and implications arising from proposed new technology research projects.
Metric	Number of proposals evaluated. Percentage of proposals approved.

Practice	Promote informed risk-taking by recognizing that discontinued projects are not failures, but rather opportunities to inform learning.
Outcome	The morale of employees involved in new technology research is improved, and employees are encouraged to propose new ideas and projects.
Metric	Number of new ideas or projects proposed. Number of awards given for failed projects that generated key learnings.
Practice	Measure the performance impact of major new technology research projects.
Outcome	The transparency of major new technology research projects is increased, leading to improvements in areas such as resource allocation.
Metric	Percentage of new technology research projects with appropriate metrics assigned.

Level 3 POMs

Practice	Define a process to record and develop new technology research concepts, to record decisions, and to identify risks.
Outcome	The rationale and implications of all new technology research projects are articulated, agreed, and clearly documented. IT and business benefits are taken into account.
Metric	Number and percentage of new technology research projects tracked.
Practice	Formally set aside resources and funding for new technology research projects.
Outcome	New technology research is perceived at all levels as a worthwhile and distinct activity, attracting commensurate attention and resources.
Metric	Percentage of the IT budget formally allocated to new technology research activity.
Practice	Standardize a business case template for new technology research in conjunction with other business units.
Outcome	New technology research projects can be more easily compared on a like-for-like basis.
Metric	Number and percentage of new technology research projects using an approved business case template.
Practice	Encourage employees from the IT function and other business units to suggest potential usage scenarios for new technologies.
Outcome	There is timely identification of new technologies that may be of benefit to the organization.
Metric	Number of new ideas or projects proposed by employees.

Level 4 POMs

Practice	Engage with key technology suppliers on their research activities and new technology offerings.
Outcome	The choice of what new technology research projects to pursue is better informed in relation to emerging opportunities.
Metric	Number of engagements and resulting opportunities identified.
Practice	Collate lessons learned from ongoing and completed new technology research projects.
Outcome	The governance process for managing ongoing and future new technology research is improved.
Metric	Number of insights collected across the IT function from new technology research projects.
Practice	Communicate an integrated approach throughout the organization for identifying and evaluating new technologies.
Outcome	Duplication of research effort is avoided and research expertise is enhanced.
Metric	Percentage of employees who are aware of approaches for identifying and evaluating new technologies.

Level 5 POMs

Practice	Engage with industry networks in setting standards/regulations for emerging technologies.
Outcome	The organization will be more informed of technology trajectories, and may be able to exert influence on its direction.
Metric	Representation on relevant industry boards. Number of industry network events attended.
Practice	Continually evaluate and refine new technology research activities across the organization.
Outcome	The performance of new technology research improves continually – for example, in the results it delivers, in its use of resources, and in its timeliness.
Metric	Frequency of review meetings to evaluate contributions of new technology research activities across the organization.

Addressing Typical Challenges

Some typical challenges that can arise in attempting to develop maturity in the Research, Development and Engineering (RDE) capability are set out below.

Challenge	Lack of constructive collaboration between the IT function and other business units when initiating new technology research projects.
Context	Other business units fail to see the potential value of proposed new technology research projects.
Action	Use business language (as opposed to technical terms) to communicate the potential value to management regarding new technology research projects.
Challenge	Cancelling unpromising new technology research projects at the appropriate time.
Context	Many projects continue past the point when they are no longer viable, due to poor levels of oversight.
Action	Define minimum criteria that a project must meet to progress, and ensure adequate levels of governance are brought to bear.
Challenge	Ambiguous definition of new technology research deliverables.
Context	Definition of deliverables is unclear leading to overspend or time overrun on new technology research projects.
Action	Raise awareness among senior management of the importance of ensuring project deliverables are clearly outlined and documented from the beginning, along with relevant details of resource requirements and timelines.
Challenge	Lack of an isolated environment in which to test new technologies.
Context	Technologies that seem promising, but are as yet unproven within the organization, don't have a suitable technical platform within which they can be field tested. For that reason, they are not investigated further.
Action	Promote the benefits of maintaining a suitable technical environment to enable new technologies to be field-tested.
Challenge	Employee antipathy to submitting of new technology/project proposals.
Context	While employees might have good ideas, they are inhibited from progressing them by a fear-of-failure culture.
Action	Instil a culture that encourages employees to take informed risks, and reward projects that inform learning even if the project fails (as opposed to only rewarding successful technologies).

Management Artefacts

Management artefacts that may be used to develop maturity in the Research, Development and Engineering (RDE) capability include:

▸ Guidelines for new technology research intelligence gathering.
▸ A repository of new technology research projects.
▸ An ideation platform.
▸ A new technology research performance report.
▸ An innovation lab.

Guidelines for New Technology Research Intelligence Gathering

The purpose of guidelines on intelligence gathering for new technology research is to describe how resources are to be deployed to gather and categorize intelligence/information on new technology opportunities, solutions, and usage models that might offer value to the organization in the future.

Intelligence may be gathered using a variety of mechanisms and sources including benchmarking of industry peers, collection of information from trade fairs/events, technology vendor briefings, technology/horizon scanning, and so on. Insights derived from this process are then fed back to the appropriate point of use within the organization. Having intelligence gathering guidelines can help ensure that business goals are considered from the outset.

Repository of New Technology Research Projects

A repository of new technology research projects is a structured collection of all documentation relating to active and proposed research projects. The following are some of the documents it might contain.

▸ *Project Proposal:* Project proposals may arise from multiple sources including:
  ▸ Consideration of intelligence discovered through activities such as industry benchmarking, industry networking, technology/horizon scanning, and so on.
  ▸ A directive from senior management to investigate the feasibility of a particular concept or idea.
  ▸ A request for assistance with innovation projects, for example from those involved in innovation management.
▸ *Business Case:* A business case is a document that describes the potential value of a proposed research project, outlining how it will address such things as customer needs, market analysis, alignment with the technical strategy, financial analysis, business relevance, and so on. Business cases will be assessed for 'go/no-go' by the research governance process.
▸ *Project Tracking Report:* A project tracking report provides management with a status report on active new technology research projects as they move through their various stages – research, prototyping, proof-of-concept testing, and recommendations.
▸ *Research Outcomes Report:* A research outcomes report may be produced shortly after project initiation (for example, where a proposal is discontinued during the up-front-analysis process) or more commonly following the prototyping and testing conducted during the phased delivery stage. Its purpose is to report on the findings and recommendations, and to give the rationale for these recommendations.

Ideation Platform

An ideation platform is a popular type of social collaboration platform that enables the collection of innovative ideas from a wide variety of sources, including employees, customers, and partners, who are encouraged to contribute their own ideas and to discuss and develop those of others. Ideas are typically ranked according to a number of criteria, including the reputation of the individual submitting the idea, responses to that idea, and the feasibility of acting on the suggestion. Ideation platforms often make use of behavioural science methods, software algorithms, and game mechanics to encourage participation and collaboration.

New Technology Research Performance Report

A new technology research performance report is used to monitor and evaluate the impact and performance of new technology research activities. Metrics might include assessing the impact on product development roadmaps, product revenues, organizational operating costs, and perhaps the impact on stock price.

Innovation Lab

An innovation lab is a platform for IT to showcase novel or unique approaches to how emerging technologies and technology-driven innovations can enable business units overcome specific challenges. Innovation labs can take many forms – for example, product demonstrations, presentations, focus groups, or town hall-style forums. The purpose is to provide an opportunity for the IT function to engage with other business units, to share knowledge about business challenges, and to identify opportunities for IT to address them innovatively.

26.5 REFERENCE

See Also

Other capabilities of IT-CMF that have a particularly close relationship with the Research, Development and Engineering (RDE) capability include:

Capability	What it provides
07. Green Information Technology (GIT)	Direction on how research into emerging technologies could assist environmentally sensitive computing
08. Innovation Management (IM)	Details on activities to encourage IT-enabled innovation
09. IT Leadership and Governance (ITG)	Guidelines for governance of research and establishing a decision-making process
14. Strategic Planning (SP)	Direction and information about potential themes, ideas, and opportunities for research
20. Enterprise Architecture Management (EAM)	Guidelines and rules derived from the enterprise architecture, within which new technologies should eventually operate
22. Knowledge Asset Management (KAM)	Access to knowledge assets to support research
28. Solutions Delivery (SD)	Development of new technologies for enterprise deployment

Further Reading

Cooper, R.G., and Edgett, S.J., 2012. The Innovation Diamond™: an executive framework. Product Development Institute. Available at: <http://www.prod-dev.com/innovation_diamond.php>.

Day, G., Schoemaker, P., and Gunther, R., 2000. *Wharton on managing emerging technologies.* Hoboken, NJ: Wiley.

iSixSigma, 2012. Design for Six Sigma (DFSS) versus DMAIC. Available at: <http://www.isixsigma.com/library/content/c020722a.asp>.

Notes

[1] Jensen, R., 2007. The digital provide: information (technology), market performance, and welfare in the south Indian fisheries sector. *The Quarterly Journal of Economics,* 122(3), 879–924.

[2] Ogunyemi, A., and Johnston, K.A., 2012. Towards an organizational readiness framework for emerging technologies: an investigation of antecedents for South African organizations' readiness for server virtualization. *The Electronic Journal on Information Systems in Developing Countries,* 53(5), 1–30.

SRP
27. Service Provisioning

27.1 OVERVIEW

Goal

The Service Provisioning (SRP) capability aims to identify, deliver, and manage the IT services that enable the organization to meet its defined business objectives.

Objectives

▸ Implement a transparent process for monitoring the services that the IT function provides to its customers in the organization and address any problems as soon as they appear.
▸ Improve IT helpdesk productivity by quickly resolving any requests from customers, preferably during the initial contact with the customer.
▸ Where IT services do fail, restore them as quickly as possible, and plan proactively for any necessary IT service disruptions.
▸ Support business change while maintaining a stable IT service environment.
▸ Promote active stakeholder management of users and customers.
▸ Maintain the services portfolio so that it is fit for purpose and aligned to the organization's objectives.

Value

The Service Provisioning (SRP) capability helps to ensure that the organization's strategy and objectives are supported by reliable and effective IT services.

Relevance

Many businesses rely on the availability of internal and external facing business services to compete successfully. These business services are typically enabled by interconnected IT services and applications, whose stability and scalability are critical to successful business operations and competitive advantage [1]. For example, a survey of over two hundred organizations estimated that the financial impact per annum of business disruption due to the unplanned unavailability of IT services is on average more than US$100 million per organization [2].

By developing an effective Service Provisioning (SRP) capability, an organization can unify the necessary production/operation components of IT service delivery so that the IT function can provide more reliable and more effective IT services.

27.2 SCOPE

Definition

The Service Provisioning (SRP) capability is the ability to manage the life cycle of IT services to satisfy business requirements. This includes ongoing activities relating to operation, maintenance, and continual service improvement, and also transitional activities relating to the design and introduction of services, their deployment, and their eventual decommissioning. The Service Provisioning (SRP) capability includes:

▶ Defining and describing the services provided by the IT function.
▶ Managing the IT services catalogue.
▶ Managing IT service configuration.
▶ Managing IT service availability.
▶ Managing the IT service desk.
▶ Managing requests, incidents, and problems.
▶ Managing access to IT services.
▶ Addressing requests for new IT services and decommissioning unwanted IT services.
▶ Managing IT service levels and service level agreements (SLAs).

Other Capabilities

The following are addressed by other capabilities of IT-CMF:

For...	Refer to...
Managing the IT services portfolio	05. Demand and Supply Management (DSM)
Providing the overall architectural guidelines on the design of IT services	20. Enterprise Architecture Management (EAM)
Developing and releasing software applications	28. Solutions Delivery (SD)
Managing the physical infrastructural assets	30. Technical Infrastructure Management (TIM)

27.3 UNDERSTANDING MATURITY

Recognizing Excellence

When the Service Provisioning (SRP) capability is well-developed or mature:

▸ Stakeholders are satisfied with the availability and reliability of IT services.
▸ IT service levels are proactively reported and IT service failures are quickly resolved with minimal business disruption.
▸ IT services, including their key performance indicators (KPIs), are well defined and documented in a services catalogue that is integrated with relevant IT processes.
▸ IT service requirements are regularly reassessed to confirm that they are fit for purpose.
▸ There are appropriate channels for prioritizing IT service change requests based on their business relevance.
▸ IT service management is highly automated.
▸ Customers are aware of the costs relating to their usage of IT services.

Maturity at the Critical Capability Level

The following statements provide a high-level overview of the Service Provisioning (SRP) capability at successive levels of maturity:

Level 1	The service provisioning processes are ad hoc, resulting in unpredictable IT service quality.
Level 2	Service provisioning processes are increasingly defined and documented, but execution is dependent on individual interpretation of the documentation. Service level agreements (SLAs) are typically defined at the technical operational level only.
Level 3	Service provisioning is supported by standardized tools for most IT services, but may not yet be adequately integrated. SLAs are typically defined at the business operational level.
Level 4	Customers have access to services on demand. Management and troubleshooting of services are highly automated.
Level 5	Customers experience zero downtime or delays, and service provisioning is fully automated.

Maturity at the Capability Building Block (CBB) Level

The Capability Building Blocks (CBBs) associated with the Service Provisioning (SRP) capability fall into two categories:

▸ Category A: three CBBs associated with *Transitional Execution* – these manage the design, deployment, and decommissioning of IT services.
▸ Category B: two CBBs associated with *Operational Execution* – these manage the operations, maintenance, and continual improvement of IT services.

These are described below, together with a summary of the different maturity levels for each.

Category A: CBBs Associated with *Transitional Execution*

CBB A1: Service Definition

Identify and describe each IT service offering and its components – these include Service Level Agreements (SLAs), Operational Level Agreements (OLAs), and Underpinning Contracts (UPCs).

Level 1   If there is an IT service definition, it is agreed on an ad hoc basis.

Level 2   A limited number of IT services are defined and documented.

Level 3   The majority of IT services are defined and consistently documented, including details of their key performance indicators (KPIs) and enabling processes.

Level 4   All IT services are comprehensively defined and documented, and are prioritized based on their importance or relevance to the business.

Level 5   All IT services are continually assessed, created, updated, and removed to remain relevant to business needs and to take advantage of innovations across the business ecosystem.

CBB A2: Service Architecture

Define the service architecture and all its component parts, their interrelationships, and the operational processes through which they interface with surrounding processes, supporting activities, and business ecosystem partners.

Level 1   There are ad hoc basic definitions of IT service components (hardware, software, processes, OLAs, UPCs, and so on), but the relationships between them are not properly defined and are based on ad hoc or informal knowledge.

Level 2   The architecture of a limited number of key IT services is consistently defined. The documentation of the interfaces to the surrounding processes has begun.

Level 3   The architecture of most IT services is defined. Interfaces to more and more key surrounding processes are increasingly and consistently documented. Definitions and documentation are regularly updated as service components change.

Level 4   The architecture of all IT service components across the business is comprehensively defined and documented. The relationships between the IT service components are documented and updated in a timely manner to handle any changes that directly or indirectly impact on these relationships.

Level 5   The architecture of all IT service components is continually reviewed, including the links that connect them to relevant business ecosystem partners.

CBB A3: IT Service Life Cycle Management

Manage the life cycle flow of each IT service from its introduction through deployment to eventual decommissioning.

Level 1   The service life cycle from introduction to decommissioning is generally managed in an ad hoc and largely uncoordinated manner. Disruption to business operations is common.

Level 2   IT service life cycle management generally includes a testing phase for larger projects. Some obsolete services are decommissioned, but associated components are left active even if they are not needed. Disruption to business operations is decreasing but is typically managed reactively.

Level 3   Most new IT services are managed using a formal release management process. Most obsolete services and related components are actively decommissioned. Disruption to business operations is proactively managed.

Level 4   Well-functioning IT service life cycle processes are in place across the whole organization, where the potential impact of introducing or decommissioning IT services is understood in advance, keeping disruption to business operations to a minimum.

Level 5   IT service life cycle management causes no disruption to business operations and is continually reviewed for alignment with the business needs and inputs of the relevant business ecosystem partners.

Category B: CBBs Associated with *Operational Execution*

CBB B1: Customer-Facing Service Operation

Manage customer access to IT assistance – for example, IT helpdesk support, requests for IT services, and IT service performance reporting.

Level 1   Customer access to assistance is ad hoc.

Level 2   Customers can access assistance across multiple service channels – for example, by person, email, phone, or web interface. However, the service experience varies.

Level 3   Customers can access increasingly standardized levels of service across most channels.

Level 4   Customers can access standardized levels of service across all channels.

Level 5   Access channels are continually optimized based on their effectiveness and customer feedback.

CBB B2: Internal Service Operation

Manage all non-customer-facing activities relating to IT service operation – for example service request fulfilment, incident/problem management, and service level management.

Level 1   There is no defined process in place for managing internal service operations.

Level 2   There are defined approaches emerging for managing a limited number of internal service operations. However, they are typically manual and prone to being overwhelmed.

Level 3   There are standardized approaches for managing most internal service operations. There is a shift in balance from manual to automated operations.

Level 4   There are comprehensive tool-supported approaches to managing internal service operations, and these can scale to meet variations in the workload.

Level 5   Internal service operations are continually reviewed for improvement opportunities.

27.4 IMPROVEMENT PLANNING

Capability Evaluation

Two summary assessment questions are set out below, along with the typical response associated with each level of maturity.

How does the IT function develop and deploy IT services?

Level 1   IT service development and deployment are ad hoc.

Level 2   IT service development and deployment have begun to be standardized. However, it is occasionally driven by the demands of individual business units and one-off projects.

Level 3   IT service development is carried out in accordance with a centralized IT services catalogue, and services are deployed following a formal release process.

Level 4   IT services are developed and deployed in a modular way. Roll-out of services is proactively monitored, and there are comprehensive service level agreements (SLAs) in place.

Level 5   Business targets and conformance to SLAs sytematically drive IT service development. Services can be deployed on demand.

How are the operations of IT services reviewed and adapted?

Level 1	There is little or no focus on IT service operation improvement.
Level 2	There are defined IT service operation improvement approaches in parts of the IT function.
Level 3	There are standardized IT service operation improvement approaches across the IT function.
Level 4	Comprehensive improvement approaches are fully integrated across the organization
Level 5	IT service operation improvement approaches are continually reviewed and regularly extended to include relevant business ecosystem partners.

Key Practices-Outcomes-Metrics (POMs)

Some useful POMs for developing the Service Provisioning (SRP) capability are summarized below.

Level 2 POMs

Practice	Define the key IT services of the organization.
Outcome	Service definitions for key services are available to customers.
Metric	Percentage of services that are formally defined.
Practice	Identify and document all underlying components for key IT services.
Outcome	An understanding emerges of the interdependency of components that support key services.
Metric	Percentage of services that are documented to the component level.
Practice	Formally manage service introduction for larger projects.
Outcome	There is a greater chance that services will be more stable (and less disruptive to other services) when they are released.
Metric	Percentage of service introductions that include a test phase.
Practice	Establish basic service-level measurement for key services.
Outcome	Objective monitoring of service levels aids the dialogue with customers.
Metric	Percentage of services that support service-level reporting.
Practice	Ensure that IT service incidents are tracked, recorded, and reported in a satisfactory manner.
Outcome	The availability of current and historical incident data informs IT service improvement initiatives.
Metric	Number of incidents logged, fixed, and open per calendar month. Percentage of recurring versus non-recurring incidents.

Level 3 POMs

Practice	Expand service definition to all IT services, and validate KPIs for key services.
Outcome	Customers have a greater understanding of the services available to them.
Metric	Percentage of services that are formally defined and that include validated KPIs.
Practice	Expand the identification and documentation of components to all IT services. Keep the definitions and documentation up to date as service components change.
Outcome	There is a comprehensive understanding of the relationships between the components and the IT services that depend on them. There is improved traceability of any changes made to services and their underlying components.
Metric	Percentage of services with up-to-date documentation for their underlying components.
Practice	Mandate all new services to use a formal release management process. Ensure a roll-back procedure is available and tested before a new service is introduced or an existing service is modified.
Outcome	The organization has the capability to introduce and roll back releases and upgrades to IT services, reducing the risk of negative impact on business operations.
Metric	Percentage of services introduced using formal release management protocols. Percentage of attempted roll-backs that complete successfully.
Practice	Standardize the reporting of IT service quality levels.
Outcome	The impact of IT service levels is clarified.
Metric	Percentage of services for which quality is reported using a standard format/content.
Practice	Record, track, and report on all incidents. Prioritize and manage incidents based on the urgency to restore services as defined by SLAs.
Outcome	Incidents are systematically managed and the organization is aware of any SLA violations.
Metric	Percentage of incidents that have an SLA assigned. Percentage of SLA violations.

Level 4 POMs

Practice	Expand the definition of IT services so that they are expressed in business terms. Define business KPIs for all IT services.
Outcome	Customers can make more informed decisions regarding IT service selection.
Metric	Percentage of services with business-assigned metrics (KPIs).

Practice	Define and document all underlying components for all IT services across the organization. Manage the relationships between components and services in an integrated way.
Outcome	All service components for all IT services are linked within a database, and they are managed in an integrated manner.
Metric	Percentage of unscheduled service interruptions to IT services that result from changes to unidentified service components.
Practice	Mandate the use of a comprehensive change management process to accompany the introduction of an IT service. Establish interfaces to the key surrounding processes – for example, asset management, demand and supply management, and people management.
Outcome	Service introduction is likely to cause minimal or no disruption to the business.
Metric	Mean time taken to introduce an IT service. Percentage of IT service requests that result from IT service changes or introductions.
Practice	Map IT service-level reporting to business operational metrics (for example, end-to-end availability) and enable it with tool-supported reporting.
Outcome	Stakeholders can readily prioritize service improvements.
Metric	Percentage of IT services incorporated in the organization's business operational metrics.
Practice	Proactively collect event-monitoring data to ensure that all incidents are swiftly addressed.
Outcome	Service availability and reliability are increased.
Metric	Percentage of automated service restorations.

Level 5 POMs

Practice	Continually review service provisioning practices and document service improvements.
Outcome	Helpdesk requests for information on IT services decrease, and change control is enhanced.
Metric	Frequency of service documentation updates.
Practice	Implement an integrated approach to maintaining relationships between IT service components.
Outcome	Change control is enhanced when the connections between related infrastructure and applications are clearer.
Metric	Percentage of unscheduled service interruptions to key services that result from changes to unidentified service components.
Practice	Proactively review the scheduling and effectiveness of releases to accommodate business needs and schedules.
Outcome	New IT services or service upgrades are introduced into operations with no business disruption.
Metric	Amount of business service time lost because of release activity.

Practice	Implement automated reporting for key stakeholders and for the service level management functions.
Outcome	Service level transparency is maximized.
Metric	Percentage of services that have automated service-level reporting to stakeholders.

Practice	Complement the existing incident management system with self-healing processes.
Outcome	The majority of potential incidents are averted before they become significant issues. Those incidents that do occur are remedied automatically.
Metric	Percentage of unplanned versus planned impacts on IT services. Mean time to achieve incident resolution.

Addressing Typical Challenges

Some typical challenges that can arise in attempting to develop maturity in the Service Provisioning (SRP) capability are set out below.

Challenge	Lack of an overall vision or plan for IT services.
Context	The absence of a customer-focused capability to deliver IT services results in unstructured IT activities and poor interactions between IT technical personnel and customers and clients.
Action	In consultation with the rest of the organization, define a service architecture so that the business needs are the driving force in defining the requirements for IT services.

Challenge	Customers are unable to comprehend available IT service offerings, what the services include, their limitations, the associated costs, how to request services, and how to get help to resolve issues.
Context	IT services are poorly catalogued because of inadequate approaches to service identification and documentation.
Action	Work with stakeholders across the organization to emphasize the benefits of using consistent service definition methods to validate the IT services catalogue.

Challenge	Available KPIs don't support objective decision-making regarding goal setting and monitoring of IT services.
Context	There is limited stakeholder enthusiasm for investing time and energy into defining robust customer-centric KPIs to express business value.
Action	Promote senior management discussion on the benefits to having quality KPIs that are relevant and tailored to ensure that IT services are achieving the desired results.

Challenge	A lack of senior management ownership for service provisioning.
Context	Service provisioning is considered a low priority by the senior management team, who regard it as the domain of engineers from the IT function.
Action	Stimulate senior management discussion and raise awareness of how the day-to-day operations of service provisioning are critical to the ability of individuals and the organization to deliver on their commitments, and of how service provisioning should be strategically managed to maximize value.

Management Artefacts

Management artefacts that may be used to develop maturity in the Service Provisioning (SRP) capability include:

- An IT services catalogue.
- A service level agreement (SLA).
- An operational level agreement (OLA).
- A configuration management database (CMDB).
- An IT service management software suite.

IT Services Catalogue

The IT services catalogue is a list of customer-facing IT services provided by the IT function to the organization. It facilitates central registration of IT services, the finding and requesting of IT services by consumers, and service fulfilment tracking. Each service within the catalogue typically includes a description of the service, how it can be requested, how to get support, available service level options and associated costs (if applicable), details of who is responsible for the service, plus other information regarding the specific attributes of the service. Increasingly, IT services catalogues are accessible via online self-service portals – for example, via cloud-based services. They can also be filtered and grouped in various ways – for example, by a particular theme (such as the most popular applications, CRM applications, desktop publishing software), by applicability to specific job functions, and so on. Such catalogues can help simplify the provision of IT services.

Service Level Agreement (SLA)

A service level agreement provides a formalized record of the customer's expectations regarding the level of service from a supplier. Typically, it can include:

- A general definition of the service to be provided.
- Service level measurement methods for capacity, response time (latency), availability (up-time), reliability (mean-time between failures and mean-time to resolution), control limits on process variances, and so on.
- Remedies or penalties that apply if service levels are not achieved.
- Responsibilities of each party – for example, support and escalation procedures.
- A service performance reporting process, its contents and frequency.
- A dispute resolution process.
- Indemnification against third-party costs resulting from service level breaches.
- A process for updating the agreement.

Having effective SLAs defined for IT services will help manage expectations of both the supplier and customer.

Operational Level Agreement (OLA)

An operational level agreement sets out how different sub-groups in an IT service provider's organization share responsibility for delivering the components of the end-to-end service described in the service level agreement. OLAs can also be implemented with external organizations upon whom the service provider relies. Key elements of an OLA include:

▸ Expectations and performance targets for each element in the supply chain for the service.

▸ Clear descriptions of service ownership, accountability, roles, and other responsibilities.

▸ Key interaction elements of the service provider's sub-groups.

The OLA helps ensure that activities performed by different groups and individuals in the service provider's organization are clearly aligned to satisfy the service level agreement.

Configuration Management Database (CMDB)

The configuration management database is a repository of information or metadata on all significant IT components. Typically a CMDB includes details of:

▸ IT assets and applications, collectively referred to as configuration items (CIs).

▸ The relationship between the CIs.

▸ The CIs' life cycle stage – for example, whether it is active or retired.

▸ Changes made – for example, changes to a CI's status or relationship to other CIs.

The CMDB helps in understanding interconnections between IT assets and applications, allowing the impact of proposed changes to be modelled, root cause analysis of service level issues to be performed, and the reconstruction of software and hardware configurations.

IT Service Management Software Suite

An IT service management software suite can support effective IT operations by helping to automate IT service management processes using proven practices. It can include:

▸ *Service Request/Ticket Management:* supports logging tickets through to issue resolution.

▸ *Incident Management:* categorizes issues and automates resolution workflows.

▸ *Problem Management:* supports root-cause analysis to minimize problems recurring.

▸ *Change Management:* automates standards and procedures for making changes.

▸ *Release Management:* supports distributing releases and communicating changes.

▸ *Availability Management:* provides information on configuration and services availability.

▸ *Service Level Management:* maintains and improves IT services, and manages services catalogues.

▸ *Self-Service Management:* allows customers to submit and track the status of their issues, and use the knowledge base to perform self-service actions.

▸ *Knowledge Base:* creates a knowledge base of resolutions and how-to solutions for use by both IT helpdesk agents and end users via self-service.

▸ *Configuration Management:* identifies configuration items and requests for change (RFCs).

▸ *Remote Control:* allows IT helpdesk agents to securely resolve end-user issues from anywhere.

▸ *Analytics and Reporting:* generates reports on IT helpdesk performance and service quality – for example, incident analysis, service requests, and problem and change records.

27.5 REFERENCE

See Also

Other capabilities of IT-CMF that have a particularly close relationship with the Service Provisioning (SRP) capability include:

Capability	What it provides
01. Accounting and Allocation (AA)	Charge-back (or show-back) information pertaining to the cost of individual IT service consumption
05. Demand and Supply Management (DSM)	Information on the business demand for IT services; management and communication of the IT services portfolio
12. Service Analytics and Intelligence (SAI)	Detailed visibility of actual consumption patterns and their impact on the performance of business operations
13. Sourcing (SRC)	Sourcing decisions that may affect the provision of IT services
20. Enterprise Architecture Management (EAM)	Definition of the standards and policies to guide the planning and provision of IT services
28. Solutions Delivery (SD)	Conversion of business requirements into IT services
29. Supplier Management (SUM)	Support for planning activities with external suppliers to enable robust predictions of service quality and availability
30. Technical Infrastructure Management (TIM)	Status updates on technical problem management and solutions for tickets originally logged by service provisioning
31. User Experience Design (UED)	Guidance on improving the usability of IT services and solutions

Further Reading

Cabinet Office, 2011. *ITIL lifecycle suite*. London: The Stationery Office.

Grönroos, C., 2007. *Service management and marketing: customer management in service competition*. Chichester: Wiley.

International Organization for Standardization (ISO), 2011. *ISO/IEC 20000 Information Technology – Service Management*. Geneva, CH: ISO.

Notes

[1] BCS, 2009. The increasing importance of business service management. Available at: <http://www.bcs.org/content/conWebDoc/24352>.

[2] CA Technologies, 2011. *The avoidable cost of downtime: phase 2.* [pdf]. Available at: <http://www.arcserve.com/us/lpg/~/media/Files/SupportingPieces/ARCserve/avoidable-cost-of-downtime-summary-phase-2.pdf>.

SD

28. Solutions Delivery

28.1 OVERVIEW

Goal

The Solutions Delivery (SD) capability aims to develop IT solutions that are effective in meeting business needs.

Objectives

▸ Manage business requirements, contain development costs, and reduce the time to market for IT solutions.

▸ Adopt flexible solutions development and delivery methodologies based on the project context – for example, waterfall, agile, or a hybrid of the two.

▸ Ensure that IT solutions follow agreed development methodologies regardless of where they are developed within the organization – within the IT function or within other business units.

▸ Employ built-in assurance mechanisms that enhance the quality of IT solutions to better meet business requirements and service standards.

▸ Design and develop stable and flexible IT solutions that can easily be maintained and updated to meet future demands of the organization.

Value

The Solutions Delivery (SD) capability ensures a balance between quality, costs, and schedule during the development of IT solutions to meet organizational objectives.

Relevance

Up to two-thirds of technology-related projects end in failure. Reasons regularly cited include project team inexperience, large project size, unclear and complex requirements, inadequate testing, poor change management, and lack of stakeholder communication. Typically, successful projects can spend up to 40 per cent of the total project effort in a design phase (requirements analysis and planning). This is the case regardless of whether they adopt waterfall, incremental, or agile project delivery methodologies – the latter two typically cycling through multiple design-develop-deploy phases. They can spend up to another 40 per cent in a deploy phase (releasing and validating), with the remaining 20 per cent in a develop phase (building and testing).

Organizations that rush into a develop phase without thoughtful consideration of design can suffer unforeseen consequences. For example, finding and fixing a problem in a later phase is more expensive than finding and fixing it during a design phase. Additionally, there will be implications relating to the maintainability of inefficiently designed solutions when they are deployed. Such challenges underscore the need for the development of IT solutions to be better managed so that they achieve more predictable and successful outcomes [1].

By establishing an effective Solutions Delivery (SD) capability, an organization can more effectively manage IT solutions during the design, development, and deployment phases, and control costs and schedules while minimizing the risk of failure. Consequently, the organization can more readily leverage the resultant IT solutions to deliver business value.

28.2 SCOPE

Definition

The Solutions Delivery (SD) capability is the ability to design, develop, validate, and deploy IT solutions that effectively address the organization's business requirements and opportunities. The Solutions Delivery (SD) capability covers:

▸ Managing requirements (functional and non-functional) and their traceability throughout the IT solution's delivery life cycle.
▸ Developing IT solutions based on the output from requirements analysis and the solution's architecture.
▸ Selecting appropriate methods and IT solutions delivery life cycle models (for example, waterfall, incremental, agile).
▸ Reviewing and testing IT solutions throughout the development process.
▸ Managing changes and releases that occur during the IT solution's delivery life cycle.

Other Capabilities

The following are addressed by other capabilities of IT-CMF:

For...	Refer to...
Prioritizing and deprioritizing programmes for investment funding	18. Portfolio Planning and Prioritization (PPP)
Managing project delivery methodologies	24. Programme and Project Management (PPM)
Managing IT solutions when in operation	27. Service Provisioning (SRP)
Managing the technical Infrastructure	30. Technical Infrastructure Management (TIM)
Conducting in-depth investigations of end-user preferences, usability, and prototyping	31. User Experience Design (UED)
Tracking delivery across multiple programmes	34. Portfolio Management (PM)

28.3 UNDERSTANDING MATURITY

Recognizing Excellence

When the Solutions Delivery (SD) capability is well-developed or mature:

▸ IT solutions are specified, designed, developed, and deployed in a consistent but flexible manner to ensure that cost, scheduling, functionality, and quality are optimized to satisfy business needs.

▸ Solutions delivery methodologies guide the development of technology correctly on the first attempt, keeping errors and unplanned rework to a minimum.

▸ Development of IT solutions is not forced into unsuitable delivery methodologies.

▸ The activities of implementation and testing are performed independently of each other, ensuring solutions are robust and reliable before being released.

Maturity at the Critical Capability Level

The following statements provide a high-level overview of the Solutions Delivery (SD) capability at successive levels of maturity:

Level 1   There is ad hoc use of solutions delivery methodologies. IT solutions are typically delivered with wide variations in quality, schedule, and cost expectations.

Level 2   Basic solutions delivery methodologies are defined and applied to a limited number of IT solution projects, which are beginning to meet expectations, but variations in quality, schedule, and cost still occur.

Level 3   Standardized solutions delivery methodologies are applied to most IT solution projects, enabling many of them to regularly meet expectations for quality, schedule, and cost.

Level 4   Comprehensive and flexible project delivery methodologies are applied to all projects, enabling most projects to meet expectations for quality, schedule, and cost.

Level 5   Solutions delivery methodologies are continually analysed and refreshed. Solutions delivery expectations for quality, schedule, and cost are nearly always met.

Maturity at the Capability Building Block (CBB) Level

The Capability Building Blocks (CBBs) associated with the Solutions Delivery (SD) capability fall into four categories:

▶ Category A: two CBBs associated with the *Design Phase* – these manage requirements and IT solution conceptualization.

▶ Category B: two CBBs associated with the *Develop Phase* – these build and test the IT solution.

▶ Category C: two CBBs associated with the *Deploy Phase* – these manage the deployment/roll out of the IT solution.

▶ Category D: two CBBs associated with *Adoption of Solution Delivery Methodologies* – these promote the organizational uptake of methods and practices to support solutions delivery.

These are described below, together with a summary of the different maturity levels for each.

Category A: CBBs Associated with the *Design Phase*

CBB A1: Requirements

Manage requirements and their traceability throughout the IT solutions delivery life cycle to serve business needs.

Level 1	Any requirements that are gathered are vaguely defined, are not well understood, and are limited, typically, to functional requirements.
Level 2	Defined methods for conducting interviews and workshops for eliciting functional and non-functional requirements are applied to a limited number of larger IT solutions development projects.
Level 3	A standardized method for eliciting requirements is applied to most IT solutions development projects.
Level 4	A comprehensive suite of methods and techniques for requirements gathering and analysis (for example, interviewing, prototyping, scenario generation, modelling, use cases, checklists, and so on) are consistently used for each IT solutions development project organization-wide.
Level 5	New and emerging innovative methods and techniques for requirements gathering and analysis are continually researched, regularly involving input from the relevant business ecosystem partners.

CBB A2: Design Conceptualization

Apply architecture principles and guidelines to inform the design of IT solutions to meet requirements.

Level 1 Design is performed in an informal or ad hoc manner. There are few or no standards in place – for example, just those relating to safety or tolerances.

Level 2 The IT function promotes a primary standard or criterion to control the design process – for example, scalability.

Level 3 A suite of common design standards (relating, for example, to safety and design tolerances) and criteria (relating, for example, to modularity, portability, scalability, and maintainability) are agreed between the IT function and some other business units.

Level 4 Compliance criteria are enforced organization-wide to ensure the selection of the most suitable design solution and compatibility with design architecture guidelines.

Level 5 New standards and techniques for design are continually evaluated for introduction into the solutions delivery life cycle. Regular insights gleaned from relevant business ecosystem partners are part of the evaluation.

Category B: CBBs Associated with the *Develop Phase*

CBB B1: Fabricate

Construct IT solutions based on design principles and standards – for example, multi-tier architecture, coding, and security.

Level 1 IT solutions are constructed on an informal or ad hoc basis, with little or no use of common principles or standards.

Level 2 Defined principles and standards for the construction of IT solutions are consistently applied to a limited number of projects.

Level 3 Standardized principles and standards for the construction of IT solutions are consistently applied to most projects within the IT function.

Level 4 A comprehensive set of principles and standards for the construction of IT solutions are consistently applied to virtually all projects across the organization.

Level 5 IT solution construction principles and standards are continually reviewed, benchmarked, and regularly informed by insights from relevant business ecosystem partners.

CBB B2: Test

Conduct validation testing to ensure that IT solutions meet specified requirements. This can include unit, integration, system, user acceptance, and regression testing.

Level 1	Little or no test planning occurs, with testing carried out on an ad hoc basis, if at all.
Level 2	Testing activities are managed within the IT function, with test cases normally developed after the IT solutions are implemented. A growing emphasis is placed on ensuring that adequate test resources are available.
Level 3	The IT function promotes multi-level testing – for example, unit, integration, system, and acceptance test levels with regression testing. Testing is performed in accordance with an agreed test strategy, identifying the test levels to be performed and the independence required between development and testing.
Level 4	Testing is performed consistently organization-wide in accordance with an agreed life cycle model, with test planning and control, test analysis, test design, and test execution perceived as distinct testing phases. A comprehensive set of test measures is captured and analysed to track progress and the quality of testing.
Level 5	Testing is continually monitored and optimized organization-wide, includes regular input from relevant business ecosystem partners, and consists of all life cycle activities concerned with the checking of IT solutions. Actions can be swiftly taken to remedy any deviations that begin to occur.

Category C: CBBs Associated with the *Deploy Phase*

CBB C1: Release Management

Manage the deployment of IT solutions into the operational environment.

Level 1	No formal release management approach is in place. Solutions are deployed in an uncontrolled, disorganized manner.
Level 2	Releases occur using basic procedures that are not yet consistently applied – for example, limited evaluations of proposed changes occur but without involvement of all relevant stakeholders, or most proposed changes are recorded but not in a standardized manner.
Level 3	There is a standardized release management approach for most releases, with validated release procedures and templates. The potential impact of releases is consistently evaluated and involves stakeholders from both the IT function and a growing number of other affected business units.
Level 4	All releases are comprehensively managed and deployed in alignment with an organization-wide version control approach, where changes are assessed for their positive/negative impact and prioritized accordingly.
Level 5	Release management approaches are continually improved to allow the seamless flow of new IT solutions into the operational environment.

CBB C2: Version Control

Manage the control of versions that occur during the solution's delivery life cycle using appropriate methods – for example, methods for initiating, defining, evaluating, and approving/disapproving proposed changes.

Level 1   Any version control that occurs during the solution's delivery life cycle is informal or ad hoc.

Level 2   Defined version control approaches are in place for a limited number of larger projects. Revision histories for changes may not be maintained consistently.

Level 3   A standardized version control approach is in place for most projects. Most revision histories are recorded in a consistent manner.

Level 4   Organization-wide tools (for example, for recording change requests, decision-making, and revision history) support the version control approach. All relevant stakeholders affected by changes are involved as necessary.

Level 5   The version control approach is continually reviewed and improved, and regularly includes input from the relevant business ecosystem partners.

Category D: CBBs Associated with *Adoption of Solutions Delivery Methodologies*

CBB D1: Methods and Practices

Ensure the availability and use of IT solutions delivery methods and practices – for example, requirements management, configuration management, and release management.

Level 1   There may be methods and practices in place, but they are seldom used and are normally abandoned in times of crisis. Compliance monitoring is not a regular activity and is usually only instigated on failure of delivery.

Level 2   Defined solutions delivery methods and practices are beginning to emerge for a limited number of projects. There is some compliance monitoring, but use of it still varies across projects.

Level 3   Standardized methods and practices are in place for most projects across their solutions delivery life cycle. Compliance monitoring is growing.

Level 4   Comprehensive and flexible methods and practices are in place for all projects across their solutions delivery life cycle. End-to-end compliance monitoring occurs with necessary corrective action taken as required.

Level 5   Continual compliance monitoring ensures that available methods and practices remain fit for purpose.

CBB D2: Practice Evolution

Evolve IT solutions delivery approaches and methodologies in response to business needs and in line with industry practices.

Level 1   No continual improvement initiatives are in place. Lessons learned and deficiencies are seldom captured.

Level 2   Basic continual improvement efforts are emerging where basic lessons learned are captured; however, there is likely to be fragmented implementation of new/improved approaches across parts of the IT function.

Level 3   A continual improvement programme is in place by which lessons are captured and improvements/deficiencies are consistently identified. The implementation of new/improved approaches is more consistent across the IT function.

Level 4   Commitment and resources are obtained from all relevant stakeholders organization-wide to ensure all improvements are comprehensively implemented.

Level 5   Continual practice evolution is based on a blended use of quantitative measures of performance and qualitative input obtained from continual improvement initiatives, from industry benchmarking, and from relevant business ecosystem partners.

28.4 IMPROVEMENT PLANNING

Capability Evaluation

Two summary assessment questions are set out below, along with the typical response associated with each level of maturity.

To what extent are IT solutions development approaches in place across requirements gathering, design, building, testing, and deployment/release?

Level 1   Any development approaches in place for solutions delivery are informal and (typically) are inconsistently applied.

Level 2   Basic development approaches for solutions delivery are emerging in limited areas of the IT function.

Level 3   Standardized development approaches are in place across the IT function and are consistently used for most projects during their solutions delivery life cycle.

Level 4   Comprehensive development approaches for solutions delivery are adopted organization-wide and consistently used.

Level 5   The development approaches for solutions delivery are continually reviewed based on past performance and regular input from relevant business ecosystem partners.

How is the governance of IT solutions development managed?

Level 1   Any governance of IT solutions development is largely informal and ad hoc in nature.

Level 2   Basic governance is in place for a limited number of IT solutions development projects.

Level 3   A standardized governance approach is applied to most IT solutions development projects across the IT function.

Level 4   There is a comprehensive governance approach organization-wide and it is applied to all IT solutions development projects.

Level 5   The governance approach is continually reviewed to establish its fitness for purpose and alignment with the latest proven approaches.

Key Practices-Outcomes-Metrics (POMs)

Some useful POMs for developing the Solutions Delivery (SD) capability are summarized below.

Level 2 POMs

Practice	Elicit functional and non-functional requirements in a suitable format through, for example, qualitative data collection techniques such as interviews and workshops.
Outcome	Requirements are documented and stored in a format that ensures they are clear, correct, unambiguous, and testable.
Metric	Number of requirements specified in desired formats.
Practice	Prioritize and define implementation standards – for example, coding standards and integration standards.
Outcome	Agreement on appropriate guidelines is reached in advance to ensure that the solutions design adequately satisfies all system requirements.
Metric	Percentage of applicable design guidelines correctly implemented by project.
Practice	Define and agree testing procedures.
Outcome	Ability to perform testing in accordance with agreed testing procedures will help to improve the appropriateness and effectiveness of the testing performed.
Metric	Number of solutions where agreed testing procedures are used during the testing process.
Practice	Identify and agree a formal release management approach with procedures and templates for releases.
Outcome	A release schedule that specifies the date of each release is in place.
Metric	Percentage of releases performed in accordance with the defined release management approach.

Practice	Define and agree core elements of solutions delivery processes – for example, requirements management, design, building, testing, and configuration management processes.
Outcome	Stable processes are provided to support delivery of appropriate IT solutions. These processes help to ensure consistency in the approach used to deliver solutions and prevent the need to create processes from scratch for each solution delivered.
Metric	Number of processes that are defined and agreed.

Level 3 POMs

Practice	Promote involvement of relevant stakeholders in analysing business requirements and converting them into an agreed set of system requirements. Include relevant business and user representatives as well as representatives from those areas responsible for design, development, testing, deployment, and maintenance of the proposed solution.
Outcome	This helps to ensure that a complete set of functional and non-functional requirements is accurately specified, and the quality of the proposed IT solution is improved.
Metric	Percentage of relevant stakeholders participating in requirements specification.
Practice	Agree a test strategy that identifies the test levels to be performed. For each test level (for example, those that relate to unit, integration, system, and user acceptance), clearly specify the defined objectives, scope, and assigned responsibilities.
Outcome	The test strategy is the starting point for testing. Test levels are unambiguously defined, and this reduces the likelihood of overlap between the test levels and leads to a more efficient test process.
Metric	Percentage of IT solutions delivered in accordance with a test strategy.
Practice	Agree criteria for selecting an appropriate solutions delivery life cycle model – for example, those that might apply to waterfall, incremental, or agile models.
Outcome	Appropriate life cycle models are considered, allowing pros and cons to be objectively considered, so that the best outcome can be delivered.
Metric	Percentage of projects that use suitable life cycle models.
Practice	Ensure key stakeholders are allocated appropriate levels of authority for evaluating, and approving or rejecting proposed changes to IT solutions.
Outcome	Releases are appropriately governed and controlled.
Metric	Percentage of changes evaluated that had involvement from necessary stakeholders.

Practice	Establish and maintain the test environments within which the necessary testing can be carried out prior to implementation.
Outcome	Stable test environments are provided for each level of testing, ensuring the separation of development, system, and user testing environments.
Metric	Percentage of releases tested in correct test environments prior to release.

Level 4 POMs

Practice	Implement methods to facilitate the tracing of requirements from their source to design, implementation, and testing (in both directions).
Outcome	Methods are available to enable requirements to be traced in both directions throughout the solutions delivery life cycle, thereby enabling the validation of specified requirements by relevant users.
Metric	Percentage of requirements traceability methods that support bi-directional traceability throughout the full solutions delivery life cycle.

Practice	Expand the portfolio of design methods – for example, these could include prototypes, structural models, design thinking, design reuse, design patterns, and entity relationship models.
Outcome	The quality of designs is enhanced, productivity is improved, and the likelihood of errors and rework downstream is reduced.
Metric	Number of effective design methods used.

Practice	Fully integrate release management and version control processes.
Outcome	The delivery of IT solutions into the operational environment is improved.
Metric	Percentage of version control and release activities that are integrated.

Practice	Promote integrated tools that can assist in the execution of solutions delivery processes – for example, these could include requirements modelling, test automation, defect management, and measurement capture, storage, and analysis.
Outcome	Greater levels of productivity can be supported, and errors can be reduced.
Metric	Percentage of processes supported by integrated tools.

Practice	Measure the performance of the solutions delivery processes against specific targets and KPIs.
Outcome	Transparency is increased and process predictability is improved.
Metric	Percentage of solutions delivery processes that have specific targets and KPIs.

Level 5 POMs

Practice	Investigate innovative methods and techniques for requirements gathering, analysis, design, development, and deployment of solutions on a continual basis.
Outcome	The quality of IT solutions benefits from the latest proven practices.
Metric	Number of innovative methods and techniques introduced into the solutions delivery processes.

Practice	Continually monitor and optimize testing in accordance with test plans. Mandate that all testing activities conform to an organization-wide test strategy.
Outcome	All test processes, scripts, tools, and environments support optimization of testing. Actions are taken without delay if any deviations are found during testing.
Metric	Number of IT solutions where testing is continually monitored in accordance with test plans. Percentage of testing activities that adhere to a test strategy.
Practice	Mandate a continual improvement programme by which deficiencies in approaches are identified and improvements are implemented through incremental and innovative change.
Outcome	Approaches are reviewed and adapted consistently in an effective and efficient manner.
Metric	Percentage of improvement requests that are reviewed and implemented.
Practice	Continually analyse and review performance measures relating to the solutions delivery processes. Feed information back into a continual improvement and benchmarking initiative.
Outcome	The performance of solutions delivery processes is objectively evaluated. Corrective and preventative actions can be taken to optimize these processes.
Metric	Frequency of review of performance measures relating to the solutions delivery processes.

Addressing Typical Challenges

Some typical challenges that can arise in attempting to develop maturity in the Solutions Delivery (SD) capability are set out below.

Challenge	IT solutions fail to satisfy users' needs or are considered not fit-for-purpose.
Context	Requirements gathering does not gather input from relevant stakeholders or adequately reflect their inputs.
Action	Raise awareness among senior management of the importance of adopting a robust process for requirements gathering, one in which the needs of all users, from both the IT function and the rest of the business, are gathered and clearly understood.
Challenge	Some of the solutions delivered are not stable, maintainable, or upgradeable.
Context	There are no common design standards in place to provide guidance on issues such as safety and design tolerances; and criteria such as modularity, portability, scalability, maintainability, and organization architecture are not considered in advance.
Action	Highlight to senior management the importance of identifying and agreeing applicable design standards in advance of developing IT solutions.

Challenge	The development and delivery of major IT solutions are often abandoned as management loses confidence midway through the project that it can deliver the desired outcomes.
Context	When a robust solutions delivery process is not considered and agreed in advance, the project is likely to be beset by poor understanding of requirements and ineffective use of resources, leading to a solution that does not address the needs of users, or is terminated before completion.
Action	Stimulate senior management discussion on the importance of a robust solutions delivery process to increase project success rates.
Challenge	Lack of a formal organizational test strategy.
Context	General awareness of the importance of a robust test strategy is often lacking. Some testing may be undertaken but this is often limited to such things as functional testing, and other areas such as user testing are often overlooked.
Action	Initiate an awareness campaign on the importance of adopting a robust test strategy before the IT solution is released.
Challenge	Scope creep and constantly shifting requirements make it more difficult to deliver against defined project objectives.
Context	Scope creep and shifting requirements can often arise from poor change control approaches, from lack of proper initial identification of what is required, from a weak project manager or executive sponsor, or from poor communication between parties.
Action	Stimulate discussion among senior management on the value of adopting a formal version control process across the solutions delivery life cycle and of allocating responsibility for this activity.

Management Artefacts

Management artefacts that may be used to develop maturity in the Solutions Delivery (SD) capability include:

▸ Solutions development methodologies.
▸ A systems requirements log.
▸ A functional and non-functional requirements log.

Solutions Development Methodologies

IT solutions development methodologies are accepted practices for producing high quality systems that meet or exceed customer expectations (based on their requirements). These include agile methodologies (such as XP and Scrum), iterative methodologies (such as Rational Unified Process and Dynamic Systems Development Method), and sequential methodologies (such as waterfall). Each methodology specifies different practices and supporting templates to manage systems through clearly defined phases, such as:

▸ Project Planning.
▸ Requirements and Specification.
▸ Architecture and Design.
▸ Programming and Testing.
▸ Deployment and Installation.
▸ Operations and Support.

Among the factors that might determine the choice between agile, iterative, and sequential methodologies are:

▸ The type of project – for example, a minor upgrade of an existing solution versus a brand new system built from scratch.
▸ Upfront clarity on project requirements.
▸ Level of client involvement.
▸ Project size and complexity.
▸ Level of integration with existing systems.
▸ Tolerance for scope and cost changes.
▸ Time to market.
▸ Location of project teams, including their cultural backgrounds, linguistic abilities, and time zones.

After the basic methodology is chosen, it is sometimes adapted to fit better with the project goals and organizational context.

Systems Requirements Log

The purpose of a systems requirements log is to enable business analysts to capture the user's expectations of the required IT solution and how it will solve the user's problem or achieve a particular objective. Business analysts typically meet with system owners, users, and project stakeholders to define the IT solution's context of use. They may use methods and techniques such as interviewing, direct observation, prototyping, scenario generation, modelling, use cases, and so on to elicit and validate user requirements. The systems requirements log forms the basis for estimating project costs and scheduling, and a reference for validating the IT solution during testing and peer reviews in advance of the IT solution's formal release. It is a useful artefact to help ensure that a project remains under control and within budget.

Functional and Non-Functional Requirements Log

Once the systems requirements log is approved, the next step is to define the internal workings of the IT solution, typically in the form of functional and non-functional requirements.

Functional Requirements

Functional requirements specify a behaviour or function, what the system should do – for example, 'add customer' or 'print invoice'. Some of the more typical functional requirements include:

▸ Business rules and administrative functions.
▸ Transaction corrections, adjustments, and cancellations.
▸ Authentication, authorization levels, and audit tracking.
▸ External interfaces and certification requirements.
▸ Reporting requirements, and legal or regulatory requirements.

Non-functional Requirements

Non-functional requirements describe how the system works, how it should behave, or its quality characteristics. Non-functional requirements specify criteria that judge the operation of a system, rather than specific behaviours – for example, 'Modified data in a database should be updated for all users accessing it within 2 seconds'. Some typical non-functional requirements are:

▸ Performance – for example, response time.
▸ Availability, reliability, recoverability.
▸ Manageability – for example, maintainability, serviceability, interoperability, scalability, capacity.
▸ Security, regulatory, data integrity.
▸ Usability.

28.5 REFERENCE

See Also

Other capabilities of IT-CMF that have a particularly close relationship with the Solutions Delivery (SD) capability include:

Capability	What it provides
03. Business Process Management (BPM)	Understanding of the underlying business process context that a proposed IT solution may have to comprehend
06. Enterprise Information Management (EIM)	Details on the quality of information that the development of a proposed IT solution may have to comprehend
09. IT Leadership and Governance (ITG)	Guidance on governance to inform stakeholder and requirements management
20. Enterprise Architecture Management (EAM)	Architectural principles and designs for informing the software architecture design
21. Information Security Management (ISM)	Security policies that IT solutions development methodologies may have to incorporate
24. Programme and Project Management (PPM)	Appropriate project delivery methodologies to support the IT solutions development process
26. Research, Development and Engineering (RDE)	Details on the investigation and validation of new technologies
30. Technical Infrastructure Management (TIM)	The underlying computing infrastructure to develop IT solutions
31. User Experience Design (UED)	In-depth analysis of usability and user preferences
33. Benefits Assessment and Realization (BAR)	A validated business case to justify proposed IT solutions

Further Reading

Capability Maturity Model Integration Institute (CMMI-I), 2013. Get started – begin your CMMI journey. Available at: <http://cmmiinstitute.com/get-started>.

Isaias, P., and Issa, T., 2014. *High level models and methodologies for information systems*. New York, NY: Springer.

Larman, C., 2003. *Agile and iterative development*. Boston, MA: Addison Wesley.

Meyer, B., 2014. *Agile: the good, the hype, and the ugly*. Cham, CH: Springer.

Notes

[1] Office of the Chief Information Officer (OCIO, Newfoundland Labrador, Canada), 2014. Solution delivery framework. Available at: <http://www.ocio.gov.nl.ca/ocio/pmo/sdf.html>.

SUM
29. Supplier Management

29.1 OVERVIEW

Goal

The Supplier Management (SUM) capability aims to manage interactions between the IT function and its suppliers.

Objectives

▸ Translate the sourcing strategy into supplier performance objectives and relationship management activities.

▸ Strike an appropriate balance between cost efficiency and supply/service quality.

▸ Foster collaboration, trust, empathy, open communication, and a desire for mutual benefit to encourage co-innovation with preferred suppliers.

▸ Ensure the integrity of supplier performance monitoring.

▸ Identify constraints and scope for manoeuvre when (re)negotiating supplier contracts.

▸ Use suppliers' expertise and innovation to support and inform the IT services' development roadmap.

▸ Engage proactively with suppliers to resolve incidents, problems, or poor performance.

▸ Manage supply risks across the portfolio of suppliers.

Value

The Supplier Management (SUM) capability helps the IT function to build cooperative relationships with its suppliers, with a view to optimizing costs, creating shared value, and reducing supply-related risks.

Relevance

After the IT sourcing strategy has been defined and the suppliers have been selected, the relationships with the suppliers have to be managed. Failure to manage these relationships can result in adversarial interactions with the suppliers. Managing them effectively can result in collaborative partnerships that reduce costs and risks, and create opportunities for joint innovation and value creation [1].

By developing a Supplier Management (SUM) capability, an organization can have an effective approach to supplier management in which individual behaviours and organizational practices are fair, open, and honest, so that the business and operational interests of both the organization and its suppliers mutually respect each other. Ultimately, the organization can build trust and create an environment in which the organization and its suppliers collaborate to their mutual benefit.

29.2 SCOPE

Definition

The Supplier Management (SUM) capability is the ability of the IT function to manage interactions with its suppliers in line with the sourcing strategy. The Supplier Management (SUM) capability covers:

▶ Developing relationships with suppliers to improve levels of performance, quality, and innovation.

▶ Managing risks associated with the organization's use of outside suppliers.

▶ Validating that suppliers' performance is in accordance with contract terms.

▶ Facilitating lines of communication with suppliers.

▶ Managing procurement activities with suppliers.

▶ Building two-way performance evaluation between the IT function and its suppliers.

Other Capabilities

The following are addressed by other capabilities of IT-CMF:

For...	Refer to...
Carrying out organizational design activities so as to streamline engagement interfaces	10. Organization Design and Planning (ODP)
Establishing risk management practices for IT-related risks	11. Risk Management (RM)
Managing all strategic sourcing decisions, selecting IT service suppliers, and migrating IT services	13. Sourcing (SRC)

29.3 UNDERSTANDING MATURITY

Recognizing Excellence

When the Supplier Management (SUM) capability is well-developed or mature:

▸ Relationship objectives and contractual deliverables between the organization and its suppliers are consistently met.

▸ Robust and efficient communication with suppliers ensures that disagreements are resolved through collaborative and creative problem-solving, rather than coercion.

▸ Conflicts and tensions are raised at an early stage, with clear escalation paths (within both organizations) for discussing and resolving them.

▸ Preferred suppliers treat the organization as a priority customer, for example by offering preferential pricing, early exposure to innovative products and services, or ideas to promote continual improvement.

▸ There is a high degree of trust, mutual understanding, empathy, and respect between the organization and its suppliers.

▸ Opportunities for improving the cost-effectiveness and innovation of services delivered by suppliers are regularly explored and progressed.

▸ Risks associated with the continuity and integrity of supply are effectively managed.

Maturity at the Critical Capability Level

The following statements provide a high-level overview of the Supplier Management (SUM) capability at successive levels of maturity:

Level 1   Suppliers are typically viewed as utility providers, with only ad hoc monitoring of their performance. There is a limited supplier engagement model, if any, and limited opportunities for supplier development.

Level 2   A defined supplier engagement model is in place for a limited number of key suppliers. Supplier monitoring is primarily based on performance to cost criteria, but may also occasionally include some tactical supplier development opportunities.

Level 3   A standardized supplier engagement model is in place covering most suppliers, significantly reducing exposure to supplier risk. Monitoring goes beyond managing supplier performance to costs, and increasingly fosters supplier development opportunities.

Level 4   The supplier engagement model covers all suppliers, and facilitates tailored engagement with preferred suppliers. Supplier performance is consistently monitored and developed to facilitate innovation.

Level 5   The supplier engagement model and monitoring of supplier performance are continually reviewed and improved to maintain innovation across the supply chain. The organization is considered a priority customer by its preferred suppliers.

Maturity at the Capability Building Block (CBB) Level

The Capability Building Blocks (CBBs) associated with the Supplier Management (SUM) capability fall into three categories:

▶ Category A: two CBBs associated with **Supplier Alignment** – these are used to manage engagement and communication with suppliers.

▶ Category B: three CBBs associated with **Supplier Operations** – these are used to manage orders and contracts, and to co-develop supplier capabilities.

▶ Category C: two CBBs associated with **Performance and Risk Monitoring** – these are used to measure, monitor, and manage risks and performance.

These are described below, together with a summary of the different maturity levels for each.

Category A: CBBs Associated with *Supplier Alignment*

CBB A1: Supplier Engagement

Define and manage the supplier engagement model to be adopted with suppliers.

Level 1	There is an ad hoc approach to supplier engagement, if any.
Level 2	A defined supplier engagement model is in place for a limited number of key suppliers, primarily focusing on performance in relation to cost. The relationship, however, is rarely grounded in mutual trust, so that if things go wrong, time and energy can be wasted in assigning blame, rather than addressing the issue.
Level 3	A standardized supplier engagement model is in place covering most suppliers. If things go wrong, interactions are primarily solution-driven rather than fault-driven. Resolving problems is treated as a joint responsibility. Open knowledge sharing results in increasing levels of trust.
Level 4	A comprehensive supplier engagement model covers all suppliers, and facilitates tailored engagement with preferred suppliers. Engagement is focused on meeting both parties' needs in a sustainable way, with mutually beneficial outcomes, and high levels of trust.
Level 5	The supplier engagement model is continually reviewed to ensure that innovative partnerships are established and maintained. Tailored supplier engagement ensures optimal allocation of management time and resources.

CBB A2: Supplier Communications

Plan, manage, and execute the exchange of information that may be useful to both the organization and the supplier.

Level 1 Any information exchange is ad hoc and limited, due to lack of trust between the parties.

Level 2 Information exchange protocols are defined for a limited number of suppliers. These may include, for example, performance criteria, common vocabulary, nominated contact lists, roles and responsibilities, standardized documentation, and escalation paths.

Level 3 Information exchange protocols are standardized for most suppliers. Sensitive information is beginning to be shared more openly with preferred suppliers to enhance levels of mutual trust and commitment.

Level 4 Comprehensive information exchange protocols are in place, covering all suppliers. Important (even proprietary) information is shared willingly with preferred suppliers, such as jointly providing demand and supply forecasts, co-involvement in product design, or sharing of cost information.

Level 5 Information exchange protocols cover the extended supply chain and are continually reviewed. Senior executives meet regularly with their counterparts in supplier organizations to review their respective behaviours and to jointly devise improvements.

Category B: CBBs Associated with *Supplier Operations*

CBB B1: Order and Fulfilment Management

Manage interactions with suppliers so as to facilitate procurement and service delivery.

Level 1 Any interaction with suppliers is ad hoc. Operating and switching costs are a major concern for the IT function.

Level 2 Common order and fulfilment practices are emerging for a limited number of suppliers. Operating and switching costs are beginning to reduce, but remain a concern.

Level 3 Standardized order and fulfilment practices are in place, facilitating similar operational practices across most suppliers. Operating and switching costs continue to decrease.

Level 4 Comprehensive order and fulfilment practices are in place for all suppliers, and allow for tailored practices within defined threshold tolerances for preferred suppliers in order to encourage innovation. Operating and switching costs are of low concern.

Level 5 Order and fulfilment practices are continually reviewed to maintain high levels of efficiency and innovation, while minimizing switching costs for both parties.

CBB B2: Contract Compliance

Manage the obligations and responsibilities of both parties (as specified in the contract) to avoid or address incidents of non-compliance.

Level 1	Management of contract compliance is ad hoc and typically adversarial in nature.
Level 2	Management of contract compliance focuses primarily on negative reinforcement, such as penalties for missing minimum performance thresholds.
Level 3	Management of contract compliance increasingly focuses on positive reinforcement – for example, incentivizing quality and performance in excess of minimum thresholds.
Level 4	Management of contract compliance responds flexibly to changing conditions, encouraging and rewarding spontaneous innovation.
Level 5	Management of contract compliance is non-antagonistic, and is continually reviewed to ensure that it continues to support innovation and collaboration.

CBB B3: Supplier Development

Work with suppliers to identify opportunities for mutually beneficial development, such as by adapting processes and products/services, improving performance levels, co-investing in research and development, joint marketing activities, or temporarily exchanging or transferring staff.

Level 1	Practices for developing suppliers are non-existent or ad hoc.
Level 2	Defined supplier development practices are emerging for a limited number of suppliers. These are typically introduced in response to incidents.
Level 3	Standardized supplier development practices are in place for most suppliers, focused on monitoring performance in accordance with service level agreements.
Level 4	Comprehensive supplier development practices are in place for all suppliers. The procuring organization's IT services development roadmap is supported and influenced by IT suppliers' innovative capabilities. The organization and the suppliers equitably share the risks associated with adapting processes and products/services.
Level 5	Supplier development practices are continually reviewed to reinforce collaboration, innovation, and shared objectives.

Category C: CBBs Associated with *Performance and Risk Monitoring*

CBB C1: Continuity of Supply

Manage risks associated with the continuity of supply from external sources.

Level 1	Any continuity and integrity of supply risk evaluations are ad hoc. Any contingency plans regarding alternative sources of supply are also ad hoc.
Level 2	Continuity and integrity of supply risks are beginning to be evaluated, typically with a focus on tactical risks, such as variances in supply availability and/or quality, price inflation, or the impact of legislative changes. For a limited number of suppliers, a contingency plan is beginning to be defined for switching to alternative sources.
Level 3	Continuity and integrity of supply risk evaluations include addressing operational risks, such as over-dependence on key suppliers, service discontinuation, proprietary methods underpinning services, switching-costs, and vendor lock-in. There are contingency plans in place for most products and services should original supply be compromised.
Level 4	Continuity and integrity of supply risk evaluations include addressing increasingly more strategic objectives, such as information-sharing/collaboration, supplier innovation, evolution of supplier rivals, and the impact of discontinuous innovations. There are comprehensive contingency plans in place for all products and services to transition to alternative suppliers should the need arise.
Level 5	Continuity and integrity of supply risk evaluations and contingency plans are continually reviewed and take the extended supply chain into consideration where appropriate.

CBB C2: Performance Measurement and Monitoring

Manage key performance indicators (KPIs) to inform decision-making in relation to supplier management.

Level 1	If there is any monitoring of supplier performance, it tends to be ad hoc and reactive.
Level 2	Basic performance measures (such as service availability) are defined and occasionally reported. Corrective action is occasionally triggered.
Level 3	Critical performance measures (such as quality, performance, and qualitative feedback) are standardized and periodically reported. Corrective action is usually taken, but not always.
Level 4	The suite of performance measures is extended to include non-contractual items (such as relationship trust, goodwill, innovativeness, adaptability). Corrective action is virtually always taken.
Level 5	Management of performance measures is continually reviewed, and improved based on feedback and lessons learned.

29.4 IMPROVEMENT PLANNING

Capability Evaluation

Two summary assessment questions are set out below, along with the typical response associated with each level of maturity.

To what extent are supplier relationships managed to create shared value?

Level 1	Supplier relationship management is non-existent or ad hoc.
Level 2	Supplier relationship management strategies are emerging, primarily focused on satisfying the objectives of the procuring organization, sometimes resulting in adversarial, win-lose relationships.
Level 3	Supplier relationship management strategies are standardized for most suppliers, and building shared value is increasingly sought with a limited number of preferred suppliers.
Level 4	Supplier relationship management strategies are comprehensively implemented for all suppliers, with advanced strategies for developing shared value with all preferred suppliers.
Level 5	Supplier relationship management strategies are continually reviewed to ensure that they continue to maximize shared value.

How are contracts managed across the supplier base?

Level 1	Contract management approaches are non-existent or ad hoc.
Level 2	Basic contract management approaches are in place for a limited number of suppliers, primarily focused on penalizing suppliers for poor performance.
Level 3	Standardized contract management approaches are in place for most suppliers, increasingly focused on rewarding performance excellence.
Level 4	Comprehensive contract management approaches are in place for all suppliers, focused on supplier collaboration and innovation.
Level 5	Contract management approaches are continually reviewed to identify improvement opportunities.

Key Practices-Outcomes-Metrics (POMs)

Some useful POMs for developing the Supplier Management (SUM) capability are summarized below.

Level 2 POMs

Practice	Define the supplier engagement model to include, for example, contact points, escalation procedures, the frequency of operational and strategic planning and review meetings, and a description of roles and responsibilities.
Outcome	Interactions are more efficient, and problems and conflicts can be more easily resolved.
Metric	Percentage of supplier relationships managed using the defined supplier engagement model.

Practice	Implement processes for ensuring efficient interaction with suppliers on procurement, status tracking, fulfilment, and so on.
Outcome	The operational costs and errors associated with interacting with suppliers are reduced.
Metric	Percentage of suppliers following the defined processes.
Practice	Hold regular performance review meetings with suppliers – for example, in relation to service quality, change management, and incident and problem management.
Outcome	Better understanding of performance is promoted across both parties. Conflicts and tensions are identified and dealt with early.
Metric	Percentage of suppliers with whom regular reviews are held. Number of problems identified early (before significant costs are incurred) and resolved effectively.
Practice	Provide remedial training courses or workshops for suppliers in response to major incidents.
Outcome	The risk of major incidents recurring can be minimized.
Metric	Number of major incidents recurring. Number of remedial training courses or workshops delivered.
Practice	Define contingency plans for alternative sources of supply, in case the existing supply base is compromised.
Outcome	The time required to switch to alternative sources, if required, is reduced.
Metric	Percentage of contracts for which alternative sources have been identified.

Level 3 POMs

Practice	Implement a supplier segmentation policy covering, for example, spend, business criticality of services, strategic importance, complexity/frequency of changes in requirements, and switching costs.
Outcome	Relationship management can be effectively focused on prioritized and preferred suppliers.
Metric	Percentage of the supply base that is segmented.
Practice	Assign relationship manager or supplier account manager roles for preferred suppliers.
Outcome	There is greater potential for idea-sharing, and a reduction in information bottlenecks. Issues can be understood increasingly from the supplier's point of view, while communicating the procuring organization's own requirements and priorities.
Metric	Percentage of preferred suppliers for whom relationship managers or supplier account managers have been assigned. Number of major incidents with suppliers.

Practice	Regularly benchmark all key supplier contracts against alternative suppliers using standardized criteria.
Outcome	Suppliers are continually encouraged to improve in order to meet or exceed industry standards.
Metric	Percentage of contracts that are benchmarked externally. Percentage of suppliers showing performance improvements.
Practice	Track the performance of individual suppliers using transparent performance tracking methods.
Outcome	Poor performing suppliers can be identified and encouraged to improve.
Metric	Percentage of suppliers that meet performance objectives.
Practice	With preferred suppliers, seek opportunities for mutually beneficial interactions (other than traditional buy-sell transactions), such as joint product development.
Outcome	The innovative capabilities of suppliers can be harnessed to create product and service offerings that are ideally suited to the business.
Metric	Number of active project collaborations with suppliers. Business value delivered to the organization through supplier project collaborations.

Level 4 POMs

Practice	Invite suppliers to send a representative to the organization's strategic and operational meetings, and arrange for reciprocal representation at their meetings.
Outcome	Greater levels of understanding and empathy are fostered between the organization and its suppliers. Opportunities for innovation are more readily identified.
Metric	Percentage of relevant in-house meetings attended by suppliers. Number of supplier meetings at which the organization is represented.
Practice	Ensure that there are inter-supplier Operational Level Agreements (OLAs) in place across the supply chain for business critical services.
Outcome	There is increased confidence in the continuity and integrity of service supply.
Metric	Percentage of business critical services with OLAs in place.
Practice	Ensure supplier management practices are harmonized across all suppliers organization-wide, using, for example, supplier segmentation, customer/supplier perception surveys, performance scorecards, improvement charters, structured meeting templates, and benefits tracking tools.
Outcome	Relationship management becomes more cost effective, while knowledge sharing and collaboration are encouraged across the organization.
Metric	Percentage of suppliers managed using harmonized practices.

Practice	Establish guidelines for fostering collaborative relationships with preferred suppliers.
Outcome	Innovative partnerships are systematically created.
Metric	Number of product/service innovations arising from collaboration with suppliers.

Practice	Collate relationship management feedback across the supplier base.
Outcome	The supplier base can be managed holistically, rather than in silos, so that recurring issues can be dealt with efficiently.
Metric	Percentage of suppliers for whom relationship management feedback is collated centrally.

Level 5 POMs

Practice	Continually review suppliers for switching flexibility and redundancy in their products and services.
Outcome	Vulnerability and exposure to supply disruptions can be reduced.
Metric	Duration since a review was conducted for switching flexibility and redundancy in suppliers' products and services.

Practice	Regularly benchmark relationship management practices and performance by comparing with peer organizations.
Outcome	The ability to identify opportunities for improvement is enhanced.
Metric	Number of practices benchmarked.

Practice	Implement a strategic development programme for key suppliers.
Outcome	In the longer term, mutually beneficial relations can be established with suppliers.
Metric	Key supplier turnover rate. Number of suppliers that identify the organization as a priority customer.

Addressing Typical Challenges

Some typical challenges that can arise in attempting to develop maturity in the Supplier Management (SUM) capability are set out below.

Challenge	Relationships with suppliers are primarily adversarial in nature.
Context	An exclusive focus on minimum price delivery can create adversarial relationships, and limit the possibilities for collaboration.
Action	Formalize and communicate guidelines to encourage more open information flow and advocacy between the organization and its suppliers, to promote higher levels of trust and collaboration.

Challenge	Supplier management activities incur high overhead costs.
Context	With a large, heterogeneous supplier base, it can be challenging to monitor performance and remedy underperformance.
Action	Use a central system to hold all suppliers accountable to their individual service level agreements. Such a system enables all parties to view the same data, and facilitates collaborative identification and improvement of problem processes or business activities.
Challenge	One-sided control mechanisms over suppliers creates an atmosphere of mutual distrust and of divergent interests.
Context	Supplier relationships are characterized by measures and controls dominated by the procuring organization, and are not designed to produce mutual benefit.
Action	Discuss with stakeholders the merits of two-way measurement mechanisms and a balanced scorecard to encourage commitment by both parties to agree to shared performance indicators.
Challenge	The organization lacks the skills necessary for managing suppliers.
Context	Supplier management is often assigned to individuals with procurement responsibilities. However, building and managing partnerships often requires different skills from those associated with negotiating price and contracts.
Action	Discuss with stakeholders the need to shift focus from traditional buying practices towards relationship management practices. The shift in focus should be reflected in the time allocated to such activities and in training programmes, and should be integrated into performance appraisals.
Challenge	Inflexible contracts stifle collaboration with and innovation by suppliers.
Context	An over-emphasis on removing ambiguity during contractual negotiations often reduces opportunities for innovation during the contract's lifetime. This results in the supplier's potential to add value being neglected in favour of short-term gains.
Action	Work with stakeholders to ensure contracts allow for supplier performance on non-price differentiators, such as product/service innovation, joint collaboration, or influence on IT service development roadmaps.

Management Artefacts

Management artefacts that may be used to develop maturity in the Supplier Management (SUM) capability include:

- Supplier relationship management systems.
- Supplier management balanced scorecards.
- Service level agreements (SLAs).
- Operational level agreements (OLAs).

Supplier Relationship Management Systems

Supplier relationship management systems can facilitate the planning and management of activities such as performance reviews, supplier development, and remedial actions. They can be used to examine and forecast purchasing behaviour, and to shorten procurement cycles.

These systems facilitate training and access to standardized tools and templates across the organization, while reducing reliance on non-standard practices and tools developed by individuals. They provide a single view of supplier relationships, enabling relevant people to access a common and consistent repository of information, and they facilitate a common understanding of the status of current relationship activities. They can also be used to manage and audit supplier relationships, by providing access to consistent reports of supplier performance and other relationship factors, such as risk and resource allocation.

Supplier Management Balanced Scorecards

The objective of a supplier management balanced scorecard is to comprehensively characterize the customer-supplier performance and to identify the potential for a long-term relationship based on value added. A balanced scorecard approach adds strategic non-financial performance measures to traditional cost metrics, and includes performance measures from the supplier's perspective to provide a more 'balanced' view of the customer-supplier relationship and create joint ownership of performance outcomes. In defining what metrics to track, it is recommended to identify the five or six critical or catalytic criteria that have most influence on customer-supplier performance.

Service Level Agreements (SLAs)

A service level agreement provides a formalized record of the customer's expectations from the supplier regarding the level of service, and the penalties that may apply if the expected service is not delivered (and/or the rewards if expectations are exceeded). Typically, it can include:

- A general definition of the service to be provided.
- Service level measurement methods for response time, availability, and so on.
- Remedies or penalties if service levels are not achieved.
- Incentives for exceeding expectations.
- Responsibilities of each party – for example, support and escalation procedures.
- Service performance reporting processes, their content, and frequency.
- A dispute resolution process.
- Indemnification for third-party costs arising from service level breaches.
- A process for updating the agreement.

Having effective SLAs defined for IT services will help manage expectations of both the supplier and customer.

Operational Level Agreements (OLAs)

An operational level agreement sets out how different sub-groups in an IT service provider's organization share responsibility for delivering the components of the end-to-end service described in the service level agreement. OLAs can also be implemented with external organizations upon whom the service provider relies. Key elements of an OLA include:

▸ Expectations and performance targets for each element in the supply chain for the service.

▸ Clear descriptions of service ownership, accountability, roles, and other responsibilities.

▸ Key interaction elements of the service provider's sub-groups.

The OLA helps ensure that activities performed by different groups and individuals in the service provider's organization are clearly aligned to satisfy the Service Level Agreement (SLA).

29.5 REFERENCE

See Also

Other capabilities of IT-CMF that have a particularly close relationship with the Supplier Management (SUM) capability include:

Capability	What it provides
08. Innovation Management (IM)	Guidance on stimulating innovation to deepen relationships between entities
13. Sourcing (SRC)	The sourcing strategy for IT services, and how the initial selection of suppliers for IT services is conducted
25. Relationship Management (REM)	Overarching relationship management practices for the IT function itself and for other business units and external entities
27. Service Provisioning (SRP)	Management of IT services

Further Reading

Blokdijk, G., 2008. *Supplier management best practice handbook*. Brisbane, AU: Emereo Publishing.

Emmett, S., and Crocker, B., 2009. *Excellence in supplier management.* Cambridge: Cambridge Academic.

ITSQC, 2015. *The eSourcing capability model for client organizations (eSCM-CL).* Available at: <http://www.itsqc.org/models/escm-cl/>.

Laseter, T.M., 1998. *Balanced sourcing: cooperation and competition in supplier relationships.* San Francisco, CA: Jossey-Bass.

Notes

[1] Wade, M., Piccoli, G., and Ives, B., 2011. IT-dependent strategic initiatives and sustained competitive advantage: a review, synthesis, and an extension of the literature. In: W.L. Currie and R.D. Galliers, eds. 2011. *The Oxford handbook of management information systems: critical perspectives and new directions*. Oxford: Oxford University Press, Ch. 14.

TIM

30. Technical Infrastructure Management

30.1 OVERVIEW

Goal

The Technical Infrastructure Management (TIM) capability aims to holistically manage all physical and virtual components of the IT infrastructure to support the introduction, maintenance, and retirement of IT services.

Objectives

▸ Provide technical infrastructure stability, availability, and reliability through effective operation, maintenance, and retirement of infrastructure components.

▸ Provide technical infrastructure adaptability and flexibility through forward-planning when creating, acquiring, improving, and disposing of infrastructure components.

▸ Provide seamless interoperability across different kinds of infrastructure components.

▸ Protect technical infrastructure and the data that flows through it.

▸ Make provision for effective infrastructure utilization.

Value

The Technical Infrastructure Management (TIM) capability provides a reliable, flexible, secure, and operationally efficient IT infrastructure to meet business requirements.

Relevance

Almost every aspect of modern business has come to rely on business capabilities enabled by IT services, which in turn run on IT infrastructure. Indirectly, IT infrastructure has become the backbone to supporting interactions across customers, suppliers, employees, and partners. Therefore, the management of the IT infrastructure will have significant impact on the success or failure of an organization.

By establishing an effective Technical Infrastructure Management (TIM) capability, an organization can provide appropriate infrastructure that will support current and future needs. In doing so, the capability helps organizations become more efficient, redefine their business models, and improve their customer experiences [1].

30.2 SCOPE

Definition

The Technical Infrastructure Management (TIM) capability is the ability to manage an organization's IT infrastructure across the complete life cycle of:

▶ Transitional activities including building, deploying, and decommissioning infrastructure.
▶ Operational activities including operation, maintenance, and continual improvement of infrastructure.

IT infrastructure is comprised of:

▶ Physical devices – for example, servers, storage, and mobile devices.
▶ Virtual devices/resources – for example, virtual storage and virtual networks.
▶ Infrastructure-related software – for example, middleware, operating systems, and firmware.
▶ Communications components – for example, LAN/WAN, Wi-Fi, MPLS, and voice infrastructure.
▶ Platform services – for example, content management and web services.
▶ IT infrastructure governance – for example, asset management and configuration management.

Related Capabilities

The following are addressed by other capabilities of IT-CMF:

For...	Refer to...
Performing capacity planning	04. Capacity Forecasting and Planning (CFP)
Diagnosing IT infrastructure constraints	12. Service Analytics and Intelligence (SAI)
Defining architecture guidelines for the design of IT infrastructure	20. Enterprise Architecture Management (EAM)
Ensuring information security	21. Information Security Management (ISM)
Managing IT services	27. Service Provisioning (SRP)
Designing and developing IT solutions	28. Solutions Delivery (SD)

30.3 UNDERSTANDING MATURITY

Recognizing Excellence

When the Technical Infrastructure Management (TIM) capability is well-developed or mature:

▸ The IT infrastructure delivers and maintains a reliable, secure, and agile environment that can meet the changing needs of the organization.

▸ The IT infrastructure supports innovation and the ability to quickly introduce, test, and try out new applications and new ways of doing business.

▸ The IT infrastructure is cost-effective and can readily scale to meet fluctuating business demands.

Maturity at the Critical Capability Level

The following statements provide a high-level overview of the Technical Infrastructure Management (TIM) capability at successive levels of maturity:

Level 1   Management of the IT infrastructure is reactive or ad hoc.

Level 2   Documented policies are emerging relating to the management of a limited number of infrastructure components. Predominantly manual procedures are used for IT infrastructure management. Visibility of capacity and utilization across infrastructure components is emerging.

Level 3   Management of infrastructure components is increasingly supported by standardized tool sets that are partly integrated, resulting in decreased execution times and improving infrastructure utilization.

Level 4   Policies relating to IT infrastructure management are implemented automatically, promoting execution agility and achievement of infrastructure utilization targets.

Level 5   The IT infrastructure is continually reviewed so that it remains modular, agile, lean, and sustainable.

Maturity at the Capability Building Block (CBB) Level

The Capability Building Blocks (CBBs) associated with the Technical Infrastructure Management (TIM) capability fall into four categories:

▶ Category A: nine CBBs associated with *Overarching Activities* – these manage activities applicable or common to all IT infrastructure components – for example, integration, problem management, and change management.

▶ Category B: four CBBs associated with *Decentralized Infrastructure* – these manage IT infrastructure items that are not located in central IT facilities – for example, hardware, software, configuration switch settings, and firmware.

▶ Category C: three CBBs associated with *Communications Infrastructure* – these manage all of the components that provide the telephony, computer, and wireless networks for voice, data, and audio-visual services.

▶ Category D: four CBBs associated with *Data Centre Services* – these plan, design, integrate, and operate the IT data centre environment.

These are described below, together with a summary of the different maturity levels for each.

Category A: CBBs Associated with *Overarching Activities*

CBB A1: IT Operations Management

Manage IT infrastructure activities in support of business activities – for example, the processing, storage, and transmission of data.

Level 1	IT operations management is ad hoc, and business operations are frequently disrupted.
Level 2	Approaches for IT operations management are beginning to be defined and are focused on removing siloed infrastructure management. Disruption to business operations is decreasing.
Level 3	Approaches for IT operations management are standardized across the IT infrastructure, providing management with an end-to-end view across various IT infrastructure components. Disruption to business operations is minimal.
Level 4	Information is shared between the IT function and the rest of the business (for example, through the use of a shared operations calendar), and this helps ensure that the IT infrastructure is managed effectively and with virtually no disruption to business operations.
Level 5	Approaches for IT operations management are continually reviewed and optimized.

CBB A2: Infrastructure Integration

Develop skills, policies, and approaches to enable the infrastructure to work cohesively as a whole.

Level 1   Integration planning is non-existent or ad hoc.

Level 2   Integration policies, approaches, and competences are emerging for limited parts of the IT infrastructure. Integration is a highly manual process, sometimes prone to delays and errors.

Level 3   Integration policies, approaches, and competences are standardized for most parts of the IT infrastructure. Integration is partly automated, enabling improved cohesion and troubleshooting.

Level 4   Policy-based integration management and troubleshooting are performed with high levels of automation, enabling automatic and trustworthy integration of the infrastructure.

Level 5   Policies, approaches, and competences are continually reviewed to optimize IT infrastructure integration.

CBB A3: Incident and Problem Management

Implement workarounds, repairs, and root cause analysis (where needed), facilitated by appropriate diagnostic practices.

Level 1   Incident and problem management is non-existent or ad hoc.

Level 2   Defined practices for incident and problem management are emerging for a limited number of IT services. Basic diagnostic metrics that measure why a process is not performing to expectations assist root cause analysis.

Level 3   Standardized incident and problem management practices are applied for most IT services. Diagnostic metrics focus on control limits to prevent and detect issues.

Level 4   Comprehensive incident and problem management practices are applied to all IT services. Diagnostic metrics focus on minimizing repeat incidents and the advanced detection of potential incidents before they occur.

Level 5   Incident and problem management is continually reviewed and optimized.

CBB A4: Infrastructure Performance Management

Manage infrastructure performance in support of service levels agreements (SLAs) – for example, in relation to availability and response time.

Level 1   Infrastructure performance management is ad hoc and reactive.

Level 2   Infrastructure performance levels are managed at an individual infrastructure component level.

Level 3   End-to-end SLAs are agreed across most infrastructure components.

Level 4   Business-level SLAs are agreed between the IT function and the rest of the business.

Level 5   Infrastructure performance management approaches are continually reviewed and optimized.

CBB A5: Asset Management

Manage the deployment and utilization of IT infrastructure assets, including software licenses, networks, physical devices, and virtual devices. Redeploy, retire, and acquire assets as needed.

Level 1 — Asset management is ad hoc and highly manual.

Level 2 — Defined approaches and tools for asset management are emerging. However, manual asset management approaches dominate.

Level 3 — Standardized approaches and tools for asset management are in place, enabling increasing levels of automation to accurately record life cycle state data.

Level 4 — Comprehensive levels of automation across approaches and tools for asset management enable real-time recording of asset life cycle, depreciation, and vulnerability status.

Level 5 — Approaches and tools for asset management are continually reviewed and optimized.

CBB A6: Infrastructure Change Management

Manage major technology infrastructure changes – for example, the transition to cloud, major hardware refreshes, firmware upgrading, introduction of a bring-your-own-device policy, and so on.

Level 1 — IT infrastructure change management is ad hoc and locally driven.

Level 2 — IT infrastructure changes are planned but some business disruptions do occur.

Level 3 — The IT infrastructure change management processes are well defined and consistently used. There is a roll-back facility for major changes to the IT infrastructure.

Level 4 — IT infrastructure changes are planned, and delivered with minimal disruptions across the organization. There is a roll-back facility provided for all changes to the IT infrastructure.

Level 5 — IT infrastructure changes are systematically planned and delivered without disruption across the organization.

CBB A7: Data Centre Environment

Manage all aspects of the data centre environment, including power efficiency and availability, network, cooling, fire-suppression, physical access controls, and security.

Level 1 — There is an ad hoc approach to management of the data centre environment.

Level 2 — Data centre efficiency is beginning to be considered by the IT and Facilities functions. However, partitioned or disjointed approaches still remain.

Level 3 — Joint management of the data centre environment is emerging between the IT and Facilities functions. Data centre efficiency is increasingly taken into account in the development of relevant policies and procedures.

Level 4 — A holistic management approach takes full advantage of the close relationship between the IT and Facilities functions.

Level 5 — Management of the data centre environment is continually reviewed for improvement.

CBB A8: Business Continuity Planning

Manage IT infrastructure to support business continuity planning.

Level 1   Business continuity planning is limited to ad hoc backups and ad hoc restorations.

Level 2   Basic business continuity plans are emerging, primarily based on dependable restoration for a limited number of IT infrastructure services. Utility supply disruptions can be managed to avoid systems or data damage.

Level 3   Business continuity planning is standardized for most areas of IT infrastructure – including, for example, the sequence in which infrastructure services should be restored. Resilience or fault tolerance features have been built around infrastructure supporting critical business activities.

Level 4   Business continuity planning covers all areas of the IT infrastructure – including, for example, the ability to deal with the failure of independent infrastructure components. Robust, resilient, fault tolerant, and fault handling system designs are in place, and there are site failover capabilities for critical and core business activities.

Level 5   Business continuity planning is continually reviewed to leverage the latest business recovery configuration options.

CBB A9: Configuration Management

Implement overarching policies, approaches, and tools for joined-up configuration management across the IT infrastructure – including, for example, allocation of CPU, memory, and storage to a virtual server, configuration of the laptop build image for a group of end customers, and so on.

Level 1   Any configuration management that takes place is ad hoc. It typically takes place locally and is often incomplete.

Level 2   Defined configuration management policies and approaches are emerging for a limited number of areas, primarily focusing on configuration management governance and access controls.

Level 3   Standardized configuration management policies, approaches, and tools are applied to most areas. The focus of configuration management is expanded to include version control of configuration data.

Level 4   Comprehensive configuration management policies, approaches, and tools are applied to all areas.

Level 5   Configuration management policies, approaches, and tools are continually reviewed and optimized.

Category B: CBBs Associated with *Decentralized Infrastructure*

CBB B1: Support Infrastructure

Develop overarching approaches and policies for the life cycle management of decentralized infrastructure equipment.

Level 1   The life cycle management of the infrastructure is ad hoc and reactive.

Level 2   Defined life cycle management approaches and policies are emerging in a limited number of areas. However, the consistency of their use may still vary.

Level 3   Standardized life cycle management approaches and policies are used in most areas. The consistency of their use is improving.

Level 4   Comprehensive life cycle management approaches and policies are consistently used in all areas.

Level 5   Life cycle management approaches and policies are continually improved and optimized across all areas.

CBB B2: User, Mobile, and Personal Devices

Implement approaches and policies for the life cycle management of mobile and personal devices.

Level 1   The set-up, ongoing maintenance, and support of mobile and personal devices is ad hoc.

Level 2   Basic management and support for a bring-your-own-device (BYOD) programme are emerging for a limited set of devices.

Level 3   Standardized management and support for a BYOD programme are in place for a growing set of devices.

Level 4   Comprehensive management and support for a BYOD programme are in place for virtually all relevant devices across the organization.

Level 5   The management and support for a BYOD programme are continually reviewed based on industry-proven practices.

CBB B3: Peripherals

Implement approaches and policies for the life cycle management of peripherals and consumables – including, for example, printers, scanners, monitors, and other devices.

Level 1   The set-up, ongoing maintenance, and support of peripheral devices is ad hoc.

Level 2   There is defined set-up, configuration management, and support for a limited set of peripheral devices.

Level 3   There is standard set-up, configuration management, and support for most of the peripheral devices used in the organization.

Level 4   There is comprehensive set-up, configuration management, and support for all peripheral devices used in the organization.

Level 5   The management of all peripheral devices is continually reviewed based on industry-proven practices.

CBB B4: Endpoint Devices

Implement approaches and policies for the life cycle management of endpoint devices – including, for example, thin clients, POS terminals, and so on.

Level 1   The set-up, on-going maintenance, and support of endpoint devices is ad hoc.

Level 2   There is defined setup, configuration management, and support for a limited number of endpoint devices.

Level 3   There is standard setup, configuration management, and support for most of the endpoint devices used in the organization.

Level 4   There is comprehensive set-up, configuration management, and support for all endpoint devices used across the organization.

Level 5   The management of all endpoint devices is continually reviewed based on industry-proven practices.

Category C: CBBs Associated with *Communications Infrastructure*

CBB C1: Wide Area Networks (WAN)

Develop and implement policies and procedures for the life cycle management of in-house and vendor services and the associated equipment – including for example routers, firewalls, and so on.

Level 1   A WAN service is available, but its management is ad hoc.

Level 2   Applicable standards, architecture rules, and regulations are being identified to guide the development of policies and procedures for the WAN within a defined risk management approach. Adoption of policies and procedures may still be limited.

Level 3   Policies and procedures are standardized, and use toolsets to monitor and manage the WAN and to enforce some elements of those policies and procedures.

Level 4   All elements of policies and procedures are enforced using configured tools to monitor network issues and invoke appropriate actions automatically.

Level 5   Policies and procedures are continually reviewed for improvement. Tools can pre-empt network management issues.

CBB C2: Local Area Networks (LAN)

Develop and implement approaches and policies for the life cycle management of local area networks, including Wi-Fi.

Level 1	Both the procurement and management of the LAN is ad hoc.
Level 2	Applicable standards, architecture rules, and regulations are being identified to guide the development of policies and procedures for the LAN within a defined risk management approach.
Level 3	Policies and procedures are standardized, and use toolsets to monitor and manage the LAN and to enforce some elements of those policies and procedures.
Level 4	All elements of policies and procedures are enforced using configured tools to monitor network issues, and invoke appropriate actions automatically.
Level 5	Policies and procedures are continually reviewed for improvement. Tools can pre-empt network management issues.

CBB C3: Voice, Video, and Convergent Services

Develop and implement approaches and policies for the life cycle management of voice, video, and other services where technology convergence is a factor.

Level 1	Standards identification and policy development are ad hoc in relation to voice, video, and convergent services.
Level 2	Applicable standards, architecture rules, and regulations are being identified to guide the development of policies and procedures for voice, video, and convergent services within a defined risk management approach.
Level 3	Policies and procedures are standardized, and use toolsets to monitor and manage the voice, video, and convergence environment and to enforce some elements of those policies and procedures.
Level 4	All elements of policies and procedures are enforced using configured tools to monitor voice, video, and convergence environment issues, and invoke appropriate actions automatically.
Level 5	Policies and procedures relating to voice, video, and convergence are continually reviewed for improvement. Tools can pre-empt management issues relating to the voice, video, and convergence environment.

Category D: CBBs Associated with *Data Centre Services*

CBB D1: High Performance, Server, and General Purpose Computing

Develop and implement approaches and policies for the life cycle management of the processing infrastructure.

Level 1	Life cycle management of the processing infrastructure is ad hoc. Activities tend to be reactive.
Level 2	Life cycle management is emerging for limited areas of the processing infrastructure. Business units are beginning to show savings based on their use of different processing infrastructures.
Level 3	Life cycle management and tool sets have been standardized for most areas of the processing infrastructure in the IT function and some other business units. There is focused investment in processing infrastructure to contain costs.
Level 4	Life cycle management and tool sets cover virtually all areas of the processing infrastructure. There is focused investment in matching workloads to appropriate processing infrastructure to maximize utilization and efficiency.
Level 5	Life cycle management and tool sets are continually reviewed for improvement and optimization.

CBB D2: Storage

Develop and implement approaches and policies for the life cycle management of storage – including, for example, computer memory, disk drives, solid state disks, and so on.

Level 1	Life cycle management of storage is non-existent or ad hoc. Activities tend to be reactive.
Level 2	Life cycle management is emerging for a limited number of storage areas. Business units are beginning to show savings based on their use of different storage tiers.
Level 3	Life cycle management and tool sets have been standardized for most storage areas in the IT function and some other business units. There is focused investment in storage technologies to contain costs.
Level 4	Life cycle management and tool sets cover virtually all areas of storage. There is focused investment in storage for business protection.
Level 5	Storage life cycle management is continually reviewed for improvement and optimization.

CBB D3: Mainframe Computing

Develop and implement approaches and policies for the life cycle management of mainframe computers.

Level 1	Life cycle management of mainframe computers is non-existent or ad hoc. Activities tend to be reactive.
Level 2	Life cycle management is emerging for a limited number of mainframe areas. Some other business units are beginning to show value from their use of mainframe services.
Level 3	Life cycle management and tool sets have been standardized for most mainframe computers. There is focused investment in the containment of mainframe costs.
Level 4	Life cycle management and tool sets cover virtually all areas of mainframe computing. There is focused investment in mainframe computing to enable business services.
Level 5	Mainframe computing life cycle management is continually reviewed for improvement and optimization.

CBB D4: Infrastructure Related Software

Develop and implement approaches and policies for life cycle management of infrastructure-related software – for example, application integration and middleware software, information management software, storage management software, and IT operations management and security software.

Level 1	Life cycle management for infrastructure-related software is ad hoc. Activities tend to be reactive.
Level 2	Life cycle management is emerging for a limited number of infrastructure-related software areas.
Level 3	Life cycle management and tool sets have been standardized for most infrastructure-related software areas.
Level 4	Life cycle management and tool sets comprehensively cover virtually all infrastructure-related software areas.
Level 5	Infrastructure-related software life cycle management is continually reviewed for improvement and optimization.

30.4 IMPROVEMENT PLANNING

Capability Evaluation

Two summary assessment questions are set out below, along with the typical response associated with each level of maturity.

To what extent is the technical infrastructure managed to deliver robust, IT-enabled business services – using, for example, criteria such as reliability, scalability, availability, and cost efficiency?

Level 1	The technical infrastructure's support of IT-enabled business services is managed in an ad hoc manner.
Level 2	Service level agreements (SLAs) are in place for a limited number of IT infrastructure components regarding support of IT-enabled business services.
Level 3	End-to-end SLAs are mapped to most IT infrastructure components to support IT-enabled business services.
Level 4	SLAs are mapped to all IT infrastructure components to support IT-enabled business services. Operational level agreements (OLAs) are defined for the entire IT infrastructure.
Level 5	IT infrastructure is self-healing – in other words, infrastructure components have the ability to know when they are not working correctly, and (without human intervention) make the necessary adjustments to restore themselves to normal operation levels.

How is the IT infrastructure managed?

Level 1	Management of the IT infrastructure is reactive or ad hoc.
Level 2	Documented policies are emerging in relation to the management of a limited number of infrastructure components. Predominantly manual procedures are used for IT infrastructure management. Visibility of utilization across infrastructure components is emerging.
Level 3	Management of infrastructure components is increasingly supported by standardized tool sets and partly integrated practices, resulting in decreased execution times and improving infrastructure utilization.
Level 4	Policies relating to IT infrastructure management are implemented automatically, promoting execution agility and achievement of infrastructure utilization targets.
Level 5	The IT infrastructure is continually reviewed so that it remains modular, agile, lean, and sustainable.

Key Practices-Outcomes-Metrics (POMs)

Some useful POMs for developing the Technical Infrastructure Management (TIM) capability are summarized below.

Level 2 POMs

Practice	Develop standards and policies relating to IT infrastructure life cycle management and select appropriate tools to implement them.
Outcome	A consistent, repeatable, and reliable approach emerges to design, implement, and support the IT infrastructure across its various component categories.
Metric	Percentage of IT infrastructure component types whose life cycles are documented and are covered by standards and policies.
Practice	Develop or join communities of practice to grow IT infrastructure competences.
Outcome	Skills and competences are consistently applied to develop and support a more responsive and cost-effective IT infrastructure.
Metric	Percentage of IT infrastructure personnel who are members of a community of practice.
Practice	Define and plan IT infrastructure change management to reduce/minimize disruption to business operations.
Outcome	Changes to the IT infrastructure are planned, communicated to stakeholders, are generally predictable, and can be reversed if necessary.
Metric	Percentage of changes to the IT infrastructure that have to be temporarily rolled back.
Practice	Work with the other relevant business units to improve the governance and budget control for IT infrastructure management.
Outcome	The design, support, and maintenance of the IT infrastructure become more predictable, and developers, support personnel, and customers have a clearer understanding of what is possible, and in what timeframes.
Metric	Percentage of IT infrastructure expenditure formally approved within agreed governance and budget control practices.
Practice	Define IT infrastructure roles and the skills associated with them across IT infrastructure component categories.
Outcome	IT infrastructure personnel can increase their skill levels and plan their careers; and this in turn will improve the development and support of the IT infrastructure.
Metric	Number of IT infrastructure roles with defined skills/competences. Percentage of IT infrastructure employees with training plans and career paths.

Practice	Divide IT services into those that are, and those that are not, business critical. Standardize and optimize the business critical services and segment them into service tiers.
Outcome	Reduced cost, lower risk, and reduced management complexity are experienced. This prepares the groundwork for automation, and to take advantage of emerging technologies such as social, mobile, data analytics, and cloud computing.
Metric	Percentage of IT services that are business critical. Percentage of IT services that are standardized.

Level 3 POMs

Practice	Audit the IT infrastructure against agreed policies, approaches, and life cycle management protocols.
Outcome	Assurance increases on the design, implementation, and support of the IT infrastructure.
Metric	Number of IT infrastructure non-compliance incidents identified.
Practice	Standardize practices for incident management and problem resolution.
Outcome	Incidents and problems are handled correctly and cause minimum disruption.
Metric	Number and percentage of incidents resolved per day. Incident mean time to repair (MTTR). Number and percentage of problems resolved per month.
Practice	Standardize targets for the IT infrastructure (relating, for example, to availability, utilization, and response times), and measure and report on them in both technical and business service terms.
Outcome	SLAs are in place that track the effectiveness and efficiency of the IT infrastructure.
Metric	Percentage coverage of SLAs across the IT infrastructure.
Practice	Promote IT infrastructure management for environmental sustainability.
Outcome	The IT infrastructure is managed for triple bottom-line impact – that is, its social, environmental, and financial impact.
Metric	Power usage effectiveness (PUE). Percentage of IT infrastructure components disposed of in a compliant manner.
Practice	Use IT infrastructure technology roadmaps to discuss, agree, and plan the future IT infrastructure.
Outcome	The planning of IT infrastructure is transparent and takes account of enterprise architecture requirements.
Metric	Number and availability of approved IT infrastructure roadmaps.
Practice	Analyse and rationalize the organization's IT services and workloads to consolidate and virtualize the underlying infrastructure.
Outcome	IT services are optimized to save on energy, costs, space, and resources, and asset utilization is improved.
Metric	Percentage of IT services that are rationalized and virtualized.

Level 4 POMs

Practice	Prioritize the utilization and availability of the IT infrastructure.
Outcome	The IT infrastructure scales to match the business needs of the organization.
Metric	Percentage total downtime broken down by service. Frequency of SLAs being broken. Utilization rates across IT infrastructure components.
Practice	Automate, where appropriate, IT infrastructure process execution (for example account provisioning, software distribution, and intrusion detection).
Outcome	Higher levels of automation makes real-time IT infrastructure provisioning increasingly viable.
Metric	Percentage of relevant IT infrastructure processes that are automated.
Practice	Ensure that feedback from business units and users informs the development, improvement, and utilization of the IT infrastructure.
Outcome	The IT infrastructure can be proactively planned to meet the operational, tactical, and strategic objectives of the business.
Metric	The frequency of meetings relating to IT infrastructure between IT and other business units. The level of agreement that the IT infrastructure can meet business objectives.
Practice	Create and use a standard catalogue of IT infrastructure services and make it accessible to users through a self-service portal.
Outcome	Users can access IT infrastructure resources more efficiently.
Metric	Percentage of IT infrastructure services that are available via a standard catalogue. Percentage of IT services that are available via a self-service portal.

Level 5 POMs

Practice	Continually improve the architecture of all IT infrastructure components to enhance agility and integration.
Outcome	The IT infrastructure continues to be modular, agile, lean, and sustainable.
Metric	IT infrastructure modularity (coupling effort across components). IT infrastructure agility/flexibility across component configurations. Sustainability (power usage effectiveness (PUE) across components).
Practice	Manage the IT infrastructure to support optimal availability and utilization.
Outcome	The IT infrastructure complies with SLAs, and any breaches are immediately reported and corrected.
Metric	Number of SLA breaches by service.
Practice	Implement automatic monitoring of the IT infrastructure, supported by a self-healing capability.
Outcome	Very high service quality arises from automatic response to alerts and self-healing.
Metric	System uptime. Mean time to recover (MTTR).

Practice	Continually investigate and take advantage of new technologies that improve levels of automatic infrastructure orchestration, such as Intelligent Infrastructure Management Systems or Software Defined Infrastructure.
Outcome	The complete infrastructure can be automatically controlled and managed.
Metric	Percentage of the IT infrastructure that is automatically managed.

Addressing Typical Challenges

Some typical challenges that can arise in attempting to develop maturity in the Technical Infrastructure Management (TIM) capability are set out below.

Challenge	Difficulty in quantifying the business value of IT infrastructure investments can lead to situations where infrastructure investments are inadequate or are made without understanding of the likely consequences.
Context	The benefits of IT infrastructure investments tend to be difficult to quantify. Such investments are often foundational and serve multiple IT services, with the object of providing flexibility, scalability, or agility for the future.
Action	Encourage investment planners to explore ways of mapping intangible infrastructure benefits to tangible business results. Consider financial modelling techniques such as 'real options' to model the value of future options enabled by infrastructure investments.
Challenge	Lack of suitably trained/qualified IT infrastructure experts.
Context	The organization is not attracting or recruiting suitably qualified IT personnel, or once recruited, they are not receiving adequate training and development to keep abreast of technology changes. The consequence is that the IT infrastructure capability within the organization is hampered by a lack of personnel with the required levels of experience and expertise.
Action	Ensure recruitment targets suitably qualified IT infrastructure experts. Implement a mentoring network and a continuous professional development programme to ensure appropriate technical infrastructure skills are kept up to date.
Challenge	The IT function and the rest of the business are not sufficiently engaged to set priorities for the IT infrastructure planning.
Context	The IT function is not sufficiently connected with the strategic priorities of the organization. This can result in IT infrastructure planning that is not aligned with the objectives of the entire organization.
Action	Have the IT function and the rest of the business jointly plan and set IT infrastructure objectives. This activity can be greatly enhanced when senior representatives from different business units are jointly responsible for planning outcomes.

Challenge	Reduced efficiency of IT operations arising from the need to support a disparate and heterogeneous IT infrastructure.
Context	IT infrastructure environments tend to evolve over time, accumulating an array of different infrastructure components from different vendors – for example, server, storage, network, and purpose-specific support tools. Supporting such a heterogeneous infrastructure environment can be a complex endeavour, can make it difficult to be flexible, and can drive up maintenance and support costs.
Action	Promote management discussion regarding the merits of various strategic options to manage the IT infrastructure – for example, moving to a more homogenous IT environment, finding a solutions provider that can cover multiple technologies, or implementing software-defined infrastructure practices.

Management Artefacts

Management artefacts that may be used to develop maturity in the Technical Infrastructure Management (TIM) capability include:

▶ Documentation of the policies and approaches for life cycle management of the IT infrastructure.
▶ An IT infrastructure roadmap.
▶ A remote infrastructure management (RIM) platform.
▶ A configuration management database (CMDB).
▶ A mobile device management (MDM) platform.

Documentation of the Policies and Approaches for Life Cycle Management of the IT Infrastructure

Documenting the life cycle management of the IT infrastructure involves describing the technology infrastructure domains, the standards and guidelines to be followed within each domain, and ongoing operations. Such documentation can provide higher levels of productivity, reduced complexity, improved operational efficiency, and better communication. It can also give assurance on the continued availability of infrastructure services, and can help deliver more consistent technical support. Documentation objectives can include:

▶ Ensuring adherence to agreed infrastructure standards and monitoring compliance.
▶ Defining acceptable infrastructure management behaviours and eliminating non-compliant activities.
▶ Defining minimum hardware and software requirements.
▶ Ensuring safeguards to protect the integrity and availability of the technology infrastructure.
▶ Implementing and maintaining disaster recovery protocols.
▶ Ensuring seamless interoperability among internal and external organizational entities.
▶ Maintaining effective change management policies and practices.
▶ Defining, implementing, and maintaining the security of the IT infrastructure.

IT Infrastructure Roadmap

The IT infrastructure roadmap documents how the technology infrastructure is expected to evolve in supporting the business strategy. It helps drive investment priorities typically over the next one to three years. Often it contains the following:

- ▶ A strategy statement with a list of the strategic priorities for the business (not IT-specific).
- ▶ A timeline of major infrastructure transformation initiatives with approximate start and end dates.
- ▶ A high-level justification for each transformation initiative.

The roadmap serves a number of functions, including the facilitation of investment discussions and improvement in planning activities.

Remote Infrastructure Management (RIM) Platform

The objective of a RIM platform is to ensure compliance with corporate policies through:

- ▶ Remote management of IT infrastructure components such as servers, storage, networked devices, desktops, and so on.
- ▶ Automation of infrastructure management processes – for example, configuration management, incident management, problem management, change management, capacity management, security management, performance management, recovery management, and so on.

A RIM platform can assist with consolidating and integrating IT operations management and IT service management approaches. RIM platforms can reside internally within the organization or can be outsourced to a third-party specializing in this activity.

Configuration Management Database (CMDB)

The configuration management database is a repository of information or metadata on all significant IT components. Typically a CMDB includes details of:

- ▶ IT assets and applications, collectively referred to as configuration items (CIs).
- ▶ The relationship between the CIs.
- ▶ The CIs' life cycle stage – for example, whether it is active or retired.
- ▶ Changes made – for example, changes to a CI's status or relationship to other CIs.

The CMDB helps in understanding interconnections between IT assets and applications, allowing the impact of proposed changes to be modelled, root cause analysis of service level issues to be performed, and the reconstruction of software and hardware configurations.

Mobile Device Management (MDM) Platform

A mobile device management platform is a specific type of RIM platform that helps with policy enforcement across heterogeneous mobile devices, segregating corporate data from personal data on mobile devices. A MDM platform provides device platform specific features including encryption, geo-location, data wiping, device lock, passcode reset, security patching, and authentication for access to corporate applications such as email, calendar, contacts, intranet, and so on. The benefit of a MDM platform is that it enables productive use of mobile devices within the organization (for example, through a BYOD programme), while at the same time protecting organizational assets. Mobile devices can include smartphones, tablets, laptops, and e-book readers that are provided by the organization or individually owned.

30.5 REFERENCE

See Also

Other capabilities of IT-CMF that have a particularly close relationship with the Technical Infrastructure Management (TIM) capability include:

Capability	What it provides
02. Business Planning (BP)	Programmes to inform how the technical infrastructure should be developed to support current and future business objectives
04. Capacity Forecasting and Planning (CFP)	Forecasts for the services supported by the technical infrastructure – for example, storage
07. Green Information Technology (GIT)	Policies for managing the IT infrastructure in an environmentally sensitive manner
11. Risk Management (RM)	Guidance on identifying risks and risk handling strategies
12. Service Analytics and Intelligence (SAI)	Perspectives regarding an end-to-end view of IT services
14. Strategic Planning (SP)	The IT strategy to inform the long-term evolution of the technical infrastructure roadmaps
20. Enterprise Architecture Management (EAM)	Standards, directions, policies, frameworks, and roadmaps to guide technical infrastructure planning
26. Research, Development and Engineering (RDE)	Insights on new technologies that could benefit management of the IT infrastructure more efficiently and effectively
27. Service Provisioning (SRP)	Functional and non-functional requirements for consideration when planning the technical infrastructure
28. Solutions Delivery (SD)	Infrastructure requirements to support new IT services and solutions
32. User Training Management (UTM)	Training on configuring and managing IT infrastructure components

Further Reading

Estall, H., 2012. *Business continuity management systems: implementation and certification to ISO 22301*. Swindon: BCS.

Josyula, V., Orr, M., and Page, G., 2011. *Cloud computing: automating the virtualized data centre*. Indianapolis, IN: Cisco Press.

Laan, S., 2013. *IT infrastructure architecture – infrastructure building blocks and concepts.* 2nd ed. Raleigh, NC: Lulu Press.

Notes

[1] Luftman, J., Zadeh, H.S., Derksen, B., Santana, M., Rigoni, E.H., and Huang, Z.D., 2013. Key information technology and management issues 2012–2013: an international study. *Journal of Information Technology*, 28(4), 354–66.

UED
31. User Experience Design

31.1 OVERVIEW

Goal

The User Experience[*] Design (UED) capability aims to address both the usability and the usefulness of IT services and solutions across various audiences, purposes, and contexts of use.

▸ Usability relates to the ease with which IT services and solutions can be used from a user's perspective.

▸ Usefulness relates to how well IT services and solutions serve their intended purposes.

Objectives

▸ Shift from technology-centric to user-centric design of IT services and solutions; in other words, make the transition from designing within the engineering boundaries or limitations of the technology to designing IT services and solutions around the needs of those who will use them.

▸ Place the user's experience of the IT service or solution (rather than the service or solution itself) at the centre of design and development – for example, a user's experience of email may rely on computer hardware performance, network connectivity, email client usability, user proficiency, purpose of the task, and the environment/context of access.

▸ Consider users' experiences across their interactions with IT services and solutions – including their knowledge about the range of services available, their experiences of taking delivery of services and using services, the training and support they require or receive, how upgrades are handled, and how redundant services are removed.

▸ Adopt a user experience design approach that reduces development time and cost, and produces IT services and solutions that satisfy both business and user objectives.

Value

The User Experience Design (UED) capability helps increase levels of proficiency and productivity by using actionable information obtained from users in the design and maintenance of IT services and solutions.

---

[*] User Experience is also sometimes called UX.

Relevance

User experience design is not the same as user interface design; it extends beyond promoting visual consistency and simplification of design elements for an IT service or solution, to also cover user needs, wants, and limitations – and it does this in different contexts, with different purposes, and across different audiences. Typically, failure to take a user-centred approach to design has consequences *after* the deployment of an IT product or solution, and shows up in recurring IT helpdesk calls, disappointing usage levels, the need for additional user training, continual change requests and upgrades, lost employee productivity, and poor satisfaction levels. An IT product or solution that fails to take all aspects of the users experience into account can end up being very costly.

By establishing an effective User Experience Design (UED) capability, an organization can help ensure that IT services and solutions are fit-for-purpose – that they make sense (are more usable) and solve real problems (are more useful). It can facilitate a common understanding regarding the goals users need to accomplish in pursuit of their business objectives, and then enables design of a user experience that directly supports achievement of those objectives. IT services and solutions should be designed from the very beginning to bridge the gap between the user and the business objectives, with the aim of reducing costs, increasing employee productivity and satisfaction levels, and boosting organizational competitiveness.

31.2 SCOPE

Definition

The User Experience Design (UED) capability is the ability to proactively consider the needs of users at all stages in the life cycle of IT services and solutions. The User Experience Design (UED) capability covers:

▸ Designing IT services and solutions that both meet business objectives and satisfy user needs.

▸ Arriving at an understanding of users' preferences in their interactions with IT services and solutions.

▸ Designing 'mock' environments of IT services and solutions to enable evaluation from a user experience perspective.

▸ Gathering users' experiences through qualitative and quantitative methods – for example, through surveys, focus groups, and interviews.

Related Capabilities

The following are addressed by other capabilities of IT-CMF:

For…	Refer to…
Developing IT employees' skills	23. People Asset Management (PAM)
Evaluating the potential business impact of new technologies	26. Research, Development and Engineering (RDE)
Designing and developing functional and non-functional requirements	28. Solutions Delivery (SD)
Providing user training on IT services and solutions	32. User Training Management (UTM)

31.3 UNDERSTANDING MATURITY

Recognizing Excellence

When the User Experience Design (UED) capability is well-developed or mature:

▸ The organization can consistently design user experiences that successfully balance business, technical, and user needs, reducing the need for re-work post deployment.
▸ The quality of design is continually improved through evaluation and feedback from users.
▸ User experience is continually considered in the development of IT services and solutions throughout their life cycles.
▸ User input informs the acquisition of new technology, and the redevelopment and/or replacement of legacy IT services and solutions.
▸ IT solutions have easy-to-learn and easy-to-use interaction methods, increasing productivity and reducing training needs, and with a focus on eliminating or reducing opportunities for user error.

Maturity at the Critical Capability Level

The following statements provide a high-level overview of the User Experience Design (UED) capability at successive levels of maturity:

Level 1	There is no official recognition of user experience as a discipline within the organization. IT services and solutions are not typically considered user-friendly.
Level 2	Defined user experience approaches are emerging in the design and development of a limited number of IT services and solutions. The user experience of most IT services and solutions is improving.
Level 3	Standardized user experience approaches guide the design and development of most IT services and solutions, which increasingly enable users to accomplish their tasks and goals easily, efficiently, and accurately.
Level 4	Comprehensive user experience approaches are used during the design and development of all IT services and solutions, so that they are generally suitable for their audiences, purposes, and contexts of use.
Level 5	User experience approaches are adopted, and are continually reviewed for improvement opportunities. IT services and solutions offered/brokered by the IT function consistently provide richer user experiences when compared to market alternatives.

Maturity at the Capability Building Block (CBB) Level

The Capability Building Blocks (CBBs) associated with the User Experience Design (UED) capability fall into two categories:

▶ Category A: two CBBs associated with *Measuring and Understanding User Experiences* – these manage how user experiences might be gathered and communicated to inform the design of IT services and solutions.

▶ Category B: three CBBs associated with *Designing, Testing, and Improving User Experiences* – these use the collated user experience data to explore and evaluate how future user experiences might be improved.

These are described below, together with a summary of the different maturity levels for each.

Category A: CBBs Associated with *Measuring and Understanding User Experiences*

CBB A1: Researching User Experiences

Assess user behaviours, needs, and motivations – for example, through surveys, focus groups, individual interviews, direct observation, and usability testing.

Level 1   Any approaches to capturing user experiences and assessing responses are ad hoc and tend to be used only where they are necessary to meet a compliance requirement.

Level 2   A defined user experience assessment approach is used in a limited number of higher profile IT services and solutions. Typically only a limited number of users are assessed, and the focus is generally on user testing and setting basic metrics.

Level 3   A standardized user experience assessment approach is applied to most IT services and solutions. Users are regularly assessed as a representative sample of all users, and the focus is on visual elements and physical interaction.

Level 4   A comprehensive user experience assessment approach is applied to all IT services and solutions. Consistent sampling of users focuses on elements such as observation or context of use.

Level 5   User experience assessment approaches are continually reviewed, with a systematic focus on assessing the consistency of user experiences between (as well as within) IT services and solutions.

CBB A2: Communicating User Experiences

Convey user behaviours, needs, and motivations to stakeholders to enable informed action – for example, by using personas, user scenarios, storyboarding, use cases, and storytelling.

Level 1   Any methods that are in place to communicate user experiences are ad hoc.

Level 2   Defined communication methods are emerging to communicate minimum user experiences across a limited number of key IT services and solutions.

Level 3   Standardized communication methods are in place to communicate above-the-minimum user experiences across most IT services and solutions.

Level 4   A comprehensive suite of communication methods are in place to communicate advanced user experiences across all IT services and solutions.

Level 5   Communication methods are optimized across all IT services and solutions, are continually evaluated, and regularly include input from relevant business ecosystem partners.

Category B: CBBs Associated with *Designing, Testing, and Improving User Experiences*

CBB B1: Designing User Experiences

Conceptualize design options for enhancing the user experience of IT services and solutions – using abstraction methods such as drawings, sketches, blueprints, wireframes, prototypes, papers, and formulas.

Level 1	Conceptualization of user design options is non-existent or ad hoc. Design is based primarily on technical integration.
Level 2	Conceptualization of user design options is increasingly considered for a limited number of major IT services and solutions, primarily focusing on visual elements.
Level 3	Conceptualization of user design options is considered for most IT services and solutions, focusing on visual elements and physical interaction.
Level 4	Conceptualization of user design options is considered for all IT services and solutions, focusing on qualitative methods such as observation or contexts of use.
Level 5	Conceptualization of user design options is continually refined to systematically address various audiences, purposes, and contexts of use.

CBB B2: Evaluating User Experiences

Apply evaluation methods and criteria to assess user experience of IT services and solutions, and to assess design options relating to them. Evaluation methods might include, for example, surveys, interviews, focus groups, walkthroughs, productivity studies, and usability tests. Evaluation criteria might include, for example, system performance, task success rate, time on task, error rate, and satisfaction ratings.

Level 1	Evaluation methods are non-existent or ad hoc. Criteria are typically limited to a system's technical performance.
Level 2	Defined evaluation methods and criteria to evaluate user experience are applied to a limited number of design options and IT services and solutions, and are beginning to be mapped to IT project impact measures.
Level 3	Standardized evaluation methods and criteria to evaluate user experience are applied to most design options and IT services and solutions, and can be regularly mapped to IT service impact measures.
Level 4	Comprehensive evaluation methods and criteria are applied to all design options and IT services and solutions, and can be systematically mapped to business impact measures.
Level 5	Evaluation methods and criteria are continually reviewed for improvement opportunities.

CBB B3: Informing User Experience Design

Make available and implement feedback to improve the user experience of design options and IT services and solutions.

Level 1   Availability of feedback is ad hoc or anecdotal, and rarely acted upon.

Level 2   Semi-structured feedback is occasionally available for a limited number of design options and IT services and solutions. Feedback may not always be acted upon.

Level 3   Structured feedback is regularly available for most design options and IT services and solutions. Feedback is acted upon in most instances.

Level 4   Comprehensive feedback is continually available for all design options and IT services and solutions. Feedback is always acted upon.

Level 5   The availability of feedback systematically shapes strategic choices for the design of IT services and solutions.

31.4 IMPROVEMENT PLANNING

Capability Evaluation

Two summary assessment questions are set out below, along with the typical response associated with each level of maturity.

How is user experience taken into account in the organization?

Level 1   User experience is never or only rarely considered.

Level 2   User experience is beginning to be considered in parts of the IT function. Often approaches are limited to usability testing.

Level 3   User experience design is recognized as a formal discipline within the IT function, with approaches regularly applied in advance of software coding activities commencing.

Level 4   User experience design is comprehensively applied throughout the life cycle of most IT services and solutions, with employees across the organization consistently seeing tangible improvements.

Level 5   User experience design is considered a core strength of the IT function, and is continually reviewed for improvement opportunities.

How, in general, do users perceive IT services and solutions?

Level 1   The experience for users is generally one of frustration across IT services and solutions.

Level 2   IT services and solutions increasingly provide more technically useful features, but still require significant learning and training efforts before they are regarded as usable by users.

Level 3   Many IT services and solutions are increasingly created with the user experience in mind from the outset, providing more intuitively usable services and solutions that increasingly meet business and user objectives.

Level 4   The user experience of internally sourced IT services and solutions is at least as good as that for bought-in services and solutions. Usability is a key consideration in the creation of IT services and solutions.

Level 5   Users report a high level of satisfaction with the usability of IT services and solutions, and the user experience is continually reviewed for improvement opportunities.

Key Practices-Outcomes-Metrics (POMs)

Some useful POMs for developing the User Experience Design (UED) capability are summarized below.

Level 2 POMs

Practice	Define a user experience vision for IT services and solutions, and communicate it with stakeholders and project teams.
Outcome	The core characteristics of the desired user experience are communicated, and provide the foundation upon which future design decisions are based.
Metric	Percentage of stakeholders and project team members to whom the user experience vision has been communicated.
Practice	Provide training on the user experience assessment methods – for example, using focus groups, surveys, usability tests, A/B benchmarking, eye-tracking, and accessibility analysis. Begin to roll out user experience assessments across IT services and solutions.
Outcome	A consistent approach emerges for capturing the user experience across IT services and solutions.
Metric	Percentage of relevant stakeholders trained in the use of user research and validation methods.

Practice	Promote the use of user experience design methods in the (re)design of IT services and solutions – for example, through the use of sketches, wireframes, prototypes, and storyboards.
Outcome	Comprehension of user experience is embedded into the creation of IT services and solutions.
Metric	Percentage of users who can perform a core set of tasks faster than they could with a previous version. Percentage of users who can perform a core set of tasks with no help or training. Percentage of users who rate an IT solution's ease-of-use as acceptable. Percentage of users who call support when using a new or redesigned IT service or solution.
Practice	Equip users with training, documentation, and social/collaborative crowd-sourcing platforms for guidance on how to use IT services and solutions more effectively.
Outcome	Users have the self-directed means to increase their proficiency and deal with deficiencies in usability.
Metric	Percentage of IT services and solutions that are supported by appropriate documentation, user training, and problem-resolution guidance.

Level 3 POMs

Practice	Formally incorporate user experience design practices into IT project delivery methodologies.
Outcome	Project timelines and methodologies can be extended to allow for the incorporation of user experience design practices.
Metric	Percentage of projects with user experience design activities built into their project plans.
Practice	Segment and profile users, and ensure appropriate sampling occurs to capture representative feedback.
Outcome	The (re)development of IT services and solutions will more broadly reflect various user needs and goals, and result in better success in addressing them.
Metric	Percentage of users sampled across profiles. Percentage of users (by segment) who rate an IT service's or solution's ease-of-use as acceptable.
Practice	Standardize master guidelines on usability principles (for example, across criteria such as accessibility, the level of information provided, the quality of the interaction, and the visual design) for developing internal and assessing external IT services and solutions.
Outcome	Guidance is available to help ensure increasingly consistent user experiences.
Metric	Percentage of IT services and solutions that are compliant with usability guidelines.

Practice	Standardize the business impact criteria used to measure improvements to the user experience.
Outcome	Understanding the business value of better user experiences helps ensure that an improved user experience is prioritized for new IT services and solutions or for changes to existing IT services and solutions.
Metric	Quantification of the business value/impact of improving the user experience.

Level 4 POMs

Practice	Empower users to suggest designs for better experiences for IT services and solutions – for example, through user networks, special interest groups, themed competition challenges, and hackathons.
Outcome	Allowing users to collaborate with each other on ideas to improve their user experiences may lead to fresh insights not possible with more traditional approaches.
Metric	Implemented user-generated ideas relating to the user experience as a percentage of all such user-generated ideas.
Practice	Formalize an organization-wide community of practice on user experience.
Outcome	Lessons learned and proven practices can be readily shared across individuals and projects, and can help improve practitioner expertise.
Metric	Community participation levels by relevant employees – for example, levels of membership and growth.
Practice	Track comparative survey results relating to user experiences of IT services and solutions over time.
Outcome	The quality of the user experience of IT services and solutions (as reported by users themselves) can be tracked over time and benchmarked to support decisions on what improvements to make.
Metric	Percentage of IT services and solutions with user experience data.

Level 5 POMs

Practice	Set up a continual improvement programme to enhance the methods used to capture and integrate information about user experience. This might include, for example, knowledge sharing with external peers, assessing the organizational impact of user experience practices, and acting upon lessons learned.
Outcome	The organization can benefit by improving existing and incorporating the latest approaches.
Metric	Number of updates made to the approved suite of user experience design practices.

Practice	Assign executive ownership for the continual improvement of the user experience for individual IT services and solutions.
Outcome	Insights about user needs, attitudes, and behaviours drive strategic decision-making for IT services and solutions.
Metric	Yes/no indicator regarding the assignment of executive responsibility. Percentage of users who rate their satisfaction with IT services and solutions as high or very high.

Addressing Typical Challenges

Some typical challenges that can arise in attempting to develop maturity in the User Experience Design (UED) capability are set out below.

Challenge	Pressure to meet budgets and deadlines often means that user experience is one of the first elements to be sacrificed to deliver an IT solution on time/within budget.
Context	Culturally and politically across the organization, adhering to budget and delivering on time are valued more than delivering a good user experience. This can result in user experience not being addressed prior to the IT solution's release.
Action	Raise with senior management the principle that delivering a good user experience should be regarded as an intrinsic part of any release and should be allowed for in all project timelines. Ensure that those who develop IT solutions are incentivized to take account of user experience metrics.
Challenge	While the IT function invests heavily in developing IT services, the services are generally considered 'clunky' and not user-friendly.
Context	When designing IT services, functional and non-functional requirements are focused on satisfying the objectives of business sponsors, with little consideration given to the users' point of view – for example, users' tasks and goals, and questions such as the following: ▸ How can the design of a service facilitate users' cognitive processes? ▸ What are the users' experience levels with similar services? ▸ How do users think this service should work?
Action	Initiate awareness among developers of the importance of achieving a balance between business objectives and user objectives in the delivery of highly relevant and usable services.
Challenge	A belief that once initial user requirements are captured in the early project phases, there is no further need to engage with users.
Context	Although initial requirements may be documented, there is likely to be ambiguity remaining about what exactly users want, and this can lead to misinterpretation of requirements and a solution that does not satisfy users' needs.
Action	Advocate for methodologies that allow requirements to be clarified as users interact with early prototypes based on the initial requirements gathered (but without encouraging feature creep). This will result in more usable IT solutions that can support better user experiences.

Challenge	Once an IT service or solution is deployed, little attention is paid to whether or not it remains relevant and usable.
Context	Post deployment, little or no resources are invested into understanding how users' experience might degrade as their objectives and work contexts change over time.
Action	Stimulate senior management awareness that understanding the quality of the user experience should not be confined to the development of new IT services and solutions or the upgrading of existing ones. Advocate for a user experience strategy that monitors user experience before, during, and after deployment – to check on the continuing relevance of IT services and solutions for users.

Management Artefacts

Management artefacts that may be used to develop maturity in the User Experience Design (UED) capability include:

▸ Artefacts to support user experience research methods.
▸ Artefacts to support user experience communication methods.
▸ Artefacts to support user design conceptualization methods.

Artefacts to Support User Experience Research Methods

The main purpose of user experience research methods is to determine who the users are and what their experiences are. Artefacts (for example, software, tools, and documentation) that support research methods fall into two broad approaches:

▸ *Quantitative research:* this generates data about behaviours or attitudes based on indirect observation of users – for example, using eye tracking, clickstream analysis, A/B benchmarking, survey tools, and web-server logs. This approach typically requires pre-formulated questions or investigation topics to capture large amounts of highly structured data.
▸ *Qualitative research:* this generates data about behaviours or attitudes based on direct observation of users – for example, using interviews, focus groups, or field studies. This approach typically gives more freedom to the researcher to ask open-ended questions, follow interesting lines of enquiry, probe on behaviour, or flexibly adjust the study based on early insights to better satisfy the study's objectives. The resulting collected data is typically less structured than for quantitative research methods.

The choice of which method to use and what supporting artefacts to use will usually be guided by the objectives of the user experience research. Generally speaking, qualitative methods are better suited for exploratory purposes, while quantitative methods are typically better suited for confirmatory purposes – for example, where the researcher is seeking to confirm or disconfirm a hypothesis. However, both approaches can be applied in either context.

Artefacts to Support User Experience Communication Methods

Artefacts (for example, software, tools, and documentation) that support communication of user experiences to the development team and other stakeholders can be found across the following approaches:

▸ *Story telling:* describes real people in real places doing real things, which can be a much more powerful depiction than an abstract list of functional requirements.

▸ *Persona:* a persona is the description of an ideal or archetypal user used in a development or testing environment as a representative of a group of users with shared characteristics. Using personas can help make the user experience more tangible to the development team and create empathy with users.

▸ *A user scenario:* a brief statement that details how a system might be interpreted, experienced, and used. It is often written in narrative form and told from a persona's point of view. There may be several user scenarios attached to each persona group.

▸ *A use case:* a written description of how users perform tasks in order to achieve a defined objective. It provides a list of goals which can be used to establish the scope of the IT solution and describe functions which in turn become solution requirements.

▸ *A storyboard:* a pictorial representation of a service concept or flow. Storyboards are shown to users so they can provide feedback on how well the proposed model fits their needs, and how it could be improved.

Artefacts to Support User Design Conceptualization Methods

User design conceptualization methods are used by developers to build representations of the user experience. Such representations can then be modified and improved based on user feedback before the entire system or solution is built. Artefacts (for example, software, tools, documentation) that support conceptualization methods can be found across the following popular approaches:

▸ *Wireframe:* an illustration of the primary interface elements regarding space allocation, placement of content, and functions. This typically excludes styling elements.

▸ *Prototype:* a rudimentary simulation of a proposed information system or IT solution, built for demonstration purposes to test and validate the user experience before fully developing the actual information system or IT solution.

31.5 REFERENCE

See Also

Other capabilities of IT-CMF that have a particularly close relationship with the User Experience Design (UED) capability include:

Capability	What it provides
08. Innovation Management (IM)	Ideas for improving the user experience of IT services and solutions
24. Programme and Project Management (PPM)	Project delivery methodologies that can incorporate user experience design practices
26. Research, Development and Engineering (RDE)	Investigation of new technologies and their potential usage models
28. Solutions Delivery (SD)	Requirements management and (re)development of IT solutions

Further Reading

Courage, C., and Baxter, K., 2005. *Understanding your users: a practical guide to user requirement methods, tools and techniques*. San Francisco, CA: Morgan Kaufmann.

International Organization for Standardization (ISO), 2015b. *ISO 13407 1999 Human-centred design processes for interactive systems*. Available at: <http://www.iso.org/iso/catalogue_detail.htm?csnumber=21197>.

Preece, J., Rogers, Y., and Sharp, H., 2011. *Interaction design: beyond human–computer interaction*. 3rd ed. Chichester: Wiley.

UTM

32. User Training Management

32.1 OVERVIEW

Goal

The User Training Management (UTM) capability aims to ensure that users acquire the skills they need to use business applications and other IT-supported services effectively.

Objectives

- ▶ Enhance the organization's efficiency and productivity by ensuring users receive the training they need to use business applications and other IT-supported services.
- ▶ Reduce disruption to the organization's operations due to retraining or upskilling when business applications and other IT-supported services are deployed or upgraded.
- ▶ Improve user satisfactions levels with business applications and other IT-supported services.
- ▶ Reduce user support costs in, for example, helpdesk and related areas.

Value

The User Training Management (UTM) capability ensures that users are proficient and productive in their use of business applications and other IT-supported services.

Relevance

Effective user training is key to the successful implementation and use of IT-supported services. Users must be adequately trained and educated in the use of new software and IT systems if the expected return on IT investments is to be realized. However, user training is often poorly executed, with the result that the IT function receives many unanticipated requests for support whenever new systems or upgrades are rolled out.

By developing an effective User Training Management (UTM) capability, an organization can deliver appropriate training and support content, and is able to improve user proficiency in the use of business applications and other IT-supported systems.

32.2 SCOPE

Definition

The User Training Management (UTM) capability is the ability to provide training that will improve user proficiency in the use of business applications and other IT-supported services. The User Training Management (UTM) capability covers:

▸ Ensuring that users achieve the required level of proficiency by providing appropriate training to those users who need it, when they need it, in a way that supports the organization's operational needs cost-efficiently.

▸ Delivering user training on business applications, other IT-supported services, and applications used for IT service and hardware management.

▸ Delivering training associated with IT-supported security, governance policies, industry regulations, acceptable use policies, and so on.

▸ Assessing the impact of IT-supported training on user proficiency and productivity in the work environment.

Other Capabilities

The following are addressed by other capabilities of IT-CMF:

For...	Refer to...
General skills development for employees	23. People Asset Management (PAM)
Managing requests for case-by-case IT assistance via helpdesk support	27. Service Provisioning (SRP)
Improving user experience of business applications and other IT-supported services	31. User Experience Design (UED)

32.3 UNDERSTANDING MATURITY

Recognizing Excellence

When the User Training Management (UTM) capability is well-developed or mature:

▸ Users acquire the skills they need to achieve proficiency in the use of business applications and other IT-supported services.

▸ Training requests are prioritized at an organizational level based on strategic IT development/deployment and business requirements.

▸ Training programmes ensure users have access to appropriate, targeted, and timely content.

Maturity at the Critical Capability Level

The following statements provide a high-level overview of the User Training Management (UTM) capability at successive levels of maturity:

Level 1   Training is provided on an ad hoc basis, if at all.

Level 2   Training is emerging for a limited number of business applications and other IT-supported services.

Level 3   Training is provided for the majority of business applications and other IT-supported services. Tailored training is emerging for a limited number of users.

Level 4   Training is available for virtually all business applications and other IT-supported services, and training can be tailored to the needs of various users and operational circumstances.

Level 5   All training is available on demand, in personalized formats, and is continually updated to satisfy changing needs.

Maturity at the Capability Building Block (CBB) Level

The Capability Building Blocks (CBBs) associated with the User Training Management (UTM) capability fall into two categories:

▶ Category A: three CBBs associated with **Development of Training Methodology** – these define the resources, and the mechanisms or methods for developing and delivering training content.

▶ Category B: one CBB associated with **Training Impact Assessment** – this looks at the impact of training on user proficiency and productivity levels.

These are described below, together with a summary of the different maturity levels for each.

Category A: CBBs Associated with *Development of Training Methodology*

CBB A1: Training Resources

Identify resources, including people, processes, and systems that are necessary to meet current and future training requirements.

Level 1   Resources are made available informally for the purposes of user training, if at all.

Level 2   Defined but limited resources within the IT function are available for user training. They tend to be allocated on a first-come, first-served basis.

Level 3   Resources available for user training include allocations from some other business units.

Level 4   Resources for user training are managed at an organizational level. Allocation is based on prioritized operational needs across the whole organization.

Level 5   Resources, both from within the organization and from external sources, are continually reviewed in line with strategic objectives and operational needs.

CBB A2: Delivery Methods

Identify and employ the training delivery methods that are most likely to achieve the desired levels of user proficiency (for example, face-to-face learning, web-based learning, self-paced learning).

Level 1	Delivery methods are chosen in an ad hoc manner, and may be inconsistent.
Level 2	Most user training takes place in face-to-face training sessions.
Level 3	User training is increasingly delivered using automated delivery methods.
Level 4	The training catalogue has an appropriate balance of automated and manual delivery methods, with material tailored to the needs of defined user groups.
Level 5	Delivery methods are dynamically reconfigured to provide a blended training experience, combining online and face-to-face interaction, and are personalized to the needs of individual users.

CBB A3: Training Material Development

Adopt a methodology for developing training content that will meet the requirements of the users and fit the training delivery methods.

Level 1	No formal design methodology is considered when developing training content.
Level 2	The use of design methodologies is emerging in the development of user training content for a limited number of business applications and other IT-supported services.
Level 3	Specific design methodologies are mandated for the development of user training content for most business applications and other IT-supported services, but they may not yet be consistently applied everywhere.
Level 4	Design methodologies are consistently applied in the development of all user training content for all business applications and other IT-supported services.
Level 5	Design methodologies are continually reviewed to confirm that they are resulting in the optimal design of training programmes and materials.

Category B: CBB Associated with *Training Impact Assessment*

CBB B1: Impact of Training on User Proficiency and Productivity

Evaluate the impact of training on user proficiency and productivity levels.

Level 1   Any training impact assessments are informal and conducted in an ad hoc manner.

Level 2   The IT function is starting to conduct increasingly regular training impact assessments. However, the results of assessments have only limited effect on training development.

Level 3   Standardized training impact assessments are conducted across the IT function and some other business units. These are taken into account in subsequent training content development and delivery.

Level 4   Results of training impact assessments systematically inform the planning of skills development for employees across the whole organization.

Level 5   Results of training impact assessments inform a cycle of continual improvement across the whole organization and, where appropriate, with relevant business ecosystem partners.

32.4 IMPROVEMENT PLANNING

Capability Evaluation

Two summary assessment questions are set out below, along with the typical response associated with each level of maturity.

How is IT-related training developed to address user needs?

Level 1   Any user training developed is ad hoc and typically driven in isolation for other similar efforts.

Level 2   Basic user training materials is emerging for a limited number of targeted business applications and other IT-supported services.

Level 3   There is a structured approach for generating standard training materials for many of the business applications and other IT-supported services.

Level 4   There is a comprehensive approach for generating customizable training materials for all of the business applications and other IT-supported services.

Level 5   Individual user needs and learning flexibility are central to how training is continually reviewed for improvement opportunities.

How is IT-related user training delivered, and its impact assessed?

Level 1	Training delivery and impact assessments are ad hoc, and are generally one-off events rather than routine ones.
Level 2	The frequency of training delivery is increasing, but the resulting improvements in proficiency levels may not be measured.
Level 3	There is a standardized schedule of training delivery, with a growing focus on systematic evaluation of user proficiency before and after training.
Level 4	Training is delivered on demand. The impact of training on business productivity is comprehensively measured.
Level 5	Training comprehensively addresses precise gaps in user proficiency. Impact assessments continually improve the training portfolio mix.

Key Practices-Outcomes-Metrics (POMs)

Some useful POMs for developing the User Training Management (UTM) capability are summarized below.

Level 2 POMs

Practice	Undertake assessments of user training needs within the IT function.
Outcome	Strengths and weaknesses in proficiency levels are known for the IT function. This forms a basis for action, and generates a baseline to measure the effect of improvement actions.
Metric	Percentage of users within the IT function who have had their training needs assessed.
Practice	Develop user training content for a targeted number of key business applications and other IT-supported services to increase user proficiency levels.
Outcome	Limited resources can be targeted on improving user productivity on key applications. Early successes can generate the business case for additional resources.
Metric	Percentage of prioritized business applications for which user training content is developed.
Practice	Deliver training using resources available internally within the IT function – for example, more experienced employees train the less experienced employees.
Outcome	Basic training needs are met using cost-effective internal resources.
Metric	Percentage of employees qualified as trainers.
Practice	Provide a training schedule with a repeating cycle.
Outcome	Training demand can be aggregated, and users that require training can plan in advance when to take training, minimizing disruption to their normal responsibilities.
Metric	Percentage of users satisfied with training availability.

Practice	Assess user satisfaction with the quality of training provided.
Outcome	There is better understanding of where the training needs to be improved.
Metric	Percentage of users who feel that the training met their needs.

Level 3 POMs

Practice	Develop a standardized approach for evaluating training delivery methods. Consider factors such as cost, speed of delivery, and access.
Outcome	Economies of scale and scope can be identified.
Metric	Availability of cost breakdown by training delivery method.

Practice	Identify appropriate authors for developing bespoke training material for the organization's needs. Take input from other business units into consideration during training development.
Outcome	Responsibility for the development of training material is in place, resulting in improved quality and relevance of training material/content.
Metric	Number of individuals from within the IT function who have responsibility for developing training material. Number of individuals from other business units who provide input into the development of training material.

Practice	Apply standardized approaches to assess the quality and relevance of current training offerings for the user.
Outcome	The fitness-for-purpose of current training is consistently considered and improvements can be planned.
Metric	Percentage of users who are satisfied with the breadth and depth of the training catalogue.

Practice	Apply standardized approaches to assess users in their work environments against desired training outcomes (such as speed or productivity) before and after training.
Outcome	The impact of the training can be objectively expressed.
Metric	Percentage of persons trained who have been assessed before and after training.

Level 4 POMs

Practice	Undertake employee proficiency assessments organization-wide.
Outcome	Training delivery can be prioritized according to the greatest organizational needs.
Metric	Percentage of employees across the organization who have had their proficiency levels assessed.

Practice	Introduce more flexible approaches to how training is delivered, and how the content is provided/accessed.
Outcome	Increased flexibility results in greater uptake of training across the organization and training better matches the users' demands.
Metric	Percentage of users who are satisfied with training availability.

Practice	Allocate responsibility for the development of training to a cross-organizational training group.
Outcome	The quality and relevance of the training are improved by taking the perspectives of multiple stakeholders into consideration.
Metric	Percentage of relevant business units participating.

Level 5 POMs

Practice	Continually assess proficiency levels using inputs from job roles, skill profiles, and job families.
Outcome	Current and future training programmes can be broken down by user job type, position, previous training, and business unit requirements.
Metric	Percentage of employees who have had proficiency levels assessed using input from job roles, skill profiles, and job families.
Practice	Capture input from across the business ecosystem in relation to the continual improvement of training delivery.
Outcome	The quality and relevance of the training increase, as training benefits from more diverse inputs.
Metric	Diversity of channels/stakeholders offering input to training.

Addressing Typical Challenges

Some typical challenges that can arise in attempting to develop maturity in the User Training Management (UTM) capability are set out below.

Challenge	Inadequate understanding of user proficiency needs across the organization.
Context	The focus typically tends to be on ensuring service availability, while little attention is paid to educating users on how they can maximize their use of those services.
Action	Generate awareness of the benefits of having an organization-wide understanding of user proficiency needs, and the contribution that increasing proficiency levels makes to improving both job satisfaction and business productivity.
Challenge	Lack of adequate resources (people, financial, and so on) for training design, development, and delivery.
Context	User training is not regarded as high-priority.
Action	Generate awareness at senior management level of the potential impact on key business performance indicators that raising of user proficiency levels can have.

Challenge	The quality of training across different delivery methods varies considerably.
Context	Training delivery methods tend to be chosen based on localized needs and without adherence to common guidelines. This can result in large variations in the quality of training.
Action	Stimulate discussion with senior management regarding the importance of having guiding principles in place for selecting training delivery methods, so that key factors such as quality, cost, speed of delivery, and access are systematically considered.
Challenge	Poor or limited uptake in the training offered to users.
Context	Users often have diverse preferences for when and how they would like to access training.
Action	Raise awareness at senior management level of the importance of taking users' preferences into account when selecting delivery method(s), and how increased flexibility can improve training uptake.
Challenge	Difficulty in communicating the potential impact of training.
Context	Training is delivered, but little effort is made to assess whether it meets the needs of users and business units, in terms of quality or relevance.
Action	Work with business units to track improvements in user proficiency levels and the effect on key performance indicators.

Management Artefacts

Management artefacts that may be used to develop maturity in the User Training Management (UTM) capability include:

▸ A user training management plan.
▸ A training content knowledge base.
▸ A database of training needs.
▸ A training impact assessment method.

User Training Management Plan

The user training management plan outlines the overall plan for training development and delivery, and the resources (financial, personnel, systems, material, and so on) required for them. At a more detailed level, the plan outlines:

▸ The goals and training needs.
▸ The learning objectives.
▸ The learning methods and activities.
▸ The documentation or evidence of learning.
▸ The training evaluation process to ensure quality and relevance of the training content.

The plan also specifies criteria for the selection of training delivery methods, such as quality, cost, speed of delivery, access (for example, face-to-face, virtual, blended), and content customization or personalization.

Training Content Knowledge Base
As training content is developed, a system or knowledge base should be implemented to ensure ease of access to content, and to encourage a consistent approach to the design and re-use of content to improve organizational efficiencies and to reduce costs. This knowledge base may take the form of an internal 'wiki', intranet, or cloud-based system with adequate security to enable different levels of access (for example, read only, or read/write access) depending on the type of user.

Database of Training Needs
The database consists of quantitative and qualitative data on user training needs collected from across the organization. This data is communicated to relevant stakeholders to help in the prioritization, design, development, and delivery of training material. Training requests may be prioritized at an organizational level, based on strategic IT deployments and business requirements, and translated into training programmes.

Training Impact Assessment Method
The training impact assessment method documents how users are formally assessed before and after training, and how feedback is obtained and used to improve the quality and relevance of future training content and delivery. Proficiency assessments before and after training help to determine and enhance training quality and relevance.

32.5 REFERENCE

See Also

Other capabilities of IT-CMF that have a particularly close relationship with the User Training Management (UTM) capability include:

Capability	What it provides
23. People Asset Management (PAM)	Development of employees and their skillsets
27. Service Provisioning (SRP)	User proficiency levels and potential training gaps shown up by recurring user issues
28. Solutions Delivery (SD)	Information about user training required for upcoming releases
31. User Experience Design (UED)	Information about the usability of IT services and solutions, which may inform user training needs

Further Reading

Curtis, B., Hefley, W.W., and Miller, S.A., 2009. *The people capability maturity model (P-CMM) Version 2*, 2nd ed. [pdf] Software Engineering Institute. Available at: <http://www.sei.cmu.edu/reports/09tr003.pdf>.

Beaudoin, M., Kurtz, G., Jung, I., Suzuki, K., and Grabowski, B., 2013. *Online learner competencies: knowledge, skills, and attitudes for successful learning in online settings*. Charlotte, NC: Information Age Publishing.

Managing IT for Business Value

Investments in IT must be linked to overall business benefits. This means that the investments should not be viewed simply as technology projects, but as projects that generate business value and innovation across the organization. The **Managing IT for Business Value** macro-capability provides a structure within which the IT function provides the rationale for investment in IT and measures the business benefits accruing from it.

Contents: Managing IT for Business Value

BAR

33. Benefits Assessment and Realization

33.1 OVERVIEW

Goal

The Benefits Assessment and Realization (BAR) capability aims to forecast, crystalize, and sustain the business benefits arising from IT-enabled change initiatives.

Objectives

- Increase organizational awareness, understanding, and commitment to the importance of creating a value mind-set/culture and sustaining business value from IT-enabled change.
- Promote the message that benefits do not come from technology in and of itself, but rather from the change that technology shapes and enables – change that must be led and managed.
- Focus management on outcomes of IT-enabled change initiatives and measurable benefits rather than on activities.
- Create management approaches to assess potential benefits and likely costs in a transparent and inclusive manner, with a focus on continual learning and improvement.
- Define transparent links between IT services and solutions (that is, what is produced or delivered) and their business impact (that is, their expected contribution to business objectives).
- Manage organizational interactions across complementary actions, such as process redesign, training, cultural/behavioural change, and incentive structures, to deliver and sustain the business benefits enabled by IT.
- Create a common language for describing business benefits arising from technology – for example, achievement of a business result (or end-outcome) that a stakeholder perceives to be of value (which may not necessarily be of financial value).
- Broaden employees' focus beyond efficient implementation and operation of technology to include the effective delivery of business benefits from technology implementation and operation across the full life cycle of the investment.

Value

The Benefits Assessment and Realization (BAR) capability helps an organization forecast and manage the realization of benefits from IT-enabled change initiatives.

Relevance

The purpose of investing in technology is to enable the organization to do new things or to do existing things more efficiently or effectively [1]. Technology adds value by supporting business continuity and business change [2]. However, the realization of the potential value depends not so much on the size of the investment, as on management's effectiveness in leveraging the investment to achieve business results. There is considerable variance in the effectiveness of different organizations in this regard [3], and a robust benefits management approach can help ensure that IT resources are used to deliver business value to the organization.

By establishing a mature Benefits Assessment and Realization (BAR) capability, an organization can identify, plan for, and manage the delivery of business benefits arising from technology expenditure. It can look beyond the tactical execution of individual IT projects (that is, a focus on the outputs) to the actual achievement of the business benefits (that is, a focus on the outcomes). In summary, a benefits realization capability helps an organization to confirm that it is deriving the expected benefits from IT-enabled change initiatives [4].

33.2 SCOPE

Definition

The Benefits Assessment and Realization (BAR) capability is the ability to forecast, realize, and sustain value from IT-enabled change initiatives. The Benefits Assessment and Realization (BAR) capability covers:

▶ Establishing systematic, objective, and consistent approaches to managing benefits across the full investment life cycle for IT-enabled change – that is, from benefits forecasting and planning, to benefits reviewing and reporting.
▶ Identifying and advocating cultural and behavioural changes to maximize the value of IT-enabled change.

Other Capabilities

The following are addressed by other capabilities of IT-CMF:

For...	Refer to...
Assessing risks to the realization of benefits	11. Risk Management (RM)
Formulating strategic options	14. Strategic Planning (SP)
Prioritizing the investment portfolio	18. Portfolio Planning and Prioritization (PPP)
Executing delivery of individual programmes and projects	24. Programme and Project Management (PPM)
Tracking direct and indirect costs	35. Total Cost of Ownership (TCO)

33.3 UNDERSTANDING MATURITY

Recognizing Excellence

When the Benefits Assessment and Realization (BAR) capability is well-developed or mature:

▶ There is a shared understanding throughout the organization of how IT-enabled change contributes to the realization of business value.

▶ Stakeholders agree on how to create and sustain business value from IT-enabled change.

▶ A consistent set of benefits management methods and business performance indicators underpins decision-making throughout the investment life cycle.

Maturity at the Critical Capability Level

The following statements provide a high-level overview of the Benefits Assessment and Realization (BAR) capability at successive levels of maturity:

Level 1   The organization typically focuses on delivering to technical project criteria, such as delivering on time, to budget, and to specification, rather than on realizing business benefits. Post-implementation reviews to evaluate organizational benefit are rarely conducted.

Level 2   Some larger IT-enabled change programmes are beginning to use limited forms of benefits management methods. Post-implementation reviews are occasionally conducted, mainly to evaluate technology deployment efficiency.

Level 3   Most programmes are described in terms of business value and consistently use benefits management methods. Post-implementation reviews are conducted on most programmes – these include an evaluation of the organizational changes needed to realize the value of technology deployment.

Level 4   The organization has developed deep expertise in applying benefits management methods, and responsibility for realizing value is spread across the organization. Business value reviews are conducted throughout the investment life cycle, from conceptualizing to deployment to eventual retirement.

Level 5   Management continually monitors, reviews, and improves benefits management methods across the organization, and exchanges insights with relevant business ecosystem partners. Post-implementation reviews of IT-enabled change consistently contributes to better subsequent use of resources.

Maturity at the Capability Building Block (CBB) Level

The Capability Building Blocks (CBBs) associated with the Benefits Assessment and Realization (BAR) capability fall into five categories:

▶ Category A: two CBBs associated with *Leadership* – these are concerned with developing a business value mind-set among stakeholders.

▶ Category B: four CBBs associated with *Governance* – these deal with the scope of business value management in the organization.

▶ Category C: three CBBs associated with *Benefits Process* – these deal with establishing operational practices to support benefits management.

▶ Category D: three CBBs associated with *Management of Change* – these determine how organizational change is effected.

▶ Category E: one CBB associated with *Organizational Learning* – this determines the ability of the organization to improve and develop its management of benefits.

These are described below, together with a summary of the different maturity levels for each.

Category A: CBBs Associated with *Leadership*

CBB A1: Value Culture

Create a shared understanding of what constitutes business value for the organization, and a culture focused on creating and sustaining that value.

Level 1	The organizational culture focuses on value only in an ad hoc manner.
Level 2	A shared value culture is emerging across a limited number of IT-enabled change programmes.
Level 3	Most IT-enabled change programmes share a common value culture.
Level 4	A comprehensive value culture is embedded throughout the organization for all IT-enabled change programmes.
Level 5	The organization's value culture is continually reviewed and reinforced.

CBB A2: Common Purpose

Create a shared understanding and acceptance of how IT-enabled change programmes contribute to the realization of business value in support of the organization's mission and vision.

Level 1	There is no understanding of how IT-enabled change contributes to the realization of business value, or any such understanding is limited to an individual's knowledge of specific programmes that have local impact.
Level 2	Business value drivers are emerging for the IT function, resulting in a growing understanding in parts of the IT function of how IT-enabled change contributes to the realization of business value. However, instances of specific links between business value drivers and individual IT-enabled change programmes may be limited.
Level 3	The IT function and some other business units use business value language to actively promote a common understanding of how IT-enabled change contributes to the realization of business value.
Level 4	Employees across the organization understand the contribution of IT-enabled change to business value, and are strongly committed to working together to deliver that value.
Level 5	Employees' understanding of how IT-enabled change contributes to the realization of business value and their commitment to delivery are continually validated. The organization proactively collaborates with relevant business ecosystem partners to realize business value from IT-enabled change.

Category B: CBBs Associated with *Governance*

CBB B1: Life Cycle Governance

Establish governance structures (evaluation, direction, and monitoring) for benefits management throughout the investment life cycle, from decision-making on the initial concept through to the eventual retirement of assets.

Level 1	Governance mechanisms are in place primarily for technology delivery, with no consideration of benefits management.
Level 2	An emerging benefits management governance approach is used for a limited number of key investments, but there is often a lack of consistency.
Level 3	A standardized benefits management governance approach is used across the IT function and in some other business units, resulting in consistent planning and delivery for most investments.
Level 4	A comprehensive benefits management governance approach is embedded throughout the life cycle of all investments in the organization.
Level 5	Benefits governance is continually reviewed to confirm its effectiveness and alignment with all other governance processes in the organization, and, where appropriate, with the processes in relevant business ecosystem partners.

CBB B2: Business Case Objective

Use the business case as an aid to management decision-making throughout the investment life cycle.

Level 1   Business cases, if they are developed at all, are typically developed simply for the purpose of obtaining funding, rather than justifying expenditure in terms of business value.

Level 2   A defined business case template is beginning to be used to justify expenditure in larger project proposals. However, it may be used inconsistently, thereby limiting the effectiveness of comparative evaluations.

Level 3   A standardized business case template is mandatory for justifying expenditure in key project proposals across the IT function and some other business units. Previously approved business cases are occasionally reviewed to check that the forecasted benefits are delivered.

Level 4   A single comprehensive business case template is required to justify expenditure in all investments across the organization. Previously approved business cases are regularly reviewed to check that the forecasted benefits continue to materialize.

Level 5   The business case template is continually reviewed for effectiveness, based on the outcomes of past investment decisions. The review of previously approved business cases continues until the relevant technology assets are retired or replaced.

CBB B3: Responsibility and Accountability

Assign individuals who will work to achieve the benefits (responsibility), and assign individuals who will ultimately be answerable for the delivery of benefits (accountability).

Level 1   The IT function is typically consumed with efficiently implementing new IT services and maintaining the continuity of existing IT services. Responsibility and accountability for realizing business benefits are not formally considered.

Level 2   Responsibility for realizing benefits for a limited number of projects is typically assigned to project managers. The IT function accepts a limited scope of accountability for realizing benefits. There may still be no significant engagement with business units on the topic of responsibility and accountability.

Level 3   The IT function and some other business units are beginning to jointly assign responsibility and accountability for realizing the benefits of IT-enabled change.

Level 4   There is a clear understanding and acceptance of responsibilities and accountabilities for realizing the benefits of IT-enabled change across the entire organization.

Level 5   The sharing of responsibility and accountability is continually reviewed for effectiveness, based on the outcomes of previous IT-enabled change programmes.

CBB B4: Relevant Metrics

Define and apply metrics that facilitate management oversight of benefits throughout the investment life cycle.

Level 1	Only basic financial cost metrics are typically used, such as numbers of full-time equivalent employees (FTEs) or IT funding levels. There is no effective tracking of benefits in place.
Level 2	Simple business impact metrics are beginning to be applied to a limited number of programmes. However, consistency across programmes may still be lacking.
Level 3	A standardized range of metrics for expressing business value (financial and non-financial), cost, and risk is consistently applied to most programmes, allowing benefits to be consistently expressed and compared across programmes.
Level 4	A comprehensive range of leading and lagging metrics is applied to all programmes, so that corrective action can be taken as necessary to safeguard benefits.
Level 5	The catalogue of metrics in use is continually reviewed for effectiveness, based on the benefit outcomes of previous investments.

Category C: CBBs Associated with *Benefits Process*

CBB C1: Benefits Planning

Identify, map, and communicate the interdependent outcomes that may affect the business benefits arising from IT-enabled change.

Level 1	There is little or no formal benefits planning in the organization. The main focus is on managing deployment of technology solutions and controlling deployment costs.
Level 2	A defined benefits planning approach is beginning to be used for a limited number of investment proposals. The benefit estimates may not be sufficiently validated with appropriate stakeholders, or may be too high-level, and lack appropriate levels of detail.
Level 3	Standardized benefits planning approaches are used in most investment proposals, with, for example, methods and templates for benefits mapping, a benefits register, business cases, and so on. This enables broader stakeholder engagement and more comprehensive understanding of benefits, costs, risks, and the extent of business change required.
Level 4	Comprehensive benefits planning approaches are integrated into all planning activities organization-wide, resulting in a clear shared understanding of how IT-enabled change will deliver business benefits.
Level 5	The benefits planning approaches are continually evaluated and improved based on past experiences and on insights exchanged with key business ecosystem partners.

CBB C2: Benefits Enablement

Detemine the wider organizational change necessary to realize the intended benefits from IT-enabled change.

Level 1	The focus is typically limited to technology implementation, with little consideration given to the wider organizational changes needed.
Level 2	A limited number of programmes and projects have the associated business benefits clearly articulated, with the required organizational changes incorporated into the implementation plan. The affected business units are increasingly engaged in planning and implementing the necessary organizational changes.
Level 3	Most programmes and projects have the associated business benefits clearly articulated from the outset. The affected business units are fully engaged in managing the full scope of the organizational changes required.
Level 4	The benefits arising from the organizational changes that technology enables are recognized organization-wide. The IT function and other business units are accountable for and incentivize the organizational changes needed to realize these benefits.
Level 5	The organization consistently benefits from IT-enabled change programmes and projects. The aggregate benefit accruing from all IT-enabled change programmes and projects is greater than the benefit from the individual programmes and projects.

CBB C3: Benefits Review and Harvesting

Establish oversight mechanisms to ensure that the forecasted benefits are delivered, and that the organization avails of any unexpected benefits that arise.

Level 1	There are no formal safeguards in place to detect and respond to the threat of benefits being eroded. Harvesting of any benefits accruing is ad hoc or non-existent.
Level 2	Post-implementation reviews for a limited number of larger programmes and projects consider the accrual of benefits. This typically occurs 'once off' at programme or project closure.
Level 3	Regular stage gate reviews are conducted throughout the programme or project deployment life cycle, from approval to completion, to ensure that benefits are safeguarded and enhanced when opportunities allow.
Level 4	Benefits oversight extends beyond the programme or project deployment life cycle and into its operational life cycle. Benefits accrual targets are integrated into performance appraisals.
Level 5	Benefits oversight is continually reviewed for effectiveness, based on the organization's past experiences and those of relevant business ecosystem partners.

Category D: CBBs Associated with *Management of Change*

CBB D1: Behavioural Change

Recognize, accomplish, and sustain the behavioural changes needed to achieve business benefits.

Level 1	There is limited clarity about the behavioural changes needed to realize business benefits from IT-enabled change.
Level 2	The required behavioural changes are identified in a limited number of larger programmes and projects. In some cases, there may be a lack of expert knowledge, organizational authority, and/or available resources to deliver those changes.
Level 3	Standardized planning of behavioural change is in place for most programmes and projects across the IT function and some other business units. It covers communication, skills training, and incentive schemes.
Level 4	There are comprensive programmes in place across the organization to support behavioural change. Desired behavioural changes are formally linked to personal performance objectives and reviews.
Level 5	Behavioural change is sustained by continually improving supporting approaches based on their effectiveness.

CBB D2: Stakeholder Engagement

Identify and engage relevant stakeholders to achieve the changes necessary for benefits realization.

Level 1	Most change programmes and projects have only a limited understanding of the need to engage stakeholders who could impede or accelerate the delivery of business benefits.
Level 2	Programme and project plans are beginning to include a list of relevant stakeholders and some rudimentary actions to engage them. However, a detailed stakeholder impact analysis is typically not carried out.
Level 3	Stakeholder engagement is a recognized work stream in most programmes and projects. It typically takes into consideration the ability of different stakeholders to influence change and their likely attitude to the change programme or project.
Level 4	For all programmes and projects, there is a tailored engagement strategy that takes into account how stakeholders are likely to respond to change, and how best to deal with their response.
Level 5	Stakeholder engagement methods are continually reviewed for improvements. Insights are exchanged with relevant business ecosystem partners.

CBB D3: Communication

Communicate the messages needed, and elicit and respond to feedback in order to secure commitment to the benefits realization effort.

Level 1	Communication is limited to basic project management and oversight reporting. The need to address the organizational and people aspects of change is not recognized.
Level 2	The vision for the programme or project and its general business benefits are typically communicated at the programme or project launch. However, the specific changes required at the individual stakeholder level to secure commitment to the benefits realization effort are not typically communicated.
Level 3	Throughout the programme or project delivery, there is communication aimed at securing commitment to the benefits realization effort, and it is tailored to the needs and interests of individual stakeholder groups.
Level 4	Communication aimed at securing commitment to the benefits realization effort continues beyond the programme or project delivery and into its full operational life cycle.
Level 5	Communication practices are continually reviewed to sustain stakeholder commitment to the benefits realization effort.

Category E: CBB Associated with *Organizational Learning*

CBB E1: Practice Evolution, Innovation, and Sharing

Encourage the adoption and development of benefits management practices.

Level 1	There are no defined approaches for sharing benefits management practices. Any sharing that does occur is typically unplanned – for example as people move across roles and/or projects.
Level 2	Reviews are occasionally organized to share insights and promote basic benefits management practices.
Level 3	New and improved benefits management practices are routinely disseminated, with practitioners coached in how to adapt them to their specific programme and project contexts.
Level 4	There is deep and comprehensive expertise in the use of benefits management practices across the organization, with effective networks of learning and support in place.
Level 5	There is active experimentation and exploration of new and improved approaches to tackling benefits management challenges.

33.4 IMPROVEMENT PLANNING

Capability Evaluation

Two summary assessment questions are set out below, along with the typical response associated with each level of maturity.

To what extent does the organization focus on realizing demonstrable business value from technology expenditure?

Level 1   The primary management focus is on minimizing technology implementation costs, rather than on realizing business benefits.

Level 2   Discussion of technology expenditure in terms of business benefits or outcomes that it delivers is emerging in parts of the IT function.

Level 3   The IT function and some other business units jointly assign responsibility and accountability for realizing the benefits arising from technology expenditure.

Level 4   Assignment of responsibility and accountability for realizing the benefits arising from technology expenditure is appropriately shared across the entire organization.

Level 5   The assignment of responsibility and accountability is continually reviewed to embed the organization-wide understanding that benefits accrue from the business changes that technology enables, and not from technology alone.

To what extent are business cases managed as decision-making aids?

Level 1   Business cases focus primarily on the initial deployment costs. They are typically developed simply for the purpose of obtaining funding, rather than justifying expenditure in terms of business value.

Level 2   A defined business case approach is increasingly applied to justifying expenditure for larger proposals. However, business benefits are not documented in any depth.

Level 3   Business cases for most investments are standardized to include details of the expected business benefits, along with robust analysis of the necessary business changes, the associated risks, and the costs.

Level 4   Business cases for all investments provide comprehensive support for evaluating the business benefits arising from technology expenditure by, for example, accounting for tangible and intangible benefits.

Level 5   Business cases are continually updated to reflect lessons learned from past experience to systematically inform technology investment decisions.

Key Practices-Outcomes-Metrics (POMs)

Some useful POMs for developing the Benefits Assessment and Realization (BAR) capability are summarized below.

Level 2 POMs

Practice	Promote agreement among relevant stakeholders on the definition of business value.
Outcome	Consensus grows that technology is only a means to an end – its purpose is to contribute to specified business objectives.
Metric	Percentage of heads of business units that sign-off on a common definition of business value.
Practice	Mandate a standard business case template for all IT investments.
Outcome	A common format for business plans allows investments to be compared on a cost/benefit basis.
Metric	Percentage of investments using the approved business case template.
Practice	Assign accountability for realizing benefits to IT programme managers.
Outcome	Benefits are actively considered before, during, and after project implementation. Consistent benefits management practices are gradually adopted.
Metric	Percentage of programmes with formal accountability assigned.
Practice	Establish a benefits plan to record and monitor forecasted benefits, identify their owners, and track results.
Outcome	Benefits can be actively managed while the programme is in progress (as opposed to only at the end).
Metric	Percentage of programmes for which a benefits plan is available.
Practice	Include details of how benefits were managed in the post-implementation reviews for all major programmes.
Outcome	Lessons learned can inform the management of future programmes.
Metric	Percentage of programmes/projects on which a review of benefits is carried out within six months of implementation.

Level 3 POMs

Practice	Express the impact of technology expenditure on business value, using widely understood business-relevant language.
Outcome	IT-enabled change programmes are consistently linked to their business objectives.
Metric	Percentage of IT-enabled change programmes that articulate their contribution to business value.

Practice	Engage stakeholders by using a benefits plan, highlighting the need for behavioural change to ensure successful delivery of business value.
Outcome	Adequately engaged stakeholders understand how benefits can be realized and are more likely to be committed to making the necessary organizational changes.
Metric	Percentage of key stakeholder groups engaged.
Practice	Establish a standardized governance framework for benefits planning, enablement, and review. This should include approaches/practices, roles and responsibilities, organizational structures, information requirements, and supporting tools.
Outcome	Major programmes can be managed as programmes of business change, with clear ownership of and accountability for benefits realization.
Metric	Percentage of programmes managed under a standardized governance framework.
Practice	Require a benefits map and benefits plan to be included as part of the standard business case.
Outcome	A robust business plan is created, with a focus on the realization of business benefits. Risks and dependencies that have the potential to affect the realization of benefits are identified.
Metric	Percentage of business cases that include a benefits map and a benefits plan.
Practice	For larger projects, conduct a baseline measurement on indicators defined in the business case before technology deployment, and another measurement after deployment.
Outcome	The forecasted benefits are objectively validated and confirmed.
Metric	Percentage of projects with pre- and post-deployment indicator measurements. Realized value as a percentage of forecasted value.

Level 4 POMs

Practice	Assign and incentivize accountability for realizing the benefits of technology expenditure across relevant business units.
Outcome	Benefits realization is likely to be more successful, as it depends on wider organizational change.
Metric	Percentage of programmes where accountability for achieving benefits has been accepted by relevant stakeholders. Percentage of projects where benefits are fully realized.
Practice	Require business cases to be revisited during and after project deployment to confirm that the forecasted benefits are actually accruing.
Outcome	Business cases become more thorough and realistic, because of the increased likelihood of them being revisited during and after deployment.
Metric	Percentage of approved programmes whose business case forecasts are checked during and after deployment.

Practice	Train change agents and benefits owners to deal with behavioural issues relating to organizational change and development.
Outcome	Expertise is developed to support stakeholder engagement and behavioural change initiatives.
Metric	Percentage of trained benefits delivery stakeholders.
Practice	Implement education, mentoring, and reward/sanction systems to discourage 'old' behaviour and encourage and embed 'new' behaviour to align with IT-enabled change.
Outcome	Business benefits are increasingly realized as individuals understand what is expected of them, and have the skills, knowledge, and motivation to perform their roles in the new way.
Metric	Percentage of employees who have received appropriate support. Percentage of employees whose personal objectives are linked to the achievement of business benefits.

Level 5 POMs

Practice	Actively promote participation in benefits management communities of practice.
Outcome	By sharing benefits management practices with others, the organization can learn from others' experiences and adapt its practices as appropriate.
Metric	Percentage of proven practices from external sources validated for potential use internally.
Practice	Recognize and celebrate successful demonstrations of business value delivery.
Outcome	The business value culture is continually reinforced as people learn of and from success stories.
Metric	Number of exemplars that are showcased.
Practice	Regularly review the effectiveness and relevance of the business value indicators.
Outcome	Technology investments continue to target the objectives of the organization.
Metric	Number of reviews of business value indicators.
Practice	Continually record the actual realization rate for forecasted benefits.
Outcome	The accuracy of past forecasts affects the organization's confidence in the business cases for future investment.
Metric	Percentage of projects where benefits are tracked throughout their life cycle.

Addressing Typical Challenges

Some typical challenges that can arise in attempting to develop maturity in the Benefits Assessment and Realization (BAR) capability are set out below.

Challenge	The IT function's culture is focused on technology delivery, with little consideration for the creation of business value.
Context	The IT function may have a legacy role and remit that are limited to technology implementation, and may not appreciate the need for organizational change to harvest the technology's potential benefits.
Action	Promote the principle that value is created by organizational change enabled by technology, rather than by technology itself. Encourage the organization to adopt a culture that is benefits-led rather than just concentrating on technology delivery.
Challenge	There is no common library of business value indicators (KPIs), and this hampers the expression and understanding of how technology expenditure impacts business value.
Context	Different business units measure and report performance in different ways. This makes it difficult for IT-enabled change programmes to express consistently their expected impact on business unit performance.
Action	Ascertain how different business unit leaders measure their operational and strategic performance. Draw up a draft library of business value indicators for review by the business units and agree an approved list. Then require these indicators to be used in all business cases as the basis for how business impact forecasts are expressed.
Challenge	The uptake of benefits management practices across programmes is slow.
Context	Programme managers and stakeholders generally feel that they don't have the necessary time or support to adopt such practices.
Action	Initiate an awareness-raising campaign on the importance of business value management in day-to-day activities. Promote benefits management practices, and regularly check compliance across programmes.
Challenge	Joint ownership for delivering business value from IT-enabled change is not readily accepted by the affected business units. There is difficulty in managing benefits realization because of the cross-functional nature of benefits management.
Context	Other business units may be unwilling to accept joint responsibility for realizing business value if they lack confidence in the programme delivery management, or in the abilities of the IT function or an external service provider.
Action	Work on establishing trust between all parties by seeking to identify and address concerns early in a programme. Consider establishing a joint oversight committee of relevant stakeholders to rapidly troubleshoot issues as they arise.

Management Artefacts

Management artefacts that may be used to develop maturity in the Benefits Assessment and Realization (BAR) capability include:

▸ A library of business value indicators.
▸ A benefits plan.
▸ A business case template.
▸ A benefits dependency map.

Library of Business Value Indicators

Defining and using standard indicators establishes a common language for describing specific, observable, and quantifiable impacts on business goals. Value indicators are financial and non-financial measurements of business value, against which all initiatives can be measured – if the impact of a proposed project cannot be expressed in terms of one or more value indicators, then it should not proceed. The specific value indicators for each organization will vary, but they are likely to be related to such items as cash cycle, efficiency, time to market, customer growth/retention, compliance with regulations, and so on. Each value indicator will typically have a title, description, and calculation formula. Value indicators provide a framework for understanding and quantifying business benefits from IT-enabled change.

Benefits Plan

The benefits plan documents the ownership of expected benefits and the responsibilities for delivering them. It identifies the organizational changes that are required to realize the benefits and who is responsible for making them happen. It is separate from the technical implementation plan but depends on it to introduce the enabling technology. The plan supports tracking of benefits over time to determine the business value effectiveness of IT-enabled change.

Business Case Template

The business case template outlines how the financial and business justification for a proposed IT-enabled change programme is to be presented. It sets out the format for presenting the analysis of costs, benefits, risks, and underlying assumptions, and describes how the proposed investment should be related to its strategic context. The template should cover all topics that are taken into account in making a decision about whether a project should proceed. Business cases constructed using a common template are easily compared with one another, so that informed choices can be made.

The business case remains important throughout the entire life cycle of an IT investment – from the initial decision to proceed to the decisions made at periodic project reviews to continue, modify, or terminate the project. The template should thus cover items that are of relevance throughout the life cycle.

Benefits Dependency Map

In many projects, the link between business drivers and intended benefits to be derived from the IT solution's functionality is not always clear. As a result, many projects end up focusing simply on technology implementation. A benefits dependency map is a graphic illustration of the cause and effect links between overall investment objectives, intended benefits, underlying organizational changes needed, and the enabling technology. A benefits dependency map can promote a common understanding among stakeholders that, to realize intended benefits, everyone involved must treat the project as an organizational change project, and not just a technology implementation project.

33.5 REFERENCE

See Also

Other capabilities of IT-CMF that have a particularly close relationship with the Benefits Assessment and Realization (BAR) capability include:

Capability	What it provides
09. IT Leadership and Governance (ITG)	Defined guidelines for establishing the accountability framework for business value realization
11. Risk Management (RM)	Insights on risks that could threaten the realization of benefits
14. Strategic Planning (SP)	The strategic context and objectives, to inform how business value should be expressed
18. Portfolio Planning and Prioritization (PPP)	Oversight on approving/rejecting and prioritizing proposed business cases
35. Total Cost of Ownership (TCO)	Necessary input on the total cost of IT investments, to enable business case evaluations

Further Reading

Ashurst, C., 2011. *Benefits realization from information technology.* New York, NY: Palgrave Macmillan.

ISACA, 2010. *Enterprise value: governance of IT investments. The Val IT Framework 2.0.* Rolling Meadows, IL: ISACA.

Jenner, S., 2012. *Managing benefits.* London: The Stationery Office.

Schryen, G., 2013. Revisiting IS business value research: what we already know, what we still need to know, and how we can get there. *European Journal of Information Systems,* 22, 139–69.

Sward, D., 2006. *Measuring the business value of information technology.* Hillsboro, OR: Intel Press.

Ward, J., and Daniel, E., 2006. *Benefits management.* Chichester: John Wiley.

Notes

[1] Peppard, J., Ward, J., and Daniel, E., 2007. Managing the realization of business benefits from IT investments. *MIS Quarterly Executive*, 6(1), 1–11.

[2] Markus, M.L., and Soh, C.,1995. How IT creates value, a process theory synthesis. In: *Proceedings of the 16th International Conference on Information Systems*, Amsterdam.

[3] Jurison, J., 1996. Toward more effective management of information technology benefits. *Journal of Strategic Information Systems*, 5(4), 263–74.

[4] Thorp, J., 2003. *The Information Paradox – realizing the business benefits of information technology*. Toronto, CA: McGraw-Hill.

PM

34. Portfolio Management

34.1 OVERVIEW

Goal

The Portfolio Management (PM) capability aims to monitor and report on the status of an investment portfolio of IT programmes.

Objectives

▶ Monitor ongoing risks, progress deviations, and other factors that might impact on the portfolio's success.
▶ Improve consistency in the evaluation of the portfolio's current status.
▶ Support timely delivery of programmes within the portfolio through effective monitoring of resource allocation and use.
▶ Improve confidence that the programmes in the portfolio remain aligned with the organization's overall strategy and business objectives.
▶ Amplify business value realization across related programmes.

Value

The Portfolio Management (PM) capability helps ensure that the status of programmes is closely tracked to support early identification of potential issues and to minimize programme delivery conflicts.

Relevance

Many IT functions are reputed to under-deliver across their IT investment portfolios. An investment programme portfolio is likely to consist of complex and interdependent programmes, which compete for finite financial, technical, and people resources. A portfolio approach to managing programmes should be developed to closely monitor progress, and to ensure that planned resource allocations remain on track to deliver business value.

By establishing an effective Portfolio Management (PM) capability, an organization can closely monitor and track the progress of programmes that are part of the portfolio. Additionally, past experiences on the performance of previous portfolios can be fed forward to support the current portfolio's delivery [1] [2], enabling more effective decisions to be taken that help minimize resource demand conflicts and support balanced portfolio execution.

34.2 SCOPE

Definition

The Portfolio Management (PM) capability is the ability to monitor, track, and analyse the programmes in the IT portfolio, and to report on their status. The Portfolio Management (PM) capability covers:

▸ Monitoring and tracking the progress and impact of programmes within the portfolio.

▸ Reviewing the programmes in the portfolio for adherence to the original business case.

▸ Monitoring utilization rates against planned resource allocations, including financial, technical, and people resources.

▸ Providing the Portfolio Planning and Prioritization (PPP) capability with an up-to-date portfolio status, including any deviations beyond a defined threshold on progress and expected impact.

Related Capabilities

The following are addressed by other capabilities of IT-CMF:

For...	Refer to...
Modelling and planning the availability of resources for the IT function	04. Capacity Forecasting and Planning (CFP)
Procuring services or suppliers	13. Sourcing (SRC)
Deciding on which programmes to invest in, continue, or stop	18. Portfolio Planning and Prioritization (PPP)
Setting up and executing individual programme tasks	24. Programme and Project Management (PPM)
Managing suppliers	29. Supplier Management (SUM)
Benefits forecasting and business case development	33. Benefits Assessment and Realization (BAR)

34.3 UNDERSTANDING MATURITY

Recognizing Excellence

When the Portfolio Management (PM) capability is well-developed or mature:

▸ Systematic approaches are in place for tracking and monitoring programmes within a defined portfolio.

▸ Timely reporting on the portfolio's progress is regularly provided to executive-level management, and when warranted, corrective action can be taken swiftly.

▸ Impact analysis on interdependent programmes is readily available when there are progress deviations.

▸ Resource allocations are monitored for alignment with the organization's overall strategy.

▸ Past portfolio performances help inform how the current portfolio is managed.

Maturity at the Critical Capability Level

The following statements provide a high-level overview of the Portfolio Management (PM) capability at successive levels of maturity:

Level 1   Portfolio management activities are non-existent or are performed in an ad hoc manner.

Level 2   A portfolio approach is emerging for a limited number of key programmes in the IT function, tracking basic data on high-level milestones and resource utilization versus allocation.

Level 3   A portfolio approach is firmly established for programmes in the IT function and for some other business units, modelling interdependencies with other programmes, critical paths, and resource utilization.

Level 4   A comprehensive suite of performance metrics is tracked for the IT portfolio across the organization, and what-if scenario analysis can be readily modelled.

Level 5   Portfolio management approaches are continually improved, and involve key business ecosystem partners when relevant.

Maturity at the Capability Building Block (CBB) Level

The Capability Building Blocks (CBBs) associated with the Portfolio Management (PM) capability fall into two categories:

▶ Category A: two CBBs associated with **Appraisal** – these deal with monitoring the status and resource usage of programmes within the portfolio.

▶ Category B: two CBBs associated with **Sensitivity Analysis and Communication** – these deal with possible deviations from planned forecasts, and communicate portfolio status to support timely decision-making and future planning activities.

These are described below, together with a summary of the different maturity levels for each.

Category A: CBBs Associated with *Appraisal*

CBB A1: Progress Monitoring

Monitor and track the progression of programmes within the portfolio.

Level 1   Status tracking of programmes is non-existent or ad hoc.

Level 2   High-level milestones for a limited number of programmes within the IT function are tracked using an emerging portfolio approach.

Level 3   Critical path activities are tracked across most programmes within the IT function and for some other business units using common portfolio approaches (for example, a portfolio dashboard).

Level 4   Critical path activities for programmes across the organization are tracked using comprehensive portfolio approaches.

Level 5   Critical path tracking approaches are continually improved, and when appropriate may reflect input from relevant business ecosystem partners.

CBB A2: Resource Monitoring

Monitor the utilization of financial, technical, and people resources against planned allocations for programmes within the portfolio.

Level 1	Resource allocation and utilization are monitored in an ad hoc manner, if at all.
Level 2	Basic data on resource allocation and utilization is collected for a limited number of programmes within the portfolio. Typically, however, poor performance only comes to light when it deviates significantly beyond defined thresholds.
Level 3	Monitoring of resource utilization against planned allocations occurs for most programmes across the IT function. Performance that is outside defined thresholds can be readily assessed and reported on.
Level 4	There is organization-wide monitoring regarding resource utilization against planned allocations for all programmes.
Level 5	Resource allocation and utilization rates are continually improved, and input from relevant business ecosystem partners is received where necessary.

Category B: CBBs Associated with *Sensitivity Analysis and Communication*

CBB B1: Impact Modelling and Scenario Analysis

Conduct 'what if' analysis to determine the impact potential scenarios might have on the portfolio's collective resources, schedules, and business value. Monitor corrective actions taken within the portfolio.

Level 1	Modelling of the business impact of the portfolio is non-existent or ad hoc.
Level 2	Changes in the business impact or value-at-risk are modelled for a limited number of programmes within the IT function using emerging analysis approaches.
Level 3	Changes in the business impact or value-at-risk are modelled for most programmes across the IT function and for some other business units using standardized analysis approaches.
Level 4	Regular modelling occurs for programmes across the organization using comprehensive analysis approaches.
Level 5	Changes in the business impact or value-at-risk for the portfolio are continually reviewed and dynamically updated with corrective feedback loops.

CBB B2: Status Reporting

Report on the current portfolio status, including significant progress deviations, emergent risks, and business value threats.

Level 1	Reporting on the programmes in the portfolio is non-existent or ad hoc. Reports may be inaccurate, incomplete, and unreliable.
Level 2	Reports on the current status and schedule of the portfolio are available, but not in a standardized format. Typically, they arise from direct requests rather than as part of a planned cycle.
Level 3	A standardized format is used for reporting current status on most programmes within the portfolio. This includes, for example, details of status, schedule, progress, resourcing levels, and risks. The reports are circulated to key stakeholders at an agreed frequency – for example, weekly, bi-weekly, or monthly.
Level 4	A comprehensive and formal approach is in place for organization-wide reporting on the current status of all programmes in the portfolio across the organization. These reports are provided to a centralized board with appropriate decision-making authority.
Level 5	Timely decision-making on the portfolio is supported by flexible reporting options (for example, dynamic drill-down on data, custom what-if analysis).

34.4 IMPROVEMENT PLANNING

Capability Evaluation

Two summary assessment questions are set out below, along with the typical response associated with each level of maturity.

To what extent does the organization track the status of IT programmes using a portfolio approach?

Level 1	Status tracking of programmes is non-existent or ad hoc.
Level 2	High-level milestones for a limited number of programmes are tracked inside the IT function using an emerging portfolio approach.
Level 3	Critical path activities are tracked across most programmes within the IT function and for some other business units using a standardized portfolio approach.
Level 4	Critical path activities and other performance metrics for all programmes across the wider organization are tracked using a comprehensive portfolio approach.
Level 5	Portfolio status tracking is continually reviewed for improvements, frequently involving input from relevant business ecosystem partners.

To what extent are the current status, progress deviations, and risks of programmes in the portfolio reported upon to support decision-making?

Level 1	Reporting on programmes in the portfolio is non-existent or ad hoc. Reports may be inaccurate or incomplete, and do not generally support effective decision-making or trigger corrective actions.
Level 2	Reports are available, but not in a standardized format. Typically, they arise from direct requests rather than as part of a planned cycle.
Level 3	A standardized template is used for reporting on most programmes within the portfolio. The reports are circulated to key personnel at an agreed frequency.
Level 4	A comprehensive and formal reporting approach is in place for all programmes across the organization. Reports enable timely actions to be taken.
Level 5	Timely decision-making on the portfolio is supported by flexible reporting options – for example, dynamic drill-down, custom what-if analysis. Reporting approaches are continually examined for improvement opportunities.

Key Practices-Outcomes-Metrics (POMs)

Some useful POMs for developing the Portfolio Management (PM) capability are summarized below.

Level 2 POMs

Practice	Centrally track the high-level delivery milestones for key programmes within the IT function.
Outcome	An overview of the current delivery status against the original plan facilitates improved decision-making in relation to managing the portfolio.
Metric	Percentage of programmes with milestone tracking.
Practice	Apply office productivity applications to support portfolio management approaches – for example, define templates using spreadsheet and document applications.
Outcome	Portfolio management is facilitated through the use of basic templates.
Metric	Percentage of programmes tracked using defined templates.
Practice	Monitor the current against the planned spend for key programmes in the portfolio.
Outcome	Basic budget data is available, and can be used to support future portfolio decision-making.
Metric	Percentage of programmes with financial resource monitoring.

Practice	Establish a basic reporting approach that outlines the status of key programmes within the portfolio to key stakeholders.
Outcome	There is growing transparency on fundamental portfolio data such as current status, resource utilization, and any issues that might impact the portfolio's success.
Metric	Percentage of programmes with status reporting.

Level 3 POMs

Practice	Promote the central monitoring of standardized variables such as business value, risks, and resource utilization for most programmes in the portfolio – for example, by using a portfolio dashboard.
Outcome	There is increasing transparency on most programmes which can help initiate corrective actions.
Metric	Percentage of programmes with monitoring of standardized variables.
Practice	Regularly track defined success metrics for all programmes.
Outcome	Wider compliance to status reporting provides better visibility on the portfolio's entire progress, and the impact of any progress deviations.
Metric	Percentage of programmes with milestone tracking. Percentage of programmes with status reporting.
Practice	Use a standard approach for reporting on the portfolio's status to key stakeholders at an agreed frequency.
Outcome	Visibility on the portfolio's progress is increased, supporting decisions on reprioritization if required.
Metric	Percentage of programmes with standardized status reporting.

Level 4 POMs

Practice	Monitor the impact of corrective actions taken to ensure that appropriate variables are being tracked.
Outcome	The timely execution of corrective actions can prevent negative impacts.
Metric	Percentage of corrective actions that ensured the achievement of the original programme objectives.
Practice	Conduct scenario analysis across the entire portfolio, and consider the consequences that failure of key programmes or changes in strategic direction might have on the portfolio.
Outcome	Decision-making and planning are enhanced with better understanding of the key influencing variables.
Metric	Percentage of programmes on which scenario analysis is conducted.

Practice	Provide reports on the portfolio's status to key stakeholders across the organization.
Outcome	Distribution of reports to stakeholders with appropriate authority ensures clear transparency on all issues that might impact the portfolio's success. The impact of these issues is highlighted earlier and can be dealt with in a way that will not adversely impact the critical path activities.
Metric	Percentage of programmes with a current status report.

Level 5 POMs

Practice	Make co-sharing of relevant portfolio programmes with key business ecosystem partners systematic.
Outcome	The impact of potential deviations across relevant business ecosystem partners is better understood.
Metric	Percentage of the portfolio for which key business ecosystem partners provide status report inputs. Percentage of the portfolio on which status reports are shared with key business ecosystem partners.
Practice	Continually evaluate the value-at-risk for the entire portfolio.
Outcome	There is clearer understanding of variables that could lead to potential business value loss, especially where these are trending outside defined safe limits.
Metric	Percentage of programmes that use value-at-risk and scenario analysis monitoring.
Practice	Monitor resource utilization across the portfolio, and redistribute unused resources to other programmes when such requirements arise.
Outcome	Resources can be temporarily or permanently diverted to support opportunities or challenges in other programmes.
Metric	Percentage of programmes with forward-looking resource monitoring.
Practice	Continually update the assumptions that underlie the portfolio to ensure that the full range of possible portfolio outcomes is covered.
Outcome	Underlying outcome scenarios are continually stress-tested to support timely decision-making.
Metric	Frequency of reviews of underlying assumptions (and updates as appropriate) for differing scenarios.

Addressing Typical Challenges

Some typical challenges that can arise in attempting to develop maturity in the Portfolio Management (PM) capability are set out below.

Challenge	Lack of senior management support for portfolio management activities.
Context	Portfolio management may not be regarded as being of strategic importance – for example, when scarce resources are exclusively devoted to individual programmes, rather than being considered where they might have the biggest impact across the programme portfolio.
Action	Promote the value of a portfolio approach to senior management as the most efficient and effective approach for deploying the organization's resources.
Challenge	Inadequate investment of resources in portfolio management activities.
Context	Individual business units are reluctant to invest in portfolio management activities, as they view this as a cross-organizational activity that should be centrally coordinated.
Action	Promote the idea that portfolio management will be successful only if individuals and business units across the organization jointly contribute to it.
Challenge	Inadequate visibility of the delivery status of programmes across the portfolio.
Context	Progress, risks, progress deviations, and other metrics in relation to programmes are not adequately tracked owing to fragmented oversight approaches and a reluctance to report activities.
Action	Raise awareness at a senior management level of the importance of portfolio oversight in informing programme reprioritization, and future portfolio planning activities.
Challenge	Inability to reallocate resources between programmes in the portfolio in a timely manner.
Context	There is inadequate utilization monitoring for financial, technical, and people resources across programmes in the portfolio.
Action	Raise awareness at a senior management level of the importance of clear visibility on resources' availability in order to adjust allocation as required, and minimize resource wastage.
Challenge	Failure to adopt a balanced and holistic view of the entire portfolio.
Context	Too much emphasis is placed on individual programmes, rather than optimizing outcomes across the entire portfolio.
Action	Promote to senior management the value of using balanced criteria to evaluate the entire portfolio – where such criteria encompass the organization's strategic direction and business objectives.
Challenge	Poor organizational awareness of the benefits from portfolio management activities.
Context	Portfolio management activities are poorly monitored and communicated.
Action	Promote widespread awareness among stakeholders of successes and quick wins arising from portfolio management activities.

Management Artefacts

Management artefacts that may be used to develop maturity in the Portfolio Management (PM) capability include:

▸ A portfolio report.
▸ A portfolio dashboard.
▸ A scenario analysis model.

Portfolio Report

A portfolio report includes a detailed overview of all programmes in the portfolio and is updated over time to reflect the portfolio's current status, to track actual versus planned progress, and to record progress deviations, risks, and other issues that may impact the successful completion of programmes. Financial, technical, and people resource utilization is tracked, compared to the plan, thereby providing visibility into resource constraints and conflicts. The portfolio report will inform decision-making to improve programme success rates.

Portfolio Dashboard

A portfolio dashboard provides a clear, visual summary of the portfolio's overall health, and as such is a useful tool to support the management team in portfolio monitoring and control. The dashboard should highlight the key performance metrics in relation to all programmes in the portfolio. These might include, for example, overall status, scope, schedule, budget, resource utilization, risk exposure, portfolio changes, stakeholder satisfaction, strategic alignment, and so on.

Typically, a dashboard displays data in a graphical format. A simple and useful visual approach is to adopt red (critical), amber (attention required), and green (on target) status symbols for the dimensions being measured. In this way, an organization might graphically record the number of programmes in the portfolio that are on track, off track because of minor issues, and off track because of significant issues. This quick, visual summary of the entire portfolio means that detailed status reports need to be read only for those programmes that require attention.

Scenario Analysis Model

A scenario analysis model supports decision-making in relation to a programme based on the analysis of different possible future scenarios, and by identifying and challenging the key assumptions and variables upon which the programme plan was originally based. An organization develops a series of scenarios that reflect possible future situations and outcomes, based on certain trends continuing or on certain conditions being met. These scenarios may be developed by gathering data on factors that might impact on the portfolio's composition, resources, and schedules. Through conducting 'what if' analysis, the impact of different scenarios on programmes can be reflected, and an organization can adjust the plan to reflect the most likely future scenario.

34.5 REFERENCE

See Also

Other capabilities of IT-CMF that have a particularly close relationship with the Portfolio Management (PM) capability include:

Capability	What it provides
11. Risk Management (RM)	Information on proactively assessing, managing, and handling exposure, on the potential outcomes of portfolio risks, and on scenario models
14. Strategic Planning (SP)	Details on business objectives and plans
18. Portfolio Planning and Prioritization (PPP)	Prioritization of IT programmes for investment, and approval of the allocation of resources among them
24. Programme and Project Management (PPM)	Support for programme execution and generation of individual status reports
33. Benefits Assessment and Realization (BAR)	Evaluation of potential benefits accruing from the programmes in the portfolio mix

Further Reading

Kaplan, J.D., 2009. *Strategic IT portfolio management: governing enterprise transformation.* Waltham, MA: PRTM.

Levin, G., and Wyzalek, J. (eds.), 2014. *Portfolio management: a strategic approach* (Best Practices and Advances in Programme Management Series). Boca Raton, FL: CRC Press.

Maizlish, B., and Handler, R., 2008. *IT (information technology) portfolio management step-by-step: unlocking the business value of technology.* Hoboken, NJ: Wiley.

Project Management Institute, 2013. *The standard for portfolio management.* 3rd ed. Newtown Square, PA: Project Management Institute.

Notes

[1] Project Management Institute, 2013. *The standard for portfolio management.* 3rd ed. Newtown Square, PA: Project Management Institute.

[2] Kaplan, J.D., 2009. *Strategic IT portfolio management: governing enterprise transformation.* Waltham, MA: PRTM.

TCO
35. Total Cost of Ownership

35.1 OVERVIEW

Goal

The Total Cost of Ownership (TCO) capability aims to collect, analyse, and disseminate data on all costs associated with an IT asset or IT-enabled business service throughout its life cycle, from initial acquisition, through deployment, operations, and maintenance, to its eventual removal.

Objectives

▶ Establish a standardized method of estimating, tracking, comparing, and managing the life cycle costs of IT assets and IT-enabled business services.

▶ Improve IT investment decisions by systematically comparing the incremental costs (direct and indirect) of competing systems to the full costs of existing systems.

▶ Raise awareness in the organization of the full costs of IT, and promote strategic budgeting by collecting and disseminating data on the full life cycle costs of technology.

▶ Improve the accuracy of total cost of ownership forecasts based on lessons learned from comparing forecasted and actual costs incurred.

Value

The Total Cost of Ownership (TCO) capability analyses the life cycle costs associated with IT assets and IT-enabled business services. It facilitates investment selections, drives service improvements, and helps control costs.

Relevance

The total cost of owning or operating an IT asset or IT-enabled business service includes not only the initial cost of acquisition and deployment, but also ongoing recurring costs, such as those associated with operations, support, and maintenance – for example, training, upgrades, licences, replacements, consumables, retirements, and disposals. Over the lifetime of the asset or service, these costs can greatly exceed the initial cost of acquisition. When these costs are fully understood, investment decisions are better informed, and overall costs within the IT function are more easily controlled [1].

By developing an effective Total Cost of Ownership (TCO) capability, an organization can make more informed decisions on the management of legacy IT costs and the selection of new investments. For example, taking total cost of ownership into account when evaluating alternative systems leads to a more realistic assessment of their value to the business, and can lead to considerable savings over the lifetime of the chosen system.

35.2 SCOPE

Definition

The Total Cost of Ownership (TCO) capability is the ability to identify, compare, and control all direct and indirect costs associated with IT assets and IT-enabled business services. The Total Cost of Ownership (TCO) capability covers:

▸ Identifying and analysing IT costs across asset and service life cycles, from acquisition to operations, enhancements, and end of life.

▸ Identifying all costs that both directly and indirectly affect the bottom line – for example hardware and software acquisition, management and support, communications, training, end-user expenses, the opportunity cost of downtime, and other productivity losses.

▸ Establishing a common methodology for comparing costs within and across IT assets, processes, and services.

Other Capabilities

The following are addressed by other capabilities of IT-CMF:

For...	Refer to...
Allocating/charging back direct and indirect costs	01. Accounting and Allocation (AA)
Refining the IT spending plan based on the calculated total cost of ownership	15. Budget Management (BGM)

35.3 UNDERSTANDING MATURITY

Recognizing Excellence

When the Total Cost of Ownership (TCO) capability is well-developed or mature:

▸ The organization is able to identify opportunities for reducing costs by reliably tracking the total cost of ownership across all classes of IT assets and IT-enabled business services.

▸ Total cost of ownership models incorporate a comprehensive set of direct and indirect costs, and are continually refreshed based on actual costs realized.

▸ Strategic portfolio decisions, including investment and retirement decisions, are better informed.

▸ The total cost of ownership approach is fully aligned with the wider organizational finance systems and IT asset and software licensing databases for costs and asset tracking.

▸ Total cost of ownership methods are clear and transparent. Decisions based on total cost of ownership also consider business benefits and are made jointly with relevant business stakeholders.

Maturity at the Critical Capability Level

The following statements provide a high-level overview of the Total Cost of Ownership (TCO) capability at successive levels of maturity:

Level 1	Total cost of ownership concepts and methodologies are loosely applied, if at all.
Level 2	Defined methods are emerging for establishing total cost of ownership for a limited number of key IT projects and IT-enabled business services. Actual cost data is rarely used to refresh estimated total cost of ownership data.
Level 3	Standardized total cost of ownership is tracked for most IT assets and services. Total cost of ownership data reflects direct costs and an increasing proportion of indirect costs. Data is occasionally refreshed (typically annually) based on actual costs.
Level 4	Comprehensive total cost of ownership tools and methods are used to collect relevant direct and indirect cost data for all IT assets and services. Data is periodically refreshed (typically monthly) based on actual costs.
Level 5	Total cost of ownership tools and methods are continually reviewed to reflect industry best-known practice. Total cost of ownership data is updated to reflect actual costs in near real time via database linkages.

Maturity at the Capability Building Block (CBB) Level

The Capability Building Blocks (CBBs) associated with the Total Cost of Ownership (TCO) capability fall into three categories:

▶ Category A: three CBBs associated with **Models, Tools, and Methods** – these develop the approaches for estimating and calculating costs, tracking cost drivers, and enabling comparisons within and across IT assets and IT-enabled business services.

▶ Category B: two CBBs associated with **Adoption and Impact** – these promote the widespread adoption/use of total cost of ownership approaches to inform decision-making.

▶ Category C: two CBBs associated with **Stakeholder Management** – these deal with including key stakeholders in total cost of ownership decision-making.

These are described below, together with a summary of the different maturity levels for each.

Category A: CBBs Associated with *Models, Tools, and Methods*

CBB A1: Cost Coverage

Identify cost drivers throughout the life cycle of the asset or IT-enabled business service, to include direct and indirect costs involved in acquisition, operations, enhancements, and end of life.

Level 1	Only the most obvious of direct costs for IT assets and services are typically considered.
Level 2	Most direct costs and some indirect costs are identified, and these are refreshed using actual cost data once annually for a limited number of key IT assets and services.
Level 3	All direct costs and most indirect costs are identified, and these are refreshed using actual cost data at least quarterly for most IT assets and services.
Level 4	All direct and indirect costs are identified, and these are refreshed using actual cost data at least monthly for all IT assets and services.
Level 5	Continual improvements are applied to the collection of actual cost data, and the total cost of ownership data is refreshed in near real time as costs are incurred.

CBB A2: Tracking Methods

Establish methods to track total cost of ownership, and integrate them into the financial accounting systems of the organization.

Level 1	There is no or ad hoc use of total cost of ownership tracking methods.
Level 2	A standard manual approach is emerging for tracking total cost of ownership in parts of the IT function.
Level 3	There is a partly automated, standard method for tracking total cost of ownership across the IT function which is designed to support investment, retirement, and strategic planning decisions. It has some linkages with the wider organizational accounting systems.
Level 4	Total cost of ownership methods are adequately automated, effectively support investment, retirement, and strategic planning decisions, and seamlessly integrate with the wider organizational accounting systems.
Level 5	The total cost of ownership methods and their linkages with relevant business ecosystem partners are continually reviewed for improvement.

CBB A3: Data Reliability

Create reliable total cost of ownership analysis for IT assets and IT-enabled business services.

Level 1	IT assets and services are typically tracked on an ad hoc basis, if at all. There is little confidence in the reliability of results.
Level 2	A defined approach is emerging for tracking total cost of ownership for a limited number of IT assets and services. The accuracy of projections is improving but still varies.
Level 3	The method of tracking total cost of ownership is standardized for most IT assets and services. The accuracy of projections is increasing.
Level 4	Comprehensive total cost of ownership tracking is applied to all IT assets and services. Projections are accurate within acceptable tolerance/confidence levels.
Level 5	Total cost of ownership projections are considered robust and reliable. They are continually revised in light of experience.

Category B: CBBs Associated with *Adoption and Impact*

CBB B1: Adoption

Promote organizational uptake of total cost of ownership models, tools, and methods.

Level 1	Total cost of ownership models, tools, and methods are adopted on an ad hoc basis, if at all.
Level 2	Parts of the IT function make purposeful efforts to use total cost of ownership models, tools, and methods, reflecting an emerging cost management culture.
Level 3	The entire IT function has adopted a standard set of total cost of ownership models, tools, and methods, in order to manage IT costs.
Level 4	The IT function, along with the rest of the business, uses a comprehensive suite of total cost of ownership models, tools, and methods, reflecting an organization-wide cost management culture.
Level 5	Total cost of ownership models, tools, and methods are continually reviewed for improvements, and are used jointly with relevant business ecosystem partners.

CBB B2: Impact on Decision-Making

Use total cost of ownership data to inform business decisions, such as decisions to invest in, retire or replace systems, and also decisions relating to budget planning, and evaluation of competing options and business cases.

Level 1	There may be some informal and ad hoc use of total cost of ownership data for cost control.
Level 2	Total cost of ownership data is increasingly used on a limited number of IT assets and IT-enabled business services, resulting in the identification of a limited number of cost control opportunities.
Level 3	Total cost of ownership data for most IT assets and services is regularly used to build a portfolio of opportunities for cost control.
Level 4	Total cost of ownership data is systematically used to restructure the entire cost base across all IT assets and services.
Level 5	Total cost of ownership data is continually reviewed to deliver informed financial decisions across the entire organization, frequently leveraging insights from relevant business ecosystem partners.

Category C: CBBs Associated with *Stakeholder Management*

CBB C1: Communication

Communicate total cost of ownership activities and outcomes with key stakeholders.

Level 1	Total cost of ownership activities and outcomes are reported in an ad hoc manner, if at all.
Level 2	Total cost of ownership activities and outcomes are beginning to be communicated more reliably in some parts of the IT function.
Level 3	Total cost of ownership activities and outcomes are communicated in a consistent manner across the IT function and to some other business units.
Level 4	The communication of total cost of ownership activities and outcomes reaches stakeholders organization-wide, and becomes embedded in the organization's culture.
Level 5	Total cost of ownership communication regularly extends to relevant business ecosystem stakeholders.

CBB C2: Inclusion

Involve stakeholders in relevant total cost of ownership calculation decisions to support the financial management of IT.

Level 1   Some informal stakeholder involvement may occur in an ad hoc manner.

Level 2   A defined approach is beginning to be adopted for engaging with a limited number of IT stakeholders regarding total cost of ownership calculation decisions.

Level 3   A standard approach is adopted for engaging with all relevant stakeholders across the IT function regarding total cost of ownership calculation decisions.

Level 4   There is a comprehensive approach for engaging with relevant stakeholders across the organization regarding total cost of ownership calculation decisions.

Level 5   The engagement approach is continually reviewed for inclusiveness, and relevant business ecosystem partners are included when appropriate.

35.4 IMPROVEMENT PLANNING

Capability Evaluation

Two summary assessment questions are set out below, along with the typical response associated with each level of maturity.

How is the total cost of ownership for IT assets and IT-enabled business services calculated to identify IT cost drivers?

Level 1   There is no or limited cost tracking, resulting in unreliable cost projections.

Level 2   There is basic tracking for a limited number of IT assets and services in parts of the IT function. The reliability of cost projections is improving.

Level 3   There is structured cost tracking for most IT assets and services across the IT function. Cost projections are accurate most of the time.

Level 4   Automated cost tracking is in place for all IT assets and services across the organization. Cost projections are accurate within broad tolerance ranges.

Level 5   Near real-time cost tracking extends to relevant business ecosystem partners. Cost projections are accurate within tight tolerance ranges.

To what extent do total cost of ownership activities support decision-making?

Level 1   Total cost of ownership activities may support decision-making, but mostly in an ad hoc manner.

Level 2   Defined total cost of ownership activities are used in parts of the IT function to inform a limited number of cost management targets and investment decisions.

Level 3   Standardized total cost of ownership activities are regularly used across the entire IT function to inform most cost management targets and investment decisions.

Level 4   Comprehensive total cost of ownership activities inform all cost management targets and investment decisions across the organization.

Level 5   Total cost of ownership activities are continually reviewed to ensure they remain a systematic part of all cost management programmes and strategic investment decision-making.

Key Practices-Outcomes-Metrics (POMs)

Some useful POMs for developing the Total Cost of Ownership (TCO) capability are summarized below.

Level 2 POMs

Practice	Prioritize an inventory list of IT assets and IT-enabled business services for collating life cycle costs.
Outcome	There is an emerging database for querying costs associated with IT assets and services.
Metric	Percentage of IT assets and services covered.
Practice	Refresh total cost of ownership models by linking into the organization's financial system of record.
Outcome	Confidence is emerging that total cost of ownership models are underpinned by actual cost data.
Metric	Percentage of total cost of ownership models underpinned by actual (versus estimated) cost data.
Practice	Define a standardized total cost of ownership calculation template for proposed investments.
Outcome	A common total cost of ownership methodology allows prospective investments to be evaluated consistently.
Metric	Percentage of proposed investments for which total cost of ownership is calculated using a standard template.
Practice	Communicate total cost of ownership benchmarking outcomes to key business unit stakeholders.
Outcome	Value-for-money discussions with stakeholders are better informed.
Metric	Number of benchmark studies that lead to cost improvement initiatives.

Level 3 POMs

Practice	Formally initiate tracking of direct and indirect costs across all IT assets and IT-enabled business services.
Outcome	The cost of ownership database is expanded, enabling improved cost management of IT assets and services.
Metric	Percentage of IT assets and services whose total cost of ownership is tracked.
Practice	Automate the tracking of costs.
Outcome	Total cost of ownership modelling becomes timelier, less onerous and less prone to error.
Metric	Percentage of data that is collected via automated means.
Practice	Motivate and incentivize employees to meet cost management targets.
Outcome	Cost management goals are distributed across the wider organization.
Metric	Percentage of IT total cost of ownership targets realized.
Practice	Fully integrate total cost of ownership activities with the organization's financial system of record, and with IT asset and software licensing databases.
Outcome	Data can be centrally managed and refreshed in a timely manner to calculate and track costs.
Metric	Percentage of total cost of ownership data that is sourced from the organization's financial system of record.

Level 4 POMs

Practice	Ensure total cost of ownership projections are within acceptable tolerance ranges – for example, in the range of 3 to 5 per cent.
Outcome	Decision makers are confident that total cost of ownership projections are accurate and can be used in decision-making.
Metric	Percentage of projections that are within tolerance limits.
Practice	Measure and recognize the success of business units in meeting cost management targets.
Outcome	Stakeholders engage more readily in cost management activities.
Metric	Percentage of IT total cost of ownership targets realized.
Practice	Ensure that total cost of ownership data is used in developing strategic plans.
Outcome	Systematic use of total cost of ownership data informs strategic investment choices.
Metric	Percentage of strategic portfolio/investment decisions supported by total cost of ownership data.
Practice	Promote the use of total cost of ownership data in all investment decisions organization-wide.
Outcome	Decisions about proposed investments consistently take both direct and indirect costs into account.
Metric	Percentage of investment decisions supported by total cost of ownership data.

Level 5 POMs

Practice	Continually review total cost of ownership approaches.
Outcome	There is a high degree of confidence that the costs of IT are managed appropriately.
Metric	Percentage of actual costs that differ from projections by more than agreed tolerances.
Practice	Regularly revise and update the IT assets and IT-enabled business services list in a Configuration Management Database (CMDB).
Outcome	The list of assets and services reflects actual cost drivers.
Metric	Frequency of review of the IT assets and services list.
Practice	Continually refresh total cost of ownership data with actual costs.
Outcome	Total cost of ownership data remains accurate.
Metric	Frequency with which the data is refreshed.

Addressing Typical Challenges

Some typical challenges that can arise in attempting to develop maturity in the Total Cost of Ownership (TCO) capability are set out below.

Challenge	Concerns that additional overheads may be associated with total cost of ownership activities.
Context	Although likely to reduce long-term costs, total cost of ownership modelling itself initially adds cost by gathering and considering more information.
Action	Engage leaders in simplifying the tracking of total cost of ownership.
Challenge	Lack of belief in the benefits associated with total cost of ownership activities.
Context	Collecting accurate total cost of ownership data can be cost prohibitive if such data is fragmented across the organization.
Action	Use any cost data available, including that from industry peers and vendors, to estimate rough cost models and to identify quick wins.
Challenge	Stakeholder commitment to achieving cost management goals wanes after initial successes.
Context	Organizational fatigue prevails following initial achievements, leading to a failure to identify new opportunities to challenge cost drivers.
Action	Continually promote recent case studies and the benefits of understanding total cost of ownership across the organization.

Management Artefacts

Management artefacts that may be used to develop maturity in the Total Cost of Ownership (TCO) capability include:

▸ Total cost of ownership policy and models.
▸ A cost tracking database.
▸ A configuration management database (CMDB).

Total Cost of Ownership Policy and Models

A total cost of ownership policy provides an overview of how total cost of ownership will be applied in the organization. It comprises the scope, methods, and tools that will be used in calculating and tracking costs, and in engaging with stakeholders on total cost of ownership results and their potential impact on the organization. A total cost of ownership policy is implemented via models that identify the elements that contribute to the full costs of IT assets and IT-enabled business services. These models are used to systematically analyse all costs related to an IT asset or service for the purpose of supporting investment decisions (such as make or buy, invest, retire an asset, or alternative options for asset use). Models are used to track current costs and predict future cost trajectories. Modelling should allow significant cost trends and issues to be readily highlighted, and should also identify areas in which cost-savings could be made. More sophisticated approaches may provide 'what if' analysis, allowing management to look at the impact of different scenarios on total cost of ownership.

Cost Tracking Database

A cost tracking database is a data repository of IT asset and IT-enabled business service costs. It includes all costs (direct and indirect) that are incurred throughout the life cycle of an IT asset or service, including acquisition and procurement, operation and maintenance, and end-of-life management. The database is updated over time, tracking the actual costs against the forecasts, and recording any deviations. Ideally, the cost tracking database is aligned with the organization's financial systems of record, enabling frequent updates to maintain cost data reliability.

Configuration Management Database (CMDB)

The configuration management database is a repository of information or metadata on all significant IT components. Typically a CMDB includes:

▸ A collection of IT assets and applications, collectively referred to as configuration items (CIs).
▸ The relationship between the CIs.
▸ The CI's life cycle (for example active, retired, and so on).
▸ A change log – for example, one that records changes to a CI's status or relationship to other CIs.

The CMDB helps in understanding the interconnections between IT assets and applications, thereby enabling the financial management tools to model and analyse cost data and determine appropriate service level costs.

35.5 REFERENCE

See Also

Other capabilities of IT-CMF that have a particularly close relationship with the Total Cost of Ownership (TCO) capability include:

Capability	What it provides
01. Accounting and Allocation (AA)	Insight into the processes for allocating IT costs across the business
12. Service Analytics and Intelligence (SAI)	Insight into the relationships between cost drivers and IT assets and services
15. Budget Management (BGM)	Input on actual costs to refresh assumptions of the total cost of ownership model

Further Reading

McKeen, J.D., and Smith, H., 2010. Developments in practice XXXVII: Total cost of ownership. *Communications of the Association for Information Systems*, 27(32).

Steinberg, R.A., Cannon, D., and Hunnebeck, L., 2011. *ITIL Life Cycle Suite*. 2nd ed. London: The Stationery Office.

Notes

[1] Mieritz, L., and Kirwin, B., 2005. Defining Gartner total cost of ownership. Gartner. Available at: <https://www.gartner.com/doc/487157/defining-gartner-total-cost-ownership>.

Going forward with IT-CMF

Next Steps

The Innovation Value Institute has a dual mandate – facilitating the ongoing development of IT-CMF, and promoting its adoption globally. IT-CMF is a flexible and adaptable framework that can be used in a variety of ways by different organizations to improve their IT capabilities, depending on their situation and their ambitions [1][2][3]. The Institute has developed a range of enabling structures and artefacts to help organizations maximize their benefit from using the framework. These structures and artefacts have been tried and tested in a variety of environments, and so they work as design patterns that enable any organization to deploy them with confidence, instead of trying to reinvent their own individual approaches. In developing these supports, IVI recognizes that organizations require a solution template to improve their capability, but that it must be sufficiently flexible and adaptable to be useful in each individual context.

Some of the ways in which organizations typically use IT-CMF include[1]:

- IT-CMF assessment and benchmarking.
- IT-CMF critical capability mapping onto the IT operating model.
- IT-CMF critical capability mapping onto management roles.
- IT-CMF mapping to incumbent/legacy frameworks.
- IT-CMF as a platform for targeting IT and business problems/opportunities.
- IT-CMF as a platform for employee training and skills development.

These are described below. In all instances, we recommend that an organization considering adopting IT-CMF should engage with IVI or with one of its certified partners, so that their individual needs can be assessed, and IT-CMF can be applied optimally to drive increased levels of agility, innovation and value for the organization.

IVI's certified international partner network is growing steadily. The Institute has trained and certified thousands of professional service providers, educational institutions and training organizations who provide competence services associated with IT-CMF. If you are interested in joining this network, please contact the IVI via the website, www.ivi.ie.

IT-CMF Assessment and Benchmarking

A core function of IT-CMF is to provide an assessment (or reference) framework along with associated improvement roadmaps to help an organization continually manage and develop the IT capability in support of agility, innovation and value. Assessment can range from the formal – where IT-CMF is used by a certified third-party to audit the organization, to the informal – where IT-CMF guides general management discussion. As IT-CMF is a cross-industry approach, it can be supplemented with benchmarking insights from peer organizations. Capability maturity comparisons with industry peer groups can prove very informative.

---

[1] For the latest on IT-CMF adoption and usage techniques, see www.ivi.ie.

When more granular insights on a critical capability are sought, an organization should consider a 'deep-dive' assessment with IVI or with one of its certified partners, in which a critical capability's context and complexity are examined in more detail.

IT-CMF Critical Capability Mapping onto the IT Operating Model

An IT operating model defines how the critical work of the IT function is carried out. By mapping IT-CMF's critical capabilities onto the IT function's operating model, the operating model is clarified, and the actions needed to drive continual improvement can be more easily identified. Similarly, IT-CMF's critical capabilities can be mapped onto the organization's IT value chain.

IT-CMF Critical Capability Mapping onto Management Roles

IT-CMF can be used to assign executive sponsorship for developing each of the critical capabilities that are key to success for the organization, and a framework for assessing performance and progress. This ensures that there is clear ownership and accountability for the ongoing development of critical capabilities, and also helps to identify overlapping responsibilities and gaps in the responsibility and accountability coverage for critical capabilities.

IT-CMF Mapping to Incumbent or Legacy Frameworks

Organizations can use IT-CMF as a strategic umbrella framework, allowing discrete IT management frameworks and approaches already in use within the organization for specific areas to be used in a unified manner, integrating and filling gaps between such approaches. IT-CMF provides the holistic view that systematically identifies weaknesses in the value delivery chain, and helps derive improvement plans.

IT-CMF as a Platform for Targeting IT and Business Problems/ Opportunities

IT-CMF's critical capabilities can be combined and configured to target specific challenges and opportunities in the IT function and in the wider business, such as high costs, limited innovation, the adoption of emerging technologies, and so on. IVI is continually working to determine the combinations of critical capabilities that are particularly applicable to specific types of problems and opportunities.

IT-CMF as a Platform for Employee Training and Skills Development

IT-CMF's critical capabilities represent organization-level behaviours and outcomes. Once the organization has agreed the critical capabilities that it wishes to develop, it can quickly deduce its human resource needs and prioritize the development of the employee competences that are needed to enhance and sustain organization-level behaviours and outcomes.

Organizations using IT-CMF can avail of IVI's certified *Capability Improvement Programme* – in which all the enabling tools, training, and artefacts are integrated for seamless execution. This is available through multiple channels, including online and through IVI's certified international partner network. In addition, IVI has a comprehensive suite of training and education offerings, ranging from executive overviews to a university master's degree, designed for managers, practitioners, consultants, and academics. See www.ivi.ie for more details.

Continuous Development of IT-CMF and IVI

The growth and reach of IVI in the development and promotion of IT-CMF continues at an accelerated pace. Ongoing development of IT-CMF has remained critical to ensuring its currency and relevance to a growing ecosystem. As technology continues to evolve, and as academic researchers and industry practitioners continue to develop and share new practices for the management of IT, IT-CMF continues to be developed as a living body of knowledge. While this book presents a guide to IT-CMF's body of knowledge as it is today, new practices and learnings are continually added to the body of knowledge upon which IT-CMF is based.

One of the strengths of IT-CMF is the user community that has grown up around it. IVI's member organizations and users continually share their experiences of using IT-CMF and of the particular challenges they face in their day-to-day work. This results in continual re-evaluation and refinement of the framework and the various elements within it, so that it is constantly relevant and useful. The latest developments are always published on the IVI's website, www.ivi.ie. The website also has more information on the background and history of IT-CMF, and additional tools, tips and templates to assist in its effective deployment.

IVI has attracted a community of users who are committed to improving their management of technology. It includes many of the world's leading organizations and academic institutions who openly share information, insights, lessons learned and challenges faced, so that all can benefit. You are welcome to join in this exciting, challenging and rewarding work.

Similarly, if you have any questions about IT-CMF or about how it might be applied in your organization, contact us at IVI. We also welcome any comments on this book or suggestions for improvement in future editions.

To get involved, email ivi@nuim.ie, visit www.ivi.ie or call IVI on +353 (0)1 708 6931.

Martin Delaney
General Manager and
Technology Leader
Innovation Value Institute

Prof. Martin Curley
Vice President, Intel Labs
Senior Principal Engineer
Director, Intel Labs Europe,
Intel Corporation
Co-Founder, Innovation
Value Institute

Prof. Brian Donnellan
Academic Director
Innovation Value Institute
Professor of Information
Systems Innovation
Maynooth University

Notes

[1]. Curley, M. and Kenneally, J., 2011. Using the IT Capability Maturity Framework to improve IT capability and value creation: An Intel IT case study. In: *Proceedings of the15th IEEE International Conference on Enterprise Distributed Object Computing (EDOC 2011).* Washington, DC: IEEE Computer Society.

[2]. Curley, M. and Kenneally, J., 2007. Methods and metrics to improve the yield of IT using the IT-CMF – an Intel case study. In *Proceedings of the 2007 IEEE International Conference on Exploring Quantifiable IT Yields (EQUITY '07).* Washington, DC: IEEE Computer Society.

[3]. Kenneally, J., Curley, M., Wilson, B., Buddrus, U., Porter, M., Murnane, S., McLaughlin, S., Boutemy-Deniau, M. and Hoyt, J., 2014. Accelerating electronic medical record adoption and innovation with targeted IT capabilities. In: *Proceedings of the 25th ISPIM Conference, Innovation for Sustainable Economy and Society.* Lappeenranta University of Technology Press.

Appendices

Contents: Appendices

Bibliography

Agarwal, R., and Sambamurthy, V., 2002. Principles and models for organizing the IT function. *MIS Quarterly Executive,* 1(1), 1–16.

Ahlemann, F., Stettiner, E., Messerschmidt, M., and Legner, C., 2012. *Strategic enterprise architecture management: challenges, best practices, and future developments.* Berlin: Springer.

Van Aken J.E., 2005. Management research as a design science: articulating the research products of mode 2 knowledge production in management. *British Journal of Management,* 16(1), 19–36.

Alavi, M., and Leidner, D.E., 2001. Review: knowledge management and knowledge management systems: conceptual foundations and research issues. *MIS Quarterly*, 25(1), 107–36.

Alexander, C., Ishikawa, S., and Silverstein, M., 1977. *A pattern language*. New York, NY: Oxford University Press.

Ali, S., and Green, P., 2012. Effective information technology (IT) governance mechanisms: an IT outsourcing perspective. *Information Systems Frontiers,* 14(2), 179–193.

Allen, T., and Henn, G., 2007. *The organization and architecture of innovation: managing the flow of technology.* New York, NY: Routledge.

Anderson, K., 2010. Implementing enterprise information management: a research-based approach in two Swedish municipalities: Part 2. *IQ (InfoRMAA Quarterly)* 26, 34–7.

Ariss, A., 2014. *Global talent management: challenges, strategies and opportunities*. Cham: Springer.

Ashurst, C., 2011. *Benefits realization from information technology.* New York, NY: Palgrave Macmillan.

Baldwin, E., and Curley, M., 2007. *Managing IT innovation for business value: practical strategies for IT and business managers.* (IT Best Practices Series). Hillsboro, OR: Intel Press.

Barney, J.B., 1991. Firm resources and sustained competitive advantage. *Journal of Management,* 17(1), 99–120.

BCS, 2009. The increasing importance of business service management. Available at: <http://www.bcs.org/content/conWebDoc/24352>.

Beaudoin, M., Kurtz, G., Jung, I., Suzuki, K., and Grabowski, B., 2013. *Online learner competencies: knowledge, skills, and attitudes for successful learning in online settings*. Charlotte, NC: Information Age Publishing.

Becker, J., Niehaves, B., Poppelbus, J., and Simons, A., 2010. Maturity models in IS research. In: *Proceedings of the 18th European conference on information system.* Available at: <http://www.researchgate.net/publication/221408759_Maturity_Models_in_IS_Research>.

Bhattacharyya, D.K., 2009. *Organizational systems, design, structure and management.* Mumbai: Himalaya Publishing House.

Blevins, T.J., Spencer, J., and Waskiewicz, F., 2004. *TOGAF ADM and MDA.* [pdf] The Open Group and OMG. Available at: <http://www.opengroup.org/cio/MDA-ADM/MDA-TOGAF-R1-070904. pdf>.

Bloch, M., Blumberg, S., and Laartz, J., 2012. Delivering large-scale IT projects on time, on budget, and on value. McKinsey & Company. Available at: <http://www.mckinsey.com/insights/ business_technology/delivering_large-scale_it_projects_on_time_on_budget_and_on_value>.

Blokdijk, G., 2008. *Supplier management best practice handbook.* Brisbane, Australia: Emereo Publishing.

Boots, J., 2012. *BPM boots on the ground: how to implement strategic business process management.* Tampa, FL: Meghan Kiffer Press.

Brinckmann, J., Salomo, S., and Gemuenden, H.G., 2011. Financial management competence of founding teams and growth of new technology-based firms. *Entrepreneurship Theory and Practice,* 35, 217–243.

British Computer Society, 2004. *The challenges of complex IT projects. The report of a working group from the Royal Academy of Engineering and the British Computer Society.* London: The Royal Academy of Engineering.

Brock, J., Saleh, T., and Iyer, S., 2015. Large-scale IT projects – from nightmare to value creation. *BCG Perspectives.* Available at: <https://www.bcgperspectives.com/content/articles/technology-business-transformation-technology-organization-large-scale-it-projects/>.

Brown, E.J., and Yarberry, W.A., 2008. *The effective CIO: how to achieve outstanding success through strategic alignment, financial management, and IT governance.* Boca Raton, FL: CRC Press.

Browning, T., 2014. *Capacity planning for computer systems.* London: Academic Press.

Brynjolfsson, E., 1998. Information technology and organizational design – evidence from micro data. MIT Sloan School of Management. Available at: <http://digital.mit.edu/erik/ITOD.htm>.

Burton, R.M., Obel, B., and DeSanctus, G., 2011. *Organizational design: a step-by-step approach.* 2nd ed. Cambridge: Cambridge University Press.

Bustin, G., 2014. Why most company strategic plans fail. *Forbes.* Available at: <http://www.forbes. com/sites/forbesleadershipforum/2014/09/15/why-most-company-strategic-plans-fail/>.

CA Technologies, 2011. The avoidable cost of downtime: phase 2. [pdf]. Available at: <http:// www.arcserve.com/us/lpg/~/media/Files/SupportingPieces/ARCserve/avoidable-cost-of-downtime-summary-phase-2.pdf>.

Cabinet Office, 2011. *ITIL lifecycle suite.* London: The Stationery Office.

Cannon, D., Wheeldon, D., Lacy, S., and Hanna, A., 2011. *ITIL service strategy.* London: The Stationery Office.

Cao, L., Mohan, K., Ramesh, B., and Sarkar, S., 2013. Adapting funding processes for agile IT projects: an empirical investigation. *European Journal of Information Systems,* 22, 191–205.

Capability Maturity Model Integration Institute (CMMI-I), 2013. Get started – begin your CMMI journey. Available at: <http://cmmiinstitute.com/get-started>.

Carcary, M., Doherty, E., and Thornley, C., 2015. Business innovation and differentiation: maturing the IT capability. *IT Professional*, 17(2), 46–53.

Case, G., Du Moulin, T., and Spalding, G., 2007. *Service management strategies that work – guidance for executives.* Zaltbommel NL: Van Haren.

Castellina, N., 2014. Improving planning, budgeting, and forecasting with advanced analytics. The Aberdeen Group. Available at: <http://www.aberdeen.com/research/9565/RR-planning-budgeting-forecasting-analytics.aspx/content.aspx>.

Chan, Y.E., 2002. Why haven't we mastered alignment? The importance of the informal organization structure. *MIS Quarterly Executive,* 1(2), 97–112.

Chesbrough, H.W., 2003. *Open innovation: the new imperative for creating and profiting from technology*. Boston, MA: Harvard Business School Publishing.

Chesbrough, H.W., 2003. The era of open innovation. *Sloan Management Review*, 44(3), 35–41.

Christensen, C.M., 1997. *The innovator's dilemma: when new technologies cause great firms to fail*. Boston, MA: Harvard Business Review Press.

Cooper, R.G., and Edgett, S.J., 2012. The Innovation Diamond™: an executive framework. Product Development Institute. Available at: <http://www.prod-dev.com/innovation_diamond.php>.

Costello, T. et al., 2013. IT frameworks. *IEEE IT Professional*, 15(5).

Coughlan, J., Lycett, M., and Macredie, R.D., 2005. Understanding the business–IT relationship. *International Journal of Information Management,* 25(4), 303–19.

Council on CyberSecurity, 2013. *Critical controls for effective cyber defense*. Available at: <http://www.counciloncybersecurity.org/critical-controls/>.

Courage, C., and Baxter, K., 2005. *Understanding your users: a practical guide to user requirement methods, tools and techniques*. San Francisco, CA: Morgan Kaufmann.

Cross, R., and Parker, A., 2004. *The hidden power of social networks: understanding how work really gets done in organizations*. Boston, MA: Harvard Business School Publishing.

Curley, M., 2004. *Managing information technology for business value*. Hillsboro, OR: Intel Press.

Curley, M., 2006. The IT transformation at Intel. *MIS Quarterly Executive,* 5(4).

Curley, M., 2007. Introducing an IT capability maturity framework. In J. Cardos, J. Cordeiro, and J. Filipe (eds.) *Enterprise Information Systems*. Berlin: Springer.

Curley, M., 2008. *The IT capability maturity framework: A theory for continuously improving the value delivered from IT capability*. Ph.D. National University of Ireland, Maynooth.

Curley, M., 2012. The emergence and initial development of a new design pattern for CIOs using design science. In: *Practical aspects of design science* (Communications in Computer and Information Science Series, Volume 286). Berlin: Springer.

Curley, M., and Kenneally, J., 2007. Methods and metrics to improve the yield of IT using the IT-CMF – an Intel case study. In *Proceedings of the 2007 IEEE International Conference on Exploring Quantifiable IT Yields (EQUITY '07)*. Washington, DC: IEEE Computer Society.

Curley, M., and Kenneally, J., 2011. Using the IT Capability Maturity Framework to improve IT capability and value creation: An Intel IT case study. In: *Proceedings of the 15th IEEE International Conference on Enterprise Distributed Object Computing (EDOC 2011)*. Washington, DC: IEEE Computer Society.

Curley, M., Kenneally, J., and Dreischmeier, R., 2012. Creating a new IT management framework using design science: a rationale for action and for using design science. In: *Practical aspects of design science* (Communications in Computer and Information Science Series, Volume 286). Berlin: Springer.

Curley, M., and Salmelin, B, 2014. Open innovation 2.0: a new milieu. In: *EU Open Innovation 2.0 Yearbook*. Luxembourg: European Commission.

Curry, E., Guyon, B., Sheridan, C., and Donnellan, B., 2012. Developing a sustainable IT capability: lessons from Intel's journey. *MIS Quarterly Executive*, 11(2), 61–74.

Curtis, B., Hefley, W.W., and Miller, S.A., 2009. The people capability maturity model (P-CMM). Version 2, 2nd ed. [pdf] Software Engineering Institute. Available at: <http://www.sei.cmu.edu/reports/09tr003.pdf>.

DAMA, 2009. *The DAMA guide to the data management body of knowledge (DMBOK)*, 1st ed. Bradley Beach, NJ: Technics Publications.

DAMA, 2011. *The DAMA dictionary of data management*. 2nd ed. Bradley Beach, NJ: Technics Publications.

Datar, S.M., Rajan, M.V., Wynder, M., Maguire, W., and Tan, R., 2013. *Cost accounting: a managerial emphasis*. Melbourne, AU: Pearson Higher Education.

Davenport, T.H., 1993. *Process innovation: reengineering work through information technology*. Boston, MA: Harvard Business School Press.

Davenport, T.H., 2006. Competing on analytics. *Harvard Business Review*, 84, 98–107.

Davenport, T.H., De Long, D.W., and Beers, M.C., 1998. Successful knowledge management projects. *Sloan Management Review*, 39, 43–57.

Davenport, T.H., Harris, J., and Morison, R., 2010. *Analytics at work: how to make better decisions*. Boston, MA: Harvard Business School.

Day, G., Schoemaker, P., and Gunther, R., 2000. *Wharton on managing emerging technologies*. Hoboken, NJ: Wiley.

Dosi, G., Nelson, R.R., and Winter, S.G. (eds.), 2000. *The nature and dynamics of organizational capabilities*. Oxford: Oxford University Press.

The Economist (green.view), 2009. Computing climate change. 24 August 2009. Available at <http://www.economist.com/node/14297036>.

Eisenhardt, K.M., and Martin, J.A., 2000. Dynamic capabilities: what are they? *Strategic Management Journal*, 21(10/11), 1105–21.

Elky, S., 2006. *An introduction to information systems risk management*. [pdf] SANS Institute. Available at: <http://www.sans.org/reading_room/whitepapers/auditing/introduction-information-system-risk-management_1204>.

Emmett, S., and Crocker, B., 2009. *Excellence in supplier management.* Cambridge: Cambridge Academic.

Energy Information Administration (US), 2009. *Annual energy outlook 2009 – with projections to 2030.* [pdf] DOE/EIA-0383. Available at: <http://www.eia.gov/forecasts/archive/aeo09/pdf/0383(2009).pdf>.

Eppler, M., and Helfert, M., 2004. A classification and analysis of data quality costs. In: *Proceedings of the Ninth International Conference on Information Quality (ICIQ-04).* Cambridge, MA. November 5th–7th, 2004.

Ernst and Young, 2013. *Under cyber attack: EY's global information security survey.* [pdf]. Available at: <http://www.ey.com/Publication/vwLUAssets/EY_-_2013_Global_Information_Security_Survey/$FILE/EY-GISS-Under-cyber-attack.pdf>.

Estall, H., 2012. *Business continuity management systems: implementation and certification to ISO 22301.* Swindon: BCS.

Esty, D., and Winston, A., 2009. *Green to gold: How smart companies use environmental strategy to innovate, create value, and build competitive advantage.* Hoboken, NJ: Wiley.

Evans, J., and Lindsay, W., 2015. *An introduction to Six Sigma and process improvement.* 2nd ed. Boston, MA: Cengage Learning.

Fahey, L., and Prusak, L., 1998. The eleven deadliest sins of knowledge management. *California Management Review*, 40, 265.

Fraser, J., Simkins, B. and Narvaez, K, 2014. *Implementing enterprise risk management: case studies and best practices.* Hoboken, NJ: Wiley.

Gartner, 2005. Business process management's success hinges on business-led initiatives. Available at: <http://www.gartner.com/doc/483847/business-process-managements-success-hinges>.

Gartner, 2015. *Gartner IT Glossary.* Available at: <http://www.gartner.com/it-glossary>.

Giachetti, R.E., 2004. A framework to review the information integration of the enterprise. *International Journal of Production Research*, 42(6), 1147–66.

Granados, N., and Gupta, A., 2013. Transparency strategy: competing with information in a digital world. *MIS Quarterly*, 37(2), 637–42.

Grönroos, C., 2007. *Service management and marketing: customer management in service competition.* Chichester: Wiley.

Gunther, N.J., 2006. *Guerrilla capacity planning: a tactical approach to planning for highly scalable applications and services.* Secaucus, NJ: Springer-Verlag.

Hallinan, E., 2004. Tracking your cost management performance. *Reeves Journal,* 84.

Harris, M.D., Herron, D., and Iwanicki, S., 2008. *The business value of IT: managing risks, optimizing performance and measuring results.* Boca Raton, FL: CRC Press.

Harry, M., and Schroeder, R., 2006. *Six Sigma: the breakthrough management strategy revolutionizing the world's top corporations*. New York, NY: Crown Business.

Helfat, C.E., and Peteraf, M.A., 2003. The dynamic resource-based view: capability lifecycles. *Strategic Management Journal*, 24(10), 997–1010.

Helfert, M., and Curley, M., 2012. Design science in action: researching and developing the IT-CMF. In: *Practical aspects of design science* (Communications in Computer and Information Science Series, Volume 286). Berlin: Springer.

Hevner, A., March, S., and Park, J., 2004. Design science in information systems research. *MIS Quarterly*, 28(1), 75–105.

Hills, A., 2009. Succession planning – or smart talent management? *Industrial and Commercial Training*, 41(1), 3–8.

Holt, A.L., 2013. *Governance of IT – an executive guide to ISO/IEC 38500*. Swindon: BCS.

Hope, J., 2009. *Target-setting: focus on medium-term stretch goals that drive continual improvement.* [pdf] IBM, Actions in Innovation Series. Available at: <ftp://ftp.software.ibm.com/software/data/sw-library/cognos/pdfs/articles/art_target_setting_focus_on_mediumterm_stretch_goals_that_drive_continuous_improvement.pdf>.

Humphrey, W.S., 1988. Characterizing the software process: a maturity framework. *IEEE Software*, 5(2), 73–79.

International Association of Outsourcing Professionals (IAOP), 2014. *The outsourcing professional body of knowledge (OPBOK)*. Zaltbommel, NL: Van Haren.

International Board of Standards for Training, Performance, and Instruction (IBSTI), 2015. New set of competencies for online learners. Available at: <http://ibstpi.org/new-set-of-competencies-for-online-learners/>.

International Organization for Standardization (ISO), 2004. *ISO 14001:2004 Environmental management systems – requirements with guidance for use*. Available at: <http://www.iso.org/iso/home/store/catalogue_tc/catalogue_detail.htm?csnumber=31807>.

International Organization for Standardization (ISO), 2009. *ISO 31000 – Risk management*. Available at: <http://www.iso.org/iso/home/standards/iso31000.htm>.

International Organization for Standardization (ISO), 2011. *ISO/IEC 20000 Information Technology – Service Management*. Geneva, CH: ISO.

International Organization for Standardization (ISO), 2012. *ISO/IEC 15504-5:2012. Information technology – process assessment – part 5: an exemplar software life cycle process assessment model*. Available at: <http://www.iso.org/iso/catalogue_detail.htm?csnumber=60555>.

International Organization for Standardization (ISO), 2015a. *Information technology – governance of IT for the organization (ISO/IEC 38500).* Available at: <http://www.iso.org/iso/home/store/catalogue_tc/catalogue_detail.htm?csnumber=62816>.

International Organization for Standardization (ISO), 2015b. *ISO 13407 1999 Human-centred design processes for interactive systems*. Available at: <http://www.iso.org/iso/catalogue_detail.htm?csnumber=21197>.

IT Systems Audit and Control Association (ISACA), 2009. *Risk IT framework*. Available at: <http://www.isaca.org/Knowledge-Center/Research/ResearchDeliverables/Pages/The-Risk-IT-Framework.aspx>.

IT Systems Audit and Control Association (ISACA), 2010. *Enterprise value: governance of IT investments. The Val IT Framework 2.0.* Rolling Meadows, IL: ISACA.

IT Systems Audit and Control Association (ISACA), 2012. *COBIT 5.0 – A business framework for the governance and management of enterprise IT*. Available at: <http://www.isaca.org/COBIT/Pages/COBIT-5-Framework-product-page.aspx>.

IT Systems Audit and Control Association (ISACA), 2013. *COBIT 5 for risk*. Available at: <http://www.isaca.org/cobit/pages/risk-product-page.aspx>.

Isaias, P., and Issa, T., 2014. *High level models and methodologies for information systems*. New York, NY: Springer.

iSixSigma, 2012. Design for Six Sigma (DFSS) versus DMAIC. Available at: <http://www.isixsigma.com/library/content/c020722a.asp>.

ITSQC, 2015. *The eSourcing capability model for service providers (eSCM-SP) v2*. Available at: <http://www.itsqc.org/models/escm-sp/>.

Jaquith, A., 2007. *Security metrics: replacing fear, uncertainty, and doubt,* Upper Saddle River, NJ: Pearson Education.

Jarratt, D., 2008. Testing a theoretically constructed relationship management capability. *European Journal of Marketing,* 42(9/10), 1106–32.

Jenner, S., 2012. *Managing benefits*. London: The Stationery Office.

Jensen, R., 2007. The digital provide: information (technology), market performance, and welfare in the south Indian fisheries sector. *The Quarterly Journal of Economics,* 122(3), 879–924.

Joint Task Force Transformation Initiative, 2013. *Security and privacy controls for federal information systems and organizations*. Gaithersburg, MD: National Institute of Standards and Technology. Available at: <http://dx.doi.org/10.6028/NIST.SP.800-53r4>.

Josyula, V., Orr, M., and Page, G., 2011. *Cloud computing: automating the virtualized data center*. Indianapolis, IN: Cisco Press.

Jurison, J., 1996. Toward more effective management of information technology benefits. *Journal of Strategic Information Systems*, 5(4), 263–274.

Kaplan, J.D., 2009. *Strategic IT portfolio management: governing enterprise transformation*. Waltham, MA: PRTM Inc.

Kaplan, R.S., and Norton, D.P., 1996. *The balanced scorecard: translating strategy into action*. Boston, MA: Harvard Business School Press.

Kaplan, R.S., and Norton, D.P., 2004. *Strategy maps: converting intangible assets into tangible outcomes*. Boston, MA: Harvard Business School Press.

Keeley, L., Walters, H., Pikkel, R., and Quinn, B., 2013. *Ten types of innovation: the discipline of building breakthroughs*. Hoboken, NJ: Wiley.

Keen, P., and Williams, R., 2013. Value architectures for digital business: beyond the business model. *MIS Quarterly*, 37(2), 643–8.

Kenneally, J., Curley, M., Wilson, B., Buddrus, U., Porter, M., Murnane, S., McLaughlin, S., Boutemy-Deniau, M., and Hoyt, J., 2014. Accelerating electronic medical record adoption and innovation with targeted IT capabilities. In: *Proceedings of the 25th ISPIM Conference, Innovation for Sustainable Economy and Society.* Lappeenranta, FI: Lappeenranta University of Technology Press.

Kerzner, H., 2005. *Using the project management maturity model: strategic planning for project management.* 2nd ed. Hoboken, NJ: Wiley.

Kerzner, H., 2013. *Project management: a systems approach to planning, scheduling, and controlling.* 11th ed. Hoboken, NJ: Wiley.

Kiron, D., Prentice, P.K., and Ferguson, R.B., 2014. The analytics mandate. *MIT Sloan Management Review,* 55, 29–33.

Klosterboer, L., 2011. *ITIL capacity management.* Boston, MA: Pearson Education.

Kraus, S. Reiche, B.S., and Henning Reschke, C., 2007. Implications of strategic planning in SMEs for international entrepreneurship research and practice. In M. Terziovski (ed.) 2007. *Energizing Management through Innovation and Entrepreneurship: European Research and Practice.* London: Routledge. pp 110–27.

La Rosa, M., and Soffer, P., 2015. Special issue on best papers from the 'BPM 2012' workshops. *Information Systems and e-Business Management,* 13, 1–3.

Laan, S., 2013. *IT infrastructure architecture – infrastructure building blocks and concepts.* 2nd ed. Raleigh, NC: Lulu Press.

Lacity, M., and Hirschheim, R., 1993. *Information systems outsourcing: myths, metaphors, and realities.* Chichester: Wiley.

Lacity, M., Willcocks, L., and Feeny, D., 1996. The value of selective outsourcing. *MIT Sloan Management Review.* Spring 1996. Available at: <http://sloanreview.mit.edu/article/the-value-of-selective-it-sourcing/>.

Larman, C., 2003. *Agile and iterative development.* Boston, MA: Addison Wesley.

Laseter, T.M., 1998. *Balanced sourcing: cooperation and competition in supplier relationships.* San Francisco, CA: Jossey-Bass.

Levin, G., and Wyzalek, J. (eds.), 2014. *Portfolio management: a strategic approach (Best Practices and Advances in Programme Management Series).* Boca Raton, FL: CRC Press.

Lu, Y., and Ramamurthy, K., 2011. Understanding the link between information technology capability and organizational agility: an empirical examination. *MIS Quarterly*, 35(4), 931–54.

Luftman, J., Zadeh, H.S., Derksen, B., Santana, M., Rigoni, E.H., and Huang, Z.D., 2013. Key information technology and management issues 2012–2013: an international study. *Journal of Information Technology,* 28(4), 354–66.

McDermott, R., 2000. Why information technology inspired but cannot deliver knowledge management. *Knowledge and Communities*, 41, 21–35.

McGittigan, J., 2014. *IT budgeting key initiative overview*. Gartner Research. Available at: <https://www.gartner.com/doc/2701817/it-budgeting-key-initiative-overview>.

McKeen, J.D., and Smith, H., 2010. Developments in practice XXXVII: Total cost of ownership. *Communications of the Association for Information Systems*, 27(32).

McLaughlin, S., 2012. *Positioning the IT-CMF: a capability versus process perspective.* [pdf] IVI executive briefing. Available at: <http://ivi.nuim.ie/sites/ivi.nuim.ie/files/publications/IVI%20Exec%20Briefing%20-%20Positioning%20IT-CMF,%20v0.5%20(no%20mark-ups).pdf>.

McLaughlin, S., Sherry, M., Doherty, E., Carcary, M., Thornley, C., Wang, Y., CEPIS, IDC, and empirica, 2014. *European Commission DG Enterprise and Industry. e-Skills: the international dimension and impact of globalization.* [pdf]. Available at: <http://www.eskills-international.com/files/FINAL_INTERNATIONAL_e_Skills_report_Aug_14.pdf>.

Maizlish, B., and Handler, R., 2008. *IT (information technology) portfolio management step-by-step: unlocking the business value of technology*. Hoboken, NJ: Wiley.

Manfreda, A., and Štemberger, M.I., 2011. Partnership between top management and IT personnel: is it really beyond the reach? In *Proceedings of the European, Mediterranean & Middle Eastern Conference on Information Systems, May 30–31, Athens, Greece*, 523–30.

Marchewka, J., 2014. *Information technology project management: providing measurable organizational value*. 5th ed. Hoboken, NJ: Wiley.

Mark, D., and Rau, D.P., 2006. Splitting demand from supply in IT. *The McKinsey Quarterly*, September 2006, 22–29.

Markus, M.L., and Soh, C., 1995. How IT creates value, a process theory synthesis. In *Proceedings of the 16th International Conference on Information Systems*, Amsterdam.

Mentzas, G., 1997. Implementing an IS strategy – a team approach. *Long Range Planning*, 1(1), 84–95.

Mettler, T., 2009. A design science research perspective on maturity models in Information Systems. St Gallen: Institute of Information Management. University of St Gallen, CH.

Meyer, B., 2014. *Agile: the good, the hype, and the ugly*. Cham, CH: Springer.

Microsoft, 2012. *Microsoft Operations Framework (MOF) 4.0*. Available at: <http://www.microsoft.com/en-ie/download/details.aspx?id=17647>.

Mieritz, L., and Kirwin, B., 2005. Defining Gartner total cost of ownership. Gartner. Available at: <https://www.gartner.com/doc/487157/defining-gartner-total-cost-ownership>.

Mithas, S., Ramasubbu, N., and Sambamurthy, V., 2011. How information management capability influences firm performance. *MIS Quarterly*, 35(1), 237–56.

Nelson, R.R., and Winter, S.G., 1982. *An evolutionary theory of economic change*. Cambridge, MA: Belknap Press.

Nevo, S., and Wade, M.R., 2010. The formation and value of IT-enabled resources: antecedents and consequences of synergistic relationships. *MIS Quarterly,* 34(1), 163–83.

Nevo, S., and Wade, M.R., 2011. Firm-level benefits of IT-enabled resources: a conceptual extension and an empirical assessment. *Journal of Strategic Information Systems*, 20, 403–18.

Niemann, K.D., 2006. *From enterprise architecture to IT governance.* Wiesbaden, DE: Vieweg & Sohn.

North, K., and Kumta, G., 2014. *Knowledge management: value creation through organizational learning.* Cham, CH: Springer.

Office of Cybersecurity and Communications National Cyber Security Division, 2008. *Information technology (IT) security essential body of knowledge (EBK): a competency and functional framework for IT security workforce development*, Washington, DC: United States Department of Homeland Security.

Office of Government Commerce, 2011. *Management of risk – guidance for practitioners.* 3rd ed. London: The Stationery Office.

Office of the Chief Information Officer (OCIO, Newfoundland Labrador, Canada), 2014. Solution delivery framework. Available at: <http://www.ocio.gov.nl.ca/ocio/pmo/sdf.html>.

Ogunyemi, A., and Johnston, K.A., 2012. Towards an organizational readiness framework for emerging technologies: an investigation of antecedents for South African organizations' readiness for server virtualization. *The Electronic Journal on Information Systems in Developing Countries*, 53(5), 1–30.

Open Group, 2011a. *Open information security management maturity model (O-Ism3).* Zaltbommel NL: Van Haren.

Open Group, 2011b. *TOGAF Version 9.1.* Zaltbommel, NL: Van Haren Publishing.

Pasher, E., and Ronen, T., 2011. *The complete guide to knowledge management: a strategic plan to leverage your company's intellectual capital.* Hoboken, NJ: Wiley.

Patching, K., and Chatham, R., 2000. *Corporate politics for IT managers.* Oxford: Butterworth Heinemann.

Paulk, M.C., Curtis, B., Chrissis, M.B., and Weber, C., 1993. Capability maturity model for software (Version 1.1). Software Engineering Institute. Available at <http://resources.sei.cmu.edu/library/asset-view.cfm?assetID=11955>.

Pavlou, P.A., and El Sawy, O.A., 2010. The 'third hand': IT-enabled competitive advantage in turbulence through improvisational capabilities. *Information Systems Research*, 21(3), 443–71.

Pendharkar, P.C., 2014. A decision-making framework for justifying a portfolio of IT projects. *International Journal of Project Management,* 32(4), 625–39.

Pennypacker, J., and Retna, S. (eds.), 2009. *Project portfolio management: a view from the management trenches.* Hoboken, NJ: Wiley.

Peppard, J., and Ward, J., 1999. 'Mind the gap': diagnosing the relationship between the IT organization and the rest of the business. *Journal of Strategic Information Systems,* 8(1), 29–60.

Peppard, J., Ward, J., and Daniel, E., 2007. Managing the realization of business benefits from IT investments. *MIS Quarterly Executive*, 6(1), 1–11.

Perrin, A., Vidal, P., and Mc Gill, J., 2004. *Valuing knowledge management in organizations, from theory to practice: the case of Lafarge Group.* [pdf]. Available at: <http://km.typepad.com/index/files/valuing_km_in_organizations_the_lafarge_case_perrin_vidal_mcgill.pdf>.

Porter, M.E., 1991. Towards a dynamic theory of strategy. *Strategic Management Journal*, 12, 95-117.

Preece, J., Rogers, Y., and Sharp, H., 2011. *Interaction design: beyond human–computer interaction*. 3rd ed. Chichester: Wiley.

Project Management Institute, 2013a. *A guide to the project management body of knowledge*. 5th ed. Newtown Square, PA: Project Management Institute.

Project Management Institute, 2013b. *The standard for portfolio management*. 3rd ed. Newtown Square, PA: Project Management Institute.

Quintas, P., Lefrere, P., and Jones, G., 1997. Knowledge management: a strategic agenda. *Long Range Planning*, 30, 385–91.

Reich, B.H., and Benbasat, I., 2000. Factors that influence the social dimension of alignment between business and information technology objectives. *MIS Quarterly*, 24(1), 81–113.

Ross, J.W., Beath, C.M., and Goodhue, D.L., 1996. Develop long-term competitiveness through information technology assets. *Sloan Management Review*, 38(1), 31–42.

Ryan, R., and Raducha-Grace, T, 2009. *The business of IT: how to improve service and lower costs*. Upper Saddle River, NJ: IBM Press.

Schniederjans, M.J., Schniederjans, D.G., and Starkey, C.M., 2014. *Business analytics principles, concepts, and applications: what, why, and how*. Upper Saddle River, NJ: Pearson Education.

Schryen, G., 2013. Revisiting IS business value research: what we already know, what we still need to know, and how we can get there. *European Journal of Information Systems*, 22, 139–69.

Schwalbe, K., 2013. *Information technology project management*. 7th ed. Boston, MA: Cengage Learning.

Schwienbacher, A., 2014. Financing the business. In T. Baker and F. Welter, *The Routledge companion to entrepreneurship*. Abingdon: Routledge, 193–206.

Scullion, H., Collings, D.G., and Caligiuri, P., 2010. Global talent management. *Journal of World Business*, 45(2), 105–8.

Seddon, P.B., Calvert, C., and Yang, S., 2010. A multi-project model of key factors affecting organizational benefits from enterprise systems. *MIS Quarterly*, 34, 305–328.

Silicon Republic, 2010. Closing the gaps between ICT and enterprise risk management. *Silicon Republic*. Available at: <http://www.siliconrepublic.com/news/item/16901-closing-the-gaps-between-ic>.

Sing, A.N., Gupta, M.P., and Ojha, A., 2014. Identifying factors of 'organizational information security management'. *Journal of Enterprise Information Management Decision*, 27.

Software Engineering Institute, 2011. *Standard CMMI appraisal method for process improvement (SCAMPISM) A. Version 1.3. Method definition document*. [pdf]. Available at: <http://www.sei.cmu.edu/reports/11hb001.pdf>.

Sparrow, P., Scullion, H., and Tarique, I., 2014. *Strategic talent management: contemporary issues in an international context*. Cambridge: Cambridge University Press.

Stamp, M., 2011. *Information security: principles and practice*. Hoboken, NJ: Wiley.

Suby, M., 2013. *The 2013 (ISC)2 global information security workforce study*. [pdf] *Frost and Sullivan*. Available at: <https://www.isc2.org/giswsrsa2013>.

Sward, D., 2006. *Measuring the business value of information technology*. Hillsboro, OR: Intel Press.

Tallon P., and Short, D.J., 2010. *Data migration practices and tiered storage management: challenges and opportunities*. [webinar paper]. Available at: <http://hmi.ucsd.edu/pdf/DataMigrationSept_2010_webinar.pdf>.

Tallon. P., and Scannell, R.W., 2007. Information life cycle management, *Communications of the ACM,* 50(11), 65–9.

Teece, D., and Pisano, G., 1994. The dynamic capabilities of firms: an introduction. *Industrial and Corporate Change*, 3(3), 537–56.

Teece, D.J., 2007. Managers, markets, and dynamic capabilities. In C. Helfat, S. Finkelstein et al. (eds.), *Dynamic capabilities: understanding strategic change in organizations*. Oxford: Blackwell.

Teichroew, D., Robichek, A.A., and Montalbano, M., 1965. An analysis of criteria for investment and financing decisions under certainty. *Management Science,* 12, 151–79.

Thorp, J., 2003. *The Information Paradox – realizing the business benefits of information technology*. Toronto, CA: McGraw-Hill.

Tidd, J., and Bessant, J., 2013. *Managing innovation: integrating technological, market and organizational change*. Chichester: Wiley.

Turel, O., and Bart, C., 2014. Board-level IT governance and organizational performance. *European Journal of Information Systems,* 23, 223–39.

US Government, 2002. *Public Printing and Documents, Coordination of Federal Information, Subchapter III – Information Security*. (44 U.S.C. § 3542(b)). [pdf]. Available at: <https://www.law.cornell.edu/uscode/pdf/uscode44/lii_usc_TI_44_CH_35_SC_III_SE_3542.pdf>.

Venkatraman, N.N., and Loh, L., 1994. The shifting logic of the IS organization: from technical portfolio to relationship portfolio. *Information Strategy: The Executive's Journal*, 10(2), 5–11.

Wade, M., Piccoli, G., and Ives, B., 2011. IT-dependent strategic initiatives and sustained competitive advantage: a review, synthesis, and an extension of the literature. In: W.L. Currie and R.D. Galliers (eds.), 2011. *The Oxford handbook of management information systems: critical perspectives and new directions*. Oxford: Oxford University Press, Ch. 14.

Ward, J., and Daniel, E., 2006. *Benefits management*. Chichester: Wiley.

Ward, J., and Peppard, J., 1996. Reconciling the IT/business relationship: a troubled marriage in need of guidance. *Journal of Strategic Information Systems,* 5(1), 37–65.

Ward, J., and Peppard, J., 2002. *Strategic planning for information systems,* 3rd ed. Hoboken, NJ: Wiley.

Weill, P., and Ross, J., 2004. *IT governance: how top performers manage IT decision rights for superior results*. Boston, MA: Harvard Business School Press.

Weill, P., and Ross, J., 2005. A matrixed approach to designing IT governance. *MIT Sloan Review.* Available at: <http://sloanreview.mit.edu/article/a-matrixed-approach-to-designing-it-governance/>.

Westerman, J., 2009. *The case for business process management.* [pdf] BPTrends. Available at: <http://www.bptrends.com/publicationfiles/04-09-CS-Case-for-BPM-TIBCO.doc.pdf>.

Whelan, E., and Carcary, M., 2011. Integrating talent and knowledge management: where are the benefits? *Journal of Knowledge Management,* 15(4), 675–87.

Whitman, M., and Mattord, H., 2011. *Principles of information security.* Boston, MA: Cengage Learning.

Whitman, M., and Woszczynsk, A., 2003. *Handbook of information systems research.* Hershey, PA: Idea Group Publishing.

Wisner, J., Tan, K.C., and Leong, G., 2015. *Principles of supply chain management: a balanced approach.* Boston, MA: Cengage Learning.

Wixom, B.H., and Markus, M.L., 2015. Data value assessment: recognizing data as an enterprise asset. *Centre for Information Systems Research (CISR) Research Briefing,* vol.XV.

Zwass, V., 2015. Planning for Information Systems. In: W.R. King (ed.) 2015. *Planning for Information Systems (Advances in Management Information Systems).* London: Routledge.

Glossary B

360 degree feedback	360 degree feedback is feedback on an employee's performance from the employee's immediate work circle – for example, from colleagues, subordinates, supervisors, and managers. It typically also includes a self-evaluation by the employee.
A/B benchmarking	A/B benchmarking is a user experience testing technique that compares user responses to alternative design elements within a controlled environment.
Access control	Access control refers to the ways in which users must identify themselves in order to gain access to a given area or resource, such as by password, biometrics, or other tokens. Authorization and access control lists are consulted to verify that the requested access is authorized by the appropriate authority. Details of the access request are often logged for audit purposes.
Access rights	Access rights define the level of permission that different users have to an application, service or data. They can be based on allowed actions, such as create, read, update, or delete. Access can also be system-wide or restricted to specific files, databases, records, or customized views, showing only what is needed to perform a specific task. Finally, access rights may be restricted in other ways, such as being only allowed from specific devices or locations, only for specific time slots, or limited to accessing a limited number of records over a given time period.
Accounting model	An IT accounting model shows specific links between the cost of an IT asset or service and its consumption – for example, the unit-cost per service.
Architecture components	Architecture components include both *information* artefacts – such as principles, business process models, a vision statement, and roadmaps – and *process* artefacts, such as application assessments, infrastructure assessments, and so on.
Architecture layers	Architecture layers are views taken by IT architects to simplify understanding and assist in representation and planning. A layer may be thought of as a view of a single floor in a multi-storey building rather than trying to depict the detail of all floors on one diagram. Typical IT layers include database server views, application server views, network connectivity views, location views, business process views, and so on.
Assessment sponsor	An assessment sponsor is an individual who represents the organization being assessed, who requires the assessment to be performed, and who provides the necessary resources for its execution.

Asset	An IT asset refers to the hardware, software, applications, and other IT resources owned or controlled by an organization.
Authentication	Authentication is the process of validating an individual's purported identity (Whitman and Mattord, 2011).
Authorization	Authorization is the giving to individuals, groups, or other legal entities, and/or other devices, software agents, and systems, of official permission (usually based on rules) to access data, programs, or information or their supporting systems and infrastructure (DAMA, 2011).
Availability	Availability is the characteristic of an information resource that determines the period of time within which a service, interface, or channel must be accessible and usable upon demand with minimal or no interruption.
Benefit	A benefit is an end-state outcome that represents an improvement in nature and value, which is considered to be a desired advantage by the organization.
Benefits accrual	Benefits accrual refers to ensuring that benefits are realized as soon as possible and that they are sustained for as long as possible.
Benefits harvesting	Benefits harvesting refers to organizing for the delivery of planned and emerging benefits and, when necessary, taking action to ensure that they are delivered.
Benefits management	Benefits management refers to the way in which an organization identifies, defines, tracks, realizes, and optimizes benefits at an initiative or portfolio level.
Benefits map	A benefits map is a graphical illustration of benefits and related change initiatives, the relationships between them, and how they individually and collectively contribute to one or more investment objectives.
Benefits plan	A benefits plan is a policy document to guide planning and tracking the realization of expected benefits across an initiative or programme, and to set appropriate review controls.
Benefits realization	Benefits realization is the techniques, disciplines, and mind sets that an organization must adopt to maximize the business value of projects and investments.
Benefits register	A benefits register is used to track the progress and outcomes of forecasted benefits. For each benefit, the register includes information such as the benefit title, how it is measured, measurement results, and who is responsible and accountable for individual benefits.
Big data	Big data refers to large amounts of varied data and data sources that are acquired, processed, and analysed promptly to generate actionable business insights.
Bottom-up data valuation	Bottom-up data valuation uses microeconomic approaches to data valuation.

Bring-your-own-device (BYOD)	'Bring-your-own-device' (BYOD) is the practice of allowing employees to use their personally owned devices (such as laptops, tablets or smart phones) within the work environment.
Budget	A budget is the financial resource allocated to a defined activity or business unit.
Budget plan	A budget plan is a detailed financial plan that quantifies future resource requirements.
Business benefit	A business benefit delivered by an investment is an end outcome that stakeholders seek to realize and own as an advantage. Business benefits map to strategic business objectives and ultimately to the wider delivery of business value.
Business case	A business case sets out the justification for an organizational activity (such as a project), based on its alignment with business objectives, priorities, and expected value. Typically it outlines costs, benefits, risks, and timescales, and is the basis against which continuing viability is tested. An outline business case provides a preliminary justification for a programme or project.
Business continuity	Business continuity is the aggregate of processes, approaches, material, and personnel that are put in place to ensure that either: ▶ Essential functions, IT services, and projects can continue during and after a disaster –or– ▶ Partially or completely interrupted functions and services, above a defined degree of business relevance (criticality), can be recovered and restored within a predetermined time after a disaster or extended disruption.
Business ecosystem	The business ecosystem is a superset including the 'organization'. It includes the value chain of a business, and also those with indirect roles, such as companies from other industries producing complementary products or equipment, and even competitors.
Business intelligence	Business intelligence is the collection of knowledge and data that enables an organization to make better informed business decisions.
Business process modelling notation (BPMN)	Business process modelling notation (BPMN) is a standard for business process modelling that provides a graphical notation for specifying business processes based on a flowcharting technique. The objective of BPMN is to support business process management, for both technical users and business users. The notation is intuitive to business users, while at the same time it can represent complex process semantics.
Business unit	A business unit is part of an organization treated for any purpose as a distinct entity – for example, HR, Sales, Legal, IT, and Marketing.

Business value	Business value is the overriding gain that accrues to the organization as a whole, such as increase in market share, better operating margins, or increased profit. Business value is created to support the business objectives, and is the sum of realized business benefits.
Capability	Capability is the quality of being capable; of having the capacity or ability to do something; of being able to achieve declared goals and objectives.
Capability Building Block (CBB)	A Capability Building Block (CBB) describes the key components of a critical capability (CC) that enable a CC's goals and objectives to be achieved efficiently and effectively.
Capability framework	A capability framework is a mental model that identifies and organizes various capability elements, and supports the undertaking of capability improvement.
Capability target	A capability target is the desired state – for example, the target maturity level – for a particular capability or a specific part of a capability.
Capacity model	A capacity model is used to calculate the capacity required by an organization to meet demands for IT services, infrastructure, facilities, and people under different scenarios.
Capacity plan	A capacity plan is a forecast of the future capacities that will be required in the context of a particular defined scenario, with details of the resources required to supply those capacities when they are needed.
Capacity planning headroom	Capacity planning headroom is the spare capacity currently available to handle short-term or known usage spikes as they occur – for example, those that arise at financial year-end, or those related to increased customer activity. Headroom is usually expressed as a percentage of current capacity.
Capital expenditure (CAPEX)	Capital expenditure (CAPEX) refers to the funds used by an organization to acquire or upgrade physical assets such as property, industrial buildings, or equipment. It is also termed 'above the line' expenditure.
Carbon footprint	Carbon footprint is a measure of the total set of greenhouse gases or atmospheric carbon dioxide emissions caused directly and indirectly by human activities, organizations, or products. It includes energy consumption and emissions over a period of time.
Career development model	A career development model is a model that outlines the career paths open to IT employees. It supports the proactive planning and implementation of actions enabling IT employees to achieve their career goals.
Chargeback	Chargeback is the allocation of costs associated with providing IT services to the individuals or departments that use them.

Classification scheme (Knowledge)	A classification scheme is a structured system, using a defined and controlled vocabulary, for grouping, organizing, and labelling knowledge assets or information items. It facilitates finding/retrieval of items by clearly indicating their content, and also reveals the relationship between items by, for example, grouping similar items under one subject heading.
Clickstream analysis	Clickstream analysis is an approach that records the paths that users take through a system based on their mouse-clicks.
Community of practice	A community of practice is a group of people who share a concern or a passion for something they do, who engage in a process of collective learning, and learn how to do it better as they interact regularly.
Competence	Competence is the ability of an individual to apply knowledge, skills and attitudes to achieving observable results.
Compliance	Compliance is the act of conforming, submitting, or adapting to a legal regulation or internal policy (Office of Cybersecurity and Communications National Cyber Security Division, 2008).
Confidentiality	Confidentiality is the characteristic of an information resource that preserves authorized restrictions on information access and disclosure, including the means for protecting personal sensitive and proprietary information (Office of Cybersecurity and Communications National Cyber Security Division, 2008).
Configuration management	Configuration management is a process used to establish and maintain information about infrastructure components, and their relationships to each other, with a view to ensuring consistency of performance in the delivery of an IT service throughout its life cycle.
Confirmative data analysis	Confirmative data analysis focuses on upholding or rejecting a hypothesis. (For example, do first-quarter sales figures support the sales forecast for the year?) A deductive approach using inferential statistics is typically taken.
Convergent services	Convergent services are those that have evolved to use a common infrastructure for services delivery – for example, voice, data and video services.
Cost driver	A cost driver refers to any root cause resulting in cost occurrence. For example, a cost driver for labour wages is labour hours worked.
Cost management	Cost management is the analysis of planned and actual expenditure to identify opportunities for savings.
Cost model	Cost models provide a means of calculating the expected cost of products or services.
Critical Capability (CC)	A Critical Capability (CC) is a defined IT management domain that can help mobilize and deploy IT-based resources to effect a desired end, often in combination with other resources and capabilities.

Critical path	Critical path refers to the set of project activities that must be delivered on time, if the overall project is not to be delayed.
Culture (organizational)	Organizational culture is the set of common attitudes, values, and behaviours of employees within an organization.
Current state evaluation	Current state evaluation is the gathering and documenting of data about the organization's actual performance in a specific capability at a given point in time.
Dashboard (management)	A management dashboard is a visual display of the key performance indicators that monitor an organization's progress in achieving one or more objectives – for example, budget or schedule. It is typically presented on a single screen in a format that makes it easier for management to quickly and easily make informed decisions – for example, using red, amber, and green status symbols.
Data	Data consists of facts represented as text, numbers, graphics, images, sound, or video. Data is the raw material used to represent information, or from which information can be derived (DAMA, 2011).
Data centre	A data centre is a facility used to house computer systems and associated components such as telecommunications and storage systems. It generally includes redundant or backup power supplies, redundant data communications connections, environmental controls (for example, air conditioning, fire suppression), and various security devices.
Data classification	Data classification is the conscious decision to assign a level of sensitivity to data as it is being created, amended, enhanced, stored, or transmitted. The classification of data should then determine the extent to which the data needs to be controlled and secured and is also indicative of its value in terms of business assets (Office of Cybersecurity and Communications National Cyber Security Division, 2008).
Data glossary	A data glossary is a dictionary for a limited subject area. In metadata management, it may be an extract of business terms and their meaning from the metadata.
Data pattern	A data pattern is a simple way of prescribing how particular types of data should be presented. For example, *dd/mm/yyyy* is a data pattern for presenting dates, and *€9,999.99* is a pattern for presenting currency values.
Data/information valuation	Data/information valuation can refer to the cost to replace data, the value at risk if data is not accessible when needed, its resale value, or its error costs. The perceived value changes with the life cycle stage and the stakeholder role.
Decision rights	Decision rights, in relation to a specific task, are rights that empower an individual to make decisions to accomplish that task.

Depth of defence	Depth of defence is the concept of protecting a computer network with a series of defensive mechanisms such that if one mechanism fails, another will already be in place to thwart an attack (Office of Cybersecurity and Communications National Cyber Security Division, 2008).
Design principle, IT	An IT design principle is a high-level guideline for making fundamental decisions regarding hardware and software infrastructure.
Direct costs	Direct costs are those costs that are specifically and exclusively associated with a particular cost object – for example, the cost of purchasing hardware components for providing IT services.
Disaster recovery	Disaster recovery is the approaches, policies, and procedures for restoring the organization's IT services (IT infrastructure, applications, and data) following the occurrence of a disruptive event/incident.
Earned value	Earned value is a trend analysis technique for measuring project progress and performance and predicting future outcomes. It reflects measures of actual work completed, actual time taken, and actual cost incurred, compared with what was planned or budgeted for.
Effectiveness	Effectiveness refers to the extent to which the effort put into an activity delivers the desired results.
Efficiency	Efficiency refers to completing activities or achieving outcomes in an economical manner; it is the ratio of inputs to outputs.
Employment life cycle	The employment life cycle is a model reflecting all stages of an employee's career from recruitment to termination.
Endpoint devices	Endpoint devices are typically network-attached human interface devices or other device interfaces with device-to-device interactions, and are often the origins or final destinations for messages.
Enterprise architecture (EA) domain	An enterprise architecture domain is an architectural view of interrelated areas. Common examples include business, data, application, and technical domains, but these EA domains could be divided according to different schemata.
Enterprise risk management (ERM)	Enterprise risk management (ERM) consists of the approaches and methods used to identify the potential risks to the organization, to understand and manage the identified risks in an integrated way so that they fit within the organization's risk tolerance, and to provide assurance regarding the achievement of the organization's objectives.
Environmental factors	Environmental factors include the physical space, air humidity and temperature, dust and pollution levels including ozone levels, utility supplies such as power and network, radio frequency isolation, geostability, vibrations, and so on.
Explicit knowledge	Explicit knowledge is structured facts that can be articulated in a formal language, codified or encoded, stored in certain media, and readily transmitted to others for sharing and use.

Exploratory data analysis	Exploratory data analysis focuses on identifying new information or insights in the data. An inductive approach using descriptive statistics is typically taken.
Eye tracking	Eye tracking is a user experience testing technique that tracks the eye movements of users while they are using an IT system.
Far-shoring	Far-shoring is offshoring located in a country distant from the organization's field of operation.
Financing	Financing is the process of establishing possible sources of financial resources to meet the organization's funding requirements. These may include a centrally allocated IT budget, allocations from business units, and external sources such as joint ventures, vendor and supplier leasing, and clients.
Firmware	Firmware is software that is embedded in hardware, typically in non-volatile memory.
Forensic (data)	Many applications, systems, and devices create audit logs with elevated levels of security and integrity that make them acceptable as evidence in a court of law, and in this sense the data they contain may be regarded as 'forensic'. For example, analysis of usage or audit logs may enable an investigator to establish definitively and verifiably the timing and sequence of system activities carried out by a particular person. In some countries, such data may be subject to discovery (disclosure) or to a court order.
Full investment life cycle	The full investment life cycle refers to the period from the initial concept/idea through to the eventual retirement of the asset.
Funding	Funding is the process of identifying and setting the overall level of financial resources required to meet the organization's needs, based on, for example, strategic priorities or competitive benchmarks.
Gantt chart	A Gantt chart is a visual representation of a project schedule, in which a series of horizontal lines depicts the duration of activities to be performed, and their start and finish dates. The Gantt chart also supports the sequencing of (interdependent) project activities, allocation of resources, and tracking of project progress.
Gap (demand–supply)	A demand–supply gap is the difference between the business demand for IT service and the available supply at any given time.
Governance, IT	IT governance is a framework of decision rights and accountability, designed to foster desirable behaviour in the development and use of IT.
Incident	An incident is any unplanned interruption to or deterioration in the quality of an IT service. In the context of security or risk management, an incident could be a violation, or imminent threat of a violation, which could have an impact on the business now or provide the potential for an impact in the future.

Incident management	Incident management takes responsibility for logging, recording and resolving any unexpected operational events or interruptions to IT services, and for returning them to normal as quickly as possible with as little impact on the business as possible.
Incident response	Incident response is the definition and execution of a set of instructions or procedures to detect, respond to, and limit consequences of any incident which affects the security or availability of systems, services, or information.
Indirect costs	Indirect costs are those costs that are not specifically and exclusively associated with a particular cost object.
Industrialized IT	Industrialized IT refers to the standardizing of IT services by predesigning/preconfiguring solutions that are automated, scalable, repeatable, and reliable to meet the organization's needs at a reasonable cost.
Information	Information is the interpretation of data (or combinations of data elements) based on its context, including the business meaning of data elements and related terms, the format in which the data is presented, the timeframe represented by the data, and the relevance of the data to a given usage (DAMA, 2009).
Information fragment	An information fragment is a piece of information isolated from its context.
Information security governance	Information security governance is the process of setting, controlling, administering, and monitoring conformance with security policy (DAMA, 2011).
Information type	Information may be classified or assigned to different types based on a variety of criteria, such as confidentiality (secret, proprietary, internal use only, general business use, etc.), file extension (.docx, .xlsx, .fm, .pdf, etc.), legal status (personal, sensitive personal, non-personal, etc.), usage areas (technical, forensic, audit, life cycle, etc.), artefact type (invoice, goods received note, timesheet, tender, etc.), and so on.
Infrastructure component	An infrastructure component is a specific IT component, such as a network, storage device, or CPU.
Inherent risk	Inherent risk is the risk of loss or damage materializing in the event that no actions are taken to prevent that happening.
Innovation centre	An innovation centre is an entity that supports business activity by developing and commercializing new ideas in pursuit of competitive advantage, including the development of new or enhanced products, services, and/or processes.
Innovation framework	An innovation framework is a set of tools and methodologies used to manage or direct innovation activity.

Innovation network	An innovation network is a formal or informal grouping of people who come together to jointly seek out innovative practices or solutions. Members may be drawn from the IT function, from other business units, and from other organizations. Innovation networks emphasize the value of cross-functionality, multi-disciplinarity, and diversity among members. They also enable collaboration and economies of scale, they share knowledge and learning, and they mitigate the risks of innovation by distributing them among their members.
Integrity (Information)	Integrity is the characteristic of an information resource that is guarded against improper modification or destruction, and for which non-repudiation and authenticity are ensured (US Government, 2002).
IT function	The IT function is the department or business unit within an organization charged with managing information technology services and solutions on behalf of the organization.
IT infrastructure	IT infrastructure is the collection of physical components and services, telecommunications, operating systems, monitoring, and security sub-systems that make up the organization's IT assets.
IT posture	IT posture represents an organizational attitude towards the use of IT in an organization. Some organizations may view IT as a real source of competitive advantage whilst others may view IT purely as a cost to be minimized.
IT service	IT services are the services that IT provides to the business. They may be comprised of several infrastructure components and applications – for example, email, helpdesk, financial account processing, and customer relationship management. An IT service contributes towards a customer realizing business/mission value by facilitating outcomes they want to achieve.
IT service provider	An IT service provider is any person or company that supplies IT services to the organization. A provider may be known as a supplier, vendor, or sourcing partner.
IT vision	The IT vision is the desired future state of the IT function and its positioning towards stakeholders. The IT vision provides the direction and a reference for functional goal-setting.
Job family	A job family is a series of progressively more senior, related jobs in which similar work is performed, similar skills, knowledge, and expertise are required, and comparable responsibilities, salary ranges, and duties exist.
Key performance indicator (KPI)	A key performance indicator (KPI) is a quantifiable metric of performance, usually against a predetermined target for an individual, a team, or a campaign. KPIs are used to track progress towards goals; they can be financial or non-financial in nature.
Knowledge	Knowledge is a collection of organized and integrated facts (such as formulae, numbers, and procedures/rules), expert opinions, skills and/or expertise about a subject.

Knowledge asset	A knowledge asset is an organized collection of explicit and tacit knowledge captured from employees, processes, practices, products, services, stakeholders, external sources, and lessons learned from actions.
Knowledge profiling	Knowledge profiling is a systematic procedure/technique for developing detailed descriptions of individual knowledge assets and relationships between sets of knowledge assets (for example, by their basic types of identity, structure, and possible uses). The aim is to enable decisions based on combinations of attributes – for example, their use based on value to particular stakeholders.
Layered defence	Layered defence is an approach to security whereby different types of obstacles are used to protect information from attack. Obstacles can include firewalls, intrusion detection systems, malware scanners, integrity auditing procedures, and storage and network encryption tools. Each can protect information in ways the others cannot.
Lead (capability) framework	A lead framework is the central reference onto which all other (capability) frameworks are mapped. It provides a common language for describing specific capabilities when several frameworks are used simultaneously in the organization.
Lean	Lean describes a philosophy and a set of tools devoted to the identification and elimination of waste.
Life cycle	A life cycle represents activities grouped into phases at a reasonable level of granularity (for example, design, build, deploy, operate, and decommission; or initiate, plan, execute, monitor, control, and close).
Local area network (LAN)	A local area network (LAN) is a network that uses network media to interconnect devices within a limited area such as a home, school, computer laboratory, or office building. The defining characteristics of LANs, in contrast to wide area networks (WANs), include their smaller geographic area, and non-inclusion of leased telecommunication lines.
Master data	Master data is the data that provides context for business activity data in the form of common and abstract concepts relating to the business activity (DAMA, 2011).
Maturity	Maturity is the state of completeness of an individual's or an organization's ability to achieve a desired end or outcome.
Metadata	Metadata is 'data about data' – data that defines and describes the characteristics of other data. It is used to develop business and technical understanding and improve data-related processes (DAMA, 2009).
Multi-protocol label switching (MPLS)	Multi-protocol label switching (MPLS) is an IEFT-approved standard for directing packets in a wide area IP network. Operating below the IP layer and above the optical layer, MPLS is used to ensure that packets take the same route.
Near-shoring	Near-shoring is using service providers in locations that are near to where the service is likely to be consumed. This model is typically used to minimize communication and management barriers, such as language, culture, time differences, or distance.

Non-repudiation	Non-repudiation is the ability to assert the authorship of a message or information authored by a second party, preventing the author from denying his/her own authorship or actions (Open Group, 2011).
Off-shoring	Off-shoring is the practice of using service providers in locations that are distant from where the service is likely to be consumed. This model is typically used to take advantage of market arbitrage – for example, labour costs.
On-shoring	On-shoring is the practice of using service providers located in the same country as the contracting organization.
Operational expenditure (OPEX)	Operational expenditure refers to expenditure that a business incurs as a result of performing its normal business operations. It is also termed 'below the line' expenditure.
Operational level agreement (OLA)	An operational level agreement (OLA) is an agreement between internal support groups, defining how the groups share responsibilities in delivering a service with a given service level.
Operational services	Operational services are processes and services delivered by the IT function, primarily focused on the day-to-day running of the organization.
Opportunity cost	Opportunity cost measures the cost that is lost or sacrificed when the choice of one course of action requires that an alternative course of action (the opportunity) be given up.
Organization (business)	An organization is a unit of people and other resources structured and managed to meet a need or to pursue collective goals (often defined in a legal arrangement).
Organization structure	An organization structure is the hierarchical arrangement of lines of authority, and the information flows between different managerial positions and roles. It typically outlines roles, responsibilities, accountabilities, and span of control, and can be visually depicted in an organization chart.
Over-run	An over-run is an instance of spending exceeding the budgeted provision.
Peer review	A peer review is an evaluation of a work product performed by peers of the producer of the work product for the purpose of identifying defects and possible improvements. A peer review may take a number of forms, including an inspection, a technical review, or a walkthrough.
Peripheral device	A peripheral device is a device that can be attached to, and used with, a computer, without being an integral part of it – for example a printer, scanner or bar code reader.
Physical infrastructure	Physical infrastructure refers to buildings, fire prevention and suppression systems, cabling, power supplies, temperature control systems, computer and network patch panels and centres, off-site storage, physical security and access control systems, etc.

Platform (software, infrastructure)	A platform consists of hardware and software acting as a base set of technologies on which other technologies or processes are built and operated. A platform is designed to provide interoperability, simplified implementation, and streamlined deployment and maintainability of solutions. Types of platforms can include data platforms, computing platforms, and so on (DAMA, 2011).
Portfolio	A portfolio is a collection of programmes and projects that an organization is executing or planning to execute to contribute to the achievement of its objectives.
Portfolio investment board	A portfolio investment board is a centralized planning and prioritization committee that approves the programme investment portfolio. The board should make decisions in line with the strategic direction provided by the senior management of the organization.
Portfolio prioritization framework	A portfolio prioritization framework is an established set of guidelines and practices used to guide the organization in the prioritization of a programme, project, or portfolio.
Power usage effectiveness (PUE)	Power usage effectiveness (PUE) is the proportion of total energy used by a data centre facility that is delivered to the computing equipment.
Problem management	Problem management is the process responsible for resolving incidents and problems that interrupt or degrade IT services. It proactively attempts to prevent problems from occurring, reduces the impact of unavoidable problems, and finds solutions to prevent problems recurring.
Process interface	A process interface is a point in a process where responsibility for an activity passes from one organizational entity to another. This can be from one person to another, from one department or group to another, or from one organization to another.
Process modelling	Process modelling involves creating a symbolic representation of an organization's activities. In doing so, it can help to present activities in ways that makes them clearer and easier to analyse and discuss, and that also makes them easier to improve and redesign.
Process modelling notation	Process modelling notation is a visual and usually symbol-and-text-based representation of activities that follows a standard set of rules. Examples of common notations are business process modelling notation (BPMN), unified modelling language (UML), and universal process notation (UPN).
Process owner	A process owner is a person with responsibility for process design, enablement, and performance. He or she typically oversees day-to-day performance of a process and authorizes changes and improvements to the process, perhaps acting as project manager for improvement efforts.
Programme	A programme is a collection of related projects that are centrally managed in a coordinated manner to attain business objectives and benefits – for example, establishing a shared services centre.

Programme/project issues log	A programme/project issues log is a spreadsheet or database recording all unexpected problems or issues on a project, their severity, allocated responsibility, and resolution, among other factors.
Programme/project risk scorecard	A programme/project risk scorecard is a visual tool that plots the impact and likelihood of risks occurring on a chart, thereby supporting identification of risks that are critical, moderate, and low level in nature.
Project	A project is a unique set of coordinated activities, with defined start and end points, that are undertaken to meet specific objectives and attain desired results. End points can include time, cost, or performance targets.
Project management office (PMO)	A project management office (PMO) is a department or group within an organization that acts as a centre of excellence to promote and facilitate the use of proven project management practices.
Project sponsor	A project sponsor is a senior representative from a business unit who funds the execution of a specific project. The project sponsor is the main point of contact for the project manager in relation to high-level project definition, requirements assessment, and project approval.
Prototype	A prototype is any low resolution/fidelity representation of a proposed solution. This can range from a paper-based storyboard through to a complex hardware/software/firmware system.
Real options valuation	Real options valuation involves examining the alternatives presented by a business investment opportunity. Real options might, for example, include expanding production, buying in from an external source, diverting resources to a different project, or ceasing an activity.
Regression testing	Regression testing is software testing that seeks to uncover software errors by partially retesting a modified program.
Request for information (RFI)	A request for information (RFI) is a request addressed to potential service providers seeking written information about their capability to deliver a service. In a tendering process, the RFI is usually followed by a request for proposal (RFP).
Request for proposal (RFP)	A request for proposal (RFP) is a request addressed to potential service providers seeking a competitive, structured proposal for the delivery of a service to meet a client's specified requirements.
Residual risk	A residual risk is the risk remaining after all mitigation actions have been taken. It is essentially the risk accepted by the business.
Resource	A resource refers to assets (tangible, including financial, physical/infrastructural, human; or intangible, including software, data, intellectual property, branding, culture) that an organization owns, controls, or has access to on a semi-permanent basis.
Resource levelling	Resource levelling is a technique in which project start and finish dates are adjusted based on resource constraints with the goal of balancing demand for resources with the available supply.

Resource smoothing	Resource smoothing is a project management technique which aims to complete the work by a required date, while avoiding peaks and troughs in resource utilization.
Responsibility matrix	A responsibility matrix is a graphic representation that identifies who is responsible for specific activities or deliverables.
Retained organization	The retained organization refers to an organization's services and employees that are not outsourced or transferred to a shared services centre as part of the shift to a shared services model.
Return on assets (ROA)	Return on assets (ROA) is a performance measure of management's efficiency in using its assets to generate earnings. It is calculated by dividing the organization's annual earnings by its total assets. ROA is displayed as a percentage.
Return on investment (ROI)	Return on investment (ROI) is a performance measure used to evaluate the efficiency of an investment or to compare the efficiency of a number of different investments.
Risk	Risk is the possibility of suffering loss or damage as the result of a future event which may or may not happen.
Risk acceptance/ absorption	Risk acceptance/absorption is a risk handling strategy where the possibility of a risk occurrence is accepted, often because the severity of the risk is lower than the organization's risk tolerance level.
Risk assessment	Risk assessment is the process through which risks are identified for a particular scenario. They can then be assessed according to (a) the severity or scale of the loss or damage that would be caused by the unfavourable event (the risk incident), and (b) the probability of the risk incident actually happening.
Risk avoidance	Risk avoidance is a risk handling strategy which aims to eliminate the possibility of the risk incident occurring.
Risk handling strategy	A risk handling strategy is the approach the organization adopts to address identified and prioritized risks, to ensure they do not exceed the organization's risk tolerance level. These strategies include risk acceptance/absorption, risk avoidance, risk mitigation/reduction, and risk transfer. Note: Risk handling is sometimes also referred to as risk treatment.
Risk incident	A risk incident is an event that causes an operational and/or strategic business impact.
Risk management policy	A risk management policy is a document that defines how risks are assessed, prioritized, handled, monitored, and communicated.
Risk management programme	A risk management programme is the culture, structures, and approaches necessary for the effective management of risk.
Risk mitigation/ reduction	Risk mitigation/reduction is a risk handling strategy which involves taking action to reduce either the probability of unacceptable risks or their impact, to a point where their severity falls below the organization's maximum risk tolerance threshold.

Risk profile	A risk profile is the various risks that the organization may face, such as IT security risks, data protection and information privacy risks, operations/business continuity risks, IT investment risks, IT service contracts/supplier risks, IT reputation/brand risks, or regulatory/ legal and ethics policy compliance risks; these risks are collected in assessments and used to determine the risk management policy.
Risk register	A risk register is a database of risks with results of their assessment (including description and quantification) that is used, for example, in decision-making and mitigation tracking.
Risk tolerance	Risk tolerance is an organization's capacity and willingness to absorb risk. It reflects the degree of uncertainty an organization is willing to accept with respect to negative impacts on the business, and is typically set in alignment with the relative importance of its business objectives.
Risk transfer	Risk transfer is a risk handling strategy that involves allocating liability for the risk to another party.
Risk-adjusted return on capital (RAROC)	Risk-adjusted return on capital (RAROC) refers to an adjustment to the return on an investment that accounts for the element of risk. RAROC gives decision makers the ability to compare the returns on several different projects with varying risk levels.
Root cause analysis	Root cause analysis is a problem-solving approach that seeks to identify the core underlying causes of issues or failures.
Run rate	The run rate is an estimate of financial performance based on an extrapolation of current results and trends into the future.
Scenario planning	Scenario planning is the use of empirical modelling to compute possible future scenarios and outcomes. Scenario planning is conducted to analyse the implications of envisaged changes.
Scope creep	Scope creep is uncontrolled change or growth in a project's scope caused by an accumulation of often small adjustments to the project's initial scope or objectives. This sometimes happens when the scope of a project is ill defined, poorly documented, or weakly controlled.
Search procedures	Search procedures are methods of searching a database, such as Boolean searching (using AND, OR, NOT) using combinations of keywords, or free text searching.
Security	Security is a discipline concerned with ensuring that information is adequately protected for confidentiality, that system, data, and software integrity is maintained, and that information and system resources are protected against unplanned disruptions.
Security architecture	Security architecture is the structure of security layers deployed in an organization. Security architecture provides security views of the overall architecture to aid and assist in security planning and implementation.
Security audit	A security audit is a systematic evaluation of the security of an organization's information systems by measuring how well they conform to a set of established criteria (Office of Cybersecurity and Communications National Cyber Security Division, 2008).

Security classes	Security classes are classes or categories to which data can be assigned – for example, secret, proprietary confidential, internal business only, and general business use.
Security threat profile	A security threat profile characterizes the likely intent, capability, and target of threats to the business (Joint Task Force Transformation Initiative, 2013). Expanded threat profiles might include detection and neutralization techniques.
Security tools	Security tools include access control testing software, anti-virus and anti-spyware tools, log analysis and reporting tools.
Server	A server provides a specific kind of service to a client running on the same computer or on other computers on a network. Examples include: ▶ A network server for managing network traffic. ▶ A name server for mapping user and computer names to machine addresses. ▶ A database server for enabling clients to interact with a database. ▶ An application server that runs applications for clients.
Service level agreement (SLA)	A service level agreement (SLA) is an agreement between a service provider and a customer, defining the minimum or target level of a service in terms of measurable indicators, such as availability, performance, operation, and so on.
Service life cycle management (SLM)	Service life cycle management (SLM) is a holistic approach that helps organizations look at service management as an end-to-end process rather than a series of discrete events.
Shadow IT	Shadow IT includes IT expenditure within the organization that is outside the ownership or control of the IT function.
Showback	Showback is similar to chargeback, but the metrics are for informational purposes only, and no one is billed.
Simple network management protocol (SNMP)	Simple network management protocol (SNMP) is a set of internet standard protocols governing the monitoring and configuring of network devices, including printers, servers, switches, and routers.
Six Sigma	Six Sigma is a business management strategy that seeks to improve processes through the removal of variation and defects.
Software defined infrastructure	Software defined infrastructure is a collective term used to refer to software defined storage, software defined networks, and virtualization, in which resources can typically be reassigned without the need for manual intervention.
Solution	A solution is a product and/or service that is provided to address a specific business problem or other need.
Solutions delivery life cycle	A solutions delivery life cycle describes the various phases executed in delivering an IT solution, from requirements capture and analysis through to design, implementation, testing, and release into the operational environment.

Sourcing	Sourcing is the procurement of goods and/or services either from inside the organization or from an outside supplier.
Sourcing governance model	A sourcing governance model sets out how to integrate the governance of IT service providers into the overall IT governance model.
Sourcing model	A sourcing model is the mechanism used to source goods or services for the organization.
Span of control	Span of control refers to the number of employees a manager has reporting to him/her.
Strategic objective	An IT strategic objective is the long/medium-term tangible goal that, once reached, results in the realization of the IT vision.
Strategic plan	An IT strategic plan is the description of activities to be undertaken in pursuit of the IT strategic objective. Typically, it defines IT's value proposition, mission, vision, and targets, but provides only general guidance on how the targets will be met.
Strategic workforce management	Strategic workforce management is the development of plans, policies, and systems to support the establishment and maintenance of a productive workforce.
Subscription IT services	Subscription IT services are those that are offered on a subscription basis.
Succession plan	A succession plan is a plan for identifying and developing employees who are capable of providing continuity by filling key organizational positions when they become open.
Supplier engagement model	A supplier engagement model is a high-level approach that defines how the organization manages its relationship with a supplier. It may reflect, for example, contact points, escalation procedures, the frequency of operational and strategic planning and review meetings, a description of roles and responsibilities, penalties for late delivery, and so on.
Sustainability metric	A sustainability metric is a measurement used to assess an organization's level of success in achieving its defined goals for sustainability. Such metrics may include percentage of assets recycled, organization-wide power consumption per day, or CO_2 generated per employee.
System architecture	The system architecture describes the fundamental concepts or properties of a system embodied in its components, their relationships to each other and to the environment, and the principles guiding its design and evolution.
Tacit knowledge	Tacit knowledge is the combination of knowledge and know-how that is embodied in individual expertise and that contains subjective insights gained from personal beliefs, experiences, or work routines.
Technical architecture	The technical architecture is a formal description of an IT system, which defines and documents the set of rules governing the arrangement, interaction, and interdependence of the parts or elements of the system.

Technology-driven innovation	Technology-driven innovation is the exploitation of technology to enable new or different ways of working in pursuit of a competitive advantage. It includes the development of new or enhanced products, services, and/or processes.
Test level	A test level is the level at which groups of test activities are organized and managed together. Examples of test levels are the unit level, integration level, system level, and acceptance test level.
Top-down data valuations	Top-down data valuation uses macroeconomic approaches to data valuation.
Total cost of ownership model	A total cost of ownership model is a framework for defining the elements that contribute to the full costs of IT assets and services, and for tracking and analysing them to reveal areas where savings can be made, or where investment is lacking.
Triple bottom line (TBL)	Triple bottom line (TBL) is an evaluation of organizational activities using a comprehensive assessment of performance across financial (profit), environmental (planet), and social (people) dimensions.
Unauthorized access	Unauthorized access refers to approaching, trespassing within, communicating with, storing data in, retrieving data from, or otherwise intercepting and changing computer resources without consent (Office of Cybersecurity and Communications National Cyber Security Division, 2008).
Underpinning contract (UPC)	An underpinning contract (UPC) is an agreement on the level of IT services that a service provider will provide, and at what price to the service recipient. A UPC is a supporting document for the service level agreement (SLA), and is the external equivalent of an operational level agreement (OLA).
Under-run	An under-run is an instance of spending less than the budgeted provision.
Unified modelling language (UML)	Unified modelling language (UML) is a general-purpose graphical modelling language that uses a set of symbols and connectors to create process diagrams to model workflows, and provides a standard way to visualize the design of a system.
Unit cost	A unit cost is the average total cost of producing one unit of output. A unit cost is calculated by dividing the total cost of production by the total number of units produced.
Unit testing	Unit testing is a software testing technique that focuses on exercising the features of individual functions or modules in isolation.
Universal process notation (UPN)	Universal process notation (UPN) is a business process notation designed to provide usable process information to the executors of a business process, and to address the technical needs of an IT audience.
Upward feedback	Upward feedback is performance evaluation feedback provided to managers by their direct reports.

Usability	Usability relates to the ease with which IT services and solutions can be used from a user's perspective.
Usefulness	Usefulness relates to how well IT services and solutions serve their intended purposes.
User acceptance testing (UAT)	User acceptance testing (UAT) is the testing of the IT solution for its functionality and usability prior to customer delivery. It uses real-world scenarios that resemble how the application might be used by the user.
User account	A user account is the representation of a user in an information system; it can be linked to a specific person (Open Group, 2011).
User experience	User experience is the aggregate of users' perceptions and responses arising from their use or anticipated use of a product, system, or service.
User interface	A user interface is the means by which the user and a computer system interact, in particular through the use of input devices and software.
User proficiency	User proficiency is the level of knowledge or aptitude a user has in effectively using business systems, IT supported services, or a particular system.
Value chain	A value chain is a series of activities that, when combined, define how a business adds value.
Value-at-risk	Value-at-risk is a metric used to quantify the potential loss of business value if IT services were to fail and cause significant business disruption.
Variance analysis (budgeting)	Variance analysis is the examination of the difference between budgeted costs and the actual costs incurred.
Virtualization	Virtualization refers to the act of creating a virtual (rather than actual) version of something, including but not limited to a virtual computer hardware platform, operating system (OS), storage device, or computer network resources.
Walkthrough	Walkthrough is a thorough demonstration or explanation detailing each step of the IT solution. Its purpose is to identify errors and learn from the user's experience.
Wide area network (WAN)	A wide area network (WAN) is a geographically dispersed telecommunications network. The term distinguishes a broader telecommunication structure from a local area network (LAN).

Acronyms and Abbreviations

C

AA	**Accounting and Allocation**
API	Application programming interface
ATM	Asynchronous transfer mode
BAR	**Benefits Assessment and Realization**
BGM	**Budget Management**
BOP	**Budget Oversight and Performance Analysis**
BP	**Business Planning**
BPM	**Business Process Management**
BPMN	Business process modelling notation
BYOD	Bring-your-own-device
CAM	**Capability Assessment Management**
CAPEX	Capital expenditure
CBB	Capability building block
CC	Critical capability
CEO	Chief executive officer
CFO	Chief financial officer
CFP	**Capacity Forecasting and Planning**
CI	Configuration item
CIO	Chief information officer
CMDB	Configuration management database
CMIS	Capacity management information system
CMMI	Capability Maturity Model Integration
CO_2	Carbon dioxide
COBIT	Control Objectives for Information and Related Technology
COO	Chief operations officer

CPU	Central processing unit
CRM	Customer relationship management
DSM	**Demand and Supply Management**
EA	Enterprise Architecture
EAM	**Enterprise Architecture Management**
EIM	**Enterprise Information Management**
ERM	Enterprise risk management
ERP	Enterprise resource planning
FF	**Funding and Financing**
FTE	Full-time equivalent
GIT	**Green Information Technology**
HCI	Human–computer interaction
HR	Human resources
IAOP	International Association of Outsourcing Professionals
IaaS	Infrastructure as a service
IETF	Internet Engineering Task Force
IM	**Innovation Management**
IP	Internet protocol
IS	Information systems
ISM	**Information Security Management**
ISP	Internet service provider
IT	Information technology
IT-CMF	Information Technology Capability Maturity Framework
ITG	**Information Technology Leadership and Governance**
ITIL	Information Technology Infrastructure Library
ITSQC	IT Service Quality Certification
IVI	Innovation Value Institute
KAM	**Knowledge Asset Management**

KPI	Key performance indicator
LAN	Local area network
MDM	Mobile device management
MPLS	Multi-protocol label switching
MTBF	Mean time between failures
MTTR	Mean time to repair/recover/resolution
ODP	**Organization Design and Planning**
OLA	Operational level agreement
OPEX	Operational expenditure
OS	Operating system
PAM	**People Asset Management**
PM	**Portfolio Management**
PMO	Project Management Office
POM	Practice–Outcome–Metric
PPM	**Programme and Project Management**
PPP	**Portfolio Planning and Prioritization**
PUE	Power usage effectiveness
RAID	Redundant array of inexpensive disks
RAROC	Risk-adjusted return on capital
RDE	**Research, Development and Engineering**
REM	**Relationship Management**
RFC	Request for change
RFI	Request for information
RFP	Request for proposal
RFQ	Request for quote
RIM	Remote infrastructure management
RM	**Risk Management**
ROA	Return on assets
ROI	Return on investment

SaaS	Software as a service
SAI	**Service Analytics and Intelligence**
SD	**Solutions Delivery**
SLA	Service level agreement
SNMP	Simple network management protocol
SOX	Sarbanes–Oxley Act
SP	**Strategic Planning**
SRC	**Sourcing**
SRP	**Service Provisioning**
SUM	**Supplier Management**
TBL	Triple bottom line
TCO	**Total Cost of Ownership**
TIM	**Technical Infrastructure Management**
UAT	User acceptance testing
UED	**User Experience Design**
UML	Unified modelling language
UPC	Underpinning contract
UPN	Universal process notation
UPS	Uninterruptible Power Supply
UTM	**User Training Management**
UX	User experience
VRIN	Valuable, rare, inimitable, non-substitutable
WAN	Wide area network
XaaS	*Everything*-as-a-service

Management Artefacts **D**

Management Artefact	CC where mentioned
Access controls policy	06-EIM
Account management plan	25-REM
Accounting model, IT	01-AA
Annual report, IT	25-REM
Analytics software	12-SAI
Architecture development methodology	20-EAM
Assessment guideline document	19-CAM
Assessment methodology	19-CAM
Benefits dependency map	33-BAR
Benefits plan	33-BAR
Budget analysis tool, IT	16-BOP
Budget plan, IT	15-BGM 16-BOP 17-FF
Budget review charter, IT	15-BGM
Business-as-usual commitments database	02-BP
Business case, outline	14-SP
Business case template	33-BAR
Business plan, IT	02-BP
Business process management governance model	03-BPM
Business process management policy	03-BPM
Business process management technology suite	03-BPM

Management Artefact	CC where mentioned
Business process model and notation	03-BPM
Business process to IT service maps	12-SAI
Business relationship call logs	25-REM
Business strategic plan	14-SP
Business (unit) profiles	25-REM
Business value indicators, library of	33-BAR
Capability-based framework	19-CAM
Capacity management information system	04-CFP
Career development model	23-PAM
Cash flow/operating budget statement	15-BGM 17-FF
Chargeback/showback model	01-AA
Configuration management database (CMDB)	12-SAI 35-TCO 27-SRP 30-TIM
Corporate steering committee, IT	09-ITG
Cost tracking database	35-TCO
Database of training needs	32-UTM
Decision-making process, IT	09-ITG
Decision-making responsibility and accountability matrix	09-ITG
Demand models	05-DSM
Development roadmap	19-CAM
Enterprise architecture deliverables	20-EAM
Enterprise architecture tool set and repository	20-EAM
Environmental sustainability strategy	07-GIT
Enterprise governance council, IT	09-ITG
Financial audit report, IT	15-BGM 16-BOP
Forecast plan, IT	04-CFP
Funding benchmark data, IT	17-FF

Management Artefact	CC where mentioned
Funding models, IT	17-FF
Functional and non-functional requirements log	28-SD
Global requirements catalogue	02-BP
Green information technology roadmap	07-GIT
Green information technology targets	07-GIT
HR policies	23-PAM
Ideation platform	26-RDE
Incident log	21-ISM
Information governance policy	06-EIM
Information management strategy	06-EIM
Information security management policy	21-ISM
Innovation facilitation portal	08-IM
Innovation lab	25-REM 08-IM 26-RDE
Innovation pipeline dashboard	08-IM
Innovation recognition rewards	08-IM
Infrastructure roadmap, IT	30-TIM
IT infrastructure, policies and approaches for life cycle management	30-TIM
Job families	23-PAM
Knowledge asset repository	22-KAM
Knowledge domain experts register	22-KAM
Knowledge strategy document	22-KAM
Mobile device management (MDM) platform	30-TIM
New technology research intelligence gathering, guidelines for	26-RDE
New technology research performance report	26-RDE
New technology research projects, repository of	26-RDE
Operational level agreement (OLA)	27-SRP 29-SUM
Organization charts	10-ODP
Organization design guidelines	10-ODP

Management Artefact	CC where mentioned
Organization design effectiveness indicators	10-ODP
Organization structure templates	10-ODP
Portfolio dashboard	34-PM
Portfolio plan	18-PPP
Portfolio prioritization criteria	18-PPP
Portfolio prioritization framework	18-PPP
Portfolio report	34-PM
Programme performance dashboard	24-PPM
Programme/project issues log	24-PPM
Programme/project risk scorecard	24-PPM
Project schedule/Gantt chart	24-PPM
Remote infrastructure management (RIM) platform	30-TIM
Risk management policy	11-RM
Risk profiling and scoring approach	11-RM
Risk register	11-RM 21-ISM
Scenario analysis model	34-PM
Security management software, IT	21 ISM
Service level agreement (SLA)	12-SAI 27-SRP 29-SUM
Service management software suite, IT	27-SRP
Services catalogue, IT	01-AA 05-DSM 25-REM 27-SRP
Services portfolio, IT	05-DSM
Shared operations calendar	05-DSM
Social collaboration platform	08-IM
Solutions development methodologies	28-SD
Sourcing contract	13-SRC

Management Artefact	CC where mentioned
Sourcing methodology, IT	29-SUM
Sourcing model templates	13-SRC
Sourcing readiness checklist	13-SRC
Strategic options, IT	14-SP
Strategic plan, IT	14-SP
Strategic sourcing plan, IT	13-SRC
Supplier management balanced scorecards	29-SUM
Supplier relationship management systems	29-SUM
Supply models	05-DSM
Systems requirements log	28-SD
Total cost of ownership framework and models	35-TCO
Training catalogue	23-PAM
Training content knowledge base	32-UTM
Training impact assessment method	32-UTM
User design conceptualization methods	31-UED
User experience communication methods	31-UED
User experience research methods	31-UED
User training management plan	32-UTM
Utilization report, IT	04-CFP
Vision statement, IT	14-SP 09-ITG
Vulnerabilities and patch availability database	21-ISM
Workforce strategy, IT	23-PAM